Forensic Computing

Tony Sammes and Brian Jenkinson

Forensic Computing

Second edition

 Springer

Tony Sammes, BSc, MPhil, PhD, FBCS, CEng, CITP
The Centre for Forensic Computing
DCMT
Cranfield University
Shrivenham, Swindon, UK

Brian Jenkinson, BA, HSc (hon), MSc, FBCS, CITP
Forensic Computing Consultant

British Library Cataloguing in Publication Data
A catalogue record for this book is available from the British Library

Library of Congress Control Number: 2006927421

ISBN-13: 978-1-84628-397-0   e-ISBN-13: 978-1-84628-732-9
ISBN-10: 1-84628-397-3   e-ISBN 10: 1-84628-732-4
ISBN 1-85233-299-9 1st edition

Printed on acid-free paper

© Springer-Verlag London Limited 2007

First published 2000
Second edition 2007

9 8 7 6 5 4 3 2 1

Springer Science+Business Media
springer.com

Dedication

To Joan and Val

Acknowledgements

The authors would like to thank all the members and former members of the FCG Training Committee for the very valuable contributions that they made to the first edition of this book. In particular, our grateful thanks go to Steve Buddell, Tony Dearsley, Geoff Fellows, Paul Griffiths, Mike Hainey, Dave Honeyball, Peter Lintern, John McConnell, Keith McDonald, Geoff Morrison, Laurie Norton, Kathryn Owen and Stewart Weston-Lewis. For this second edition we would, in addition, like to thank Lindy Sheppard, Dr Tristan Jenkinson and John Hunter for their kind support. Our thanks also go to the students of the 30 or so Forensic Computing Foundation Courses that have now been run for all their helpful comments and suggestions. We would like to add a sincere word of thanks to our publisher and editors, to Catherine Brett, Wayne Wheeler, Helen Callaghan and Beverley Ford, all of Springer, who, after much chivvying, eventually managed to get us to put pen to paper for this second edition, and a most important thank you also to Ian Kingston of Ian Kingston Publishing Services, who has made the result look so good. Finally our contrite thanks go to our families, to whom we did sort of promise that the first edition would be the last.

Contents

1. Forensic Computing

Introduction

Throughout this book you will find that we have consistently referred to the term "Forensic Computing" for what is often elsewhere called "Computer Forensics". In the UK, however, when we first started up, the name "Computer Forensics" had been registered to a commercial company that was operating in this field and we felt that it was not appropriate for us to use a name that carried with it commercial connotations. Hence our use of the term "Forensic Computing". Having said that, however, we will need on occasion to refer to "Computer Forensics", particularly when quoting from overseas journals and papers which use the term, and our use in such circumstances should then be taken to be synonymous with that of "Forensic Computing" and not as a reference to the commercial company.

In point of fact, we will start with a definition of Computer Forensics that has been given by Special Agent Mark Pollitt of the Federal Bureau of Investigation as: "*Computer forensics is the application of science and engineering to the legal problem of digital evidence. It is a synthesis of science and law*" (Pollitt, undated). In his paper he contrasts the problems of presenting a digital document in evidence with those of a paper document, and states: "*Rarely is determining that the [paper] document physically exists or where it came from, a problem. With digital evidence, this is often a problem. What does this binary string represent? Where did it come from? While these questions, to the computer literate, may seem obvious at first glance, they are neither obvious nor understandable to the layman. These problems then require a substantial foundation being laid prior to their admission into evidence at trial.*" These are questions for which we try to provide the requisite technical knowledge in Chapters 2, 3, 4, 5 and 6.

In a second paper (Pollitt, 1995), Special Agent Mark Pollitt suggests that in the field of computer forensics: "*Virtually all professional examiners will agree on some overriding principles*" and then gives as examples the following three: "*... that evidence should not be altered, examination results should be accurate, and that examination results are verifiable and repeatable*". He then goes on to say: "*These principles are universal and are not subject to change with every new operating system, hardware or software. While it may be necessary to occasionally modify a principle, it should be a rare event.*" In Chapters 7 and 8 we will see that these overriding principles are in complete accord with the practices that we recommend and with those that have been put forward in the Good Practice Guide for Computer based Electronic Evidence (ACPO, 2003) of the UK Association of Chief Police Officers (ACPO).

In short, it is the essence of this book to try to provide a sufficient depth of technical understanding to enable forensic computing analysts to search for, find and confidently present any form of digital document[1] as admissible evidence in a court of law.

■ ■

Origin of the Book

The idea for the book sprang originally from a course that had been developed to support the forensic computing law enforcement community. The then UK Joint Agency Forensic Computer Group[2] had tasked its Training Sub-Committee with designing and establishing education and training courses for what was seen to be a rapidly developing and urgently needed discipline. The first requirement was for a foundation course that would establish high standards for the forensic computing discipline and would provide a basis for approved certification. The Training Sub-Committee, in collaboration with academic staff from Cranfield University, designed the foundation course such that it would give successful candidates exemption from an existing module in Forensic Computing that was available within the Cranfield University Forensic Engineering and Science MSc course programme. The Forensic Computing Foundation course (FCFC) was thus established from the outset at postgraduate level and it continues to be formally examined and accredited at this level by the university.

The FCFC, of two weeks duration, is jointly managed and delivered by staff from both the forensic computing law enforcement community and the university. It covers the fundamentals of evidence recovery from mainly PC-based computers and the successful presentation of that evidence before a court of law. The course does not seek to produce computer experts. Rather, it sets out to develop forensic computing analysts who have a proven capability for recovering evidential data from computers whilst preserving the integrity of the original and who are fully competent in presenting that evidence in an understandable form before a court of law.

At the time of writing, some 30 cohorts have successfully completed the FCFC since its inception in March 1998, and the taught material of the course has been continually revised and updated in the light of much useful feedback and experience. A full MSc in Forensic Computing is now offered by the university, of which the FCFC is a core module, and the first cohort of students on this program graduated with

---

1   Document here refers to a document in the widest sense. It includes all forms of digital representations: photographic images, pictures, sound and video clips, spreadsheets, computer programs and text, as well as fragments of all of these.

2   The Joint Agency Forensic Computer Group was made up of representatives from ACPO, the Inland Revenue, HM Customs and Excise, the Forensic Science Service and the Serious Fraud Office. It has now been renamed the Digital Evidence Group and still retains a similar composition.

their MScs in 2005. It is the material from the FCFC that forms much of the substance of this book.

The structure of the book differs a little from the way in which the material is presented on the course itself, in order to make the sequencing more pertinent to the reader. Nevertheless, it is intended that the book will also serve well as a basic textbook for the FCFC.

Structure of the Book

Picking up on one of the key questions raised by Special Agent Mark Pollitt in the earlier quotes – "... *What does this binary string represent?*" – we start our investigation in Chapter 2 by considering what information is and just what binary strings might represent. We look at number systems in some detail, starting with decimal and then moving to binary, ranging through little endian and big endian formats, fixed point integers and fractions, floating point numbers, BCD and hexadecimal representations. We then look at characters, records and files, file types and file signatures (or magic numbers) and hexadecimal listings. A number of file formats are then considered, with particular reference to some of the better known word processing, graphic and archive file formats. To complement this chapter, the ASCII, Windows ANSI and IBM Extended ASCII character sets are listed at Appendix 1, where mention is also made of UCS, UTF and Unicode, and the magic number signatures of many of the standard file formats are listed at Appendix 2. In addition, the order code for the Intel 8086 processor is listed in hexadecimal order at Appendix 7. These appendices provide a useful reference source for the analysis of binary sequences that are in hexadecimal format.

In Chapter 3, we look at fundamental computer principles: at how the Von Neumann machine works and at the stored program concept. The basic structure of memory, processor and the interconnecting buses is discussed and a worked example for a simplified processor is stepped through. The ideas of code sequences, of programming and of breaking sequence are exemplified, following which a black box model of the PC is put forward.

Although the material in Chapters 2 and 3 has altered little, apart from some minor updating, from that of the first edition, that of Chapter 4 has had to be significantly updated to take account of the changes in technology that have occurred since 2000. Chapter 4 continues on from Chapter 3 and aims to achieve two goals: to put a physical hardware realization onto the abstract ideas of Chapter 3 and to give a better understanding of just what is "inside the box" and how it all should be connected up. We need to do this looking inside and being able to identify all the pieces so that we can be sure that a target system is safe to operate, that it is not being used as a storage box for other items of evidential value, and that all its components are connected up and working correctly. We again start with the black box model and relate this to a modern motherboard and to the various system buses. Next we look at the early Intel processors and at the design of the PC. This leads on to the development of the Intel processors up to and including that of the Pentium 4 and then a brief look at some other compatible processors. Discussion is then centred on memory chips, and this is followed by a brief mention of disk drives, which receive a very much more detailed treatment in a chapter of their own. Finally, a number of other peripheral devices and expansion cards are discussed. Diagrams and photographs throughout this chapter aim to assist in the recognition of the various parts and their relative placement in the PC.

Chapter 5, on disk geometry, provides the real technical meat of the book. This is the largest chapter by far and the most detailed. It too has been significantly updated to reflect the advent of bigger and faster disks and to examine FAT32 systems in more detail. In order to understand the second question posed by Special Agent Mark Pollitt in the above quotes – "*Where did it* [this binary string] *come from?*" we need to know a little about magnetic recording and rather a lot about disk drives. The chapter opens with an introduction to five main issues: the physical construction of disk drives; how addressable elements of memory are constructed within them; the problems that have arisen as a result of rapid development of the hard drive and the need for backward compatibility; the ways in which file systems are formed using the addressable elements of the disk; and where and how information might be hidden on the disk. Discussion initially centres on the physical construction of disks and on CHS addressing. Encoding methods are next considered, together with formatting. This leads on to hard disk interfaces and the problems that have been caused by incompatibility between them. The 528 Mbyte barrier is described and the workaround of CHS translation is explained, together with some of the translation algorithms. LBA is discussed and a number of BIOS related problems are considered. New features in the later ATA specifications, such as the Host Protected Area, are mentioned and a summary of the interface and translation options is then given. Details of fast drives and big drives are given, with particular reference to 48 bit addressing, and mention is made of Serial ATA. This is followed by a detailed explanation of the POST/Boot sequence to the point at which the bootstrap loader is invoked. A full discussion of the master boot record and of partitioning then follows and a detailed analysis of extended partitions is presented. Since our explanations do not always fully conform with those of some other authorities, we expand on these issues in Appendix 6, where we explain our reasoning and give results from some specific trials that we have carried out. Drive letter assignments, the disk ID and a brief mention of GUIDs is next made and then directories, and DOS and Windows FAT (16 and 32) file systems, are described, together with long file names and additional times and dates fields. We then give a summary of the known places where information might be hidden and discuss the recovery of information that may have been deleted. We conclude the chapter with a short section on RAID devices. Three appendices are associated with this chapter: Appendix 3, which lists a typical set of POST codes; Appendix 4, which gives a typical set of BIOS beep codes and error messages; and Appendix 5, which lists all currently known partition types.

One of the major changes to the FCFC, made in recent years, has been to include the practical analysis of NTFS file systems. We have had to find space to include this in addition to the analysis of FAT-based file systems, as we now note an almost equal occurrence of both file systems in our case work. In recognition of this, we have introduced, for this second edition, a completely new Chapter 6 on NTFS. Some of this material has been developed from an MSc thesis produced by one of the authors (Jenkinson, 2005). Following a brief history of the NTFS system and an outline of its features, the Master File Table (MFT) is examined in detail. Starting from the BIOS Parameter Block, a sample MFT file record with resident data is deconstructed line by line at the hexadecimal level. The issue with Update Sequence Numbers is explained and the significance of this for data extraction of resident data from the MFT record is demonstrated. The various attributes are each described in detail and a second example of an MFT file record with non-resident data is then deconstructed line by line at the hexadecimal level. This leads to an analysis of virtual cluster numbers and data runs. Analysis continues with a sample MFT directory record with resident data and then an examination of how an external directory listing is created. A detailed analysis of INDX files follows and the chapter concludes with the highlighting of a number of issues of forensic significance. Three new appendices have also been added: Appendix 8 provides an analysis of the NTFS boot sector, and BIOS parameter block; Appendix 9 provides a detailed analysis of the MFT header and the attribute maps; and Appendix 11 explains the significance of alternate data streams.

A detailed technical understanding of where and how digital information can be stored is clearly of paramount importance, both from an investigative point of view in finding the information in the first place and from an evidential point of view in being able to explain in technically accurate but jury-friendly terms how and why it was found where it was. However, that admitted, perhaps the most important part of all is *process*. Without proper and approved process, the best of such information may not even be admissible as evidence in a court of law. In Chapter 7, the Treatment of PCs, we consider the issues of process. We start this by looking first at the principles of computer-based evidence as put forward in the ACPO Good Practice Guide (ACPO, 2003). Then we consider the practicalities of mounting a search and seizure operation and the issues that can occur on site when seizing computers from a suspect's premises. The main change here from the first edition is that today more consideration may have to be given to some aspects of live analysis; in particular, for example, where a secure password-protected volume is found open when seizure takes place. Guidelines are given here for each of the major activities, including the shutdown, seizure and transportation of the equipment. Receipt of the equipment into the analyst's laboratory and the process of examination and the production of evidence are next considered. A detailed example of a specific disk is then given, and guidance on interpreting the host of figures that result is provided. Finally, the issues of imaging and copying are discussed.

In the treatment of PCs, as we see in Chapter 7, our essential concern is not to change the evidence on the hard disk and to produce an image which represents its state exactly as it was when it was seized. In Chapter 8 we look at the treatment of organizers and we note that for the most part there is no hard disk and the concern here has to be to change the evidence in the main memory as little as possible. This results in the first major difference between the treatment of PCs and the treatment of organizers. To access the organizer it will almost certainly have to be switched on, and this effectively means that the first of the ACPO principles, not to change the evidence in any way, cannot be complied with. The second major difference is that the PC compatible is now so standardized that a standard approach can be taken to its analysis. This is not the case with organizers, where few standards are apparent and each organizer or PDA typically has to approached differently. The chapter begins by outlining the technical principles associated with electronic organizers and identifying their major characteristics. We then go on to consider the application of the ACPO Good Practice Guide principles and to recommend some guidelines for the seizure of organizers. Finally, we discuss the technical examination of organizers and we look particularly at how admissible evidence might be obtained from the protected areas.

The final chapter attempts to "look ahead", but only just a little bit more. The technology is advancing at such an unprecedented rate that most forward predictions beyond a few months are likely to be wildly wrong. Some of the issues that are apparent at the time of writing are discussed here. Problems with larger and larger disks, whether or not to image, the difficulties raised by networks and the increasing use of "on the fly" encryption form the major topics of this chapter.

Throughout the book, we have included many chapter references as well as a comprehensive bibliography at the end. Many of the references we have used relate to resources that have been obtained from the Internet and these are often referred to by their URL. However, with the Internet being such a dynamic entity, it is inevitable that some of the URLs will change over time or the links will become broken. We have tried to ensure that, just before publication, all the quoted URLs have been checked and are valid but acknowledge that, by the time you read this, there will be some that do not work. For that we apologise and suggest that you might use a search engine with keywords from the reference to see whether the resource is available elsewhere on the Internet.

References

ACPO (2003) *Good Practice Guide for Computer Based Electronic Evidence V3*, Association of Chief Police Officers (ACPO), National Hi-Tech Crime Unit (NHTCU).
Jenkinson, B. L. (2005) The structure and operation of the master file table within a Windows 2000 NTFS environment, *MSc Thesis*, Cranfield University.
Pollitt, M. M. (undated) *Computer Forensics: An Approach to Evidence in Cyberspace*, Federal Bureau of Investigation, Baltimore, MD.
Pollitt, M. M. (1995) Principles, practices, and procedures: an approach to standards in computer forensics, *Second International Conference on Computer Evidence*, Baltimore, Maryland, 10–15 April 1995. Federal Bureau of Investigation, Baltimore, MD.

2. *Understanding Information*

Introduction

In this chapter we will be looking in detail at the following topics:

- What is information?
- Memory and addressing
- Decimal and binary integers
- Little endian and big endian formats
- Hexadecimal numbers
- Signed numbers, fractions and floating point numbers
- Binary Coded Decimal (BCD)
- Characters and computer program codes
- Records, files, file types and file signatures
- The use of hexadecimal listings
- Word processing and graphic file formats
- Archive and other file formats

We note that the fundamental concern of all our forensic computing activity is for the accurate extraction of information from computer-based systems, such that it may be presented as admissible evidence in court. Given that, we should perhaps first consider just what it is that we understand by this term *information*, and then we might look at how it is that computer systems are able to hold and process what we have defined as information in such a wide variety of different forms.

However, deciding just what it is that we really mean by the term *information* is not easy. As Liebenau and Backhouse (1990) explain in their book *Understanding Information*: "*Numerous definitions have been proposed for the term 'information', and most of them serve well the narrow interests of those defining it.*" They then proceed to consider a number of definitions, drawn from various sources, before concluding: "*These definitions are all problematic*" and "*... information cannot exist independently of the receiving person who gives it meaning and somehow acts upon it. That action usually includes analysis or at least interpretation, and the differences between data and information must be preserved, at least in so far as information is data arranged in a meaningful way for some perceived purpose.*"

This last view suits our needs very well: "*... information is data arranged in a meaningful way for some perceived purpose*". Let us take it that a computer system holds *data* as suggested here and that any *information* that we (the receiving persons) may extract from this data is as a result of our analysis or interpretation of it in some meaningful way for some perceived purpose. This presupposes that we have to hand a set of interpretative rules, which were intended for this purpose, and which we apply to the data in order to extract the information. It is our application of these rules to the data that results in the intended information being revealed to us.

This view also helps us to understand how it is that computer systems are able to hold information in its multitude of different forms. Although the way in which the data is represented in a computer system is almost always that of a *binary* pattern, the forms that the information may take are effectively without limit, simply because there are so many different sets of interpretative rules that we can apply.

Binary Systems and Memory

That computer manufacturers normally choose to represent data in a two-state (or *binary*) form is an engineering convenience of the current technology. Two-state systems are easier to engineer and two-state logic simplifies some activities. Provided that we do not impose limits on the sets of interpretative rules that we permit, then a binary system is quite capable of representing almost any kind of information. We should perhaps now look a little more closely at how data is held in such binary systems.

In such a system, each data element is implemented using some physical device that can be in one of two stable states: in a memory chip, for example, a transistor switch may be on or off; in a communications line, a pulse may be present or absent at a particular place and at a particular time; on a magnetic disk, a magnetic domain may be magnetized to one polarity or to the other; and, on a compact disc, a pit may be present or not at a particular place. These are all examples of two-state or binary devices.

When we use such two-state devices to store data we normally consider a large number of them in some form of conceptual structure: perhaps we might visualize a very long line of several million transistor switches in a big box, for example. We might then call this a *memory*. We use a notation borrowed from mathematics to symbolize each element of the memory, that is, each two-state device. This notation uses the symbol "1" to represent a two-state device that is in the "on" state and the symbol "0" to represent a two-state device that is in the "off" state. We can now draw a diagram that symbolizes our memory (or at least, a small part of it) as an ordered sequence of 1s and 0s, as shown in Fig. 2.1.

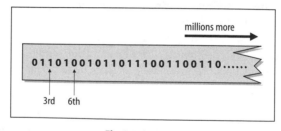

Fig. 2.1 Memory.

Each 1 and each 0 is a symbol for one particular two-state device in the structure and the value of 1 or 0 signifies the current state of that device. So, for example, the third device from the left in the sequence is "on" (signified by a "1") and the sixth device from the left is "off" (signified by a "0").

Although we can clearly observe the data as an ordered sequence of 1s and 0s, we are not able from this alone to determine the information that it may represent. To do that, we have to know the appropriate set of interpretative rules which we can then apply to some given part of the data sequence in order to extract the intended information.

Before we move on to consider various different sets of interpretative rules however, we should first look at some fundamental definitions and concepts that are associated with computer memory. Each of the two symbols "1" and "0", when representing a two-state device, is usually referred to as a *binary digit* or *bit*, the acronym being constructed from the initial letter of "binary" and the last two letters of "digit". We may thus observe that the ordered sequence in Fig. 2.1 above has 24 bits displayed, although there are millions more than that to the right of the diagram.

Addressing

We carefully specified on at least two occasions that this is an *ordered* sequence, implying that position is important, and this, in general, is clearly the case. It is often an ordered set of symbols that is required to convey information: an ordered set of characters conveys specific text; an ordered set of digits conveys specific numbers; an ordered set of instructions conveys a specific process. We therefore need a means by which we can identify position in this ordered sequence of millions of bits and thus access any part of that sequence, anywhere within it, at will. Conceptually, the simplest method would be for every bit in the sequence to be associated with its unique numeric position; for example, the third from the left, the sixth from the left, and so on, as we did above. In practical computer systems, however, the overheads of uniquely identifying every bit in the memory are not justified, so a compromise is made. A unique identifying number, known as the *address*, is associated with a group of eight bits in sequence. The group of eight bits is called a *byte* and the bytes are ordered from address 0 numerically upwards (shown from left to right in Fig. 2.2) to the highest address in the memory. In modern personal computers, it would not be unusual for this highest address in memory to be over 2000 million (or 2 Gbyte; see

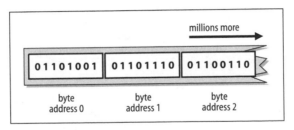

Fig. 2.2 Byte addressing.

Table 2.1 Units of memory.

● Nibble	= half a byte	= 4 bits
● Byte	= 1 byte	= 8 bits
● Word	= 2 bytes	= 16 bits
● Double word	= 4 bytes	= 32 bits
● Kilobyte	= 1024 bytes	= 2^{10} bytes
● Megabyte	= 1,048,576 bytes	= 2^{20} bytes
● Gigabyte	= 1,073,741,824 bytes	= 2^{30} bytes
● Terabyte	= 1,099,511,627,776 bytes	= 2^{40} bytes
● Petabyte	= 1,125,899,906,842,624 bytes	= 2^{50} bytes

Table 2.1). Our ordered sequence fragment can now be represented as the three bytes shown in Fig. 2.2.

Today the byte is used as the basic measure of memory size, although other terms are still often met: a *nibble* is half a byte = 4 bits; a *word* is 2 bytes = 16 bits; a *double word* is 4 bytes = 32 bits. As computer memory and disk sizes have become very much larger, so the byte has become a comparatively small unit, and various powers of two are now used to qualify it: a kilobyte is 2^{10} = 1024 bytes; a megabyte is 2^{20} = 1,048,576 bytes; a gigabyte is 2^{30} = 1,073,741,824 bytes; a terabyte is 2^{40} = 1,099,511,627,776 bytes; and a petabyte is 2^{50} = 1,125,899,906,842,624 bytes. This sequence of powers of 2 units continues further with exabyte, zettabyte and yottabyte. Traditionally, computing scientists have always based their memory units on powers of 2 rather than on powers of 10, though this is a matter of some contention within the standards community[1]. In *Data Powers of Ten* (Williams, 1996), the practical implications of some of these units are compared: a kilobyte is likened to a very short story, a megabyte to a small novel, 5 megabytes to the complete works of Shakespeare and a gigabyte to a truck filled with paper.

We can now move on to another very important idea. We can associate a particular set of interpretative rules with a particular sequence of byte addresses in the memory. This then tells us how the patterns of 1s and 0s at those addresses are to be interpreted in order to extract the information that the data held there is intended to represent[2]. It is important to note that these associations of rule sets with addresses

---

1   The issue is whether the prefixes kilo, mega, giga etc. should be raised to powers of two as traditionally implemented by the computing fraternity or to powers of ten as decreed by the General Conference of Weights and Measures for SI units. If they were to be changed to powers of ten, kilo would become 10^3 = 1000 and mega would become 10^6 = 1,000,000. See Williams (1996).

2   The association of a set of interpretative rules with a sequence of memory addresses is known as *typing*. In a *strongly typed* system, the computer programs will not only contain rules about the interpretation that is to be applied to data at given memory addresses, but will also contain rules that limit the ways in which that data may be manipulated to those appropriate to the interpretation.

are completely flexible; in general, in a computer system any associations can be made with any sequence of bytes, and these can be changed at any time.

There are, however, some standard interpretative rule sets which all computer systems share and we will start by considering the most commonly used of these: the interpretation of a binary data pattern as a decimal number.

Number Systems

Before we look at the interpretative rules for binary data patterns we should remind ourselves of the rules for decimal data patterns. In the representation of numbers generally, we use a notation that is positional. That is, the position of the digit in the pattern is significant and is used to determine the multiplying factor that is to be applied to that digit when calculating the number. In the Western decimal system, each digit in the pattern can range in value from 0 to 9 and the multiplying factor is always some power of 10 (hence the *decimal* system).

The particular power of 10 depends on the actual position of the digit relative to a *decimal point*. The powers of 10 start from 0 immediately to the left of the decimal point, and increase by one for each position we move to the left and decrease by one for each position we move to the right. When writing down whole numbers, we tend not to write down the decimal point itself, but assume it to be on the extreme right of the positive powers of 10 digit sequence. Hence we often write down "5729" rather than "5729.0". All of this, which is so cumbersome to explain, is second nature to us because we have learned the interpretative rules from childhood and can apply them without having to think. As an example of a whole number, we read the sequence "5729" as five thousand, seven hundred and twenty-nine. Analysing this according to the interpretative rules we see that it is made up of:

$$5 \times 10^3 + 7 \times 10^2 + 2 \times 10^1 + 9 \times 10^0$$

or, in terms of the expanded multiplying factors, as shown in Fig. 2.3:

$$5 \times 1000 + 7 \times 100 + 2 \times 10 + 9 \times 1$$

As we described above, the powers of 10 which form the multiplying factors, increase by one for every move of digit position to the left and decrease by one for every move of digit position to the right. The use of this style of interpretative rule set is not limited to decimal numbers. We can use the concept for any number system that we wish (see Table 2.2). The number of different digit symbols we wish to use (known as the *base*) determines the multiplying factor; apart from that, the same

10^4	10^3	10^2	10^1	10^0	10^{-1}	10^{-2}	10^{-3}
10 000	1000	100	10	1	1/10	1/100	1/1000
	5	7	2	9 . 0			

decimal point

Fig. 2.3 Rules for decimal numbers.

Table 2.2 Other number systems.

Binary	Base 2	0 and 1
Ternary	Base 3	0, 1 and 2
Octal	Base 8	0 to 7
Decimal	Base 10	0 to 9
Hexadecimal	Base 16	0 to 9 and a to f

rules of interpretation apply. In the case of the decimal system (base 10) we can see 10 digit symbols (0 to 9) and a multiplying factor of 10. We can have an *octal* system (base 8) which has 8 digit symbols (0 to 7) and a multiplying factor of 8; a *ternary* system (base 3) that has 3 digit symbols (0 to 2) and a multiplying factor of 3; or, even, a *binary* system (base 2) that has 2 digit symbols (0 and 1) and a multiplying factor of 2. We will later be looking at the *hexadecimal* system (base 16) that has 16 digit symbols (the numeric symbols 0 to 9 and the letter symbols A to F) and a multiplying factor of 16.

Binary Numbers

Returning now to the binary system, we note that each digit in the pattern can range in value from 0 to 1 and that the multiplying factor is always some power of 2 (hence the term "binary"). The particular power of 2 depends on the actual position of the digit relative to the *binary point* (compare this with the decimal point referred to above).

The powers of 2 start from 0 immediately to the left of the binary point, and increase by one for each position we move to the left and decrease by one for each position we move to the right. Again, for whole numbers, we tend not to show the binary point itself but assume it to be on the extreme right of the positive powers of 2 digit sequence (see Fig. 2.4). Now using the same form of interpretative rules as we did for the decimal system, we can see that the binary data shown in this figure (this is the same binary data that is given at byte address 0 in Fig. 2.2) can be interpreted thus:

$$0 \times 2^7 + 1 \times 2^6 + 1 \times 2^5 + 0 \times 2^4 + 1 \times 2^3 + 0 \times 2^2 + 0 \times 2^1 + 1 \times 2^0$$

which is equivalent, in terms of the expanded multiplying factors, to:

$$0 \times 128 + 1 \times 64 + 1 \times 32 + 0 \times 16 + 1 \times 8 + 0 \times 4 + 0 \times 2 + 1 \times 1$$

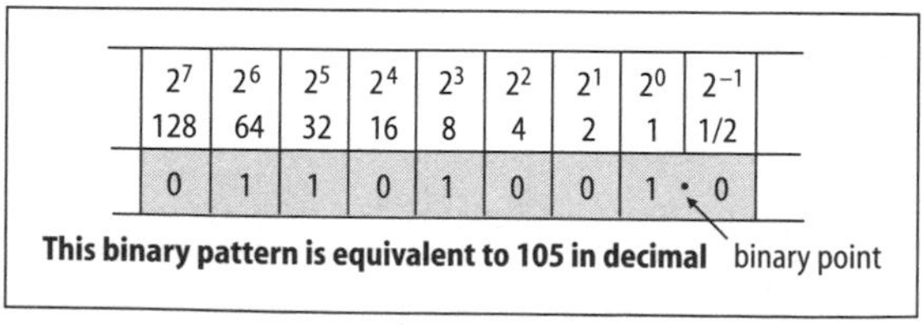

2^7	2^6	2^5	2^4	2^3	2^2	2^1	2^0	2^{-1}
128	64	32	16	8	4	2	1	1/2
0	1	1	0	1	0	0	1	0

This binary pattern is equivalent to 105 in decimal   binary point

Fig. 2.4 Rules for binary numbers.

and this adds up to 105. It is left for the reader to confirm that the data in the other two bytes in Fig. 2.2 can be interpreted, using this rule set, as the decimal numbers 110 and 102.

Taking the byte as the basic unit of memory, it is useful to determine the maximum and minimum decimal numbers that can be held using this interpretation. The pattern 00000000 clearly gives a value of 0 and the pattern 11111111 gives:

$$1 \times 2^7 + 1 \times 2^6 + 1 \times 2^5 + 1 \times 2^4 + 1 \times 2^3 + 1 \times 2^2 + 1 \times 2^1 + 1 \times 2^0$$

which is equivalent to:

$$1 \times 128 + 1 \times 64 + 1 \times 32 + 1 \times 16 + 1 \times 8 + 1 \times 4 + 1 \times 2 + 1 \times 1$$

and this is equal to 255. The range of whole numbers that can be represented in a single byte (eight bits) is therefore 0 to 255. This is often found to be inadequate for even the simplest of arithmetic processing tasks and two bytes (a word) taken together are more frequently used to represent whole numbers. However, this poses a potential problem for the analyst as we shall see. We can clearly implement a number in a word by using two bytes in succession as shown in Fig. 2.5.

However, we need to note that byte sequences are shown conventionally with their addresses increasing from left to right across the page (see Figs. 2.2 and 2.5). Contrast this with the convention that number sequences increase in value from right to left (see Fig. 2.4). The question now arises of how we should interpret a pair of bytes taken together as a single number. The most obvious way is to consider the two bytes as a continuous sequence of binary digits as they appear in Fig. 2.5. The binary point is assumed to be to the right of the byte at address 57. As before, we have increasing powers of 2 as we move to the left through byte 57 and, at the byte boundary with byte address 56, we simply carry on. So, the leftmost bit of byte address 57 is 2^7 and the rightmost bit of byte address 56 continues on as 2^8. Using the rules that we established above, we then have the following interpretation for byte address 57:

$$0 \times 128 + 1 \times 64 + 1 \times 32 + 0 \times 16 + 1 \times 8 + 1 \times 4 + 1 \times 2 + 0 \times 1$$

together with this for byte address 56:

$$0 \times 32768 + 1 \times 16384 + 1 \times 8192 + 0 \times 4096$$
$$+ 1 \times 2048 + 0 \times 1024 + 0 \times 512 + 1 \times 256$$

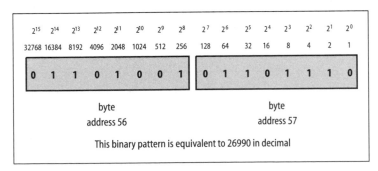

Fig. 2.5 A number in a word.

The decimal number interpretation of the two bytes taken together in this way is the total of all the individual digit values and is equal to the value 26990.

The range of numbers for the two bytes taken together can now readily be established as 00000000 00000000 to 11111111 11111111. The first pattern clearly gives 0 and the pattern 11111111 11111111 gives 65535. The range of whole numbers using this system is therefore 0 to 65535 and this is left for the reader to confirm. It is evident that we could use a similar argument to take more than two bytes together as a single number; in fact, four bytes (a double word) are often used where greater precision is required.

Little Endian and Big Endian Formats

The approach adopted here of taking the two bytes as a continuous sequence of binary digits may seem eminently sensible. However, there is an opposing argument that claims that the two bytes should be taken together the other way round. The lower powers of 2, it is claimed, should be in the lower valued byte address and the higher powers of 2 should be in the higher valued byte address. This approach is shown in Fig. 2.6 and is known as *little endian* format as opposed to the first scheme that we considered, which is known as *big endian* format[3].

Here we see that the digit multipliers in byte address 56 now range from 2^0 to 2^7 and those in byte address 57 now range from 2^8 to 2^{15}. Using this little endian format with the same binary values in the two bytes, we see that from byte address 56 we have:

$$0 \times 128 + 1 \times 64 + 1 \times 32 + 0 \times 16 + 1 \times 8 + 0 \times 4 + 0 \times 2 + 1 \times 1$$

and from byte address 57 we have:

$$0 \times 32768 + 1 \times 16384 + 1 \times 8192 + 0 \times 4096$$
$$+ 1 \times 2048 + 1 \times 1024 + 1 \times 512 + 0 \times 256$$

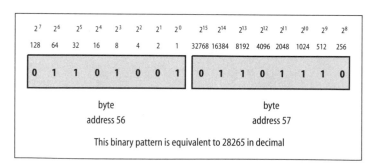

Fig. 2.6 Little endian format.

---

3   The notion of big endian and little endian comes from a story in *Gulliver's Travels* by Jonathan Swift. In this story the "big endians" were those who broke their breakfast egg from the big end and the "little endians" were those who broke theirs from the little end. The big endians were outlawed by the emperor and many were put to death for their heresy!

The decimal number interpretation of these same two bytes taken together in this little endian format is 28265, compared with the 26990 which we obtained using the big endian format.

The problem for the forensic computing analyst is clear. There is nothing to indicate, within a pair of bytes that are to be interpreted as a single decimal number, whether they should be analyzed using little endian or big endian format. It is very important that this issue be correctly determined by the analyst, perhaps from the surrounding context within which the number resides or perhaps from a knowledge of the computer program that was used to read or write the binary data. It is known, for example, that the Intel 80x86 family of processors (including the Pentium) use little endian format when reading or writing two-byte and four-byte numbers and that the Motorola processors use big endian format for the same purpose in their 68000 family[4]. Application software, on the other hand, may write out information in little endian or big endian or in any other formats that the programmer may choose.

In order to examine this matter a little more closely, it is appropriate at this time to consider another important number system: hexadecimal. We will return to our examination of decimal numbers after this next section.

Hexadecimal Numbers

As we mentioned earlier, the hexadecimal number system uses base 16. It therefore has 16 digit symbols: the numeric symbols 0 to 9 and the letter symbols A to F and it has a multiplying factor of 16.

Its real value to the analyst is that it provides a much more compact and convenient means of listing and interpreting binary sequences. It is more compact because every four binary digits may be replaced by a single hexadecimal digit and it is more convenient because translation between binary and hexadecimal can be done (with a little practice) quickly and easily by inspection. At Table 2.3 we have shown the binary equivalent for each of the 16 hexadecimal digits and we note that we need exactly four binary digits to give each one a unique value. This, of course, should not surprise us, since 2^4 is 16. We might also note that the decimal equivalent of each 4 bit binary sequence is the actual value (0, 1, 2, 3 etc.) for the hexadecimal symbols 0 to 9, and the values 10, 11, 12, 13, 14 and 15 for the hexadecimal symbols A, B, C, D, E and F respectively.

Table 2.3 Hexadecimal code table.

Hex	Binary	Hex	Binary	Hex	Binary	Hex	Binary
0	0000	4	0100	8	1000	C	1100
1	0001	5	0101	9	1001	D	1101
2	0010	6	0110	A	1010	E	1110
3	0011	7	0111	B	1011	F	1111

---

4   As reported on page 61 of Messmer (2002).

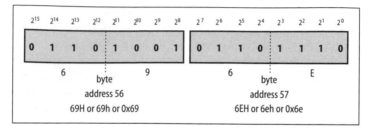

Fig. 2.7 Hexadecimal representation.

We note from this that each 4 bit half byte (that is, each nibble), can be represented by exactly one hexadecimal digit and a full byte can therefore be exactly represented by two hexadecimal digits.

Returning again to the two bytes that we were examining in Figs. 2.5 and 2.6 above, we can see, at Fig. 2.7 how the values in these two bytes can equally well be represented by the four hexadecimal digits: 69H and 6EH. Two digits are used for the value of the byte at address 56 and two digits for the value of the byte at address 57 and, in each case, a trailing "H" has been added to signify that these sequences are to be interpreted as hexadecimal, rather than decimal. You may note from the figure that either upper or lower case can be used both for the letter symbols and for the "H" marker. Alternatively, 0x may be put in front of the number, thus: 0x69 and 0x6e. Throughout the book, we use a variety of forms for representing hexadecimal numbers, in line with the screen shots from different software packages.

Prior to becoming practised, the simplest means of translation is to look up the values in Table 2.3. From this we can easily see that "6" is "0110" and "E" is "1110", and so 6EH is 01101110. We can also easily see the 4 to 1 reduction in size in going from binary to hexadecimal.

More Little Endian

Now that we have at least a nodding acquaintance with hexadecimal, we can more easily consider some of the issues surrounding the Intel processors, application programmers and little endian. What we, as analysts, have to examine are often sequences of binary (or more likely hexadecimal) digits that have been extracted from memory or from disk. In interpreting these, we need to determine in what order they should be examined, and that order will depend upon the type of processor and the program that wrote them.

Consider, for example, that a program is designed to write out to disk a sequence of four bytes that have been produced internally. Let us say that these four bytes are (in hexadecimal) "FB 18 7A 35". The programmer, when designing the program, may decide that the Intel processor is to write out the sequence of four bytes, one byte at a time, as four separate bytes. The result written out would be exactly as the sequence is held internally:

FB 18 7A 35

This is because little endian is not an issue at the level of the byte. Consider, now, that the programmer, when designing the program, decided that the Intel processor is to write out the sequence of four bytes as two *words*. To do this, the programmer would use different instruction codes in this new program compared with the previous program. Each word (of two bytes) would be written out by the Intel processor in little endian format, reversing the order of each pair. The sequence on the disk would then become:

18 FB 35 7A

Finally, consider that the programmer, when designing the program, decided that the Intel processor is to write out the sequence of four bytes as a *double word*. Again, the programmer would use different instruction codes, and this time the sequence would be written out as:

35 7A 18 FB

Here, the order of all four bytes has been reversed. This is not the end. The processor does the same with, for example, 8 byte date and time sequences, and we must know enough to re-order such sequences before we attempt to interpret them.

What becomes very clear from this is that as analysts we must know the context that is associated with any given binary sequence if we are to interpret the sequence correctly.

A Simple Rule of Thumb for Numbers in Words

If the format is little endian, take the value of the left-hand byte and add to it 256 times the value of the right hand byte. Decimal value = LH + (256 × RH).

If the format is big endian, take the value of the left hand byte times 256 and add to it the value of the right hand byte. Decimal value = (LH × 256) + RH.

Signed Numbers

So far we have only considered the representation of positive whole numbers. Negative numbers are also required and these can be represented by taking out of use one of the digit positions and re-employing it as a *sign bit*. This means, of course, that it cannot then be used as part of the number itself. The digit position that is chosen is always the leftmost bit in the sequence; in the case of a single byte, this is the 2^7 digit position. If this particular bit is set to 1, by definition, the number is negative; if it is set to 0, by definition the number is positive, as indicated in Fig. 2.8. In this figure we have shown two bytes, which, unlike previous figures, are not to be taken together or considered as a single number. Instead, for this example, each byte is to be interpreted as a separate signed number. The left-hand byte represents +1 and the right-hand byte represents −1.

The data pattern in the right-hand byte may not appear as expected for a representation of −1 and this may need some explanation. In order to ensure that the mathematics of positive and negative numbers works systematically we have to have a representation where the binary number +1 when added to the binary number −1

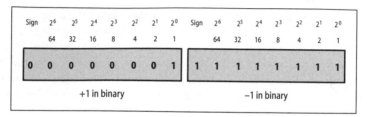

Fig. 2.8 Two signed numbers.

gives us the binary number 0. In a single byte, the binary number +1 is represented as expected, and as shown in Fig. 2.8, by:

Sign 2^6 2^5 2^4 2^3 2^2 2^1 2^0

0   0   0   0   0   0   0   1   +1 in binary

The number is positive because the sign bit is 0 and it is of value 1 because only the 2^0 column is set. Now we have agreed that negative numbers by definition will have the sign bit set, so the most obvious pattern for –1 might simply be:

Sign 2^6 2^5 2^4 2^3 2^2 2^1 2^0

1   0   0   0   0   0   0   1   a suggestion for –1 in binary

This number is negative because the sign bit is set to 1 and it would seem to be of value 1 because only the 2^0 column is set. Hence, it is a possible –1. However, when we add the +1 and the suggested –1 patterns together using the rules[5] of binary addition, the result is:

Sign 2^6 2^5 2^4 2^3 2^2 2^1 2^0

0   0   0   0   0   0   0   1   +1 in binary

1   0   0   0   0   0   0   1   a suggestion for –1 in binary

_____

1   0   0   0   0   0   1   0

which, according to our same rules appears to be –2: a negative number because the sign bit is set to 1 and of value 2 because the 2^1 column is set. This clearly does not work. We now need to ask ourselves what pattern, when added to +1, would result in 0? There is only one such pattern, and it is as shown below. It works because 1 + 1 results in 0 with a 1 carried into the next left-hand column. We see that this sequence causes a carry to occur from column to column until the last (2^7) column is reached, whereupon the sign bit becomes a 0 and the final carry "falls off the end" or *overflows*. This condition will be detected by most arithmetic units and in the case of signed binary arithmetic would be classed as an acceptable result.

_____

5   In binary addition: 0 + 0 = 0; 0 + 1 = 1; 1 + 0 = 1; and 1 + 1 = 0 carry 1 to the next digit
     on the left.

Sign	2^6	2^5	2^4	2^3	2^2	2^1	2^0	
0	0	0	0	0	0	0	1	+1 in binary
1	1	1	1	1	1	1	1	a pattern that sums to zero (the real −1)
0	0	0	0	0	0	0	0	

This structure for negative numbers is in what is known as *two's complement* form. As an analyst, it can be very useful to know how to determine the value of a negative binary number that is held in two's complement form, since it is not easy to see by inspection.

A Simple Rule of Thumb for Negative Numbers

The rule is very simple. First write down the negative binary number, and then, on the next line, we write down the inverted pattern with all the 0 digits replaced by 1s and all the 1 digits replaced by 0s. Finally, to this result, we add the value of +1 in binary. This sum is the equivalent positive number for the given negative number. As an example, consider the value 1110 1101 as a signed number. It is clearly negative since the 2^7 position is 1. We apply the rules as follows:

Sign	2^6	2^5	2^4	2^3	2^2	2^1	2^0	
1	1	1	0	1	1	0	1	write down the negative number in binary
0	0	0	1	0	0	1	0	change all the 1s to 0s and all the 0s to 1s
0	0	0	0	0	0	0	1	add 1 in binary
0	0	0	1	0	0	1	1	the result is $16+2+1=19$

The value 1110 1101 is therefore equivalent to −19. It is interesting to note that this process works both ways. We can take the positive number +19 and determine the pattern for −19 by following exactly the same rules, as follows:

Sign	2^6	2^5	2^4	2^3	2^2	2^1	2^0	
0	0	0	1	0	0	1	1	write down the positive number 19 in binary
1	1	1	0	1	1	0	0	change all the 1s to 0s and all the 0s to 1s
0	0	0	0	0	0	0	1	add 1 in binary
1	1	1	0	1	1	0	1	and the result is what we started with

Sample Negative Number in a Word

When we are looking at signed numbers in hexadecimal (and we certainly have to do that when we are examining NTFS MFT records) we have to remember that they are probably stored in little endian and that they are sometimes negative. As an example consider examining the two-byte hexadecimal sequence "74 FE", which we are told is a signed integer in little endian word format. What is its value?

We start by noting that it is a little endian word, so the pattern needs to be re-ordered to "FE 74". Next we note that the leading hexadecimal digit is "F", which is 1111, so the most significant bit of the word is a 1, indicating that the result is a negative number. Now we write down the binary for this and follow the rules we described above[6]

Sign	2^{14}	2^{13}	2^{12}	2^{11}	2^{10}	2^9	2^8	2^7	2^6	2^5	2^4	2^3	2^2	2^1	2^0	
1	1	1	1	1	1	1	0	0	1	1	1	0	1	0	0	write down the number FE 74 in binary
0	0	0	0	0	0	0	1	1	0	0	0	1	0	1	1	change all the 1s to 0s and all the 0s to 1s
0	0	0	0	0	0	0	0	0	0	0	0	0	0	0	1	add 1 in binary
0	0	0	0	0	0	0	1	1	0	0	0	1	1	0	0	the result is 256 + 128 + 8 + 4 = 396

The value FE 74 is therefore equivalent to –396.

Range of Signed Numbers

The range of *signed numbers* that can be represented in a single byte (the range we considered previously was that of *unsigned numbers*) can now be seen to be from:

Sign	2^6	2^5	2^4	2^3	2^2	2^1	2^0	
0	1	1	1	1	1	1	1	+127, the largest positive integer, to
1	0	0	0	0	0	0	0	–128, the largest negative integer

that is, from +127 (sign bit is zero) to –128 (sign bit is 1) and the range of signed integers for two bytes can just as readily be calculated as +32,767 to –32,768. This is an exercise left for the reader. At Table 2.4 we show a summary of the ranges for signed and unsigned integers in one and two bytes.

Table 2.4 Signed and unsigned integer ranges.

● Range of unsigned integers in one byte	0 to 255
● Range of signed integers in one byte	+127 to –128
● Range of unsigned integers in two bytes	0 to 65,535
● Range of signed integers in two bytes	+32,767 to –32,768

---

6   It is possible to perform these calculations in hexadecimal without converting first to binary.

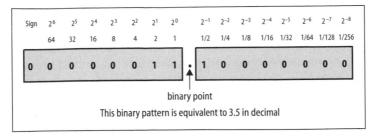

Fig. 2.9 Mixed numbers.

Fractions and Mixed Numbers

So far we have only looked at the representation of whole numbers or *integers* and the form of representation that we have been considering is generally known as *fixed point*. Although we will only touch on this here, fixed point representation can be used for fractions and mixed numbers as well simply by considering the binary point to be at some position other than at the extreme right-hand side of the digit sequence. So, for example, in Fig. 2.9 the binary point is considered to be in between the two bytes that are to be taken together as a single number.

As a result, the rightmost digit of the left-hand byte has a multiplying factor of 2^0 (which is 1) and the leftmost digit of the right-hand byte has a multiplying factor of 2^{-1} (which is ½). With all that has gone before we can readily see that the left-hand byte may be interpreted as:

$$0 \times \text{Sign} + 0 \times 64 + 0 \times 32 + 0 \times 16 + 0 \times 8 + 0 \times 4 + 1 \times 2 + 1 \times 1$$

and the right-hand byte may be interpreted, using vulgar fractions, as:

$$1 \times 1/2 + 0 \times 1/4 + 0 \times 1/8 + 0 \times 1/16 + 0 \times 1/32 + 0 \times 1/64 + 0 \times 1/128 + 0 \times 1/256$$

In decimal, the right-hand byte becomes:

$$1 \times 0.5 + 0 \times 0.25 + 0 \times 0.125 + 0 \times 0.0625 + 0 \times 0.03125$$
$$+ 0 \times 0.015625 + 0 \times 0.0078125 + 0 \times 0.00390625$$

and, by adding all the digits from this pair of bytes, we see that this represents the number +3½ or +3.5.

As an exercise, attempt the interpretation of the two bytes in Fig. 2.7 as a mixed decimal number with the binary point assumed to be between byte address 56 and byte address 57. The result, you will find, is +105.4296875. A simpler way of calculating the mixed number value than adding up all the fractional parts is to take the whole number value and *scale* it. In decimal arithmetic, dividing the number by ten is equivalent to shifting the decimal point one position left. Similarly, in binary arithmetic, dividing the number by two is equivalent to shifting the binary point one position left. Using big endian interpretation, the whole number value for Fig. 2.7 was found to be 26,990. If we wish the binary point to be between the two bytes, this is equivalent to shifting the binary point 8 positions to the left (the width of a byte) which is also equivalent to dividing the number by $2^8 = 256$. The number 26,990 divided by 256 does indeed result in +105.4296875.

Floating Point

All the forms of number representation that we have so far considered belong to the family of *fixed point* numbers. Another common form of number representation is that of *floating point*. In this format, several bytes are used to represent a number. The basis for this representation is the so-called *scientific notation* (also known as *exponential notation*). In this notation, numbers are represented (on paper) in a form such as $+2.5 \times 10^{+2}$, which is equivalent to $+2.5 \times 100 = +250.0$. The signed mixed number (+2.5), which is limited by *normalization* to be greater than 1.0 and less than 10.0, is known as the *mantissa* or *significand*, and the signed power of 10 (+2) is known as the *exponent* or *characteristic*. In order to represent a number in this format, the mantissa has to be adjusted until there is just one digit before the decimal point and the remaining digits are after it (normalization). To maintain the overall value of the number, the exponent then has to be increased or decreased accordingly. It is this adjustment of the position of the decimal point that results in the term "floating point", as opposed to our earlier considerations of fixed point format.

In representing floating point numbers in a binary system, one sequence of bits is used for the exponent and another sequence of bits is used for the mantissa. The base to which the exponent is raised is 2 in the binary system, as opposed to 10 in the decimal system. Both the mantissa and the exponent may have positive or negative values so the problem of representing negative numbers in binary patterns arises in both cases. In the case of the mantissa, a separate sign bit is used to indicate positive or negative values. However, it is important to note that a 2's complement format is not used for the rest of the mantissa, which is always left as a positive number (unlike the fixed point representation that we considered above). For the sign of the exponent, a so-called *bias* is used. In this form of representation, a fixed value (the bias) is added to the exponent value prior to writing the data and subtracted from the value immediately after reading the data. By this means, the data placed in the exponent field is always kept positive. For example, with a bias of 127 and an exponent value of 42, the value placed in the exponent field would be $127 + 42 = 169$. On reading the exponent field of 169, the bias would immediately be subtracted giving $169 - 127 = 42$. This results, of course, in the original exponent value. For a negative exponent value of, say, –5, the value placed in the exponent field would be $127 + -5 = 122$ and the exponent read out from the field would be $122 - 127 = -5$. In this way, all values stored in the exponent field are positive.

Complications arise because there are several different formats. Most systems comply with the IEEE formats which define three floating point types: short real (1 bit for the sign of the mantissa, 8 bits for the exponent, and 23 bits for the mantissa itself), long real (1 bit for the sign of the mantissa, 11 bits for the exponent, and 52 bits for the mantissa itself) and temporary real (1 bit for the sign of the mantissa, 15 bits for the exponent, and 64 bits for the mantissa itself)[7]. In addition, Microsoft have traditionally used their own (different) floating point formats in their BASIC

---

7   ANSI/IEEE Standard 754-1985 Standard for Binary Floating Point Arithmetic.

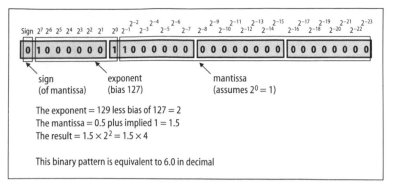

Fig. 2.10 Floating point.

programming interpreters. Figure 2.10 shows the format for the IEEE short real representation.

The sign bit refers to the mantissa and therefore, in this case, indicates a positive number. The exponent is not signed but has a 127 bias as explained above. This means that the value of the exponent is the binary value of the data held in the exponent field with the value of 127 subtracted from it. The binary value of the data in the exponent field is clearly: $1 \times 2^7 + 1 \times 2^0 = 128 + 1 = 129$. The value of the exponent is therefore $129 - 127 = 2$. The binary value of the mantissa field is clearly $1 \times 2^{-1} = 0.5$. However, with this format, by definition and as indicated in the diagram, the value of the mantissa always has an implied $2^0 = 1$ added to it (note that it starts at 2^{-1} in the diagram). As a result, the actual value of the mantissa is $0.5 + 1 = 1.5$. The overall decimal value of the number is thus: $1.5 \times 2^2 = 1.5 \times 4 = 6.0$.

As we have seen above, the IEEE standard for floating point arithmetic requires, for single precision (short real) floating point numbers, a 32 bit word, which may be represented as shown below:

S EEEEEEE FFFFFFFFFFFFFFFFFFFFFFF

In this, the leading bit position is the sign bit, "S", the next eight bits are the exponent bits, "E", and the final 23 bits are the mantissa or fractional part, "F". Special cases for the value of the floating point number, "V", are then given in the IEEE standard by the rules shown in Table 2.5.

Most modern computer systems have a mathematical co-processor which implements floating point arithmetic in the IEEE formats (see Table 2.6) and uses these floating point representations for storing and manipulating so-called *real* numbers.

Binary Coded Decimal

Another number format which is often used is that of *binary coded decimal*, or BCD. In this interpretation, the binary value of each byte in a sequence of bytes represents directly a single decimal digit. So the decimal number 105 would be represented in BCD by the three bytes shown in Fig. 2.11. The problem with this approach is that it is very wasteful of storage. Each byte is capable of holding 256 different values (0 to

Table 2.5 Rules and examples of IEEE single precision format.

- If E = 255 and F is not zero, then V = "Not a Number" (NaN)
  0 11111111 00000100000000000000000 = NaN
  1 11111111 00100010001001010101010 = NaN
- If E = 255 and F is zero and S is 1, then V = −Infinity
  1 11111111 00000000000000000000000 = −Infinity
- If E = 255 and F is zero and S is 0, then V = +Infinity
  0 11111111 00000000000000000000000 = +Infinity
- If E = 0 and F is zero and S is 1, then V = −0
  1 00000000 00000000000000000000000 = −0
- If E = 0 and F is zero and S is 0, then V = +0
  0 00000000 00000000000000000000000 = +0
- If 0 < E < 255 then V is a normalized number (implied leading 1.0)
  0 10000000 00000000000000000000000 = $+1 \times 2^{(128-127)} \times 1.0 = 2$
  0 10000001 10100000000000000000000 = $+1 \times 2^{(129-127)} \times 1.101 = 6.5$
  1 10000001 10100000000000000000000 = $-1 \times 2^{(129-127)} \times 1.101 = -6.5$
  0 00000001 00000000000000000000000 = $+1 \times 2^{(1-127)} \times 1.0 = 2^{(-126)}$
- If E = 0 and F is not zero then V is an "unnormalized" number (no leading 1.0)
  0 00000000 10000000000000000000000 = $+1 \times 2^{(-126)} \times 0.1 = 2^{(-127)}$

Table 2.6 IEEE floating point formats.

● Short real	4 bytes	1 sign, 8 exponent, 23 mantissa
● Long real	8 bytes	1 sign, 11 exponent, 52 mantissa
● Temporary real	10 bytes	1 sign, 15 exponent, 64 mantissa

255) and this form of BCD only uses 10 different values (the digits 0 to 9). A more efficient use is known as *packed BCD* where each decimal digit is held in a nibble (4 bits) instead of a byte. A byte in this representation can therefore hold two decimal digits, as shown in Fig. 2.12.

All that has been done here is that the value 00000001 from the first byte of Fig. 2.11 has been reduced to a nibble of value 0001 and placed in the first nibble of the first byte of Fig. 2.12. The value 00000000 from the second byte of Fig. 2.11 has been

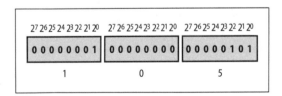

Fig. 2.11 Binary coded decimal.

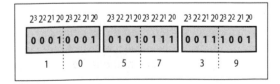

Fig. 2.12 Packed binary coded decimal.

reduced to a nibble of value 0000 and placed in the second nibble of the first byte of Fig. 2.12. The value 00000101 of the third byte of Fig. 2.11 has been reduced to a nibble of value 0101 and placed in the first nibble of the second byte of Fig. 2.12. All that has been lost in each case are leading zeros, which do not contribute to the value of the digit. What was in three bytes has now been *packed* into the three nibbles, leaving room for another three digits to be represented (I have arbitrarily chosen "7", "3" and "9" in the figure). Figure 2.12 therefore represents the decimal number 105,739 held in three successive bytes in packed BCD form.

Characters

After numbers, the next most obvious sets of interpretative rules are those for characters. By "character" we mean a single symbol that is to be printed on a printer or displayed on a visual display unit and which includes within the set of all characters, the letters of the alphabet, both upper and lower case, and the digits 0 to 9. In most binary representations, a single character is represented by the data pattern in a single byte. Since a byte can hold 256 different patterns (recall that the range of numbers in a byte is 0 to 255) then up to 256 different characters can be defined.

American Standard Code for Information Interchange

Any character we wish could be associated with any of the 256 binary patterns. So, for example, we could define quite arbitrarily that the character "A" be represented by "00001000" and the character "B" be represented by "00001001" and so forth. In practice, the association between a particular character and particular binary pattern has to be standardized so that, for example, printers and display units will operate compatibly between different systems. The most common set of associations is the American Standard Code for Information Interchange, or *ASCII* as it is universally known. The ASCII code only actually defines characters for the first 128 binary values (0 to 127), and of these the first 32 are used as non-printing *control characters* originally intended for controlling data communications equipment and computer printers and displays. IBM introduced for their personal computer (PC), an *extended ASCII* code which is also in common use, as is the *Windows ANSI* code, which is used in Microsoft Windows. In addition to the original ASCII meanings, these codes each assign (typically different) particular character symbols to all those binary values in the range 128 to 255. These two sets of extended ASCII character codes are given at Appendix 1.

At Fig. 2.13, we have shown the three bytes we started with at Fig. 2.2, interpreted now as three ASCII characters in sequence. The result of this interpretation is the three letter sequence "inf". Clearly, given the page layout and punctuation characters that are available in ASCII, this approach can be used for representing arbitrarily long text documents. A sequence of characters such as this is often known as a *string*. In many systems, the end of a text string is marked by a binary all zeros byte (ASCII code 0) and this is often referred to as an *ASCIIZ string*.

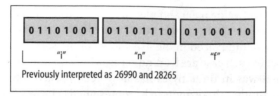

Fig. 2.13 ASCII characters.

Although ASCII code is certainly the most widely used representation for characters, one other is still sometimes met with, particularly on IBM mainframes. This is known as extended binary coded decimal interchange code or *EBCDIC*. In addition, many personal information managers and electronic organizers use their own particular modified versions of ASCII, which are often not published. An analyst will need to know these when looking at internal memory.

Universal Character Set, Unicode and UTF-8

From the late 1980s onwards, work has been carried out by two independent organizations to try to create a single unified character set that would embrace all possible languages and dialects. The *Unicode Project*[8] was established by a consortium of manufacturers, mainly concerned with the development of multilingual software, and the *ISO 10646 Project* was set up by the International Organization for Standardization (ISO)[9]. Fortunately, in the early 1990s, members of the two project teams commenced working together on creating a single code table, and the two standards are now compatible.

The *Universal Character Set* (*UCS*), defined by ISO 10646, is a superset of all other character set standards. It contains those characters that are required to represent practically all known languages. It was originally defined as a 31 bit character set and sub-sets within it which differ only in the least significant 16 bits are known as planes. The most commonly used characters have been placed into what is called the *Basic Multilingual Plane* (*BMP*) or Plane 0, and, within that plane, the UCS characters U+0000[10] to U+007F are identical to those of ASCII. The value U+005A, for example, refers to the character "Z".

The encodings UCS-2 and UCS-4 refer to code sequences of 2 and 4 bytes respectively. Unless otherwise stated, such sequences are big endian in order, with the most significant byte coming first. ASCII characters can be converted to UCS-2 encoding simply by inserting a 00H byte before the ASCII byte and can be converted to UCS-4 encoding simply by inserting three 00H bytes before the ASCII byte.

---

8 See http://www.unicode.org/

9 See http://www.iso.org/iso/en/ISOnline.frontpage

10 UCS characters in plane 0 are shown as "U+" followed by the two-byte (16 bit) hexadecimal value of the character code

The original Unicode is, in effect UCS-2 encoding, and this is what we will find in use when we consider, in a later section, the issue of long file names in Microsoft Windows. However, UCS-2 is not a suitable encoding system for Unicode when it is used in Unix systems. For this reason, other encoding systems were devised, and the most prominent of these is the *Unicode* (some say *UCS*) *Transformation Format-8* (*UTF-8*). This uses a variable number of bytes, depending upon the character. Characters in the range U+0000 to U+007F are simply encoded as single bytes in the range 00H to 7FH, exactly as for ASCII. Characters greater than U+007F are encoded as a sequence of two or more bytes, with the first byte indicating how many more bytes follow in the sequence.

UTF-16 provides what is in effect a 21 bit character set by reserving certain 16 bit codes as the first word of a *surrogate pair*. The presence of such a 16 bit word signals that a second 16 bit word follows, and this combined encoding then represents the character. Clearly, this technique extends the range of characters that can be represented.

It has become customary, particularly in Microsoft Windows systems, to specify whether the Unicode bytes are to be read in little endian or big endian order by starting the file with a *Byte Order Mark* (*BOM*). This is the sequence FEFFH, which, when seen in this order, indicates big endian interpretation. When seen as FFFEH it indicates little endian interpretation. For a good explanation of all of these issues, see Kuhn (2005).

Computer Programs

There is one more standard form of interpretative rule set which we need to mention before leaving this section. That is the interpretation of binary byte sequences as a program of instructions to the computer. Because of the complexity of this topic, however, detailed discussion is best left until we have considered the way in which a computer operates. Suffice to say here that the binary patterns in a sequence of bytes may be interpreted by the processor as an ordered sequence of operations that it must perform. There are therefore sets of interpretative rules that the processor follows to interpret the bit patterns as instructions to itself. We will consider this further in a later chapter.

Records and Files

We have now looked at a number of different interpretations for the eight bit binary patterns that can be held in one, two, three or four bytes (see Table 2.7).

The interpretations for one, two, three and four bytes that we have looked at are by no means exhaustive, even for the very limited set of interpretative rules that we have considered. Clearly, for example, we could have a mixed number or a fraction in a single byte and we could have a fixed point whole number in four or even eight bytes. As we have also seen, we can have a sequence of bytes of arbitrary length to represent a string of characters of arbitrary length.

Table 2.7 Some possible interpretations.

● One byte	One fixed point unsigned whole number (0 to 255)
	One fixed point signed whole number (+127 to –128)
	One ASCII character
● Two bytes	One fixed point unsigned whole number (0 to 65535)
	One fixed point signed whole number (+32767 to –32768)
	One fixed point mixed number or fraction
	Four hexadecimal digits
● Three bytes	Three BCD digits
	Six packed BCD digits
	Three ASCII characters
● Four bytes	One IEEE "short real" floating point number

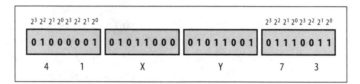

Fig. 2.14 Military vehicle registration record.

The byte is often (though not always) used as the fundamental unit for making more useful structures such as *records* and *files*. A record is a sequence of bytes, which typically will have different sets of interpretative rules associated with different parts of the byte sequence. Say, for example, we require to hold a military vehicle registration number in a record. Such registration numbers are made up of a two-digit decimal number followed by two letters followed again by another two-digit decimal number, thus: 41 XY 73. We could choose to define a military vehicle registration record in four bytes as follows. The first two-digit decimal number is held as packed BCD in the first byte; then there are two ASCII character bytes, and finally the second two-digit decimal number is again held as packed BCD in the fourth byte, as shown in Fig. 2.14.

Our definition above defines the interpretative rules for both the construction and the interpretation of our military vehicle registration record. In order to make "sense" of these four bytes, the analyst must know, or be able to deduce, the interpretative rules for this particular record. Clearly, there is no limit to the different types of record that are possible nor to the complexity of any given record structure. If the wrong[11] interpretation is not to be made, it is essential that the analyst is able to prove that the interpretative set of rules applied to the four bytes is that intended by the originator for that record structure.

A sequence of records may be called a *file*. The records in the file may all be of the same type, or they may be of a variety of types; they may be very complex or they may be as simple as a single byte each. Again, there is no limit on the different types of file

---

11 By "wrong" here we mean "not that intended" by the originator of the record.

possible. A file is the basic element that is normally stored in a *file system*. In most file systems the file is given a name and often a type description. So, for example, in the MS-DOS[12] file system, a file is given a file name of up to eight characters and a file type of up to three characters. When written down, it is normal practice to show the file name separated from the file type by a period thus: TEST.TXT signifies a file of file name "TEST" and of file type "TXT".

File Types and Signatures

File types may be used to signify the types of record that are held in the file. This is useful to the analyst as a starting point for deducing the appropriate set of interpretative rules for the file. Some software packages might use this file type to confirm initially that a suitable file is being processed, but this is never a sufficient test and further checks are invariably made of the actual data. There is no guarantee that any particular system will conform to the file typing practice and, indeed, a conscious attempt to deceive subsequent analysis may have been made by deliberately misusing a particular known file type. In addition, some files may have a sequence of bytes at the beginning of the file that specifically indicate the type of file. This is known as the *file signature* or *magic number* (see later section). Although this too can be deliberately changed to hinder recognition by the analyst, it is less likely to be done, since the associated application software would then be unable to recognize the file until the correct signature had been restored. At Appendix 2 we have listed some of the more common file signatures.

Use of Hexadecimal Listings

One of the simplest and most common forms of file is that of the *plain text file*. In this, all the records are single bytes and each byte represents one ASCII character. Such files are sometimes called *ASCII files* or *text files* and they are often signified by a file type of "TXT". Even with something as simple as this there are variations: the end of each line of text in the file may be indicated by the two byte values 0DH followed by 0AH, which represent the characters "carriage return" and "line feed" respectively, or it may be indicated by the single byte 0AH, or it may be indicated by the single byte 0DH. All three approaches are in common use, but few application software packages recognize all three. Figure 2.15 shows an example of an ASCII text file (TEST.TXT) in the form of a so-called *hexadecimal listing*. This form of listing is very useful to the analyst and it is displayed here by means of a shareware program called Gander for Windows produced by Dave Lord in 1991. This uses lower-case letters for hexadecimal values and, to make the point that both cases are equally acceptable, we use lower case in the rest of this section when referring to the figures.

---

12 Microsoft Disk Operating System.

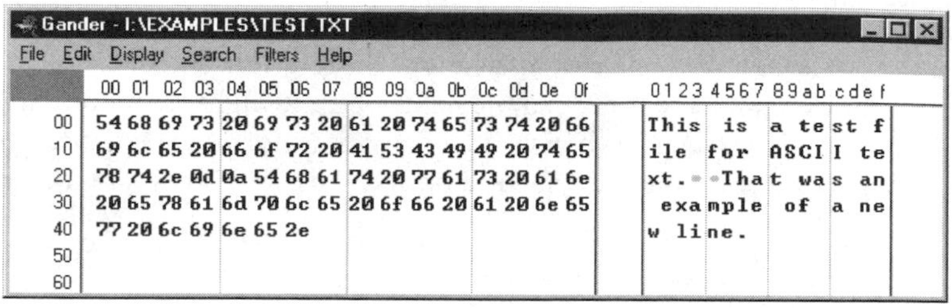

Fig. 2.15 Hexadecimal listing of TEST.TXT.

The listing of Fig. 2.15 shows the actual byte values in the file: in hexadecimal number form in the left-hand panel and in ASCII character form in the right-hand panel. If we examine the left-hand panel, we can see that the address of each byte is given, also in hexadecimal number form, by the sum of the row and column numbers. So, for example, the third byte in the sequence (of value 69H) is at address row 00H + column 02H = 02H (remember addresses start from 0); the sixteenth byte (of value 66H) is at address row 00H + column 0fH = 0fH; and the thirty-sixth byte (of value 0dH) is at address row 20H + column 03H = 23H. It is at addresses 23H and 24H that we see an example of the carriage return (0dH) line feed (0aH) sequence that we referred to above. In the right hand-panel of the listing, we see the ASCII character interpretation for each byte, but only where that interpretation results in a visible character. So, for example, the effects of the ASCII characters associated with addresses 23H and 24H (carriage return 0dH and line feed 0aH respectively) are not implemented (we would get a new line of text in the display, if they were) but instead a blob is put in their place, and this is repeated for all non-visible characters. The ASCII text file, when printed out, displays the visible text shown in Fig. 2.16.

> This is a test file for ASCII text.
> That was an example of a new line.

Fig. 2.16 Printout of TEST.TXT.

Word Processing Formats

In practice, there is not much to gain from using a hexadecimal viewer with a plain text ASCII file. The real benefits come when the file is not made up solely of ASCII characters. One type of word processor replaces some of the ASCII characters and embeds its own word processing codes directly into the text of the file. These codes signify, for example, the page layout, the type of printer and all those other elements that determine the appearance of the document, such as bold, italic, underline and the font types and point sizes etc. A second type of word processor leaves the text alone but generates separate tables of codes that point to various elements of the text and define the specific layout, appearance and edits that are to be applied. Both types normally also include a file signature at the beginning of the file.

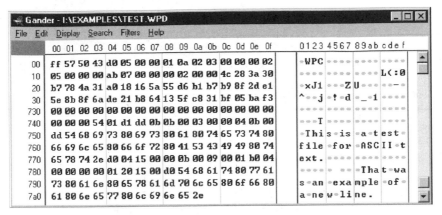

Fig. 2.17 Hexadecimal listing of WordPerfect file.

WordPerfect

At Fig. 2.17 we have shown a hexadecimal listing of some of the byte patterns that result when the same text as that shown at Fig. 2.16 is processed using the Corel® WordPerfect® version 8 word processing application (later versions are not significantly different). The listing has been limited to two small parts: the first part is from addresses 00H to 3fH and the second part is from addresses 730H to 7aaH. The detail between addresses 3fH and 730H has been deliberately omitted in this example for the purposes of clarity.

The first point to note is the significant increase in size of the word processor file over that of the original ASCII file. The word processor file is 7abH bytes long (equal to 1,963 bytes) and the ASCII file is only 47H bytes long (equal to 71 bytes). The second point to note is the presence of a file signature in the first few bytes of the file. Here we see in the first four bytes of this file the hexadecimal codes: "ff 57 50 43"[13], which is the known signature[14] for a Corel WordPerfect word processor document file. The third point we may note is that the ASCII text, which starts at 751H with the byte value 54H for the character "T", has been modified. The space character in ASCII is 20H (for an example, see byte address 04H in Fig. 2.15), but here the space character has been replaced with 80H (see, for example, byte address 755H in Fig. 2.17). In addition, there is nothing recognizable as a carriage return or a line feed character, 0dH and 0aH respectively, between the two lines of ASCII text, in the area of addresses 774H to 788H.

---

13 The WordPerfect signature is often written as –1, "WPC".

14 Many file signatures are listed in books such as *The File Formats Handbook* (Born, 1997) and *Encyclopedia of Graphics File Formats* (Murray and vanRyper, 1996). See Appendix 2 for some examples.

As mentioned above, this word processor replaces some ASCII character codes and uses embedded file format codes. The Software Development Kit[15] provided with Corel WordPerfect Suite 8 includes full details of all these codes. Using this information, we are able to interpret the entire file should we so wish. This we will not do, but a few simple examples will make the point. The four byte sequence "01 0a 02 03" at addresses 08H to 0bH specifies that the document was written by a WordPerfect program, that it is a WordPerfect document and that the application program was WordPerfect version 8. The two byte sequence "ab 07" at addresses 14H and 15H is in fact the file size in little endian fixed point integer format. That is, it is the number 07abH which is equal to 1,963 bytes, as we noted above. Finally, the sequence of bytes that starts "d0 04" at addresses 774H and 775H and ends "00 d0" at addresses 787H and 788H is called an "end-of-line group" and represents the end of line characters between the two lines of text.

Provenance of Documents

Some important points for the analyst may be drawn from this limited analysis. One of the most difficult issues for the analyst is in determining provenance for documents which may have been deleted and subsequently partially overwritten. Typically, a "cookie" file downloaded as a result of Internet browsing would only overwrite the first sector (512 bytes) of a deleted file whose space had been reallocated. This would certainly cause the file signature to be overwritten, but, specifically for a WordPerfect file, it might not affect the text portions, which are located towards the end of the deleted file. These text portions would be uniquely recognizable by the embedded 80H codes present in place of spaces and the file format code sequences indicating end of line, etc. A report that explained this analysis could well give sufficient credibility to relevant text fragments for them to be admissible in court.

Microsoft Word for Windows

Of course, not all word processors are the same, and at Fig. 2.18 we see a hexadecimal listing of some of the byte patterns that result when the ASCII text shown at Fig. 2.16 is processed using Microsoft Word for Windows 95 version 7 (newer versions are similar). The listing this time has been limited to three small parts: the first part is from addresses 00H to 1fH, the second part is from addresses 4f0H to 54fH, and the third part is from addresses 2be0H to 2bffH. Here we note that the Microsoft Word for Windows file is very much larger: 2c00H bytes (which is equal to 11,264 bytes) compared with the WordPerfect file size of 1,963 bytes and the ASCII file size of 71 bytes (see Table 2.8). We also note that the signature for a Microsoft Word for Windows file appears to extend from addresses 00H to 07H and to consist of the eight hexadecimal codes: "d0 cf 11 e0 a1 b1 1a e1". At address 507H we note that the space

---

15 See WordPerfect Document File Format, Corel WordPerfect Suite 8 Software
  Development Kit in Corel/SDKs/Suite8/DOCS/A_FRNTFF.htm on the WordPerfect CD-
  ROM.

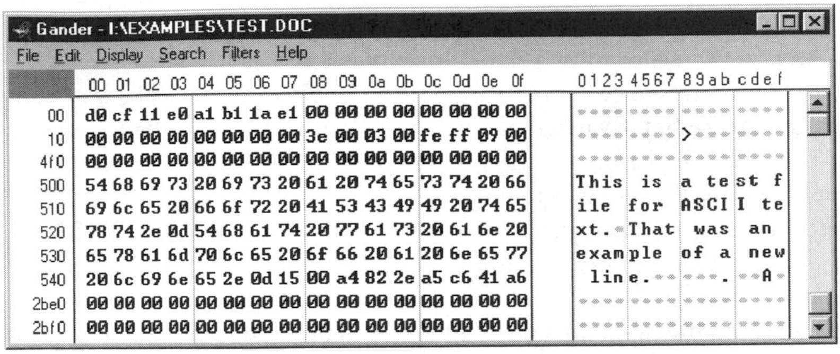

Fig. 2.18 Hexadecimal listing of MS Word for Windows file.

Table 2.8 Typical file sizes.

● ASCII text file	71 bytes
● WordPerfect 8	1963 bytes
● Word for Windows 7	11264 bytes

character is held using its ASCII value of 20H and that at address 523H the end of line is indicated by an ASCII carriage return character with a byte value of 0dH.

This word processor is of the second type that we referred to above. It leaves the text alone but generates tables of codes that point into the text and define the layout, appearance and edits that are to be applied to it. This latter point is important, in that we cannot assume that the form and order of the text that we see in the hexadecimal listing is the form and order that will be displayed by the word processor application. This is because there is what is called a *piece table*, which is generated during the editing of the document, and which specifies how the text is to be broken up into pieces and in what order those pieces are to be used. In *non-complex* documents there is only one piece and so the problem does not arise, but the analyst needs to be able to analyse the Word[16] document in detail in order to be sure of this in the case of a partially overwritten fragment.

Compound Documents

The file signature "d0 cf 11 e0 a1 b1 1a e1" is not, however, the particular signature for a Microsoft Word document. It is instead the general signature for a Microsoft *compound document*[17], sometimes known as an *OLE2* container. Compound

---

16 Born notes in *The File Formats Handbook* (Born, 1997) that "... *the complete structure of the Winword format is confidential and may not be published here*". More recently, however, detailed specifications have appeared on the Internet under the title "Microsoft Word 97 Binary File Format".

17 No details of this format were found in the public domain until relatively recently. Now a number of sites are providing access to a Microsoft document entitled "Compound File Binary File Format". The URL of one such site, at the time of writing, is http://www. aafassociation. org/html/specs/aafcontainerspec-v1.0.1.pdf (Microsoft, 2004).

documents are used throughout the Microsoft Office range, including Word, Excel and PowerPoint. The concept was devised by Microsoft to permit many different types of data objects to be contained within a single document. The idea is that the tools required to edit the various objects can be automatically called up through the *object linking and embedding* (OLE) mechanisms so that the user can concentrate on the document itself rather than on the various applications associated with it. The approach has evolved through a number of developments from OLE itself, through OLE2 and a generic architecture known as the *Component Object Model (COM)* to *Distributed COM (DCOM)*.

In order to do this, each document contains structured storage and is similar to a volume that has been set up with a FAT file system (see Chapter 5). The document contains a root directory and a number of folders (known as *storages*) and a number of files (known as *streams*). One such stream in a Word document container is the current "WordDocument" stream, and it is this that contains the text we have been looking at in Fig. 2.18. The Word document itself, however, also contains a number of other streams, including standard streams (such as "SummaryInformation") that specify the properties of the document. Some of these values are displayed when, in Windows, a right mouse button context menu is opened on the document and the "properties" item is selected. Such data is often called *metadata*. In addition to the standard streams, it is sometimes the case that previous versions of the Word document are still present in the container as well as metadata that is not accessible through normal application software.

There have also been reports of so called *trash blocks* being noted which hold data from other applications and from other parts of the disk and the memory. This appears to be an issue whereby the application does not clear newly allocated blocks of their current content when, for example, extending the size of the file. The effect of this is that sensitive data could become inadvertently saved within the Word file. Examination of such blocks could provide useful additional information to an analyst about other applications that have been run on the target machine, and this can be done using a hexadecimal viewer such as Gander. There is also the possibility that such data could be passed inadvertently from one system to another when Word documents are enclosed in email messages. Of course, it would also be possible for sensitive data to be hidden deliberately within a Word file and sent openly as an email enclosure.

Although the authors have carried out a great deal of forensic case work involving the analysis of OLE2 container documents, and currently run a course for forensic practitioners on Microsoft Office Document Analysis and Reconstruction, we do not feel that it would be appropriate to give a more detailed treatment here. It is a complex subject and we believe that to do it justice would probably require a complete book in itself.

Rich Text Format

In the previous two word processor examples we have been seeing a mixture of binary control codes and ASCII text. For the last example in this section, we note at

```
Gander - I:\EXAMPLES\TEST.RTF                                            _□×
File  Edit  Display  Search  Filters  Help

     00 01 02 03 04 05 06 07 08 09 0a 0b 0c 0d 0e 0f   0123 4567 89ab cdef
00   7b 5c 72 74 66 31 5c 61 6e 73 69 20 5c 64 65 66   {\rtf1\ansi \def
10   66 30 7b 5c 66 6f 6e 74 74 62 6c 0d 0a 7b 5c 66   f0{\fonttbl··{\f
20   30 5c 66 72 6f 6d 61 6e 20 54 69 6d 65 73 20 4e   0\froman Times N
30   65 77 3b 7d 7d 5c 63 6f 6c 6f 72 74 62 6c 0d      ew;}}\colortbl·
40   0a 5c 72 65 64 30 5c 67 72 65 65 6e 30 5c 62 6c   ·\red0\green0\bl
d0   5c 70 61 72 64 20 5c 73 6c 30 20 0d 0a 7b 5c 70   \pard \sl0 ··{\p
e0   6c 61 69 6e 20 54 68 69 73 20 69 73 20 61 20 74   lain This is a t
f0   65 73 74 20 66 69 6c 65 20 66 6f 72 20 41 53 43   est file for ASC
100  49 49 20 74 65 78 74 2e 5c 70 61 72 20 0d 0a 7d 7b  II text.\par ··}{
110  5c 70 6c 61 69 6e 20 54 68 61 74 20 77 61 73 20   \plain That was
120  61 6e 20 65 78 61 6d 70 6c 65 20 6f 66 20 61 20   an example of a
130  6e 65 77 20 6c 69 6e 65 2e 7d 7d                   new line.}}
```

Fig. 2.19 Hexadecimal listing of RTF file.

Fig. 2.19 the same information encoded in *Rich Text Format* (RTF) which was designed to use only the displayable ASCII characters[18].

In this example the listing has been limited to two parts: from addresses 00H to 4fH and from addresses d0H to 13aH. The file signature is evident at the beginning of the file as "{\rtf1\ansi" and the text clearly starts at address e5H. In addition, it is apparent that the formatting information is also held in text form; thus we see ASCII character details about font and colour as well. Many applications support RTF, so it can be a useful exchange medium between different products.

Magic Numbers

It is not just word processing packages that use file signatures to identify their application files. The idea has been around since the very early days of computing, and in the *Unix* community, in particular, the first few bytes of a binary file are often used to indicate type. This is generally referred to as its "magic number" and is defined as: "*Special data located at the beginning of a binary data file to indicate its type to a utility... once upon a time, these magic numbers were PDP-11 branch instructions that skipped over header data to the start of executable code*"[19]. There are now thousands of such magic numbers, many not documented, many proprietary and many simply picked at random. An attempt[20] was being made to document and standardize magic numbers as well as to specify basic rules for their future selection, but little action seems to have been taken since 1998. A preliminary draft document[21], dated

---

18 This format was designed by Microsoft as a method of encoding formatted text and graphics for ease of transfer between different applications. It is used by the clipboard in Windows. From (Born, 1997).

19 Quoted from URL http://www.science.uva.nl/~mes/jargon/m/magicnumber.html.

20 See URL http://www.catb.org/~esr/magic-numbers/ for the Magic Numbers Group Home Page.

21 Rfc-draft, v1.2 1996/11/20 available at URL http://www.catb.org/~esr/magic-numbers/rfc-draft.

November 1996, is still in existence which states: "*... it is very desirable that files should generally present themselves as self-describing objects from which an application launcher or navigation tool can readily deduce both their uses and at least some of the semantics of their contents.*" Clearly, this work would be of much interest to the forensic computing analyst, since it could assist in making the recognition and interpretation of well-behaved files a routine activity[22]. We consider in a later section the problem of badly behaved files and deliberate attempts to hide information.

Graphic Formats

It is in the digital representation of graphic images that we find perhaps the greatest range of different file formats. Just to give a flavour for some of these graphic formats, we will use the digital image of a Zeon Tech digital diary, shown at Fig. 2.20, as our example. A high-resolution digital image was first taken with a digital camera and then processed using a graphics software package (Paint Shop Pro) to give a series of lower resolution 256 greyscale images in a number of different graphic formats. The first of these that we will consider is that of the Graphics Interchange Format, or GIF. developed by CompuServe in 1987 to permit the passing of graphic images by email.

Fig. 2.20 Zeon Tech digital diary (photograph: Tony Sammes and Brian Jenkinson).

---

22 In Unix, there is a special program, `file(1)`, which attempts to identify the type of any given file from its magic number.

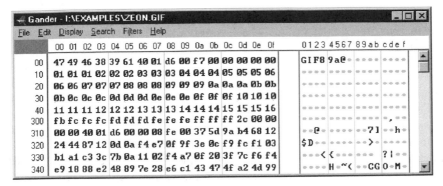

Fig. 2.21 Hexadecimal listing of GIF file.

Graphic Interchange Format

GIF enables several pictures to be stored in one file and it uses a loss-free compression algorithm[23] to reduce the file size. The specification, published in 1987, is referred to as "GIF87a" and an extended version published in 1989 is known as "GIF89a". In the case of our example, the resulting GIF file is 64 kilobytes in size and two small segments of the file, examined using the Gander hexadecimal viewer, are shown at Fig. 2.21.

The file signature (or magic number) can readily be seen in the first few bytes as "47 49 46 38 39 61" or "GIF89a". This is followed immediately by the *logical screen descriptor block*, starting at address 06H, which specifies the width of the logical screen in pixels as "40 01" (translated from little endian this becomes 0140H = 320 decimal) and the height of the logical screen in pixels as "d6 00" (again, translated from little endian, this is 00d6H = 214 decimal). It also shows at address 0aH that there is a *global colour table* and that the colour resolution is 8 bits for each primary colour in the colour table[24]. The global colour table starts at address 0dH with "00 00 00" and consists of 256 triples, each triple representing the red, green, blue (RGB) intensity values of one of the 256 possible colours in the colour palette. In this case, the colours in the palette are all greyscale colours. We can tell this because the intensities of each of the R, G and B values for each colour triple are identical, thus resulting in a palette of grey/black tones.

Two small segments of the file have been shown. The second segment, starting with address 300H, shows the last entry of the colour table at address 30aH with R, G, B values "ff ff ff". The next value, at address 30dH, is "2c" and this signals the start of a GIF picture (there may be more than one). This is the first byte of the *image descriptor block* which defines at address 30eH the left coordinate of the picture in pixels, 0000H, at address 310H the top coordinate of the picture in pixels, 0000H, at

---

23 Lempel–Ziv–Welch (LZW) compression. See Blackstock (undated) for an outline of the process.

24 For these and similar details see page 684 *et seq.* of Born (1997)

address 312H the width of the picture in pixels (again, to be translated from little endian, thus 0140H = 320 decimal) and at address 314H the height of the picture in pixels (also, to be translated from little endian, 00d6H = 214 decimal). Immediately following this is a single flags byte and then, starting from address 317H, is the first *raster data block*. This will typically be followed by a number of *raster data sub-blocks*.

In constructing the GIF file, the original picture has been analysed, starting in the top left-hand corner, and working, pixel by pixel, from left to right and from top to bottom. Each pixel of the picture has been coded as a colour byte, the value of which is the relative entry in the colour table of value 0 to 255. This stream of pixel bytes has then been encoded using LZW compression and the resulting output stream has been used to form the raster data block and sub-blocks, the first bytes of which are the block lengths. Each data block therefore contains LZW compressed data, which we will not attempt to analyse here. The first of the data blocks commences with a *code size* byte which is used in the decompression process. In our example, this byte is at address 317H (of value 08H) and the first raster data block starts at address 318H and has a length of feH. The compressed data for this block starts at address 319H.

LZW Legal Problems

Although GIF became one of the most widely used formats for graphic files, legal difficulties have arisen in recent years. In 1977, Abraham Lempel and Jakob Ziv (Ziv and Lempel, 1977) developed the first of the LZ compression algorithms (LZ77) which are found in archiving programs such as *zoo*, *lha* and *pkzip*. In 1984, Terry Welch, whilst working for Sperry Corporation, produced a modified version of the LZ compression algorithm known as the LZW algorithm. It is this algorithm which is used today in the GIF and TIFF graphic file formats. In 1983, Sperry Corporation (and possibly IBM) applied for patents for the LZW algorithm in a number of countries and the patent ownership was transferred from Sperry Corporation to Unisys when the new company was formed. In 1994, CompuServe and Unisys came to an agreement whereby the use of the LZW algorithm would be licensed for application in the GIF file format. However, this was not as beneficial as it at first seemed and it created many problems for the user community, who had understood from CompuServe that the GIF format was freely available for unrestricted use. Up until recently, licences have been required from Unisys for all software that reads or writes the GIF format. The latest position is given in this quote from "The Free Software Foundation" (Free Software Foundation, 2006): *"We were able to search the patent databases of the USA, Canada, Japan, and the European Union. The Unisys patent expired on 20 June 2003 in the USA, in Europe it expired on 18 June 2004, in Japan patent expired on 20 June 2004 and in Canada it expired on 7 July 2004. The U.S. IBM patent expires 11 August 2006, (we are still searching the databases of other countries)."* It may well be that the GIF format makes a full come back in the near future.

Portable Network Graphic

The reaction of many in the graphics community to this problem, and, in particular, that of the Free Software Foundation, was to drop GIF altogether and to embrace a new format called Portable Network Graphic (PNG)[25]. This format uses an LZ77 variant of the compression algorithm which is not part of the Unisys patent and the unofficial expansion of the acronym "PNG" is "PNG's Not GIF".

The PNG work has been well received by the graphics community and many graphics packages now support it. Murray and vanRyper (Murray and vanRyper, 1996) state: "*We are happy to report that the PNG specification is one of the most complete, well-thought-out, and well-written file format specifications yet examined by the authors of this book.*"

Our second graphics example of the picture at Fig. 2.20 shows at Fig. 2.22 one small segment of a PNG file, again examined using the Gander hexadecimal viewer. This file is 44 kilobytes in length. The file signature is the first eight bytes and is always "89 50 4e 47 0d 0a 1a 0a". This is not a random choice of values, since the bytes are used to assist in detecting various kinds of errors. The value 89, for example, is used to detect whether the file has passed through a 7 bit data transmission channel, in which case the 89 would become 09. The characters "PNG" give an immediately recognizable text signature. The byte pair 0d 0a is used to determine whether or not the file has been manipulated by software that alters carriage return and newline sequences, and the byte 1a prevents the listing of the file on MS-DOS operating systems, since this byte value is the MS-DOS end of file marker, Control-Z.

Immediately after the signature is the Header *chunk*. The length of the data in the chunk is given by the double word starting at address 08H and of value "00 00 00 0d". Note that this format uses big endian storage, and thus the value is equivalent to 0000000dH, which is decimal 13. Next follows the signature for the chunk, which are the characters "IHDR" at address 0cH and then the 13 data bytes of the chunk starting at address 10H. These take the form of a double word for the width of the image in pixels "00 00 01 40" (big endian format of 00000140H results in 320 decimal) followed by a double word for the height of the image in pixels "00 00 00 d6" (big

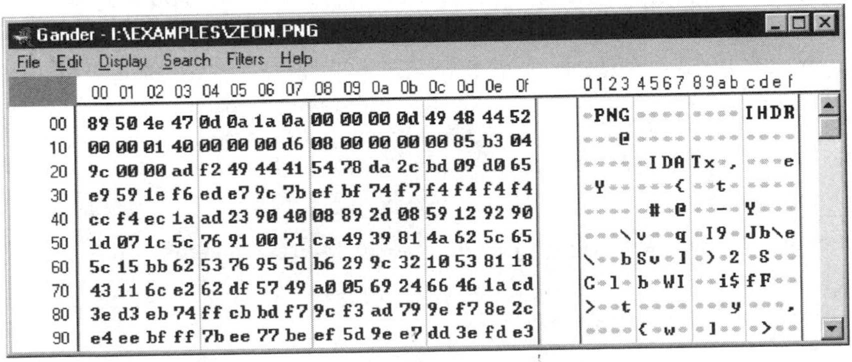

Fig. 2.22 Hexadecimal listing of PNG file.

25 See article by Atzberger and Zolli (Atzberger and Zolli, 1996)

endian format of 000000d6H results in 214 decimal). Finally, the last five bytes "08 00 00 00 00", starting from address 18H, indicate an 8 bit per pixel greyscale colour depth[26]. These are exactly the same results as we obtained from interpreting the equivalent GIF file.

The chunk ends at 1dH with a double word cyclic redundancy check and the next chunk starts at address 21H with a chunk data length of "00 00 ad f2", which is equivalent to 44530 in decimal. The signature for this chunk, the Image Data chunk, is the characters "IDAT" and the 44530 bytes of compressed data start at address 29H. The image data is laid out as a bitmap which has been scanned from left to right and from top to bottom and it is compressed using a variation of the *deflate*[27] compression method developed by Phil Katz, the author of the *pkzip* archiving program. Again, we will not attempt to decode the compressed data of this example.

JPEG Compression

Both the graphic formats so far considered use lossless[28] compression methods and, at best, in practice, will only achieve an approximate halving of the file size. The final example we will look at is a graphic format that utilises lossy compression methods and one that can achieve much higher compression ratios. The Joint Photographic Experts Group (JPEG) is a standards committee that was formed in 1987 from two separate bodies, a CCITT (International Telegraph and Telephone Consultative Committee) sub-group and an ISO (International Organization for Standardization) sub-group. The two sub-groups had both been researching compression methods for the transmission of graphic images and the combining of the two sub-groups permitted the establishment of a single standard.

JPEG, unlike the previous formats, is not based on a single compression method[29]. Rather it is a toolkit of methods that may be altered to fit the needs of the user. Different compression methods may be used to trade quality of image against file size. As mentioned above, JPEG also differs in that it primarily uses lossy methods of compression. These work by discarding information that normally goes unnoticed by the human eye. As a result, there need be no perceptible degradation in quality despite achieving compression ratios of the order of 20:1. The JPEG ISO standard (ISO, undated) describes the compression methods for images, but it does not define a common file interchange format which will enable JPEG bitstreams to be exchanged between a variety of platforms and applications. The JPEG File Interchange Format (JFIF) has been designed to meet just this need. In the 1992 specification (Hamilton, 1992), the author states: "... *the only purpose of this simplified*

---

26 For these and similar details see page 700 *et seq.* of (Murray and vanRyper, 1996)

27 See the file Application.txt available from URL: http://www.pkware.com/ documents/casestudies/APPNOTE.TXT.

28 In a lossless system, the original bit pattern can be restored in its entirety from the compressed version.

29 See page 191 *et seq.* of Murray and vanRyper (1996) for a discussion of JPEG compression.

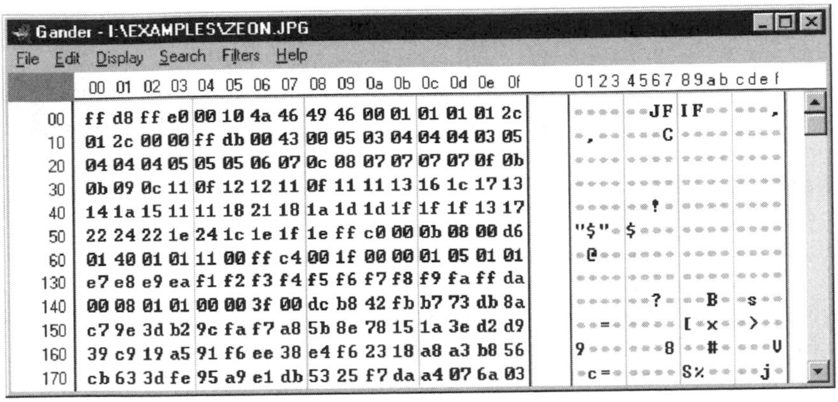

Fig. 2.23 Hexadecimal listing of JPG file.

format is to allow the exchange of JPEG compressed images". Image files with file types such as JPG, JIF, JPEG or JFIF are usually to be found in JFIF format (but see section on EXIF below), and our final example of the picture at Fig. 2.20 is in just this format.

JPEG File Interchange Format (JFIF)

At Fig. 2.23 two small segments of the JPG file are shown, again examined using the Gander viewer. This file is only 17 kilobytes in length as a result of the lossy compression. The quality of the image, however, is little different from that of the GIF and PNG versions. The file signature is effectively the first four bytes "ff d8 ff e0" although these are made up of two separate blocks. The *start of image (SOI) marker* block, "ff d8", is required by the JPEG standard to signal the start of a JPEG file and the "ff e0" indicates an *application (APP0) marker* block which, together with the characters "JFIF", starting at address 06H identify this as a JFIF file[30]. Although not shown, the file ends with "ff d9", the *end of image (EOI) marker*.

Also of interest is the sequence that starts at address 59H of value "ff c0". This is a *start of frame marker* block which at address 5dH has the bits per pixel value of 08. At address 5eH is a two-byte word giving the height of the image in pixels "00 d6" (big endian format of 00d6H results in 214 decimal) and at address 60H is a two byte word giving the width of the image in pixels "01 40" (big endian format of 0140H results in 320 decimal). Once again, these are exactly the same results as we obtained from interpreting the equivalent GIF and PNG files. In the second segment of the file, starting with address 13eH, we see the *start of scan marker*, "ff da", and this is then followed at 148H by the compressed image data, also scanned from left to right and from top to bottom. It is at this point, once again, that we will leave the analysis[31].

---

30 Compare this with the explanation for EXIF files below.

31 For more detail see page 895 *et seq.* of Born (1997).

Exchangeable Image file Format (ExIF)

Every JPEG file begins with the SOI (start of image) marker, "ff d8", and ends with the EOI (end of image) marker, "ff d9". In between these two markers are a series of blocks, each of which is defined by a specific marker. The size of each block is specified within the block and this allows applications that do not understand a particular marker to skip over the block concerned. It also provides considerable flexibility in the overall structure of the file.

As we have seen, the first JPEG file format standard (JFIF), defined in 1992, provides for the interchange of JPEG bit streams. It also permits key information to be added to the file, such as resolution, colour space and a thumbnail image. As a matter of interest, the thumbnail image can also be very useful to the analyst. Where, perhaps, the actual JPEG file is damaged and cannot be displayed using standard graphics software, it may be possible to extract the thumbnail as a separate JPEG file and view, in miniature, what the larger picture would have shown.

In 1998, the Japanese *Electronic Industry Development Association* (*JEIDA*) developed a new standard called the *Exchangeable Image file Format* (*ExIF*). This has been designed to allow camera and image metadata to be stored in JPEG (and TIFF) files. This different form of a JPEG file is indicated by the APP0 marker, "ff e0", being replaced by a new application marker, APP1, of value "ff e1" and the letters "JFIF" being replaced by the letters "Exif". Such a file is easily recognizable using a hexadecimal viewer.

The metadata stored may provide very valuable evidence to an investigator, since it can include such details as when the picture was taken, what camera make and model was used, what the camera settings were, whether the camera was on self timer, and whether a flash was used. This information can be extracted using a viewer designed for the purpose (one such is Exif Reader[32]) or by analyzing the metadata directly using a hexadecimal viewer. Full details of this structure, including all the metadata tags, are given in Brown (2004).

Other Graphic File Formats

There are many other graphic file formats: BMP, FLI, FLC, MAC, ICO, IMG, PAL, PIC, PCX and TIF to name but a few. Some file signatures are listed at Appendix 2, but reference books such *as The File Formats Handbook* (Born, 1997) and *Encyclopedia of Graphics File Formats* (Murray and vanRyper, 1996) are essential for a detailed analysis. The full specifications for many of these formats are also freely available on the Internet[33].

---

32 See http://www.takenet.or.jp/~ryuuji/minisoft/exifread/english/.

33 See, for example, "The Graphics File Format Page": http://www.dcs.ed.ac.uk/home/ mxr/gfx/.

Archive Formats

The file archive program *pkzip* has already been mentioned in the context of the LZ compression algorithms, as have similar products such as *zoo* and *lha*. Archivers such as these carry out two separate functions: they compress one or more files using lossless compression and they archive the resulting compressed files into a single archive file, which, in the case of *pkzip*, is given a file type of "ZIP". Although this is one of the most common archive systems in use today, implementations of it are generally proprietary and licensed application programs have to be obtained. An exception to this is *gzip*[34], which is an open-source, patent-free variation of the LZ77 algorithm. This system is commonly used by HTTP servers to compress HTML web pages and is also much in favour with the Unix community. Files compressed using gzip are normally allocated a "Z" or "GZ" file type.

Pkzip

To demonstrate an archive format, the two word processing files TEST.DOC and TEST.WPD, were archived using *pkzip* to form the file TEST.ZIP. At Fig. 2.24, two small segments of the resulting file are shown, using the Gander hexadecimal viewer. The ZIP file is 2597 bytes long compared with the 11,264 bytes of TEST.DOC and the 1963 bytes of TEST.WPD. The file signature can be seen in the first four bytes as "50 4b 03 04" and this is most readily recognized as starting with the characters "PK". This signature is part of the *local file header* and is repeated for every file in the archive. Immediately after the signature are a series of bytes detailing the *pkzip* version number, general purpose flags, the compression method used, the last modified date and time of the file, a cyclic redundancy check, the compressed and uncompressed file sizes and the file name in characters[35].

The name of the first file in the archive starts at address 1eH and is seen to be "TEST.DOC". The length of this file name is confirmed at addresses 1aH and 1bH as

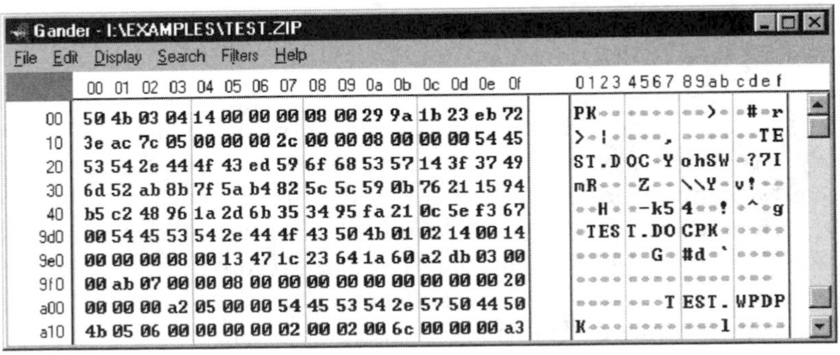

Fig. 2.24 Hexadecimal listing of ZIP file.

34 See RFC 1952 (Deutsch, 1996).

35 For these, and details of the compression algorithms, see PKWARE (2006).

the two bytes "08 00", which translated from little endian is 0008H, equal to 8 characters. The compressed file size is the four bytes "7c 05 00 00" starting at 12H, which translated from little endian is 0000057cH, equal to 1404 in decimal. The original file size is the four bytes "00 2c 00 00" starting at 16H, which translated from little endian is 00002c00H, equal to 11,264 in decimal (entirely as we expect). The compression method is given at addresses 08H and 09H as the two bytes "08 00", which translated from little endian is 0008H; this value specifies "deflation". It is interesting to note the very significant reduction in file size that is possible with compressing this kind of word processing file. The last modified file time is given at addresses 0aH and 0bH as the two bytes "29 9a" and the last modified file date is given at addresses 0cH and 0dH as the two bytes "1b 23". Taken together, after translation from little endian, these four bytes specify a DOS date and time of 27/08/1997 at 19:17:18, which is the last modified date and time value found on the file itself. Starting at address 0eH are the four byte values "eb 72 3e ac", and these, translated from little endian to be ac3e72ebH, are the 32 bit cyclic redundancy check for the uncompressed file. Immediately following the file name at address 26H is the start of the compressed data of the file itself.

Each of the files in the archive follows a similar pattern: a local file header followed by the compressed file data. At the end of the sequence of files, a *central directory record* is established. In the second segment of the ZIP file, starting with address 9d9H, we see the signature "50 4b 01 02" of the second (and last)[36] *file header* in this central directory record. Each of these headers contains very similar information to that held in the local file header, including, as can be seen starting at address a07H, the file name in character form. The central directory record (and the ZIP file) is terminated by an *end of central directory record*, starting at address a0fH with signature "50 4b 05 06". From the viewpoint of the forensic computing analyst, it is useful to note that even if the ZIP file has been password protected, the file names and other details are still available, both in the local file headers and in the central directory record.

Other Applications

The final format considered in this chapter is the record structure found in the memory of some Sharp organizers. The structure, shown at Fig. 2.25, takes the form of a record signature, made up of the three bytes "20 07 00", which is preceded by two counts, each of which are two bytes in length held in little endian format. Immediately after the signature are the character bytes of the record itself. The first two-byte count specifies the length of the record, including the count bytes, and the second two-byte count specifies the length of the preceding record.

In the first entry of the example shown in Fig. 2.25, the first count is "15 00", which, translated from little endian format gives 0015H, equal to 21 in decimal, and, taking

---

36 The start of the first file header of the central directory structure occurs at an address not shown in Fig. 2.24.

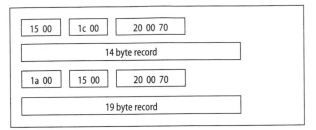

Fig. 2.25 Structure of a Sharp organizer record.

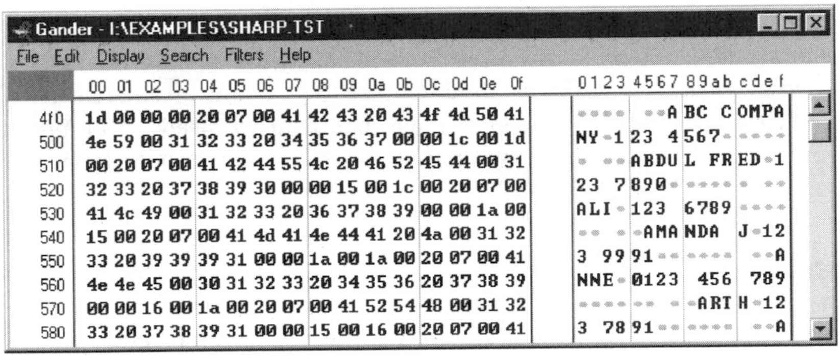

```
Gander - I:\EXAMPLES\SHARP.TST                                          _ □ ✕
File  Edit  Display  Search  Filters  Help
      00 01 02 03 04 05 06 07 08 09 0a 0b 0c 0d 0e 0f     0 1 2 3 4 5 6 7 8 9 a b c d e f
4f0   1d 00 00 00 20 07 00 41 42 43 20 43 4f 4d 50 41     • • • •    • •A BC  C OMPA
500   4e 59 00 31 32 33 20 34 35 36 37 00 00 1c 00 1d     NY •1 23  4 567 • • • • •
510   00 20 07 00 41 42 44 55 4c 20 46 52 45 44 00 31     •  • •A BDU L  FR ED •1
520   32 33 20 37 38 39 30 00 00 15 00 1c 00 20 07 00     23  7 890 • • • • •  •  • •
530   41 4c 49 00 31 32 33 20 36 37 38 39 00 00 1a 00     ALI •1 23  6789 • • • •
540   15 00 20 07 00 41 4d 41 4e 44 41 20 4a 00 31 32     •• •  •AMA NDA  J •12
550   33 20 39 39 39 31 00 00 1a 00 1a 00 20 07 00 41     3 99 91 • • • • •   • •A
560   4e 4e 45 00 30 31 32 33 20 34 35 36 20 37 38 39     NNE• 0123  456  789
570   00 00 16 00 1a 00 20 07 00 41 52 54 48 00 31 32     • • • • • • •  •ART H •12
580   33 20 37 38 39 31 00 00 15 00 16 00 20 07 00 41     3  78 91 • • • • •   • •A
```

Fig. 2.26 Hexadecimal listing of part of a Sharp organizer memory dump.

into account the seven bytes of the two counts and the signature, gives a text character record size of 14 bytes. The second count of this record indicates that the *previous* record is "1c 00" (or 001cH translated from little endian), which is equal to 28 (in decimal) bytes long.

The second entry shows the first count as "1a 00" (or 001aH translated from little endian), which is equal to 26 (in decimal) and, once again, taking into account the seven bytes, gives a text character record size of 19 bytes. The second count of this record is, of course, the same as the first count of the previous record.

Finally, at Fig. 2.33 is shown a hexadecimal listing of part of the memory of a Sharp organizer which uses this format for its record structure. Starting from address 529H can be seen the two counts of values, "15 00" and "1c 00", followed by the signature at address 52dH of "20 07 00". Following this are the 14 text character bytes of the record. In this particular format, the value 00H is used to represent a newline. The next record then starts at 53eH with the counts of values "1a 00" and "15 00". Of interest to the forensic computing analyst is the fact that the signature in this format is changed for secret records to "A0 07 00", although the text characters remain unchanged. Direct access to the memory and a knowledge of the record structure permits the analyst to extract password-protected records from this model of organizer.

Quick View Plus

This chapter would not be complete without reference to the file utility Quick View Plus[37]. This program uses the file signature in a file to identify the file format and then display it in accordance with the rules of that format. The outline specification for the most recent version (9.0) at the time of writing, states: *"Quick View Plus provides real benefits by enabling you to access information in over 250 file types without the native applications. Email attachments, Web files, legacy documents, and more"*.

A utility such as this, together with a hexadecimal viewer, is an essential tool for the forensic computing analyst. It should be noted, however, that some members of the forensic computing community take the view that computer output that is to be presented in evidence should always be produced using the application software that was used to create it. Quick View Plus and other tools are thus seen to be useful for rapid review and to assist in identification, but evidence needs to be produced, wherever possible, using the original software installed on the suspect machine.

Exercises

2.1   Interpret each of the pairs of binary byte patterns that follow as:

(1) a little endian unsigned decimal integer
(2) a little endian signed decimal integer
(3) a big endian unsigned decimal integer
(4) a big endian signed decimal integer
(5) two signed decimal integers
(6) a big endian unsigned mixed decimal number with the binary point between the two bytes
(7) a packed binary coded decimal number
(8) a hexadecimal number
(9) two ASCII characters

Where a value is not relevant, such as a non-printing ASCII character or a BCD digit outside of the range 0 to 9, write a "?" symbol.

(a) 01010111 01110110
(b) 10000000 01111111
(c) 01000110 01011001
(d) 00000101 10001000
(e) 00110111 10011001
(f) 01110010 00111111
(g) 10010001 01000010
(h) 01010101 01100001

---

37 This is a commercial product produced by Stellent Corporation, and distributed by Avantstar, Inc. (Avanstar, undated).

2.2 Write down the binary patterns in two bytes for the following:

  (a) 7f 43 hexadecimal little endian
  (b) 18ab hexadecimal big endian
  (c) "Az" ASCII characters
  (d) 1904 packed BCD
  (e) 18956 unsigned decimal big endian
  (f) 51423 unsigned decimal little endian
  (g) –4 and –60 two signed decimal numbers
  (h) 103.75 unsigned mixed decimal big endian with the binary point between the two bytes

2.3 Write down the binary patterns in four bytes for the following short real floating point numbers:

  (a) +12.0
  (b) +16.0
  (c) +127.0
  (d) –127.0

2.4 Write down the short real floating point numbers represented by the following four byte sequences:

  (a) 41 c6 00 00H
  (b) c1 c6 00 00H
  (c) 44 f8 40 00H
  (d) c5 9d 08 00H

2.5 Examine the partial hexadecimal listing at Fig. 2.27 and answer the following questions about the file to which it relates:

  (a) Can you confirm that this is a graphics file?
  (b) What are the dimensions of the image?
  (c) Is the image colour or greyscale?

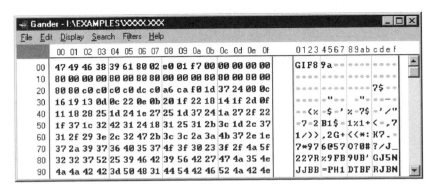

Fig. 2.27

References

Atzberger, P. and Zolli, A. (1996), Portable Network Graphics, *Trincoll Journal*. URL: `http://www.trincoll.edu/~tj/tj10.31.96/articles/tech.html`.

Avanstar Inc. (undated), *Quick View Plus from Stellent Corporation*, republished under licence by Avanstar, Inc., Corporate Headquarters, 18986 Lake Drive East, Chanhassen, MN 55317, USA. URL: `http://www.avantstar.com/`.

Blackstock, S. (undated) *LZW and GIF Explained*. URL: `http://www.cis.udel.edu/~amer/CISC651/lzw.and.gif.explained.html`.

Born, G. (1997) *The File Formats Handbook*, International Thompson Publishing, London.

Brown, C. L. T. (2004) Exchangeable Image file Format (ExIF), *Technical White Paper*, Technology Pathways LLC. URL: `http://www.TechPathways.com/uploads/Exif.pdf`.

Deutsch, P. (1996) *RFC 1952, GZIPfile format specification version 4.3*, Network Working Group.

Free Software Foundation (2006) *Why There Are No GIF files on GNU Web Pages*. URL: `http://www.gnu.org/philosophy/gif.html`.

Hamilton, E. (1992) *JPEG File Interchange Format Version 1.02*, C-Cube Microsystems, 1778 McCarthy Blvd, Milpitas, CA 95035, USA.

ISO (undated) ISO DIS 10918-1.

Kuhn, M. (2005) *UTF-8 and Unicode FAQ*. URL: `http://www.cl.cam.ac.uk/~mgk25/unicode.html`.

Liebenau, J. and Backhouse J. (1990) *Understanding Information – An Introduction*, Macmillan Press Ltd, Basingstoke and London, pp. 1–3.

Messmer, H.-P. (2002) *The Indispensable PC Hardware Book*, 4th edn, Addison-Wesley, Reading, MA.

Microsoft Corporation (2004) *Compound File Binary File Format*. Issued under licence to the Advanced Authoring Format (AAF) Association and currently available as Low-Level Container Specification v1.0.1 at `http://www.aafassociation.org/html/specs/aafcontainerspec-v1.0.1.pdf`.

Murray, J. D. and vanRyper, W. (1996) *Encyclopedia of Graphics File Formats*, O'Reilly & Associates, Sebastopol, CA.

PKWARE Inc. (2006) *APPNOTE.TXT – .ZIP File Format Specification*, Version: 6.3.0, Revised: 29 September 2006. URL: `http://www.pkware.com/documents/casestudies/APPNOTE.TXT`.

Williams, R. (1996) *Data Powers of Ten*. Although the original page has now expired, a similar version is available at URL: `http://www2.sims.berkeley.edu/research/projects/how-much-info/datapowers.html`.

Ziv, J. and Lempel, A. (1977) A universal algorithm for sequential data compression, *IEEE Transactions on Information Theory*, **23**(3), 337–343.

3. IT Systems Concepts

Introduction

In this chapter we will examine the following topics:

- The memory and the processor
- Address and data buses
- The stored program concept
- Format of instructions
- The processor mechanism
- A worked example of processor execution
- Stepping through the worked example
- Program and data and rules and objects
- Software and programming
- Breaking sequence
- A black box model of the PC

In the previous chapter we have seen how we can use binary patterns, physically implemented as the two-state devices of a computer memory, to represent information in a wide variety of forms. We have looked, in some detail, at the representation of numbers, of text, and of pictures, and briefly at some other complex file structures, and we may well have come to the conclusion that perhaps we really *can* represent any real-world object by means of binary patterns in a computer memory. For all practical purposes, this is indeed the case. We may recall that the reason for this unbounded diversity of what can be represented from such simple patterns stems from the limitless sets of rules that we may use to interpret and manipulate them. In all that we have talked about so far, however, the processes of applying the different rules of interpretation to the various binary patterns have all been carried out, by each one of us individually, in our minds. These processes have then revealed to each one of us the "meaning" of a particular pattern given a particular interpretation. Another way of looking at this is that we have extracted *information* from *data*.

In this next chapter, we examine the idea that the rules of interpretation and manipulation, instead of just being in our minds for us to apply, might also be held in the memory of a computer as a sequence of binary patterns. These patterns could then be interpreted by the computer, as an ordered set of instructions which, when executed, cause the computer to carry out a series of actions. If, in carrying out these actions, the computer were to manipulate and interpret other binary patterns of data in its memory, we might see this as little different in principle from our own interpretations of such patterns. We might then view the computer, when executing instructions, as a device that is capable of extracting information from data.

The part of the computer that carries out the function of executing instructions is called the *processor* and the relationship between this element and the memory is what we now need to examine in more detail. We will do this by means of a worked example, showing step by step the principles involved and how data in the memory is interpreted and manipulated by the processor. In order not to confuse the reader with unnecessary detail at this stage, some simplifying assumptions will initially be made, but these do not alter the principles that will be described.

Two Black Boxes

We start with a very simple diagram (Fig. 3.1) showing a processor and a memory as two black boxes connected together by two arrowed lines. The black boxes are shown as separate because it is very likely that they will be implemented using different electronic chips: a processor chip and a memory chip (or possibly a set of memory chips). They are connected together by flexible cables (or tracks on a printed circuit board) which are made up of several wires in parallel. Such multiple connections are called *buses*.

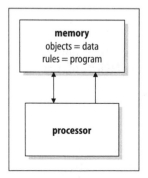

Fig. 3.1 Processor and memory.

Buses

One bus (the *address bus*) has a single arrow on it, indicating a one-way transfer of data and the second bus (the *data bus*) has two arrows, indicating a two-way transfer of data. If we think about the requirement to pass binary patterns between the processor and the memory we might consider an appropriate unit as being the byte. Recalling that a byte consists of eight binary bits, a suitable form of connection that would permit all eight bits of a byte to be transferred in one go would be eight parallel lines: a separate line for each bit. This is precisely the form that a bus takes: a set of parallel lines that permits the transfer of several bits of data all at once. Buses come in many sizes, and the eight bit data bus suggested by this example is now rather dated. However, it will serve our purposes well enough here and we will consider bus sizes again in a later chapter.

The Stored Program Concept

Within the memory box we have indicated binary patterns that represent both *objects* and *rules*. The objects are typified by the real-world objects that we were considering in Chapter 2: numbers, text, pictures, record structures etc. It is perhaps unfortunate that in this context such objects are also sometimes referred to as "data", an association that should not be confused with our earlier use of the word. The rules are ordered sequences of instructions that are to be interpreted by the processor and which will cause it to carry out a series of specific actions. Such sequences of rules are called *programs* and the idea that the computer holds in its memory instructions to itself is sometimes referred to as the *stored program concept*.

So we have the situation where the first of the two black boxes in the diagram, the memory, contains not only the binary patterns that represent the real world objects (the data) but also the binary patterns that represent the rules (the program). These rules specify what is to be done to the binary patterns that are the data, and it is these program rule patterns that are to be interpreted by the second of the two black boxes shown in the diagram: the processor.

The idea can be quite difficult to grasp. There are binary patterns in one part of the memory. These binary patterns are interpreted by the processor as a sequence of rules. The processor executes this sequence of rules and, in so doing, carries out a series of actions. These actions, typically, manipulate binary patterns in another part of the memory. These manipulations then confer specific interpretations onto the manipulated binary patterns. This process mimics, in a very simple form, our mental interpretation of a binary pattern.

Instructions

Now let us consider the form that one such instruction or rule might take. Keeping our example as uncomplicated as possible, we will define a rule as consisting of the binary patterns in two consecutive bytes in memory, as shown in Fig. 3.2.

For our simplified processor, we will decree that the pattern in the first byte of the pair (and we will take the diagram as being big endian) is to represent a *doing* code to

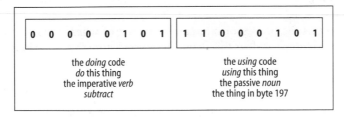

Fig. 3.2 An instruction.

Table 3.1 Example doing codes.

Action	Doing code
Load a byte	00000001
Store a byte	00000010
Add a byte	00000100
Subtract a byte	00000101

the processor. This is an imperative: *do this thing*; the actual details of what particular thing is to be done are to be determined by the binary pattern in the doing byte. In Fig. 3.2 this pattern is 00000101 and we have arbitrarily decided that this should represent the action *subtract* one byte pattern from another.

We will further decree that the pattern in the second byte is to represent the object on which the doing code action is to be carried out. We have called this the *using* code. In Fig. 3.2 this pattern is 11000101, which in decimal is 197. In many cases, the value of this second byte will refer to a starting place in memory where the object to be manipulated resides; that is, it will often be a memory byte address.

The two-byte pattern may therefore be interpreted as an instruction, or rule, which states: "subtract the thing in byte 197". In a practical processor, we would probably have a wide variety of different doing codes available, known collectively as the *order code* for the processor, and these would associate specific patterns in the doing byte with specific actions available in the hardware of the processor. Typical examples might include: add a byte, subtract a byte, multiply a byte, divide a byte, input a byte, output a byte, move a byte, compare a byte and so forth.

There may be similar actions which relate to two or more bytes taken together. The range and functionality of these doing codes are defined by the hardware of the processor[1]. For our example processor, however, we will only consider four such doing codes – *load a byte*, *store a byte*, *add a byte* and *subtract a byte* – and we will decree that load a byte is to be 00000001, store a byte is to be 00000010, add a byte is to be 00000100, and subtract a byte is to be 00000101, as shown in Table 3.1.

The Processor

The basic mechanism for our example processor is very simple. The idea of the stored program concept, as implemented in a modern computer, was first expounded by John Von Neumann (1945). This idea decrees that instructions are held sequentially in the memory and that the processor executes each one, in turn, from the lowest address in memory to the highest address in memory, unless otherwise instructed.

To achieve this the processor maintains a record of where it has got to so far in executing instructions. It does this using an internal store that is variously called the

---

1   Two approaches have been adopted by processor chip manufacturers: designs with large numbers of complex instructions, known as Complex Instruction Set Computers (CISC), and designs with a minimal set of high-speed instructions, known as Reduced Instruction Set Computers (RISC).

counter register or the *sequence control register* or the *program counter*. This is a small element of memory, internal to the processor, which normally holds the address in the main memory of the next instruction that the processor is about to execute. The processor will go through a series of steps to execute an instruction. Again, for the purposes of our example, we have simplified this sequence into four steps: *fetch*, *interpret*, *update* and *execute*. In the *fetch* step, the processor will first of all use its program counter to send a signal to the main memory requesting that it be sent a *copy* of the next instruction to be executed. It will do this using the address bus. The memory will then respond by sending back a copy of the binary patterns that it holds at the address it has been given. It will do this using the data bus. The processor will then take the binary patterns that represent the instruction from the data bus and place them in its *instruction registers* in readiness for decoding. Once the transfer is complete, the processor will then enter the *interpret* step, where it will interpret or *decode* the patterns as an imperative instruction. Part of the pattern will be used to select the action that the processor should perform, and part will be used to determine the object to which this action should be applied, as we described above. On completion of its preparations to perform the instruction, the processor will then enter the *update* step. In this step, the processor prepares its program counter so that it is ready for the next instruction in sequence.

In general, it does this by calculating the length in bytes of the current instruction and adding that value to its program counter. Given that the system is set up to obey a sequence of instructions, one after the other, from lower address to higher address, the program counter, having had this length added, will thus be pointing to the start of the next instruction in the sequence. Finally, the processor enters the *execute* step, where the action defined in the interpret step is applied to the object defined in the interpret step. To do this, it may well use an additional register as a scratchpad for interim results, and this is sometimes known as an *accumulator* or *general purpose register*. After that, the processor repeats the cycle starting with the fetch step once again.

The Worked Example

Fig. 3.3 shows a more detailed view of the two black boxes that we considered earlier, now rotated through 90° and expanded so that we can see something of what they contain. Here we are able to see into a small portion of the main memory on the left-hand side and observe exactly what patterns are in the bytes with addresses 3, 4 and 5 and 31 through to 36.

All that we require for the processor, on the right-hand side, is a small element of internal memory for the registers and a four-step cyclic control mechanism which we find useful to compare with the four stroke internal combustion engine. Where we have "suck", "squeeze", "bang" and "blow" for the four strokes of the internal combustion engine we have "fetch", "interpret", "update" and "execute" for the four steps of the processor cycle. One rather important difference between the two models, however, is their rotational speed. In the case of a typical modern processor,

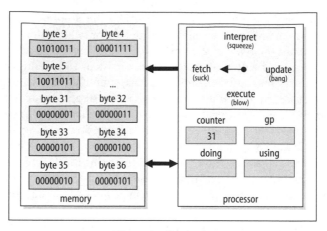

Fig. 3.3 Looking inside.

the Intel Pentium 4 for example, the speed of operation can be as high as 10 000 MIPs[2] or more. This suggests that, since each "revolution" causes one instruction to be carried out, the equivalent "rotational speed" is 10 000 million revolutions per second, compared with the 4000 or so *revolutions per minute* of an internal combustion engine.

The processor is shown connected to the main memory by the two buses, the address bus at the top and the data bus at the bottom. There is a third bus, not shown on the diagram for the sake of clarity, known as the *control bus*, and this is concerned with control activities, such as the direction of data flow on the data bus and the general timing of events throughout the system.

As was described above, the program counter in the processor holds the address of where in main memory the next instruction that the processor is to execute can be found (in this example, address 31[3]) and the *doing* and *using* registers are our versions of the instruction registers used by the processor to interpret the current instruction. The *gp* register is the general purpose scratchpad register that was also referred to earlier. We have used throughout registers that are only one byte in size so as to keep the example simple. Again, this does not affect the principles, but modern practical processors are likely to have two, four and even eight byte registers.

The in-built control mechanism of our example processor causes it to cycle clockwise through the four steps: fetch, interpret, update and execute, over and over again, repeating the same cycle continuously all the while that the processor is switched on. We have earlier likened this to the four strokes of the internal combustion engine (suck, squeeze, bang and blow), and these are also shown on the diagram. The rate at which the processor cycle is executed is controlled by a system

2   MIPs stands for *Millions of Instructions Per Second* or, as some would have us say, *Meaningless Indicators of Performance*.

3   This number would be held in the register in binary, but we have shown it here in decimal so as not to over-complicate the example.

clock and, as mentioned above, this might well be running at several thousands of millions of cycles per second[4].

Executing the Worked Example

Using our example machine, we can now step through the processor cycle for ourselves and determine exactly what happens at each stage and how each pattern in memory is interpreted by the system. We start with the beginning of the fetch step, as shown in Fig. 3.4.

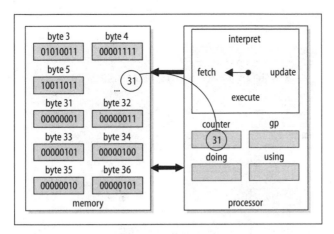

Fig. 3.4 Processor puts 31 on address bus.

Here the value of the program counter, shown as decimal 31 in the diagram, is placed on the address bus by the processor and sent across to the memory in binary by means of the eight parallel connections referred to earlier[5]. The memory is by this means requested to transfer a copy of what is in bytes 31 and 32, that is, the patterns of the next instruction, to the processor[6].

In Fig. 3.5 we see copies of the two bytes being passed across the data bus in binary, one after the other, back to the processor. As these copies are received so the processor places them in its doing and using registers respectively. On completion, the processor then moves on to the interpret step, as shown in Fig. 3.6.

---

4   One point arises from this speed of operation. Should you happen to note that your PC is starting to behave suspiciously and you try to stop the current operation as quickly as you can, you are almost certainly many thousands of millions of instructions too late in the most rapid action that you could possibly take!

5   A modern processor is more likely to have an address bus of 32 bits.

6   The assumption is made here that the memory somehow "knows" that instructions are two bytes long. In practice, the processor would request the appropriate number of bytes for the particular instruction. This simplification does not affect the principles of the example.

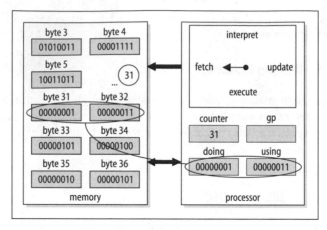

Fig. 3.5 Memory sends copies of bytes 31 and 32.

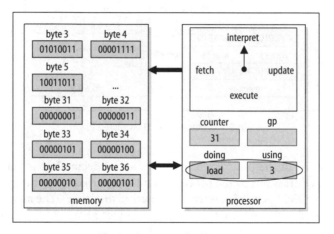

Fig. 3.6 Interpret as load byte 3.

The "handshaking" process we have seen here is typical of the way in which the various parts of the computer system interact with one another. Requests are sent across the address bus and results are returned across the data bus, with control being exercised by signals on the control bus, which for clarity we have not shown on our diagrams. For example, signals on the control bus will indicate when the address and data buses contain valid values and can therefore be read.

In Fig. 3.6, we see that the patterns in the doing and using registers have been interpreted as the instruction "load byte 3". We can interpret the doing code 00000001 from Table 3.1 as "load a byte" and the using code 00000011 as the "address of byte 3".

The processor would now, at this step, have prepared its internal circuitry so as to be ready to carry out the action "load address byte 3" when it reaches the execute step.

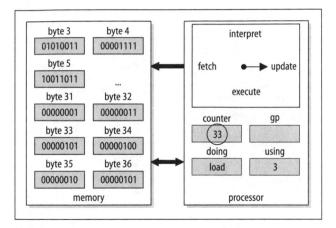

Fig. 3.7 Update counter to 33.

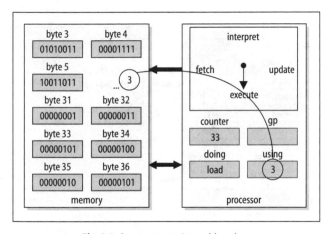

Fig. 3.8 Processor puts 3 on address bus.

In Fig. 3.7, we see the effect of the update step. Here the value 2 has been added to the program counter so that it now holds the address of the next instruction in the sequence, address 33. In our example, we decided to make all instructions of the same length, that is two bytes, and so arranging for the program counter to point to the next instruction in the sequence is achieved simply by adding 2 to its value. As we will see later, the update sequence occurs at this point in the cycle, because we may, for certain functions, wish to modify the program counter in the execute step.

In the execute step, the instruction "load address byte 3" is carried out by the processor. First of all a copy of the using register, shown as decimal 3 in Fig. 3.8, is placed on the address bus by the processor and sent across to the memory in binary[7].

_____

7   Like the value for the program counter, this number would be held in the register in
    binary, but we have shown it here in decimal so as not to over-complicate the example.

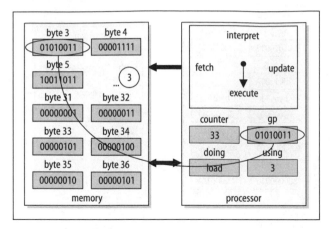

Fig. 3.9 Memory sends copy of byte 3 to processor.

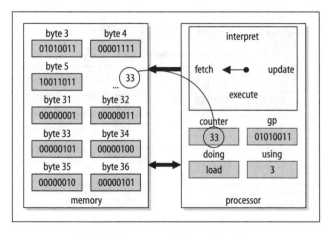

Fig. 3.10 Processor puts 33 on address bus.

This requests the memory to transfer a copy of byte 3 to the processor over the data bus. We see this happening in Fig. 3.9. When the processor receives the copy of byte 3, it places the binary value, 01010011, into its general purpose (gp) register as shown in the diagram. This completes the execution of the first instruction. The processor then moves on to the next step which is the fetch step for the next instruction as shown in Fig. 3.10.

Here we see the start of a similar cycle of events as before. The processor places the value of the program counter, shown as decimal 33 in the diagram, onto the address bus, thus requesting the memory to transfer a copy of what is in bytes 33 and 34, the patterns of the next instruction, to the processor.

The memory responds, in a similar manner to that shown before, by transferring copies of bytes 33 and 34 across the data bus. In this case 00000101 is sent first, followed by 00000100, and these are written by the processor into its doing and using

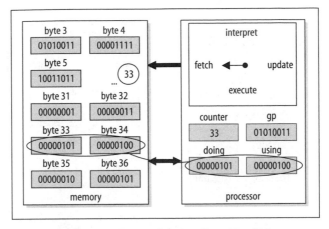

Fig. 3.11 Memory sends copies of bytes 33 and 34.

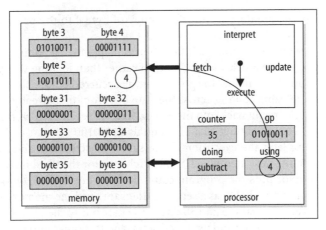

Fig. 3.12 Processor puts 4 on address bus.

registers respectively. This situation is then as shown at Fig. 3.11. From all that has gone before, it is not difficult to work out what will happen at the interpret step, which we have not shown as a separate diagram. The processor, at this step, decodes the doing register as "subtract a byte" (see Table 3.1) and the using register as "address byte 4". The instruction set up internally by the processor is therefore "subtract address byte 4".

For the update step, which we have also not shown as a separate diagram, the processor simply adds 2 to the program counter, which then becomes 35, to take account of the fact that this is a Von Neumann sequential machine and that each instruction is of two bytes in length.

Given all of that, the start of the execute step "subtract address byte 4" is then as shown in Fig. 3.12. As before, a copy of the using register, shown as decimal 4 in Fig. 3.12, is placed on the address bus by the processor and sent across to the memory in binary.

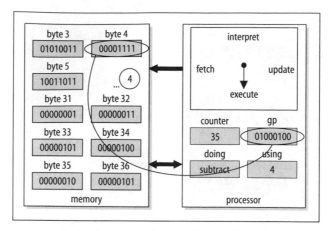

Fig. 3.13 Memory sends copy of byte 4 to processor.

This requests the memory to transfer a copy of byte 4 to the processor over the data bus, and we see this happening in Fig. 3.13.

This time, however, something a little different happens. The doing action here is not "load a byte" but "subtract a byte" and so rather than loading the value coming across the data bus straight into the gp register, as occurred before, the processor this time *subtracts* the value coming across the data bus from that already held in the gp register, putting the result back into the gp register. We see, therefore, that the action, in binary, of 01010011 subtract 00001111 equals 01000100.

This then completes the execution of the second instruction, and the processor now moves on to the next step, which is the fetch step for the third instruction. Once again, the processor puts the program counter value, decimal 35, onto the address bus (which we have not shown as a separate diagram) and the memory sends copies of the two bytes at addresses 35 and 36 across the data bus to the processor. As before, these are placed in the doing and using registers, and this outcome can be seen in Fig. 3.14.

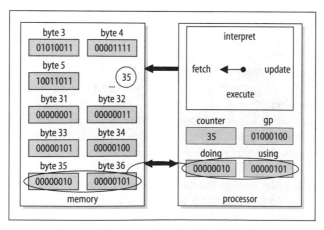

Fig. 3.14 Memory sends copies of bytes 35 and 36.

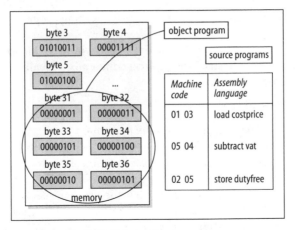

Fig. 3.18 Object and source programs.

convenient-to-us binary form that the computer needs, and to place the resulting binary patterns in the appropriate places in memory for us.

Perhaps the simplest form of external representation that we might use is the hexadecimal equivalent of the binary values. We could then lay the three instructions out on a piece of paper or type them it in at a terminal in the following format:

```
01 03 <newline>
05 04 <newline>
02 05 <newline>
```

We have here arranged for the doing code to be separated from the using code by a space and for each separate instruction to start on a new line. We would also need to specify to the translator program where in memory the sequence was to be placed (in our example, from bytes 31 onwards). All that we have done is to use an external abstraction that is a little more readable to us than the binary patterns the computer uses. We have in fact defined a very simple *programming language* and in this format the program statements would be known as *machine code*.

There is no reason, however, why we should limit ourselves to a numeric language representation. We know that 00000001 means "load a byte", 00000101 means "subtract a byte" and 00000010 means "store a byte", so we could use the words "load", "subtract" and "store" to represent the equivalent doing codes. In addition, we could replace the byte addresses 3, 4 and 5 with suitably chosen names to give us a much more readable format, thus:

```
load       costprice
subtract   vat
store      dutyfree
```

We really do not mind which actual addresses in memory are used for the data, provided that they are accessed consistently, so we can name them costprice, vat and dutyfree and permit the translator to decide exactly where in memory they are to be put. One of the benefits of this is that the purpose of the rules can become much clearer if the names are sensibly chosen. In this format the program statements would be known as *assembly language* and the translating program would be called an *assembler*.

It is possible to go further and develop a much more complex programming language together with its translating program, then more usually called a *compiler*, that permits statements such as:

```
dutyfree := costprice - vat;
```

These may then be *compiled* into the internal binary patterns that the machine requires. Such statements are typical of so called *High Order Languages* (HOLs); that is, languages that have been specifically designed to assist programming at a high level of abstraction. Some examples of these are: ALGOL, COBOL, FORTRAN, Pascal, C, C++ and Ada. It should be noted that what the programmer writes down in the programming language is often called the *source code* and what is actually executed by the computer, after translation or compilation, may be called the *object code*.

Practical Programming Systems

In a practical programming system, such as an *integrated development environment* (IDE; see, for example, Borland (1994)), there will be more complications than this, of some of which the forensic computing analyst needs to be aware. Source code files will often have a file type that indicates the programming language in which they have been written: PAS for Pascal, C for C, and CPP for C++ for example. Such files will invariably be in ASCII text format. Many systems will also use ASCII text files of type H for configuration and header information. In practice, most compilers do not compile source code directly into the object code of the computer, but rather generate an intermediate or *semi-compiled* file format that permits the linking of library and other files to this semi-compiled file before the generation of the final executable program. Such semi-compiled files often have the file type OBJ. Files of type OBJ may also be grouped into library files of type LIB using *library manager* software. The final executable program, of file type COM or EXE, is normally produced by the *linker*. This takes the semi-compiled OBJ file and embeds within it all the necessary library files and any other specified OBJ files to produce the final executable form that we called above the object code.

However, this method can be wasteful when many EXE files all have copies of the same library files within them. To overcome this, the concept of *Dynamic Link Library* files or *DLLs* was conceived, and these are loaded by the operating system as needed and provide common access to library files dynamically for all those EXE files that support the facility.

If, during forensic analysis, a programming system is met with, all of these types of files are likely to be found. In addition there may be DSK, PRJ and TC files which are used by the programming environment to control the desktop, the project and the programming environment configurations respectively[11].

---

11 For details of these and other file signatures see Appendix 2.

Breaking Sequence

In all that has been described so far, the processor has had no option but to execute one instruction after the other in sequence through the memory. This occurs because the program counter is automatically incremented by two within the processor control cycle, and the program counter always points to the next instruction that the processor is to execute. In practice, however, this is not very useful by itself. Many processes are highly repetitive and we would often like to be able to repeat a sequence of instructions many times. This can be achieved if we provide instructions which have doing actions that change the value of the program counter. This can be made even more useful if we make the carrying out of these doing actions conditional on some other register value.

So, we might invent a new instruction for the processor with doing code 00001000, say, which has the following doing action: *"if the gp register is not equal to zero then subtract the value of the using code from the program counter"*.

How might this work? Before we look at an example, it would be as well to establish a method that avoids us having to draw quite so many diagrams as we used for the previous example.

Finger Checks

When programming at very low level or when attempting to deal with a particularly elusive bug, programmers will sometimes use what used to be known as *finger checks*. As shown at Table 3.2 for the worked example of Fig. 3.4, the current values of the processor registers and of any relevant memory addresses are placed in the columns of a table and each row of the table is used to represent the execution of a single instruction. In this way, the effects of the execution of each instruction by the processor can be examined in detail without the need for all the diagrams that we used above. In this instance, Table 3.2 encapsulates the effects of the execution of the three instructions from our worked example.

In this table we have drawn up five columns. The first column shows the current value of the program counter. For each program counter value we show a line of values, with, in separate columns, the doing code (and its equivalent action), the using code, and the current value in the gp register. We also show the values in all the relevant memory addresses, 3, 4 and 5.

Table 3.2 Finger check of the worked example.

Program counter	Doing		Using code	gp	Address		
	Code	Action			03	04	05
31	01	load	03	53	53	0f	9b
33	05	subtract	04	44	53	0f	9b
35	02	store	05	44	53	0f	44
37							

For this example, the program counter starts at 31, which refers to a doing code of 01H and a using code of 03H, resulting in the instruction "load 03". The execution of this instruction results in the gp register being set to 53H[12]. The memory addresses 3, 4 and 5 contain 53H, 0fH and 9bH respectively. Meanwhile, the program counter has been stepped to 33 and this refers to a doing code of 05H and a using code of 04H, resulting in the instruction "subtract 04". The execution of this instruction results in the value 0fH being subtracted from the 53H in the gp register giving the result in the gp register of 44H. No changes occur to the memory bytes of 3, 4 or 5. Finally, the program counter has been stepped to 35 and this refers to a doing code of 02H and a using code of 05H, resulting in the instruction "store 05". The execution of this instruction results in the value in the gp register, 44H, being written into memory address 5. No changes occur to the memory bytes of 3 or 4. Now we find that the program counter has been stepped to 37, where we leave the example.

A Revised Example

Let us now consider a revised example, shown at Fig. 3.19, which incorporates our new break sequence instruction, 00001000. We need to give this new instruction a name, and in most programming languages it will be called something like: *jump*, *branch* or *goto* and the conditional versions would be called *jump if* etc. We will call ours "*jump back if gp not zero*" to describe its action and then use an acronym such as "jbnz". This is typical of the kinds of names that are given by processor manufacturers to their assembly language codes.

Now we will use our finger check technique to step through the actions of the example in Fig. 3.19, the relevant table for which is shown at Table 3.3.

The program counter starts at 31, referring to the instruction "load 07" and the execution of this results in the gp register being set to 03H. Meanwhile, the program

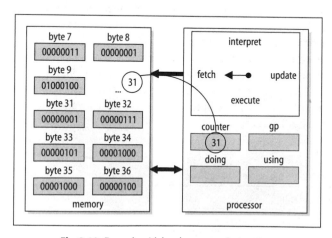

Fig. 3.19 Example with break sequence instruction.

---

12 Note that we have used here hexadecimal format (hence the "H") rather than the binary format that appears in the worked example.

Table 3.3 Finger check of the new example.

Counter register	Doing		Using code	gp	Address		
	Code	Action			07	08	09
31	01	load	07	03	03	01	44
33	05	subtract	08	02	03	01	44
35	08	jbnz	04	02	03	01	44
37 – 4 = 33	05	subtract	08	01	03	01	44
35	08	jbnz	04	01	03	01	44
37 – 4 = 33	05	subtract	08	00	03	01	44
35	08	jbnz	04	00	03	01	44
37							

counter has been stepped to 33. The next instruction, at 33, is "subtract 08" and the result of this execution is that 01H (the value in byte address 08) is subtracted from 03H in the gp register, giving 02H. Again, the program counter has been stepped, now to 35, whence our new instruction "jbnz 04" comes into effect. By this time, the program counter has already been stepped to 37[13] when the action "*if the gp register is not equal to zero then subtract the value of the using code from the program counter*" is carried out. The gp register is 02H, which is not zero, so the program counter is changed to 37 – 4 = 33, which has the effect of executing the "*jump back if gp not zero*" doing code. The instruction at 33, "subtract 08", is therefore repeated and the result of this execution is that once again the value 01H is subtracted, this time from the value 02H in the gp register, giving the value 01H. Again, we find that the program counter has been stepped to 35, and our new instruction "jbnz 04" comes into effect once more. This time the gp register is 01H, which is still not zero, so the program counter is changed once more to 37 – 4 = 33.

So the process repeats again. The instruction at 33, "subtract 08", is executed once more and the result of this execution is that the value 01H is subtracted, this time from the value 01H in the gp register, giving a value of 00H. Again, the program counter has been stepped to 35 and our new instruction "jbnz 04" comes into effect. This time, however, the gp register is 00H, which is indeed zero. So, on this occasion, the value of the using code is *not* subtracted from the program counter, which therefore remains at 37. From here on the processor continues to execute instructions in sequence through the memory *until instructed otherwise by some other jump type instruction*.

Some analysis of this construct is useful. The two instructions at 33 and 35 were executed in sequence three times; precisely the number of times that is specified by the value in byte 7. The gp register was used as a counter. It was set initially to the value of byte 7, and was then reduced by one each time the *loop* of instructions was

---

13 Recall that the update step takes place before the execute step, so the program counter is set to the *next* instruction *before* the current instruction is executed.

executed until it reached zero, This is a typical construct for controlling a loop. What has been demonstrated with this example is a *counter-controlled loop*.

This loop has not done anything interesting, and that is simply in order to keep the example clear and to limit the number of instructions that we would have to examine each time we worked round the loop. In practice, we might think of a small program that repeats a sequence of operations on a very large database. Let us say that, the sequence is, for every record in the database (perhaps 1 000 000 records or more):

open the next record
extract the name field
print the name field

Now we can conceive of first writing the relatively few instructions needed to carry out this sequence of operations once. Then we put, at the beginning of those instructions, code that loads a counter with 1 000 000 and, we put, at the end of those instructions, code that subtracts 1 from the counter. Finally, we put at the very end a jbnz command to jump back to the start of "open the next record" if the new value of the counter is not yet zero. In this way, the sequence of instructions to open a record and extract and print the name field would be carried out exactly 1 000 000 times, once for each record in the database.

An Information Processing System

If what has been covered to this point is clear, then a very reasonable understanding of the principles by which all Von Neumann architecture computers operate and are programmed should have been gained. In a later chapter we will examine the specific architecture and workings of the PC, but this should not now hold any surprises in store for us. To complete this chapter, we should now develop our two black boxes of processor and memory into a complete system.

Expanding on our two black boxes of Fig. 3.1, we now include an input device, an output device and a backing store to obtain the black box model of a complete information processing system, as shown in Fig. 3.20. This is a typical black box model of a PC.

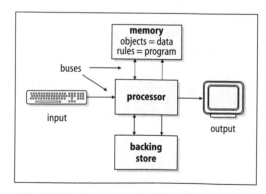

Fig. 3.20 Black box model of an information processing system.

A typical input device would be a *keyboard* and a typical output device would be a *visual display unit* (*VDU*) or *monitor*. Up until relatively recently most monitors would have been based on the *cathode ray tube* (*CRT*) display, but today a flat screen panel *liquid crystal display* (*LCD*), is much more likely. Many other kinds of input and output devices may of course be connected, ranging for example from *printers* and *sound cards* to *modems* and *mice*. All have access to the processor and memory, either directly or indirectly, through the address, data and control buses.

Because the main memory is usually volatile and loses all information at power down, it is essential that we are able to load previously developed programs and data from some external source into the main memory and save our programs and data that we wish to use again onto a more permanent medium. A device which provides this facility is called a *backing store*, and this is the lower black box in our diagram. In principle, at least, a backing store is very simple. When it is required to save a program or a piece of data, the binary patterns in memory representing the relevant information are transferred, for example, to a magnetic disk, where they are used to record equivalent magnetic patterns on the surface of the disk. When it is required to restore the program or piece of data, then the relevant part of the magnetic disk is played back and the resulting binary patterns are used to reset the memory addresses to their original values. In this way, any information may be saved and reloaded from disk. In Chapter 5 we will examine this process in much more detail.

Several forms of magnetic disk have become available over the years, including various sizes of *floppy disk*, various sizes of *hard disk* and several versions of *Zip disk*. However, magnetic disk is not the only medium for backing store. Magnetic tape was first used, with rows of large reel-to-reel systems once typifying the layman's image of a computer centre. Today magnetic tape is still used, though more usually in the form of *cartridge tapes*.

Non-magnetic systems are also widely used, the most common of these being CD-ROM devices, where the binary patterns are implemented as pits in the surface of the disk and are read back by laser light. Originally these were classed as WORM[14] systems that could not be rewritten to, but nowadays so-called *rewritable CD-ROM* devices have become very common. *DVD* (which originally stood for *Digital Video Disc* but is now more usually called *Digital Versatile Disc*) has become the major substitute for CD-ROM drives on all modern systems. DVD operates in a similar manner to CD-ROM, using lasers to read pits on the surface of the disk, and it is of the same physical dimensions. The major differences, however, are that it uses a higher frequency laser, has a smaller track pitch and pit size and can be double-layered and double-sided. In comparison with a CD-ROM, which has a capacity of around 700 Mbyte, the single-sided, single-layered DVD has a capacity of 4.7 Gbyte, and a double-sided, double-layered DVD can hold up to 17 Gbyte.

---

14 This acronym stands for "Write Once Read Many".

References

Borland (1994) *Borland C++ User's Guide, Version 4.5*, Borland International, Inc., Scotts Valley, CA 95067-0001.

Von Neumann, John (1945), *First Draft of a Report on the EDVAC*, 30 June 1945, Contract No W-670-ORD-492, Moore School of Electrical Engineering, University of Pennsylvania, Philadelphia.

Exercises

3.1   Using Table 3.1 and a finger check table as required, determine the actions that will occur when the instructions shown in Fig. 3.21, from address 31 onwards, are executed.

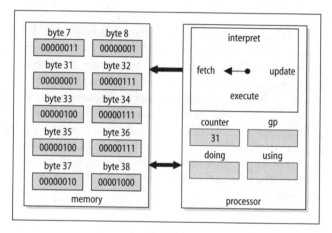

Fig. 3.21

3.2   Examine the diagram at Fig. 3.22. This is a more extensive piece of program code and data than we have used before. For this reason, a diagram such as Fig. 3.21 has not been used, but rather the program code and data segments have been written down in a tabular form, much as early programmers used programming sheets. Assuming that the program counter starts at 31, and using the doing codes that we have defined, determine the final value of memory address 09. What process is carried out by this code?

3.3   List a sequence of instructions, using only "jbnz" and those listed in Table 3.1, that will result in the value in memory address 05 being *multiplied* by the value in memory address 06 and the byte result left in memory address 07. Assume that memory address 05 contains the value 3 and that memory address 06 contains the value 7. Confirm, after execution of the program using a finger check, that memory address 07 contains 21. Because this is quite difficult, three hints are given as follows: (1) Note that multiplication can be implemented by

program			data	
Memory address	Doing code	Using code	Memory address	Value
31	01	05	05	04
33	02	06	06	00
35	01	07	07	01
37	04	08	08	01
39	02	09	09	00
3b	01	08	0a	01
3d	02	07		
3f	01	09		
41	02	08		
43	01	06		
45	05	0a		
47	02	06		
49	08	16		

Fig. 3.22

successive addition. (2) You will need to use some additional memory bytes for temporary storage. (3) The program is at least 11 instructions long.

4. PC Hardware and Inside the Box

Introduction

In the previous two chapters we have looked first at how information can be represented and then at how the principles of a von Neumann machine may be used to
construct an information processing system. In this chapter we will take the black
box model of chapter 3 and develop from that the actual hardware of a modern PC.
As we do that, we will look inside the box so that we can identify all the pieces. This is
an important part of an analyst's task. A detailed internal examination of a PC is
invariably going to be required since we will wish to know firstly that it is safe to
operate, and then to see whether it is being used as a storage box for other items of
possible evidential value, and finally whether all its components are connected up
correctly. An ability to recognize what should be there and how the bits should be
connected together is therefore of some considerable importance. This is summa-
rized as follows:

- Revision of the black box model
- The mother board and all the buses
- Packaging of chips
- The 8088 and the design of the PC
- System resources
- The Intel processors
- Static RAM, dynamic RAM and ROM
- Connection of backing store devices
- Connection of peripherals
- Expansion cards

The Black Box Model

Just to remind us, the black box model of Chapter 3, has been shown again as Fig. 4.1.
We can use this to identify the elements of a real PC that we will need to look at. The

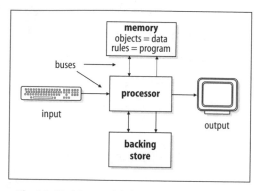

Fig. 4.1 Black box model of an information processing system.

first element we are going to consider, rather surprisingly perhaps, is the mechanism by which the major elements are connected up.

We have shown in the diagram the interconnections between the major elements: we referred to these in Chapter 3 as the address and data buses. Recalling that they are simply sets of electrical connections, it will be no surprise to note that they tend to be implemented as parallel tracks on a printed circuit board (PCB). This brings us then to the most important component of all, the *motherboard*. This normally hosts the processor and the memory chips, and as a result the buses between them are usually just parallel tracks on the motherboard. Also on the motherboard is the *chipset* that carries out all the housekeeping needed to keep control of the information transfers between the processor, the memory and all the peripheral devices. In addition, the motherboard hosts the real-time clock, which contains within it the battery-backed memory known as the *CMOS or Complementary Metal Oxide Semiconductor* memory, and the *Basic Input Output System (BIOS) Read-Only Memory (ROM)*. One particularly clever idea in the original design of the PC was to arrange for the various buses to be accessible in a standard form so that *expansion cards* could be fitted into *expansion slots* on the motherboard and thus gain access to all the buses. The motherboard normally has a number of these expansion slot connectors either directly fitted onto the motherboard itself, or fitted onto a separate *riser board* or *daughterboard* that may be connected at right angles to the motherboard.

The next item we need to look at is the processor. This technology has advanced at an unprecedented rate, in terms of both performance and price, over the past 25 years, and a little bit of the history of the PC needs to be covered because of the way that various legacy issues still affect us today. Then we must look at the memory, and this too has advanced rapidly both in performance and price, resulting in very much greater capacities becoming the norm. We need also to look at the backing store, of which the floppy disk and the hard disk are the most common examples. Although we will examine these in much greater detail in Chapter 5, we need here to note the various other kinds of backing store that we might come across, and to be able to recognize them and understand how they are connected into the system.

For the external peripherals of the system, such as the display, the mouse, the keyboard, the printer and the scanner, we will do no more than mention how they are connected. Finally, we need to look at some of the possible expansion cards, such as the video card, the network card and the sound card, at least in enough detail to be able to recognize them.

The Buses and the Motherboard

We start our exploration with the buses. As we have seen earlier, the buses are no more than a set of parallel electrical connections: one connection for each bit of information. Hence an eight bit bus can transfer eight bits or one byte of information at a time. From this, it becomes apparent that although the speed at which the processor operates is a very important factor in the overall performance of the system, it is the data transfer rates across the system buses which effectively act as bottlenecks and limit the performance of the whole. For this reason, there has been much development of buses throughout the life of the PC to try to overcome these various performance bottlenecks as the major elements of the system have all become so much faster.

Three Buses

A simplistic view of the PC considers the major elements to be interconnected by means of three main buses: the *address bus*, the *data bus* and the *control bus*. In Fig. 4.2 we have taken as an example the interconnections of these three buses between the processor unit and the memory unit.

Here the address bus provides the means by which, for example, the processor can signal the memory with the address of a byte to which it wants access. We saw this in action in Chapter 3. More generally, the address bus is used by any autonomous[1]

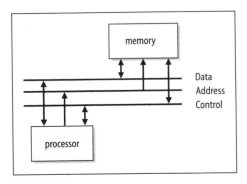

Fig. 4.2 Three buses.

---

1   Autonomous devices are devices that can operate without every action being controlled by the main processor. The writing of a memory block to a hard disk drive, for instance, would be initiated by the processor, but the disk controller might then carry out the detailed transfer of each byte of memory autonomously, referring back to the processor with an interrupt only when the transfer was complete. This is sometimes also referred to as Direct Memory Access (DMA).

device to specify the address of some other device (or the address of part of some other device such as a memory byte) with which it wishes to communicate. The data bus, in the above diagram, provides the means by which the data bits are passed, in parallel, between the memory and the processor after the address of the required byte has been specified by the address bus. Again, we saw this in action in Chapter 3. The control bus carries, as you might expect, a number of control lines concerned with the housekeeping that is necessary to make this all work. Examples of such control lines include signals to indicate that the data bus is being used to *read* a byte from memory, the data bus is being used to *write* a byte into memory, the values on the address bus are currently valid, the processor is using the system buses, and so forth. In addition, a number of clock timing signals are also distributed by means of the control bus.

The three-bus model derives from the early processors, with their sets of data, address and control pins, which were used to construct the first PCs. The buses are implemented in such a way as to provide a standard interface to other devices. Using this standard interface, expansion cards containing new devices can easily be slotted into spare sockets on the motherboard and be connected directly to the three buses.

Size of Buses

Clearly the size of the data bus, that is, the number of bits that can be transferred in parallel, is going to be a major factor in determining overall system performance. The wider the bus, the more data that can be passed in parallel on each machine cycle and hence the faster the overall system should be able to run. The data bus width is often used to categorize processors. Very early processors are known as *8 bit*, because they have only 8 pins for access to their external data bus. In the mid- to late 1970s came the first of the *16 bit* processors, and the Intel Pentium processors of today are *64 bit*, which means that they can transfer 8 *bytes* at a time over their external data bus. One point worth noting, in passing, is that modern processors are likely to have much larger internal data buses, which interact with their on-chip *caches*, than the external data buses that are evident to the rest of the system. In the case of the Intel Pentium 4, the internal data bus, on the chip itself, is 256 bits wide.

The width of the address bus, on the other hand, determines the maximum number of different devices or memory bytes that can be individually addressed. In practice, it imposes a limit on the size of the memory that is directly accessible to the processor, and thus dictates the memory capacity of the system.

Packaging of Chips

Obviously then, for high performance and high capacity, we want the data and address buses to be as large as possible. One limitation that is imposed on the size of these buses is the need to connect each separate contact point on the tiny processor chip to a corresponding pin on some supporting container package and then to be able to plug that package into a suitable socket on the motherboard.

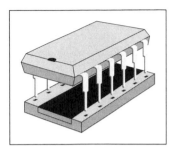

Fig. 4.3 A typical DIL chip.

One standard packaging arrangement that has been around since the early days of the PC is for the *Dual In Line* (*DIL*) chip as shown at Fig. 4.3 (from Microsoft ClipArt Gallery 2.0), and this is often known as a *Dual In line Package* (*DIP*). For the processor at the heart of the original IBM PC, the Intel 8088, the DIL package has 40 pins, with 20 down each side. The data bus is 8 bits wide and the address bus is 20 bits wide, but 20 pins on the package are also needed for control signals and for the power supply. In order to fit all of this onto a 40 pin package, many of the pins have to be used for more than one purpose at different times in the processor cycle. With the Intel 8088, the address pins 0 to 7 also double up as the eight data bus pins and the address pins 16 to 19 carry status information as well. This technique is known as *multiplexing* and obviously adds additional complication to the motherboard in having to separate out the various signals. DIL packages with more than 40 legs were found to be very unwieldy and difficult to plug into their sockets, although the Texas Instruments TMS9900 had 64 pins in a DIL package (see Adams, 1981). In later processor systems, as the number of pin connections required increased, the DIL packaging was found to be too limiting and was replaced by a square- or rectangular-shaped package with several rows of pins on each side, known as a *Pin Grid Array* (*PGA*).

With this packaging, now often referred to as the *form factor* of the chip, we see the more frequent use of *Zero Insertion Force* (*ZIF*) sockets, which allow the relatively easy replacement and upgrading of pin grid array processor chips. A ZIF socket allows a chip to be inserted into the socket without using any significant force. When the chip is properly seated in the socket, a spring-loaded locking plate is moved into place by means of a small lever, which can be seen to the left of Fig. 4.4, and this grips all the pins securely making good electrical contact with them. In Fig. 4.4 the lever is shown in the down (locked) position on a Socket 939 ZIF socket. The form factors of processor chips for the PC introduced by Intel over the years have seen a variety of pin grid array systems, initially known as *Socket 1* through to *Socket 8*, as shown at Table 4.1[2]. Socket 8 is a *Staggered Pin Grid Array* (*SPGA*), which was specially designed for Pentium Pro with its integrated L2 cache.

Intel also introduced what they called a *Single Edge Contact* (*SEC*) cartridge for some of the Pentium II and III processors. This form factor is called *Slot 1* and is a 242 contact daughter card slot. They then increased the number of contacts on the SEC

---

2 See http://en.wikipedia.org/wiki/CPU_socket.

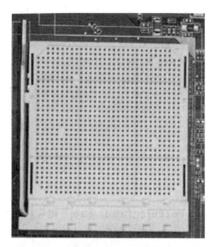

Fig. 4.4 A Socket 939 ZIF socket (photograph: Tony Sammes and Brian Jenkinson).

Table 4.1 Initial Socket numbers.

Socket	No. of pins	Layout	Processor types
Socket 1	169	17 × 17	486SX, SX2, DX, DX2, DX2 and DX4 Overdrive
Socket 2	238	19 × 19	486SX, SX2, DX, DX2, DX2 and DX4 Overdrive 486 Pentium Overdrive
Socket 3	237	19 × 19	486SX, SX2, DX, DX2, DX4 486 Pentium Overdrive
Socket 4	273	21 × 21	Pentium 60, 66 and Pentium 60, 66 Overdrive
Socket 5	320	37 × 37	Pentium 75–133, Pentium 75 + Overdrive
Socket 6	235	19 × 19	486DX4, 486 Pentium Overdrive
Socket 7	321	37 × 37	Pentium 75–200, Pentium 75 + Overdrive
Socket 8	387	34 × 37	Pentium Pro

cartridge to 330 and this became known as *Slot 2*. Other manufacturers produced *Slot A* and *Slot B* SEC form factors.

Subsequently, for the Pentium III and Pentium 4, the Socket form factor returned to favour and a variety of different Socket numbers were produced by Intel with the Socket number indicating the number of pins on the PGA. Some examples are: Socket 370, Socket 423, Socket 478, Socket 479, Socket 775 and so forth. In addition, other manufacturers produced their own versions, such as: Socket 754, Socket 939 (the one shown in Fig. 4.4 for an AMD chip), Socket A, Socket F and so forth.

A more radical approach to the packaging problem is to place the die (or silicon chip) directly onto the printed circuit board and bond the die connections straight onto lands set up for that purpose on the PCB. The die is then covered with a blob of resin for protection. This technique is known as *Chip on Board* (*COB*) or *Direct Chip Attach* (*DCA*) and is now frequently found in the production of *Personal Digital Assistants* (*PDAs*) and electronic organizers.

Bus Routes

As the PC developed, the simple idea of having just one set of buses (the address bus, the data bus and the control bus) which connected everything to everything was found wanting. The problem is that different parts of the system operate at different speeds and require different bus widths, so the "one size fits all" approach leads to unacceptable data transfer bottlenecks.

In order to try to reduce these bottlenecks, a number of different buses were introduced which were tailored to connect particular parts of the system together. In the early designs, these buses might be called, for example, the *processor bus*, the *I/O (input–output) bus* and the *memory bus*.

At Fig. 4.5 we see a typical case, where the processor bus connects the processor both to the bus controller chipset and to the external cache memory (ignoring for the moment the connection to the local bus). This processor bus is a high-speed bus, which for the Pentium might have 64 data lines, 32 address lines and various control lines, and would operate at the external clock rate. For a 66 MHz motherboard clock speed, this means that the maximum transfer rate, or *bandwidth*, of the processor data bus would be $66 \times 64 = 4224$ Mbit per second.

Continuing with our example case, the memory bus is used to transfer information from the processor to the main *dynamic random access memory (DRAM)* chips of the system. This bus is often controlled by special memory controller chips in the bus controller chipset because the DRAM operates at a significantly slower speed than the processor. The main memory data bus will probably be the same size as the processor data bus, and this is what defines a *bank* of memory. When adding more DRAM to a system, it has to be added, for example, 32 bits at a time if the processor has a 32 bit data bus. For 30 pin, 8 bit SIMMs (see later section on memory),

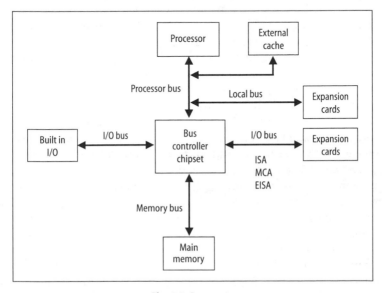

Fig. 4.5 Bus routes.

four modules will be required to be added at a time. For 72 pin, 32 bit SIMMs, then only one module is required to be added at a time.

In our example case, the I/O bus is the main bus of the system. It connects the processor, through the chipset, to all the internal I/O devices, such as the primary and secondary *IDE* (*Integrated Drive Electronics*) controllers, the floppy disk controller, the serial and parallel ports, the video controller and, possibly, an integrated mouse port. It also connects the processor, through the chipset, to the expansion slots. Newer chipsets were designed to incorporate what is called *bus mastering*, a technique whereby a separate bus controller processor takes control of the bus and executes instructions independently of the main processor.

I/O bus architectures have evolved since the first PC, albeit rather slowly. The requirement has always been quite clear. In order to capitalize on the rapid improvements that have taken place in chip and peripheral technologies, there is a need to increase significantly the amount of data that can be transferred at one time and the speed at which it can be done. The reason for the relatively slow rate of change in this area has been the need to maintain backward compatibility with existing systems, particularly with respect to expansion cards.

The original IBM PC bus architecture used an 8 bit data bus which ran at 4.77 MHz and became known as the *Industry Standard Architecture* (*ISA*). With the introduction of the PC AT, the ISA data bus was increased to 16 bits and this ran first at 6 MHz and then at 8 MHz. However, because of the need to support both 8 bit and 16 bit expansion cards, the industry eventually standardized on 8.33 MHz as the maximum transfer rate for both sizes of bus, and developed an expansion slot connector which would accept both kinds of cards. We rarely see ISA connector slots on motherboards today.

When the 32 bit processors became available, manufacturers started to look at extensions to the ISA bus which would permit 32 data lines. Rather than extend the ISA bus again, IBM developed a proprietary 32 bit bus to replace ISA called *Micro Channel Architecture* (*MCA*). Because of royalty issues, MCA did not achieve wide industry acceptance and a competing 32 bit data bus architecture was established called *Extended Industry Standard Architecture* (*EISA*) which can handle 32 bits of data at 8.33 MHz.

All three of these bus architectures (ISA, MCA and EISA) run at relatively low speed and as Graphical User Interfaces (GUIs) became prevalent, this speed restriction proved to be an unacceptable bottleneck, particularly for the graphics display. One early solution to this was to move some of the expansion card slots from the traditional I/O bus and connect them directly to the processor bus. This became known as a *local bus*, and an example of this is shown in our example at Fig. 4.5. The most popular local bus design was known as the *Video Electronics Standards Association* (*VESA*) *Local Bus* or just *VL-Bus* and this provided much improved performance to both the graphics and the hard disk controllers.

Several weaknesses were seen to be inherent in the VL-Bus design. In 1992 a group led by Intel produced a completely new specification for a replacement bus architecture. This is known as *Peripheral Component Interconnect* (*PCI*). Whereas VL-Bus links directly into the very delicate processor bus, PCI inserts a bridge between the processor bus and the PCI local bus. This bridge also contains the memory controller that connects to the main DRAM chips. The PCI bus operates at 33 MHz and at the full data bus width of the processor. New expansion sockets that connect directly to

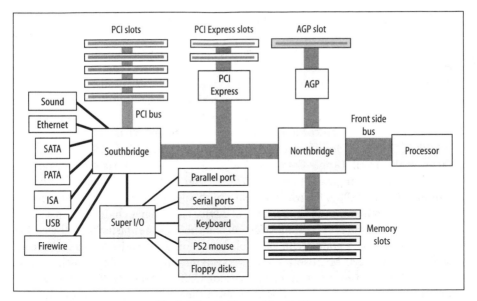

Fig. 4.6 Northbridge and Southbridge.

the PCI bus were designed and these, together with expansion sockets for updated versions of this bus, are what are likely to be found on most modern motherboards. The design also incorporates an interface to the traditional I/O bus, whether it be ISA, EISA or MCA, and so backward compatibility is maintained.

Further development of this approach led to the *Northbridge* and *Southbridge* chipset that we find in common use today. At Fig. 4.6 we show a typical layout diagram of a motherboard that uses these chipsets. The Northbridge chip connects via a high-speed bus, known as the *Front Side Bus* (*FSB*) directly to the processor. We have attempted, in the diagram, to give some idea of relative performance of the various buses by making the thickness of the connecting lines indicative of their transfer rates. We may note that the memory slots are connected to the Northbridge chip, as is the *Accelerated Graphics Port* (*AGP*). More recently, we may find high-performance *PCI Express* slots connected to both the Northbridge and Southbridge chips. This is a very fast serial bus consisting of between 1 and 32 *lanes*, with each lane having a transfer capability of up to 2.5 gigabits per second.

The Northbridge chip is connected to the Southbridge chip, which in turn connects to a wide variety of devices, such as the PCI expansion slots, the *Serial ATA* (*SATA*) disk interface, the *Parallel ATA* (*PATA*) disk interface, the sound system, Ethernet, the ISA bus (if one exists) and so forth. In addition, the slower speed devices, such as the parallel port (for printers), the serial communication ports, the PS2 mouse port, the floppy disks and the keyboard, are often connected to the Southbridge chips via a *Super IO* chip, as shown in Fig. 4.6.

Intel then introduced the *Intel Hub Architecture* (*IHA*)[3] where, effectively, the Northbridge chip is replaced by the *Memory Controller Hub* (*MCH*) and the

---

3 See http://www.intel.com/design/chipsets/840/.

Southbridge chip is replaced by the *I/O Controller Hub* (*ICH*). There is also a *64 bit PCI Controller Hub* (*P64H*). The Intel Hub Architecture is said to be much faster than the Northbridge/Southbridge design because the latter connected all the low-speed ports to the PCI bus, whereas the Intel architecture separates them out.

Finally, before leaving this section, we should mention two other technologies which are in widespread use. *FireWire* is a serial bus technology with very high transfer rates which has been designed largely for audio and video multimedia devices. Most modern camcorders include this interface, which is sometimes known as i.Link. The official specifications for Firewire are IEEE-1394-1995, IEEE 1394a-2000 and IEEE 1394b (Apple Computer Inc., 2006), and it supports up to 63 devices daisy chained to a single adapter card. The second technology is that of *Universal Serial Bus* (*USB*) (USB, 2000), which is also a high-speed serial bus that allows for up to a theoretical maximum of 127 peripheral devices to be daisy chained from a single adapter card. The current version, USB 2.0, is up to 40 times faster than the earlier version of USB 1.1. A good technical explanation of USB can be found in Peacock (2005). With modern Microsoft Windows systems, "hot swapping[4]" of hard disk drives can be achieved using either Firewire or USB connections. This is of significance to the forensic analyst in that it enables the possible collection of evidence from a system that is kept running for a short while when first seized. This might be required when, for example, an encrypted container is found open on a computer that is switched on (see Chapter 7 for more details).

A Typical Motherboard

At Fig. 4.7 is shown a typical modern motherboard, an Asus A8N32-SLI (Asus, 2005). On the left-hand side of the diagram we can see clearly the three PCI expansion slots. This modern board, as expected, has no ISA or VESA slots, but it does have three of the relatively new PCI Express slots. Two of these slots are PCI Express × 16 with what is known as *Scalable Link Interface* (*SLI*)[5] support, and this provides the motherboard with the capability for fitting two identical graphics cards in order to improve overall graphics performance. These two slots are of a darker colour than the PCI slots and slightly offset from them. One is located between the first and second PCI slot and the other, which is marked "PCI Express" in the diagram, is to the right of the third PCI slot. The third PCI Express slot is a × 4 slot, which is much smaller and is located just to the right of this second PCI Express slot.

We can also clearly see the ZIF Socket 939 for the AMD processor. The two IDE sockets for the ribbon cables to the Primary and Secondary parallel ATA hard disks are at the bottom of the diagram close to the ATX power socket and the floppy disk controller socket. This motherboard also has four Serial ATA sockets to the left of the Primary IDE parallel socket, and at the top of the diagram can be seen in addition a Serial ATA RAID socket.

---

4   This is where a hard disk drive may be connected or disconnected without rebooting or logging out of the system.

5   See http://en.wikipedia.org/wiki/Scalable_Link_Interface.

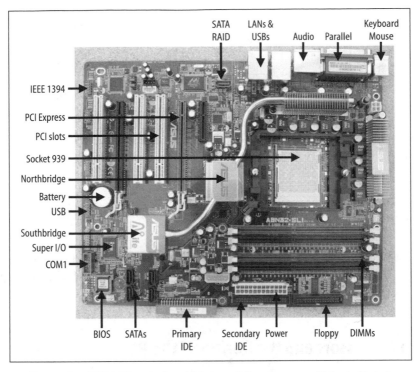

SATA
RAID

LANs &
USBs

Audio Parallel

Keyboard
Mouse

IEEE 1394

PCI Express

PCI slots

Socket 939

Northbridge

Battery

USB

Southbridge

Super I/O

COM1

BIOS   SATAs   Primary   Secondary Power   Floppy   DIMMs
                 IDE   IDE

Fig. 4.7 Asus A8N32-SLI motherboard (photograph: Tony Sammes and Brian Jenkinson).

At the bottom left of the diagram can be seen an 8 Mbyte flash EPROM, which contains the BIOS, and the motherboard is controlled by Northbridge and Southbridge chips which, as can be seen, are connected together by a copper *heatpipe*. This is said to be provide a innovative fanless design for a much quieter motherboard. This motherboard is also fitted with a Super I/O chip, as we discussed above.

Along the left-hand side of the diagram we note the COM1 port socket, USB and FireWire (IEEE 1394) sockets, and the CR2032 lithium cell battery which provides power for the real-time clock and the CMOS memory. Along the top we note gigabit Local Area Network (LAN) sockets, more USB sockets, the audio sockets, the parallel port and the PS2 mouse and keyboard sockets.

The main random access memory is fitted into *DIMM* (*Dual In-line Memory Module*) slots, of which four 184 pin *Double Data Rate* (*DDR*) slots can be seen in the diagram, although two are darker in colour and are not quite so evident. This motherboard supports a maximum of 4 Gbyte of memory and, as for most motherboards, there are various rules about what mix of memory modules are permitted in the four memory slots.

In recent years, motherboards have been designed so that the sockets for many of the peripheral devices can be brought out on the rear panel of a computer in a standardized way without the requirement for a plethora of connecting cables. These sockets are set at right angles to the motherboard and fit through a template on the

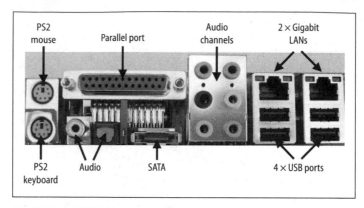

Fig. 4.8 Asus A8N32-SLI motherboard rear panel sockets (photograph: Tony Sammes and Brian Jenkinson).

rear computer panel. A typical set is shown for the Asus A8N32-SLI motherboard at Fig. 4.8 and this is the rear panel view of the sockets that are shown at the top right-hand side of Fig. 4.7.

Intel Processors and the Design of the PC

The original IBM PC architecture, dating from 1981, was based on the Intel 8088 processor chip. This architecture became known as the *PC/XT* with XT referring to *Extra Technology*. The Intel 8088 is a later version of the Intel 8086, a processor chip that was first produced in 1976. Microcomputer systems of this time were all 8 bit and the 8086, which was one of the first chips to have an external data bus of 16 bits, did not immediately gain widespread support, mainly because both the chip and the 16 bit motherboard designed to support it were, at the time, very expensive. In 1978, Intel introduced the 8088, which is almost identical (Intel, 1979) to the 8086, but has an 8 bit external data bus rather than the 16 bits of the 8088. Both these processors have a 16 bit internal data bus and fourteen 16 bit registers. They are packaged as 40 pin DIL chips and have an address bus size of 20 bits, enabling them to address up to 2^{20} bytes; that is, up to 1,048,576 bytes or 1 Mbyte. With the XT architecture designed round the 8088 chip it was able to use the then industry standard 8 bit chip sets and printed circuit boards that were in common use and relatively cheap. Bus connections in the original XT architecture were very simple. Everything was connected to every thing else using the same data bus width of 8 bits and the same data bus speed of 4.77 MHz. This was the beginning of the 8 bit ISA bus that we discussed above.

The PC Memory Map

The layout of the PC memory map (see Fig. 4.9) and part of the basic design of the PC is a consequence of the characteristics of these Intel 8088 and 8086 processors. The memory map is, of course, limited to 1 Mbyte, which is the address space of this

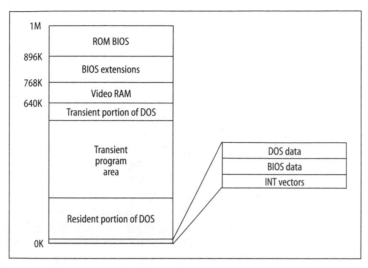

Fig. 4.9 The PC-XT system memory map.

processor family (20 bits). The first 1024 bytes of this address space are reserved by the processor for its *interrupt vectors*, each of which is a four byte pointer to an interrupt handling routine located elsewhere in the address space. To ensure a flexible and upgradeable system, the interrupt vectors are held in RAM so that they can be modified. In addition, when the processor is first switched on, and before any volatile memory has yet been loaded with programs, it expects to start executing code from an address that is 16 bytes from the top of the address space. This indicates that this area will have to be ROM.

The memory map that results is thus not surprising. The entire address space of 1 Mbyte cannot all be allocated to RAM. The compromise made was to arrange for the lower 640 kbyte to be available as the main RAM[6] and the upper part of the address space to be taken up with the ROM BIOS, with the video RAM and to give room for future expansion with BIOS extensions. The reason for the 640 kbyte figure is said to be that the original designers looked at the then current microprocessor systems[7], with their address buses of 16 bits and their consequent user address spaces of 64 kbyte of RAM, and felt that ten times this amount was a significant improvement for the new PC. In practice, of course, the *transient program area* in which the user 's application programs run does not get the whole of the 640 kbyte. Some is taken up by the interrupt vectors and by the BIOS data, and some by the *disk operating system (DOS)*, as shown in Fig. 4.9.

---

6   Because of cost, many early systems did not have the whole of the 640 kbyte populated with memory chips.

7   One of the most popular chips of the time was the Zilog Z80 using the CP/M operating system.

Design of the PC

The basic philosophy behind the design is very sound. The ROM BIOS, produced for the manufacturer of the motherboard, provides the programs for dealing in detail with all the vagaries of the different kinds and variations of the specific hardware related to that motherboard. The operating system and the application programs can interact with the standard interface of the BIOS and, provided that this standard is kept constant, both the operating system and the application programs are transportable to any other PC that observes this same standard. The standard BIOS interface utilises yet another feature of this processor family, that of the *software interrupt*. This works in a very similar manner to the hardware interrupt. On detection of a particular interrupt number, the processor saves the current state of the system, causes the interrupt vector associated with that number to be loaded and then transfers control to the address to which the vector points. In the case of a hardware interrupt, this will be to the start location of where code to deal with some intervention request from the hardware resides. In the case of a software interrupt, which calls on the BIOS, this will have been issued as an *INT* instruction code by some calling program, and will cause an appropriate part of the BIOS ROM code to be executed. In both cases, when the interrupt is complete, the original state of the system, saved at the time of the interrupt, will be restored. One of the major benefits of this approach is the ability to change the interrupt vectors, because they are held in RAM. Let us consider, for example, that we are using the original BIOS to control our graphics display and that this therefore contains a set of programs which control the actual display controller chip which is on our motherboard. When one of our applications uses the display, it will issue a standard BIOS software interrupt and the associated interrupt vector will have been set up to transfer control to where these original BIOS graphics programs reside. Now consider the case where we purchase a super, high-performance, modern graphics controller expansion card and fit that into one of the expansion slots on our PC. On the graphics expansion card will be new BIOS programs for dealing with the high-performance graphics controller that is fitted to this card. What is arranged for us by the system, during the bootstrap sequence, is that the graphics controller interrupt vector is changed from pointing to the original BIOS addresses to now pointing to the appropriate addresses in the BIOS extensions area of the memory space where our new graphics card BIOS has been installed. Precisely how the interrupt vectors are changed we will see when we look at the bootstrap sequence in Chapter 5. It is enough for now to recognize that the same application, issuing the same software interrupt as before, now automatically gets access to the new high performance graphics controller system.

PC System Resources

Hardware interrupts are transmitted along *Interrupt Request channels* (IRQs) which are used by various hardware devices to signal to the processor that a request needs to be dealt with. Such a request may arise, for example, because input data is now available from the hardware and needs processing, or because output data has now been dealt with by the hardware and it is ready for the next tranche. There are a limited number of IRQs available and each has its own specific address in the interrupt vector table which points to the appropriate software driver to handle the hardware that is assigned to that IRQ. Many IRQs are pre-assigned by the system to internal devices and allocation of IRQs to expansion cards has to be carried out with great care, since the system is not able to distinguish between two hardware devices which have been set to use the same IRQ channel. Often, an expansion card will have *DIP* (*Dual Inline Package*) switches which enable one of a number of different IRQ channels to be selected for a given configuration in an attempt to avoid IRQ conflicts.

Autonomous data transfer, which is the sending of data between a hardware device and the main memory without involving the main processor, is provided by *Direct Memory Access* (*DMA*) channels, and these too are a limited resource. Again, some of the channels are pre-assigned by the system and others are available for use by expansion cards and may also be set by DIP switches on the card. Conflicts can arise if two different hardware devices are trying to use the same DMA channel at the same time, though it is possible for different hardware devices to share channels providing that they are not using them at the same time.

The third system resource is the *I/O port address*. The Intel 8088 processor, in addition to being able to address 1 Mbyte of main memory, can also address, quite separately, up to 65,535 I/O ports. Many hardware device functions are associated with an I/O port address. For example, the issuing by the processor of an IN instruction to a particular port address may obtain from the hardware associated with that address the current contents of its status register. Similarly, the issuing by the processor of an OUT instruction to a port address may transfer a byte of data to the hardware. This type of activity is known as *Programmed I/O* (*PIO*) or *Processor I/O* as opposed to *Memory Mapped I/O* (*MMIO*), where the 65,535 port addresses are each assigned space in the overall main memory map. Using MMIO, any memory access instruction that is permitted by the processor can be used to access a port address. Normally a particular hardware device will be allocated a range of port addresses.

The final system resource, and perhaps the one in greatest demand, is that of main memory address space itself (see Fig. 4.9). MMIO is rarely used in the PC because it unnecessarily takes up valuable main memory address space in the upper part of the memory map, space that is required for the use of any BIOS extensions in particular.

When a new expansion card is fitted, therefore, consideration has to be given to what of these limited system resources it is going to require. It may have to be allocated an IRQ, a DMA channel, a set of port addresses and, possibly, some address space in the upper part of the memory map for a BIOS extension. The concept of *Plug and Play* (*PnP*) was introduced with Microsoft Windows 95 to try to automate this process of assigning these limited system resources. The system BIOS, the operating system and the PnP-compatible hardware devices have to collaborate in order to identify the card, assign and configure the resources and find and load a suitable driver.

The Intel 80286 and the AT Architecture

In 1981 a new processor chip was introduced by Intel, the 80286[8] (often just called the 286). This offers an external data bus of 16 bits and a wider address bus of 24 bits. The 24 bits of the address bus potentially gives access to 2^{24} bytes of memory, that is, to 16 Mbyte, and the resulting memory above the 1 Mbyte region became known as *Extended Memory*. The 80286 chip is fully compatible with the 8086 and 8088 chips and it adds a new mode of operation called *Protected Mode*, which enables access to this extended memory. The original mode of operation then became known as *Real Mode*.

IBM developed the *AT* (*Advanced Technology*) architecture, based on this new chip, because it was fully compatible with the 8088 and all software that ran on the earlier systems should be able to run on the AT. The new chip was much faster than the 8088, and the original AT, which first ran at 6 MHz, was some five times faster than the 8088 running at 4.77 MHz. In practice, the AT systems using the 80286 were seen, from a user viewpoint, to be little more than very fast XTs, though there were some other important changes in the architecture. For example, combined 8 bit and 16 bit ISA expansion slots were introduced to take advantage of the new 16 bit data bus, without losing the legacy 8 bit systems. The IRQ and DMA channel allocations set by the system were changed and an increased range of both IRQ and DMA channels was made available. However, because the operating system and much of the available software was unable to use the new protected mode of the chip, useful advantage could not be taken of the additional memory access that the system could provide.

The 80386 Chip

When Intel introduced the 80386 (often just called the 386) in 1985, it rightly promised a vast improvement in the performance of PCs. The chip can operate at clock speeds from 16 MHz up to 33 MHz. With its 32 bit address bus it provides an address space of 4 Gbyte, and with a 32 bit internal and a 32 bit external data bus it can transfer 4 bytes of data at a time. It is fully backward compatible with the 8086, 8088 and the 80286 processors and it adds yet a further mode to the protected and real modes of its predecessor, that of *Virtual 8086 Mode*, which is sometimes called *Virtual Real Mode*. This new mode allows a control program to create what are in effect a series of "virtual" 8086 systems on the one PC, each of which is operating in a protected mode which prevents it from interfering with the others.

Many variations of the 386 chip exist. The original 80386 became known as the 386DX when Intel introduced a cheaper version of the chip known as the 386SX. Whilst retaining the internal 32 bit data bus, the external data bus on the 386SX was reduced to 16 bits. This move took advantage of the large number of 16 bit ISA

---

8   Before this Intel had produced the 80186 and 80188 chips. These were very similar to
    their 8086 and 8088 predecessors, but incorporated on the same chip several others of
    the 8086 family of components. This provided for a reduced chip count over the original
    8086 family.

cards, which by that time were in common use, and 386SX-based systems rapidly became popular entry level computers. A *coprocessor*, used to perform floating point arithmetic in hardware, thus improving the performance of scientific and engineering calculations, was produced for the 80386, and this was designated the 80387.

The 80486 Chip

The 80486, which is normally called the 486, is essentially an 80386 with an enhanced 80387 coprocessor built onto the chip. It also incorporates enhanced memory management, 8 kbyte of internal *cache* memory and a more efficient design. A 486 will run, for the same clock speed, about twice as fast as the equivalent 386, and the chip is fully compatible with the 8086, 8088, 80286 and 80386 processors. Initial chips ran at a clock rate of 25 MHz, but later ones were available in 33 MHz and 50 MHz versions. The 486 effectively created a revolution. Before its introduction, *Graphical User Interfaces* (*GUIs*), such as those used by Microsoft Windows, had not achieved widespread, popularity largely because of performance limitations, often characterized by the appearance of the dreaded hourglass icon. The 486 changed that, providing a performance that made GUIs more acceptable.

Many variations of the 486 chip also exist. The original 80486 chip became known as the 486DX when the cheaper 486SX was introduced. This 486SX is essentially a 486DX without the onboard maths coprocessor, and the early 486SXs were simply 486DXs with their maths coprocessor element disabled, although the chip later became established as a design in its own right. Intel also produced the 487SX as a separate maths coprocessor for those who wished subsequently to upgrade their 486SX systems. Motherboards of upgradeable systems were fitted with an extra socket into which this 487SX could be fitted. In practice, the 487SX is a fully functional 25 MHz 486DX, and when it is installed in its socket it completely disables the original 486SX via a new signal from one of its pins, and takes over all processor functions from the 486SX.

The big advance, based on this same idea, was the introduction of the *OverDrive* processor. This was before the widespread use of ZIF sockets, and the exercise of prising out a 169 pin processor chip and replacing it with another was not a recommended practice. Instead, the idea of fitting a new processor chip into a separate upgrade socket which automatically disabled the existing processor seemed like a very sensible strategy. The 486DX2 overdrive processor uses the same pinout as the 487SX and therefore can be fitted into the same upgrade socket. The 486DX2 achieves clock speed doubling by running at twice the speed of the motherboard clock. For a 33 MHz clock this means that the 486DX2 runs internally at 66 MHz. In a similar manner, the 486DX4 triples the clock speed.

None of these chips is being marketed today, although forensic computing analysts may still come across systems using them. The separate OverDrive socket idea has also now been dropped in favour of the ZIF socket. The original OverDrive socket is now called Socket 1 (see Table 4.1), and the current upgrade strategy is to remove the processor chip from its ZIF socket and replace it with the upgrade rather than to add a second chip which disables the first.

The Pentiums – Through Pro to 4

In 1993, Intel shipped the first of what they designated the Pentium processor. As part of a natural progression, it might well have been called the 80586, but, since a number cannot be trademarked, Intel chose this time to give the chip a name in order to try to protect themselves against possible future clones. The original chip was about twice as fast as the 80486 for the same clock rate. It can effectively be thought of as two 80486 processors with separate 8 kbyte code and 8 kbyte data caches connected internally by a 256 bit data bus. The chip has an external data bus of 64 bits and an address bus of 32 bits, and is fully software compatible with the 386 and 486 processors. Like the 486DX, the Pentium incorporates an internal maths coprocessor, which is much improved over its predecessors. As mentioned above, the Pentium processor is designed to connect to the rest of the system through the PCI bus, which runs at 33MHz and can be 32 or 64 bits wide.

The first generation systems ran at 60 MHz and 66 MHz clock speeds. Second generation systems run at 75, 90, 100, 120, 133, 150,166 and 200 MHz from basic motherboard speeds of 50, 60 and 66 MHz. This range is achieved by on chip clock multiplication, which is activated by two pins on the chip labelled BF1 and BF2. The four combinations possible with these two pins give clock multipliers of 1.5, 2, 2.5 and 3, resulting in the variety of Pentium speeds quoted. Most motherboards have jumper pins which allow these settings to be changed. Selecting a setting that is above that recommended for the processor is known as *overclocking*. The third generation of Pentium processors incorporates *MMX* (*Multi Media eXtension*) technology and has additional instructions and data types that have been designed for high-performance multimedia and communications applications. These run at 166, 200 and 233 MHz.

The Pentium Pro was introduced in 1995 with clock speeds of 150, 166 and 200 MHz. They became commercially available in early 1996, but were rapidly replaced by the Pentium IIs in 1997, with clock speeds from 233 MHz to 450 MHz. The Pentium III was being offered from early 1999 with clock speeds ranging from 550 MHz to 1.0 GHz and, at the time of writing (March 2007) we currently have the Pentium 4 processor with clock rates from 1.30 GHz to 3.80 GHz and *dual core*, which has two complete processor chips in the one package.

Compatible Processors

A number of compatible processors have been produced by manufacturers other than Intel, the most notable being AMD (Advanced Micro Designs) and Cyrix (now taken over by VIA).

These chips are fully compatible in terms of emulating the processor instructions, and some are also pin-compatible. For those that are not pin-compatible, specialist motherboards are provided. Recent versions of the AMD chips are the Athlon 64 FX which operates at up to 2.80 GHz, and the AMD Sempron, which operates at up to 2.0 GHz. At Fig. 4.10 we have shown the top and bottom views of an AMD Athlon 64 FX processor.

Fig. 4.10 The AMD Athlon 64 processor (photograph: Tony Sammes and Brian Jenkinson).

A Few Words about Memory

Memory chips are made up of an array of transistor type cells each of which can be in one of two states: either on or off, representing the values 1 or 0. *Random access memory* (*RAM*) is characterized by being *volatile* (that is, it loses its information when power is removed) and by being capable of easy modification (that is, it accepts both read and write operations).

SRAM and DRAM

Static RAM (*SRAM*) uses between 4 and 6 transistor memory elements for each switch cell[9] to form a logical unit known as a bistable flip-flop. The flip-flop may be in one of two stable states and, once set in a particular state, and provided the power remains applied, it will continue in that state until a new state is set. *Dynamic RAM* (*DRAM*), on the other hand, uses a single transistor-based capacitor[10] for each switch cell and the small charge on the capacitor is used to determine its state. As a result of leakage current, however, the charge on each capacitor dissipates quite quickly, and thus has to be refreshed at regular intervals, of the order of a few tens of microseconds or so. It is this characteristic that gives it the name *dynamic* RAM. Because of the need for this regular refresh, additional circuitry is required, internal addressing is much more complicated and the speed of access is reduced. However, DRAM is much cheaper to manufacture than SRAM, since DRAM requires only one memory element to every six required for SRAM.

These characteristics determine the way in which we use the two kinds of RAM in the PC. Since DRAM is relatively cheap, it is used for the whole of the main RAM memory, which today might be as much as 4 Gbyte. However, since its performance is

---

9   IBM uses 6 transistor memory elements for an SRAM cell. See IBM (1997).

10 In IBM DRAM this is known as a *trench capacitor*. See IBM (1996a).

slow compared with SRAM and it would significantly delay the modern processor, a *cache memory* is often provided, the purpose of which is to provide a high-speed buffer between the processor and the slower main memory. In the past, two levels of cache were often found: L1 (or Level 1) SRAM cells built onto the processor chip itself and L2 (Level 2) SRAM chips that were installed on the motherboard. More recently, processors such as the Pentium 4 have contained both L1 and L2 caches on the processor chip itself, and where a further SRAM cache is installed on the mother-board, this is then known as L3 (Level 3) cache.

Memory chips are packaged in many ways. Older chips still use the DIL standard package that we have referred to before, and we may still find some SRAM in sockets on the motherboard in this form. More likely today, however, SRAM will be in *PLCC* (*Plastic Leaded Chip Carrier*) or *TQFP* (*Thin Quad Flat Plastic*) packages, that are surface mounted onto the motherboard. For the DRAM we may find 100, 168, 184 or 240 pin *DIMMs* (*Dual Inline Memory Modules*) or 72, 144 or 200 pin *SODIMMs* (*Small Outline DIMMs*) in sockets on the motherboard. Typical memory module sizes currently range from 168 Mbyte to 4 Gbyte, and, as we discussed above, various rules as to the mix of modules permitted are associated with each motherboard. You may recall that our example motherboard of Fig. 4.7 has four 184 pin DDR (*Double Data Rate*) DIMM sockets. We show an example of a 1 Gbyte 184 pin DIMM memory module at Fig. 4.11.

Advances in the performance of DRAMs have come over the last few years as a result of making changes to the basic DRAM architecture of the chip. The internal layout of a DRAM chip can be likened to that of a spreadsheet with all of its cells in a series of columns and rows. Access to any particular cell may then be made by selecting a specific column and row address. Because of the refresh cycles that have to take place, selecting both the column and the row address takes time. One improvement in the design of the DRAM is to arrange for the rows to have a relatively large number of columns and then to ensure that successive data items are held in the same row. This has the benefit of saving the time needed to select the row address when accessing successive data items, since it already remains selected. Each row can be considered to be a page, and chips using this mode of operation are often called *Fast Page Mode* (*FPM*) DRAMs. A further extension to this idea is implemented in *Extended Data Out* (*EDO*) DRAMs (IBM, undated). Normally, the cell data is only available while the row and column addresses remain selected. We have seen that with FPM, the row address remains selected between accesses, but clearly the column address cannot if we want to select another element. With EDO, the DRAM holds the data valid on its output pins, even after the column selection has become invalid for the current element and we are starting to access the next element. This speeds up the rate of access and gives an extended period of time over which the processor can

Fig. 4.11 A 184 pin 1 Gbyte DDR DIMM (photograph: Tony Sammes and Brian Jenkinson).

access the data. Clearly the motherboard must be "EDO aware" for this to work. EDO is also sometimes called *Hyper Page Mode*.

Another advance occurred with the development of *Synchronous DRAM* (*SDRAM*) (IBM, 1996b). Where FPM and EDO DRAMs are driven asynchronously, with each access being initiated by control signals from the processor, SDRAM is operated synchronously with all its accesses controlled by the same external clock as that used by the processor. This, together with a burst capability, permits much faster consecutive read and write operations compared with FPM and EDO. In addition, SDRAM may have two internal banks, so that while one bank is being accessed, the other is being prepared.

Double Data Rate (*DDR*) *SDRAM* is essentially an improvement over the earlier SDRAM. It is very similar to SDRAM in design and operation, the main difference being that it can transfer data on both the rising and falling edges of a clock cycle. Compared with traditional SDRAM, which can only transfer on the rising edge, this gives DDR SDRAM effectively twice the bandwidth, and by 2005 it had become the mainstream memory technology to be found on most motherboards. From 2003, however, development had started on the next generation of memory, *Double Data Rate 2* (*DDR2*) *SDRAM*, and this improves performance by permitting faster clock rates whilst still maintaining a clean data output. Several motherboards were available at the time of writing which were fitted for DDR2 SDRAM.

Video RAM (*VRAM*) and *Synchronous Graphics RAM* (*SGRAM*) (IBM, 1996c) are DRAMs that have been designed specifically for graphics applications. VRAM is based on the standard asynchronous DRAM architecture, but has the addition of a high-speed serial port and a serial access memory (SAM) that is designed to hold part of a page of data from the internal DRAM array. The VRAM has a standard DRAM interface as well and this permits data to be read from or written to the VRAM whilst serial data is continuously being written to the video interface. Such an approach is sometimes referred to as *dual port*. SGRAM is video RAM that is very similar in operation to that of SDRAM but has been optimized for graphics-intensive operations. More recently, high-performance graphics cards are beginning to be found with *Double Data Rate 3* (*DDR3*) *SDRAM* fitted.

ROM

Read-Only Memory (ROM) is characterized by being non-volatile and read-only. The information stored in it may be built into the chip during manufacture or it may be subsequently placed there by *programming* the chip. Chips that are capable of being programmed after manufacture are known as *Programmable ROMs* (*PROMs*) and the simplest form is programmed by permanently fusing selected links in the memory chip so that it retains the required binary pattern. This is a one-time process, and such chips cannot be reused.

Reusable read-only memory chips are called *Erasable PROMs* (*EPROMs*) or *Electrically Erasable PROMs* (*EEPROMs*). EPROMs, together with a later development known as *Flash Memory*, are looked at in more detail in Chapter 8, when we consider the significance of the memory type in the treatment of organizers. An example of a Flash EPROM is the BIOS chip seen on the motherboard of Fig. 4.7.

Backing Store Devices

A variety of devices can be used for backing store, of which the most familiar are probably the standard 3.5 inch *floppy disk* drive and the *hard disk* drive. We devote the main chapter of the book, Chapter 5, to the topic of magnetic disk drives, since it is of such fundamental importance to the forensic computing analyst. Other backing store devices of some importance include 120 Mbyte floppy disk drives, *CD-ROM* (*Compact Disc Read-Only Memory*) drives, *DVD* (*Digital Versatile Disk*) drives, *Iomega ZIP* drives, and a wide assortment of magnetic tape units. Most of these devices come in one of two flavours: internal fitting, where they are connected to an IDE slot or to a SCSI card, and external fitting, where they may be connected via a USB or FireWire port. Some external drives, in the past, could be connected via a parallel printer port, and we may even still see the old 5.25 inch floppy disk drive on some elderly systems. Becoming increasingly popular in the last few years is the so-called *Thumb Drive*. This is also normally connected via a USB port and appears to the PC as another ATA hard drive. It is made up of flash memory and to date the largest size in production is 64 Gbyte[11].

Hard Disk Drive Units

At Fig. 4.12 we have shown a picture of a (now) relatively small hard disk drive. It is a Seagate Medalist 8641, Model ST38641A, and the CHS parameters are given on the label as Cylinders 16,383, Heads 16 and Sectors 63. The disk has an 8.4 Gbyte capacity. On the right-hand side of the figure, in the top corner, can be seen fitted a typical standard power supply connector, recognizable by its four coloured leads: a red, two blacks and a yellow.

The connector is shaped so that it will only fit in the socket one way round. Immediately beneath the power connector can be seen fitted the IDE ribbon cable connector. The ribbon cable is 2 inches wide and contains 40 parallel lines[12]. One line is invariably coloured red and this is line 1 of the cable. Current ribbon cable sockets and connectors tend not to be shaped or to have guards which prevent incorrect connection and it is thus very important to match the red line of the cable with pin number one in the sockets at both ends of the cable. Incorrect connection will certainly ensure that the disk drive does not work and may damage it. The other end of the ribbon cable, of course, connects to one of the two IDE slots that we saw in Fig. 4.7 on the motherboard, or, possibly, to an IDE expansion card. Most motherboards have at least two slots, which permit up to four IDE devices, such as hard drives, CD-ROM and DVD drives, and 120 Mbyte floppy disks, to be connected to the system. One slot is the IDE primary and the other is the IDE secondary. From each slot, the ribbon cable can connect up to two devices, a master and a slave. Which is master and

---

11 See http://www.buslink.com/B1/ProductDetails.asp?id=148 (retrieved 19 February 2007) where a 64 Gbyte thumb drive is currently on offer at $5000.

12 Later ribbon cables have 80 slightly thinner conductors, and we discuss this in Chapter 5.

Fig. 4.12 A Seagate Medalist 8641 hard disk drive (photograph: Tony Sammes and Brian Jenkinson).

which is slave is determined not by position on the cable, as it is in the case of floppy disks, but by jumper settings on the disk itself.

We have also shown at Fig. 4.13 details of the type of socket found on the Seagate Medalist drive of Fig. 4.12. On the left-hand side of the figure can be seen the 40 pin socket for the IDE ribbon cable, with pin number 1, the one associated with the red line, on the right-hand side of the socket.

On the right-hand side of the figure can be seen the power socket and the shaped surround that ensures that its connector can only be fitted one way round. In between the two sockets can be seen three pairs of jumper pins with a jumper set on the left-hand side. A jumper is set by sliding a small connector over both the top and bottom pins of a pair, which then makes electrical connection between the two. Reference to the disk manufacturer's documentation for the particular drive should provide details of what all the various jumper settings do. In the case of this disk, the jumper as fitted sets the disk up as a master. Other settings would switch it into slave mode or to cable select. A check of these jumper settings is of much importance to

Fig. 4.13 Parallel ATA disk drive sockets and jumpers (photograph: Tony Sammes and Brian Jenkinson).

Fig. 4.14 Serial ATA disk drive sockets and jumpers (photograph: Tony Sammes and Brian Jenkinson).

the forensic computing analyst in order to ensure that the disk has been set up correctly.

Increasingly, we are seeing more and more Serial ATA (SATA) disks. At Fig. 4.14 we show the connections for such a disk, which are quite different from those for Parallel ATA (PATA). The power cable socket is the bigger of the two, shown on the left of the diagram, and the serial signal cable socket is shown in the centre. According to current specifications, the jumpers are "for factory use only", as each device has its own cable and is designated a master on that cable.

Floppy Disk Drive Units

These are connected via a ribbon cable similar to those used for parallel ATA disks. In this case the cable is 1.75 inch width, and connects the (up to two) floppy disks to the Floppy Disk Controller (FDC) slot on the motherboard. This slot can be seen marked "Floppy" in Fig. 4.7. The ribbon cable again has one line coloured red to identify pin 1, and it has a total of 34 lines. It is easily recognizable in the system because the cable is split and has 8 lines that have one full twist in them just before it connects to one of the two floppy disk units that it supports. It is this set of twisted cables that allow the two floppy drives, A: and B:, to be separately identified. Power connectors are identical to those for hard drive units in the case of 5.25 inch floppy drives and similar, but slightly smaller for 3.5 inch floppy drives.

External Peripherals

Most of the external peripherals connect to the buses of the motherboard by means of appropriate sockets, connectors and cables. The keyboard may have its own PS/2 socket on the motherboard, and this is shown in Fig. 4.7. In some older systems, the PS/2 socket on the motherboard might not be accessible from outside the casing and a short connecting cable then had to be fitted from the PS/2 socket on the mother-board to an external PS/2 socket on the casing of the main unit.

The mouse may also have a socket on the motherboard for a PS/2 cable connection. This too, on older systems, might require a cable to the casing of the main unit, as described for the keyboard connection. Similarly, short ribbon cables might be needed to connect the serial port sockets and the parallel port socket, seen in Fig. 4.7, to the appropriate serial and parallel port sockets on the main casing. It was to avoid all these cables that the standardized set of sockets mounted directly on the motherboard and designed to fit through the rear panel of the PC was introduced (see Fig. 4.8). The serial ports were once widely used for devices such as the mouse, modems, digital cameras and perhaps PC links to organizers, mobile phones and other electronic equipment. These days, such devices are more likely to be connected via USB or FireWire ports. The parallel port was once used for devices such as printers, plotters and scanners, and sometimes even for interconnecting with other PCs. Again, printers are now often connected via USB ports and the parallel port is less frequently used.

The only major peripheral not so far dealt with is the display. For this motherboard, the display will have its own expansion card, slotted into one of the PCI Express expansion slots, and a socket on the card will provide the video connection to the display. Some older motherboards have their own onboard display controllers, and then there will be a video socket for this purpose on the motherboard.

Expansion Cards

A very brief look at some typical expansion cards now follows. The first of these is shown at Fig. 4.15: an ASUS EAX1300PRO graphics card.

One point is particularly noteworthy with respect to this example. Although not obvious at first sight, this is a PCI Express card and not a PCI card. The clues are in the positioning of the space between the two sets of contacts on the connector and in the tail on the right-hand side of the connector, just under the centre of the fan. Ordinary PCI cards do not have tails, and it is this tail, trapped by the retention mechanism on the PCI Express x16 socket on the motherboard, that locks the card in place, a feature that has been found necessary for graphics cards. Although a similar retention system is used with the older AGP sockets, the positioning of the space between the two sets of contacts is different between the AGP cards and the PCI Express x16 cards. Close examination of the PCI and PCI Express x16 sockets in Fig. 4.7 shows that these

Fig. 4.15 ASUS EAX1300PRO graphics card (photograph: Tony Sammes and Brian Jenkinson).

Fig. 4.16 AWE32 Sound Blasfer card (photograph: Tony Sammes and Brian Jenkinson).

too have different spaces between the two sets of contacts, and this spacing can be used to aid identification of the different expansion cards.

At Fig. 4.16 we have shown an old AWE32 Sound Blaster card. Although these are now obsolete, as we would expect audio to be implemented directly on the motherboard these days, we have shown this card for two main reasons.

First of all it is a good example of a 16 bit ISA card, and this can be recognized by the position of the split between the two sets of contacts seen at the bottom of the figure. Also just visible on the right-hand side of the figure is the metal plate, which forms part of the outer casing, and a number of sockets through which various sound connections can be made. The second reason for showing this card is that this model, in common with many sound cards that were manufactured before the IDE CD-ROM drive interface had been developed, has three different CD-ROM interface sockets on the left-hand side of the figure. These enable a CD-ROM drive to be fitted which interfaces through the Sound Blaster card, the technique that was most frequently used on older systems to provide a CD-ROM facility.

The final picture, at Fig. 4.17, is that of a simple network card. Again, this has a PCI connection, shown at the bottom of the picture, and we can just see a network cable plugged into a 10BaseT socket on the left-hand side of card.

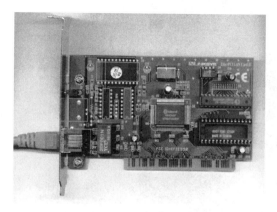

Fig. 4.17 Simple network card (photograph: Tony Sammes and Brian Jenkinson).

Although there are very many different kinds of expansion card, these three examples should give a reasonable view of what to expect inside the box. Often the purpose of an expansion card becomes evident from the connections that are made to it. Equally often, there is useful information screen printed on the printed circuit board which will help identify the manufacturer of the card and its type.

References

Adams, C. K. (1981) *Master Handbook of Microprocessor Chips*, Tab Books Inc., New York.

Apple Computer Inc. (2006) *Device Drivers FireWire*. URL: `http://developer.apple.com/hardwaredrivers/fireWire/Index.html`.

ASUS (2005) *ASUS Motherboard A8N32-SLI*, E2280, Second Edition V2, October 2005, ASUSTeK Computer Inc.

Freer, J. (1987) *Systems Design with Advanced Microprocessors*, Pitman, London.

IBM (1996a) *Understanding DRAM Operation*, IBM Applications Note, 12/96, International Business Machines Corp. URL: `http://www.cs.albany.edu/~sdc/CSI404/dramop.pdf`.

IBM (1996b) Synchronous DRAMs: the DRAM of the future, *IBM MicroNews*, First Quarter, 4–6.

IBM (1996c) *Understanding VRAM and SGRAM Operation*, IBM Applications Note, 12/96, International Business Machines Corp. URL: `http://www.ee.surrey.ac.uk/Personal/R.Webb/13a15/extras/vrmsgrm.pdf`.

IBM (1997) *Understanding Static RAM Operation*, IBM Applications Note, 03/97, International Business Machines Corp. URL: `http://www.ee.surrey.ac.uk/Personal/R.Webb/13a15/extras/sramop.pdf`.

IBM (undated) *Understanding EDO (Hyper Page Mode)*, IBM Applications Note, International Business Machines Corp. URL: `http://www.chips.ibm.com/` (no longer available).

Intel (1979) *The 8086 Family User's Manual*, Intel Corporation.

Khambata, A. J. (1982) *Microprocessors/Microcomputers Architecture, Software, and Systems*, John Wiley & Sons, New York.

Mueller, S. (1998) *Upgrading and Repairing PCs*, 8th edn, Macmillan Computer Publishing, New York.

Peacock, C. (2005) *USB in a Nutshell, Making Sense of the USB Standard*, 15 June 2005. URL: `http://www.beyondlogic.org/usbnutshell/usb1.htm`.

USB (2000) *Universal Serial Bus Specification Revision 2.0*, Compaq, Hewlett-Packard, Intel, Lucent, Microsoft, NEC, Philips, 27 April 2000. URL: `http://www.usb.org/developers/docs/usb_20_05122006.zip`.

5. *Disk Geometry*

░ ░

Introduction

In this chapter we look in detail at the geometry of floppy and hard disk drives to find out exactly how information is stored and how it might be hidden. The topics we are going to consider are the following:

- The development of the hard disk
- Physical construction – heads, tracks and cylinders
- Formation of addressable elements
- Encoding methods and formats for floppy disks
- Encoding methods and formats for hard disks
- The formatting process
- Hard disk interfaces
- IDE/ATA problems and workarounds
- The boot sequence and POST
- The master boot record and partitions
- Directories and file systems
- Hiding information

░ ░

A Little Bit of History

One of the most important devices from a forensic computing viewpoint is the hard disk drive, which today may contain hundreds of gigabytes of information. It is of more than passing historical interest to note, however, that the very early IBM Personal Computers, released in 1981, were not provided with any kind of hard disk drive; indeed there was no program code (Majors, 1995) in their BIOS that could recognize a hard drive nor any provision in the early versions of their operating systems for hard disk support. PC-DOS versions 1.0 and 1.1 and MS-DOS versions 1.0 and 1.25 had no support at all.

It was not until MS-DOS version 2.0, released in March 1983, that hard disk support was provided in the operating system code (Duncan, 1988). In addition, the lack of any subdirectory facilities in the file structure of these operating systems meant that there was a very low upper limit (Duncan, 1988) on the numbers of files that could be stored on a disk. MS-DOS 1.0 and its file system was based on the 16 bit operating system 86-DOS, and this in turn had been designed by Seattle Computer Products to be upwards compatible with C/PM-80, the Digital Research 8 bit operating system, which was then the current standard for the Intel 8080 and Zilog Z-80 microprocessors. In the CP/M file systems, the directory area on the disk is of fixed size and typically can contain only some 64 entries. This does not necessarily represent even 64 files, since multiple directory entries may be needed for a single file (Clarke and Powys-Lybbe, 1986). However, since these file structures were designed solely for floppy disk support and these, at the time, had a capacity of only 160 kbyte per disk, this did not pose a real problem. Even with support for hard disks in MS-DOS 2.0, the amount of data on a disk did not pose the problem that it does today.

Five Main Issues

From a forensic computing viewpoint, there are five main issues that we need to consider with respect to disk drive units. These are:

- the physical construction of the unit itself
- the way in which addressable elements of memory are formed within the unit
- the variety of interfacing issues and problems that have arisen as a result of rapid development
- the implementation of file systems using the addressable elements of memory
- the ways in which information might be hidden on the disk

In this chapter, we will consider each of these five issues in turn.

Physical Construction of the Unit

We will start with floppy disk units, not only because these were the sole forms of backing store available on the early PCs, but also because they are the simplest in structure and in concept.

We see at Fig. 5.1 a simple conceptual model of a floppy disk drive unit. A magnetic disk or *platter*, contained in a protective envelope or hard plastic case, is inserted into the drive and automatically locked onto a spindle. It is then rotated at a constant speed by means of a spindle motor. The disk itself is a circular piece of very flexible plastic (hence the term *floppy* disk), coated on both sides with a magnetic material. A *head assembly*, consisting of two magnetic read/write heads, one in contact with the upper surface of the disk and one in contact with the lower surface of the disk, may be moved in discrete steps across the disk by means of a stepper motor.

Because the magnetic read/write heads are in contact with the two surfaces of the disk, physical wear occurs and the rotational speed has to be limited to ensure a reasonable life for the disk and drive unit. For the standard 3.5 inch, 1.44 Mbyte floppy, the rotational speed is limited to 360 revolutions per minute.

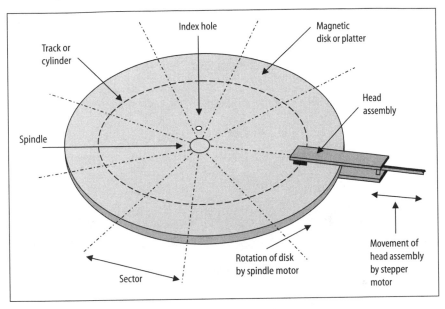

Fig. 5.1 Physical construction.

Tracks and Cylinders

Given that the head assembly is held at some particular position in its series of steps across the surface of the disk, the area of magnetic material that is passing under the upper head as a result of the rotation of the disk is seen to be a very narrow circular strip.

This is shown as a dashed oval in Fig. 5.1. The strip is called a *track*, and, since there is one track swept out by the upper head and a second track swept out by the lower head, the two tracks taken together are referred to as a *cylinder*. The number[1] of possible cylinders for a given drive is clearly determined by the number of discrete steps available to the stepper motor. This concept of a cylinder is more explicitly illustrated in Fig. 5.2, where three disk platters and six tracks are shown[2].

Clearly, information may be magnetically recorded onto a given track by moving the head assembly to the appropriate step position, switching to one of the two heads electronically, and writing electromagnetically to the disk surface for the period of one rotation. Similarly, the information may be "played back" by moving the head assembly to the appropriate step position, switching to the appropriate head, and reading electromagnetically from the disk surface for a period of one rotation.

---

1   For the standard 3.5 inch, 1.44 Mbyte floppy, the number of possible steps and hence the number of cylinders is 80.

2   We will use the terms *track* and *cylinder* from now onwards, usually without distinguishing between them, to mean a particular positioning of the head assembly.

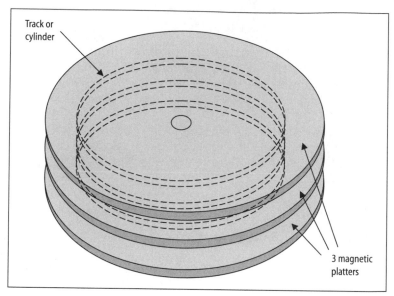

Track or cylinder

3 magnetic platters

Fig. 5.2 A cylinder.

One problem that becomes evident from this simple approach is the determination of where a track, which is circular, begins and ends. This is where the index hole (see Fig. 5.1) comes in for older floppy disks; it helped to mark the beginning and end of a track.

For the standard 3.5 inch, 1.44 Mbyte floppy, a metal slot on the floppy disk is mated with a pin on the drive spindle, which registers the disk in relationship to the spindle motor. Given this registration, timing pulses can be used to help determine the start and end of tracks.

Formation of Addressable Elements

In practice, the track is found to be too large a unit for storing information, so it is divided into a number of equal sized *sectors*. Shown in Fig. 5.1 are 9 *sectors per track* (*spt*), which is typical for the older 5.25 inch floppy disks. The later ones use 15 sectors per track whilst the standard 3.5 inch, 1.44 Mbyte floppy has 18 sectors per track.

The position of each sector can be determined by timing pulses that are generated in conjunction with the index hole and the rotation of the spindle motor. In this way, any information unit on the disk can be uniquely identified and accessed. First the head assembly must be moved to the correct cylinder position, then the appropriate head must be switched in electronically to access the correct track, and then the read process must start when the timing pulses indicate that the correct sector is passing under the head.

CHS Addressing

This led to the use of so-called *CHS addressing*: C for the cylinder number (starting from 0), H for the head number (starting from 0) and S for the sector number (starting from 1). The formation of addressable elements of disk memory is achieved by means of this *physical CHS address*, which uniquely identifies every sector on the disk[3]. Although this form of addressing has today become obsolete for the majority of modern hard disks, we cannot, as forensic analysts, ignore how it works. This is because CHS addressing is still used by most bootstrap programs when the computer first starts up. It is also used by most floppy disks and other media such as thumb drives and CF cards, and we may well come across some older hard disks for analysis that can only be addressed in this way.

Reading from or Writing to a CHS Disk

We can now visualize the way in which an operating system might read from or write to a CHS addressed disk. The operating system would need first to send a "command" to the disk controller to move the head assembly by means of the stepper motor to the required cylinder (or track) position; the "C" of the CHS address. It would then need to send a second "command" to the controller to switch in the required head electronically; the "H" of the CHS address. Then it would need to send a third "command" to the controller to allow the disk to rotate until the particular required sector was coming under the head assembly; the "S" of the CHS address. The operating system would then need to send a "command" instructing the controller to read from or write to the sector as it passes under the head assembly. In practice these "commands" are all loaded into the registers of the processor and are passed to the disk controller by means of an INT 13h software interrupt, which we discuss in more detail later. Part of the CHS address design is to place on the surface of the disk, in each sector, a copy of the actual CHS address for that sector known as the ID Address Mark (IDAM). The disk controller, when instructed to read from or write to a sector at a specific CHS address, first reads the IDAM at the sector it has selected to confirm that carrying out these three physical CHS commands has resulted in the correct sector being accessed. This is an important part of the controller's error-checking mechanism.

Encoding Methods and Formats for Floppy Disks

The *format* of the information recorded on the track and on each sector within the track is very important in helping to identify sector addresses. A track consists of a serial sequence of bits which are all interpreted as 8 bit bytes. One might reasonably assume that these bit patterns are simply recorded directly onto the magnetic platter

---

3   The outermost cylinder on the disk is normally cylinder 0 and the topmost head is normally head 0.

as a sequence of small magnetized areas, with a "0" being represented by, say, a "north–south" magnetized area and a "1" by a "south–north" magnetized area.

In practice this is not done, because the magnetic heads operate by detecting *changes* in magnetization, so a long run of 1s or 0s using our simple-minded approach would not generate any signals. Instead, an *encoding* method is used which ensures that there are plenty of changes in the magnetization, whatever the bit pattern of our track data happens to be.

To clarify the distinction between the encoding method and the format we should note that the *encoding method* determines how a *bit* is actually encoded on the magnetic surface of the disk and the *format* determines what sequences of *bytes* are used to represent the various data structures that are required. These data structures include, for example, the CHS address for each sector, the sector data blocks and any error-detecting or correcting codes.

FM and MFM Encoding

Two encoding methods exist for floppy disks: Frequency Modulation (FM) and Modified Frequency Modulation (MFM). At Fig. 5.3 we see FM and MFM encoding methods compared for the same data pattern. This data pattern is an example byte of value 41h representing the character "A". The byte is shown, for example purposes, with a leading and trailing 0 to make it up to the ten bit sequence: 0010000010. The information is written as a continuous bit stream onto the magnetic surface.

In the case of FM, information is stored in a *bit cell* and this consists of a *clock bit* and a place for a *data bit*. Electromagnetic theory tells us that only a flux change can create a signal, so every bit needs to be implemented by some kind of flux change, usually a reversal of magnetization. Each set clock or data bit is therefore established by a reversal of magnetization. Typical of FM is a clock bit present for every bit cell and a data bit present only where there is a 1 in the data stream and absent where there is a 0 in the data stream. In the FM encoding section of Fig. 5.3 we can see, as magnetic flux density reversals, the clock bits for each bit cell and the two set data bits for the byte 41h (0100 0001).

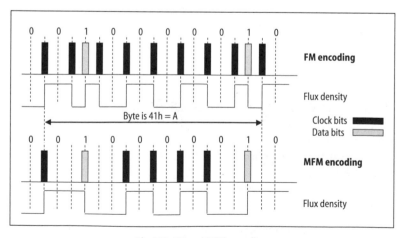

Fig. 5.3 FM and MFM encoding.

Table 5.1 Rules for MFM encoding.

- A data bit is always written if it is equal to 1.

- A clock bit is only written if the preceding bit cell as well as the current bit cell does not have a data bit set.

It was very soon recognized that, for FM encoding, many of the clock bits are, in fact, redundant. Their presence is only required to identify the start of a bit cell, thus helping to maintain synchronization of the controller with the data stream. However, synchronization is only a problem where the data stream consists of a series of 0s together and a reversal does not occur for some time. Provided that reversals occur frequently enough, synchronization can be maintained.

In the MFM encoding method, two simple rules were established that determined when a clock bit needs to be written in order to maintain synchronization and when it can be ignored. The rules are shown in Table 5.1. What these rules are doing is to set a clock bit whenever a run of two 0 data bits occurs. This can be clearly seen from the MFM encoding section of Fig. 5.3, which shows the same byte, 41h, encoded using these rules.

By comparing the flux reversals in the two sections it is not difficult to see that MFM will permit, on average, twice the information density over that of FM for the same recording density. As a result, FM encoding is almost never used today.

Floppy Disk Low-Level Format

A slightly different low-level format is specified for the two encoding methods, but both of these formats require, for each track on the disk, a *start of track* sequence of bytes, a *sector format* sequence which includes the CHS address and the data block for each of the sectors, and an *end of track* sequence of bytes.

As mentioned earlier, bytes are recorded sequentially along the track, with each byte itself being recorded as eight serial bits. At Table 5.2 (Messmer, 2002, p. 791) we have shown the sequence of bytes that are required for a 5.25 inch floppy disk track in IBM format using the MFM (Modified Frequency Modulation) encoding method that we discussed in the previous section.

Referring to Table 5.2, we note that a track always starts with a so-called GAP 4A sequence, which consists of 80 bytes each of value 4eh. This is the hex value that is used for all gaps in this format. Although early floppy disk controllers could recognize the beginning of the track by means of the index hole on the floppy, as we mentioned above, the physical size of this hole is far too large and its physical position is far too imprecise to determine precisely where the track on more modern disks begins[4]. The 80 byte 4eh pattern warns the disk controller that the track is about to start and gives the electronics time to synchronize with the 12 byte sequence of 00h which follows. This is known as the *synchronization* (SYNC) block.

The four bytes of the *Index Address Mark* (IAM) tell the controller that the sectors of the track are about to follow, and immediately after this there is another gap of 50

---

4   Data bits on a 15 sector per track floppy are only about 2 microns apart, whereas the index hole is about 1 mm in diameter.

Table 5.2 5.25 inch floppy disk format MFM encoding.

GAP 4A	80 bytes 4eh	Start of track
SYNC	12 bytes 00h	
IAM	4 bytes c2h c2h c2h fch	
GAP 1	50 bytes 4eh	
SYNC	12 bytes 00h	Start of sector 1
IDAM	4 bytes a1h a1h a1h feh	
ID	4 bytes cylinder head sector sector-size *1024 cylinders, 256 heads, 63 sectors*	
CRC	2 byte CRC value	
GAP 2	22 bytes 4eh	
SYNC	12 bytes 00h	
DAM	4 bytes a1h a1h a1h fbh (or f8h)	
Data	512 bytes data	
CRC	2 byte CRC value	
GAP 3	80 bytes 4eh	End of sector 1
...		Sectors 2 to 15
GAP 4B	?? bytes 4eh	End of track

bytes of 4eh, GAP 1. It is this Index Address Mark that signals the true start of the track[5].

After the start of track sequence, the sectors proper begin. Each of the sectors (and in this format there are 15 of them) has ten sections, of which only those for sector 1 are shown in the diagram. After another synchronization (SYNC) sequence of 12 bytes of 00h, the *ID Address Mark* (IDAM), which we mentioned above, follows; this indicates the start of the ID or identification field for the sector concerned and is where the CHS address is held. The ID field is made up of four bytes, of which three are used for *cylinder*, *head* and *sector* addressing and the fourth is used to indicate the *sector size* for floppy disks and as a *flag* byte for hard disks, the details of which we will look at later. At Fig. 5.4 we have shown the layout of the first three of the four ID bytes which provide the CHS address for the sector. Ten bits are used for the cylinder[6] address with the *leading* two bits of that address being taken from the high end of the sector byte (the third byte). This gives a maximum cylinder address of 1023, and since the cylinder count starts from 0, we may address up to 1024 cylinders. Eight bits are used for the head address (the whole of the second byte) giving a maximum value of 255, and since the head count starts from 0 we may address up to 256 heads. Only six bits are used for the sector address (the remainder of the third byte), giving a

---

5 Floppy disks used to fail rather more frequently than today, and one error message would often be "Missing index address mark".

6 Recall that *cylinder* numbers are the same as *track* numbers; they represent the position of the head assembly.

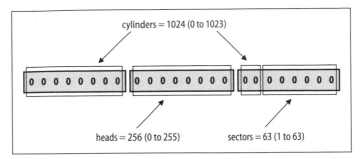

Fig. 5.4 CHS of ID field.

maximum value of 63, and, since the sector count conventionally always starts from 1, we may address up to 63 sectors.

Because of the importance of these ID marks, a two-byte *Cyclic Redundancy Check* (CRC)[7] is calculated and stored at format time for the IDAM and ID fields. Another gap then follows of 22 bytes of 4eh, GAP 2, which is deliberately put there to give the controller time to check this CRC, and then there is another synchronization (SYNC) sequence of 12 bytes of 00h. This is followed by the *Data Address Mark* (DAM), which signals the start of the actual 512 bytes of data[8].

After this data block comes another two-byte CRC, calculated for the whole of the data area, and the sector is finally terminated by another gap, GAP 3, of 80 bytes of 4eh. This gap is designed to be long enough to allow for any variations in recording speed and thus avoid the inadvertent overwriting of the following sector. This first sector is then followed by the other 14 sectors, using exactly the same format, and then the *End of Track* is written as GAP 4B, a variable number of 4eh bytes forming a flexible buffer which finally links up with GAP 4A. With all of this laid down during formatting, we can easily see why a formatted disk has less usable data space than an unformatted disk. We can also see how a disk controller can confirm that it has accessed the correct CHS address by checking the sector ID field.

The 8.4 Gbyte Barrier

Having discussed track and sector formatting now in some detail, it might be useful at this point to consider what implications, if any, these data structures could have on hard disk capacity. Although there is not going to be any problem for current floppy disks, with their very limited capacity, it is important to understand that we have, at the level of the disk format itself, imposed limits on the range of CHS addresses that are possible. This is because we have used fixed sizes for the numbers of bits that have

---

7 A cyclic redundancy check is a form of checksum that can be used to detect certain kinds of error. For a good detailed explanation, see Messmer (2002, pp. 796–800).

8 Data sizes other than 512 bytes are possible for floppy disks and these would be indicated appropriately by the setting in the fourth byte of the ID. However, 512 bytes is the size most usually adopted.

been allocated to each of the three CHS parameters, namely: 1024 cylinders (0 to 1023 in 10 bits), 256 heads (0 to 255 in 8 bits) and 63 sectors (1 to 63 in 6 bits).

The maximum number of sectors it is thus possible to address is $1024 \times 256 \times 63$, and given that the normal sector data size is 512 bytes, we can calculate the theoretical maximum size of a formatted disk as $1024 \times 256 \times 63 \times 512$ bytes = $8,455,716,864$ = 8.4 Gbyte[9]. Here is one of the factors that originally resulted in the so-called *8.4 Gbyte barrier*. This ID field structure is the structure of the original low-level format design for floppy disks which was carried over with little modification into the ST412/506 low-level format design when hard disks first became available. It is also precisely the same structure that is used for the INT 13h[10] disk access mechanism where the three bytes of Fig. 5.4 equate to the three registers CH, DH and CL respectively. We will be looking at this in detail in a later section in order to understand many of the hard disk design concepts. Hard disk manufacturers have tended subsequently, in their low-level formatting design, to utilize these four ID bytes in rather different ways in order to help overcome this barrier, as we shall note later. However, since the low-level format structure is completely hidden from the outside world by the disk controller in modern hard disks, some manufacturers[11] have radically revised the data structures which they use in their low-level formats. As a result, the four ID bytes are no longer a factor in the 8.4 Gbyte barrier.

Construction of Hard Disk Systems

One of the big differences between floppy disks and hard disks is that the heads do not (normally) touch the surface of a hard disk except when at rest. The hard disk is, as the name suggests, made up of a number of rigid hard *platters* and the *head–disk assembly* is enclosed in a dust-free environment.

All the heads are fixed to the same *actuator* and fly free just above the surface of the disk, held up by aerodynamic pressure (Fig. 5.5). At the time of writing, a common size of disk platter, usually referred to as the *form factor*, is 3.5 inches, although 2.5 inches is often used for notebook computers and is becoming more common for standalone drives. The number of heads is likely to be between two and six and the rotational speeds are typically from 3,600 to 7,200 revolutions per minute[12]. Servo control circuits are used to position the head assembly and to reduce

---

9   Note that this figure is calculated using powers of ten units for kilo, mega and giga, for which we divide by $1000 \times 1000 \times 1000$. If we were to use powers of two units, more normal for computer work, we would divide by $1024 \times 1024 \times 1024$ and get a result of 7.87 Gbyte, a number which is also sometimes used.

10 Throughout we have used "INT 13h" to refer to the legacy disk interrupt mechanism and "INT 13h extensions" to refer to the extended system.

11 IBM have designed a new low-level format which does not use ID bytes at all. It is called the No-ID™ sector format; see IBM (1995).

12 At the time of writing, disks from a number of manufacturers now have rotational speeds of 15,000 rpm.

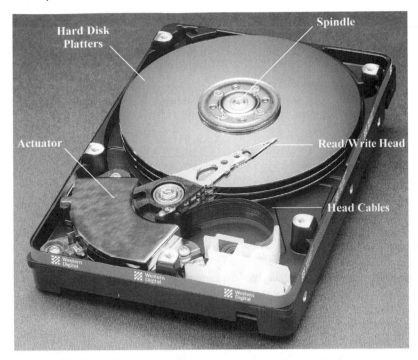

Fig. 5.5 Western Digital Caviar (with kind permission of Western Digital Corporation).

any rotational variations in speed to approximately ±0.1%. A nice analogy for the standard of engineering required is quoted here from Seagate (1995a): *"Today's new generation of disc drives achieve the engineering equivalent of a Boeing 747 flying at Mach 4 just two meters above the ground, counting each blade of grass as it flies over."*

As in the case of floppy disks, except for high-performance systems and RAID (see later section), only one head is active at any one time for reading or writing data. Having said that, in some hard disk systems, one of the disk surfaces[13] may be used for holding pre-formatted control information, and thus its associated head is also in use at the same time as the data head for servo control purposes. Tracks on this surface are called *servo tracks* or *index tracks* and the head itself is known as the *servo head* or the *index head*. Disks that use this technique often appear to have an odd number of real physical heads, since one has been reserved for servo use. Other systems may instead embed the servo information into the data tracks as *servo sectors* (IBM, 1995). The head assembly, instead of being positioned by a stepper motor actuator[14] is controlled by a linear motor system which is often referred to as a *voice coil actuator*. In this system, the head reads the preset data on the servo tracks and uses this with a feedback loop to position the voice coil actuator and the head

---

13 Usually the topmost.

14 An outdated mechanical head positioning system that was used with early hard disks drives and is still used for floppy disk drives.

assembly very accurately to any particular cylinder position. It is this approach that has led to a rapid expansion in the capacity of hard disks by radically increasing the number of real physical cylinders[15]. This development was apparently not foreseen by the early designers who, if the low-level format ID data structure sizes are any indication, expected instead the number of heads to increase towards 256. We recall from our discussion above of the 8.4 Gbyte barrier that the ID field in a sector only has scope to specify up to 1024 cylinders, rather than the many thousands that we may find in modern hard disks. This is yet another limitation to which we will return shortly.

When the drive is switched off, the heads rest on the surface. Most modern disks "park" their heads automatically onto an unused track as they power down, though earlier disks had a special PARK program designed for this purpose. It is certainly unwise practice to use any version of this program with a modern self-parking disk! Typical distances for heads flying free are 0.2 to 0.5 microns above the surface, or some 12 millionths of an inch. By comparison, a fingerprint and a smoke particle are some five to ten times thicker at 3 microns and a hair is some thirty times thicker at 10 microns. Contamination can therefore be a serious potential problem.

Hard disks have an internal air filter which is used for filtering the air already in the case. To avoid the head–disk assembly exploding as a result of low external air pressure, such as might occur in an aircraft cabin at high altitude, the case has a venti-lation slit which is also protected by an air filter.

Note, however, that it is not a good idea to place your laptop in the hold baggage compartment when flying without first removing the hard disk(s) and carrying them in the cabin with your hand baggage. It is not that the decompression of the hold will itself damage the disks; air will simply be forced out of the ventilation slits. The problem occurs on returning to normal atmospheric pressure. Air will then be forced back into the disk, and this air may contain contaminants which the simple filters cannot handle. The result can be a catastrophic head crash. Another problem that can arise is that of thermal shock. The temperature may change from about –25 °C in the hold at cruising height to +20 °C on the ground over a period of about half an hour, and this may result in severe physical damage to the disk.

Encoding Methods and Formats for Hard Disks

A very similar approach to that used for floppy disks was originally adopted for the encoding and low-level formatting of hard disks. Indeed, the approaches can be seen to have developed directly from their floppy disk controller antecedents. Three encoding methods may be met with: *Modified Frequency Modulation* (*MFM*) encoding, *Run Length Limited* (RLL) encoding and *Advanced Run Length Limited* (ARLL) encoding. Again slightly different low-level formats are used for the different encoding methods and also between hard disk manufacturers.

---

15 The Cheetah from Seagate has 6,526 cylinders; see Seagate (1997a).

RLL Encoding

We will first look briefly at RLL encoding and compare it with MFM. It is an area that tends to be shrouded in mystery, quite unjustifiably so as it turns out.

We saw earlier how MFM can provide, on average, a 2 to 1 improvement over FM by writing a clock bit only if two 0 data bits occur in succession. However, if we were to have all 512 data bytes in a sector filled with 0s we would still have 4096[16] clock bits using MFM. With RLL, there are no clock bits, but this means that with long sequences of 0 data bits we would have no 1 bits set at all in the recorded stream and the controller would quickly lose synchronization.

What *Run Length Limited* means is that although there might be no clock bits in the stream to be recorded, we first encode that stream, before recording, into one which does have 1s at sufficiently small intervals to maintain synchronization. We do this by limiting the *run length* of any sequence of 0s to something that is short enough for the controller to maintain synchronization; hence *run length limited*. With one of the most widely used RLL methods[17], there are, by definition, at least two and at most seven 0 bits between any two 1 bits in the recorded stream. This is achieved by encoding the original data bit pattern in terms of a well-defined set of (what we have called here) *data chunks*. These data chunks, together with their appropriate RLL 2,7 codes are shown in Table 5.3. You will note if you look at the resultant code fragments that you can never have sequences that have less than two or more than seven 0s, no matter what sequences of RLL 2,7 code you use. If, as shown in the example, we wanted to encode a sequence of nine 0s we would use the 000 chunk three times, thus generating: 000100 000100 000100. We note two things from this: first that the largest run length that has been generated is five and the smallest run length is two, fulfilling the required conditions, and that there has been a significant increase in size, with 9 bits becoming 18. In fact, we find that RLL 2,7 doubles the number of bits needed for any given data sequence.

If we now consider Fig. 5.6 we see the same example that we used before in Fig. 5.3 to compare FM with MFM; that is, the data bits 0010000010, representing the

Table 5.3 Code for RLL 2,7.

Data chunk	RLL 2,7 code
000	000100
10	0100
010	100100
0010	00100100
11	1000
011	001000
0011	00001000

---

16 512 bytes × 8 bits = 4096 bit cells, each requiring a clock bit.

17 Known as RLL 2,7.

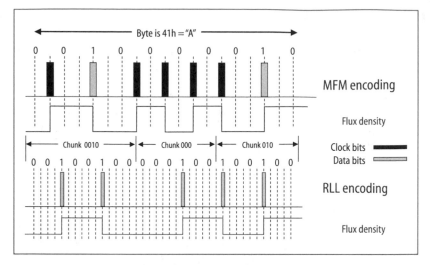

Fig. 5.6 RLL encoding.

character "A" of byte value 41h with a leading and trailing 0. The MFM flux density encoding for the character "A", in the upper half of the diagram, can be clearly seen to require seven flux reversals. In the lower half of the diagram, the data bits have been re-encoded into RLL 2,7 form using the three chunks – 0010, 000 and 010 – resulting in the RLL 2,7 recorded bit stream of 00100100 000100 100100. The flux density for this same character "A", encoded using RLL, can be seen in the lower half of the diagram to require only five flux reversals.

From this we can clearly see the advantage when we look at the two flux densities. For RLL we have no clock bits at all and hence there is a significant saving of the order of 3 to 1 over the equivalent MFM. However, because we have increased the recorded bit pattern size by re-encoding it into RLL 2,7 code, there is also a loss of the order of 2 to 1 through using RLL. Combining these two, we find a net gain on average, using RLL 2,7 over MFM, of about 1.5 to 1.

One problem with the RLL method is that if the system does lose synchronization, a burst error of up to five bits can result. This requires much more sophisticated error detection and correction, so RLL controllers tend to use *error-correcting codes* (ECC) in their formats rather than the simpler CRC codes we saw in the MFM format. Other RLL methods exist which may be referred to as *Advanced RLL* or *ARLL*. Examples include RLL 1,7 and RLL 3,9. In both these cases the encoding overhead is even higher and the larger number of 0 bits permitted between two 1 bits makes greater demands on system synchronization. The payoff, however, is that data density improvements of up to 90% over that of MFM can be realized.

Hard Disk Low-Level Format

As in the case of the floppy disk low-level format, the original hard disk low-level format requires, for each track on the disk, a start of track sequence of bytes, a sector

Table 5.4 ST412/506 hard disk format RLL encoding.

SYNC	11 bytes 00h	Start of track
IAM	2 bytes a1h fch	
GAP 1	12 bytes ffh	
SYNC	10 bytes 00h	Start of sector 1
IDAM	2 bytes 5eh a1h	
ID	4 bytes cylinder head sector flags *1024 cylinders, 256 heads, 63 sectors*	
ECC	4 byte ECC value	
GAP 2	5 bytes 00h	
SYNC	11 bytes 00h	
DAM	2 bytes 5eh a1h	
Data	512 bytes data	
ECC	4 byte ECC value	
GAP 3	3 bytes 00h and 17 bytes ffh	End of sector 1
...		Sectors 2 to 26
GAP 4B	approx. 93 bytes 00h	End of track

format sequence which includes the CHS address and the data block for each of the sectors, and an end of track sequence of bytes. As before, bytes are recorded sequentially along the track, with each byte itself being recorded as eight serial bits. It should be noted that for hard disks the actual format is very controller dependent, and this usually means that the format performed by one controller cannot be utilized by another.

At Table 5.4 (see Messmer, 2002, p. 859) is shown the hard disk format for an ST412/506 controller using RLL encoding. As can be seen, the fields and sectors are very similar to those for the 5.25 in floppy disk format using MFM encoding that we saw at Table 5.2.

The first point to note is that all the gaps are very much smaller (GAP 1 is 12 bytes instead of 50, GAP 2 is 5 bytes instead of 22, and GAP 3 is 20 bytes instead of 80). This reduction in gap size is made possible because the rotation of the disk is much more stable, partly because of the lack of any friction between the surface of the disk and the heads and partly because of the servo feedback loop that we referred to earlier. We might also note the 4 byte error-correcting code (ECC) fields in place of the 2 byte cyclic redundancy checks (CRCs) that we saw with MFM encoding.

When discussing RLL encoding above, we identified the need for more extensive error correction in order to deal with the burst errors that can be a feature of this form of encoding. Some formats use 6 bytes for the ECC fields, permitting the controller electronics to detect and correct an even greater range of errors. The ID fields again use four bytes and the first three bytes specify cylinder, head and sector numbers exactly as for the MFM encoded format (see Fig. 5.4). The implication is, of

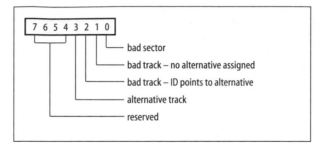

Fig. 5.7 Sector flag details.

course, that the 8.4 Gbyte barrier will still apply to hard disks that are formatted in this way.

The fourth byte is not used to specify sector size, as is the case with the floppy disk MFM encoded format, but instead it is used as a *sector flag* which enables the controller to perform *bad sector mapping*. The details of this sector flag are shown at Fig. 5.7.

Bad Sector Mapping and Defect Lists

The need for bad sector mapping and the sector flag arises because of micro-defects that are found to exist on the magnetic surface of the disk at the time of manufacture. Seagate (1995a) states that there should be less than one defect per formatted megabyte and that the disk should be defect-free for the first two cylinders. The defects are of two types: hard, which usually relate to a surface problem, and soft, which is normally some kind of magnetic anomaly. Although hard defects can be discovered relatively easily with low-level formatting software, soft defects can only be found after much testing with very sophisticated test equipment. The manufacturer used to perform such tests over a period of several hours and from these tests would determine a *manufacturer's defect list* of all the bad sectors. Such lists were often marked on the casing of the drive as a *defect label* in a form similar to that shown in Table 5.5.

With modern Zoned Bit Recording disks (see later section), defect labels are no longer used and bad sector mapping strategies, as described in this section, are completely hidden by the internal controller. The issues, however, are still relevant and are described here for two reasons: firstly, because it is important to understand that although hidden, bad sector mapping strategies continue to be required, with

Table 5.5 Defect label.

Cyl	Hd	BFI
72	0	5314
73	0	5315
74	0	5316
161	2	1816

more comprehensive ones now being used to give the appearance of a fault-free disk; and, secondly, because it is possible for forensic computing analysts to come across older disks which still visibly exhibit these characteristics.

In the old style of defect list, each bad sector is specified by its cylinder and head number, which defines the track, and the *bytes from index* (BFI)[18] value. This specifies the number of bytes from the start of track index mark to where the bad area exists. This index mark, which is usually generated by a Hall sensor embedded in the spindle motor or encoded onto the servo tracks, is considered the absolute point of reference for the BFI value. During the low-level formatting process, the controller performs bad sector mapping to remove the effects of these defects. This used to be achieved by a number of strategies.

If the controller identified a defect that only affected a single sector of the track it would attempt to shift the sector formatting slightly so that the defect occurred in one of the sector or track gaps, where it would have no effect. This is known as *sector slipping*. If this was not possible, the controller would mark the sector concerned as *bad* by setting bit 0 of the sector flag to 1 (see Fig. 5.7). The controller would not then permit any accesses to this bad sector. Some controllers were also able to format an additional spare sector on the track to replace this bad sector, thus ensuring that there would be no loss of formatted disk capacity.

Where there was more than one defective sector in a track, the controller could apply one of two strategies. In the first strategy, it could mark the entire track as bad by setting bit 1 of the sector flag to 1 in all the sectors of the track. The controller would not then permit any access to any of the sectors in that track. The effect of this was to reduce the formatted disk capacity and create a "hole" in the disk address space where the bad track resided.

A better strategy was to mark the complete track as bad by setting bit 2 of the sector flag to 1 in all the sectors of that track and assigning an alternative track starting from the highest numbered cylinder. The CHS address values of the ID fields in all these bad sectors were then set to point to their replacement counterparts in the alternative track. So, when a seek to a sector in a bad track was made, the controller simply looked up the alternative sector address in the ID field of the sector in the bad track and then performed a seek to that alternative sector instead. Any track that had been assigned in this way as an alternative track had bit 3 of the sector flag set to 1 in all of its sectors. This strategy could still result in a loss of formatted disk capacity, in that the alternative track would no longer be available for use in its own address position. However, it does have the benefit of ensuring that there would then be no "hole" in the disk address space, since the addresses of the bad track would all appear to work correctly using the alternative track sectors. In any case, most disks were designed to have some spare capacity, outside of the user address space, which was specifically set aside for this defective sector or defective track reallocation purpose. For example, the Seagate ST-225 had a nominal capacity of 20 Mbyte and an actual capacity of 21.4 Mbyte, making up to 1.4 Mbyte available for reallocation to defective sectors and tracks. Substantial spare capacity is normally built in to all modern hard

---

18 Sometimes also called the *byte count after index* (BCAI).

disk drives, but this is only accessible to the drive controller and is not part of the user address space.

Finally, it should be noted that there are four reserved bits in the sector flag shown at Fig. 5.7. We will return to these bits when we examine the ATA (AT Attachment) interface and LBA (Logical Block Addressing) in a later section.

A Possible Place to Hide

The reader might at this stage be wondering why it should be necessary to examine the hard disk geometry down to this level of detail. The reason is that sectors that have been marked as bad by the controller in this way could well be a very good place in which to hide information. Consider the situation where a particular track is used for storing some incriminating information and then deliberately marked as bad using, for example, the legacy controller command[19] REASSIGN ALTERNATIVE TRACK. This would not cause a new format to be laid down, so no information would be overwritten, but it would cause the controller to adjust its bad sector mapping such that all references to this track now point to the specified alternative track. Someone with a reasonable technical competence and a knowledge of the specific controller commands should certainly be able to do this. It would then not be possible for anyone else to access this incriminating information, or even necessarily be aware of its existence, without reassigning the track. Although this scenario is not a particularly likely one in practice, forensic computing analysts do need to be aware of the possibilities. One possible indicator here of something amiss is that there might then appear to be one formatted track too few for the known physical disk geometry.

Cylinder Number –1 and the Service Area

The early controllers that carried out bad sector mapping often reserved the first physical cylinder on the disk for their own use. Where this was the case, the physical cylinder was often assigned the artificial cylinder number "–1". As such, it was accessible only to the controller using specific internal commands, since it did not appear in the normal data address space of the disk. It was on this cylinder that the defect list was stored, often in two parts: the original manufacturer's defect list as described above and as illustrated at Table 5.5, and a so-called *grown defect list*, which was determined by the controller during formatting and added to by the subsequent use of manufacturer specific bad sector mapping commands.

---

19 Note that this discussion applies specifically to ST412/506 controllers which have now largely been replaced by ATA disks (see later section). However, it should be possible to obtain a similar effect with ATA disks using manufacturer-specific commands where these are known. Some modern disks can be switched into a so-called "factory mode", where a special set of diagnostic and defect management commands becomes available. Such commands might be password-protected. On floppy disks, use of the WRITE DELETED SECTOR command will permit the hiding of information that can only be read back using the READ DELETED SECTOR command.

These same techniques can still be found in modern hard disks. Cylinder –1 is now often replaced by an on-disk *service area*, which may well be larger than a single cylinder. This area may contain not only the manufacturer's defect list (now more usually known as the primary or *P-List*) and the grown defect list (now more usually known as the *G-List*), but also copies of the controller firmware, SMART[20] (Self-Monitoring, Analysis, and Reporting Technology) counters, as well as the sector translation and zone allocation tables (see later section on Zoned Bit Recording). In addition, there is likely to be a substantial part of the disk reserved for the reallocation of defective sectors.

The main difference between the two original defect lists is that the sophisticated testing that was carried out by the manufacturer was able to identify both hard and soft defects and was able to measure the exact byte positions of such defects using the bytes from index (BFI) count. It was these counts that were then placed in the manufacturer's defect list, as we have seen.

The disk controller, however, was not able to identify soft defects and did not normally measure BFIs, so the grown defect list differed in these two respects. Detailed information about the physical disk geometry together with the disk model and the manufacturer's name was also often written to cylinder –1 by the manufacturer. This was of particular importance for autoconfiguring controllers which could determine their own physical disk geometry by simply reading the first physical sector on the disk.

At Table 5.6 is shown the way in which a manufacturer's defect list, the grown defect list and the disk geometry information was typically written onto cylinder –1. Given 17 sectors per track, we note that the information was restricted to the first two heads (because these were present on all hard disks) and that more than one copy of the lists was held.

Table 5.6 Controller cylinder –1.

Sector	Head 0	Head 1
1	Disk geometry copy 1	Disk geometry copy 3
2	Disk geometry copy 2	Disk geometry copy 4
3–8	Reserved	Reserved
9–10	Manufacturer's defect list copy 1	Reserved
11–12	Manufacturer's defect list copy 2	Reserved
13–14	Grown defect list copy 1	Reserved
15–16	Grown defect list copy 2	Reserved
17	Reserved	Reserved

---

20 Most modern disk systems incorporate SMART technology. The internal operations of the disk are continuously monitored by a suite of diagnostic programs and any unusual events are recorded, analysed and, if necessary, reported to the user. This provides an early warning of impending disk failure which should be sufficient to permit the safe backing up of all user data.

Table 5.7 Disk geometry information.

Byte	Contents
0–1	Signature 0dabeh of geometric information
2–3	Number of cylinders
4	Number of heads
5	Number of sectors per track
6–7	Reserved
8	Interleave factor
9	BIOS flag byte
10	Number of cylinders for alternative tracks
11	Reserved
12–13	Start cylinder of write precompensation
14–20	Manufacturer's name (ASCII)
21–39	Product name
40–511	Reserved

A typical structure for the disk geometry information that was held in sectors 1 and 2 of tracks 0 and 1 of cylinder –1 is shown at Table 5.7. It is important to note that these details refer to the now obsolete ST412/506 controllers (Messmer, 2002, p. 866). With the more modern ATA or Integrated Drive Electronics (IDE) drives (see later section on interfacing) an IDENTIFY DEVICE command can be issued to the controller to obtain 512 bytes of detailed device information, with the interpretation to be placed on each byte defined in the ATA-2 (and later) specifications, and associated ANSI standards (ANSI, 1996). This information can be used for autoconfiguration of the disk by the BIOS. It may also be used in conjunction with specialist software made available by some disk manufacturers[21] to provide a detailed printout of an IDE hard disk as shown at Fig. 5.8.

There are a number of points that arise from the printout of Fig. 5.8 that we will be returning to later: the different cylinder, head and sector numbers in the three columns, and the meanings of the terms LBA, DMA and PIO, for example. Before we do that, however, there are still some points related to Table 5.7 that need to be discussed, the first of which is the *interleave factor*.

The Interleave Factor

This has to do with the problem of reading two successive sectors and not having enough time to transfer the buffer from the first sector across the interface into the computer before the second sector comes under the read head. This might be because error-correcting codes are being used and the controller has to wait until the whole sector is available in the buffer before it can be checked, or it might be because

---

21 See, for instance, the program FIND-ATA.EXE from Seagate (Seagate, 1994) that was used to produce Fig. 5.8.

```
                            Find-ATA v1.0

      Drive: ST32140A                        Port: Primary (01F0h)
      Serial #:            JB192001  CMOS Type: 1    Unit: 0 - Master

                  Hardware       DOS         Current        Max ECC: 22 bytes
   Cylinders: 4095            1023         4095
       Heads: 16              64           16
     Sectors: 63              63           63
    Capacity: 2,113,413,120   2,111,864,832  2,113,413,120

                        Available  Information
   R/W Multiple Mode:      Yes      32 sectors Max  Current: 32 sectors/block
            LBA Mode:      Yes      4127760
            DMA Mode:      Yes      Single: 0  (0111)  Multi: 1  (0111) 180 nsec
   Advanced PIO Mode:      Yes      (0011)    +,-IORDY: 120 nsec, 180 nsec

   Default PIO Mode: 2, 240 nsec, up to 8.33 MB/Sec

   Buffer: 128 KBytes Type: A dual ported multi-sectored buffer capable of
           simultaneous transfers with a read caching capability.

        Copyright 1994 Seagate Technology, Inc. All rights reserved
```

Fig. 5.8 Disk information from Find-ATA program.

the interface itself is too slow. The problem can be overcome by interleaving. Instead of having sector 2 physically follow sector 1 on the track, it is placed, for example, physically one sector further on. In this way there is time for the buffer to be emptied between transfers, since we now read every other sector but still receive the sectors in numerical sequence.

In Fig. 5.9 we have shown three cases: interleave factor 1:1, which means there is no interleaving; interleave factor 2:1, which is the example we described above with one sector in between; and interleave factor 3:1, where there are two sectors in between. With many older disk controllers it was possible to specify the interleave factor required when performing a low-level format. Software was available to test the effect of different interleave factors on such drives and to help determine an optimum value when fitted in particular computer systems.

Interleaving is no longer an issue when using a modern hard disk drive. Such drives normally have a memory buffer which can hold an entire track at a time,

```
Interleave factor 1:1
1   2   3   4   5   6   7   8   9   10  11  12  13  14  15  16  17

Interleave factor 2:1
1   10  2   11  3   12  4   13  5   14  6   15  7   16  8   17  9

Interleave factor 3:1
1   7   13  2   8   14  3   9   15  4   10  16  5   11  17  6   12
```

Fig. 5.9 Interleave factors.

instead of just a sector, and this completely obviates the need for any form of interleaving.

Write Precompensation

Also referred to in Table 5.7 is the *start cylinder of write precompensation*. This too applies only to older hard disk systems. These systems use the same number of sectors per track (spt), which was 17 for the earliest systems, for every cylinder on the disk. Since tracks are concentric circles, that means that as we move in closer to the spindle the physical track length gets less and hence the packing density of the bits increases[22]. This makes magnetic interactions between certain bit patterns more likely and so to limit this effect, the electronic process of write precompensation arranges for particular bits in particular bit patterns to be written to the disk a little earlier or a little later than normal. The outermost cylinder number from which these timing adjustments are to be applied is referred to as the *start cylinder of write precompensation*.

Zoned Bit Recording

The capacity and performance of hard disk systems have improved radically since those early systems that we have been talking about above, and one means by which a considerable improvement has been made is to utilize better the so-called *areal density* of the disk: that is, the number of bits that can be packed into each unit of area on the disk. As we noted above, if we keep the same number of sectors per track across the whole disk then the packing density towards the centre is much greater than the packing density at the outermost edge. If we are to make the most of the allowable areal density across the whole surface of the disk, it is essential that we have different numbers of sectors per track for different groups of cylinders on the disk. Then, as we move outwards from the centre of the disk, and the track length increases, so outer cylinders could have more sectors per track than inner cylinders for the same bit density. When using this technique, of course, write precompensation becomes less of an issue.

Having more than one set of sectors per track on the disk is known as *zoned bit recording* (ZBR)[23]. With this approach, tracks are grouped into zones and each zone on the disk has a different number of sectors per track. As we move from the innermost zone outwards so the sectors per track figure increases such that the bit packing density within all the tracks is now more even.

At Fig. 5.10 we see the 15 zones of a 3.8 Gbyte Quantum Fireball™ hard disk (Quantum, 1996), with sectors per track ranging from 122 to 232, and with each zone

---

22 Clearly, if we are to get the same number of bits (because there are the same number of sectors per track) into a smaller track length, then they have to be closer together.

23 Also known as *multiple zone recording (MZR)* and *zoned constant angular velocity* recording (ZCAV).

Zone	14	13	12	11	10	9	8	7	6	5	4	3	2	1	0
Spt	122	135	142	153	162	170	180	185	195	205	214	225	225	229	232
Tracks	454	454	454	454	454	454	454	454	454	454	454	454	454	454	454

Fig. 5.10 Zoned bit recording.

consisting of 454 tracks[24]. We may wish to note the very large number of tracks[25] (15 × 454 = 6810) on this disk and the much larger numbers for sectors per track[26] compared with the 17 of early disks. Not shown on this diagram are the different data transfer rates for the various zones. Since the angular velocity of the disk is constant and there are substantially more sectors on the outer tracks than there are on the inner ones, then the data transfer rates for the outer tracks must be higher than those for the inner ones. An interesting side effect of this feature is that benchmark tests run on the disk when new, and then again after being in use for some time, might suggest that the disk is getting slower. In fact, all that is happening is that the benchmark tests are being run on unused tracks that are now closer to the centre than when the disk was new. This is because sectors are normally assigned by the file system from the outermost cylinder inwards. What the benchmark is telling us is what we already knew: the data transfer rates of the inner zones are slower than those of the outer zones.

This ZBR approach, however, now poses us a serious problem. Our use of CHS addressing has always assumed a known constant value[27] for sectors per track across the whole of the disk. If that assumption is now no longer true, then we would need to give a fourth parameter with each CHS address: that of the sectors per track for the particular zone within which that address resided. This would significantly complicate the disk interface.

A much better solution is for the controller to *pretend* to us that there is no zoning and to provide to us a contrived sectors per track value, normally 63, that is constant for the whole disk. When the controller receives, from the outside world, a CHS address that is based on this contrived sectors per track value, it simply *translates* this external CHS address into its own internal zoned address. In this way, we need have no knowledge of the zoning within the disk system in order to address it. We also need have no knowledge of any of the low-level formatting data structures, encoding methods or bad sector mapping strategies that may be used by the manufacturer, since the controller hides all of this from us. Indeed, modern

---

24 It is not a requirement that zones be of equal numbers of tracks. This disk just happens to be built this way.

25 Just a reminder that tracks in this context is synonymous with cylinders.

26 Note that the figure of 225 for both zones 2 and 3 is correct.

27 If in doubt about this, consider repeatedly incrementing the sector count by 1 and then trying to decide when the sector count should revert to 1 and the head count should be incremented. The CHS address system only works for a fixed sector per track value across the disk.

controllers constantly monitor the internal state of the disk, using spare capacity as we have described above to re-map sectors and tracks as defects are detected, so that the disk appears "perfect" for most of its life.

Such a re-mapping strategy has important implications for forensic computing analysts. If the disk has been used to hold unlawful material, it is possible that some of the sectors holding that unlawful material might have become re-mapped internally by the disk controller following the detection of defects. Under these circumstances, the material from the bad sectors would automatically be duplicated and held in the re-mapped good sectors elsewhere. To the external world, only the good sectors would be apparent or accessible, but the disk would still contain copies in the bad sectors that were now inaccessible. This means that even the most comprehensive of normal disk wipes would not remove the bad sector copies, since they are no longer accessible outside of the controller. Although these re-mapped bad sectors might be technically quite difficult to access, knowledge of the manufacturer's controller program and, in particular, the factory mode special command set for the controller, might permit some of the material to be restored. The implications of this are that completely wiping a ZBR disk using normal processes will not guarantee the removal of all unlawful material, and therefore a hard disk which had contained such material should not be returned to a defendant. This was the ruling given in a Manchester Crown Court judgement in 2002 (R v Aslett, 2002).

However, it should be noted that later versions of the ATA specifications, which we discuss in a subsequent section, include an *optional* security feature, which is described as follows: "*When normal erase mode is selected, the SECURITY ERASE UNIT command writes binary zeroes to all user data areas. The enhanced erase mode is optional. When enhanced erase mode is selected, the device writes predetermined data patterns to all user data areas. In enhanced mode, all previously written user data is overwritten, including sectors that are no longer in use due to reallocation*" (McLean, 2001, p. 231). This implies that all disks conforming to this ATA specification can be expected to include commands for a "normal erase mode". This mode enables complete wiping, by the disk controller, of the user area, but does not include wiping of the re-mapped bad sectors. It further implies that disks conforming to this ATA specification *optionally* may include commands for an "enhanced erase mode". This mode enables complete wiping, by the disk controller, of the user area and does include wiping of the re-mapped bad sectors. However, there is no guarantee currently that any particular disk will support this optional feature.

Finally, to conclude this section, it should be noted that the *internal sector translation* that is carried out by the disk controller to convert those outside world CHS addresses that use a contrived sectors per track value to its own internal zoned address form is not to be confused with the *CHS address translation* issues that we are going to be discussing shortly in connection with the various legacy interface problems.

Head and Cylinder Skewing

The last issue that we need to consider in this section is *skewing*. If we consider a drive that has two physical heads, then the sequence for accessing consecutive sectors, assuming there are 17 to the track (given an older non-ZBR disk system), will

No skewing

Cylinder 0:

Head 0:	1	2	3	4	5	6	7	8	9	10	11	12	13	14	15	16	17
Head 1:	1	2	3	4	5	6	7	8	9	10	11	12	13	14	15	16	17

Cylinder 1:

Head 0:	1	2	3	4	5	6	7	8	9	10	11	12	13	14	15	16	17

Head skew = 2   Cylinder skew = 8

Cylinder 0:

Head 0:	1	2	3	4	5	6	7	8	9	10	11	12	13	14	15	16	17
Head 1:	16	17	1	2	3	4	5	6	7	8	9	10	11	12	13	14	15

Cylinder 1:

Head 0:	8	9	10	11	12	13	14	15	16	17	1	2	3	4	5	6	7

Fig. 5.11 Head and cylinder skewing.

be as follows: cylinder 0, head 0, sectors 1 to 17; then cylinder 0, head 1, sectors 1 to 17; then cylinder 1 head 0, sectors 1 to 17 and so forth.

Clearly, in the interests of performance, the head assembly is left at a particular cylinder position until each head has been accessed before moving it to the next cylinder position. The time taken to switch a head electronically is much shorter than the time taken to move the head assembly one cylinder position. Nevertheless, even the head switching time can be significant when compared with the speed at which sectors are passing under the heads.

If the head switching time is greater than the time it takes for the gap between sector 17 and sector 1 to pass under the heads and the sectors are physically lined up such that sector 1, head 0 is immediately above sector 1 head 1 on the platters, as shown in the upper part of Fig. 5.11, then we are going to miss reading sector 1 head 1 immediately after we have read sector 17 head 0. This means that we will have to wait an entire revolution of the disk before we can access it again. *Head skewing* recognizes this problem and arranges for sector 1 head 1 to be physically located further round the track; in the case shown in the lower half of Fig. 5.11, physically under head 0 sector 3, giving a head skew of 2. A similar problem arises with the time it takes to move the head assembly from cylinder 0 to cylinder 1. In this case the time is much longer but the principle is exactly the same. Here we apply what is known as *cylinder skew* and shown in Fig. 5.11 is a cylinder skew of 8 such that sector 1 of head 0 cylinder 1 is physically located under sector 9 head 1 cylinder 0. Hence, after we have read sector 17 head 1 cylinder 0, we have the time it takes for 8 sectors to pass before we must start to read sector 1 head 0 cylinder 1; sufficient time to move the head assembly one track position.

The Formatting Process

Another major difference between hard disks and floppy disks is to be found in the formatting process. For floppy disks we identify two stages of formatting: low-level

Table 5.8 Formatting floppy disks.

- *Low-level formatting*, which is carried out to establish the tracks and sectors with all the address marks, IDs and gaps we have discussed above.

- *High-level formatting*, during which the file system for the particular operating system is established.

Table 5.9 Formatting hard disks.

- *Low-level formatting*, which is carried out to establish the tracks and sectors with all the address marks, IDs and gaps we have discussed above.

- *Partitioning*, which enables more than one logical volume to be associated with a disk.

- *High-level formatting*, during which the file system for the particular operating system is established on a volume.

and high-level (see Table 5.8), and for hard disks there are three stages: low-level, partitioning and high-level (see Table 5.9).

Floppy Disk Formatting

The two stages for floppy disks are both carried out by the standard DOS program FORMAT. This first of all performs the low-level format function itself by writing on to the floppy disk, a track at a time, all the gaps, address marks, sectors and CRCs that we have described above, together with all the sector data areas filled with a series of f6h bytes. After writing each track, it then reads back all the sectors of that track, recalculating and checking the data area CRCs and making a note of any sectors that are *bad*[28].

The FORMAT program next performs a high-level format, which for floppy disks is invariably a FAT-based system, by setting up an MS-DOS or Windows file system on the disk (of which more in a later section). This involves writing the *boot sector*, the two *file allocation tables* (FATs) and the *root directory*. The FORMAT program then marks the FATs appropriately with any bad sectors that it identified during the low-level formatting process. We will see how this is done in more detail in a later section. Note for now that this is not the same process as the bad sector mapping that we saw carried out by the controller of the hard disk. In this case it is a part of the file system structure (the file allocation table laid down by the high-level format) that is being marked, as opposed to the sector flag bytes written by the low-level format that we saw before (see Fig. 5.7).

If, when initiating the FORMAT program, the /S option had been selected, the program then copies onto the floppy disk the system files IO.SYS, MSDOS.SYS and COMMAND.COM, making the disk *bootable*. Finally, the FORMAT program prompts for a *volume label* which is to be set on to the floppy disk, and then the process terminates.

---

28 Bad sectors in this context are those where the CRC calculated from the sector data just read does not agree with the CRC that was written to that sector during the format.

Hard Disk Formatting

What is often a source of confusion concerning the FORMAT program is that it can carry out, without intervention, both a low-level format and a high-level format on floppy disks, yet it is not able to perform a low-level format on any hard disks. It is, however, invariably used for establishing the MS-DOS file system on a hard disk; that is, performing the high-level format. In the case of hard disks, the low-level format is invariably done by the manufacturer and the general advice is never to attempt to carry out a low-level format of a hard disk unless you are an expert. There are some good reasons for wanting to do a low-level format on certain types of older hard disks and some very good reasons for not doing it on other kinds of hard disk. Amongst the very good reasons for not doing it on some early IDE disks is the risk of losing the factory written manufacturer's defect list (which includes the soft defect listings that are virtually impossible for a user to determine) and the loss of any optimized interleave and skewing values. On later disks, internal address translation (see the section on Zoned Bit Recording) and internal sector mapping may be operative. When the disk is in this mode[29] (and disks that use zoned bit recording are always in translation mode), a low-level format is harmless to the defect mapping files and the skewing values. If, however, the disk is in physical mode, the defect mapping files and skewing values may again be lost. All the low-level format might do when the disk is in translation mode is to "scrub" the data in all the sectors; it does not re-write the formatting structure. It should be noted, however, that it is completely destructive to all the data on the disk. This is sometimes referred to as *intermediate* or *mid-level formatting* (Seagate, 1997b). Amongst the good reasons for perhaps wanting to do this are the contraction of a virus, the increasing incidence of bad sectors, or the complete removal of an operating system.

Since the DOS FORMAT program cannot be used to low-level format a hard disk, the manufacturer may provide special programs[30] specifically for this purpose. Alternatively, there may be formatting utilities built into the BIOS of the PC or the BIOS of the hard disk itself which can be accessed using the DOS DEBUG[31] command. Again, none of these utilities should be invoked unless the analyst has a very high level of expertise in hard disk systems.

Partitioning

Given a hard disk with an appropriate low-level format, the next step is to *partition* it, even if only one partition is to be used. Partitioning is the process of dividing the hard disk up into a number of logical pieces, each piece being a partition. A useful

---

29 Some non-ZBR drives can be switched between a physical mode and a translation mode (non-physical geometry).

30 SGATFMT4.EXE is one such program, provided by Seagate for use on their ATA (IDE) hard drives (Seagate, 1995a).

31 This DEBUG command takes the form -G=C800:5, where G is for GO and C800 is the upper memory address of the disk BIOS.

way of thinking of a hard disk partition is to consider it as being a *big floppy*. The process of partitioning allows for a *logical volume* to be associated with each partition and for different operating systems to be associated with different volumes. The standard program that is often used to carry out partitioning is FDISK, though manufacturers sometimes provide their own utilities (Seagate, 1995b), and specialist software such as Partition Magic (PowerQuest, 1996) can make this rather arcane task much easier. We will examine the details of partitions, the *master boot record* and the whole boot process itself in a later section.

The final activity required is a high-level format of each partition. As in the case of the floppy disk, a high-level format is carried out to set up the file system for the particular operating system that is to be used with this partition. Again, as for the floppy disk, FORMAT is often used for this process and this will involve, for a FAT-based file system, writing the boot sector, the two file allocation tables (FATs) and the root directory[32]. At this stage in the floppy disk format, the FORMAT program would mark the FATs with any bad sectors that it identified during the low-level formatting process. However, in the case of modern hard disks, bad sector mapping has already been carried out by the controller internally, so the disk should appear to be perfect to the FORMAT program and there thus should be no bad sectors to report or to mark in the FATs. An analyst might reasonably take the view that any bad sectors found in the FAT tables associated with a modern ZBR disk should be treated with suspicion.

If the /S option has been selected, FORMAT then copies onto the hard disk the system files IO.SYS, MSDOS.SYS and COMMAND.COM[33], making the hard disk partition bootable under certain conditions (see later section). Finally, the FORMAT program prompts for a volume label which is to be set on to the hard disk partition and then the process terminates.

It is worth noting here that when a volume label is set at the end of the FORMAT process, the volume label text may be placed in the boot record at offset 2bh (see Table 5.18) and also as a Volume directory entry in the Root Directory (see Fig. 5.39). However, it should not be assumed that this is always so, and we recommend that tests be carried out to confirm the particular circumstances of any given case where this is of significance.

Hard Disk Interfaces

We have now seen in quite some detail how data is stored on a hard disk and how it is addressed. We now need to consider how data gets transferred between the PC and the hard disk. In other words, we need to look at the various software and hardware interfaces.

---

32 A FAT-based file system has been used here as the example. See later sections for details of the NTFS file system.

33 A DOS operating system has been used here as the example. A similar set of files would be used for Windows operating systems.

The BIOS and Interrupt Vectors

We start with a reminder of how the memory of the PC is laid out (see Fig. 5.12). As we will see later, this is how all PC systems are currently initialized. The processor *always* starts up in 16 bit real mode and uses the segment offset addressing system for which Fig. 5.12 is the memory map. It is only at some later stage that the processor may be switched to 32 bit protected mode by a command from within an appropriate operating system. We need, therefore, to know about 16 bit mode in order to understand the bootstrap sequence to which we will be returning in a later section. For now, we need to recall that the design of the PC incorporates the concept of a basic input/output system (the System BIOS) which is permanent program code held in read-only memory (ROM) in the upper memory block area. This provides us with a standardized low-level interface to the specific hardware of the computer. The particular functions of the BIOS are accessed by means of interrupt call instruction codes (INTs) and different interrupt numbers access different parts of the BIOS software that controls different parts of the hardware.

For example: INT 10h deals with the video system, INT 13h deals with the disk system, INT 14h deals with the serial communications ports and INT 16h deals with the keyboard. In addition, different function numbers within an interrupt carry out different actions. For example: INT 13h function 2 reads a disk sector, INT 13h function 3 writes a disk sector and INT 13h function 5 formats a disk track. In this way, application software that interacts with the BIOS can be independent of the specific hardware of the particular machine but instead can deal with generic hardware functions that are standardized. This makes any software that uses this BIOS interface portable across PC systems.

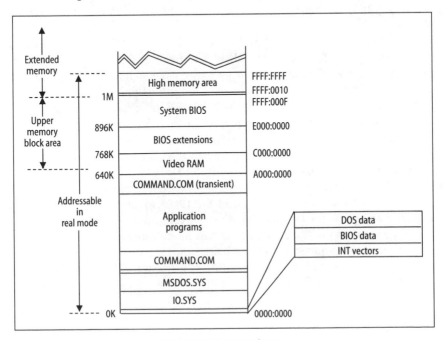

Fig. 5.12 PC memory layout.

There is considerable flexibility in the PC design for exactly where the BIOS program code that implements any particular interrupt might be located, since all interrupt calls are redirected through an *interrupt vector table* that is held in random access memory (RAM) at address 0000:0400 and below. This table has a 4 byte pointer[34] for each interrupt and is built afresh each time the PC carries out its boot-up sequence. It is therefore possible to cause any interrupt to go to any place in real mode memory simply by changing the 4 bytes of the relevant interrupt vector. This enables us to place interrupt program code anywhere in the real mode memory and, perhaps, change an interrupt from taking us to the standard BIOS code and instead going to where some revised set of functions have been placed. We will come back to this point again.

Whereas there is considerable flexibility in where the INT routines are located and in the ways in which they are implemented, and thus in the functionality that they are able to exhibit, there is little flexibility in the form of the interfaces that they present to the software that uses them. This is always the problem with any kind of interface standard: if it is to be useful it must remain constant, or, at the very least, be backward-compatible with all previous versions if legacy systems are to continue to work. Such constancy, over time, risks having to live with a dinosaur that inhibits the implementation of any new features or of any new developments.

It is this problem of standards and of legacy systems that, throughout its relatively short history, has so bedevilled the hard disk story and has caused to be imposed on the user a variety of performance and capacity limitations for which often less than elegant solutions have had to be devised. In order to make sense of this we do need to be aware of a little of this history.

The ST412/506 Interface

In the very beginning there were no hard disk drives for PCs and, as a result, no inbuilt BIOS support for them. Hard disks had been available to mainframe and minicomputer systems for many years prior to this time, so it was not long before this technology was targeted at the new Personal Computer. It initially came in the form of a separate cabinet which contained the hard disk drive itself, the disk controller electronics, and an internal power supply. In addition, an 8 bit *host adaptor expansion card* would be fitted inside the PC in a spare expansion slot, and this would be connected by cables to the disk controller in the cabinet. The controller in turn was connected to the hard disk drive (see Fig. 5.13).

Hard disks such as these became known as *Winchester Drives*. The term seems to have been taken from an old IBM drive of the 1960s which had 30 Mbyte of fixed storage and an option for a further 30 Mbyte of removable storage. This drive was informally known as the "30-30" and from this name came an association with the calibre (.30) and the number of grains of black powder (30) used by the famous "30-30" Remington rifle, otherwise known as the "Winchester". The term "Winchester" soon came to signify any fixed disk for the PC.

---

34 These are *far pointers*; see later section.

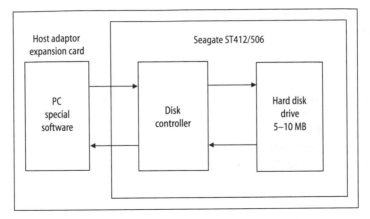

Fig. 5.13 ST412/506 hard disk drives.

There were no INT 13h BIOS functions for the PC at this time, so special-purpose software had to be provided. The host adaptor in the expansion slot would be addressed by this special software, through which would be sent appropriate commands to the disk controller. The disk controller would then transfer the required data to and from the hard disk itself.

A system typical of the time was the Seagate ST-506, introduced in 1980, which had a formatted capacity of just 5 Mbyte. At Fig. 5.14 is shown part of its specification (Seagate, 1991a). It may be noted that it used MFM encoding, had a stepper type actuator, 153 cylinders, 4 heads and 17 sectors per track. This gave it a capacity of 153 $\times$ 4 $\times$ 17 $\times$ 512 = 5,326,848 bytes. The ST-506 design incorporated a very well defined interface between the disk drive and the controller.

Introduced about a year later, its successor, the Seagate ST-412 (Seagate, 1991b), had a 10 Mbyte capacity and a slightly modified interface which added a "buffered seeks" facility. It was these two, now obsolete, systems that contributed their interface specifications and their combined names to what became the *de facto* standard for connecting hard disk drives to controllers in the early 1980s: the *ST412/506 Interface*.

```
UNFORMATTED CAPACITY (MB) _____ 6.38
FORMATTED CAPACITY (17 SECTORS) (MB) ____ 5.0
ACTUATOR TYPE _____ STEPPER
TRACKS _____ 612
CYLINDERS _____ 153
HEADS _____ 4
DISCS _____ 2
MEDIA TYPE _____ OXIDE
RECORDING METHOD _____ MFM
TRANSFER RATE (mbits/sec) _____ 5.0
INTERFACE _____ ST506
```

Fig. 5.14 Part of the ST-506 specification (with kind permission of Seagate Technology).

   In the ST412/506 design, up to two disk drives could be connected to the controller
by a single 34 line control cable and separate 20 line data cables for each drive. None
of the intelligence was in the drives, which responded to very simple control signals
from the controller, such as: switch the head assembly to move in a particular
direction, step the head assembly one step, select a particular head and so forth. The
control program for all of these actions was held in the controller itself, which was
also responsible for interpreting all commands from the PC, encoding and decoding
read and write serial data to and from the drive, transferring 8 bit bytes to and from
the PC, generating and identifying address marks and other formatting information,
and similar housekeeping activities. At the PC interface the commands to the
controller, sent by the special software referred to above, were the forerunners of the
INT 13h BIOS functions, such as: read a sector, write a sector, format a track and seek
to a specific cylinder.

   In 1983, when the *IBM XT (eXtended Technology)* became available, with its built-
in 10 Mbyte fixed disk, some of these ideas were seen to have evolved further. First of
all, the disk controller[35] had been removed from the disk drive box and built right
onto a bus interface expansion card, thus doing away with the host adaptor
expansion card. Further, program code had been provided on a ROM chip on the
controller card itself which supplemented the standard BIOS functions and obviated
the need for the special software to be installed. The design utilized interrupt request
line 5 (IRQ 5), I/O port addresses 320h to 32fh and *direct memory access* channel 3
(DMA 3). From an earlier section, we may recall that the IRQ channel permits a
hardware interrupt to be raised by the connected device, in this case the hard disk
controller. Such an interrupt will cause the processor to suspend temporarily its
current activity and execute code designed to service the device raising the interrupt.
In addition, we may recall that the port addresses are the outlets through which
commands and data are sent to and received from hardware devices, and the DMA
channel permits a hardware device to send and receive data autonomously from the
PC's memory without involving the processor.

   In 1984, the introduction of the *IBM AT (Advanced Technology)* saw a complete
overhaul of the hard disk system. The PC command interface to the controller was
now incorporated into the ROM BIOS on the motherboard of the PC as standard INT
13h functions (today known as the INT 13h *legacy* functions), thus removing the
need for a separate ROM BIOS chip on the controller card. Disk drive parameters as
well as other motherboard configuration details were held in a low-power *Complementary Metal Oxide Silicon (CMOS)* RAM chip that was used by the real-time clock
and backed up by a small battery. Some 14 different disk types were initially recognized, ranging from 10 to 112 Mbyte capacity. Any drive with physical parameters
which did not match one of the 14 had to be incorporated either by means of a ROM
extension on the disk controller card or by using special device driver software
loaded at boot time. The AT design for hard disks utilized interrupt request line 14
(IRQ 14) and I/O port addresses 1f0h to 1f8h, but did not use a direct memory access
channel at all. This was because the DMA controller and the buses to which it was

---

35 These were often called WD1003 controllers after a Western Digital design of that name.
   See Western Digital (undated a).

connected were found to be too slow for efficient disk data transfers and so *programmed input output* (*PIO*) was used instead. In this approach, the processor carries out all the transfer activity itself by means of IN and OUT instructions and no autonomous transfers take place.

This is broadly the hard disk system structure that we have today. The number of supported disk types has expanded considerably and current BIOSes provide a user-definable type which allows parameters to be set to match any drive. Most BIOSes now have an autoconfiguration mode which enables the drive to be interrogated by the BIOS and to provide its own parameter information at boot time, a facility that became standardized when the AT Attachment (ATA) specifications were implemented.

Background to the Legacy Problem

The real legacy problem of the PC disk system lies in the INT 13h BIOS functions that provide the standard command interface between any software that requires disk facilities and the disk controller. This includes the structure of a CHS address that has to be passed from the BIOS to the controller. This structure[36] exactly mimics that of the CHS address held in the ID field of the hard disk sector format (see Fig. 5.4) and therefore permits a maximum CHS address of 1024 cylinders, 256 heads and 63 sectors. This interface has had to remain constant[37] since 1984 despite some quite radical changes in the physical interfaces between the PC and the controller and the controller and the disk drive. The bus architecture linking the PC to the controller, and the interface between the controller and the hard drive, have both been changed a number of times in the past 20 years or so in order to take advantage of advances in technology and to improve performance and cost effectiveness. We will look first, very briefly, at the changes in bus architectures.

Bus Architectures

The original bus architecture of the PC-AT, although not formally specified by IBM, eventually evolved into what is now known as the *Industry Standard Architecture* (*ISA*). This has the ability to transfer data at a maximum speed of 8.33 Mbyte/s and has a data bus width of 16 bits. With the introduction of the 386 and 486 processors, which have a 32 bit data bus, an extension to the ISA architecture was made and this is called the *Extended Industry Standard Architecture* (*EISA*). This can transfer data at up to 33 Mbyte/s and has a 32 bit data bus. Meanwhile, IBM had continued development of the PC and produced the PS/2 which utilized a new bus architecture that

---

36 As described earlier, the CH register holds 8 bits of the cylinder value, the DH register holds the 8 bits of the head value, and the CL register holds the two most significant bits of the cylinder value and the 6 bits of the sector value, all in accord with Fig. 5.4. In addition, the DL register holds the drive number.

37 In 1995, extensions to the INT 13h interface were defined (Phoenix, 1995). These extensions are now to be found as standard in modern BIOSes.

they called *Micro Channel Architecture* (*MCA*). This too has a 32 bit data bus and can transfer data at up to 20 Mbyte/s or 40 Mbyte/s for short periods.

As the technology continued to develop, so even these buses were found wanting, particularly in the area of graphics and disk activity. The *Video Electronics Standards Association* (*VESA*) developed a Local Bus, bypassing the main buses, which became known as *VESA Local Bus* or just *VLB*, to address this performance problem. It too has a 32 bit data bus but can transfer data at 133 Mbyte/s or 160 Mbyte/s, depending on version.

With the introduction of the Pentium processor, Intel developed a new bus architecture that they designated *Peripheral Component Interconnect* (*PCI*). This 32 bit standard bus can transfer data at 133 Mbyte/s and this can be expanded to 64 bits with a data rate of 266 Mbyte/s. Most modern Pentium systems use this bus architecture today. However, more recent developments have included *PCI-X, PCI-X 266, PCI Express* and *InfiBand*, a comparative summary of which can be found in Mellanox (2002).

If the bus architectures have changed significantly in the past 20 years, then the disk controller to disk interfaces have changed even more significantly. The typical hard disk capacities have increased from 10 Mbyte to 400 Gbyte and the typical transfer rates have increased from 5 Mbit/s to 150 Mbyte/s (Maxtor, 2003) in the same period. In addition, the form factor has reduced from 5.25 inches to 3.5 inches[38] and the unit cost per megabyte has become significantly cheaper. We will look at some of these hard disk interface developments next.

The Enhanced Small Device Interface (ESDI)

The ST412/506 interface was soon found to be wanting. Problems arose over data integrity and speed because the raw encoded data was having to travel over lengthy cables between the read/write heads of the drive and the electronics of the controller. In addition, the controller had to be optimized by the user for the drive attached to it by setting interleave factors and so forth.

A first attempt at improving this situation was achieved by moving some of the controller electronics from the controller card on to the hard drive itself. At Fig. 5.15 we have shown a number of options for the distribution of controller functions between a separate controller card and the drive itself. The leftmost column of the table shows the ST412/506 situation with all of the controller functions on the controller card and none on the drive. The next column to the right shows the data separator electronics and the ST412/506 interface removed from the controller card and placed on the drive itself. This has the considerable advantage of getting rid of the lengthy raw data cables and thus improving both performance and error rates.

It was this approach that was adopted in the *Enhanced Small Device Interface* (*ESDI*) design. Although it was an improvement, it became obsolete very quickly because a much cheaper and more effective solution was seen to be to move *all* of the

---

38 As mentioned earlier, the form factor for notebook drives and some standalone drives is 2.5 inches.

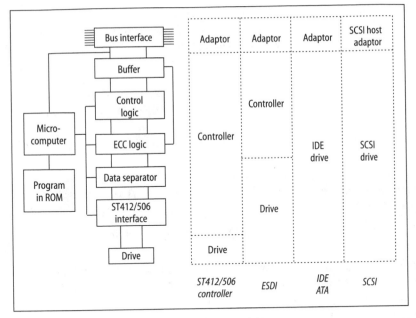

Fig. 5.15 Controllers and drives.

controller electronics except for a vestigial interface adaptor onto the drive itself. This became known as *Integrated* (or *Intelligent*) *Drive Electronics* (*IDE*).

Integrated Drive Electronics (IDE) and AT Attachment (ATA)

The name "Integrated Drive Electronics" or "IDE" was used to signify this placement of all of the controller electronics onto the drive itself, as shown in the third column of Fig. 5.15. This name is still in very common use today to identify, for example, the disk drive cables and connectors and the IDE sockets on the motherboard. The name can be misleading, since other systems, such as the *Small Computer Systems Interface* (*SCSI*)[39], also integrate the controller electronics onto the drive, as we have indicated in the fourth column of Fig. 5.15.

A better term is "*AT Attachment*" or "*ATA*", which defines the standard interface between the hard disk IDE system and the AT-style PC to which it is connected. The specification for this interface eventually became defined as an ANSI standard. This was done by the industry in an attempt to eliminate some of the incompatibility problems that surrounded the early IDE/ATA drives. These were particularly evident

39 SCSI, pronounced "scuzzy", is not just a hard disk interface. It is a flexible and powerful standard (ANSI X3T9.2) for connecting peripheral devices to computers. Up to eight intelligent devices may be connected on to the SCSI bus, one of which is the SCSI host adaptor which connects to the PC. SCSI drives are met with less frequently in PC systems than are IDE/ATA drives, and most of the problems that are identified in the next section for the IDE/ATA interface do not apply to the SCSI interface. We therefore do not consider it further here.

when attempting to install a master and slave on the same IDE/ATA channel using drives from different manufacturers. Very often the disks would not work together. The first ATA standard, drawn up in 1994, states: *"The PC AT Bus is a widely used and implemented interface for which a variety of peripherals have been manufactured. As a means of reducing size and cost, a class of products has emerged which embed the controller functionality in the drive. These new products utilize the AT Bus fixed disk interface protocol, and a subset of the AT bus. Because of their compatibility with existing AT hardware and software this interface quickly became a de facto industry standard. The purpose of the ATA standard is to define the de facto implementations"* (Lamers, 1994).

In addition to specifying a comprehensive command set and protocol that operates between the INT 13h BIOS functions and the ATA/IDE drive, this first ATA standard stipulates:

• that there is to be a single channel shared by up to two hard disks configured as master and slave;
• that programmed input–output (PIO) modes 0, 1 and 2 are to be supported, which are defined as 3.3, 5.2 and 8.3 Mbyte/s transfer rates respectively; and
• that direct memory access (DMA) modes 0, 1 and 2 for single words, defined as 2.1, 4.2 and 8.3 Mbyte/s respectively, and mode 0 for multiwords defined as 4.2 Mbyte/s, are also to be supported.

As we mentioned earlier, the basic DMA facilities provided by the standard PC-AT over ISA buses did not make DMA an attractive transfer mechanism for performance reasons and PIO tended to be used by most disk controllers instead. However, modern IDE/ATA hard disks are now likely to have their own DMA controllers on board and therefore do not need to use the slow DMA controller that is built into the PC-AT. This system is often called *bus mastering* and requires the use of a PCI bus to support it.

Although this original standard proved well suited for the early IDE/ATA disks, the rapid improvements in disk technology soon saw the need for faster transfer rates and enhanced features. An *ATA-2* specification, backward-compatible with the original standard, was drawn up in 1996.

Amongst the myriad of definitions in this second specification is the following, which we will refer back to in a later section: *"A CHS address is made up of three fields: the sector address, the head number and the cylinder number. Sectors are numbered from 1 to the maximum value allowed by the current CHS translation mode but can not exceed 255. Heads are numbered from 0 to the maximum value allowed by the current CHS translation mode but can not exceed 15. Cylinders are numbered from 0 to the maximum value allowed by the current CHS translation mode but cannot exceed 65,535"* (Finch, 1995).

This ATA-2 specification became a second ANSI standard (ANSI, 1996) and included the following features:

• faster PIO modes, 3 and 4, which are defined as 11.1 and 16.6 Mbyte/s respectively;
• faster multiword DMA modes, 1 and 2, which are defined as 13.3 and 16.6 Mbyte/s respectively;

- a new block transfer mode;
- logical block addressing (LBA), which we will be looking at later; and
- an improved IDENTIFY DRIVE (now known as IDENTIFY DEVICE) command which permits BIOS software to obtain more accurate details about the drive

Since then, the specifications have continued to be produced on a regular basis. ATA-3 was drawn up in 1995, though this was not much referred to by the disk manufacturers of the time, who invented a variety of marketing names (see below) for their drives to signify additional or enhanced features over the ATA-2 standard. ATA-3 is a minor revision of the ATA-2 standard, with which it is backward-compatible, and it defines means for improving the reliability of the higher speed transfer modes and introduces the new features of Security Mode and of Self-Monitoring, Analysis and Reporting Technology (SMART) which we referred to earlier.

Ultra-ATA is an unofficial standard of that same time which refers to the use of a higher speed DMA transfer mode (multiword DMA mode 3, sometimes called DMA-33) running at 33.3 Mbyte/s. This required a modified BIOS that supported the Ultra-ATA protocol. Ultra-ATA may also be called *Ultra-DMA* or *ATA-33*.

In addition, the *ATA Packet Interface* (or *ATAPI*) was defined as an ANSI standard, to permit CD-ROM and tape drives to be plugged into the standard IDE interface and to be configured as master or slave in just the same way as a hard disk. However, because the ATAPI protocol was not identical to the ATA-2 command set used for the hard disks, a special ATAPI driver had to be installed to communicate with these devices.

As mentioned above, a number of marketing names have been used by some of the disk manufacturers to refer to additional or enhanced features. These are not standards as such, but it is important to be aware of them because the names were in common use at the time and disks claiming these features may still be met with. *Fast ATA* and *Fast ATA-2* (Seagate, 1997c) were used by Seagate and Quantum to refer to what is essentially ATA-2. Fast ATA complies with ATA-2 except for PIO mode 4 and multiword DMA mode 2, and Fast ATA-2 appears to be no more than just ATA-2. *Enhanced IDE* or *EIDE* (Western Digital, 1997a) was used by Western Digital to refer to systems that, in addition to complying with ATA-2, included support for ATAPI and dual IDA/ATA host adaptors, permitting up to four IDE/ATA/ATAPI devices to be used. This is now the norm for most systems.

In due course the ATA specifications caught up with the various approaches adopted by the manufacturers and the majority of these features have now been incorporated into published ANSI standards based on *ATA/ATAPI-4, ATA/ATAPI-5, ATA/ATAPI-6 and ATA/ATAPI-7*. These standards are intended to be backward-compatible as evidenced by this statement from the T13 Technical Committee web site[40], which refers to the ATA/ATAPI-7 standard: "*This standard maintains a high degree of compatibility with the AT Attachment – 6 with Packet Interface (ATA/ATAPI-6), 1410D, and while providing additional functions, is not intended to require*

---

40 See *T13 Technical Committee – AT Attachment*, dated 1 August 2005, at http://www.t13.org/.

changes to presently installed devices or existing software". Similar statements are given for each of the three earlier standards. At the time of writing, the T13 Technical Committee is currently reviewing, in draft form, the *ATA/ATAPI-8* (Stevens, 2005) standard. Landis (2005) suggests that ATA-6 is the last of the PATA (Parallel ATA) interface standards that should be used, in that ATA-7 attempts to describe both PATA and SATA (Serial ATA), resulting in what "... *can be a confusing mess*".

At Annex C to ATA/ATAPI-6 (McLean, 2001) can be found an explanation of UDMA which is typical of the kind of additional functions that have been incorporated. The explanation includes the statement: "*With the advent of faster host systems and devices, the definition of the bus has been expanded to include new operating modes. Each of the PIO modes, numbered zero through four, is faster than the one before (higher numbers translate to faster transfer rates). PIO modes 0, 1, and 2 correspond to transfer rates for the interface as was originally defined with maximum transfer rates of 3.3, 5.2, and 8.3 megabytes per second (MB/s), respectively. PIO mode 3 defines a maximum transfer rate of 11.1 MB/s, and PIO mode 4 defines a maximum rate of 16.7 MB/s. Additionally, Multiword DMA and Ultra DMA modes have been defined. Multiword DMA mode 0, 1, and 2 have maximum transfer rates of 4.2, 13.3, and 16.7 MB/s, respectively. Ultra DMA modes 0, 1, 2, 3, 4, and 5 have maximum transfer rates of 16.7, 25, 33.3, 44.4, 66.7, and 100 MB/s, respectively*".

Host Protected Area (HPA)

Since ATA-4, there has been specified a little known facility called the *Host Protected Area feature set* which permits the reservation of a protected area of the disk that cannot be accessed by conventional methods. The specification states: "*The SET MAX ADDRESS or SET MAX ADDRESS EXT*[41] *command allows the host to redefine the maximum address of the user accessible address space... when the SET MAX ADDRESS or SET MAX ADDRESS EXT command is issued with a maximum address less than the native maximum address, the device reduces the user accessible address space to the maximum specified by the command, providing a protected area above that maximum address... the device shall report only the reduced user address space in response to an IDENTIFY DEVICE command... Any read or write command to an address above the maximum address specified by the SET MAX ADDRESS or SET MAX ADDRESS EXT command shall cause command completion with the IDNF bit set to one and ERR set to one, or command aborted*" (Stevens, 2005).

In February 2002, Paul Sanderson, of Sanderson Forensics[42], drew attention to a possible forensic imaging problem that could arise from this feature. Some imaging software, at that time, did not take the Host Protected Area feature into account and, if a maximum address had been set on the disk that was less than the native address of the disk, imaging occurred only up to the address that had been set and not to the end of the disk. Most imaging software producers, at the time of writing, now take

---

41 The EXT versions of these commands are used for the 48-bit addressing feature (see
  section on Fast Drives and Big Drives).

42 See http://www.sandersonforensics.co.uk/.

this feature into account in their imaging software, but it is still important, from a forensic viewpoint, to be aware if the maximum address has been changed. One means by which this can be checked is by the use of a software product called BXDR[43] that is produced by Paul Sanderson for this purpose. Consistency checks should also be made between the manufacturer's label, the model details from the manufacturer's web site and the reported parameters obtained from the BIOS or the IDENTIFY DEVICE command.

Device Configuration Overlay (DCO)

An even less well known facility was introduced in ATA-6 called the *Device Configuration Overlay feature set*. This states: *"The optional Device Configuration Overlay feature set allows a utility program to modify some of the optional commands, modes, and features sets that a device reports as supported in the IDENTIFY DEVICE or IDENTIFY PACKET DEVICE command response as well as the capacity reported"*. What this means in practice is that a DEVICE CONFIGURATION SET command may also be used to change the effective disk size, and this is more powerful than the HPA SET MAX ADDRESS command. A very useful paper which covers some of the forensic implications of both the HPA and the DCO is that of (Vidström, 2005). This outlines the possible forensic use of SMART and gives some limited advice on defect sectors.

IDE/ATA Problems and Workarounds

Having now looked a little at both the INT 13h BIOS interface and the plethora of standards that make up the IDE/ATA hard disk interface (see Table 5.10) we will now consider in the next section what the problems have been in bringing the two

Table 5.10 A plethora of standards.

Bus architectures
    Industry Standard Architecture (ISA)
    Extended Industry Standard Architecture (EISA)
    Micro Channel Architecture (MCA)
    Video Electronics Standards Association (VESA) Local Bus (VLB)
    Peripheral Component Interconnect (PCI), PCI-X, PCI-X 266, PCI-Express and Infiband

Drive interfaces
    Seagate Technologies ST412/506
    Enhanced Small Drive Interface (ESDI)
    Integrated Drive Electronics (IDE) and AT Attachment (ATA)
    Small Computer System Interface (SCSI)
    ATA, ATA-2, ATA-3, ATA-4, ATA-5, ATA-6, ATA-7, ATA-8
    Ultra-ATA, Ultra-DMA, ATA-33, DMA-33, ATA-33, DMA-33, Ultra-DMA, ATA/66. ATA
       100, ATA/133
    ATA Packet Interface (ATAPI)
    Fast ATA and Fast ATA-2, Enhanced IDE (EIDE)

---

43 See http://www.sandersonforensics.com/bxdr.htm.

together. The first serious problem arises from the CHS addressing structure that is used by the INT 13h BIOS interface and the way in which this differs from the CHS addressing structure that is used by IDE/ATA devices. The problem originally became known as the *528 Mbyte Barrier*.

CHS Addressing and the 528 Mbyte Barrier

The details can perhaps best be understood by reference to Table 5.11. Here we see in three columns the CHS addressing structure for the INT 13h BIOS, the IDE/ATA interface and the combined effect of the two connected together in the column labelled "Limitation".

The CHS values for the INT 13h BIOS column are easily recognizable from what has been discussed before. There are 10 bits for the number of cylinders, resulting in a maximum of 1024 (0 to 1023, because cylinder counting starts from 0); 8 bits for the number of heads, resulting in a maximum of 256 (0 to 255, because head counting starts from 0); and 6 bits for the number of sectors, resulting in a maximum of 63 (1 to 63 because sector counting starts from 1). This gives a total possible disk size in bytes, assuming 512 bytes per sector, of $1024 \times 256 \times 63 \times 512 = 8,455,716,864$. In SI units (powers of ten units) this is 8.45 Gbyte and in powers of two units we have to divide by $1024 \times 1024 \times 1024$ to get 7.87 Gbyte[44]. The CHS values for the IDE/ATA column can be determined by reference back to the quote from the ATA-2 interface specification. There we may recall that the quote states that cylinders are permitted to be of values 0 to 65,535 = 65,536 (16 bits), heads are permitted to be of values 0 to 15 = 16 (4 bits), and sectors are permitted to be of values 1 to 255 = 255 (8 bits). This gives a total possible disk size in bytes of $65,536 \times 16 \times 255 \times 512 = 136,902,082,560$. In SI units this is 136.9 Gbyte and in powers of two units it is 127.5 Gbyte. The "limitation" arises when we try to connect the two interfaces together. If we imagine that each bit is a separate water pipe[45] coming out of the interface then we would have 10 cylinder

Table 5.11 Connecting the interfaces.

	INT 13h BIOS	IDE/ATA	Limitation
Cylinders	1024 (10)	65 536 (16)	1024
Heads	256 (8)	16 (4)	16
Sectors per track	63 (6)	255 (8)	63
Bytes per sector	512	512	512
Size in bytes	8 455 716 864	136 902 082 560	528 482 304
SI units	8.45 Gbyte	136.9 Gbyte	528 Mbyte
^2 units	7.87 Gbyte	127.5 Gbyte	504 Mbyte

44 We have calculated both sets of units here because either may be quoted in the literature, often without any reference to derivation. We have also seen this value expressed as $8,455,716,864/1024 \times 1024 = 8064$ Mbyte = 8 Gbyte.

45 From an idea developed by Martyn Halsall whilst on a Forensic Computing Foundation course.

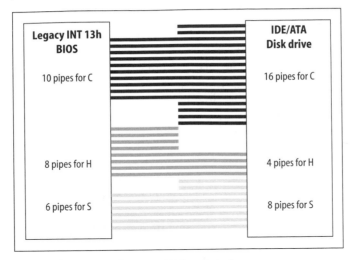

Fig. 5.16 528 Mbyte limitation.

pipes, 8 head pipes and 6 sector pipes coming out of the INT 13h BIOS interface and we would have 16 cylinder pipes, 4 head pipes and 8 sector pipes coming out of the IDE/ATA disk drive interface. If we now arrange for a plumber to connect all possible pipes coming out of the two interfaces together, we end up with the arrangement that we can see in Fig. 5.16. We see then that the only pipes that are connected up between the two interfaces are 10 cylinder pipes, 4 head pipes and 6 sector pipes.

This accounts for what we see in the "Limitation" column of Table 5.11. What have been connected are 10 pipes for the cylinders, resulting in a maximum of 1024 (0 to 1023, because cylinder counting starts from 0); 4 pipes for the number of heads, resulting in a maximum of 16 (0 to 15, because head counting starts from 0); and 6 pipes for the number of sectors, resulting in a maximum of 63 (1 to 63 because sector counting starts from 1). This gives a total accessible disk size in bytes of $1024 \times 16 \times 63 \times 512 = 528{,}482{,}304$. In SI units this is 528 Mbyte and in powers of two units it is 504 Mbyte. We can therefore see that connecting the two interfaces together limits the maximum possible disk size to 528 Mbyte. It should also be noted, since we will return to this later, that the maximum number of cylinders is limited to 1024, because only 10 of the cylinder pipes are connected.

One might be tempted to wonder why the designers of the IDE/ATA specification did not think of these problems. It is almost certain that they did. They might have chosen the design they did because disks as large as 528 Mbyte were not widely available at the time when the first ATA specification was written, but more likely it was because they recognized that future development was taking the hard disk into rapidly increasing numbers of cylinders at the expense of numbers of heads, and it was really the INT 13h BIOS structure that needed to be changed.

Whatever the reasons, the PC user of the first IDE/ATA disks was limited to 528 Mbyte of addressable space until a workaround could be established, although it was not until about 1994 that disks of that size and greater started to become available.

Extended CHS (ECHS) Translation

A possible solution to this problem can be spotted easily from Fig. 5.16. We could simply arrange to connect some of the unused head pipes at the INT 13h BIOS interface to some of the unused cylinder pipes at the IDE/ATA disk drive interface. In other words, we could try trading some of the spare head bits (4) at the INT 13h BIOS interface for some of the spare cylinder bits (6) at the IDE/ATA disk drive interface. Clearly, there are many ways in which this trade could be carried out.

One approach that was adopted by the PC industry is to take the maximum number of cylinders value at the IDE/ATA interface and, if it is greater than 1024, determine the *smallest* power of two which when divided into it makes it less than or equal to 1024. We can then think of a cylinder's address at the IDE/ATA interface as being divided by this power of two before it is passed to the cylinders register at the INT 13h BIOS interface, and, at the same time, a heads address at the IDE/ATA interface as being multiplied by the same power of two before it is passed to the heads register at the INT 13h BIOS interface. The *smallest* power of two is used because this ensures that the address space at the IDE/ATA interface that is lost by the division and rounding down process is kept to a minimum. Clearly, when moving from the INT 13h BIOS interface to the IDE/ATA interface we can think of a complementary process being carried out whereby a cylinder's address is multiplied by that same power of two and a head's address is divided by that same power of two.

This results in the same CHS address having different values at the two interfaces. In order to distinguish between a CHS address at the INT 13h BIOS interface from one at the IDE/ATA interface, we use the terms Logical-CHS (or L-CHS) for CHS addresses at the INT 13h BIOS interface and Physical-CHS (or P-CHS) for CHS addresses at the IDE/ATA interface.

In the preceding discussion, we used the phrase "we can think of" quite deliberately. The elegant idea of simply dividing and multiplying the cylinder and head components of CHS addresses by the same power of two will not work in practice because CHS addresses are whole numbers, and rounding effects of the division will not map addresses uniquely on translation. Consider, for example, a multiplying factor of 2 and the two logical CHS addresses listed below. They both translate, using the simple algorithm of doubling the cylinder number and halving the head number, to the same physical CHS address, as, of course, do many, many more.

$$\text{L-CHS}\ (4, 6, 10) \rightarrow \text{P-CHS}\ (4 \times 2, 6/2, 10) = \text{P-CHS}\ (8, 3, 10)$$

$$\text{L-CHS}\ (4, 7, 10) \rightarrow \text{P-CHS}\ (4 \times 2, 7/2, 10) = \text{P-CHS}\ (8, 3, 10)$$

A slightly more complex algorithm, based on the same idea, needs to be used in order to achieve both a unique mapping of CHS addresses and a sector ordering on the disk which is consistent[46] with logical block addressing (LBA), an alternative addressing system which we describe in a later section. This algorithm may be implemented by the following rules, for translating from L-CHS to P-CHS:

---

46 This is a requirement of the ATA specifications. We show at Appendix 10 the relationship between the two systems.

P-C = (L-C × N) + (L-H/P-Hn)
P-H = (L-H mod P-Hn)
P-S = L-S

In these rules, P-C, P-H and P-S are the components of the CHS address at the IDE/ATA or physical interface; L-C, L-H and L-S are the components of the CHS address at the INT 13h or logical interface; N is the power of two factor; P-Hn is the maximum number of heads at the physical interface; mod is the modulus function and / is the integer division function with the result rounded down. If we now consider the two translations in our example above, assuming N is 2 and P-Hn is 16, we obtain the following:

$$\text{L-CHS}\,(4,6,10) \rightarrow \text{P-CHS}\,((4 \times 2) + (6/16)), (6 \bmod 16), 10) = \text{P-CHS}\,(8,6,10)$$

$$\text{L-CHS}\,(4,7,10) \rightarrow \text{P-CHS}\,((4 \times 2) + (7/16)), (7 \bmod 16), 10) = \text{P-CHS}\,(8,7,10)$$

We now see that the mapping is unique, at least for these values. Further analysis would show that it genuinely is unique and consistent throughout. Because the factor N is always a power of two, these rules may be implemented by shifting bits the appropriate number of places left or right. For this reason it is often referred to as the *bit shifting method*.

At Fig. 5.17 we have shown the CHS values for a 540 Mbyte hard drive which, at the IDE/ATA (P-CHS) interface, requires a maximum number of cylinders of 1057 (addresses 0 to 1056), a maximum number of heads of 16 (addresses 0 to 15) and a maximum number of sectors of 63 (addresses 1 to 63). We note that, at 540 Mbyte, this drive breaches the 528 Mbyte barrier. Using the approach described above, the maximum number of cylinders value at the INT 13h BIOS (L-CHS) interface is calculated, rounding down, as 1057/2 = 528 (cylinder addresses 0 to 527) and the maximum number of heads value at the INT 13h BIOS (L-CHS) interface is calculated as 16 × 2 = 32 (heads addresses 0 to 31). The maximum number of sectors remains as 63 (sector addresses 1 to 63). The largest L-CHS address (527, 31, 63) is now well within the range of the INT 13h BIOS registers and the disk appears to the

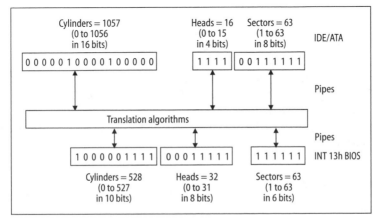

Fig. 5.17 CHS translation.

BIOS, and, of course, to all the software that uses it, to be of a quite different but entirely acceptable geometry.

It should be noted that we can lose some capacity by this translation process. The original disk geometry (P-CHS) of a maximum number of cylinders of 1057, of a maximum number of heads of 16 and of a maximum number of sectors of 63 results in a total capacity of $1057 \times 16 \times 63 \times 512 = 545,513,472$ bytes. Using a similar calculation, the INT 13h BIOS translated geometry (L-CHS) results in a total capacity of $528 \times 32 \times 63 \times 512 = 544,997,376$ bytes. This is a loss of 516,096 bytes, or about 0.1%. We also note that the largest logical CHS address translates, using the rules described above, to the following physical CHS address:

$$\text{L-CHS } (527, 31, 63) \;\rightarrow\; \text{P-CHS } ((527 \times 2) + (31/16)), (31 \bmod 16), 63)$$
$$\rightarrow \text{P-CHS } (1055, 15, 63)$$

This shows that we have lost a cylinder through translation, the largest available P-CHS cylinder number being 1056. This is a loss of 16 heads $\times$ 63 sectors per track = 1008 sectors = $1008 \times 512 = 516,096$ bytes, the figure that we have already obtained above.

We are now in a good position to interpret much of the data that was given by the Find-ATA program for the ST32140A hard disk (see Fig. 5.8). In the "Hardware" column we see that the maximum number of cylinders is 4095, the maximum number of heads is 16 and the maximum number of sectors is 63. The physical disk capacity is shown as 2,113,413,120 bytes. These figures are clearly the P-CHS values for the IDE/ATA interface and we can confirm that $4095 \times 16 \times 63 \times 512$ is indeed 2,113,413,120 bytes. In the "DOS" column we are seeing the L-CHS translated values at the INT 13h BIOS interface. The maximum number of cylinders value is calculated as 4095/4 = 1023 (rounding down) and the maximum number of heads value is calculated as $16 \times 4 = 64$, both as shown in the figure. The logical capacity can then be calculated as $1023 \times 64 \times 63 \times 512 = 2,111,864,832$ also as shown in the figure. We also note that the largest logical CHS address translates, using the rules described above, to the following physical CHS address:

$$\text{L-CHS } (1022, 63, 63) \rightarrow \text{P-CHS } ((1022 \times 4) + (63/16)), (63 \bmod 16), 63)$$
$$\rightarrow \text{P-CHS } (4091, 15, 63)$$

This shows that we have lost three cylinders through translation, the largest P-CHS cylinder number being 4094. This is a loss of 3 cylinders $\times$ 16 heads $\times$ 63 sectors per track = 3024 sectors = $3024 \times 512 = 1,548,288$ bytes, which accounts exactly for the difference between the physical capacity shown for the disk of 2,113,413,120 bytes and the logical capacity shown for the disk of 2,111,864,832 bytes.

Considering the other parameters given in Fig. 5.8, we should now be familiar with the terms DMA (Direct Memory Access) and PIO (Programmed Input Output) which we have discussed earlier. The final term, LBA, for Logical Block Addressing, we will consider very shortly.

CHS Translation Options

The translation algorithm, which operates between the two interfaces, has to reside as some form of software in the PC. There are a number of options for this. All modern BIOSes will already have the translation algorithm software built into their INT 13h functions and will automatically be capable of what is sometimes known as *Extended CHS (ECHS) Translation* or just simply *Large Mode*. Such BIOSes are often referred to as *enhanced*[47] or *translating BIOSes* and the translation algorithm as the *ECHS translation method*. If a user has an earlier BIOS, however, which does not incorporate such translation facilities, there are three possibilities for using disks larger than 528 Mbyte.

The first involves using special software drivers that do the translation for us. They are sometimes referred to as *Dynamic Drive Overlays* or *DDOs*. They are typified by EZ-Drive from Microhouse (Western Digital, 1999), and Disk Manager from Ontrack (IBM, 1999), and many hard disk manufacturers provide software of this nature with their disk products in order to deal with the non-translating BIOS problem. Both work in similar ways. During the first setting up of the disk, the DDO is placed by the initialization software in some spare disk space just after the partition table and at boot time it gets loaded into memory as the CHS translating software. We will look at this process in more detail later. Suffice to say, at this stage, that, having been loaded into memory, the CHS translating software of the DDO first adjusts the INT 13h vector in memory to point to where it, the DDO, now resides, so that all INT 13h calls thereafter are automatically handled by the translation routines.

In passing we should note the earlier comment that, without translation, the maximum number of cylinders accessible by the INT 13h BIOS is 1024. This has an important effect when we have a non-translating BIOS and are using a DDO. Prior to the DDO being activated, all INT 13h BIOS calls are subject to the non-translating BIOS limitations. In particular, this means that a boot sector, if it has to be accessed before the DDO is established[48], cannot normally reside on the disk beyond what is called the *1024 cylinder limit*.

A further important point is that DDOs are usually loaded through execution of the hard disk boot sequence. When booting from floppy disk to DOS, with a non-translating BIOS, the hard disk may not be accessible at all because the DDO has not been loaded. Most DDOs provide a workaround process for this problem, which may involve either pressing a particular key during the boot sequence or preparing a floppy disk with the DDO installed on it. This is vitally important to note from a forensic imaging viewpoint when rehosting a suspect drive that has been installed with a DDO. It is essential that the DDO is loaded from floppy disk into the forensic host machine before attempting to access the suspect drive.

The second approach to the problem is to use a disk drive unit which has its own version of the INT 13h translating BIOS routines built into its onboard ROM. During the boot process, the INT 13h vector is adjusted to point to the translating BIOS of the hard disk ROM rather than to the standard internal INT 13h BIOS routines. The 1024

---

47 Do not confuse this with the *BIOS Enhanced Disk Drive Specification* (Phoenix, 1995), which introduces entirely new INT 13h functions.

48 This depends upon the stage at which the DDO is loaded and the INT 13h vector gets changed. If this occurs during the analysis of the partition table, then boot sectors beyond the 1024 cylinder limit will be accessible. If it occurs during the sector boot sequence, they will not.

cylinder boot limit always applies here because the INT 13h vector does not get changed until after the boot sector has been accessed, but the floppy boot to DOS problem should not arise in this case as it does for the DDO. The third approach to the problem, long since outdated since all modern BIOSes now contain the updates, was to change the system BIOS. This could have been done either by obtaining an updated chip and replacing the current BIOS with it or, with the later flash BIOS systems, downloading a modification patch from the supplier and changing the flash memory.

If we refer back to Table 5.11, we may note that the total number of bits required by the ATA specification is 16 for cylinders + 4 for heads + 8 for sectors/track, giving a total of 28. In the low-level formatting discussion, we saw that three bytes (Fig. 5.4) were used for the CHS of the sector ID field, which only gives us 24 bits. However, we also saw (Fig. 5.7) that 4 bits of the sector flag in the sector ID field were "reserved", and by using these as well we can obtain the 28 bits required for P-CHS addressing. An approach used by one manufacturer (Seagate, 1995a) is shown at Fig. 5.18. Here the first two byes are used to hold the cylinders number (0 to 65,535), the last three bits of the third byte to hold the heads number (0 to 7) and the fourth byte to hold the sectors number (1 to 255).

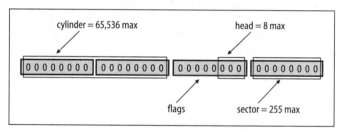

Fig. 5.18 A different use of sector ID bytes.

Logical Block Addressing (LBA)

Logical Block Addressing (LBA) is an alternative form of addressing to that of CHS and it has been included since the first ATA specification, which states: "*A drive can operate in either of two addressing modes, CHS or LBA, on a command by command basis*". In LBA, the 28 bits of the sector ID field are used as a single number, starting from 0 to identify each sector in sequence from the first to the last. The maximum possible number of sectors is, of course, $2^{28} = 268,435,456$, and this, for 512 byte sectors, results in a maximum possible size of 137,438,953,472 bytes (137 Gbyte in SI units and 128 Gbyte in powers of 2 units).

It is important to recognize that LBA is not a solution to the 528 Mbyte problem. All software which uses the INT 13h BIOS interface will be addressing the disk system using CHS addresses. Even though the IDE/ATA interface of the hard disk may be in LBA mode, all LBA addresses will have to be translated to and from the INT 13h BIOS CHS addresses that the software uses. In other words, a translating BIOS is always required, and it is the translating BIOS that provides the solution to the 528

Mbyte problem. In fact, the CHS bit shifting method described above is technically a short cut for the "correct" translating procedure, which should be the two steps:

1.   Translate the L-CHS to an LBA
2.   Translate the LBA to a P-CHS

We translate a CHS address to an LBA address by means of the following formula:

$$LBA = C \times \text{heads-per-cylinder} \times \text{sectors-per-track} + H \times \text{sectors-per-track} + S - 1$$

and we translate an LBA address to a CHS address using the following:

$$C = LBA/(\text{heads-per-cylinder} \times \text{sectors-per-track})$$

$$H = (LBA \bmod (\text{heads-per-cylinder} \times \text{sectors-per-track}))/\text{sectors-per-track}$$

$$S = ((LBA \bmod (\text{heads-per-cylinder} \times \text{sectors-per-track})) \bmod \text{sectors-per-track}) + 1$$

Using one of the bit shifting examples from above, we note an L-CHS address of (4, 7, 10), a logical heads-per-cylinder of 32, a physical heads-per-cylinder of 16 and a sectors-per-track, both logical and physical, of 63. We may now make the following calculations, where mod is the modulus function and / is the integer division function with the result rounded down, as above:

$$
\begin{aligned}
LBA &= (4 \times 32 \times 63) + (7 \times 63) + 10 - 1 \\
&= 8064 + 441 + 10 - 1 \\
&= 8514
\end{aligned}
$$

$$
\begin{aligned}
P\text{-}C &= 8514/(16 \times 63) \\
&= 8514/1008 \\
&= 8
\end{aligned}
$$

$$
\begin{aligned}
P\text{-}H &= (8514 \bmod (16 \times 63))/63 \\
&= 450/63 \\
&= 7
\end{aligned}
$$

$$
\begin{aligned}
P\text{-}S &= ((8514 \bmod (16 \times 63)) \bmod 63) + 1 \\
&= (450 \bmod 63) + 1 \\
&= 10
\end{aligned}
$$

From this we can see quite clearly that L-CHS (4, 7, 10) first translates to LBA 8514 and this then translates to P-CHS (8, 7, 10), just as we found with the bit shifting method.

Problems with Different Translation Methods

You might reasonably assume that there is only one agreed way of translating L-CHS to P-CHS and only one agreed way for converting CHS to LBA and LBA to CHS. Unfortunately, this is not the case. There is no standard algorithm and different BIOSes and different operating systems may well use different methods. As you might expect, different methods are likely also to yield different results. There is

Table 5.12 LBA assisted method.

Capacity	Sectors	Heads	Cylinders
1 < cap < 504 Mbyte	63	16	cap/(63 × 16 × 512)
504 < cap < 1008 Mbyte	63	32	cap/(63 × 32 × 512)
1008 < cap < 2016 Mbyte	63	64	cap/(63 × 64 × 512)
2016 < cap < 4032 Mbyte	63	128	cap/(63 × 128 × 512)
4032 < cap < 8032.5 Mbyte	63	255	cap/(63 × 255 × 512)

therefore a real risk when hosting a hard disk from a suspect machine that uses a non-standard BIOS on a forensic machine for imaging that the translations performed by the forensic machine may not be correct for the disk, with potentially harmful results. This will normally only apply to older disks and older BIOSes; most modern BIOSes tend to use the *de facto* (nearly) standard method that has been described above, so the problem of incorrect translation when re-hosting should not occur very often.

The second most common translation method is the so-called *LBA assisted method*, which is rather different from the bit shifting method we discussed earlier. Here the rule is to translate the CHS address at the INT 13h interface to an LBA address and use that LBA address at the IDE/ATA interface, and vice versa. This method is perhaps best understood by looking at Table 5.12. To convert an LBA address to an L-CHS address, the total capacity (cap) of the drive in bytes is first calculated. Depending upon this capacity a particular line item in Table 5.12 is selected and the cylinders, heads and sectors values are calculated according to the appropriate entries. One particular point should be noted from this figure: the heads value and the relevant cylinders divisor for 4032 to 8032.5 Mbyte capacity is 255 rather than 256. This is because of an operating system problem which we will be looking at shortly, and makes this, in point of fact, the *revised LBA assisted method*.

If we now re-consider the example of Fig. 5.8, we recall that, at the ATA/IDE interface (P-CHS), the maximum number of cylinders is 4095, the maximum number of heads is 16 and the maximum number of sectors is 63, and that this gives a disk capacity of 4095 × 16 × 63 × 512 = 2,113,413,120 bytes. From this we can determine the capacity in megabytes as 2,113,413,120/1024 × 1024 = 2015.5 Mbyte[49] and look that up in Table 5.12.

The appropriate line entry in the table is the "1008 < cap < 2016 Mbyte" line, so the cylinders become 2,113,413,120/(63 × 64 × 512) = 1023.75. Rounding down, this gives us a maximum number of cylinders of 1023, together with a maximum number of heads of 64 and a maximum number of sectors of 63. The highest available LBA address for this translation is the total number of sectors minus 1 (because LBA addresses start with 0). This is (1023 × 64 × 63) − 1 = 4,124,735. The INT 13h BIOS (L-CHS) translated address for this highest available LBA address of 4,124,735 is therefore: cylinders 1022, heads 63 and sectors 63. This is exactly the same as that obtained using the bit shifting method above for the highest CHS address at the INT 13h BIOS (DOS) interface. Note that this will not always be the case. The two

---

49 Note that Table 5.12 is in powers of two units.

translation methods produce the same CHS values in many cases, but not in all. The LBA-assisted method *always* uses 63 sectors per track. The bit shifting method uses whatever sectors per track the drive reports from the IDE/ATA interface. If this is not 63, the two algorithms will produce completely different results[50]. It can therefore be very destructive of data to change translation modes, in SETUP, between ECHS (Large) and LBA on a working drive. The actual sectors accessed could be different between the two modes for the same CHS addresses called by the software.

The 2 Gbyte Problem

Some older translating BIOSes cannot accept a cylinders value at the IDE/ATA interface that is greater than 4095 because they only allocate 12 bits for the number of cylinders in the CMOS RAM. This results in a maximum physical drive geometry of 4095 cylinders, 16 heads and 63 sectors, which is a capacity of $4095 \times 16 \times 63 \times 512 = 2,113,413,120$ bytes and is known as the *2 Gbyte problem*. Three problem scenarios have been noted (Western Digital, 1998a): the BIOS can only see a maximum of 2015.5 Mbyte and truncates the remaining space; the BIOS loses all cylinder bits above 12 and may lose 2016 Mbyte of space or more; the BIOS completely locks up at boot time. A comprehensive solution to this problem is to use a dynamic drive overlay (DDO). However, if the BIOS locks up at boot time, it will be necessary to configure the drive (incorrectly) as 1023 cylinders, 16 heads and 63 sectors in CMOS SETUP. In this way the BIOS does not see the problem and does not lock up. The DDO, when activated, fetches the true CHS parameters from the drive itself and carries out the appropriate translation. One difficulty that may have to be overcome is getting into CMOS SETUP. The option to enter SETUP comes after the BIOS has detected all the hard drives, and as the lockup will occur when the drive is detected, SETUP is not at that stage accessible. The way round this problem is to disconnect the offending drive from its cable, then boot and enter SETUP to put in the artificial safe parameters. When the drive is reconnected, it should then be possible to boot and to establish the DDO.

The 4 Gbyte Problem

Older BIOSes may exhibit another problem with disks that have a cylinders value at the IDE/ATA interface that is greater than 8191. For a drive that has 8192 cylinders, 16 heads and 63 sectors, this results in a capacity of $8192 \times 16 \times 63 \times 512 = 4,227,858,432$ bytes = 4032 Mbyte; hence this is known as the *4 Gbyte problem*. In accordance with the bit shifting method, this requires the cylinders value at the IDE/ATA interface to be divided by 16 in order for the translated cylinders value to be in the INT 13h BIOS interface range. However, this then results in a translated heads value of $16 \times 16 = 256$ and it is this translated heads value which causes the problem. This is because both MS-DOS up to version 6.22 and Windows 95 hold *the number of heads* in an 8 bit register and the maximum number of heads can then only be 255, resulting in the 4

---

50 As an example, the Western Digital WDAC2420, which is a 425 Mbyte disk, specifies 56
   sectors per track. See Western Digital (1997b).

Gbyte limit. Although this is an operating system problem, BIOS manufacturers decided to deal with it by modifications to the translating BIOS (Micro Firmware, 1998). These need to be applied both to the bit shifting or ECHS translation method and to the assisted LBA method.

The *revised ECHS translation method* makes the following adjustment. If, at the IDE/ATA interface, the number of cylinders is greater than 8191 and the number of heads is 16, then the cylinders value is multiplied by 16/15 and the heads value is set to 15 before the standard bit shifting algorithm is applied.

As an example, the Maxtor CrystalMax 1080, model number 84320A8 (Maxtor, 1996) shows 8,400 cylinders, 16 heads and 63 sectors per track as the geometry at the IDE/ATA interface. This gives us $8,400 \times 16 \times 63 \times 512 = 4,335,206,400$ bytes capacity. Using the standard bit shifting or ECHS translation method this results in $8400/16 = 525$ cylinders and $16 \times 16 = 256$ heads, causing the problem that we referred to above. The revised ECHS translation, however, first gives us $8,400 \times 16/15 = 8,960$ cylinders and 15 heads, and then this in turn is translated to $8,960/16 = 560$ cylinders and $15 \times 16 = 240$ heads. The resulting capacity is the same as before (this is not always the case), that is: $560 \times 240 \times 63 \times 512 = 4,335,206,400$ bytes. The largest L-CHS address for this disk at the INT 13h BIOS interface for the revised ECHS translation method is therefore $(559, 239, 63)$.

In the case of the LBA-assisted method, the necessary adjustment has already been built into Table 5.12. We noted in passing at the time that for the 4032 to 8032.5 Mbyte capacity the heads value and the relevant cylinders divisor are both 255 rather than the expected 256. This is, in fact, an implementation of the *revised assisted LBA method*. We can now calculate the translated CHS addresses using the revised assisted LBA method from Table 5.12 in the following manner. We again note that the total byte capacity is $8,400 \times 16 \times 63 \times 512 = 4,335,206,400$ bytes and this, divided by 1024×1024, gives us 4134.375 Mbyte. We therefore have to use the "4032 < cap < 8032.5 Mbyte" entry in the table giving us a cylinders value of $4,335,206,400/(63 \times 255 \times 512) = 527$ when rounded down. The heads figure is 255 and the sectors figure is 63, giving us a total capacity of $527 \times 255 \times 63 \times 512 = 4,334,722,560$. In addition, the largest L-CHS address for this disk at the INT 13h BIOS interface for this revised assisted LBA translation method is therefore $(526, 254, 63)$. Note that neither the total capacity for the translated disk nor the largest L-CHS address are the same as those obtained using the revised ECHS method. Here we see that the two translations are completely incompatible with one another.

Other Translation-Related Problems

It has also been found (Seagate, 1998) that some older BIOSes do not properly handle a cylinders value that is in excess of 6,322. For a drive that has 6,322 cylinders, 16 heads and 63 sectors, this results in a capacity of $6,322 \times 16 \times 63 \times 512 = 3,262,758,912$ bytes = 3,262 Mbyte (powers of ten); hence this is sometimes known as the *3.27 Gbyte problem*. It generally shows up when the cylinders value in CMOS SETUP has been set larger than 6,322. As in the case of the 2 Gbyte problem, the computer locks up at boot time and the solution options are very similar. Either set the CMOS SETUP values to 1023 cylinders, 16 heads and 63 sectors and use a DDO, or obtain an upgrade for the BIOS.

Another problem reported (Western Digital, 1998b) is that of the 240 head limitation. Many BIOSes are only able to report a maximum of 240 heads in the INT 13h function 8 call[51]. This results in a maximum recognized capacity of 1024 cylinders × 240 heads × 63 sectors × 512 bytes = 7,927,234,560 bytes = 7927 Mbyte (powers of ten) and this is sometimes called the *7.9 Gbyte problem*.

Overcoming the 8 Gbyte Barrier

At the time of writing, disks very much larger than 8.4 Gbyte have become the norm on most modern PCs. If we refer back to Table 5.11, we can readily see that it is the cylinders, heads and sectors per track maximum sizes of the original INT 13h BIOS that impose upon us this 8.4 Gbyte limit. This first has an impact when the drive is being detected and an INT 13h BIOS Function 8, "Get Drive Parameters", is invoked. This will execute code that causes an IDENTIFY DEVICE command to be issued to the IDE ATA interface. Without going into a lot of detail, the drive will respond with cylinder, head and sector information in words 1, 3 and 6 of the data structure it returns. Each of these words on the ATA interface can contain up to the value 65,535, so this is not restricting us. However, the INT 13h BIOS registers can only hold, and hence identify, maximum values for cylinders up to 1024 (0 to 1023), heads up to 256 (0 to 255) and sectors up to 63. A drive larger than 8.4 Gbyte cannot therefore be properly identified as such by the standard INT 13h BIOS functions. For the same reasons, it cannot be read from or written to above the 8.4 Gbyte limit.

This is where the *Enhanced BIOS* comes in. As is the case with so much in this field, lax use of terminology leads to so much possible confusion. The terms "enhancements" and "extensions" have both been used by different sources to apply to those modifications that were made to the original (often referred to as the *legacy*) INT 13h BIOS functions to enable CHS translation. A BIOS that can perform such translation is also sometimes known as a *translating BIOS* and contains code modifications that enable CHS translation to take place, by, for example, using the bit shifting or assisted LBA methods that we discussed earlier. Unfortunately, the same terminology tends to be applied to something that is quite different: the *INT 13h Extensions*.

The legacy INT 13h function numbers range from 00h to 1Ah; the INT 13h extensions specify completely new INT 13h function numbers which range in value from 41h to 48h. That is not all that is different. The register conventions have been changed to permit the passing of a data structure or *packet* and all addressing information is now passed via such structures rather than having to be limited by the fixed size of some register. The size of the field in the data structure used for the starting LBA address is four bytes, enabling disks as large as 2^{64} sectors to be connected. This, of course, far exceeds the capacity of the IDE/ATA interface itself, which can only handle, as we have seen in Table 5.11, a field of 28 bits for LBA, which is made up of 16 bits for the cylinders value, 4 bits for the heads value and 8 bits for the sectors value. This gives us 2^{28} sectors and the extensions thus move the barrier from 8.4 Gbyte CHS to 127.5 Gbyte LBA.

---

51 This call is the "Get Drive Parameters" function call, which the BIOS uses to build the disk parameter tables.

The INT 13h extensions Function 48h, "Get Drive Parameters", obtains its information about the drive from words 60 and 61 in the data structure that the IDE/ATA IDENTIFY DEVICE command returns. This double word value holds the drive's maximum LBA address and thus its full capacity can be recognized.

An enhanced BIOS, with the INT 13h extensions, still has the legacy INT 13h functions, so, for disks smaller than 8.4 Gbyte, it can operate as we have described earlier. For disks greater than 8.4 Gbyte, however, the operating system and all the application software using the disk must be able to make use of the INT 13h BIOS Extensions and address the disk in LBA mode.

The *Microsoft/IBM INT 13h Extensions* document describes the original *de facto* standard, and a superset of this is the *BIOS Enhanced Disk Drive Specification* (Phoenix, 1995, 1998). Most BIOS manufacturers use this *Phoenix Enhanced BIOS* specification, though a competing and incompatible version, the *Western Digital Enhanced IDE Implementation Guide*, was also published. Disks formatted using BIOS extensions based on the Western Digital specification may be unreadable on other BIOSes, the majority of which use the Phoenix specification. We have mentioned this Phoenix specification before in footnotes when we discussed the background to the legacy problem and the CHS translation options.

From all that has been said before, another obvious possibility for overcoming the 8.4 Gbyte problem is a dynamic drive overlay (DDO) such as EZ-Drive or Disk Manager which simulates these INT 13h BIOS extensions; but note that we must still have an operating system and software that is able to make use of them and can address the disk in LBA mode.

Why CHS Translation is Still Relevant

You might by this stage be justifiably thinking that all of the CHS translation issues that we have described above are now ancient history and no longer of relevance, since modern systems are fully LBA capable and can use true LBA addressing. If we examine the ATA-6 (McLean, 2001, p. 21) specification we find the following statement which seems to confirm just this view: "*All devices shall support LBA translation. In standards ATA/ATAPI-5 and earlier, a CHS translation was defined. This translation is obsolete but may be implemented as defined in ATA/ATAPI-5*".

So CHS translation is now obsolete. If we then examine the relevant part of the ATA-5 (McLean, 1999, p. 19) specification we find the following statements:

Devices shall support translations as described below:

- All devices shall support LBA translation.
- If the device's capacity is greater than or equal to one sector and less than or equal to 16,514,064 sectors the device shall support CHS translation.
- If the device's capacity is greater than 16,514,064 sectors, then the device may support CHS translation.

Up until ATA-6, it is quite clear that CHS translation was the *required* way of dealing with disks smaller than 8.4 Gbyte and was optionally supported for larger disks. This changed with ATA-6, though you might note that it is not ruled out.

There are, in fact, several very good reasons why CHS translation is still relevant even today and why an understanding of it is essential to a forensic computing analyst. The most important of these reasons include:

- The MS-DOS operating system and the Master Boot Record (see later) are still based on CHS addressing and use the INT 13h BIOS Function 8 "Get Drive Parameters" to obtain CHS addresses. Any operating system that is to be installed on the same disk must also understand CHS addressing.

- The initial bootstrap disk processing and loading of the operating system is all done in CHS mode, and, again, the INT 13h BIOS Function 8 "Get Drive Parameters" is used to obtain CHS addresses.

- Microsoft has been quoted as saying that their operating systems will not use any disk capacity that cannot also be accessed by the INT 13h BIOS legacy functions (Landis, 2001).

- Where partition tables (see later) contain CHS addresses, these are always held in L-CHS translated form.

In practice we find that the majority of hard disks continue to implement the ATA-5 CHS translation specifications for sizes less than 8.4 Gbyte. In fact, without this, those operating systems (including MS-DOS) and those software applications, of which there are still many, that are not themselves LBA-capable, could not access the disk at all.

Finally, of course, as forensic analysts, we may very well come across old hard disks that only use CHS addressing and exhibit many of the translation problems that we have described above.

It may perhaps have been thought that with modern systems all being fully LBA-capable the CHS translation problems of the past have gone away. Unfortunately, this is not the case; they have only been hidden and our modern BIOSes still do ECHS and Assisted LBA translations.

Summary of BIOS Interface Issues

At Fig. 5.19 we have shown a summary of the major interfacing issues that arise between the BIOS and IDE/ATA drives.

Communication between the applications software and the BIOS is by means of the legacy INT 13h BIOS interface. This expects CHS addressing (known as Logical CHS or L-CHS) and has cylinder, head and sector per track maximum sizes of 1024, 256 and 63 respectively. This gives us the 8.4 Gbyte limit as well as the 1024 cylinder problem. If we are to exceed the 8.4 Gbyte limit, the applications software must use the INT 13h extensions (functions in the range 41h to 48h) and Logical Block Addressing or LBA.

With a very old BIOS no CHS translation is carried out and LBA is not possible. We therefore have the 1024 cylinder problem and the 528 Mbyte limit, unless we use a dynamic drive overlay. The 528 Mbyte limit stems from having to use the minimum set of the two interface geometries: Logical CHS being 1024, 256 and 63 and Physical CHS being 65536, 16, 255, giving a minimum set of 1024, 16, 63 from which the 528 Mbyte value results. With a more recent translating or extended BIOS the limitations

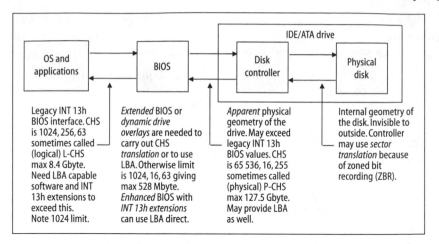

Fig. 5.19 Summary of BIOS interface issues.

of Logical CHS and Physical CHS geometries taken together no longer need apply since the BIOS can trade excess cylinder size for spare head capacity according to some agreed translation algorithm. If the drive supports LBA, similar translations can be performed by the BIOS between the legacy Logical CHS interface and LBA. A modern BIOS will provide the INT 13h extensions and these enable the direct use of LBA. The BIOS will pass LBA addresses direct to the drive, provided that the drive is also able to use LBA. If the drive is not LBA-capable, the BIOS will have to translate the LBA addresses into Physical CHS addresses before passing them to the drive, and this will again reduce the capacity to a maximum of 8.4 Gbyte.

Communication between the drive and the BIOS is across the IDE/ATA interface. This may use CHS addressing (known as Physical CHS or P-CHS) and has cylinder, head and sector per track maximum sizes of 65536, 16 and 255 respectively. This gives a theoretical maximum of 127.5 Gbyte. LBA may be used directly if the drive supports this. Big drives (see section below), however, now support a theoretical maximum of 144 Pbyte (petabytes).

Finally, for completeness, we have shown the internal interface between the controller and the disk itself. This might perform what is known as sector translation, particularly where zoned bit recording is in use. The Physical CHS addresses specified at the IDE/ATA interface are not, in such cases, an accurate representation of the physical structures internal to the drive.

Summary of BIOS Translation Options

At Fig. 5.20 is shown a summary of the translation options that might be carried out by the three different classes[52] of BIOSes. The old BIOS class can only provide a straight through capability of Logical CHS to Physical CHS. No translation or use of LBA is possible. The translating or extended BIOS class can perform translations

---

52 For a more detailed treatment of BIOS types see Landis (1995a).

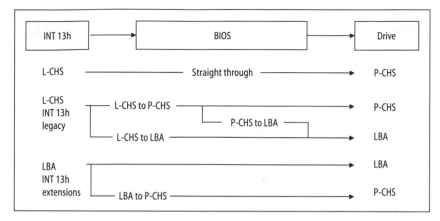

Fig. 5.20 Translation options.

from Logical CHS to Physical CHS, from Physical CHS to LBA and from Logical CHS to LBA. The enhanced BIOS or INT 13h extensions BIOS class can perform LBA direct and translation from LBA to Physical CHS. Each higher level class can, in addition, perform all the functions of the classes below it.

From a forensic computing viewpoint, we need to recall that there are a variety of possible translation algorithms and not all BIOS implementations are the same. We also need to be aware that there are at least two different and incompatible implementations of the INT 13h extensions: that of Phoenix (1995, 1998) and most other BIOS manufacturers, and that of Western Digital (1997a, undated b). The problem for the forensic computing analyst arises when there is a need to host a hard disk on a system other than the original machine. We need to be very sure that the Physical CHS or LBA addresses calculated by our host BIOS are exactly those that would have been calculated by the original BIOS given the same Logical CHS addresses, and vice versa. If we detect the presence of a DDO on the evidence disk then we must make specific arrangements to ensure that a copy of the relevant DDO software is loaded into memory on our forensic machine before trying to access the disk.

We should also be aware that some protected mode operating systems that do not use INT 13h directly have their own drivers, and these too will make assumptions about the translation that has been used in formatting and writing to the disk. Using such software, when a drive has been rehosted, needs to be done with much caution.

When a re-hosting problem arises, the first symptom is likely to be a failure by the imaging software to image the disk correctly on the forensic machine. To deal with this, the analyst will need a very good understanding of these legacy issues.

Fast Drives and Big Drives

New features called Ultra ATA/66 and ATA/100, sometimes also known as Ultra-DMA/66 or UDMA/66 and UDMA/100, provided improved performance for the

"Enhanced" IDE hard disk drive by introducing new interface cables. These contain 80 conductors in the ribbon cable that connects the disk drive to the motherboard IDE socket, as opposed to the 40 conductors of the earlier systems. The new cables are easily recognized by having twice the number of slightly thinner conductors in the ribbon. Although there are 80 conductor cables, there are still only 40 pin connections with the extra wires being used as earth returns to reduce crosstalk between the lines and hence permit the higher transfer rates. In order to use these enhanced IDE ribbon cables, both the motherboard and the hard drives themselves must support the new interface.

In July 2001, Maxtor announced the Ultra ATA/133 hard drive interface. This increased the top transfer rate to 133 megabytes per second compared with the 100 megabytes per second of the ATA/100. Maxtor referred to their Ultra-ATA/133 technology as *Fast Drives*.

At about the same time, Maxtor, Intel and Via Technologies announced the creation of the so-called Big Drive specification, which represented the first implementation of the ATA-6 specification that enabled drive capacities to exceed the 127 Gbyte barrier (Maxtor, 2001).

This specification allowed ATA drives to utilize 48-bit data addressing as opposed to the then current 28-bit addressing, thus pushing the theoretical disk capacity of an ATA drive upwards to 2^{48} sectors or 144 Pbyte (petabytes). These so-called ATAPI-6 drives also increased the maximum amount of data that could be transferred per command for ATA devices from 256 sectors (about 131 kbyte) to 65,536 sectors (about 33 Mbyte).

The relevant sections (McLean, 2001, p. 50) in the ATA-6 standard state: "*The optional 48-bit Address feature set allows devices with capacities up to 281,474,976,710,655[53] sectors or approximately 281 tera sectors. This allows device capacity up to 144,115,188,075,855,360[54] bytes or approximately 144 peta bytes. In addition, the number of sectors that may be transferred by a single command are increased by increasing the allowable sector count to 16 bits*", and: "*The 48-bit Address feature set operates in LBA addressing only. Devices implementing the 48-bit Address feature set shall also implement commands that use 28-bit addressing. 28-bit and 48-bit commands may be intermixed*".

It is also noted from the specification that the 48 bit addressing feature is implemented by converting three existing 8 bit registers, LBA Low, LBA Mid and LBA High, to first-in, first-out (FIFO) stacks that are two values deep. The three registers between them provide 24 bits[55] but each may be written to twice to provide the 48 bit address. Writing twice to the registers overcomes the 28 bit limitation that would otherwise apply across the ATA interface.

At the time of writing, 250 Gbyte hard disks have become commonplace and sizes appear set to increase well beyond that. Many hard disks larger than 127 Gbyte are

---

53 Calculated from $2^{48} - 1$.

54 Calculated from $(2^{48} - 1) \times 512$.

55 For 28 bit addressing, 4 bits of the Device register are also used.

connected via a special expansion card[56] fitted to the PCI bus, which has its own BIOS to provide enhanced services for up to four large hard drives in addition to the possible four IDE devices that are now standard on most motherboards. We are also seeing large hard drive capability being incorporated directly onto the latest motherboards.

Serial ATA (SATA)

In August 2001, a new ATA interconnection interface was published by the Serial ATA Working Group which consisted of representatives from Dell, Intel, Maxtor, Seagate, and APT Technologies. The document is known as the Serial ATA 1.0 Specification. This was followed, in October 2002, by the publication of additional new Serial ATA extensions which are defined in the Serial ATA II Specification. Copies of both of these documents may be obtained from the web site http://www.serialata.org/. Serial ATA (or SATA) has been designed to be "... *a high-speed serial link replacement for the parallel ATA attachment of mass storage devices*" (Deyring, 2003).

Useful overviews of Serial ATA can be found in a Microsoft paper (Microsoft, 2003) and a Dell White Paper (Pratt, 2003) from which the following quote is taken: "*Serial ATA eliminates the limitations of the current parallel ATA interface. Because the initial Serial ATA architecture changes the physical interface layer only, it maintains register and software compatibility with parallel ATA. No device driver changes are necessary and the Serial ATA architecture is transparent to the BIOS and the operating system*".

The main benefits of SATA would appear to be: a much thinner and more flexible cable than the 40 line parallel ATA bus, with the potential for it being significantly longer, up to 1 metre compared with 18 inches; lower operating voltages and smaller connection pin counts; and improved transfer rates of 150 Mbyte/s compared with the parallel ATA rate of 133 Mbyte/s. Future development is looking to improve the transfer rates further to 600 Mbyte/s.

SATA does not have much immediate impact on the forensic computing analyst, since the architecture is transparent to the BIOS and the operating system. We will need write blockers for hosting SATA disk drives in addition to those for parallel ATA systems and we should perhaps note that one of the changes is that the true SATA interface only permits one drive per channel and we do not have the concept of MASTER and SLAVE on the same IDE cable. We should however also note the following quote taken from Microsoft (2003): "... *the Emulating Parallel ATA mode defines a transfer level equivalent of parallel ATA for Serial ATA controllers. In this mode, a Serial ATA controller can emulate master-only (device 0) parallel ATA or shared channel parallel ATA. In master-only parallel ATA emulation, the Serial ATA controller presents itself to the computer as a parallel ATA controller with only a single master storage device attached to a channel. In shared channel parallel ATA emulation, the controller uses two Serial ATA channels, each only attach to a single*

---

56 Large drives may also be connected via USB or FireWire.

storage device, as a single parallel channel attaching two storage devices. Both forms of emulation work with Serial ATA controllers that use Windows parallel ATA (atapi.sys) drivers".

The POST/Boot Sequence

Before we start this section we need to remind ourselves of addressing in real mode and the layout of the PC memory and its use. We will then look in turn at the *start of boot* sequence, the *Power On Self Test (POST)* processes, the BIOS, the CMOS and the bootstrap loader.

Addressing in Real Mode

As we mentioned earlier, the processor always starts up in 16 bit real mode using the segment offset addressing system. We need to understand this if we are to understand the boot sequence. Internally, the Intel 8086 and 8088 microprocessor chips, on which the PC was first based, have 16 bit registers and hence the maximum number that any of them can contain is $2^{16} - 1$ which is 65,535 in decimal or FFFFh in hexadecimal. If a single register were to be used for memory addressing, the maximum size of memory that could be accessed would thus be 64 kbyte. However, the Intel 8086 and 8088 chips actually have 20 address lines (A0 to A19) in their external address bus and so are capable of accessing addresses up to $2^{20} - 1$, which is 1,048,575 in decimal or FFFFFh in hexadecimal. This permits the maximum size of memory to be 1 Mbyte.

In order to provide the external 20 bit address, two 16 bit registers are used together, as shown in Fig. 5.21. One 16 bit register is known as the *segment register* and the other as the *offset register*. The segment register value is shifted left by four

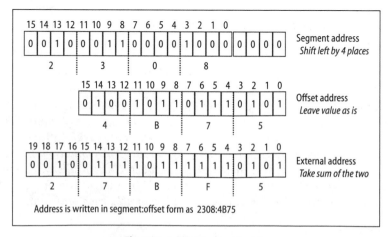

Fig. 5.21 Addressing in real mode.

places (equivalent to multiplying by 16) before being added to the offset register value to give a 20 bit external address value as shown[57].

In the example we see a segment register holding the value 2308h being shifted left by four places and then being added to an offset register holding the value 4B75h. The result forms the external 20 bit address of 27BF5h. Also shown in the figure is the standard way in which the segment and offset addresses are written. In this case we see 2308:4B75 as the segment:offset values, with no "h" being necessary since hexadecimal notation is always implied. This form of segment:offset addressing means that any given external address may be specified in a number of different ways. For example, the external address 00082 hexadecimal could be expressed as any of the following:

$$0000:0082 = 00000 + 0082 = 00082$$

$$0001:0072 = 00010 + 0072 = 00082$$

$$0002:0062 = 00020 + 0062 = 00082$$

...

$$0008:0002 = 00080 + 0002 = 00082$$

Note, as we have shown above, that the simplest way for us to translate from segment:offset form to external 20 bit address form is to take the segment value in hexadecimal, place an additional trailing zero on its right-hand side and then add the result to the offset address in hexadecimal.

In practice, PC programmers tend to use blocks of code and data which reside within 64 kbyte memory segments. The Intel 8086 and 8088 microprocessor chips have both data segment (DS) and code segment (CS) registers, amongst a number of others. It is common practice when programming to set the DS and CS registers to the start of the main data segment and the start of the main code segment memory addresses respectively[58]. That way, any references to code or data in the current code or data segments may be made by means of 16 bit offset values, sometimes called *near* or *relative pointers*. Only when it is required to refer to code or data in some other segment is it necessary to specify both the 16 bit segment and the 16 bit offset values of the address, giving rise to what is sometimes known as *far* or *absolute pointers*. What then has to happen is that the appropriate segment register, either DS or CS, depending upon whether we are dealing with data or code, has to be loaded with the 16 bit far pointer segment value before the 16 bit far pointer offset value can be used and the external address accessed.

---

57 This is a high-level explanation and is sufficient for our purposes. In fact, the segment register is made up of a number of *hidden* registers called *descriptor cache registers* which are also used in protected mode.

58 The *memory model* determines the number of code and data segments that are made available to the program. The *small* model has one 64 kbyte data segment and one 64 kbyte code segment. The *large* model has multiple 64 kbyte data segments and multiple 64 kbyte code segments. A number of other such models are defined.

We can now see, as we explained earlier, that the 4 byte entries in the interrupt vector table are actually far pointers which allow any place in the 1 Mbyte memory address space to be accessed and thus used as the starting location for the code of a device driver or interrupt handler.

Memory Layout

The original Intel 8086 and 8088 microprocessors had only the one mode of operation, and within this was implemented the segment:offset addressing architecture that we have discussed above. It is this architecture that is used by the bootstrap system and by MS-DOS, dating from the days of the original PC. In order to maintain backward compatibility with the MS-DOS operating system, all subsequent Intel microprocessor chips in the PC range have included an operating mode that provides this segment:offset addressing mechanism. It is known as *real mode*, and within it we can only address up to 1 Mbyte of memory because of the internal segment:offset design and the 20 bit external address lines of the original chips. The Intel 80286 and i386SX microprocessors have in fact 24 bit external address lines and can thus address up to $2^{24} - 1 = 16,777,215$ or 16 Mbyte of memory and the Intel i386DX, i486 and the early Pentium microprocessors have 32 bit external address lines and can thus address up to $2^{32} - 1 = 4,294,967,295$ or 4 Gbyte of memory. These greatly enhanced addressing capabilities only work, however, when the microprocessor is switched to a completely different operating mode, called *protected mode*[59], within which an entirely different form of addressing architecture is employed[60]. In protected mode, memory can be addressed right up to 4 Gbyte, and it is not unusual to find PCs these days with one or more Gbyte of RAM fitted. Any memory above the 1 Mbyte real mode limit is known as *extended memory.*

In order to discuss the various memory issues, an expanded version of Fig. 5.12 is shown at Fig. 5.22. Here we see the 1 Mbyte memory area that is addressable in real mode. In fact, it extends above the 1 Mbyte point because of a design "flaw" that was made into a feature. The segment:offset addressing scheme clearly permits at the top of the memory the following segment:offset values[61]:

FFFF:000F = FFFF0 + 000F = FFFFFh = 1,048,575   1 Mbyte − 1

FFFF:0010 = FFFF0 + 0010 = 100000h = 1,048,576   1 Mbyte exactly

---

59 There is a third mode, known as *virtual 8086* or *V86* mode, which we will not consider any further here.

60 The segment register no longer provides part of the address itself but now acts as a *selector* into one of two tables: the Global Descriptor Table (GDT), common to all applications, or the Local Descriptor Table (LDT), specific to a task. Each table contains 8 byte (64 bit) entries which include a 32 bit base address to which a 16 or 32 bit offset address may be added, a 16 bit limit address and access flags. The hidden descriptor cache registers referred to earlier are used in this process. For more details see Collins (2003).

61 Note that FFFF:000F is the same external address as F000:FFFF.

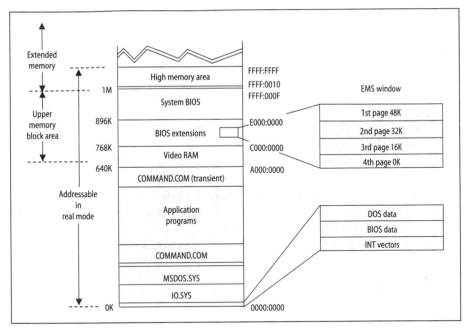

Fig. 5.22 PC memory layout.

$$FFFF:0011 = FFFF0 + 0011 = 100001h = 1,048,577 \qquad 1\ Mbyte + 1$$

...

$$FFFF:FFFF = FFFF0 + FFFF = 10FFEFh = 1,114,095$$

which is all but 16 bytes of the next 64 kbyte block above the top of memory

In the original PC there were only 20 address lines (A0 to A19), so programs which tried to address 100000h or above using the permitted segment:offset values of FFFF:0010 up to FFFF:FFFF caused a *wraparound*. That is, the leading 1 bit (which would be address line A20 if it existed) was ignored and the external memory addresses of 100000 up to 10FFEFh became 00000h up to 0FFEFh instead, resulting in a *wraparound* from the top of memory back to the bottom. This design "flaw" was turned into a useful feature when the Intel 386 microprocessor came along and memory above 1 Mbyte could be addressed in protected mode. In this case, address lines A20 and higher are physically implemented for protected mode addressing beyond 1 Mbyte and it was decided to utilize address line A20 in real mode as well. A switch was provided to activate address line A20 and with that active, instead of wraparound occurring, all but 16 bytes of the 64 kbyte segment above 1 Mbyte became addressable in real mode. This became known as the *high memory area*. The A20 switch has to be controlled carefully because some early versions of MS-DOS rely on the wraparound feature being present. Control of the switch is invested in the software driver HIMEM.SYS, which not only gives real mode access to the high memory area but also enables controlled access to the rest of the extended memory (XMS, 1991). It does this by switching the processor into protected mode in order to access data in extended memory and then back again into real mode in order to permit MS-DOS to function properly. It often does this in conjunction with another software driver, EMM386.SYS. This driver takes the extended memory provided by HIMEM.SYS and uses it to emulate *expanded memory* or to provide *Upper Memory Blocks (UMBs)* or both (EMS, 1987).

Expanded memory was a concept jointly developed by Lotus, Intel and Microsoft (LIM Expanded Memory System or LIM EMS) to provide access on the original 8086 PC to a much larger memory area than was possible using the 20 bit external address lines directly. The concept (see Fig. 5.22) entails allocating a spare 64 kbyte slot in the upper memory area where the adaptor card and BIOS extension ROMs are usually fitted. This slot is then viewed as an EMS window which contains four 16 kbyte pages. The pages can be physically mapped onto four 16 kbyte areas of memory on a card populated with up to 8 Mbyte of memory. The four pages can each be switched to access *any* 16 kbyte memory area on the card, and thus programs can have real mode access to a maximum of 8 Mbyte of memory, albeit only 64 kbyte at a time.

As mentioned above, the driver EMM386.SYS provides an emulation of the EMS card facility. Almost no systems these days have separate EMS memory cards. Instead, EMM386.SYS takes the high memory made available by HIMEM.SYS and uses that as though it were being accessed from an EMS memory card. This therefore gives us one means of providing real mode access to extended memory blocks. There are a number of other proprietary *memory managers* that operate in a similar fashion.

The expanded memory provided by EMM386.SYS may be used in a number of ways to reduce the loading of the very limited 640 kbyte region. Software drivers may be loaded in emulated expanded memory by means of the DEVICEHIGH command in CONFIG.SYS and terminate and stay resident programs may similarly be loaded in emulated expanded memory by means of the LOADHIGH command in AUTOEXEC.BAT. In addition, BIOS code can be copied into emulated expanded memory and the addressing and interrupt vectors adjusted accordingly. The advantage of this is that execution of code in, for example, 64 bit extended memory DRAM tends to be faster than execution of the same code in 8 bit BIOS ROM (Intel, 1998a, p. 12). Extended memory used in this way is often called *Shadow RAM* and this may be specified in the BIOS SETUP program. Finally, using HIMEM.SYS, parts of MS-DOS can be loaded directly into the high memory area by means of the DOS=HIGH command.

The Start of the Bootstrap Sequence

When power is first applied to the PC, tests of all the voltage and current levels are carried out by the power supply. When power is stable and all levels are acceptable, the power supply sends a Power Good (PWRGD) signal to the processor and timer chip. It might take up to half a second for the power supply to stabilize and, during this time, the timer chip has been continually sending reset signals to the processor, preventing it from executing code. When the timer chip receives the Power Good signal, it stops sending reset signals to the processor, which in turn allows the processor to commence the execution of code. The Intel processor is designed to start its execution of code from a specific place in the memory map, that is, at the segment:offset address of FFFF:0000. This is just 16 bytes from the top of the 1 Mbyte real mode memory where the start of the ROM BIOS is located.

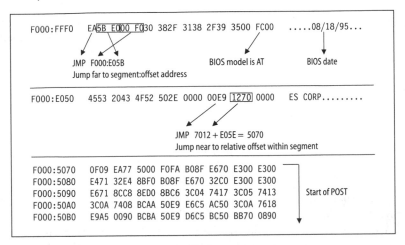

Fig. 5.23 Start of the bootstrap sequence.

At Fig. 5.23 we have shown the start of the bootstrap code sequence in three separate sections. The code sequence is shown starting in ROM BIOS at F000:FFF0, which is precisely the same external address as FFFF:0000 that is referred to in the previous paragraph. The code listing segment and offset addresses are shown in this particular format in the figure to make address references contained in the code easier to place. In the upper section of Fig. 5.23 is the commencement of the code for the *cold boot*. The instruction sequence EA 5B E0 00 F0 decodes as a far jump (code EA) to a full segment:offset address which follows in the next four bytes. However, we need to recall that Intel implements *little endian* storage, which means that the two bytes 5B E0 must be switched to become the 16 bit value E05B and the two bytes 00 F0 become F000. In addition, we need to note that the offset address is the first pair and the segment address is the second pair. Hence the jump is to the absolute address F000:E05B. The remaining ten bytes to the top of memory hold data concerning the date of the BIOS and the model of PC for which it is designed.

The middle section of Fig. 5.23 shows the code that is located at address F000:E05B, the location to which the first section has caused the microprocessor to jump. The code starts 0Bh bytes into the F000:E050 line with the sequence E9 12 70. This decodes as a near *relative* jump (code E9), meaning that the segment address value is the current segment and the offset address value is taken to be relative to the current address value. We have to note first the little endian reversal of the two address bytes from 1270 to become 7012 and then that the starting address of the *next* instruction is E05E which is the value that has to be added to the relative address 7012. This gives E05E + 7012 = 5070 using 16 bit arithmetic. The result therefore is an instruction to jump within the current segment (F000) to an offset address of 5070.

The bottom section of Fig. 5.23 shows part of the code that starts at this address. It is in fact the start of the Power On Self Test, or POST, sequence and we will be looking at some of the processes carried out by these code sequences in the next section.

Before we leave Fig. 5.23, however, it is useful to note that in some systems the EA 5B bytes at the beginning of the cold boot sequence are replaced by the code bytes CD 19 after the cold boot has completed. These translate to INT 19h, which is the *warm* boot BIOS interrupt which gets activated by the CTRL-ALT-DEL keyboard sequence on most systems. In case you might be wondering how code in read-only memory gets changed, the answer is of course, that it does not. This change can only be made if the BIOS code has been placed in shadow RAM, in which case it is the shadow RAM version that gets changed and not the ROM itself.

Typical Actions by POST

The POST sequence software, held in the ROM BIOS, initializes as necessary and then carries out diagnostic tests on each of the various hardware components of the system. Before entering each step in the sequence, the BIOS writes a one-byte identifying code, usually to I/O port 80h, which signals a successful completion of the previous step. This code is commonly referred to as a *POST code*.

By means of a special *POST code reader* the last valid code sent to the port can be observed. Such a reader may simply consist of an ISA plug-in card with a seven-segment display to show the POST code value. In the event of a hardware failure, often signalled by some kind of system lockup, the value on this display can give a good indication of the device that has failed by taking note of the last action that was successful. BIOS and motherboard handbooks often include a table of port 80h POST codes[62] and specialist software can be obtained that operates in conjunction with a POST reader to identify POST code values for a range of current BIOSes. An example screenshot from a typical program (MicroSystems, undated) of this type is shown at Fig. 5.24.

The reason for needing POST codes is not difficult to see. Because much of the POST diagnostic testing is taking place before the display system has been activated,

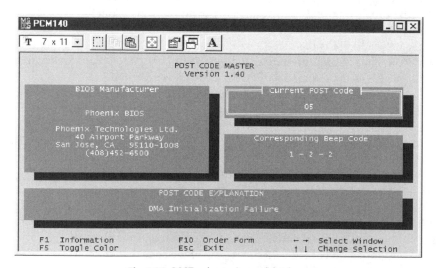

Fig. 5.24 POST code monitor and database.

---

62 The codes seem to be unique to the particular BIOS. See, for example, Appendix 3 and Intel (1998a, p. 75).

error messages cannot be written to the screen, as they would be when the display becomes active. It is for this reason that the system speaker is used to generate so called *beep codes*. As well as writing a POST code to port 80h, the BIOS will, when there is an error, send a specific sequence of beeps to the system speaker. Some beep codes are simply a number of same length beeps, some are a combination of low and high tones, some are a series of long and short beeps and some are a series of beeps and pauses. These latter are usually shown as 1-2-2-3, which is read as: 1 beep, pause, 2 beeps, pause, 2 beeps, pause, 3 beeps. The meanings of each of these beep sequences should be listed[63] in BIOS and motherboard handbooks together with any BIOS text error messages which might be written after the display becomes active.

One point of significance for the forensic computing analyst is that a successful completion of all the POST diagnostic tests normally results in a single short beep being sent to the speaker just prior to the loading of the operating system. Making a note in the log on hearing this short beep can provide some useful formal assurance that the computer concerned was operating correctly at the time that it was being used, in that it had signalled a successful passing of all of its POST diagnostic tests. At one time, a "Section 69" certificate was a legal requirement, whereby an analyst was required to certify that any computer equipment used in preparing evidence was working correctly at the time that it was used. Although this is no longer essential, it is still good practice to log such tests.

The POST first tests individual functions of the processor, its registers and some instructions; see Table 5.13. If the processor passes these tests, a checksum is then computed for each of the ROMs that form the BIOS and these computed values are compared with those that had originally been stored within the ROMs when they were programmed to give some assurance that the BIOS code has not become corrupted. A similar check is made of the CMOS RAM, which we will consider further in a moment. Each chip on the main board is then tested and initialized as necessary. These include the DMA controller, the keyboard controller, the first 64 kbyte of RAM, the interrupt controller, the cache controller and the video controller.

Table 5.13 Typical actions by POST – part I.

- Perform function check of CPU
- Test BIOS ROM checksum
- Test CMOS RAM checksum
- Test/initialize DMA controller
- Test/initialize keyboard controller
- Check first 64 kbyte RAM
- Test/initialize interrupt controller
- Test/initialize cache controller
- Test/initialize video controller

---

63 See Appendix 4 and Intel (1998b, p. 57).

Table 5.14 Typical actions by POST – part II.

- Test/initialize serial and parallel interfaces
- Check RAM above 64 kbyte
- Test/initialize floppy disk and hard drive controllers
- Set up BIOS variables
- Set up the interrupt vector table
- Search for BIOS extensions
- System and video BIOS may be transferred to shadow RAM
- Initiate bootstrap loader

Of course, once the video controller has been tested and initialized, any POST error messages can then be sent directly to the display screen.

After the main board has been tested, the POST tests the other peripherals, such as the serial and parallel interfaces and the remaining RAM above 64 kbyte; see Table 5.14. It then tests and initializes the floppy disk and hard drive controllers before setting up the BIOS variables.

The BIOS data area, as we may have noted from Fig. 5.22, is located at the very beginning of the real mode memory. It is 256 bytes long starting at address 0040:0000 (00400) and it is sometimes called the *BIOS variable range* or the *BIOS variable segment* (Tischer and Jennrich, 1996, p. 67 *et seq.*). In particular, at 0040:0072 (00472) is a marker which indicates whether this is to be a *warm boot*, for which the main memory checks are not carried out, or a *cold boot*. If the value is 1234h it is to be a warm boot; for all other values, it is to be a cold boot. The values in this segment can be examined and interpreted using specialist software such as Biosr.com (Postuma, 1995).

The CMOS RAM

The POST routines obtain some of the information that is required to establish the BIOS variables from the CMOS RAM; see Table 5.15.

The original PC-AT had 64 bytes of CMOS battery-backed RAM that was part of the Motorola MC 146818 real-time clock chip. More recent systems (Intel, 1998a, p. 18) contain 256 bytes of CMOS battery-backed RAM in the real-time clock chip which is all reserved for use by the BIOS. The CMOS RAM is not included in the real mode memory address space. but is accessed via the port addresses[64], 70h and 71h, of the real-time clock. As we saw earlier, disk drive parameters as well as many other motherboard configuration details are held in the CMOS RAM, which replaces the multitude of onboard DIP (Dual In-Line Package) switches which were to be found on the old PC-XT.

Because of the importance of this configuration information and, in particular, because the hard disk might not boot if the disk geometry parameters in the CMOS

[64] 70h is used to specify the CMOS address with an OUT instruction and 71h is used to read or write data to that address using an IN or OUT instruction respectively.

Table 5.15 CMOS RAM.

- Complementary Metal Oxide Semiconductor
  - 64 bytes of battery-backed RAM
  - Contains BIOS user-adjustable configuration details
  - Replaces multitude of DIP switches
- SETUP
  - Used to alter the CMOS settings
  - Entered during boot via F1 key, for example
- Typical settings
  - Date and time
  - Hard drive types and geometry
  - Memory configuration
  - Power management
  - Password protection

RAM become corrupted[65], it is a good idea to save the details on to a separate floppy disk. A typical example of software specially written for the purpose of saving and restoring the CMOS RAM details is the program CMOSRAM2.EXE (Mosteller, 1995).

To allow the user to alter the CMOS settings, the BIOS gives access to a program called SETUP during the boot sequence. SETUP is normally entered by pressing a special key combination such as DEL or ESC or CTRL-ESC or F1 or F2, to name but a few examples, just after the POST diagnostic sequence has completed. On the other hand, some BIOSes permit SETUP to be entered at any time by pressing, for example, CTRL-ALT-ESC.

Typically the CMOS RAM will contain information such as the date and time settings, the hard drive types and disk geometry parameters, the memory configuration (including any EMS and shadow memory), and any power management or password protection settings, as well as the checksum, referred to above, which is used by the POST routines to confirm that none of the CMOS data has become corrupted. Some SETUP programs may permit the CHS disk address translation mode to be set using terms such as NORMAL, LARGE and LBA. The meanings of these terms are as follows:

SETUP name	Translation method	Disk addressing method
NORMAL	None	CHS
LARGE	Revised ECHS	CHS or LBA
LBA	LBA Assist	LBA

Most modern BIOSes will perform an automatic translation setting using AUTO which issues the ATA command IDENTIFY DEVICE and obtains the relevant information from the disk itself.

Continuing with POST

After setting up the BIOS variables, the interrupt vector table is built; see Table 5.14. We discussed interrupts earlier and saw that they force the processor temporarily

---

65 Which, of course, will inevitably happen when the CMOS backup battery dies.

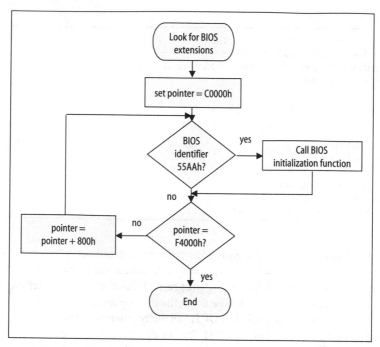

Table 5.25 Search for BIOS extensions.

to suspend the program currently being executed, saving enough information to permit a subsequent return, and then to execute some interrupt handler program associated with the interrupt number. We also saw that an interrupt may be caused either by an external hardware event or by an internal software code.

In fact, all well-behaved calls to the BIOS and the MS-DOS functions are made via internal software code interrupts. The Intel 8088 microprocessor design has some 256 interrupt vectors in its interrupt vector table and each entry in the table, as we have seen, consists of four bytes: the 16 bit offset address and the 16 bit segment address of the start of the program code for that particular interrupt. The table is located from address 0000:0000 (00000) to address 0000:03FF (003FF) and it is this table that is built at this time.

Because the vector table is held in RAM and is rebuilt each time we go through the POST/boot sequence, interrupt vectors can easily be overwritten if new or modified facilities need to be added. This is typically what happens at POST/boot time when extension cards have been added which themselves contain either replacement or updated BIOS functions in their own onboard ROM chips.

Part of the POST/boot sequence includes the search for BIOS extensions, as shown in the flowchart of Fig. 5.25, which is the next step in the process. These, you will recall, are in the memory area C000:0000 (C0000) to F400:0000 (F4000), so the search is carried out across this area by looking for the two identifier bytes 55AAh which always start a BIOS extension code sequence[66]. If a BIOS extension is found, the initialization function for that extension is called at this time. This will often add or alter a vector in the interrupt vector table thus enabling subsequent execution of code resident in the BIOS extension ROM in preference to the code of the standard BIOS function.

Once the search for BIOS extensions is complete, the POST/boot sequence may then copy BIOS program code into shadow RAM to improve performance before, finally, initiating the *bootstrap loader* as described in the next section.

Initiating the Bootstrap Loader

All bootable floppies have a *boot sector* placed by high-level formatting at the standard fixed position of cylinder 0, head 0, sector 1, on the floppy disk. Similarly, all hard disks have a *master boot record* placed at the same position of cylinder 0, head 0, sector 1 on the hard disk. In this way, both DOS and the BIOS can access floppy and hard disk bootstrap information without knowing which form of data carrier is being used. At the end of POST, the BIOS code reads the sector at cylinder 0, head 0, sector 1 by means of INT 19h[67] which in turn uses INT 13h to access a disk drive. It tries first the floppy drive[68], and if a floppy disk is present it reads from that. If a floppy disk is not present, it tries the hard disk[69], and reads from that. In either case, it loads a 512 byte sector from the disk at CHS address (0, 0, 1) into memory starting at address 0000:7C00 (07C00). Once the sector has been written into memory, the BIOS code branches to the first byte at offset 00h of the sector in memory and the processor starts to execute the values it finds there as program code.

If the sector has been loaded from a floppy disk, these first few bytes will cause a jump to the start address of the bootstrap loader, the code for which is held within the sector that has just been loaded. Also included in this sector is the *BIOS Parameter Block* or *BPB*, which is a table of values placed immediately after the jump instruction. As the bootstrap loader code for an MS-DOS system executes, it checks to see whether the hidden system files IO.SYS and MSDOS.SYS[70] are present on the disk. If the loader program finds them, they too are loaded into main memory to build the MS-DOS operating system and the bootstrap loading process continues. If these files are not found, we then get the familiar "Non-System disk or disk error..." message.

---

66 Following the two-byte 55AAh identifier is a one-byte size of ROM field in units of 512 bytes, and after this is a two-byte relative address field of the start of the initialization function.

67 It is INT 19h that is invoked when we depress the CTRL-ALT-DEL keys for a warm boot.

68 For most modern BIOSes, the order in which boot devices are to be accessed can be changed in SETUP.

69 Alternatively, the system could be set to boot from a CD or a network.

70 IBMBIOS.SYS and IBMDOS.SYS in the case of PC-DOS.

If, on the other hand, the boot is taking place from a hard disk rather than a floppy disk, the first few bytes at the beginning of the sector will cause a jump to the start address of the *partition analysis program*, the code for which is contained within the sector that has just been loaded. This program looks at the partition table, also contained within the sector that has just been loaded, and determines which (if any) is the current *active* (or *bootable*) *partition* on the hard disk. Having determined the addresses of the active partition from the partition table, it then reads the first sector of that partition, loading the 512 bytes of the sector into memory again starting at address 0000:7C00 (07C00), and overwriting what is already there. From here, it continues as for the floppy disk case, jumping to the first byte at offset 00h of the sector in memory and starting to execute the values it finds there as program code. This should be the code of a partition boot sector containing a BIOS Parameter Block, just as for the case of the floppy disk. In many ways, the hard disk partition appears to the system just like a large floppy disk. We will look at this process in some more detail when we have looked at the master boot record and the partition tables.

It is important to note that the processor is still at this stage switched to 16 bit real mode. As such, it is using the segment:offset addressing system that we have described above. Further, it should be noted that all the disk accesses have been made by means of legacy INT 13h calls. Only when the code for a more advanced operating system has been loaded and starts to execute, will there be the possibility of switching the processor to protected mode, of directly accessing the extended memory via the protected mode addressing system, of using 32 bit functions, and of using drivers that enable true LBA access. It is for these reasons that we need to be familiar with all the apparently outdated legacy issues that we have been discussing in the last few sections.

A Word About Other Systems

One of the difficulties about writing a practitioner's guide on the foundations of a rapidly changing subject is in trying to stay focused on the essential principles without becoming too sidetracked into explaining about other, less frequently encountered systems, or in becoming bogged down in a mass of technical detail about the latest technologies and developments. However, we also have to be aware that some advances do significantly change the nature of the practitioner's work and it is essential that we do cover these areas in sufficient detail.

In almost all the computers that we have encountered in our forensic case work to date, the operating systems have been Microsoft Windows-based and the platforms have been the PC-AT. It is for this reason that we have concentrated our analysis and examples on these operating systems and on this platform. That is not to say that we do not recognize the existence of Apple Macs or Unix/Linux-based systems or even Itanium microprocessors and the Extensible Firmware Interface (EFI). It is just that, at this time, in the domain within which we are operating, they are not mainstream and the fundamental principles can be better explained using the mainstream examples.

It was for a similar reason, in the first edition of the book, that we concentrated solely on the FAT-based file system, since other file systems were rarely encountered at the time of writing. Now, the NTFS (New Technology File System) has assumed a much greater prominence on the Microsoft Windows PC platform, to the point where it is probably at least as frequently encountered as the FAT-based file systems. However, FAT-based file systems are still very relevant since they are invariably used for removable devices such as floppy disks and solid state media drives, as well as providing a simpler, and sometimes preferable, alternative to NTFS for certain PC systems as well as support for those operating systems that are not able to use NTFS.

The approach we have taken in this edition is to continue to use in this chapter the FAT-based file system as our exemplar in order to explain the principles. However, we have also incorporated an entirely new follow-on chapter which is devoted to the NTFS system.

In addition, we have continued to use master boot record partitioning for our examples and only note here in passing the 128 partitions that are possible with the GUID partition table (GPT) system that is used with the Extensible Firmware Interface. We have not discussed in what follows the Dynamic Disk facility that is provided with Windows 2000, Windows XP and Windows Vista.

The Master Boot Record and Partitions

At Fig. 5.26 is shown a hexadecimal listing of part of the master boot record (MBR) from a typical hard disk. As we have seen, the MBR is held at cylinder 0, head 0, sector 1 on the hard disk and it is, like nearly all sectors on modern hard disks, 512 (or 200h) bytes long. In the listing we have shown two parts of the sector: the first part is from addresses 00h to 2fh and the second part is from addresses 160h to 1ffh, which is at the end of the sector.

As we outlined above, the POST/boot sequence causes this sector to be loaded into memory at address 0000:7C00 (07C00) onwards and it then causes a jump to the first address at offset 00h executing what it finds there as code. In fact, for the example in Fig. 5.26, all the bytes up to 1bdh form the partition analysis program, which is here

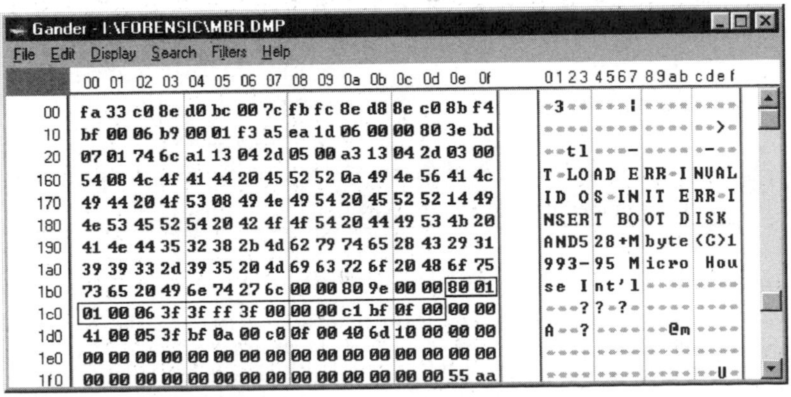

Fig. 5.26 Part of the master boot record.

different from the standard FDISK version because an EZ-Drive DDO has been installed on this disk. We can infer that this is the case by looking at the text bytes that start at 19ch and read: "(C)1993-95 Micro House Int'l". The standard FDISK version of the partition analysis program extends only from 00h to d9h with zeros from that point on to 1bdh. For an excellent exposition of how the standard partition analysis program works, see Landis (1997a).

Detailed examination of the analysis program shows that it simply searches the four entries in the partition table for an active partition. If an active partition is found, it continues to look at the remaining entries to make sure that there is only the one active entry, otherwise it displays the message "Invalid Partition Table". If there is only one active entry, it uses an INT 13h call to fetch the boot sector that is specified by the CHS start address of that entry, and it overwrites the memory area from 0000:7C00 (07C00) with this new sector. It then jumps to the first address at offset 00h of the sector keeping a pointer to the active partition table entry.

The partition table always starts at offset address 1beh in the master boot record sector. There can only be four entries in the master boot record partition table and each entry is 16 bytes long. The first entry of our example master boot record is shown outlined in Fig. 5.26. The four entries take us to offset address 1fdh in the sector and the final two bytes[71] of the partition table are always of value 55h and aah, as shown.

At Table 5.16 is shown the use of each of the bytes in the partition table entry. The first byte is the *boot flag*, which indicates whether or not the partition is active, the value being either 80h for active or 00h for not. It is useful to note that it is this boot flag value which is used to identify the device in the INT 13h call[72] to fetch the boot sector of the active partition. Because the active flag is always 80h, this is one of the

Table 5.16 Partition table entry.

Offset	Meaning	Notes
00	1 byte boot flag	80h = active (bootable) 00h = inactive (not bootable)
01–03	3 bytes start of partition	h7–h0 | c9 c8 s5–s0 | c7–c0 *max: c 1023, h 255, s 63*
04	1 byte partition type	0 = not used, 1 = DOS 12 bit FAT, 4 = DOS 16 bit FAT, 5 = Extended DOS, 6 = DOS > 32 Mbyte and many more
05–07	3 byte end of partition	h7–h0 | c9 c8 s5–s0 | c7–c0 *max: c 1023, h 255, s 63*
08–0b	4 bytes LBA address of start sector relative to start of disk (little endian)	
0c–0f	4 bytes number of sectors in the partition (little endian)	

71 Many systems will refuse to boot if these two bytes are not set to 55aah. This has been used by one imaging company in the past to set what they call a "Diblock" on a disk to prevent it from being further accessed by replacing 55aah with 55cfh in the MBR.

72 The value is loaded into the DL register.

reasons why, on some older systems, only the first hard disk, that is the device with the identifier 80h, could be used as the boot drive.

The next three bytes starting from offset 01h hold the CHS start address of the partition, that is, where the boot sector is. All eight bits of the first byte, offset 01h, are used to represent the heads value, giving a maximum of 256 heads (0 to 255). The two most significant bits of the second byte, offset 02h, together with the 8 bits of the third byte, offset 03h, form the 10 bit value for cylinders, giving a maximum of 1024 cylinders (0 to 1023). Finally, the remaining 6 bits of the second byte, offset 02h, form the sectors value with a maximum of 63 sectors (1 to 63). First we may note that this is exactly the same format as that used for the ID field at Fig. 5.4 and also the same format as that used by the INT 13h registers, where offset 01h equates to the DH register, offset 02h equates to the CL register and offset 03h equates to the CH register. This is not really surprising; the designers of the partition table decided to hold these values in a form that would simplify loading into and out of the INT 13h registers.

Secondly, we may note that we have here come up against the 528 Mbyte barrier again. More importantly we see that if the drive is larger than 528 Mbyte, then the CHS addresses that are held in the partition table must be *translated* addresses, that is, what we have earlier called L-CHS addresses rather than P-CHS addresses. Finally, we may note that the boot sector for the active partition cannot normally[73] reside beyond cylinder 1024.

The next byte, at 04h, indicates the type of partition. Although only five types are shown in Table 5.16, there are in fact many more than this, with a possible maximum of 256. Because of the importance of these types to the forensic computing analyst in helping to identify the use to which the partition is being put, a detailed list of all those currently known[74] is given at Appendix 5.

At offset 05h, another three bytes are used to specify the CHS address of the last sector of the partition, in exactly the same format as that used for the start address. Naturally, the same comments apply about this having to a be a translated CHS address if the disk size is greater than 528 Mbyte.

At offset 08h, four bytes are used to represent the start sector in LBA address form, that is, as a single number relative to the start of the disk, with the first sector on the disk being LBA 0. One word of caution might be appropriate here. In calculating this value it is essential to remember that it is held in little endian format. Finally, the last four bytes, commencing at offset 0ch, represent the number of sectors in the partition, again, held in little endian format.

This analysis allows us now to determine the meaning of all the entries in the partition table at Fig. 5.26. At 1beh the value 80h identifies this entry as the entry for the active partition. The following three bytes, at 1bfh to 1c1h, describe the starting CHS address of this active partition as cylinders 0, heads 1, sectors 1, and these may be calculated as follows:

---

73 Some more modern boot loaders are able to overcome this limitation.

74 An updated list can be found at http://www.win.tue.nl/~aeb/partitions/partition_types-1.html; see Brouwer (2005).

Address	Value	Interpretation			Result	
1bfh	01h	=	00000001	= heads	= 1	H
1c0h	01h	=	000001	= sectors	= 1	S
			00	= cylinders		
1c1h	00h	=	00000000	= cylinders	= 0	C

At 1c2h we note that the partition type is 06h, which is a DOS partition greater than 32 Mbyte, sometimes known as *BIGDOS*. Then the three bytes at 1c3h to 1c5h describe the CHS address of the end of the partition as cylinders 255, heads 63 and sectors 63 in the following way:

Address	Value	Interpretation			Result	
1c3h	3fh	=	00111111	= heads	= 63	H
1c4h	3fh	=	111111	= sectors	= 63	S
			00	= cylinders		
1c5h	ffh	=	11111111	= cylinders	= 255	C

Starting at 1c6h we have the four bytes of the LBA address as 3f 00 00 00. Recalling that this number is held in little endian format, we reorder these to be 00 00 00 3f and calculate the number as 3fh = LBA sector 63. Similarly, at 1cah we have the four bytes of the partition size as c1 bf 0f 00 and again, reordering these gives us 00 0f bf c1 which is fbfc1h = 1,032,129 sectors. With a sector size of 512 bytes this results in a partition size of $1{,}032{,}129 \times 512/(1024 \times 1024) = 504$ Mbyte.

At Fig. 5.27 is shown the Norton Disk Editor (Symantec, 1999) "partition table view" of the same partition table. It is particularly important to note that Norton Disk Editor uses *Side* for *Head* and lists the table in *Side Cylinder Sector* order and not in the CHS order that we (in common with most other writers) have been using throughout. Since Norton Disk Editor is an important tool, which we use quite frequently, this is a major potential source of confusion and should be well noted. It is

```
Physical Sector: Cyl 0, Side 0, Sector 1
+------+----+--------------------+--------------------+----------+------------+
|      |    | Starting Location  | Ending Location    | Relative | Number of  |
|System|Boot|Side Cylinder Sector|Side Cylinder Sector| Sectors  |  Sectors   |
+------+----+--------------------+--------------------+----------+------------+
|BIGDOS| Yes|  1     0      1    | 63    255     63   |    63    |  1032129   |
|EXTEND| No |  0    256     1    | 63    522     63   | 1032192  |  1076544   |
|unused| No |  0     0      0    |  0     0       0   |    0     |     0      |
|unused| No |  0     0      0    |  0     0       0   |    0     |     0      |
+------+----+--------------------+--------------------+----------+------------+
```

Fig. 5.27 Partition table entries – Norton Disk Editor partition table view.

now left as an exercise to the reader (see exercises at the end of the chapter) to confirm from Figs. 5.26 and 5.27 the details for the second (EXTEND) entry in the partition table.

Unwritten Rules for Partition Tables

As we described in the section on formatting, the partition table is constructed by the program FDISK (or some such similar utility) at the time the high-level formatting process is carried out. There do not seem to be any formal written rules laid down about how partition tables should work, although most versions of FDISK appear to conform with the set of unwritten rules (Landis, 1997b) that are shown in Table 5.17.

As we have seen, up to four 16 byte partition entries can be held in the master boot record partition table from 1beh to 1fdh. Each of these four entries may refer to a *primary* partition, that is, a partition that can contain a bootstrap loader in the first sector[75] together with associated operating system code elsewhere in the partition. There will normally be a file system, appropriate to the particular operating system, also set up in the partition. Any primary partition entry can be flagged as "active" or "bootable", but only one such partition entry can be flagged at any one time. When one primary partition is flagged as active, file systems in other primary partitions are not generally accessible; thus the file system in a primary partition is accessed, for all practical purposes, only by the operating system that is booted from that partition[76].

The partition analysis program in the master boot record looks for this one "active" or "bootable" partition entry and from this partition it loads the bootstrap loader, which in turn loads the operating system code from that partition into the

Table 5.17 Unwritten rules for partition tables.

- In the master boot record there can only be up to four *primary* partition entries *or* up to three *primary* partition entries and up to one *extended* partition entry.

- In an extended partition there can be up to one *secondary* partition entry and up to one *extended* partition entry.

- Only primary partitions can be marked as "active" (that is, bootable) and only one of them can be marked as such at any one time.

- It is usual for a partition table to start at head 0, sector 1 of a cylinder and the boot record to start at head 1, sector 1 of a cylinder.

- The slots in the partition table can be used in any order and an unused slot can occur in the middle of the table.

- Some operating systems may indicate that a partition spans or starts beyond cylinder 1024 by setting the starting and ending CHS values all to ffh.

---

75 This is the *boot sector*, sometimes also called the *boot record*.

76 More recent Microsoft Windows operating systems do now permit access to file systems that are in other primary partitions.

main memory. In this way, up to four[77] different operating systems may reside on the same hard disk, in different partitions, with only one of them being active at any one time. Special *boot manager* software (PowerQuest, 1998) may be used to select from a menu of different operating systems that may be loaded at boot time, and this is usually achieved simply by installing a modified partition analysis program in the master boot record and placing the associated boot manager code in unassigned sectors on the disk.

Extended Partitions

To overcome the limitation of having only four partitions on the disk, one of the entries in the master boot record partition table can be set instead to be an *extended* partition entry by means of the partition type values 05h or 0fh (see Appendix 5). This *first extended partition*, which takes up a primary partition slot, is essentially no more than a *container* for one or more enclosed *logical* or *secondary* partitions. The first sector of the first extended partition holds another partition table, with the rest of that sector usually set to zeros. This extended partition table (see Fig. 5.28) starts at the same offset address within the sector as the master boot record partition table, that is, at 1beh and although it is four 16 byte partition entries in length, terminated as before by 55h aah, it is only permitted to hold a maximum of *two* partition entries.

The first of these entries is likely to specify a *logical* partition, sometimes referred to as a *secondary* partition, and this partition may contain a file system and, exceptionally, an operating system. If an operating system is to be used, it must be one that is capable of being booted from a logical partition (as opposed to a primary partition). Operating systems which are believed to incorporate this feature include Windows NT, OS/2 and Linux[78]. The second entry in the extended partition table may specify another extended partition which itself starts with an extended partition table.

Terminology is likely to get in the way again here. These inner secondary extended partitions are rather different from the outer primary extended partition container,

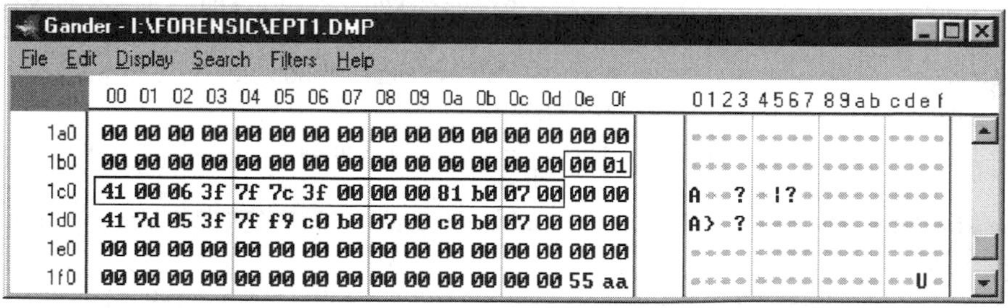

Fig. 5.28 Extended partition table.

---

77 However, some operating systems can be booted from an extended partition so it is possible to have more than four.

78 The Windows XP help file states: "*The active partition must be a primary partition on a basic disk*".

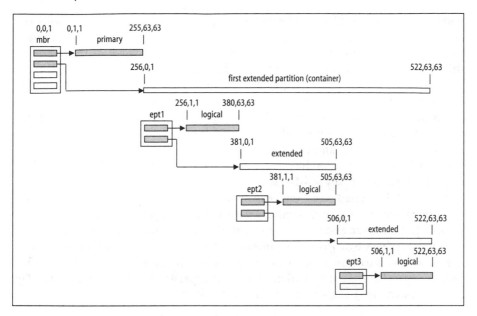

Fig. 5.29 Extended and logical partitions.

although the same partition type code is used throughout and they are all referred to simply as extended partitions. The outer or first extended partition is a container for all the logical partitions; the inner secondary extended partitions each contain just a single logical partition. This is shown diagrammatically at Fig. 5.29.

Here we see a master boot record[79] (marked mbr) at CHS 0,0,1 with two entries in the partition table. The first entry is a primary partition starting at CHS 0,1,1 and ending at CHS 255,63,63. This, in the example shown, is the active partition and contains the operating system. It would normally be assigned the drive letter "C:" by MS-DOS. The second entry is the first extended partition starting at CHS 256,0,1 and ending at CHS 522,63,63. This partition is never assigned a drive letter and, as can be seen from the diagram, it simply acts as a container for the three logical partitions. In the first sector (CHS 256,0,1) of the first extended partition we find the extended partition table[80] (marked ept1) and this contains two entries. The first is a logical partition starting at CHS 256,1,1 and ending at CHS 380,63,63. If there were no other drives with a primary partition in the system, this logical partition would be assigned the logical drive letter "D:" by MS-DOS (see following section for details of drive letter allocations). The second entry in the extended partition table at CHS 256,0,1 is a secondary extended partition. This starts at CHS 381,0,1 and ends at CHS 505,63,63. We can see from the diagram, that, unlike the first extended partition that contains all the logical partitions, this secondary extended partition only contains one logical partition. At the beginning of the partition (CHS 381,0,1), we find

---

79 This is the same master boot record as is shown in Figs. 5.26 and 5.27.

80 This is the same extended partition table as is shown at Fig. 5.28.

another extended partition table, marked ept2 in the diagram, again with two entries. The first entry is a logical partition starting at CHS 381,1,1 and ending at CHS 505,63,63. If there were no other drives with a primary partition in the system, this logical partition would be assigned the logical drive letter "E:" by MS-DOS. The second entry in the extended partition table, ept2, at CHS 381,0,1 is another secondary extended partition. This starts at CHS 506,0,1 and ends at CHS 522,63,63. At the beginning of this partition (CHS 506,0,1), we find another extended partition table, marked ept3, this time with only one entry. This entry is a logical partition starting at CHS 506,1,1 and ending at CHS 522,63,63. If there were no other drives with a primary partition in the system, this logical partition would be assigned the logical drive letter "F:" by MS-DOS.

It should be noted that our explanation of how extended partitions are constructed does not entirely conform with some of the published literature on the subject. It is, however, an accurate representation of what we have found in a series of experiments that we carried out in order to determine precisely the binary format of the extended partition structures when using the standard Micrososft FDISK functions. We have given more details of these experiments at Appendix 6, and Fig. 5.29 represents, in effect, a summary of our findings.

Drive Letter Assignments

Microsoft Knowledge Base Article 51978[81] describes in detail how MS-DOS (and this includes Windows 95, Windows 98 and Windows ME) assigns drive letters to partitions. In essence, drive letters are assigned at boot time in a fixed sequence that cannot be changed. Regardless of whether or not floppy disk drives are present (these always get assigned the drive letters A and B), MS-DOS assigns the drive letter C to the primary MS-DOS partition on the first physical hard disk. It then goes on to check for a second physical hard disk. If one is found with a primary MS-DOS partition on it, MS-DOS assigns to that partition the drive letter D. MS-DOS continues to assign successive letters of the alphabet to the first primary MS-DOS partitions found on all succeeding physical drives. When all physical drives have been checked for a first primary partition, MS-DOS returns to the first physical drive and continues to assign drive letters alphabetically to all logical drives that might be found in the extended partitions. MS-DOS repeats this process of assigning drive letters in sequence to logical drives across all the physical drives in order. Finally, MS-DOS again returns to the first physical drive and assigns drive letters to any other further primary MS-DOS partitions that might exist on the drive. It repeats this process for all the other physical drives.

From this it can be seen that MS-DOS (and Windows 95, Windows 98 and Windows ME) do not *remember* drive letter assignments between boots; rather, the drive letter assignment is re-determined for every single boot, and, given different drive configurations the drive letter assignment could well change between boots. If, for example, we had a system with two physical drives, each with a single primary

81 See http://support.microsoft.com/default.aspx?scid=kb;EN-US;51978.

partition and each with two secondary logical partitions, we would note after a boot with both disks fitted, the following drive letter assignment:

Disk 1 primary: C
Disk 2 primary: D
Disk 1 first logical: E
Disk 1 second logical: F
Disk 2 first logical: G
Disk 2 second logical: H

If, for the next boot, we removed the second disk, the drive letter assignment would become:

Disk 1 primary: C
Disk 1 first logical: D
Disk 1 second logical: E

From this, it can clearly be seen that the Disk 1 logical drive letters have both changed between the two boots, bringing with it all the attendant problems of possibly incorrect shortcuts and drive letter pointers. It may be of interest to note that some users of these early Windows systems would deliberately set the Disk 2 primary partition to be very small and hidden in order to avoid this problem. It is left as an exercise to the reader to work out what effect this would have.

This inability to remember the drive letter assignment does not occur, however, with Windows NT, Windows 2000, Windows XP and Windows Vista. With these operating systems it is possible to specify drive letter assignments using, for example, the "Disk Management" application and to know that they will be *remembered* between boots. How this is achieved is explained in the next section.

Disk ID and Partition Signature

Windows NT, 2000, XP and Vista keep a list of all mounted partitions, each identified by a unique *partition signature*, together with the assigned drive letter, in the registry key [HKEY_LOCAL_MACHINE\System\MountedDevices]. By referring to these entries the operating system is able to *remember* the drive letters assigned to each partition between boots.

The partition signature is made up of the *disk ID* (also known as the NT Serial Number) which is the four bytes that are recorded by these operating systems at address 01B8h in the master boot record, together with the starting sector number of the particular partition multiplied by 2. Shown at Fig. 5.30 is a portion of a more recent master boot record, that has been generated using Windows XP, and which incorporates this disk ID, which is seen to be of value "46 A9 46 A9".

It may also be seen that the starting sector number of the first (and only) partition, shown here in little endian, is "3F 00 00 00". The partition signature for this partition is then generated as the following construct:

```
46 A9 46 A9 00 7E 00 00 00 00 00 00
```

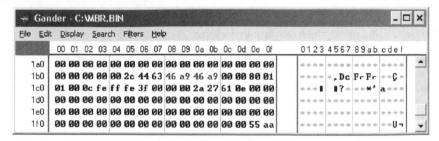

Fig. 5.30 Disk ID and Start Sector Number.

This is made up of the disk ID, "46 A9 46 A9", followed by "00", followed by the starting sector number "3F 00 00 00" doubled to give "7E 00 00 00", followed in turn by "00 00 00". If we look in the registry associated with this system, we find under HKEY_LOCAL_MACHINES\SYSTEM\MountedDevices\ the following two keys:

- The key: DosDevices\C:, which contains the value "*46 A9 46 A9 00 7E 00 00 00 00 00 00*", the partition signature that we have just constructed, and we can see that this entry defines the drive letter for this partition as C:
- The key: ??\Volume{BF77BEC6-9779-11D8-AAA6-806D6172696F}, which also contains the value "*46 A9 46 A9 00 7E 00 00 00 00 00 00*", the partition signature that we have just constructed, and we can see that this entry defines what is called the *Volume GUID* (Globally Unique Identifier) for this partition as "{BF77BEC6-9779-11D8-AAA6-806D6172696F}".

A Brief Note on GUIDs

From the "11D8" section of the GUID we can determine[82] that this is a version 1 GUID with a date and time based section of the following value: "1D8-9779-BF77BEC6". This may be interpreted as the count of 100 nanosecond intervals since 00:00:00.00, 15 October 1582 (the date of Gregorian reform to the Christian calendar). This value resolves[83] to 12:03:36 GMT on 26/04/2004, which is probably the date and time on the PC when the Volume GUID was first established. From this it can be seen that Volume IDs and GUIDs can potentially prove very useful to a forensic computing analyst.

Disk Mapping

We strongly recommend that all disks that are submitted for forensic analysis should be mapped in the detail that we have shown in Fig. 5.29. For completeness we recommend that partition size and operating system information and LBA address

---

82 For details of the structure see Leach (1998) or (Leach *et al.*, 2004).

83 This can be calculated using the "Timescale Interconverter" provided by Stockton (2005).

values are also added to such disk maps, which can then be used by the analyst to identify and investigate all the unaddressed areas on the disk. We return to this subject in Chapter 7.

Circular Extended Partitions

Mike Lambert and Charles Moore (1992) describe the effects that can occur in the presence of a so-called *circular extended partition*. This is where one of the entries in an extended partition table points back to an extended partition table that is earlier in the chain. For example, consider, in Fig. 5.29, the case where the second entry of ept3, instead of being blank, points back to ept1. We have now implemented a circular extended partition. This carries the risk that some disk analysis routines, attempting to determine how many logical drives exist on the disk, will loop forever around the sequence ept1, ept2, ept3, ept1, ept2, ept3... etc. In fact, as we describe below, many versions of IO.SYS, right up to the time of writing (2007), still do just that.

One of the tasks of IO.SYS, during the bootstrap sequence, is to mount the logical volumes. To do this, it first examines the master boot record partition table to determine whether or not an extended partition entry is specified. If one is found, it then progresses through the extended partition chain finding and mounting each logical volume in turn. If the chain is circular, however, IO.SYS might not terminate because of a coding error.

In the course of discussing the Rainbow virus, which uses the circular extended partition technique to make it more difficult to remove[84], Lambert (1995) describes the symptoms as follows: "...*when booted, the operating system load hangs and the hard disk access light stays on steadily. The kernel is hung in a loop, reading the same block (or circular chain of blocks) from the hard disk...*".

Now, the apparently obvious work around is to attempt a boot from a floppy disk. However, this will not work either if the version of IO.SYS on the floppy disk contains the same coding error. The outcome is that the PC cannot be booted with the offending disk fitted to the system. This has very important implications for the forensic analyst, since the disk appears to be unusable and therefore cannot be imaged or examined.

Lambert (1995) notes that this problem occurred with all Microsoft, IBM and DR-DOS versions implementing extended partitions up until December 1992, but that he and Moore notified all three operating system developers in September/October 1992. However, in 1995, he goes on to state (Lambert, 1995) "*Microsoft v6.0, v6.2, v6.21 and v6.22 all still have the same bug in IO.SYS, meaning that MS-DOS v3.3 to 6.22 (PC-DOS v3.3 to 5.02 and DR-DOS v6.0) will not boot in the presence of a circular extended partition. IBM v6.1 and v6.3 do not have the bug. As I have not been able to test with the latest version of DR-DOS, I do not know if the problem has been corrected as yet*".

---

84 When booted from the Rainbow infected hard disk, the virus loads first and uses the original non-circular partition table that it has stored at 0,0,6, thus hiding the problem. When booted from a clean floppy, IO.SYS may loop as described in this section.

There are two possible solutions for the forensic analyst on encountering these symptoms. One is to use a version of DOS that does not contain the IO.SYS coding error, such as FreeDOS[85] or Caldera OpenDOS[86]. The second is to use a patch for MS-DOS 6.x that has been provided by Lambert that simply prevents IO.SYS from carrying out the extended partition analysis. Using a hexadecimal editor, find in IO.SYS the sequence 07 72 03 (which should start at offset 2918h) and change the 03 at offset 291Ah to 06 and write the result back to disk. This will prevent the looping so that the hard disk can be examined and the circular extended partition removed. Note, however, that this patched version of MS-DOS will not mount the logical volumes.

Hidden Partitions

It is possible, using specialist software, to mark a partition as "hidden" such that many operating systems will no longer access it. PartitionMagic (PowerQuest, 1996) uses a partition type of 16h to hide a primary DOS partition originally of type 06h. More generally, it seems that many hidden partitions can be obtained by performing an OR function on the partition byte with the value 10h. This is certainly the case for partition bytes 01h, 04h, 06h, 07h, 0bh, 0ch, 0eh, 0fh and 83h resulting in the hidden equivalents 11h, 14h, 16h, 17h, 1bh, 1ch, 1eh, 1fh and 93h (see Appendix 5). One possible benefit of hiding a partition, apart from the obvious one of attempting to conceal information, has already been outlined in the section above on Drive Letter Assignments.

More Places to Hide

As indicated in Fig. 5.29, it is normal practice for partition tables (mbr or ept) to start at head 0, sector 1 of a cylinder, and for the first sector of the partition proper, that is the boot record, to start at head 1, sector 1 of a cylinder. The consequence of this practice is that there will invariably be a number of unused sectors at the beginning of each partition, between the partition table sector and the boot record sector. For example, in Fig. 5.29 it can be seen that sectors CHS 0,0,2 to CHS 0,0,63, sectors CHS 256,0,2 to CHS 256,0,63, sectors CHS 381,0,2 to CHS 381,0,63 and sectors CHS 506,0,2 to CHS 506,0,63 are all unused[87]. Clearly, information could be safely hidden in these sectors without any risk of it being detected by normal use of the file systems. As we described earlier (see section on CHS Translation Options), some of these sectors are precisely where software such as EZ-Drive places its Dynamic Drive Overlays (DDOs). These are also very good places to look for hidden virus code.

---

85 See http://www.freedos.org/.

86 See http://www.caldera.com/.

87 Note that the gap of 62 sectors is because of a sector per track (spt) size of 63. Some disks, for example the Western Digital WDAC2420, have 56 sectors per track and thus this will have a spacing of 55 sectors between partition table and boot record.

In addition, we may note that only the master boot record (mbr) normally contains a partition analysis program. The extended partition tables (ept1, ept2 and ept3) just contain the one or two entries of the extended partition table starting at 1beh and invariably leave the rest of the sector unused. Again, this is a possible place to hide information.

The Example Boot Sector – Windows 95 FAT16

We should now return to the example boot sector (sometimes also referred to as a *boot record*), which we considered briefly in a previous section. We may recall that floppy disks have a boot sector placed at cylinder 0, head 0, sector 1 of the disk by the high-level formatting process. Similarly, a boot sector or boot record is placed in the first sector of each primary or logical partition on a hard disk when that partition is formatted. As mentioned earlier, this means that each formatted hard disk partition looks to the system in many ways just like a big floppy disk.

At Fig. 5.31 we have shown a hexadecimal listing of the first few bytes of the actual boot sector at cylinder 0, head 1, sector 1 of the primary partition that is referred to in Figs. 5.27 and 5.29. It is shown in Fig. 5.27 as the entry marked "BIGDOS", meaning that it is an MS-DOS file partition that may exceed 32 Mbyte in size. Most of the boot sector contains the bootstrap loader program code that we referred to above, but, in addition, there is a block of data called the *BIOS parameter block* (*BPB*) that contains detailed information about the particular floppy disk or hard disk partition on which this boot sector resides. It should be noted, in passing, that although each operating system will follow the same rules for creating the master boot record and the partition tables, they can do whatever they like within the partition and they will almost certainly have their own boot sector format.

Recalling that this MS-DOS boot sector will have been loaded into memory starting from address 0000:7C00 (07C00), the first bytes to be executed as program code will be:

```
0000:7C00   EB3C   JMP to 7C02 + 3C
0000:7C02   90     NOP
0000:7C03   4D     Start of BIOS parameter block
...
0000:7C3E   FA     Start of loader program
```

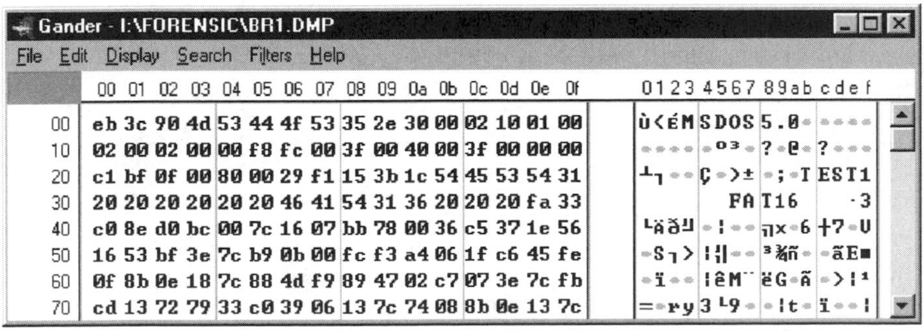

Fig. 5.31 Hexadecimal view of part of the boot sector or boot record.

This code represents a relative jump around the BIOS parameter block to the start of the loader program at 0000:7C3E (07C3E). The loader program then gets a copy of the disk parameter table, modifies it using information from the BIOS parameter block and then sets an interrupt vector to point to the altered disk parameter table. It then computes the start sector address of the root directory, and reads the first sector of the root directory into memory. It confirms that the first two entries in the root directory are the hidden system files IO.SYS and MSDOS.SYS, and if this is the case, it then reads the first three sectors of IO.SYS into memory. If this is not the case, it causes the message "Non-System disk or disk error ..." to be displayed. Finally, once the three sectors of IO.SYS have been successfully loaded into memory, the bootstrap loader transfers control to the beginning of the IO.SYS program which then proceeds to build the rest of the operating system. For an excellent analysis of the floppy disk boot sector code see Landis (1995b).

The BIOS parameter block starts at 0000:7C03 (offset 03h in the boot record) and continues to 0000:7C3D (offset 3dh in the boot record) inclusive. The details of all the information held in this parameter block are shown at Table 5.18. Listed here are the offset addresses in hexadecimal form from the boot record of Fig. 5.31 together with the use to which each field is put, the values in hexadecimal obtained from Fig. 5.31

Table 5.18 BIOS parameter block.

Offset	Use	Hex values	Meaning
00–02	Jump instruction	eb 3c 90	Jump
03–0a	OEM name and version	4d 53 44 4f 53 35 2e 30	MSDOS5.0
0b–0c	Bytes per sector	00 02	512
0d	Sectors per cluster	10	16
0e–0f	Reserved sectors	01 00	1
10	Number of FATs	02	2
11–12	Root directory entries	00 02	512
13–14	Total sectors (unused)	00 00	0
15	Media descriptor byte	f8	f8h
16–17	Sectors per FAT	fc 00	252
18–19	Sectors per track	3f 00	63
1a–1b	Number of heads	40 00	64
1c–1f	Hidden sectors	3f 00 00 00	63
20–23	Big total sectors	c1 bf 0f 00	1032129
24	Physical drive number	80	128
25	Reserved	00	0
26	Extended boot signature	29	29h
27–2a	Volume serial number	f1 15 3b 1c	1c3b15f1h
2b–35	Volume label	54 45 53 54 31 20 20 20 20 20 20	TEST1
36–3d	File system ID	46 41 54 31 36 20 20 20	FAT16

```
Sector 0
                                    OEM ID: MSDOS5.0
                           Bytes per sector: 512
                         Sectors per cluster: 16
                 Reserved sectors at beginning: 1
                                 FAT Copies: 2
                       Root directory entries: 512
                        Total sectors on disk: (Unused)
                        Media descriptor byte: F8 Hex
                              Sectors per FAT: 252
                            Sectors per track: 63
                                      Sides: 64
                        Special hidden sectors: 63
                 Big total number of sectors: 1032129
                       Physical drive number: 128
               Extended Boot Record Signature: 29 Hex
                        Volume Serial Number: 1C3B15F1 Hex
                                Volume Label: TEST1
                              File System ID: FAT16
```

Fig. 5.32 The boot sector – Norton Disk Editor boot record view.

and the interpretation that is to be placed on each field. Note, once again, that all the decimal numbers are converted using little endian format.

Although it is important to be aware of the low-level details, we do not need to do all this interpretation ourselves. At Fig. 5.32 is shown the Norton Disk Editor Boot Record view of the same boot sector listed at Fig. 5.31. From this we can obtain many of the details about the hard disk partition. The first point of interest to note is the Norton Disk Editor reference in the heading to "Sector 0". This is because Norton Disk Editor is being used in "logical" mode, that is, a mode in which the sectors are counted from zero from the beginning of the logical partition. This is in contrast with "physical" mode, where sectors are counted from the very beginning of the hard disk itself. The corresponding physical mode heading produced by Norton Disk Editor for this boot record is either "Physical Sector: Cyl 0, Side 1, Sector 1" or "Physical Sector: Absolute Sector 63".

The first item of Fig. 5.32 identifies the operating system[88] for which this partition was formatted and we note that this partition has the standard 512 bytes per sector. We also see that there are 16 sectors to the *cluster*, and this is a term which we will be discussing in a later section. The "Reserved sectors at beginning" entry refers to the number of sectors reserved for the boot record. In all the MS-DOS systems that we have seen, this has always been a single sector as it is also in the case of Windows 95 FAT16. However, for Windows 95 FAT32 and Windows 98 FAT32, more than one

---

88 For floppy disks, we will often find that this field contains ASCII characters, such as: ",&%|PIHC", the last three letters invariably being "IHC" as shown. This is a "disk id" that is written by Windows to any floppy disk that is not write protected so that Windows can detect when floppy disks are swapped. Once written by Windows, this sequence will remain the same for any further reads or writes until the disk is reformatted. Some believe that "IHC" are the first three letters, reversed, of "CHICAGO", the original code name for Windows.

sector is allocated for the boot record and we discuss the reasons for this in a later section.

Two independent copies of the *File Allocation Table* (*FAT*) are kept because this is the key means by which resources are allocated to files, and any damage to the FAT can cause serious loss of data. Keeping two copies helps reduce the risk of data loss. Again, we will discuss the FAT in more detail in a later section. The *root directory* is of fixed size in FAT16 systems and the "Root directory entries" figure defines how many directory entries can be held in this partition. Here we see a figure of 512 and since each entry is 32 bytes long, this indicates that the root directory is $512 \times 32 = 16,384$ bytes or 32 sectors in size. In passing, it is worth noting that this next field "Total sectors on disk" was one of the reasons for the infamous 32 Mbyte maximum partition size that existed for MS-DOS versions before version 3.0. Only two bytes are available for this value (see offsets 13–14h in Table 5.18), which give us 65,536 as the maximum number of sectors and results in a maximum partition size of 65,536 $\times$ 512 = 32 Mbyte. This problem was overcome in MS-DOS version 3.0 and above by using an alternative field of 4 bytes ("Big total sectors") at offsets 20–23h in the boot sector. The "Total sectors" field is now only used if the size of the volume is small enough, otherwise it is normally set to zero. The "Media descriptor byte" identifies the kind of medium that is in use; here we see f8h, which signals that this is a hard disk as opposed to some specific floppy disk. A variety of media types are defined for the various floppy disks, but only one value, f8h, is used for all hard disks. Details of the specific hard disk can, of course, be obtained from the CMOS RAM. The size of each FAT is given here as 252 sectors and then there are figures for sectors per track (63) and number of heads (64) both entirely as expected. The "Special hidden sectors" entry refers to the number of sectors on the disk before the start of the first partition and this is the "Relative Sectors" number we noted before against the BIGDOS entry in the partition table at Fig. 5.27. Similarly, we saw the "Big total number of sectors" figure of 1,032,129 as the "Number of Sectors" value for the same BIGDOS entry in the partition table at Fig. 5.27. The "Physical drive number" is 128 or 80h indicating that this is drive 0 and the next three entries are just signatures and labels. Finally, the "File System ID" signals that this is formatted as a DOS FAT16 partition.

The MS-DOS operating system uses *logical sector numbers* (*LSNs*) which start from 0 at the very beginning of the partition. Given the details from the boot record, and knowing that MS-DOS FAT16 uses a fixed structure of boot sector, FAT 1, FAT 2, root directory and files area, we can now draw up the layout of this logical partition as seen by MS-DOS. The first sector (LSN 0) contains the boot record and then there are 252 sectors for the first FAT (LSN 1 to LSN 252), followed by a further 252 sectors for the second FAT (LSN 253 to LSN 504). After this comes the root directory with 32 sectors (LSN 505 to LSN 536) and finally the start of the files area proper at LSN 537, which would appear to continue to LSN 1,032,128 (that is, the "Big total number of sectors" less 1, since LSN counting starts at 0). However, the files area only actually extends to LSN 1,032,120, and this is because of the cluster size, which we will be looking at in the next section. The details of this partition are shown at Fig. 5.33.

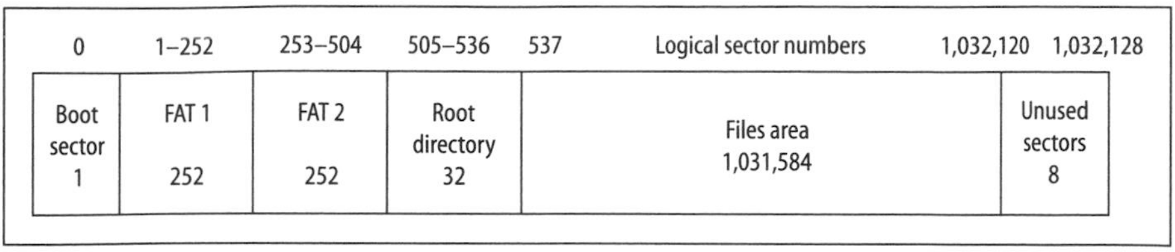

0	1–252	253–504	505–536	537	Logical sector numbers	1,032,120	1,032,128
Boot sector 1	FAT 1 252	FAT 2 252	Root directory 32		Files area 1,031,584		Unused sectors 8

Fig. 5.33 Layout of the partition.

Another Possible Hiding Place

It is possible to produce yet another hiding place on both floppy and hard disks, which cannot be addressed in the normal way through the file or operating system, by tampering with the "Total sectors" and "Big total sectors" fields in the boot record. As an example, reducing the value in the "Big total sectors" field at Fig. 5.32 from 1,032,129 to 516,065 would nearly halve the size of the volume within the partition. The last LSN for the new volume would now be 516,064, and the sectors from LSN 516,065 to LSN 1,032,128 would not be addressable by the file or operating system. It should be noted that the partition table in the master boot record has not been altered to achieve this effect (see Fig. 5.27). An analyst should be aware that it is prudent to examine these fields in the boot records of all floppy and hard disk partitions to ensure that they have not been modified to produce more possible hiding places. This applies to all FAT and NTFS disks.

FATs, Directories and File Systems

From the viewpoint of MS-DOS, each hard disk partition (or floppy disk) provides us with a set of logical sectors, each normally of 512 bytes in size, which are sequentially numbered from 0 to the end of the partition or floppy disk. However, we need more than just a sequence of sectors to make an effective file management system. We need to have structures in place that permit the sectors to be viewed as a set of files. There are two fundamental requirements here: one is for a means by which a file can be named and its characteristics be recorded, and the other is for a mechanism by which files, which use more than just a single sector, can have their sector numbers recorded in an appropriate order. A number of strategies are possible to meet these two requirements, and different operating systems typically use different approaches, with the result that they are rarely compatible with one another. MS-DOS meets the first requirement by means of the root directory[89] and the second requirement by means of the File Allocation Table or FAT. Before looking at the specific details of our example partition, we will consider the principles as outlined in Fig. 5.34.

---

89 There was only the root directory for MS-DOS version 1. Since version 2, subdirectories are also permitted as we will see later.

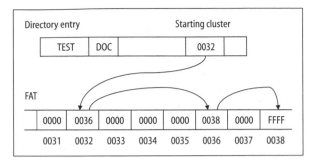

Fig. 5.34 Principles of the MS-DOS file system.

FATs and Clusters

Here we see a much simplified directory entry for a file called TEST.DOC. The original
MS-DOS file naming scheme allows for 8 upper-case[90] characters in the file name
and 3 upper-case characters in the file extension. By convention, when writing down
a reference to the file, the file name is shown separated from the file extension by a
period; hence the reference: TEST.DOC. This example directory entry has been
simplified by removing references to various file characteristics such as the file
attributes, the time and date created and the file size, for example, and we will be
coming back to all this in a moment. What is shown in the entry is a numeric pointer
to a logical starting *cluster* or *allocation unit* for the file. For the time being we will
make the assumption[91] that the cluster is equivalent to a sector. The pointer here
shows that the first part of the file TEST.DOC starts in logical cluster 0032.

The lower part of the diagram shows some of the entries in the File Allocation
Table or FAT. At entry 0032 we find a pointer to logical cluster 0036. This indicates
that the second part of the file TEST.DOC is contained in logical cluster 0036. At entry
0036 we find a pointer to logical cluster 0038. This indicates that the third part of the
file TEST.DOC is contained in logical cluster 0038. Finally, at entry 0038 we find the
value FFFF which signals the end of the cluster sequence. What the combination of
the directory entry and the FAT has told us is that the file TEST.DOC is contained in
the cluster sequence 0032–0036–0038. This system permits files to be spread over any
number of clusters, which need not be either sequential or contiguous. Clearly, there
are improvements in access time to be obtained if the clusters of a file are sequential
and contiguous since disk head movement is then minimized. After a period of use,
the file system is likely to become fragmented with portions of files spread all over
the partition. For this reason, *defrag* programs are often used to reassign, as far as
possible, sequential and contiguous cluster sequences to all files in order to improve
the file access efficiency.

Referring back to Fig. 5.33, we may note that the first logical sector number
available to the files area is LSN 537. Continuing, for the moment, with our

---

90 Together with numerals and a limited set of other symbols.

91 Which is correct for floppy disks.

assumption that clusters are equivalent to sectors, this would then form logical cluster 2. You may wonder why clusters should start at 2 and not 0. Cluster 0 in the FAT would have to have a reference to it of 0000, and since this value is used in the FAT to indicate a free cluster it could not, of course, be allocated. In addition, this first cluster was used by MS-DOS Version 1 to determine the type of disk (see later section) and is still used today to hold a copy of the Media byte value from the BPB (see offset 15h, Table 5.18) in its low 8 bits, with all other bits set to 1. Cluster 1 in the FAT is set by the FORMAT program to the end of cluster chain mark, which for FAT16 is FFFFh. In addition, the file system driver may use the two most significant bits of the Cluster 1 entry as *dirty volume flags* with all other bits left set to 1. These flags are used to indicate when a mounted volume has not been updated or dismounted cleanly and action by a disk checking program is required on the next boot. Note, from a forensic viewpoint, that when Windows mounts a volume it will very likely change these flags in the FAT unless it is prevented from doing so by some form of write blocking device. Windows might also attempt to establish recycle bins on each volume as well as altering the last accessed dates and times on many files and changing the contents of several of the system files. All of this, of course, alters the original evidence and should never be allowed to occur.

FAT12, FAT16 and FAT32

We have now made several references variously to FAT16, FAT32, 16 bit FATs and 12 bit FATs and it is perhaps useful at this stage to consider what these mean. They all simply refer to the number of bits used in the FAT table to describe one entry. So, a 12 bit FAT (FAT12 or more often just FAT) uses 12 bits (1.5 bytes) per FAT entry, a 16 bit FAT (FAT16) uses 16 bits (2 bytes) per FAT entry and a 32 bit FAT (FAT32) uses 32 bits (4 bytes) per FAT entry. Note, however, that a FAT32 entry is actually only a 28 bit entry for the FAT itself, since the four most significant bits of each entry are reserved for other purposes. The possible values that may be given to each entry in the FAT are listed at Table 5.19. In addition to what has been described before, we see that FF7h (and FFF7h and 0FFFFFF7h) are used to mark a cluster as bad, FF8h to FFEh (and FFF8h to FFFEh and 0FFFFFF8h to 0FFFFFFEh) are reserved and FFFh (and FFFFh and 0FFFFFFFh) are the markers for the last cluster in a file[92]. In passing, we may note that clusters marked in the FAT as bad are another possible place where information could be hidden.

There has been some lack of clarity in the past over precisely what FAT system type should be used for any particular disk size and it is likely that a number of disks with incompatible FAT systems exist as a result. Microsoft have produced a definitive document for their operating systems (Microsoft, 2000), and within it is the following statement: "*This is the one and only way that FAT type is determined. There is no such thing as a FAT12 volume that has more than 4084 clusters. There is no such thing as a FAT16 volume that has less than 4085 clusters or more than 65,524 clusters. There is no such thing as a FAT32 volume that has less than 65,525 clusters. If you try*

---

92 Note, however, that there are various disk utilities for Microsoft operating systems that use a different value for the last cluster in a file marker; see Microsoft (2000).

Table 5.19 FAT cluster values.

FAT12	FAT16	FAT32	Meaning
000h	0000h	00000000h	Available for allocation
001h	0001h	00000001h	Never used
002h	0002h	00000002h	Next cluster in file
...	...	...	Next cluster in file
FF5h	FFF5h	0FFFFFF5h	Next cluster in file
FF7h	FFF7h	0FFFFFF7h	Bad cluster
FFFh	FFFFh	0FFFFFFFh	Last cluster in file

to make a FAT volume that violates this rule, Microsoft operating systems will not handle them correctly because they will think the volume has a different type of FAT than what you think it does".

The original MS-DOS FAT used 12 bits per entry and the consequence of this is that only 2^{12} (that is, 4096) allocation units or clusters can be addressed. In fact the number is less than this since 000h and 001h are not used and FF6h to FFFh are reserved or used for other purposes leaving 002h to FF5h (2 to 4085) as the range of possible clusters. If we are to use one sector per cluster, as we have assumed above, the maximum number of sectors that we can address is 4084 (the maximum number of clusters for FAT12 according to the Microsoft statement above) and at 512 bytes per sector this gives us $4084 \times 512 = 2,091,008$ bytes, which is slightly less than 2 Mbyte. This would mean that the largest disk that we can deal with is only 2 Mbyte in size. This is quite satisfactory for conventional floppy disks and is precisely what is used by MS-DOS for the standard floppy disk. For larger disks, however, we need to use more than one sector per cluster.

For disks up to 16 Mbyte, Microsoft systems used to use eight sectors per cluster with a 12 bit FAT (making the cluster size $8 \times 512 = 4$ kbyte) and this gives us a maximum size of 4084 (the maximum number of clusters for FAT12 according to the Microsoft statement above) $\times$ 4096 (the cluster size in bytes) $= 16,728,064$ bytes, which is just under 16 Mbyte. However, the following statement has been included in the Microsoft (2000) document: *"If your media is larger than 4 MB, do not bother with FAT12. Use smaller BPB_SecPerClus[93] values so that the volume will be FAT16".* For example, if we had an 8 Mbyte disk (8,388,608 bytes) and specified 2 sectors per cluster (1,024 bytes), it would require 8,388,608/1,024 = 8,192 allocation units. This exceeds the 4084 maximum for FAT12 and would therefore force the format to be FAT16.

For disks between 16 Mbyte and 2 Gbyte, Microsoft systems use a series of powers of 2 sectors per cluster (see Table 5.20) up to a maximum of 64 sectors per cluster (making the cluster size $64 \times 512 = 32$ kbyte). This gives us a maximum size of 65,524 (the maximum number of clusters for FAT16 according to the Microsoft statement above) $\times$ 32,768 (the cluster size in bytes) $= 2,147,090,432$ bytes, which is just under 2 Gbyte.

---

93 This is the name given to the BPB sector per cluster field.

Table 5.20 Microsoft hard disk cluster sizes up to 2 Gbyte.

Logical drive size	FAT type	Sectors per cluster	Cluster size
0–4 Mbyte	12 bit	8	4 kbyte
4.1–15 Mbyte	16 bit	2	1 kbyte
16–127 Mbyte	16 bit	4	2 kbyte
128–255 Mbyte	16 bit	8	4 kbyte
256–511 Mbyte	16 bit	16	8 kbyte
512–1023 Mbyte*	16 bit	32	16 kbyte
1024–2047 Mbyte*	16 bit	64	32 kbyte

The significance of the cluster size is, of course, that this is the smallest unit of disk memory that can be allocated at a time. Even if we have a file of only one or two bytes, we are forced to allocate a minimum of 32 kbyte to that file if the disk is larger than 1024 Mbyte and we are using FAT16. Prior to the introduction of FAT32 there were, therefore, real advantages in partitioning a large disk into a number of smaller logical partitions in order to reduce the cluster size in each of the partitions and hence the amount of wasted space. This wasted space between the end of the file and the rest of the cluster is known as *slack space*. The cluster size and the FAT type are decided by the FORMAT program when high-level formatting is carried out on the partition and the rules applied are those that are given in the Microsoft (2000) document.

You may have noted that the largest sectors per cluster value in Table 5.20 is 64, resulting in a cluster size in bytes of 32,768. The reason for this limit, apart from not increasing further the amount of wasted space, is understood to be that some 16 bit programs make the assumption that the cluster size in bytes (which must be a power of two) will always fit into a 16 bit word. The value 32,768 (or 64 sectors per cluster) does fit, but the next power of two, 65,536 (or 128 sectors per cluster) does not, since the range in 16 bits is 0 to 65,535. The consequence of this is that no normal FAT16 partition may exceed 32,768 (the maximum cluster size in bytes that will fit into a 16 bit word) times 65,524 (the maximum number of clusters for FAT16 as given in the Microsoft (2000) document) which, as stated above, is just under 2 Gbyte. This is where the 2 Gbyte maximum partition limit comes from. Although it is possible, using Windows NT utilities, to produce FAT16 partitions which have 128 sectors per cluster (64 kbytes) and are 4 Gbyte in size, such partitions are not recommended by Microsoft (see Microsoft, 1999a) for use with MS-DOS or Windows 9x.

Returning for a moment to Fig. 5.33, we can now also see why the files area does not extend to the very end of the partition. The total number of sectors available for the files area in Fig. 5.33 is 1,032,128 − 536 = 1,031,592. Dividing this by the cluster size, 16, we obtain 64,474 clusters, with a remainder of 8 sectors. This means that the last 8 sectors in the partition cannot be addressed by the file system, which extends only to LSN 64,474 × 16 + 536 = 1,032,120. This lost area, in this case of 8 sectors, is called "Volume Slack" by some authorities and is yet another good place to hide information.

Table 5.21 Microsoft hard disk cluster sizes for FAT32.

Logical drive size	FAT type	Sectors per cluster	Cluster size
512–1024 Mbyte*	32 bit	8	4 kbyte
1–2 Gbyte*	32 bit	8	4 kbyte
2–8 Gbyte*	32 bit	8	4 kbyte
8–16 Gbyte	32 bit	16	8 kbyte
16–32 Gbyte	32 bit	32	16 kbyte
> 32 Gbyte	32 bit	64	32 kbyte

With Windows 95 OEM Service Release 2 (OSR2) and Windows 98, Microsoft (see Microsoft, 1999b) introduced an updated version of the FAT system called FAT32. This uses four bytes (32 bits) per FAT entry and can address up to $2^{28} = 268,435,456$ clusters; 2^{28} rather than 2^{32} because the most significant four bits of each entry are reserved (see section above).

Given that the maximum possible number of sectors is $2^{32} = 4,294,967,296$ (see "Big total sectors" offset 20–23 in Table 5.18) and we could address them all at 16 sectors per cluster, ($16 \times 268,435,456 = 4,294,967,296$) we could have disks as large as $4,294,967,296 \times 512 = 2,199,023,255,552$ bytes = 2 Tbyte. In practice, a number of different powers of 2 sectors per cluster are used for different disk sizes in a manner similar to that for FAT16 and the details for FAT32 are shown in Table 5.21. A cluster size of 8 sectors per cluster (4 kbyte) is used for volumes up to 8 Gbyte, 16 sectors per cluster (8 kbyte) for volumes up to 16 Gbyte, 32 sectors per cluster (16 kbyte) for volumes up to 32 Gbyte, and 64 sectors per cluster (32 kbyte) for volumes above 32 Gbyte.

In both Tables 5.20 and 5.21, the 512–1024 Mbyte and 1–2 Gbyte entries are shown marked with an asterisk. This is to indicate that although disks in these size ranges can be formatted as FAT16, they will normally be formatted by default as FAT32.

The other major difference with FAT32, is that the root directory is no longer of fixed size but is held in a cluster chain just like all other files.

Boot Sector and BPB Differences between FAT12, FAT 16 and FAT32

In the first implementation of the FAT file system (MS-DOS version 1), there was no BPB[94] in the boot sector and the determination of the media type, of which only two were possible[95], was carried out by looking at the first byte of the FAT itself as we mentioned above. This was changed in MS-DOS version 2 by placing a BPB in the boot sector. This BPB only allowed for a FAT volume with less than 65,536 sectors due to the fact that the "Total sectors" field was only two bytes in size and this resulted in the 32 Mbyte limit, again as we mentioned above. This limitation was lifted in MS-

---

94 In Microsoft (2000) a distinction is made between table entries that are deemed to be part of the boot sector and table entries that are deemed to be part of the BPB. We have not made that distinction here.

95 Either single-sided or double-sided 360 kbyte 5.25-inch floppy disks.

Table 5.22 Additional BIOS parameter block for FAT32.

Offset	FAT32
24–27	Count of sectors occupied by one FAT
28–29	Flags
2a–2b	Revision number
2c–2f	First cluster of root directory
30–31	Sector number of FSInfo (normally 1)
32–33	Sector number of copy of boot sector (normally 6)
34–3f	Reserved
40	Physical drive number (as for offset 24 in FAT16)
41	Reserved (as for offset 25 in FAT16)
42	Extended boot signature (as for offset 26 in FAT16)
43–46	Volume serial number (as for offsets 27–2a in FAT16)
47–51	Volume label (as for offsets 2b–35 in FAT16)
52–59	File system ID (as for offsets 36–3d in FAT16)

DOS 3 where the BPB was modified to include a new alternative 4 byte field for the "Big total sectors" value.

With the introduction of FAT32 in the Microsoft Windows 95 operating system (OSR2), the BPB was again modified. This new version exactly matches the FAT12 and FAT16 BPB up to but excluding offset 24h (see Table 5.18). Thereafter, the changes are as shown in Table 5.22.

It should be noted that the FAT32 boot record is contained in *three* logical sectors: 0, 1 and 2. Each of these sectors has the values "55 AA" in the last two bytes of the sector. The BPB and initial bootstrap code are contained within sector 0 and an information structure called FSInfo is normally held in sector 1 (see offset 30–31, Table 5.22). Much of the code which enables the boot record to read FAT32 entries is held in sector 2. A copy of all three sectors of the boot record is normally held in sectors 6 to 8 (see offset 32–33, Table 5.22).

The FSInfo structure contains two signatures, a lot of reserved space and two entries that might be useful for an analyst to examine, namely: a count of free clusters and the next available cluster. The count of free clusters is a 4 byte field located at offset 1E8h from the start of the sector. If the value is FFFFFFFFh, then the count is unknown, otherwise it is the last known count of free clusters on the volume. The literature helpfully tells us that it might not be correct! The four byte value at offset 1ECh is a hint to the FAT driver of where to start looking for the next free cluster. Again, if its value is FFFFFFFFh there is no hint, otherwise it might be the next available free cluster.

The Example FAT

At Fig. 5.35 we have shown, in Norton Disk Editor FAT view, a small part of the first FAT for the same example partition that we referred to in Figs. 5.31, 5.32 and 5.33 and

```
Sector 1
Clusters 2 - 255
                             3          4          5          6       <EOF>         8
                9         10         11      <EOF>         13         14         15        16
               17         18      <EOF>          0          0          0          0         0
                0          0          0      <EOF>      <EOF>      <EOF>      <EOF>         0
                0          0          0          0          0          0          0         0
                0          0          0          0          0          0          0         0
                0          0          0          0          0          0          0         0
                0          0          0          0          0          0          0         0
```

Fig. 5.35 The 1st FAT – Norton Disk Editor FAT view.

Table 5.18. From this we can readily see that one file probably starts at cluster 2, continues with clusters 3, 4 and 5, and ends with cluster 6. It is a safe bet that the next file starts with cluster 7 and continues with 8, 9 and 10 and ends with cluster 11. However, to confirm all this, we really need to examine the root directory, and it is this that we will look at next.

The Root Directory

As described earlier, MS-DOS directory entries are each 32 bytes in length. The first 8 bytes of the entry (see Table 5.23) are the eight characters of the file name, padded out, if necessary, with spaces (20h) to the end of the field.

The first byte of the file name has a special significance depending upon its value. If it is 00h, it indicates that the entry has not been used before and we have reached the last entry in the directory list. If it is e5h, which corresponds to the character "σ", then the directory entry has been deleted. We will look at file and subdirectory deletion in a later section. If it is the value 05h, then this indicates that the first file name character should be "σ", which cannot, of course be stored as itself without signalling a deleted entry! Finally, if it is the value 2eh, which corresponds to the character ".", this signifies that this entry refers to a directory, and we will say more about that in a moment.

Table 5.23 32 byte directory entry.

Offset	Meaning
00–07h	Filename 8 bytes padded with spaces
08–0ah	File extension 3 bytes padded with spaces
0bh	File attributes 1 byte
0c–15h	Reserved (MS-DOS 1.0–6.22) 10 bytes
16–17h	Time of last change 2 bytes
18–19h	Date of last change 2 bytes
1a–1bh	First cluster 2 bytes
1c–1fh	File size 4 bytes

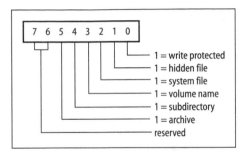

Fig. 5.36 File attributes byte.

The next three bytes are the three characters of the file extension, again padded out as necessary with spaces (20h) to the end of the field. It should be noted that the period that conventionally separates the file name from the file extension in all MS-DOS 8.3 references is not actually held in the directory entry.

The next byte in the sequence is the file attributes byte; see Fig. 5.36. This indicates whether the file is write-protected, hidden, a system file or changed since it was last backed up by an archive program. In addition, the entry may, instead of referring to a file, be a volume label or a subdirectory. If the volume label bit is set, and only one entry in the root directory may have this bit set, the file name and file extension fields are taken together without an intervening period as the 11 byte volume name for the partition. If the sub directory bit is set, the "first cluster" field points to a subdirectory rather than to a file, though in many ways a subdirectory can be considered as a special case of a file.

The next 10 bytes in the directory entry are reserved in MS-DOS 1.0 to MS-DOS 6.22. In passing, we should note that seven of these bytes are used in MS-DOS 7 and in Windows 9x for additional date and time information and two of them are used in FAT32 systems to specify the additional two bytes (making four in all) that are required for the "first cluster" value (see later section).

Following the reserved bytes are two bytes (in little endian order) used to specify the time of last change made to the file and then a further two bytes (also in little endian order) to specify the date of last change made to the file. These four bytes have a very specific structure, as shown in Fig. 5.37. Looking at them in sequence, having remembered to reorder them to account for their being in little endian, the first five bits specify the hours, the next six bits specify the minutes and the last five bits specify the number of two-second intervals. To obtain the actual seconds we need to

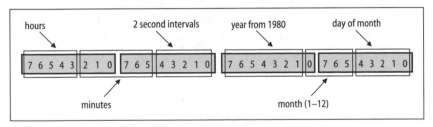

Fig. 5.37 Time and date field bytes.

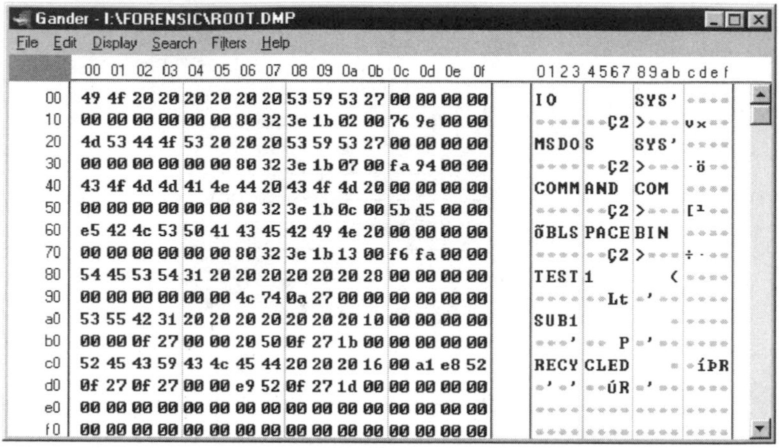

Fig. 5.38 Hexadecimal view of the root directory.

multiply the value from this field by 2. For the date fields, the first seven bits specify the number of years since 1980, the next four bits specify the month number, 1 to 12, and the last five bits specify the day of the month, 1 to 31.

The next field in Table 5.23 identifies the starting cluster for the file or subdirectory to which this entry refers. For FAT16 we simply need the two bytes as given here, but for FAT32, as mentioned above, two more bytes are needed, and these are taken from the reserved field. Note that these numbers are all little endian and that, for FAT32, the "first cluster" field contains the least significant values.

The final field in Table 5.23 is the file length in bytes and this is held little endian in the last four bytes of the entry.

At Fig. 5.38 we have shown the root directory details in hexadecimal of the example partition. Taking the first entry we see that at offsets 00–07h is the file name IO padded out with spaces and at offsets 08–0ah is the file extension SYS. At offset 0bh is the file attributes byte of value 27h, and this represents a write-protected, hidden, system file with the archive bit set. Offsets 0c–15h are not used and are set to 00h. At offsets 16–17h is the time of the last update as 3280h, reordered from little endian. In binary this is 0011 0010 1000 0000, and when divided up as in Fig. 5.37 this is equivalent to 00110 hours, 010100 minutes, and 00000 × 2 seconds, giving us 06:20:00. Similarly, the date of the last update is at offsets 18–19h and is 1b3eh, reordered from little endian. In binary this is 0001 1011 0011 1110 and when divided up as in Fig. 5.37 this is equivalent to 0001101 years from 1980, 1001 number of month, and 11110 day of month, giving us 30/09/1993. At offsets 1a–1bh is the first cluster number in little endian, that is 0002, and finally, at offsets 1c–1fh is the file size in little endian, that is 00009e76h, which is equivalent to 40,566 in decimal.

Deleted Files

Immediately below the three files IO.SYS, MSDOS.SYS and COMMAND.COM specified in this root directory, there is a deleted file which used to be DBLSPACE.BIN, starting at offset 60h. The first character of the name has been overwritten with the deleted marker e5h. When files are deleted in the MS-DOS file system, the directory entry for the file is not removed; it is simply marked as deleted in this way. If we look at the first cluster field for the file at offsets 7a–7bh we find that the value 0013 (decimal 19) is still present as is the original file size at offsets 7c–7fh of 0000faf6h (decimal 64,246). If we look, however, at the FAT table of Fig. 5.35, we see that clusters 19 to 26 are all set to 0, although clusters 27 to 30 are in use, all marked with <EOF>. This suggests that the DBLSPACE.BIN file originally used clusters 19 to 26, but these were returned to the available pool once the file had been deleted. What is important from a forensic viewpoint, however, is that on deletion of a file, MS-DOS does not delete the information contained in the clusters; it merely marks them as available for reallocation. It is therefore quite possible to restore a file that has been deleted provided that the clusters of the file have not been reused. The deleted directory entry will often contain details of the first cluster and the file length, as is the case here, and this can greatly assist the process. Utility programs, such as UNDELETE.EXE and UNERASE.EXE, attempt to automate the recovery of deleted files, but an analyst using Norton Disk Editor, for example, is likely to be much more effective in difficult cases.

The degree of success obtained in undeleting a file is obviously related to the likelihood of the original file clusters being reallocated by MS-DOS. In early versions of MS-DOS (1.0 and 2.0), a search for the next free cluster to be allocated was always made from the beginning of the FAT, but in later versions a more complicated algorithm is used, and an unused cluster near the other clusters of the file being extended is sought.

Volume Label and Subdirectory Entries

The next entry beneath the deleted file entry is a volume label, TEST1, and beneath that are two subdirectory entries, SUB1 and RECYCLED. Examination of the volume label shows that the volume name extends over the 11 bytes of offsets 80–8ah and is padded out with spaces. The file attributes byte at 8bh is of value 28h and this signifies that the volume name and the archive bits are set. The time field, at offsets 96–97h, is 744ch, and this gives 0111 0100 0100 1100 which divides up as 01110 hours, 100010 minutes and 01100 × 2 seconds, and results in 14:34:24. The date field, at offsets 98–99h, is 270ah, and this gives 0010 0111 0000 1010 which divides up as 0010011 years from 1980, 1000 number of month, and 01010 day of month, and results in 10/08/1999. The first cluster field at offsets 9a–9bh and the file size field at offsets 9c–9fh are both seen to be zero.

For the subdirectory, SUB1, a similar analysis could be performed and here we would find that the directory bit is set in the file attributes byte at offset abh (value is 10h) and that the first cluster is at 001bh (offsets ba–bbh) which is decimal 27.

Although it is important to be able to analyse the details in this way, Norton Disk Editor provides a directory view which can be used to show most of this information for us. Such a view of the example directory is given at Fig. 5.39.

From our previous analysis, all the entries in the table of Fig. 5.39 should be self-explanatory. The start sector of the root directory is 505, which conforms with our analysis at Fig. 5.33. The only unexplained item is the heading 76, which simply refers to the two reserved bits, 7 and 6, in the attribute byte.

```
Sector 505
Name      .Ext ID       Size      Date      Time     Cluster   76 A R S H D V
--------------------------------------------------------------------------------
IO         SYS  File    40566    30/ 9/93   6:20am        2      A R S H - -
MSDOS      SYS  File    38138    30/ 9/93   6:20am        7      A R S H - -
COMMAND    COM  File    54619    30/ 9/93   6:20am       12      A - - - - -
ōBLSPACE   BIN  File    64246    30/ 9/93   6:20am       19      A - - - - -
TEST1           Vol         0    10/ 8/99  14:34pm        0      A - - - - V
SUB1            Dir         0    15/ 8/99  10:01am       27      - - - - D -
RECYCLED        Dir         0    15/ 8/99  10:23am       29      - - S H D -
```

Fig. 5.39 Norton Disk Editor directory view of the root directory.

In passing, we might also note that the RECYCLED subdirectory has been added automatically to our partition by Windows 98. It is a system, hidden, directory and it is noteworthy because it breaks our forensic rules of not changing the evidence during examination. As was mentioned earlier, using Windows to examine a disk, without a write blocker in between, will result in changes such as this being made.

We should note that for FAT12 and FAT16, the size of the root directory is fixed and is given in offsets 11–12h of the BIOS Parameter Block as the number of 32 byte entries. For FAT32, however, the root directory is of variable size and is a cluster chain just like any other file. Its starting cluster is given in offsets 2c–2fh of the BIOS Parameter Block.

Subdirectories

As mentioned above, a subdirectory can be considered to be a special case of a file. It is, in fact, a file that contains directory entries in just the same format as the root directory. The contents of a subdirectory may be file entries or further subdirectory entries, but, unlike the FAT12 and FAT16 root directories, because subdirectories are specified as a cluster chain they are not constrained to being of fixed length.

At Fig. 5.40, we have shown a hexadecimal view of the subdirectory SUB1. In common with all subdirectories, the first two entries are pre-defined. The first, as can be seen from offsets 00–0ah is called "." and stands for this directory itself. Its attribute byte at offset 0bh has just the directory bit set (10h) and the first cluster value at offsets 1a–1bh is 001bh or decimal 27, which from Fig. 5.39 we can see is the first cluster of this subdirectory SUB1.

The second entry at offsets 20–2ah is similarly called ".." and this stands for the parent directory of this directory. The parent, in this case, is the root directory and the first cluster for that is shown at offsets 3a–3bh as 0000. Apart from these two entries, all the other entries in the subdirectory will either be file name entries or subdirectory entries in the form that we have seen before, with one exception, that of the *long file name* (*LFN*), which can also occur in the root directory.

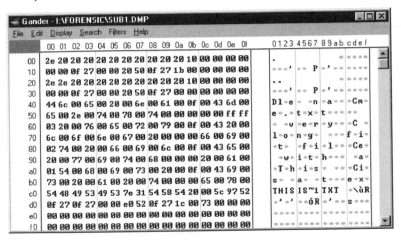

Fig. 5.40 Hexadecimal view of a subdirectory.

Long File Names

At Fig. 5.41, we have shown the Norton Disk Editor directory view of the sub directory, SUB1, that we were examining in hexadecimal form at Fig. 5.40. This shows clearly the two entries for "." and ".." and confirms the details that we established above. It also shows four entries marked LFN and a normal file entry named THISIS~1.TXT.

With Windows 95 and 98, Microsoft removed the limitation of only 8 characters for the file name and 3 characters for the file type from file and directory names and introduced the so-called *long file name*, which can be up 255 characters in length. Both upper- and lower-case letters are permitted in long file names and the range of other characters that may be used has also been increased. However, in order to maintain compatibility with MS-DOS and to continue to operate within the existing file systems, the long file name is spread over a number of standard 32 byte directory entries and it is always matched with a *short file name (SFN)* alias which conforms to the old 8.3 naming conventions. Windows automatically generates the SFN alias from the long file name. In our example case, the long file name is This is a text file with a very long file name.txt, and the SFN generated by Windows is

```
Cluster 27, Sector 937
Name      .Ext ID     Size     Date      Time     Cluster    76 A R S H D V
-------------------------------------------------------------------------------
.              Dir        0   15/ 8/99   10:01am       27      - - - - D -
..             Dir        0   15/ 8/99   10:01am        0      - - - - D -
le name.txt    LFN                                     0      - R S H - V
 very long fi  LFN                                     0      - R S H - V
t file with a  LFN                                     0      - R S H - V
This is a tex  LFN                                     0      - R S H - V
THISIS~1 TXT   File     115   15/ 8/99   10:23am       28      A - - - - -
```

Fig. 5.41 Norton Disk Editor directory view of the subdirectory SUB1.

THISIS~1.TXT. Although the actual generation algorithm is quite complicated in detail, most of the principles are clear from this example. Lower case is translated to upper case, spaces are removed and the first six characters of the resulting LFN are then used followed by a "~" and a digit to make the SFN up to 8 characters. If there is a file extension specified, the first three characters of this are used. The reason for the "~" and the digit at the end is to permit Windows to differentiate from, say, another long file name such as This is a shorter file name.txt which would then receive an SFN of THISIS~2.TXT[96].

One consequence of this approach that it is important for a forensic analyst to be aware of is that SFNs of copied files, which are generated by Windows at the time of the copy, may be different in different directories. This is because the value of the last digit in the SFN will depend upon whether there are one or more files with similar starting LFNs in the directory to which the copy is being made. Although the LFN of the copied file will always be the same as the original, the SFN of the copied file might not be the same. This means that we could have LFNs of the same name and referring to copies of the same file residing in different directories each having entirely different SFNs. We could also have SFNs of exactly the same names in different directories referring to entirely different files.

Returning to our subdirectory entry for THISIS~1.TXT at Fig. 5.41, we see that this is in exactly the same format as that for the other files we have seen at Fig. 5.39. What we do need to look at a little more closely are the four LFN entries which specify the long file name. We can see that as many 32 byte directory entries as are necessary are used to record the LFN. Each entry can hold a maximum of 13 characters of the long file name, since each of the characters is recorded in *Unicode* and requires two bytes to represent it.

A Brief Digression on Unicode and UTF

Unicode and Unicode Transformation Format (UTF) are today a rather complex subject. A useful outline of Unicode and the development of UTF is given in Davis (1999), from which the following quotes are taken: "*In the beginning, Unicode was a simple, fixed-width 16-bit encoding. Under its initial design principles, there was enough room in 16 bits for all modern writing systems. But over the course of Unicode's growth and development, those principles had to give way. When characters were added to ensure compatibility with legacy character sets, available space dwindled rapidly.... Unicode needed an extension mechanism to get up to a larger number of characters.... As a result of these different requirements, there are now three different forms of Unicode: UTF-8, UTF-16, and UTF-32*".

Continuing with the Example

We can relate the four entries of the example back to the hexadecimal view of Fig. 5.40 by noting that they start at offsets 40h, 60h, 80h and a0h respectively. The first

---

96 If we were to have more than nine files of This is ..., the tenth would become THISI~10.TXT, and so on.

Table 5.24 LFN directory entry.

Offset	Meaning
00h	Sequence number 1 byte
01–0ah	First five characters of LFN in Unicode 10 bytes
0bh	File attributes 1 byte (always 0fh)
0ch	Type indicator 1 byte
0dh	Checksum 1 byte
0e–19h	Next six characters of LFN in Unicode 12 bytes
1a–1bh	First cluster 2 bytes (always 0000h)
1c–1fh	Next two characters of LFN in Unicode 4 bytes

byte in each entry is the sequence number; that is, it specifies the order in which the entries are to be taken to restore the text of the long file name.

We can see clearly what that order should be in the example LFN by inspection of Fig. 5.41, and if we examine offsets a0h, 80h, 60h and 40h in that order we see the values 01h, 02h, 03h and 44h in the relevant first bytes The last byte in this sequence of four has bit 6 set as well as the value 04h (thus giving 44h) to indicate that it is the last entry of the long file name. All four of these bytes would have been set to E5h if the file had been deleted. These LFN slots are always directly above the regular short file name file directory entry.

At Table 5.24, we have shown the details of the LFN directory entry. Offset 0bh, the file attributes byte is always set to 0fh. This gives file attributes (see Fig. 5.36) of read-only, hidden, system and volume, as we see in Fig. 5.41.

When the LFN structures were being developed, it was found that directory entries with these attributes were generally ignored by existing software and so LFN entries such as these could safely be used with legacy systems without causing problems. At offset 0dh is a checksum byte which is the checksum of all the characters in the file name and file type fields of the associated SFN directory entry. This checksum is used by Windows to detect orphaned or corrupt LFN entries. The process involved to generate the checksum is as follows: *Take the ASCII value of the first character. Rotate all the bits of the result rightward by one bit. Add the ASCII value of the next character. Rotate all the bits of the result rightward by one bit. Add the ASCII value of the next character. Keep repeating this process until all 11 characters in the 8.3 file name have been processed.* It is left as an exercise for the reader (see exercises at the end of the chapter) to confirm that the checksum for THISIS~1TXT is 43h, as shown for the LFN entries at offsets 4dh, 6dh, 8dh and adh in Fig. 5.40.

Additional Times and Dates

Finally, as we mentioned above, it should be noted that the 10 reserved bytes in the normal file directory entry are used in MS-DOS 7 and Windows systems for additional dates and times. The details of these are shown at Table 5.25. Using the same format as that shown in Fig. 5.37, the file creation time is held in little endian form in offsets 0e–0fh, the file creation date is similarly held in offsets 10–11h and the

Table 5.25 Additional time and date fields.

Offset	Meaning
0ch	Reserved 1 byte
0dh	10 millisecond units past creation time 1 byte
0e–0fh	File creation time 2 bytes
10–11h	File creation date 2 bytes
12–13h	Last access date 2 bytes
14–15h	High word of start cluster (FAT32) 2 bytes

last access date is held in offsets 12–13h. At offsets 14–15h are the high two bytes of the 4 byte start cluster for FAT32 systems. The difference between these various times and dates is as follows: the original last modified time and date stamp of the file is that as given at offsets 16–19h; the creation time and date on the MS-DOS 7 or Windows system is that as given at 0e–11h, and the last access date made to the file is that as given at offsets 12–13h.

It is important to note that in the original date and time system, which is still used in all these fields, the time is only accurate to two seconds, since the seconds field contains a count of two second intervals (see Fig. 5.37). However, the new creation date and time has an additional field (offset 0dh) which is a count of the number of 10 millisecond units past the creation time that is given in offsets 0e–0fh. The maximum number that can be held in 1 byte is 255 and this times 10 milliseconds gives a maximum time value of 2.55 seconds. In other words, this additional field (offset 0dh) permits the accuracy of a creation time to be specified to within 10 milliseconds rather than the two seconds of the last modified field. The correct process to establish the creation date and time therefore is first to carry out the calculations on offsets 0e–0fh and 10–11h as given in Fig. 5.37 and then to add to the result the number of seconds and fractions of a second obtained from offset 0dh, *adjusting the date and time as necessary*. It is possible, for example, for the creation date and time to be two seconds before midnight and for the 10 milliseconds field to be greater than two seconds. This would require the creation date to be adjusted as well as the creation time. Not all forensic software carries out this process correctly and it would be as well for the analyst to check sample creation dates and times by hand.

If we examine the THISIS~1.TXT entry in the subdirectory at Fig. 5.40 we may note that the reserved ten bytes are in use, unlike the entries in the root directory at Fig. 5.38, which all have their corresponding ten bytes set to 0. The reason for this difference is not a function of root or subdirectories; nor is it a function of LFN or SFN entries. It is solely because the LFN entries and the associated SFN entry in the subdirectory were placed there using Windows 98, which has the additional time and date facility, whereas the entries in the root directory were placed there using MS-DOS 6.20, which does not. This can be a useful indicator on, for example, a floppy disk to determine whether or not it has been used in a Windows system.

You might note from Fig. 5.41 and Fig. 5.39 that the Norton Disk Editor directory view only appears to show the original last modified date and time. In fact, the screen may be scrolled horizontally to show all the date and time information for a directory entry.

Hiding and Recovering Information

In this section we first briefly review where information might be hidden on a disk and then we consider the possibility of recovering information that has not necessarily been deliberately hidden. A variety of opportunities exist for hiding information on hard disks, as listed below:

- With older controllers, sectors or tracks might be marked as bad within the controller when in fact they are perfectly good and are being used to hide information. This technique requires a reasonably high level of technical expertise (see Bad Sector Mapping and A Possible Place to Hide). This might also be possible with some later controllers.
- Some partitions may be deliberately marked as hidden using, for example, PartitionMagic (see Hidden Partitions).
- The accessible partitions may not use the whole of the disk. This may be accidental or deliberate. The partition table may have been modified using, for example, a disk editor so that one or more of the working partitions are no longer recorded. These conditions can be tested for by comparing the physical disk size with the sum of all the indicated partition sizes.
- The translated disk geometry may not permit access to the entire physical disk. We saw this with Fig. 5.8, where a physical geometry of 4095 cylinders and 16 heads translates to only 1023 cylinders and 64 heads. This is because 4095 is not exactly divisible by 4 and it results in a loss of $(4095 - 1023 \times 4) \times 16 \times 63 = 3024$ sectors. With a different BIOS, these sectors might have been accessible.
- Logical partitions may not fill the whole of the first extended partition (see Extended Partitions).
- Unassigned sectors following the partition tables and between partitions may have been used to hide information. Even the extended partition table sectors themselves should be examined, since only the last 66 bytes of the sector are used by the system for the partition table (see More Places to Hide)
- The usable files area may not extend to the end of the defined partition because of the cluster size (see Fig. 5.33). Any last few sectors should be checked.
- The boot record sector size field may have been altered so that the volume size is less than the partition size.
- Clusters may have been marked in the FAT as bad and then used to hide information (see FATs and Clusters).

Opportunities exist for the recovery of information that has not been deliberately hidden but has perhaps been deleted or has been saved unwittingly in various buffers or temporary files:

- It may be possible to restore some deleted files, where clusters have not yet been reused, by "following" the cluster chains in the FAT (see Deleted Files). Note that although these clusters will have all been marked as 0 (available for reallocation) in the FAT, we can often infer from the sequences of 0s that are present where a chain used to be. By examining the last few bytes in one cluster and the first few bytes in the next cluster we may be able to confirm, particularly with text files, that they used to form part of a chain.

- Where a file does not use all of the last (or only) cluster assigned to it, there may be information from previous files still accessible beyond the end of the sector in which the current file ends and up to the end of the cluster. This is known as *cluster slack space*.

- Where the last part of a file does not completely fill the standard sector buffer, there may be memory-resident data associated with some other process beyond the end of the file and up to the end of the sector buffer. This is known as *buffer slack space* or *RAM slack space*.

- Clusters currently unallocated may contain information from previous files.

- System files, such as the Windows swap file, may contain printer and other temporary file buffers that are no longer directly accessible.

At Fig. 5.42 we have shown a summary of many of these issues in diagrammatic form. The first line in the diagram shows a map of the physical disk. As expected, this starts with a master boot record (mbr) and continues with a primary partition which has been allocated the drive letter C: This is followed by a hidden partition which would appear in the partition table with the partition type byte set to hidden. Next is a partition marked "not in table". This represents a partition that has been used but whose entry has been edited out of the partition table. Then comes the first extended partition container in the form that we have seen before. This takes up the rest of the disk except for the part marked "lost". This represents those sectors that cannot be accessed because of the translated disk geometry. Between each partition and the partition tables we see unused space and this occurs because partition tables invariably start at head 0 sector 1 and boot records start at head 1 sector 1.

Within the first extended partition container we see an extended partition table followed by a logical partition that has been allocated the drive letter D:, and this is

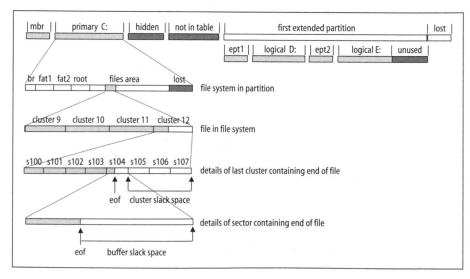

Fig. 5.42 Summary of disk and file issues.

followed by another extended partition table and another logical partition that has been allocated the drive letter E:. We also see beyond this last partition that there is unused space within the first extended partition container. In addition, we may note that once again, between each logical partition and the extended partition tables, there is unused space for precisely the same reasons as before.

The diagram also shows, for the primary C: partition an exploded view of the file system in the partition and we note the possibility of lost sectors at the end of the files area because of the need to divide sectors exactly by the sectors per cluster value (always a power of two). We have shown, in addition, an exploded view of a typical file which uses the four clusters 9 to 12 for its data. We note that the end of the file (eof) occurs part way through cluster 12 and on examining an exploded view of this cluster we see that it is made up of the eight sectors 100 to 107. Again we note that the end of file occurs in sector 104, which means that sectors 105, 106 and 107 are not used at all by this file. These three sectors are known as *cluster slack space*. Further, an exploded view of sector 104, which contains the end of file, shows that only part of the sector buffer is taken up with file data. From the end of the file to the end of the sector will be information that was in the buffer before this file update was written. This information is known as *buffer slack space* or *RAM slack space*.

RAID

Before leaving this chapter we should just make mention of *Redundant Arrays of Inexpensive Disks* or *RAID*. The concept came from the University of California at Berkeley in the mid-1980s and the original paper (Patterson *et al.*, 1988) on the subject was published at SIGMOD in 1988. Today, the word "inexpensive" that was used by the original designers is more often replaced by the word "independent".

A RAID system is a set of independent disks which appear to the operating system as a single drive. The original paper defines five levels of RAID, numbered 1 to 5, which adopt various strategies to utilize the independent disks in different ways to improve the overall reliability and performance of the RAID system. RAID is designed to improve reliability by distributing data over multiple drives and by calculating and storing parity information about it. This redundancy permits data to be restored if a drive fails. RAID is designed to improve performance by distributing the disk read processes over several disks so that transfers can take place in parallel. From a forensic viewpoint, it is best to treat a RAID unit as a single device and to image it as such. Reconstructing a RAID unit from its separately imaged components can be a difficult and time-consuming process.

Although the original paper referred only to five levels of RAID, most authorities today would list at least nine and perhaps as many as twelve levels, as outlined below.

RAID Level 0

Strictly speaking, RAID Level 0 is not a RAID system at all and it was not described in the original paper. It is however referred to as such and it has therefore been included in this brief overview. RAID Level 0 uses what is known as *sector striping* to increase performance. This means that sectors or blocks are written in turn to different drives. So, for example, given three drives, sector 1 of a file would be written to drive 1, sector 2 to drive 2, sector 3 to drive 3 and then sector 4 to drive 1 again, and so forth. The file would be *striped* across the three drives. Such striping does not need to be at the sector or block level; it can be at the byte or even the bit level. RAID Level 0 does not provide any redundancy or improved reliability, but it can be used to improve overall performance.

RAID Level 1

RAID Level 1 uses *mirroring* or *duplexing* to improve data reliability. Mirroring simply means that each drive has a duplicate, and when data is written to one drive it is simultaneously mirrored or duplicated on the second. If one drive fails, the other can be used to restore the data. Clearly the process of having to write to both drives increases the performance overheads.

RAID Level 2

This system distributes data across multiple drives at the bit level, using Hamming code error detection and correction. A system with four data drives, for example, would also require three parity drives for the error detecting and correcting codes. Because it operates at the bit level, every disk access occurs in parallel, making the transfer of large amounts of contiguous data particular efficient, and the degree of redundancy is the highest of any of the RAID levels.

RAID Levels 3 and 4

RAID Level 3 combines striping at the byte level with a single drive assigned for parity. So, typically, there might be four data drives and one parity drive in such a system. Byte 1 of a transfer would then be written to drive 1, byte 2 to drive 2, byte 3 to drive 3 and byte 4 to drive 4, then a parity value byte for those 4 bytes would be calculated and written to the parity drive; after that, byte 5 would be written to drive 1 again, and so forth.

RAID level 4 is very similar. This system combines striping at the sector or block level with a single drive assigned for parity. So, with four data drives and one parity drive, sector 1 is written to drive 1, sector 2 to drive 2, sector 3 to drive 3 and sector 4 to drive 4, then a parity sector is calculated and written to the parity drive; following that, sector 5 is written to drive 1 again, and the process continues as before.

RAID Level 5

This approach combines sector or block striping with distributed parity. In this system there is no dedicated parity disk, parity sectors or blocks are written to the next available disk in sequence. So, given, for example, five disks as before, sector 1 is written to disk 1, sector 2 to disk 2, sector 3 to disk 3, sector 4 to disk 4 and sector 5 to disk 5; then the parity sector is calculated and written to disk 1, and then sector 6 is written to disk 2 and so forth. The parity sectors are therefore distributed across all the disks.

Other RAID Levels

RAID Level 6 is similar to RAID Level 5 but incorporates a second parity scheme. RAID Level 7 is a proprietary system that incorporates a real-time embedded computer and operating system as a controller. RAID Level 10 is a combination of mirroring and striping using RAID Level 1 and RAID Level 0 (RAID-1+0) or a combination of striping and mirroring using RAID Level 0 and RAID Level 1 (RAID-0+1). RAID Level 50 is a combination of RAID Level 5 and RAID Level 0 and RAID Level 53 is a combination of RAID Level 5 and RAID Level 3. RAID Level S is another proprietary system similar to RAID Level 5. For a clear treatment of RAID see Appendix C to Zacker (1995).

Formal Specifications

Work is now in progress to establish formal industry-wide specifications for RAID systems with the "Common RAID Disk Data Format Specification", Revision 01.00.00 of which was published on 14 December 2004; see Storage Networking Industry Association (2004).

Exercises

5.1 Comparing Fig. 5.43 with Fig. 5.6, show that this RLL encoded signal represents the character "Y" and sketch the equivalent MFM encoded signal.

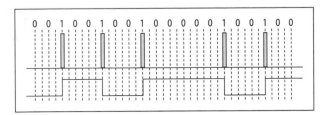

Fig. 5.43 RLL encoded signal.

5.2 At Fig. 5.44 is shown part of the listing from the Find-ATA program for a Quantum Pioneer hard disk. Using Fig. 5.8 as an example, calculate, assuming 512 bytes per sector, the capacities in bytes for the columns marked "Hardware", "DOS" and "Current" and also the number of sectors in LBA mode.

Determine the number of sectors that are inaccessible on this disk as a result of the translation shown.

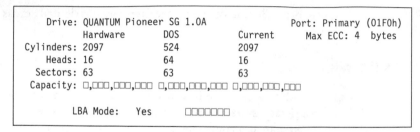

Fig. 5.44 Part of the Find-ATA analysis of a Quantum Pioneer.

5.3 Given a Logical Block Address of 1,045,721 for a disk which has 16 heads and 63 sectors per track, calculate the equivalent CHS address. Then use these CHS values to confirm the LBA address.

5.4 A Seagate ST38410A hard disk drive is marked with the following physical CHS values: cylinders 8391, heads 16, and sectors per track 63. Calculate the logical numbers of cylinders, heads and sectors per track at the INT 13h interface for this disk when it has been translated using: (a) the standard bit shifting method; (b) the revised ECHS method; and (c) the Revised LBA Assisted method. Determine the numbers of sectors lost for each form of translation.

5.5 Determine all the details of the second partition in the partition table of the master boot record shown at Fig. 5.26, starting from address 1ceh, and confirm that these are correctly given by the Norton Disk Editor view at Fig. 5.27.

5.6 Analyse the directory record for the entry "SUB1" at offset a0h in Fig. 5.38 and show that it conforms with the detail give by the Norton Disk Editor directory view in Fig. 5.39.

5.7 Using the process described below to generate an LFN checksum, show that the checksum for THISIS~1TXT is 43h. Note that the "." is not included in the calculation. A program to carry out this process, called lfn_crc.exe, is available from http://www.dmares.com/maresware/lo.htm (Mares, 2006).

Take the ASCII value of the first character. Rotate all the bits of the result rightward by one bit. Add the ASCII value of the next character. Rotate all the bits of the result rightward by one bit. Add the ASCII value of the next character. Keep repeating this process until all 11 characters in the 8.3 file name have been processed.

5.8 Analyse the subdirectory record for the entry THISIS~1.TXT at offset c0h in Fig. 5.40 and determine the values of the additional time and date fields.

References

ANSI (1996) *ANSI X3.279-1996 – AT Attachment Interface with Extensions (ATA-2)*, American National Standards Institute, 11 West 42nd Street, New York, NY 10036.

Brouwer, A. E. (2005) *Partition Types: List of Partition Identifiers for PCs*. URL: http://www.win.tue.nl/~aeb/linux/partitions/partition_types-1.html.

Clarke, A. R. M. and Powys-Lybbe, D. (1986) *The Amstrad CP/M Plus*, MML Systems Ltd, London.

Collins, R. (2003) *Dr Dobbs Microprocessor Resources, Protected Mode Basics*, Copyright © 2003 *Dr. Dobb's Journal*. URL: http://www.x86.org/articles/pmbasics/.

Davis, M. (1999) *Forms of Unicode*, President of the Unicode Consortium, IBM, 1 September. Downloaded from: http://icu.sourceforge.net/docs/papers/forms_of_unicode/.

Deyring, K.-P. (ed.) (2003) *Serial ATA: High Speed Serialized AT Attachment, Revision 1.0a*, 7 January.

Duncan, R. (1988) *Advanced MS-DOS Programming*, Microsoft Press, Redmond, WA.

EMS (1987), *LOTUS(R)/INTEL(R)/MICROSOFT(R), EXPANDED MEMORY SPECIFICATION [1]*, Version 4.0, 300275-005, October. Copyright © 1987, Lotus Development Corporation, Intel Corporation, Microsoft Corporation.

Finch, S. G. (ed.) (1995) *Information Technology – AT Attachment Interface with Extensions (ATA-2)*, Working Draft, Proposed American National Standard, X3T10 948D, Revision 3, 17 January. URL: http://alpha1.dyns.net/files/Drive/d0948r4c.pdf.

IBM (1995) *No-ID Sector Format*. Dr Steven R Hetzler, IBM Research Division, Almaden Research Center, San Jose, CA. Now Hitachi – see http://www.hitachigst.com/hdd/ipl/oem/tech/noid.htm.

IBM (1998) *IBM Deskstar 25GP and Deskstar 22GXP Hard Disk Drives*, IBM Storage Systems Division, 5600 Cottle Road, San Jose, CA 95193. Now Hitachi – see http://www.hitachigst.com/tech/techlib.nsf/techdocs/85256AB8006A31E587256A79006E5943/$file/djna_ds.pdf.

IBM (1999) *Disk Manager (version 9.47)*, 25 March, IBM Storage Systems Division, 5600 Cottle Road, San Jose, CA 95193. Now Hitachi – see http://www.hitachigst.com/hdd/support/download.htm#Diskmanager.

Intel (1998a) *SE440BX Motherboard Technical Product Specification*, March, Intel Corporation, PO Box 5937, Denver, CO 80217-9808.

Intel (1998b) *SE440BX Motherboard Product Guide*, Intel Corporation, PO Box 5937, Denver, CO 80217-9808.

Lambert, M. (1995) Circular extended partitions: round and round with DOS, *Virus Bulletin*, September, p. 14. Mike Lambert, Virus Bulletin Ltd, The Quadrant, Abingdon, Oxfordshire, OX14 3YS.

Lambert, M. and Moore, C. (1992) *Circular Extended Partitions: A DOS Vulnerability or When the Magic Floppy Won't Boot*, Mike Lambert, Before Disaster Strikes, 1153 Dublin Place, Herndon, VA 22070, and Charles Moore, Automation Mentors, Inc., 12220 Wye Oak Commons, Burke, VA 22015.

Lamers, L. J. (ed.) (1994) *Information Technology – AT Attachment Interface for Disk Drives*, Working Draft, Proposed American National Standard, X3T10 719D, Revision 4c.

Landis, H. (1995a) *How It Works – BIOS Types, CHS Translation, LBA and Other Good Stuff*, Version 4a. URL: http://www.ata-atapi.com/.

Landis, H. (1995b) *How It Works – DOS Floppy Disk Boot Sector, Version 1a*, hiw@sugs.talisman.com.

Landis, H. (1997a) *How It Works – Master Boot Record, Version 1b*, hiw@sugs.talisman.com.

Landis, H. (1997b) *How It Works – Partition Tables, Version 1e*. URL: hiw@sugs.talisman.com.

Landis, H. (2001) *How It Works: CHS Translation*. URL: http://www.ata-atapi.com/.

Landis, H. (2005) *Information, Test Software and Consulting Services for Developers of Products using ATA (PATA, IDE/EIDE), Serial ATA (SATA), ATAPI, and CE-ATA and Other ATA Related Interfaces*, 27 October. URL: http://www.ata-atapi.com/.

Leach, P. J (1998) *UUIDs and GUIDs*, Internet Draft, Network Working Group, Microsoft, Rich Salz, Certco.

Leach, P., Mealling, M. and Salz, R. (2004) *A UUID URN Namespace*, Internet Draft, Network Working Group.

Majors, N. (1995) *Technicians' Guide to PC Hard Disk Subsystems*, Data Recovery Labs. URL: http://www.programmersheaven.com/download/1471/download.aspx.

Mares, D. (2006) *Computer Forensics and Data Analysis*. Mares and Company, LLC, PO Box 464429, Lawrenceville, GA 30042-4429, USA. URL: http://www.dmares.com/.

Maxtor (1996) *Maxtor's CrystalMax 1080 Model Number 84320A8*, Rev A 3/18/96. URL: http:/
/www.mysimon.com/Hard-Drives/9025-11620_8-20142861.html.

Maxtor (2001) *Big Drives: Breaking the 137 Gigabyte Barrier*. URL: http://www.maxtor.com/
products/bigdrive/whitepaper.htm. No longer available.

Maxtor (2003) *DiamondMax Plus 9 Specification*, Maxtor Corporation, 500 McCarthy
Boulevard, Milpitas, CA, 95035. DS-DiamondMaxPlus9-5/03-CL.

McLean, P. T. (ed.) (1999) *Information Technology – AT Attachment with Packet Interface – 5*
(ATA/ATAPI-5), Working Draft, T13 1321D, Revision 1c, 31 August.

McLean, P. T. (ed.) (2001) *Information Technology – AT Attachment with Packet Interface – 6*
(ATA/ATAPI-6), Working Draft, T13 1410D, Revision 1e, 26 June.

Mellanox (2002), *Understanding PCI Bus, PCI-Express and InfiniBand Architecture*, White
Paper, Rev 1-20. Mellanox Technologies Inc, 2900 Stender Way, Santa Clara, CA 95054, USA.
URL: http://www.mellanox.com/.

Messmer, H.-P. (2002) *The Indispensable PC Hardware Book*, 4th edn, Addison-Wesley,
Reading, MA.

Micro Firmware (1998) *Issues with Hard Drives over 4GB*. Micro Firmware Tech Support, 330
W Gray Street, Norman, Oklahoma. URL: http://www.allensmith.net/Storage/
firmware/over4gb.htm.

Microsoft Corporation (1999a) *Problems Accessing FAT16 Drives Larger Than 2 GB*, Article ID:
Q127851, 15 January. URL: http://www.allensmith.net/Storage/HDDlimit/
FAT16.htm.

Microsoft Corporation (1999b) *Description of FAT32 File System*, Article ID: Q154997, 8
August, URL: http://support.microsoft.com/support/kb/Q154997.

Microsoft Corporation (2000) Hardware White Paper, *Microsoft Extensible Firmware
Initiative FAT32 File System Specification*, FAT: General Overview of On-Disk Format,
Version 1.03, December 6.

Microsoft Corporation (2003) *Serial ATA in the Microsoft Operating System Environment*, 18
July. URL: http://www.microsoft.com/whdc/device/storage/serialATA_FAQ.mspx.

MicroSystems (undated) *POST CODE MASTER Version 1.40*, MicroSystems Development, Inc.
4100 Moorpark Ave. Suite #104, San Jose, CA 95117.

Mosteller, T. (1995) *CMOSRAM2.EXE*. Tellerware, 1872 Rampart Lane, Lansdale, PA 19446-
5051.

Patterson, D. A., Gibson, G. A. and Katz, R. H. (1988) A case for redundant arrays of inexpensive
disks (RAID), *SIGMOD Conference*, pp. 109–16.

Phoenix (1995) *BIOS Enhanced Disk Drive Specification Version 1.1*, 9 May. Phoenix Technologies Ltd, 2575 McCabe Way, Irvine, CA 92714. URL: http://www.phoenix.com/.

Phoenix (1998) *BIOS Enhanced Disk Drive Specification, Version 3.0*, 12 March. Phoenix
Technologies Ltd, 2575 McCabe Way, Irvine, CA 92714. URL: http://www.phoenix.com/.

Postuma, P. (1995) *BIOS Reporter, version 1.1*. ppostuma@nbnet.nb.ca, 16 Fullyer Drive,
Quispamsis, NB, Canada E2G 1Y7.

PowerQuest (1996) *PartitionMagic 3.0 User Guide*, PowerQuest Corporation, 1083 N State
Street, Orem, UT. URL: http://www.powerquest.com/.

PowerQuest (1998) *BootMagic User Guide*, PowerQuest Corporation, PO Box 1911, Orem, UT.
Now Symantec – see http://www. symantec.com/techsupp/home_homeoffice/
products/pmagic/pmagic_8/manuals.html.

Pratt, T. (2003), *Serial ATA Interface on Client Systems*, Dell White Paper, June. URL: http://
www.dell.com/r&d.

Quantum (1996) *Quantum Fireball™ 1.0/1.2/1.7/2.1/2.5/3.2/3.8 GB AT Product Manual*,
Chapter 5, Table 5.1, Quantum Corporation.

R v Aslett (2002), IN THE CROWN COURT AT MANCHESTER, T2001/0383, Wednesday 25th
September, 2002, BEFORE: HIS HONOUR JUDGE GEAKE, *REGINA -v- JONATHAN
ASLETT*, Transcript of the Official Palantype Note of Cater Walsh & Co., Suite, 410, Crown
House, Kidderminster, DY10 2DH.

Seagate (1991a) *Specifications for ST-506*. URL: http://www.seagate.com/support/disc/
specs/mfm/st506.html.

Seagate (1991b) *Specifications for ST-412*. URL: http://www.seagate.com/support/disc/specs/mfm/st412.html.

Seagate (1994) *FIND-ATA.EXE v1.0, An ATA Interface Identify Drive Utility*. Seagate Technology, Inc., B-5 Technical Support, 920 Disc Drive, Scotts Valley, CA 95066. URL: http://www.infoatec.it/download/findat10.zip.

Seagate (1995a) *SGATFMT4.EXE v4.0, Seagate Format Drive Utility*. Seagate Technology, Inc. URL: http://www.infoatec.it/download/sgatfmt4.zip.

Seagate (1995b) *NFDisc v1.20, Partition Record Display and Maintenance*. Seagate Technology, Inc. URL: http://www.seagate-asia.com/sgt/korea/discutil.jsp.

Seagate (1997a) *Cheetah 4.5- to 9.1-Gbyte Capacity Disc Drives*. URL: http://www.seagate.com/, publication number 1480-002. No longer available.

Seagate (1997b) *Low-level Formatting an ATA (IDE) Hard Drive*. Seagate Technology, Inc., B-5 Technical Support, 920 Disc Drive, Scotts Valley, CA 95066. URL: http://www.seagate.com/ww/v/index.jsp?vgnextoid=95f0781e73d5d010VgnVCM100000dd04090aRCRD&locale=en-US.

Seagate (1997c) *Seagate Fast ATA/Fast ATA-2 Fact Sheet*. Seagate Technology, Corporate Communications. URL: http://www.seagate.com/support/kb/disc/fastfs.html.

Seagate (1998) *FAQ Disk Manager Basics, BIOS Limitations*. Seagate Technology, Inc. URL: http://www.seagate.com/support/kb/disc/bioslmt.html.

Stevens, C. E. (ed.) (2005) *Information Technology – AT Attachment – 8 ATA/ATAPI Command Set (ATA8-ACS)*, Working Draft, T13 Project 1699D, Revision 1e, 20 June.

Stockton, J. R. (2005) *Date and Time Scales*. URL: http://www.merlyn.demon.co.uk/dayscale.htm.

Storage Networking Industry Association (2004) *Common RAID Disk Data Format Specification*, Revision 01.00.00, 14 December. URL: http://www.snia.org/tech_activities/ddftwg.

Symantec (1999) *Norton Utilities Version 4, User's Guide*, Norton Disk Editor. Symantec Corporation, Peter Norton Group, 10201 Torre Avenue, Cupertino, CA 95014.

Tischer, M. and Jennrich, B. (1996) *PC Intern, The Encyclopedia of System Programming*, Abacus, Data Becker Edition.

Vidström, A. (2005) *Computer Forensics and the ATA Interface*, Technical Report FOI-R--1638--SE, February 2005, 1650-1942, Swedish Defence Research Agency, Command and Control Systems, Box 1165, SE-581 11 LINKÖPING, Sweden.

Western Digital (1997a) *Enhanced IDE Interface*. Western Digital Corporation, 8105 Irvine Center Drive, Irvine, CA 92618. URL: http://www.wdc.com/.

Western Digital (1997b) *Drive Parameters*, 25 March. Western Digital Corporation, 8105 Irvine Center Drive, Irvine, CA 92618. URL: http://www.wdc.com/.

Western Digital (1998a) *Large Disk Integration*, 7 October. Western Digital Corporation, 8105 Irvine Center Drive, Irvine, CA 92618. URL: http://www.wdc.com/.

Western Digital (1998b) *8.4 GB Capacity Barrier*. Western Digital Corporation, 8105 Irvine Center Drive, Irvine, CA 92618. URL: http://www.wdc.com/.

Western Digital (1999) *EZ-Drive FAQ Sheet*, 9 March. Western Digital Corporation, 8105 Irvine Center Drive, Irvine, CA 92618. URL: http://www.wdc.com/.

Western Digital (undated a) *User's Guide WD1003V-MM1 Winchester Disk Controller* (also MM2, SR1 and SR2). URL: http://www.wdc.com/.

Western Digital (undated b) *Enhanced IDE Implementation Guide*, Version 5, Western Digital Corporation, 8105 Irvine Center Drive, Irvine, CA 92618. URL: http://www.wdc.com/.

XMS (1991), *eXtended Memory Specification (XMS), ver 3.0*, January 1991. Copyright © 1988, Microsoft Corporation, Lotus Development Corporation, Intel Corporation, and AST Research, Inc.

Zacker, C. (1995) *Upgrading and Repairing Networks*, Que, San Francisco, CA.

6. *The New Technology File System*

Introduction

The NTFS (New Technology File System) file system has been used by Microsoft since the mid-1990s. It was rarely seen by forensic practitioners until the distribution of Windows 2000. With the introduction of Windows XP, particularly as a pre-installed operating system on new machines for use in the home, it is now encountered more often than the old FAT (File Allocation Table) based systems.

A Brief History

In the early 1990s both Microsoft and IBM recognized that the current filing system, FAT, had almost reached the end of its development road. FAT had distinct short-comings when it came to "serious" computing, particularly in the area of networks and security[1].

At that time Microsoft were using the FAT system, which they had developed in the days of DOS and the early days of Windows. They realized that to move forward into the corporate market they needed a more powerful, more reliable and more secure filing system. Further development of FAT, albeit with later "kludges and fudges", would never achieve the level of performance required for them to gain the foothold they needed in that lucrative market. They needed a filing system powerful enough and flexible enough to take on UNIX[2].

Microsoft joined forces with IBM, mainly because their futures were, at that time, inextricably linked. They developed a new filing system called HPFS (High Perfor-

---

1 See http://support.microsoft.com/kb/100108/en-us and http://www.pcguide.com/ref/hdd/file/ntfs/index.htm.

2 See http://support.microsoft.com/kb/100108/en-us and http://www.pcguide.com/ref/hdd/file/ntfs/index.htm.

mance Filing System) which was the native filing system for a new operating system, OS/2[3].

OS/2 never really took off. It is still seen on some machines, but is regarded as a "niche" operating system rather than a mainstream one. Sitting behind OS/2 was HPFS, which still had some problems and required further development. It seems that Microsoft and IBM could not reach an agreement as to the direction in which the future development of the system should go. It is also suggested in some quarters that Microsoft, having seen a vision whilst developing HPFS, decided that they needed total control and decided to go their own way. In any event the project was abandoned and OS/2 with HPFS remained with IBM alone[4].

Microsoft set out, using many ideas and concepts from the HPFS project, to develop and market a totally new filing system called NTFS (New Technology Filing System). This new system was earmarked to lie behind a new Windows product specifically aimed at the commercial market, Windows NT[5].

NTFS Features

Built into NTFS are the following features:

- *Reliability and resilience.* Although it is arguable that this has been achieved, particularly amongst those who have suffered by losing data on an NTFS system, Microsoft have made efforts within the new system to reduce data loss and improve recoverability when the system crashes or suffers from a "power-out".

- *Networking.* Microsoft recognized that networking of desktop machines in particular was going to become an important area. The networking of machines using this filing system was borne in mind as the system was developed and this has made it much easier for the operating system to integrate with the filing system for networking purposes.

- *Long file names.* The original DOS and Windows had been restricted to an 8:3 filename system. Windows 95 did manage to introduce a long file name system, but this was accomplished by a quick-and-dirty "kludge" of using additional directory entries (as we describe in Chapter 5) and all files still had to have an 8:3 name to be used by the system when accessing files. NTFS, on the other hand, allows full 255 character file names in the directory entry.

- *Storage efficiency.* By the early 1990s, FAT16 was found to be imposing severe limitations on the size of volumes. FAT32, which was introduced in the mid-1990s, did address this problem, but all FAT systems use a method of grouping a number of disk sectors into what are known as "allocation units" or "clusters". This approach can result in a loss of storage space to "slack". For example, a one byte

---

3 See http://www.millennium-technology.com/HistoryOfOS2.html.

4 See http://www.millennium-technology.com/HistoryOfOS2.html; http://www.pcguide.com/ref/hdd/file/ntfs/index.htm.

5 See http://www.pcguide.com/ref/hdd/file/ntfs/index.htm.

file could commonly be allocated a 64 sector cluster, resulting in a slack space loss of 32 kbyte less the one byte. NTFS addresses this problem by using a totally different method for file space allocation. This system also permits the existence of very large volumes.

- *Access control and security.* A major shortcoming of the FAT systems is the lack of any facility for file-level security; for example, who did and who did not have access to particular files. NTFS includes access control at the file level, and also allows the implementation of upper level access control by groups of users.

- *Future proofing.* Having learned lessons from the FAT systems, Microsoft have also built in scope for expansion of the NTFS system without the need for a major re-write. For instance, users can create their own "attributes" for inclusion within the filing system simply by defining them and placing the specifications within reserved areas of the system files. Some of these reserved areas have already been used. In particular, in the latest release, MFT record numbers have been included within MFT entries[6].

Development of NTFS continued throughout its use with Windows NT. The most common version, originally dubbed NTFS 1.1, is more commonly known as NTFS 4 because of its release with Windows NT4. In typical Microsoft style, the next version of NTFS was shipped with a new operating system. This operating system was not named Windows NT5 but Windows 2000. NTFS 5, as the filing system was officially named, contained some new elements within it, such as the Active Directory Service, Reparse Points, Change Journals, On-the-Fly Encryption and Sparse File Support[7].

With the release of Windows XP, Microsoft made clear their intention to make NTFS the filing system of preference. Users buying new systems find themselves coerced into installing NTFS in preference to FAT32. Windows XP's default filing system is NTFS, without any apparent choice. FAT32 can be forced as an option only if a FAT system is present on the hard disk before the installation of the Windows XP operating system is commenced. Normal users would not know how to create the provision of this choice. As a result, NTFS is thus growing exponentially in the home-use area[8].

NTFS – How it Works

NTFS is based around a relational database. This is the MFT or Master File Table. All "objects" stored on the volume are regarded as files, except for the Partition Boot Record. The MFT contains details of every file on the volume, including the management files that are used for the filing system. A sizeable area of the volume is reserved for the MFT to avoid it becoming fragmented as it grows in size. This area,

---

6 See http://www.pcguide.com/ref/hdd/file/ntfs/over.htm; http://support. microsoft.com/kb/100108/en-us/Q100108.

7 See http://ww.pcguide.com/ref/hdd/file/ntfs/ver.htm.

8 See Windows XP Home/Pro installation.

by default, is about 12.5% of the volume size and is known as the "MFT Reserved Area".

The filing system itself relies upon a series of management files, known as metadata files (data about data). These files are invisible to the user and manage the partition in terms of allocation of storage space, identification of space available, recovery information and descriptions of the file "attributes" available. All except the Partition Boot Record have a file record in the MFT. A detailed explanation of the MFT is given later in this chapter.

Metadata Files

As already mentioned, in addition to the MFT, there are a number of metadata files that are used by NTFS to manage the filing system, and each has a record in the MFT as follows:

- *$MFTMirr.* This file is located at the very centre of the volume where it can thus easily be found in the case of damage to the filing system. It contains duplicate MFT entries for the $MFT, $MFTMirr (itself), $Logfile and $Volume files. It is a "backup" of the first four entries of the MFT file and can be used in an attempt to recover from some system problems.

- *$Logfile.* This file is a relational database that records transactions to and from the disk. It can be used to recover from a system failure. NTFS uses a "lazy write" caching system where data is not immediately written to disk, and it also needs more than one transaction to complete a filing task. For example, two transactions are needed to update a file: one to update the file itself and a second to update the details in the MFT with respect to file dates and times and so forth. Should a power failure occur between the two transactions, recovery can be effected by completing the missed task, as indicated by the $Logfile. The size of the $Logfile depends on the volume size.

- *$Volume.* This file contains information about the volume, such as the volume label, the NTFS version number, the creation time and date and the "dirty flag". This latter item is used to indicate whether or not a clean shutdown took place on the last use of the volume.

- *$AttrDef.* This is a table of Attribute names, allocated identifier numbers, and descriptions. Its record length is 160 bytes. The most common of these Attributes are discussed later and are also listed in Appendix 9.

- *$. (dollar dot).* This is a symbol for the root directory of the volume.

- *$Bitmap.* This is a bitmap of the logical clusters on the volume. It is simply made up of binary flags, where "1" symbolizes that a cluster is in use, and "0" symbolizes that a cluster is not in use. In some respects, it is similar to a FAT but without the pointer values. $Bitmap simply records the use of the storage blocks on the volume.

- *$Boot.* This is the Boot Record for the volume. It includes the BPB (BIOS Parameter Block) which is used to mount the volume as well as additional bootstrap loader code which is used if the volume is bootable. The details of the BPB are given in Appendix 8.

- *$BadClus*. This is a file which addresses the whole volume and which reports its size as being the whole volume size. It should be noted that this file only refers to clusters and not to sectors. If one sector in a cluster is found to be bad then the whole cluster is marked as bad and an appropriate entry is made in the $Bad stream of this file. The cluster is also marked as "used" in $Bitmap to ensure that no data is stored there. NTFS does implement a feature on fault-tolerant volumes where, on identifying a bad sector, all data within the cluster concerned is moved to another location and the file details are amended appropriately. However, as a result of advanced disk management techniques at the physical level of the disk (see Chapter 5) it is rare with modern disks for the $Bad stream to contain entries.

- *$Quota*. This file was used in earlier versions of NTFS and is reportedly not used in Windows 2000 or later. The file was implemented to manage volume allocation quota sizes to users; that is, to control the amount of data that any specific user could have stored on the volume.

- *$Secure*. This file contains unique security descriptors for all the files within a volume. The security id field within the Standard Information Attribute of each file record within the MFT is an index into the file $Secure.

- *$Upcase*. This file simply contains characters in the Unicode character set. It is used to compare and sort filenames with a Unicode system without having to make reference to the code page.

- *$Extend*. This is a directory within which extended system files such as $Quota (see above), $ObjId, $Reparse and $UsnJrnl are located.

- *$ObjId*. This file is used for distributed link tracking. This allows shortcuts and OLE links to continue to work after the target file is renamed or moved. When a shortcut to a file on an NTFS volume is created, this system places a unique object identifier (ID) into the target file. The object ID is also stored within the link file and it is this object ID that is used to locate the target file. $ObjId uses a file named Tracking.log for management information.

- *$Reparse*. This file contains details of the reparse points which may be used to give additional functionality to applications that are able to make use of them. Identified within the MFT record for the application, system calls can be intercepted and then fed through further software.

- *$UsnJrnl*. This is a change journal file in which are recorded changes that are made to an "object". The changes are recorded at the end of the file, listing the file name and the time and the type of the change. No actual data that changed is kept in the file, which is a special hidden file.

The MFT in Detail

In this chapter, we set out to discuss sufficient of the low-level workings of the MFT as to enable a forensic analyst to examine in some detail the structure and working of an NTFS volume with a view to extracting evidence. It should be noted that much of the material that follows has been obtained through a series of experiments that have been carried out by the authors. Due to the limitations of both machine and man, all possible combinations of circumstances could not be tested. All direct references and examples listed here refer to a sterile, standalone, Windows 2000 installation that was created for the purpose of identifying and testing certain aspects of MFT use. It is hoped that publication of this material will precipitate feedback from readers to expand upon the base of reliable knowledge in this area. As always, the authors strongly recommend that any such findings that an analyst relies upon are retested for correctness, in the specific environment of the case, by the analyst personally.

Objects and Records

The MFT contains all details of all "objects" on the volume and thus it is the first port of call for evidence regarding the presence of files, the relevant dates and times of files, file sizes and identifications as well as their storage locations on the volume.

Each *record* within the MFT is of a fixed size and is numbered from the beginning of the MFT, starting from 0. The position of any specific record in the MFT can be found by multiplying its record number by the fixed record size and going to that byte offset within the MFT file. In earlier versions of NTFS the record number was not stored within the MFT record and its record number was determined implicitly from its physical position within the MFT file. However, the version of NTFS shipped with Windows XP does store the record number explicitly within the MFT record.

The MFT record is usually fixed at 1024 bytes. Although facilities are available to accommodate other sizes, 1024 bytes is the only size that has been seen to date within the forensic computing field.

Attributes and Resident Data

Each object, whether it be a file or directory, has its own MFT record. The object is seen as a collection of "attributes" which include details of the file or directory, the associated dates and times and the data that makes up the file. Most attributes are stored within the MFT record, including, if the data is sufficiently small in size, the file data itself. This data is known as *resident* data. For example, a record for a small .gif file of a few hundred bytes would be made up of the file details followed by the data itself, all accommodated within the 1024 byte MFT record. We shall see how this is stored in a later section.

If the amount of data for a file is too large to be accommodated within the MFT record, then the data is stored elsewhere on the volume in a separate cluster or series of clusters. Pointers within the MFT record indicate the location of this data on the volume and its size.

Directories and INDX Records

Directories are dealt with in a similar manner. If the directory listing (which is similar to a text file) can be accommodated within the MFT record then it becomes resident data. If it grows to exceed the space available it is placed out on the volume, again with pointers used to identify its location and size. The growing of files and directories is of great interest to the forensic practitioner as the majority of the resident data remains as "slack" in the record when the object is moved out of the MFT to the volume storage area. The data in the "slack" area may be of great evidential importance, as it could be the only record of details referring to deleted files. It is possible that the MFT record retains some entries as resident and some entries as non-resident. Non-resident data is stored out on the volume in "Index Buffer" files. These do not appear as files to the operating system or, indeed, to forensic software. These files start with the keyword "INDX" and are laid out internally in a similar manner to MFT records using attributes. They are pointed to by the use of data runs in the MFT record.

Pointers are used a great deal within MFT records, not only internally within the record itself, but also to point to references elsewhere. For instance, pointers are used to identify what directory a file exists in, and the MFT record for the file would contain a pointer to the MFT record which contains the *parent* directory. Thus the MFT can be used to create a screen display of a directory listing with links to the actual files contained within that directory. This permits the directory tree structure, familiar to most users, to be retained. It would be fair to say that the screen displays presented to the user are little different from those produced using a FAT system, except that more features are available, particularly in the security area.

The availability of storage space out on the volume is governed by a simple bitmap system. As explained in the section on $Bitmap above, each cluster (or storage block) is allocated one binary digit within the bitmap to signify the state of that cluster, with "1" signifying that the cluster is in use and "0" signifying that the cluster is available for use.

Storing a File

In simple terms, to store a file on the system, the following processes are carried out, though not necessarily in the order shown:

- A search is made of the MFT to find the first available record.
- If the file is small enough to fit into the MFT record together with the file Attributes it is written there; otherwise a search is made of the volume storage area bitmap to identify a location and space where the file data can be recorded out on the volume.
- The Attributes of the file are written to the MFT.
- The file data is written to the MFT or volume.
- Pointers are updated in the MFT to identify the location where the file data is stored.
- For non-resident data the bitmap is updated to show that the cluster(s) occupied by the file are now in use.
- The parent directory listing is updated and re-sorted.

Deleting a File

To delete a file on the system, the following processes are carried out, though not necessarily in the order shown:

- The MFT record is marked as deleted (a one byte flag).
- For non-resident data the bitmap is updated to show that the cluster(s) occupied by the file are now available for use.
- The file entry in the parent directory listing is removed and the listing is re-sorted. Note, however that the MFT record for the file itself will remain intact until overwritten.

The BIOS Parameter Block

Before a single, and complete, MFT record can be identified the defined size of each record must be known. This is available from the BIOS Parameter Block (BPB), which would have been created on the disk at the time of installation of the NTFS file system on the partition. The BPB is located within the Boot Record of the partition and details of the BPB are given at Appendix 8.

Table 6.1 Boot sector and BIOS parameter block.

```
Offset      0  1  2  3  4  5  6  7   8  9 10 11 12 13 14 15
00000000   EB 52 90 4E 54 46 53 20  20 20 20 00 02 08 00 00    ëR_NTFS    .....
00000016   00 00 00 00 00 F8 00 00  3F 00 80 00 3F 00 00 00    .....ø..?._.?...
00000032   00 00 00 00 80 00 80 00  40 2A 4C 00 00 00 00 00    ...._._.@*L.....
00000048   04 00 00 00 00 00 00 00  A4 C2 04 00 00 00 00 00    ........¤Â......
00000064   F6 00 00 00 01 00 00 00  B2 7C 0C D0 9E 0C D0 A0    ö.......²|.Ð_.Ð
00000080   00 00 00 00 FA 33 C0 8E  D0 BC 00 7C FB B8 C0 07    ....ú3À_Đ¼.|û_À.
00000096   8E D8 E8 16 00 B8 00 0D  8E C0 33 DB C6 06 0E 00    yØè._,.. À3ÛÆ...
00000112   10 E8 53 00 68 00 00 68  6A 02 CB 8A 16 24 00 B4    .èS.h..hj.Ë_.$._
00000128   08 CD 13 73 05 B9 FF FF  8A F1 66 0F B6 C6 40 66    .Í.s.¹ÿÿŠñf.¶Æ@f
00000144   0F B6 D1 80 E2 3F F7 E2  86 CD C0 ED 06 41 66 0F    .¶Ñ_â?÷â†ÍÀí.Af.
00000160   B7 C9 66 F7 E1 66 A3 20  00 C3 B4 41 BB AA 55 8A    ·Éf÷áf£ .Ã´A»ªUŠ
00000176   16 24 00 CD 13 72 0F 81  FB 55 AA 75 09 F6 C1 01    .$.Í.r._ûUªu.öÁ.
00000192   74 04 FE 06 14 00 C3 66  60 1E 06 66 A1 10 00 66    t.þ...Ãf`..fi..f
00000208   03 06 1C 00 66 3B 06 20  00 0F 82 3A 00 1E 66 6A    ....f;. ..,:..fj
00000224   00 66 50 06 53 66 68 10  00 01 00 80 3E 14 00 00    .fP.Sfh....>...
00000240   0F 85 0C 00 E8 B3 FF 80  3E 14 00 00 0F 84 61 00    .....è³ÿ_>....„a.
00000256   B4 42 8A 16 24 00 16 1F  8B F4 CD 13 66 58 5B 07    ´BŠ.$...‹ôÍ.fX[.
00000272   66 58 66 58 1F EB 2D 66  33 D2 66 0F B7 0E 18 00    fXfX.ë-f3Òf.·....
00000288   66 F7 F1 FE C2 8A CA 66  8B D0 66 C1 EA 10 F7 36    f÷ñþÂŠÊf‹Ðf Á ê.÷6
00000304   1A 00 86 D6 8A 16 24 00  8A E8 C0 E4 06 0A CC B8    ..†ÖŠ.$.ŠèÀä..Ì,
00000320   01 02 CD 13 0F 82 19 00  8C C0 05 20 00 8E C0 66    ..Í..,..ŒÀ. .ŽÀf
00000336   FF 06 10 00 FF 0E 0E 00  0F 85 6F FF 07 1F 66 61    ÿ...ÿ.....oÿ..fa
00000352   C3 A0 F8 01 E8 09 00 A0  FB 01 E8 03 00 FB EB FE    Ã ø.è.. û.è..ûëþ
00000368   B4 01 8B F0 AC 3C 00 74  09 B4 0E BB 07 00 CD 10    ´.‹ð¬<.t.´.»..Í.
00000384   EB F2 C3 0D 0A 41 20 64  69 73 6B 20 72 65 61 64    ëòÃ..A disk read
00000400   20 65 72 72 6F 72 20 6F  63 63 75 72 72 65 64 00     error occurred.
00000416   0D 0A 4E 54 4C 44 52 20  69 73 20 6D 69 73 73 69    ..NTLDR is missi
00000432   6E 67 00 0D 0A 4E 54 4C  44 52 20 69 73 20 63 6F    ng...NTLDR is co
00000448   6D 70 72 65 73 73 65 64  00 0D 0A 50 72 65 73 73    mpressed...Press
00000464   20 43 74 72 6C 2B 41 6C  74 2B 44 65 6C 20 74 6F     Ctrl+Alt+Del to
00000480   20 72 65 73 74 61 72 74  0D 0A 00 00 00 00 00 00     restart........
00000496   00 00 00 00 00 00 00 00  83 A0 B3 C9 00 00 55 AA    ........ƒ ³É..Uª
```

Table 6.1 shows, in a hexadecimal and ASCII display format, the boot sector and BIOS parameter block for our example system. The defined size of the MFT record on this system is specified at byte offset 64. This is a signed 8 bit number which is used in two different ways. If this number is positive (between 00–7Fh) it defines how many *clusters* there are for each MFT record. If this number is negative (80–FFh) it defines how many *bytes* there are for each MFT record. The actual value is calculated by raising 2 to the power of the absolute value of this number. In this case it may be seen that the byte at offset 64 (black background) is F6h.

The 8 bit signed value of the number, F6, is –10 and its absolute value is 10. Thus the number of *bytes* (because it is negative) in each MFT record entry is $2^{10} = 1024$ bytes. This conforms with our current experience that all systems seen to date have a 1024 byte record size.

The size of the MFT records in the example MFT has now been identified and from this we know that each record will appear at 1024 byte intervals throughout the MFT.

The location of the start of the MFT is also given within the BPB. The logical cluster number of the start of the MFT is given at byte offsets 48 to 55 as a 64 bit little-endian number. In this case the MFT is seen to start at logical cluster 4 (mid-grey background). At byte offset 13 the sector-per-cluster count is shown as 8 (light grey background), and so the MFT starts at logical sector $4 \times 8 = 32$. This is equivalent to physical sector 95, since there is normally one track from the partition table to the boot record, and this partition has 63 sectors per track. This is confirmed by byte offset 24 (double underline) which contains the value 3Fh = 63.

As might be expected, the MFT file itself is the subject of the first record in the MFT. Its size is defined within the Attribute Header for the Data Attribute within the record. In this case the physical size of the file, the logical size of the file and the initialized stream are all specified at 6,750,208 bytes, and the data run specifies a run length of 1,648 clusters starting at cluster 4. For details on how these items are identified see Appendix 9.

Types of Record

By inspection, we find that there are four types of record in our sample MFT:

- Records for files with resident data.
- Records for files with non-resident data.
- Records for directories with resident data.
- Records for directories with non-resident data.

Attribute IDs

We also note that the MFT entries are made up of a series of "Attributes" which are declared in the metadata file $AttrDef, as mentioned earlier. A scan of the $AttrDef file in our sample MFT shows that the following Attributes with their ID numbers are declared (see Table 6.2).

The ID number is a 4 byte identifier found at byte offset 129 of each record in the $AttrDef file. The record length, from inspection, is 160 bytes, the identifiers having been found to be 160 bytes apart in every case. This is easily determined using a hexadecimal viewer to view the binary layout of the file. Table 6.2 indicates that there

Table 6.2 Attributes and IDs in sample MFT.

```
Standard_Information      ID       10 00 00 00
Attribute_List           ID       20 00 00 00
File_Name                ID       30 00 00 00
Object_ID                ID       40 00 00 00
Security_Descriptor      ID       50 00 00 00
Volume_Name              ID       60 00 00 00
Volume_Information       ID       70 00 00 00
Data                     ID       80 00 00 00
Index_Root               ID       90 00 00 00
Index_Allocation         ID       A0 00 00 00
Bitmap                   ID       B0 00 00 00
Reparse_Point            ID       C0 00 00 00
EA_Information           ID       D0 00 00 00
EA                       ID       E0 00 00 00
Logged_Utility_Stream    ID       00 00 00 00
```

are 15 possible types of Attribute within the sample MFT, although it is unlikely that all will be used.

Experimentation has shown that every record in the MFT has a "FILE" Record Header which is always the same length for a given operating system. In the case of Windows 2000 it is 48 bytes, and for Windows XP its is 56 bytes. This header is followed by a number of Attributes which themselves have anAttribute Header. The Attribute header contains a field which stores the length of the Attribute. The next series of bytes following that stated length should either be the header field for the next Attribute or the end of record marker, FF FF FF FFh.

All MFT records in the sample MFT have the following overall structure:

- File Record Header
- Attribute Header
- Attribute Proper
- Attribute Header
- Attribute Proper
- Further Attribute Header and Attribute Proper pairs
- End of Record marker (FF FF FF FFh)
- Error Check Sequence (4 bytes)

It should be noted at this point that the Attribute Header can vary in size and content. The type of template to be applied depends upon bytes at offsets 8 and 9 of the header itself. These bytes indicate whether the Attribute is Resident or Non-Resident, Named or Un-Named. Details of the four templates are given in Appendix 9.

Analysis of a Sample MFT File Record with Resident Data

At Table 6.3 is shown our sample MFT record with resident data in a hexadecimal and ASCII display format. Inspection of this record shows a probable filename in Unicode at offset 234 (black background) as being immediately recognizable. To the practised eye there appears to be a set of four 8-byte Microsoft "FILETIME" date and time entries at offset 72 (light grey background) and again at offset 176 (mid-grey background). Forensic practitioners will frequently come across such date and time entries and the "C0 01" and "C4 01" values are an immediate clue as to there being a possibly correct FILETIME interpretation. Microsoft FILETIME is a date and time field that is defined as a 64 bit number (held here in little endian format) that represents the number of 100 nanosecond intervals that have elapsed since 00:00:00 GMT on 1 January 1601.

The file data itself appears to start at offset 464 with the known start string of a .gif file, GIF89a (double underline). The data appears to end at offset 727.

Table 6.3 Sample MFT record with resident data.

```
Offset      0  1  2  3  4  5  6  7   8  9 10 11 12 13 14 15
00000000   46 49 4C 45 2A 00 03 00  6D A1 8C 00 00 00 00 00   FILE*...miŒ.....
00000016   01 00 01 00 30 00 01 00  D8 02 00 00 00 04 00 00   ....0...Ø.......
00000032   00 00 00 00 00 00 00 00  05 00 03 00 84 94 00 00   ............„".
00000048   10 00 00 00 60 00 00 00  00 00 00 00 00 00 00 00   ....`...........
00000064   48 00 00 00 18 00 00 00  00 E0 48 68 B6 D7 C0 01   H........àHh¶×À.
00000080   00 E0 48 68 B6 D7 C0 01  76 2F 3F 3C 8A 57 C4 01   .àHh¶×À.v/?<ŠWÄ.
00000096   98 EF 7F 33 89 57 C4 01  20 00 00 00 00 00 00 00   ˜ïÇ3‰WÄ. .......
00000112   00 00 00 00 00 00 00 00  00 00 00 00 00 00 00 00   ................
00000128   00 00 00 00 00 00 00 00  00 00 00 00 00 00 00 00   ................
00000144   30 00 00 00 78 00 00 00  00 00 00 00 00 00 04 00   0...x...........
00000160   5A 00 00 00 18 00 01 00  48 00 00 00 00 00 01 00   Z.......H.......
00000176   60 53 63 33 89 57 C4 01  98 EF 7F 33 89 57 C4 01   `Sc3‰WÄ.˜ïÇ3‰WÄ.
00000192   98 EF 7F 33 89 57 C4 01  98 EF 7F 33 89 57 C4 01   ˜ïÇ3‰WÄ.˜ïÇ3‰WÄ.
00000208   00 01 00 00 00 00 00 00  FF 00 00 00 00 00 00 00   ........ÿ.......
00000224   20 00 00 00 00 00 00 00  0C 03 69 00 70 00 70 00    .........i.p.p.
00000240   5F 00 30 00 30 00 30 00  35 00 2E 00 67 00 69 00   _.0.0.0.5...g.i.
00000256   66 00 18 00 00 00 01 00  50 00 00 00 B0 00 00 00   f.......P...°...
00000272   00 00 00 00 00 00 03 00  94 00 00 00 18 00 00 00   ............".
00000288   01 00 04 84 78 00 00 00  88 00 00 00 00 00 00 00   ...„x...ˆ.......
00000304   14 00 00 00 02 00 64 00  04 00 00 00 00 10 18 00   ......d.........
00000320   A9 00 12 00 01 02 00 00  00 00 00 05 20 00 00 00   ©........... ...
00000336   21 02 00 00 00 10 18 00  A9 00 12 00 01 02 00 00   !.......©.......
00000352   00 00 00 05 20 00 00 00  23 02 00 00 00 10 18 00   .... ...#.......
00000368   FF 01 1F 00 01 02 00 00  00 00 00 05 20 00 00 00   ÿ........... ...
00000384   20 02 00 00 00 10 14 00  FF 01 1F 00 01 01 00 00    .......ÿ.......
00000400   00 00 00 05 12 00 00 00  01 02 00 00 00 00 00 05   ................
00000416   20 00 00 00 20 02 00 00  01 01 00 00 00 00 00 05    ... ...........
00000432   12 00 00 00 9C 52 84 94  80 00 00 00 18 01 00 00   ....œR„"€.......
00000448   00 00 18 00 00 00 01 00  FF 00 00 00 18 00 00 00   ........ÿ.......
00000464   47 49 46 38 39 61 0F 00  0F 00 C4 FF 00 C0 C0 C0   GIF89a....Äÿ.ÀÀÀ
00000480   6B 6B 39 63 63 31 73 73  39 6B 6B 31 84 8C 4A 73   kk9cc1ss9kk1„ŒJs
00000496   7B 42 7B 84 42 6B 73 39  7B 84 4A 8C 9C 52 03 00   {B{„Bks9{„JŒœR..
00000512   52 7B 8C 4A 73 84 42 9C  B5 63 94 AD 5A 8C A5 5A   R{ŒJs„Bœµc"ZŒ¥Z
00000528   94 AD 63 AD CE 7B A5 C6  73 9C BD 6B AD D6 7B B5   "cÎ{¥Æsœ½kÖ{µ
00000544   DE 84 00 00 00 00 00 00  00 00 00 00 00 00 00 00   Þ„............
00000560   00 00 00 00 00 00 00 00  00 00 00 00 00 21 F9 04   .............!ù.
00000576   01 00 00 00 00 2C 00 00  00 00 0F 00 0F 00 00 05   .....,.........
00000592   7C 20 20 8A D1 03 29 CB  A8 02 54 4B 45 D0 52 1C   | ŠÑ.)Ë¨.TKEÐR.
00000608   2B 35 DD AD B9 24 C6 68  4B 15 1C 6C C1 30 20 44   +5Ý¹$ÆhK..lÁ0 D
00000624   B6 8A 25 F8 8A 15 8C 80  C8 AF 22 99 34 77 87 80   ¶Š%øŠ.Œ€È¯"™4w‡_
00000640   E0 E1 B0 E1 1C 11 14 0F  21 80 44 BA 2D 70 8C 71   àáE á....!€Dº-pŒq
```

```
00000656   18 10 08 0A 73 64 6E 12   1B 05 82 C5 22 0E E9 EB    ....sdn...,Å".éë
00000672   13 0D 06 5A 04 00 05 7A   87 05 09 6D 01 04 02 22    ...Z...z‡..m..."
00000688   09 90 89 90 06 03 5A 78   23 06 99 99 03 08 83 8E    . ‰ ..Zx#.™™..ƒ_
00000704   2A 08 9D 01 96 97 2B 22   8D 78 84 2A 21 00 3B 00    *._.—+"_xₙ*!.;.
00000720   FF FF FF FF 82 79 47 11   00 00 00 00 00 00 00 00    ÿÿÿÿ‚yG.........
00000736   00 00 00 00 00 00 00 00   00 00 00 00 00 00 00 00    ...............
00000752   00 00 00 00 00 00 00 00   00 00 00 00 00 00 00 00    ...............
00000768   00 00 00 00 00 00 00 00   00 00 00 00 00 00 00 00    ...............
00000784   00 00 00 00 00 00 00 00   00 00 00 00 00 00 00 00    ...............
00000800   00 00 00 00 00 00 00 00   00 00 00 00 00 00 00 00    ...............
00000816   00 00 00 00 00 00 00 00   00 00 00 00 00 00 00 00    ...............
00000832   00 00 00 00 00 00 00 00   00 00 00 00 00 00 00 00    ...............
00000848   00 00 00 00 00 00 00 00   00 00 00 00 00 00 00 00    ...............
00000864   00 00 00 00 00 00 00 00   00 00 00 00 00 00 00 00    ...............
00000880   00 00 00 00 00 00 00 00   00 00 00 00 00 00 00 00    ...............
00000896   00 00 00 00 00 00 00 00   00 00 00 00 00 00 00 00    ...............
00000912   00 00 00 00 00 00 00 00   00 00 00 00 00 00 00 00    ...............
00000928   00 00 00 00 00 00 00 00   00 00 00 00 00 00 00 00    ...............
00000944   00 00 00 00 00 00 00 00   00 00 00 00 00 00 00 00    ...............
00000960   00 00 00 00 00 00 00 00   00 00 00 00 00 00 00 00    ...............
00000976   00 00 00 00 00 00 00 00   00 00 00 00 00 00 00 00    ...............
00000992   00 00 00 00 00 00 00 00   00 00 00 00 00 00 00 00    ...............
00001008   00 00 00 00 00 00 00 00   00 00 00 00 00 00 03 00    ...............
```

Normal user access to this file, via a directory folder view in Windows Explorer, shows at Table 6.4 the file details reported by the operating system, Windows 2000.

Table 6.4 Windows Explorer file directory details.

File Name & Path	\WINNT\Web\printers\images\ipp_0005.gif
Size (bytes)	255
Last Accessed	21/06/04 12:13
Last Written	08/05/01 12:00
File Created	08/05/01 12:00
Attributes	Archive bit set

With an image of the system loaded as a virtual disk, forensic software was used to examine the directory details of this file, with the results as shown at Table 6.5.

Table 6.5 Forensic software file directory details.

File Name	ipp_0005.gif
Last Access	21/06/04 12:13:45
Last Written	08/05/01 12:00:00
File Created	08/05/01 12:00:00
Entry Modified	21/06/04 12:21:10
Logical Size	255
Physical Size	255
Starting Extent	0C-C177
Physical Location	PS:1481, SO:464
Full Path	WINNT\Web\printers\images\ipp_0005.gif

Taking it Apart – the FILE Record Header

The FILE record header appears at the beginning of all MFT records. As mentioned above, its length is 48 bytes for the sample MFT because this is a Windows 2000 system. For Windows XP the header length is 56 bytes because this later version of

NTFS adds the MFT record number into the record header. In what follows, it should also be noted that almost all hexadecimal values are shown in little endian format, which is the format in which they are stored.

We now examine the header, line by line. At Table 6.6 we see that the first 4 bytes spell out the word "FILE" (black background), which identifies the entry as a file record. From an inspection of the sample MFT we note that all records start in this way.

Table 6.6 Start of file record header.

```
00000000    46 49 4C 45 2A 00 03 00  6D A1 8C 00 00 00 00 00    FILE*...miŒ.....
```

At Table 6.7 we see that the next two bytes (black background) are the value 2A 00, which in little endian is 002A = decimal 42. This is the offset pointer to the Update Sequence Number and Array and counts from the beginning of the header. It is typically different for different operating systems. In the case of Windows XP, where the MFT Record Number is allocated an additional field in this Header, the value in these two bytes will point six further bytes into the record. In what follows, we have only shown the situation for Windows 2000. See Appendix 9 for further details. Examination of the two bytes at offset 42 shows them to contain the values 03 00 and we will be discussing the significance of this in a later section.

Table 6.7 Offset to Update Sequence Number.

```
00000000    46 49 4C 45 2A 00 03 00  6D A1 8C 00 00 00 00 00    FILE*...miŒ.....
```

Byte offsets (counting from zero) 6 and 7 specify the size of the update sequence, and this is another two byte integer in little endian format. As can be seen at Table 6.8, the value here is 03 00 (black background) or decimal 3. This number here is used to represent the number of words rather than the number of bytes. It indicates that three words are used for the Update Sequence Number and the Update Sequence Array (see Tables 6.18 and 6.19). Further explanation is given below, where the update sequence itself is explored and discussed. From an inspection of the MFT, we note that all records in the sample file contain 03 00h at this location.

Table 6.8 Size of update sequence.

```
00000000    46 49 4C 45 2A 00 03 00  6D A1 8C 00 00 00 00 00    FILE*...miŒ.....
```

Highlighted (black background) in Table 6.9, the next 8 bytes (offsets 8 to 15) refer to the $Logfile sequence number (see $Logfile above).

Table 6.9 $Logfile sequence number.

```
00000000    46 49 4C 45 2A 00 03 00  6D A1 8C 00 00 00 00 00    FILE*...miŒ.....
```

Bytes 16 and 17 (black background) in Table 6.10, are referred to as the "Record Use Sequence Number", which is set to "1" when the MFT record is first used. It is subsequently incremented each time that the record is reused. It is interesting to note that the actual increment operation is made when the record is marked as deleted and available for reuse. See the item on "Identification of Files in Unallocated Space – Deleted Files" at the end of this chapter for possible other uses of this number in directory records.

Table 6.10 Record use sequence number.

```
00000016    01 00 01 00 30 00 01 00  D8 02 00 00 00 04 00 00    ....0...Ø.......
```

Bytes 18 and 19 (black background) in Table 6.11 refer to the hard link count for this file, stored as a two-byte integer number. Microsoft[9] define hard links as:

"NTFS-based links to a file on an NTFS volume. By creating hard links, you can have a single file in multiple folders without duplicating the file. You can also create multiple hard links for a file in a folder if you use different file names for the hard links. Because all of the hard links reference the same file, applications can open any of the hard links and modify the file."

Table 6.11 Hard link count.
```
00000016    01 00 01 00 30 00 01 00   D8 02 00 00 00 04 00 00    ....0...Ø.......
```

Bytes situated at offsets 20 and 21 (black background) in Table 6.12 are again a two-byte integer value specifying the "Offset to First Attribute" in this record. As with most of the pointers in the MFT, the figure is calculated from the start of the header. This pointer indicates that the first Attribute starts at 0030h which is byte offset 48.

Table 6.12 Pointer to first Attribute.
```
00000016    01 00 01 00 30 00 01 00   D8 02 00 00 00 04 00 00    ....0...Ø.......
```

The next two bytes, 22 and 23 (black background) in Table 6.13, are a set of flags. The two bytes, and in particular the byte at offset 22, refer to the current state of this particular record. The possible values are: 00 00 = a deleted FILE record, 01 00 = a FILE record in use, 02 00 = a deleted DIRECTORY record, and 03 00 = a DIRECTORY record in use. In this case we note that the value is 01 00 and that it is a FILE record in use.

Table 6.13 Record flags.
```
00000016    01 00 01 00 30 00 01 00   D8 02 00 00 00 04 00 00    ....0...Ø.......
```

Bytes at offsets 24 to 27 (black background) in Table 6.14 indicate the "real" length of the file record. To clarify this, it is referred to here as the "logical size" in keeping with the standards operated within the forensic community relating to file size and allocated space size. This "logical" size is the actual number of bytes of data stored in the record. By inspection of the sample MFT record (Table 6.3), the probable size may be identified visually as 728 bytes. Stored as a 4 byte integer in little endian format, the value 000002D8h equates to 728 decimal, exactly as expected!

Table 6.14 Logical size of record.
```
00000016    01 00 01 00 30 00 01 00   D8 02 00 00 00 04 00 00    ....0...Ø.......
```

The final four bytes of this line, from offsets 28 to 31 (black background) in Table 6.15, indicate the allocated storage size of the file record. This is referred to as the "physical" size and you will recall that this size has already been preset to 1024 bytes by the BPB. In this case translation from the little endian format gives 00000400h, which does indeed equate to 1024 decimal.

Table 6.15 Physical size of record.
```
00000016    01 00 01 00 30 00 01 00   D8 02 00 00 00 04 00 00    ....0...Ø.......
```

9 http://technet2.microsoft.com/WindowsServer/en/Library/59a9462a-cbdd-45e7-828b-12c6cd9ae4781033.mspx

The bytes at offsets 32 to 39 (black background) in Table 6.16, store the "Base File Reference" that is used when the record to be stored exceeds the allocated space of one or more MFT records. When this occurs, the succeeding records, which may be considerably detached from the first one used, contain a reference at this location to their "parent" record. It is not necessarily the case that the next record in the MFT will be used to store such "overflow" data; the record used could be anywhere in the MFT and some distance, in terms of records, from the first one used. Experiments carried out on this "Base File Reference" concept found the name to be a rather poor description of this field. The 8 byte number is actually made up of more than one value. The function of the whole number is unclear, but it seems likely that the first six bytes specifically identify the record number in the MFT of the "parent" record and the last two bytes of the field may well be a sequence number or identifier. In addition to these "backward" pointers to the parent in these Base File Reference fields, there are a series of "forward" pointers to the children (the extended records) in the parent record itself. These forward pointers are in the order that the children are to be read. In this particular case, there is no parent record and the value in the Base File Reference is 00 00 00 00 00 00 00 00.

Table 6.16 Base file reference.

00000032	00 00 00 00 00 00 00 00	05 00 03 00 84 94 00 00	............" ..

Two bytes, at offset 40 and 41 (black background) in Table 6.17, appear to be used to identify the value of the ordinal number for the next Attribute to be added to this record. In this case, the record is reported to contain four Attributes, so the next one will be the fifth. This fact will be seen to be confirmed for *this* record as the deconstruction analysis progresses. However, visual inspection of 100 other records in this MFT revealed that the value is unreliable as an indicator of the number of Attributes present. It may well be that it is a count of Attributes that have been used within the record and that it reverts to zero on record reuse. Experiments have shown that the count is incremented when an Attribute is added but does not seem to be decremented when one is removed.

Table 6.17 Possible Attribute count.

00000032	00 00 00 00 00 00 00 00	05 00	03 00 84 94 00 00	............" ..

Bytes 42 and 43 (black background) in Table 6.18 have already been identified above as the "Update Sequence Number". This is apparently used to check the integrity of each MFT record. As may be noted by inspection, this same number (in this case 03 00h) also appears as the last two bytes of each physical sector of the MFT record. The explanation for this is given in the next section.

Table 6.18 Update Sequence Number.

00000032	00 00 00 00 00 00 00 00	05 00	03 00	84 94 00 00	............" ..

The final four bytes of the "FILE" header, offsets 44 to 47 (black background) in Table 6.19, are used for the "Update Sequence Array". In this case the sequence array consists of the four bytes 84 94 00 00h. In order to check the consistency of MFT records, and other protected records, NTFS uses a "fix-up" code that it places in the final two bytes of each sector. In this case that code is 03 00h, the number that is identified as the "Update Sequence Number". The bytes which originally occupied these locations in each sector are placed in a buffer, the buffer we are now examining at bytes 44 to 47. There are two sectors in an MFT record and therefore four bytes are replaced. The four replaced bytes are 84 94h for the first sector and 00 00h for the second sector.

Table 6.19 Update Sequence Array.

00000032	00 00 00 00 00 00 00 00	05 00 03 00	84 94 00 00	.............„"..

Use of the Update Sequence Number and the Update Sequence Array

When the record is read by the operating system the sequence bytes in the last two bytes of the sector are checked to ensure that the sector has been read correctly. Once this has been done the appropriate two bytes are copied from the sequence array buffer into the correct location in the read data. As a check of this process, the file to which this record refers was copied out to a FAT-based disk. At Table 6.20 is shown the first part of the file as we found it held resident in the MFT record. We see (black background) the Update Sequence Number, 03 00h, in the last two bytes of the sector, offsets 510 and 511. The values that were originally there we see as the first two bytes of the Update Sequence Array, 84 94h, in Table 6.19.

Table 6.20 Start of GIF file resident in MFT.

00000464	47 49 46 38 39 61 0F 00	0F 00 C4 FF 00 C0 C0 C0	GIF89a....Äÿ.ÀÀÀ
00000480	6B 6B 39 63 63 31 73 73	39 6B 6B 31 84 8C 4A 73	kk9cc1ss9kk1„ŒJs
00000496	7B 42 7B 84 42 6B 73 39	7B 84 4A 8C 9C 52 03 00	{B{„Bks9{„JŒœR..
00000512	52 7B 8C 4A 73 84 42 9C	B5 63 94 AD 5A 8C A5 5A	R{ŒJs„Bœµc"-ZŒ¥Z

At Table 6.21, we show the first part of the GIF file as we found it when copied out to a FAT-based disk. Here we see, at offsets 510 and 511, the correct sequence of 84 94h, again with a black background. It is clear, that, on copying out, these two bytes are reset from the Update Sequence Number of 03 00h, present whilst they are held within the MFT record, to their correct file values of 84 94h, that had been saved in the Update Sequence Array.

Table 6.21 Start of GIF file as copied out.

00000464	47 49 46 38 39 61 0F 00	0F 00 C4 FF 00 C0 C0 C0	GIF89a....Äÿ.ÀÀÀ
00000480	6B 6B 39 63 63 31 73 73	39 6B 6B 31 84 8C 4A 73	kk9cc1ss9kk1„ŒJs
00000496	7B 42 7B 84 42 6B 73 39	7B 84 4A 8C 9C 52 84 94	{B{„Bks9{„JŒœR„"
00000512	52 7B 8C 4A 73 84 42 9C	B5 63 94 AD 5A 8C A5 5A	R{ŒJs„Bœµc"-ZŒ¥Z

The area of the MFT record beyond the "logical" record length is often (as is the case here; see Table 6.3) occupied by zeros. Therefore bytes 46 and 47 of the Update Sequence Array (see Table 6.19) are zero. These are the true values for the last two bytes of the record, which in the MFT have also been replaced with 03 00h at offsets 1022 and 1023 (see Table 6.3).

This replacement of bytes can have a significant effect on the forensic extraction of files directly from the MFT in raw form. If the file is copied out normally using the NTFS system, the last two bytes in each sector will be replaced correctly and automatically by NTFS. If, however, the file is extracted directly from the MFT record using, for example, a hexadecimal editor, this replacement process will not occur and the last two bytes of each sector will continue to contain the Update Sequence Number. This means, of course, that MD5 signatures for the two versions will be very different. Analysts must be aware of the issues surrounding the Update Sequence

Number, so that extractions of this type can be made correctly. They should also be able to explain the differences between the storage of files using this system and the storage of files in FAT-based systems.

A similar arrangement applies to other "protected" records. These include external "INDX" index records where the length of allocation blocks is fixed at 4096 bytes. A brief examination of an "INDX" record on the sample volume showed that the Size of Update Sequence here is reported to be 9. Since the record is of 4096 bytes in length, which is 8 sectors, we would expect there to be 8 pairs of bytes (one pair for each sector) to be held in the Update Sequence Array. Thus a reported length of 9 must refer to nine words, one word for the Update Sequence Number and eight words for the Update Sequence Array.

A random inspection of the records in the sample MFT showed the two bytes to be consistently present at offsets 42 and 43 with values 03 00h. They were also noted to be consistently present at record offsets 510, 511, 1022 and 1023 for every record examined.

Further experiments showed that the same cloned NTFS volume, mounted on 18 identical machines each with identical Windows 2000 operating systems, generated several different Update Sequence Numbers when they were mounted as secondary volumes. This suggests that NTFS not only checks the consistency of the MFT during a mount but may also rewrite part or all of the MFT with a different Update Sequence Number during this check. This, too, has considerable significance from a forensic viewpoint.

Taking it Apart – the Standard Information Attribute

Every MFT is made up of a series of "Attributes". Following the FILE Record header, described above, is the first of these, the Standard Information Attribute. The Attribute ID for this Attribute (see Table 6.2) is 10 00 00 00h. The first part of this Attribute follows a regular pattern known as the Attribute Header, which is here 24 bytes long. The length of this header varies according to whether or not it is Resident (offset 8 of the header) or named (offset 9 of the header).

The Attribute Header

Continuing with our sample record from Table 6.3, the bytes at offsets 48 to 51 (black background) at Table 6.22 make up the four-byte identifier for this Attribute. These Attribute IDs are defined, as already mentioned, in the $AttrDef file, and we have shown the specific ones for this sample at Table 6.2.

Table 6.22   Attribute ID.

```
00000048  10 00 00 00  60 00 00 00 00 00 00 00 00 00 00 00  ....˙...........
```

Bytes 52 to 55 (black background) at Table 6.23 define the length of this Attribute. This conforms with the common practice of defining the length of an entry immediately following the identifier. The length shown here is 00000060h, which is 96 decimal. Inspection of Table 6.3 shows that 96 bytes on from the beginning of this Attribute (offset 48), at byte offsets 144 to 147, are the four values 30 00 00 00h. This is

a set of four bytes which should be another Attribute ID. In this case it is the ID for a
File Name Attribute (see Table 6.2), which is a valid entry, as we will see later.

Table 6.23 Length of Attribute.
```
00000048    10 00 00 00 60 00 00 00  00 00 00 00 00 00 00 00    ....`...........
```

At Byte 56 (black background) at Table 6.24 is the resident/non-resident flag. This
is signified by 00h for a resident Attribute and 01h for a non-resident Attribute. The
flag refers to the body of the Attribute itself. Other Attributes will have similar
headers in which each Attribute will be defined as resident or non-resident.

Table 6.24 Resident/non-resident flag.
```
00000048    10 00 00 00 60 00 00 00  00 00 00 00 00 00 00 00    ....`...........
```

The next byte, at offset 57 (black background) at Table 6.25, is the length of the
name of the Attribute. In this case the length is zero, since this Attribute is not
allocated a name.

Table 6.25 Length of name of Attribute.
```
00000048    10 00 00 00 60 00 00 00  00 00 00 00 00 00 00 00    ....`...........
```

The bytes at offsets 58 and 59 (black background) at Table 6.26 indicate the offset
value to the start of the Attribute proper. These are not always used, as here, where
they are shown as 00 00h. It is not known why two similar fields are included in this
header; both are used in the sample MFT. See Tables 6.30 and 6.59.

Table 6.26 Offset to name of Attribute.
```
00000048    10 00 00 00 60 00 00 00  00 00 00 00 00 00 00 00    ....`...........
```

The bytes at offset 60 and 61 (black background) at Table 6.27 are identified as a set
of flags which signify the following states: 00 00h = normal, 01 00h = compressed, 40
00h = encrypted and 80 00h = sparse. It may well be, and the authors suspect this to
be the case, that this field is included in the Attribute Header for use only with a Data
Attribute. These offsets were examined right across the sample MFT and no non-
zero hits were found. However, examination of other systems revealed that files
marked as compressed did have the associated value (01 00h) stored at this location
within the relevant Data Attributes.

Table 6.27 Flags.
```
00000048    10 00 00 00 60 00 00 00  00 00 00 00 00 00 00 00    ....`...........
```

The purpose of the bytes at offsets 62 and 63 (black background) at Table 6.28 is
unclear. Some sources suggest they are used as some form of Attribute ID. Exploration of other MFTs suggest that these may be used for a number of purposes which
have not yet been sufficiently well identified by the authors. It is possible that part of
the field may be used as a flag to show virus-infected and virus-cleaned files.

Table 6.28 Not yet known.
```
00000048    10 00 00 00 60 00 00 00  00 00 00 00 00 00 00 00    ....`...........
```

The four bytes from offset 64 to offset 67 (black background) at Table 6.29 define
the length of the Attribute proper. In this case the value is 00000048h, which is 72 in
decimal. This Attribute Header is 24 bytes long and the complete Attribute, including
this header, is defined at bytes 52 to 55 (see Table 6.23) as 96 bytes. The value of the
Attribute proper should therefore be 96 − 24 = 72, which is what is stored here.

Table 6.29 Length of Attribute proper.
```
00000064    48 00 00 00  18 00 00 00   00 E0 48 68 B6 D7 C0 01    H........àHh¶×Å.
```

The next two bytes, at offsets 68 and 69 (black background) at Table 6.30, indicate the offset from the beginning of this Attribute to the start of the Attribute proper. This is where the Standard Information Attribute details start, after the header that is currently being deconstructed. The value is 0018h which equals 24 decimal. Noting from Table 6.22 that the start offset for this Attribute is 48, then the Attribute proper starts at offset 48 + 24 = 72.

Table 6.30 Offset to start of Attribute proper.
```
00000064    48 00 00 00  18 00 00 00   00 E0 48 68 B6 D7 C0 01    H........àHh¶×Å.
```

Highlighted (black background) at Table 6.31 are byte offset 70, reported to be the "indexed" flag, and byte offset 71, reported to be padding to an 8 byte boundary. As will be seen, this padding is not unusual.

Table 6.31 Indexed flag and padding.
```
00000064    48 00 00 00  18 00 00 00   00 E0 48 68 B6 D7 C0 01    H........àHh¶×Å.
```

The Standard Information Attribute Proper

The first 32 bytes of this Attribute proper from byte offset 72 to byte offset 103 (black background) at Table 6.32, refer to four dates and times.

Table 6.32 Four dates and times.
```
00000064    48 00 00 00 18 00 00 00   00 E0 48 68 B6 D7 C0 01    H........àHh¶×Å.
00000080    00 E0 48 68 B6 D7 C0 01   76 2F 3F 3C 8A 57 C4 01    .àHh¶×Å.v/?<ŠWÄ.
00000096    98 EF 7F 33 89 57 C4 01   20 00 00 00 00 00 00 00    ¯ïÇ3‰WÄ. .......
```

The values stored in these bytes are in a format known as a "FILETIME", which we mention above (see Table 6.3). This is a 64 bit number (held here in little endian format) that represents the number of 100 nanosecond intervals that have elapsed since 00:00:00 GMT on 1 January 1601. The date and time values in these 32 bytes are shown in Table 6.33.

Table 6.33 Date and time values.

Bytes 72 to 79	Creation Date and Time	08/05/01 12:00:00 GMT
Bytes 80 to 87	Last Modified Date and Time	08/05/01 12:00:00 GMT
Bytes 88 to 95	Last MFT Record Change Date and Time	21/06/04 12:21:10 GMT
Bytes 96 to 103	Last Access Date and Time	21/06/04 12:13:45 GMT

An examination of the reported times and dates by the operating system and by forensic software (see Tables 6.4 and 6.5 respectively) reveals that they are consistent with those recorded here.

Byte offsets 104 to 107 (black background) at Table 6.34 are used for File Permissions, which are similar to the FAT attribute byte in a directory entry. This attribute byte system, in the style of MS-DOS, is used on byte offset 104 with further attributes being set by byte offset 105. It is understood that the byte offsets 106 and 107 are reserved for similar use.

Table 6.34 File permissions.
```
00000096    98 EF 7F 33 89 57 C4 01   20 00 00 00 00 00 00 00    ¯ïÇ3‰WÄ. .......
```

At Table 6.35 are shown the values that we have identified. Those with an asterisk are file permissions that we have not ourselves tested.

Table 6.35 File permissions values.
```
01 00 00 00 = Read Only
02 00 00 00 = Hidden
04 00 00 00 = System
20 00 00 00 = Archive
40 00 00 00 = Device*
80 00 00 00 = Normal*
00 01 00 00 = Temporary*
00 02 00 00 = Sparse File*
00 04 00 00 = Reparse Point
00 08 00 00 = Compressed
00 10 00 00 = Offline*
00 20 00 00 = Not Content Indexed*
00 40 00 00 = Encrypted
```

Byte offsets 108 to 111 (black background) at Table 6.36 are said to be allocated for "Maximum Number of Versions". When zero, as here, it is understood that version numbering is disabled. This field is thought to be associated with Network Security, where there are multiple users and multiple files.

Table 6.36 Maximum Number of Versions.
```
00000096    98 EF 7F 33 89 57 C4 01   20 00 00 00 00 00 00 00    ˉïÇ3‰WÄ. .......
```

Byte offsets 112 to 115 (black background) at Table 6.37 are described as a "Version Number" and byte offsets 116 to 119 as a "Class ID". Experiments were carried out to try to identify useful records for these fields, but none were found. No conclusions have so far been reached regarding the proven use of these particular byte offsets.

Table 6.37 Version Number and Class ID.
```
00000112    00 00 00 00 00 00 00 00   00 00 00 00 00 00 00 00    ................
```

It is claimed that byte offsets 120 to 123 (black background) at Table 6.38 are the "Owner ID". No relevant records were found in the sample MFT.

Table 6.38 Owner ID.
```
00000112    00 00 00 00 00 00 00 00   00 00 00 00 00 00 00 00    ................
```

Byte offsets 124 to 127 (black background) at Table 6.39 are understood to be a "Security ID". Experiments were carried out to try to identify records within which these bytes are used. By extracting the record number of each successful "hit" and looking it up in the file list table of the volume, produced by forensic software, the values allocated to these bytes can be linked to the name and path of the referenced file. By sorting this combined list by the values of the bytes, a pattern of allocation is detectable. It appears that the system uses these bytes to "categorize" the file to which the value is applied. It is not known what use the system makes of this on a standalone machine, but the use of a categorized index could have a number of uses on a network. Whether these values are used as a "Security ID" has not been determined experimentally by the authors; certainly these bytes are used by the system for some purpose involving the type of file referenced, but the detail of this use is not known at the present time.

Table 6.39 Security ID.

```
00000112    00 00 00 00 00 00 00 00    00 00 00 00 00 00 00 00    ................
```

It is claimed that byte offsets 128 to 135 (black background) at Table 6.40 are the "Quota Charged". The MFT was parsed for any non-zero values in these bytes, but no relevant records were found. If of zero value, as seen here, then it is understood that Quotas are disabled.

Table 6.40 Quota charged.

```
00000128    00 00 00 00 00 00 00 00    00 00 00 00 00 00 00 00    ................
```

It is claimed that byte offsets 136 to 143 (black background) at Table 6.41 are claimed to be the "Update Sequence Number" for the file $USNJRNL. The MFT was searched for any non-zero values in these bytes, but no relevant records were found. When of zero value, as seen here, it is likely that the $USNJRNL function has not been activated.

Table 6.41 Update Sequence Number.

```
00000128    00 00 00 00 00 00 00 00    00 00 00 00 00 00 00 00    ................
```

Taking it Apart – the File Name Attribute

The start of the File Name Attribute is signalled by the identifier 30 00 00 00h at byte offset 144. This is the first field of another Attribute Header of exactly the same structure as that which we examined in Tables 6.22 to 6.31.

The Attribute Header

At byte offsets 144 to 167 (black background) at Table 6.42 are the details of this Attribute Header.

Table 6.42 Attribute header – File Name Attribute.

```
00000144    30 00 00 00 78 00 00 00    00 00 00 00 00 00 04 00    0...x...........
00000160    5A 00 00 00 18 00 01 00    48 00 00 00 00 00 01 00    Z.......H.......
```

At Table 6.43 is shown the analysis of the Attribute Header for this File Name Attribute.

Table 6.43 Attribute Header – analysis.

Bytes 144 to 147	Attribute ID	30 00 00 00
Bytes 148 to 151	Length of Attribute	00000078h = 120
		From offset 144 to 263
Byte 152	Resident/Non-Resident Flag	00h = resident
Byte 153	Length of Name of Attribute	00h = no name
Bytes 154 to 155	Offset to Start of Attribute Proper	0000h = not used
Bytes 156 to 157	Flags	0000h = normal
Bytes 158 to 159	Not Yet Known	0004h (see Table 6.28)
Bytes 160 to 163	Length of Attribute Proper	0000005Ah = 90
		From offset 168 to 257
Bytes 164 to 165	Offset to Start of Attribute Proper	0018h = 24
		144 + 24 = 168
Byte 166	Indexed flag	01h = indexed
Byte 167	Padding to 8 byte Boundary	00h

The File Name Attribute Proper

Starting from byte offset 168 is the File Name Attribute Proper. The first 8 bytes of the Attribute (black background) at Table 6.44 are a reference to the parent directory. It is believed that these bytes are in exactly the same format as those referring to the "Base File Reference" in the Attribute Header Block as described in the discussion of Table 6.16. We note that the value in these first six bytes is 0000000048h, which is equivalent to 72 in decimal. This is the record number of the directory \WINNT\Web\printers\images in which this file appears. The use of the subsequent two bytes 01 00h is not clear at this time. See the item on deleted files in unallocated space at the end of this chapter for possible other uses of this number in identifying parent directory records.

Table 6.44 Reference to parent directory.

```
00000160    5A 00 00 00 18 00 01 00   48 00 00 00 00 00 01 00    Z.......H.......
```

To the practised forensic eye four dates and times may be recognized between byte offsets 176 and 207 (black background) at Table 6.45.

Table 6.45 Four dates and times.

```
00000176    60 53 63 33 89 57 C4 01   98 EF 7F 33 89 57 C4 01    `Sc3%WÄ.¯ïÇ3%WÄ.
00000192    98 EF 7F 33 89 57 C4 01   98 EF 7F 33 89 57 C4 01    ¯ïÇ3%WÄ.¯ïÇ3%WÄ.
```

The date and time values in these 32 bytes are shown in Table 6.46.

Table 6.46 Date and time values.

Bytes 176 to 183	Creation Date and Time	21/06/04 12:13:45 GMT
Bytes 184 to 191	Last Modified Date and Time	21/06/04 12:13:45 GMT
Bytes 192 to 199	Last MFT Record Change Date and Time	21/06/04 12:13:45 GMT
Bytes 200 to 207	Last Access Date and Time	21/06/04 12:13:45 GMT

Byte offsets 208 to 215 (black background) at Table 6.47 are an 8 byte number specifying the "physical" size of the file. In this case the "physical" size is 0000000000000100h = 256 bytes.

Table 6.47 Allocated size of file.

```
00000208    00 01 00 00 00 00 00 00   FF 00 00 00 00 00 00 00    ........ÿ.......
```

Byte offsets 216 to 223 (black background) at Table 6.48 are an 8 byte number specifying the "logical" size of the file. In this case the real size is 00000000000000FFh = 255 bytes. It is thought that within the MFT record system, a padding strategy is operated such that no variable field begins or ends other than on a 4 or 8 byte boundary. This example conforms with that view, with this file being 255 bytes in real size (FFh) and 256 bytes in "physical" size (100h). This suggests that padding has taken place here.

Table 6.48 "Logical" size of file.

```
00000208    00 01 00 00 00 00 00 00   FF 00 00 00 00 00 00 00    ........ÿ.......
```

Byte offsets 224 to 227 (black background) at Table 6.49 are stated to be "Flags". These are similar to the FAT attribute byte in a directory entry, in the style of MS-DOS. We discussed these kind of flags when we examined byte offsets 104 to 107 at Table 6.34. The values which they can take are identical to those given at Table 6.35. In this case 20 00 00 00h represents a file with the Archive bit set.

Table 6.49 Flags.

```
00000224   20 00 00 00   00 00 00 00   0C 03 69 00 70 00 70 00   .........i.p.p.
```

Byte offsets 228 to 231 (black background) at Table 6.50 are reportedly used by extended attributes and reparse points. A search of the volume did not reveal any relevant records with non-zero entries at this location.

Table 6.50 Extended attributes and reparse points.

```
00000224   20 00 00 00   00 00 00 00   0C 03 69 00 70 00 70 00   .........i.p.p.
```

Byte offset 232 (black background) at Table 6.51 is a one-byte field containing the length of the filename in characters. In this case it is seen to be 0Ch, which is 12 decimal. In Unicode, which has two bytes per character, this will mean a byte length of 24. Inspection of the file name, ipp_0005.gif, which follows, shows this to be correct. The use of one byte to store this value imposes a restriction on file name length of 255 characters. *It should be noted that Unicode characters occupy 2 bytes but count as one character.*

Table 6.51 Length of file name in characters.

```
00000224   20 00 00 00 00 00 00 00   0C 03 69 00 70 00 70 00   .........i.p.p.
```

Byte offset 233 (black background) at Table 6.52 is a one-byte field that records the type of the file name. In this case it is seen to be 03h, which indicates that it is both Win32- and DOS-compliant (see Table 6.53).

Table 6.52 Type of file name.

```
00000224   20 00 00 00 00 00 00 00   0C 03 69 00 70 00 70 00   .........i.p.p.
```

Of the four categories shown in Table 6.53, the most general is that of POSIX, with value 00h, and this permits use of all Unicode characters and allows a file length of up to 255 characters. Win32, with value 01h, is a subset of POSIX and this prohibits use of a small number of Unicode characters. It is equivalent to the FAT Long File Name (LFN). DOS, with value 02h, is a subset of Win32, and this permits only single-byte upper-case characters, prohibits use of a small number of these, and requires file names to be constrained within the standard DOS 8.3 format. It should be noted that, for compatibility with other systems, it may be necessary to record both the Win32 file name and a DOS-compliant file name in two separate File Name Attributes. However, where the Win32 file name is itself DOS-compliant, this is not necessary and the name need only be recorded once. The final category, Win32 & DOS, of value 03h, is used to signal this situation; that the file name is both Win32- and DOS-compliant.

Table 6.53 File name types.

00h = Posix Type
01h = Win32 Type (Long File Name)
02h = DOS Type (8.3-compliant)
03h = Win32 & DOS Type (both Win32- and DOS-compliant)

As stated above, the value here is 03h, indicating that the filename is DOS-compliant and thus there is no need to store a Long File Name, since this would be identical. An examination of the MFT shows that where a file name is outside the constraints of the 8.3 DOS name, then two File Name Attributes are present in the record; one containing the Win32 Long File Name and one containing the DOS-compliant 8.3 file name.

As can be seen, byte offsets 234 to 257 (black background) at Table 6.54 contain the file name, the character length of which (12) is given in Table 6.51. This file name field, of value here ipp_0005.gif, has to be of variable length in order to permit the use of long file names. The six bytes from offset 258 to offset 263 are padding that has been added to ensure that the next Attribute starts on an 8-byte boundary. It appears to be standard practice for all Attributes to start on 8-byte boundaries.

Table 6.54 File name.

```
00000224   20 00 00 00 00 00 00 00   0C 03 69 00 70 00 70 00   .........i.p.p.
00000240   5F 00 30 00 30 00 30 00   35 00 2E 00 67 00 69 00   _.0.0.0.5...g.i.
00000256   66 00 18 00 00 00 01 00   50 00 00 00 B0 00 00 00   f.......P...°...
```

Taking it Apart – the Security Descriptor

At byte offsets 264 to 267 (black background) at Table 6.55 is seen to be the start of the next Attribute. The value 50 00 00 00h is its Attribute ID number and this is seen from Table 6.2 to be a Security Descriptor Attribute.

Table 6.55 Attribute ID.

```
00000256   66 00 18 00 00 00 01 00   50 00 00 00 B0 00 00 00   f.......P...°...
```

The Attributes starts with an Attribute Header and the length of the Attribute is defined in the next four bytes at offsets 268 to 271. These are highlighted (black background) at Table 6.56, and have a value of 000000B0h, which is 176 in decimal. The next Attribute therefore starts at byte 264 + 176 = 440.

Table 6.56 Length of Attribute.

```
00000256   66 00 18 00 00 00 01 00   50 00 00 00 B0 00 00 00   f.......P...°...
```

According to many sources on the Internet, this Attribute is present for backward compatibility with previous versions of NTFS. The Windows 2000 version of NTFS stores all security descriptors in the $Secure metadata file, sharing descriptors among files and directories that have the same settings. Previous versions of NTFS stored private security description information with each file and directory. The entire Attribute is shown at Table 6.57, but because it is no longer relevant we have not deconstructed it further.

Table 6.57 Security Descriptor Attribute.

```
00000256   .  .  .  .  .  .  .  .   50 00 00 00 B0 00 00 00    P...°...
00000272   00 00 00 00 00 00 03 00   94 00 00 00 18 00 00 00   ........."......
00000288   01 00 04 84 78 00 00 00   88 00 00 00 00 00 00 00   ..."x...^.......
00000304   14 00 00 00 02 00 64 00   04 00 00 00 00 10 18 00   ......d.........
00000320   A9 00 12 00 01 02 00 00   00 00 00 05 20 00 00 00   ©........... ...
00000336   21 02 00 00 00 10 18 00   A9 00 12 00 01 02 00 00   !........©......
00000352   00 00 00 05 20 00 00 00   23 02 00 00 00 10 18 00   .... ...#.......
00000368   FF 01 1F 00 01 02 00 00   00 00 00 05 20 00 00 00   ÿ........... ...
00000384   20 02 00 00 00 10 14 00   FF 01 1F 00 01 01 00 00    ......ÿ.......
00000400   00 00 00 05 12 00 00 00   01 02 00 00 00 00 00 05   ................
00000416   20 00 00 00 20 02 00 00   01 01 00 00 00 00 00 05    ... ...........
00000432   12 00 00 00 9C 52 84 94                            ....œR‖"_
```

Taking it Apart – the Data Attribute with Resident Data

This Attribute is the final Attribute within this sample record. It starts at byte offset 440 with its Attribute ID of 80 00 00 00h. This is the first field of another Attribute Header of exactly the same structure as that which we examined in Tables 6.22 to 6.31.

The Attribute Header

At byte offsets 440 to 463 (black background) at Table 6.58 are the details of this Attribute Header.

Table 6.58 Attribute Header – Data Attribute

| 00000432 | 12 00 00 00 9C 52 84 94 | 80 00 00 00 18 01 00 00 | . . . . œR„ " _ . . . . |
| 00000448 | 00 00 18 00 00 00 01 00 | FF 00 00 00 18 00 00 00 | . . . . ÿ . . . . |

At Table 6.59 is shown the analysis of the Attribute Header for this Data Attribute.

Table 6.59 Attribute Header – analysis.

Bytes 440 to 443	Attribute ID	80 00 00 00
Bytes 444 to 447	Length of Attribute	00000118h = 280
		From offset 440 to 719
Byte 448	Resident/Non-Resident Flag	00h = resident
Byte 449	Length of Name of Attribute	00h = no name
Bytes 450 to 451	Offset to Start of Attribute proper	0018h = 24
		Points to 440 + 24 = 464
Bytes 452 to 453	Flags	0000h = normal
Bytes 454 to 455	Not Yet Known	0001h (see Table 6.28)
Bytes 456 to 459	Length of Attribute Proper	000000FFh = 255
		From offset 464 to 718
Bytes 460 to 461	Offset to Start of Attribute Proper	0018h = 24
		440 + 24 = 464
Byte 462	Indexed flag	00h = not indexed
Byte 463	Padding to 8 byte Boundary	00h

The Data Attribute Proper

The Data Attribute Proper, which is the data itself starts, as we note from Table 6.59, at byte offset 464. The length of the Attribute is 280 bytes, which we may also note from Table 6.59, so the actual data run is that figure less the header length of 24, which is 256 bytes. This is the "physical" size, as we may find in Table 6.47. The length of the Attribute Proper is 255 bytes, which again is listed in Table 6.59, and we show these Attribute Proper bytes at Table 6.60 (black background). The final byte in the "physical" size of 256 bytes is slack space.

Table 6.60 The Data Attribute Proper.

00000464	47 49 46 38 39 61 0F 00	0F 00 C4 FF 00 C0 C0 C0	GIF89a....Äÿ.ÀÀÀ
00000480	6B 6B 39 63 63 31 73 73	39 6B 6B 31 84 8C 4A 73	kk9cc1ss9kk1„ŒJs
00000496	7B 42 7B 84 42 6B 73 39	7B 84 4A 8C 9C 52 03 00	{B{„Bks9{„JŒœR..
00000512	52 7B 8C 4A 73 84 42 9C	B5 63 94 AD 5A 8C A5 5A	R{ŒJs„Bœµc"–ZŒ¥Z
00000528	94 AD 63 AD CE 7B A5 C6	73 9C BD 6B AD D6 7B B5	"–c–Î{¥Æsœ½k–Ö{µ
00000544	DE 84 00 00 00 00 00 00	00 00 00 00 00 00 00 00	Þ„.............
00000560	00 00 00 00 00 00 00 00	00 00 00 00 00 21 F9 04	.............!ù.
00000576	01 00 00 00 00 2C 00 00	00 00 0F 00 0F 00 00 05	.....,..........
00000592	7C 20 20 8A D1 03 29 CB	A8 02 54 4B 45 D0 52 1C	| ŠÑ.)Ë¨.TKEÐR.

```
00000608  2B 35 DD AD B9 24 C6 68  4B 15 1C 6C C1 30 20 44   +5ÝÝ¹$ÆhK..lÁO D
00000624  B6 8A 25 F8 8A 15 8C 80  C8 AF 22 99 34 77 87 80   ¶Š%øŠ.Œ Ë¯"™4w‡_
00000640  E0 E1 B0 E1 1C 11 14 0F  21 80 44 BA 2D 70 8C 71   àáE á....! D°-pŒq
00000656  18 10 08 0A 73 64 6E 12  1B 05 82 C5 22 0E E9 EB   ....sdn...,Å".éë
00000672  13 0D 06 5A 04 00 05 7A  87 05 09 6D 01 04 02 22   ...Z...z‡..m...."
00000688  09 90 89 90 06 03 5A 78  23 06 99 99 03 08 83 8E   . _..Zx#.™™..ƒ_
00000704  2A 08 9D 01 96 97 2B 22  8D 78 84 2A 21 00 3B 00   *._.—+"_xₙ*!.;.
```

Taking it Apart – the End of Record Marker

We made mention earlier of the End of Record Marker, FF FF FF FFh, and we find this at byte offsets 720 to 723, shown in Table 6.61 (black background). As can be seen, this End of Record Marker occupies the first four bytes of a new 8-byte segment. By inspection this appears to be the norm with the use of padding, as necessary, preceding the End of Record Marker. This is followed by a further four bytes which are used as a Cyclic Redundancy Check (CRC) consistency check. It should be noted that the remainder of this particular record is almost entirely populated with zeros. This area, between the End of Record Marker (+4 bytes) and the end of the space allocated, is known as "MFT Record Slack Space". The value to the analyst of data found here is discussed in a later section.

Table 6.61 The End of Record Marker.
```
00000720   FF FF FF FF 82 79 47 11  00 00 00 00 00 00 00 00   ÿÿÿÿ‚yG.........
```

This completes the deconstruction of an MFT file record with *resident* data. By using the reference material that is provided in Appendix 9, most MFT records can be deconstructed in a similar manner.

Analysis of a Sample MFT File Record with Non-Resident Data

In order to compare and contrast an MFT record with *resident* data, the deconstruction of which we describe in detail above, with an MFT record with *non-resident* data, we now select for further examination the sample record which we show at Table 6.62. Inspection of this record shows a probable filename in Unicode starting at byte offset 234 (black background). Again, to the practised eye, there appears to be a set of four 8-byte Microsoft "FILETIME" date and time entries starting at byte offset 72 (light grey background) and again at byte offset 176 (mid-grey background).

In this case, there are no file data bytes resident and there are no further non-zero values (other than the Update Sequence Number – see Table 6.66) in the MFT record beyond byte offset 335.

Table 6.62 Sample MFT record with non-resident data.

Offset	0	1	2	3	4	5	6	7	8	9	10	11	12	13	14	15	
00000000	46	49	4C	45	2A	00	03	00	A1	3A	24	01	00	00	00	00	FILE*...¡:$.....
00000016	01	00	01	00	30	00	01	00	50	01	00	00	00	04	00	00	....0...P.......
00000032	00	00	00	00	00	00	00	00	06	00	02	00	00	00	00	00	....
00000048	10	00	00	00	60	00	00	00	00	00	00	00	00	00	00	00	....`...........
00000064	48	00	00	00	18	00	00	00	80	F3	B4	1B	8F	57	C4	01	H......._ó´._WÄ.

00000080	08	4C	2F	DE	85	57	C4	01	5E	2D	CF	1B	8F	57	C4	01	.L/þ…WÄ.^-Ï._WÄ.
00000096	5E	2D	CF	1B	8F	57	C4	01	20	00	00	00	00	00	00	00	^-Ï._WÄ. ....
00000112	00	00	00	00	00	00	00	00	00	00	00	00	0A	01	00	00	....
00000128	00	00	00	00	00	00	00	00	00	00	00	00	00	00	00	00	....
00000144	30	00	00	00	70	00	00	00	00	00	00	00	00	00	05	00	0...p..........
00000160	56	00	00	00	18	00	01	00	30	19	00	00	00	00	01	00	V.......0.......
00000176	80	F3	B4	1B	8F	57	C4	01	08	4C	2F	DE	85	57	C4	01	_ó´._WÄ..L/þ…WÄ.
00000192	08	4C	2F	DE	85	57	C4	01	5E	2D	CF	1B	8F	57	C4	01	.L/þ…WÄ.^-Ï._WÄ.
00000208	00	30	00	00	00	00	00	00	A6	26	00	00	00	00	00	00	.0......|&......
00000224	20	00	00	00	00	00	00	00	0A	03	53	00	61	00	6D	00	.........S.a.m.
00000240	70	00	6C	00	65	00	2E	00	6A	00	70	00	67	00	00	00	p.l.e...j.p.g...
00000256	80	00	00	00	48	00	00	00	01	00	00	00	00	00	04	00	_...H..........
00000272	00	00	00	00	00	00	00	00	02	00	00	00	00	00	00	00	....
00000288	40	00	00	00	00	00	00	00	00	30	00	00	00	00	00	00	@........0......
00000304	A6	26	00	00	00	00	00	00	A6	26	00	00	00	00	00	00	|&......|&......
00000320	31	03	46	E9	05	00	00	00	FF	FF	FF	FF	82	79	47	11	1.Fé....ÿÿÿÿ‚yG.
00000336	00	00	00	00	00	00	00	00	00	00	00	00	00	00	00	00	....

Normal user access to this file, via a directory folder view in Windows Explorer, shows at Table 6.63 the file details reported by the operating system, Windows 2000.

Table 6.63 Windows Explorer file directory details.

File Name & Path	\Documents and Settings\NTFS TEST\My Documents \My Pictures\Sample.jpg
Size (bytes)	9,894
Last Accessed	21/6/04 12:56
Last Written	21/6/04 11:49
File Created	21/6/04 12:56
Attributes	Archive bit set

With an image of the system loaded as a virtual disk, forensic software was used to examine the directory details of this file, with the results as shown at Table 6.64.

Table 6.64 Forensic software file directory details.

File Name	Sample.jpg
Last Access	21/06/04 12:56:03
Last Written	21/06/04 11:49:54
File Created	21/06/04 12:56:03
Entry Modified	21/06/04 12:56:03
Logical Size	9,894
Physical Size	12,288
Starting Extent	0C-C387398
Physical Location	PS:3099247, SO:0
Full Path	\Documents and Settings\NTFS TEST\My Documents \My Pictures\Sample.jpg
MFT Record Number	6489

Taking it Apart – the FILE Record Header

As with all MFT records, this record starts with a FILE Record Header and the structure and layout of this FILE Record Header is identical to the one we deconstructed above and described in Tables 6.6 to 6.19. At Table 6.65, we show (black background) the bytes of the FILE Record Header for this sample MFT record from byte offsets 0 to 47.

Table 6.65 FILE Record Header.

00000000	46 49 4C 45 2A 00 03 00 A1 3A 24 01 00 00 00 00	FILE*...:$.....
00000016	01 00 01 00 30 00 01 00 50 01 00 00 00 04 00 00	....0...P.......
00000032	00 00 00 00 00 00 00 00 06 00 02 00 00 00 00 00	....

At Table 6.66 we show the detailed analysis of this File Record Header, using the same descriptors as we used at Tables 6.6 to 6.19.

Table 6.66 FILE Record Header – analysis.

Bytes 0 to 3	Start of File Record Header	"FILE"
Bytes 4 and 5	Offset to Update Sequence Number	002Ah = 42
Bytes 6 and 7	Size of Update Sequence	0003h = 3
Bytes 8 to 15	$Logfile Sequence Number	0000000001243AA1h
Bytes 16 and 17	Record Use Sequence Number	0001h = 1
Bytes 18 and 19	Hard Link Count	0001h = 1
Bytes 20 and 21	Pointer to First Attribute	0030h = 48
Bytes 22 and 23	Record Flags	0001h = FILE Record in use
Bytes 24 to 27	Logical Size of Record	00000150h = 336
Bytes 28 to 31	Physical Size of Record	00000400h = 1024
Bytes 32 to 39	Base File Reference	0000000000000000h
Bytes 40 and 41	Possible Attribute Count	0006h = 6
Bytes 42 and 43	Update Sequence Number	0002h = 2
Bytes 44 to 47	Update Sequence Array	00 00 00 00

Taking it Apart – the Standard Information Attribute

The start of the Standard Information Attribute is signalled by the identifier 10 00 00 00h at byte offset 48. As with all Attributes, this Standard Information Attribute starts with an Attribute Header.

The Attribute Header

At byte offsets 48 to 71 (black background) at Table 6.67 are the details of this Attribute Header. Its layout is identical to the Attribute Headers that we have encountered and deconstructed above.

Table 6.67 Attribute Header – Standard Information Attribute.

00000048	10 00 00 00 60 00 00 00 00 00 00 00 00 00 00 00	....`...........
00000064	48 00 00 00 18 00 00 00 80 F3 B4 1B 8F 57 C4 01	H.......ó´.WÄ.

At Table 6.68 is shown the analysis of the Attribute Header for this Standard Information Attribute.

Table 6.68 Attribute Header – analysis.

Bytes 48 to 51	Attribute ID	10 00 00 00
Bytes 52 to 55	Length of Attribute	00000060h = 96
		From offset 48 to 143
Byte 56	Resident/Non-Resident Flag	00h = resident
Byte 57	Length of Name of Attribute	00h = no name
Bytes 58 to 59	Offset to Start of Attribute Proper	0000h = not used
Bytes 60 to 61	Flags	0000h = normal
Bytes 62 to 63	Not Yet Known	0000h
Bytes 64 to 67	Length of Attribute Proper	00000048h = 72
		From offset 72 to 143

Bytes 68 to 69	Offset to Start of Attribute Proper	0018h = 24
		48 + 24 = 72
Byte 70	Indexed flag	00h = not indexed
Byte 71	Padding to 8 byte Boundary	00h

The Standard Information Attribute Proper

The Standard Information Attribute Proper extends from byte offsets 72 to 143 as shown (black background) at Table 6.69.

Table 6.69 Standard Information Attribute Proper.

00000064	48 00 00 00 18 00 00 00	80 F3 B4 1B 8F 57 C4 01	H........ó´._WÄ.
00000080	08 4C 2F DE 85 57 C4 01	5E 2D CF 1B 8F 57 C4 01	.L/Þ..WÄ.^-Ï._WÄ.
00000096	5E 2D CF 1B 8F 57 C4 01	20 00 00 00 00 00 00 00	^-Ï._WÄ. ....
00000112	00 00 00 00 00 00 00 00	00 00 00 00 00 0A 01 00 00	....
00000128	00 00 00 00 00 00 00 00	00 00 00 00 00 00 00 00	....

At Table 6.70 is shown the analysis of the Standard Information Attribute Proper as described in Tables 6.32 to 6.41.

Table 6.70 Standard Information Attribute Proper – analysis.

Bytes 72 to 79	Creation Date and Time	21/06/04 12:56:03 GMT
Bytes 80 to 87	Last Modified Date and Time	21/06/04 11:49:54 GMT
Bytes 88 to 95	Last MFT Record Change Date and Time	21/06/04 12:56:03 GMT
Bytes 96 to 103	Last Access Date and Time	21/06/04 12:56:03 GMT
Bytes 104 to 107	File Permissions	20 00 00 00 = archive set
Bytes 108 to 111	Maximum Number of Versions	00000000h = disabled
Bytes 112 to 115	Version Number and Class ID	0000000000000000h
Byte 120 to 123	Owner ID	00000000h
Bytes 124 to 127	Security ID	0000010Ah
Bytes 128 to 135	Quota Charged	0000000000000000h
Bytes 136 to 143	Update Sequence Number	0000000000000000h

An examination of the reported times and dates by the operating system and by forensic software (see Tables 6.63 and 6.64 respectively) reveals that they are consistent with those recorded here.

Taking it Apart – the File Name Attribute

The start of the File Name Attribute is signalled by the identifier 30 00 00 00h at byte offset 144. As with all Attributes, this File Name Attribute starts with an Attribute Header.

The Attribute Header

At byte offsets 144 to 167 (black background) at Table 6.71 are the details of this Attribute Header. Its layout is identical to the Attribute Headers that we have encountered and deconstructed above.

Table 6.71 Attribute Header – File Name Attribute.

00000144	30 00 00 00 70 00 00 00	00 00 00 00 00 00 05 00	0...p..........
00000160	56 00 00 00 18 00 01 00	30 19 00 00 00 00 01 00	V.......0......

At Table 6.72 is shown the analysis of the Attribute Header for this File Name Attribute.

Table 6.72 Attribute Header – analysis.

Bytes 144 to 147	Attribute ID	30 00 00 00
Bytes 148 to 151	Length of Attribute	00000070h = 112
		From offset 144 to 255
Byte 152	Resident/Non-Resident Flag	00h = resident
Byte 153	Length of Name of Attribute	00h = no name
Bytes 154 to 155	Offset to Start of Attribute Proper	0000h = not used
Bytes 156 to 157	Flags	0000h = normal
Bytes 158 to 159	Not Yet Known	0005h = possible ID
Bytes 160 to 163	Length of Attribute Proper	00000056h = 86
		From offset 168 to 253
Bytes 164 to 165	Offset to Start of Attribute Proper	0018h = 24
		144 + 24 = 168
Byte 166	Indexed flag	01h = indexed
Byte 167	Padding to 8 byte Boundary	00h

The File Name Attribute Proper

The File Name Attribute Proper extends from byte offsets 168 to 253 as shown (black background) at Table 6.73.

Table 6.73 File Name Attribute Proper.

```
00000160    56 00 00 00 18 00 01 00   30 19 00 00 00 00 01 00    V.......0.......
00000176    80 F3 B4 1B 8F 57 C4 01   08 4C 2F DE 85 57 C4 01    _ó´._WÄ..L/Þ…WÄ.
00000192    08 4C 2F DE 85 57 C4 01   5E 2D CF 1B 8F 57 C4 01    .L/Þ…WÄ.^-Ï._WÄ.
00000208    00 30 00 00 00 00 00 00   A6 26 00 00 00 00 00 00    .0......|&......
00000224    20 00 00 00 00 00 00 00   0A 03 53 00 61 00 6D 00    .........S.a.m.
00000240    70 00 6C 00 65 00 2E 00   6A 00 70 00 67 00 00 00    p.l.e...j.p.g...
```

At Table 6.74 is shown the analysis of the File Name Attribute Proper as described in Tables 6.44 to 6.54.

Table 6.74 File Name Attribute Proper – analysis.

Bytes 168 to 175	Reference to Parent Directory	0001000000001930h = 6448
		"My Pictures"
Bytes 176 to 183	Creation Date and Time	21/06/04 12:56:03 GMT
Bytes 184 to 191	Last Modified Date and Time	21/06/04 11:49:54 GMT
Bytes 192 to 199	Last MFT Record Change Date and Time	21/06/04 11:49:54 GMT
Bytes 200 to 207	Last Access Date and Time	21/06/04 12:56:03 GMT
Bytes 208 to 215	"Physical" Size of File	0000000000003000h = 12,288
Bytes 216 to 223	"Logical" Size of File	00000000000026A6h = 9,894
Bytes 224 to 227	Flags	20 00 00 00h = archive set
Bytes 228 to 231	Extended Attributes and Reparse Points	00000000h
Byte 232	Length of File Name in Characters	0Ah = 10
Byte 233	Type of File Name	03h = Win32 & DOS
Bytes 234 to 253	File Name	"Sample.jpg"

As can be seen from Table 6.74, the reference to the parent directory is record number 6448 decimal, and this is identified in the sample MFT as the folder My Pictures, which does contain this file. It should be noted that there is a difference in the Last MFT Record Change Date and Time recorded in this attribute (Table 6.74) and the equivalent date and time recorded in the Standard Information Attribute (Table 6.70). Following a number of experiments, the authors are currently of the view that none of the dates and times in *this* attribute should be relied upon until the rules by which they are updated are fully understood.

It may be noted that the Type of File Name entry is Win32- and DOS-compliant (see Table 6.53), thus indicating that only the one File Name Attribute is required here. It may also be noted that there are two bytes of padding at byte offsets 254 to 255 to bring the next entry onto an 8-byte boundary.

Taking it Apart – the Data Attribute with Non-Resident Data

The start of the Data Attribute is signalled by the identifier 80 00 00 00h at byte offset 256. As with all Attributes, this Data Attribute starts with an Attribute Header. However, this Attribute Header is identical to previous ones encountered only for the first 16 bytes. This is because this Data Attribute is non-resident.

The Attribute Header

At byte offsets 256 to 271 (black background) at Table 6.75 are the details of the first 16 bytes of this Attribute Header. This Attribute Header is interpreted differently from the previous versions analyzed because the data is non-resident (see Appendix 9 for the template applied).

Table 6.75 First part Attribute Header – non-resident Data Attribute.

```
00000256   80 00 00 00 48 00 00 00   01 00 00 00 00 00 04 00    _...H...........
```

At Table 6.76 is shown the analysis of the first part of the Attribute Header for this non-resident Data Attribute.

Table 6.76 First part Attribute Header – analysis.

Bytes 256 to 259	Attribute ID	80 00 00 00
Bytes 260 to 263	Length of Attribute	00000048h = 72
		From offset 256 to 327
Byte 264	Resident/Non-Resident Flag	01h = non resident
Byte 265	Length of Name of Attribute	00h = no name
Bytes 266 to 267	Offset to Name of Attribute	0000h = not used
Bytes 268 to 269	Flags	0000h = normal
Bytes 270 to 271	Not Yet Known	0004h = possible ID

Byte offsets 272 to 279 (black background) at Table 6.77 are reported to record the Virtual Cluster Number (VCN) of the first virtual cluster in the data run and byte offsets 280 to 287, also highlighted (black background) at Table 6.77, are reported to record the Virtual Cluster Number of the last virtual cluster occupied by the data.

Table 6.77 Starting VCN and Last VCN.

```
00000272   00 00 00 00 00 00 00 00   02 00 00 00 00 00 00 00    ................
```

In this case the Starting VCN can be seen to be 0000000000000000h = 0 and the Last VCN can be seen to be 0000000000000002h = 2. The "logical" size of the file (see Table 6.74) is 9,894 bytes and it will therefore need a minimum of 20 sectors[10]. Since there are eight sectors per cluster on this particular disk (see offset 13 of the BIOS Parameter Block at Table 6.1) then the file will be allocated three clusters, which

---

10 Note that 19 sectors × 512 bytes per sector = 9,728 bytes and 20 sectors × 512 bytes per sector = 10,240 bytes, so 20 sectors are required for 9,894 bytes.

conforms with our findings of the data being held in VCN 0 to VCN 2. The use of three clusters results in an allocated size of $3 \times 8 = 24$ sectors = 12,288 bytes.

The two bytes at offsets 288 and 289 (black background) at Table 6.78 are used to store the offset to the data runs. In this case the offset is 0040h = 64 decimal which points to byte 256 + 64 = 320.

Table 6.78 Offset to the data runs.

```
00000288    40 00 00 00 00 00 00 00   00 30 00 00 00 00 00 00    @........0......
```

The two bytes at offsets 290 and 291 (black background) at Table 6.79 are reported as storing the compression unit size for compressed data. In this case the value is 0000h, which indicates no compression. The four bytes at offsets 292 to 295 are padding.

Table 6.79 Compression unit size.

```
00000288    40 00 00 00 00 00 00 00   00 30 00 00 00 00 00 00    @........0......
```

The four bytes at offsets 296 to 303 (black background) at Table 6.80 are reported to be the allocated size of the attribute. In this case we see that it is 0000000000003000h, which equals 12,288 decimal. This conforms with our findings above of a disk allocation of three clusters, each of eight sectors and each of 512 bytes, making a total of 12,288 bytes in length. This is the "physical" size of the file and confirms that value noted in Table 6.74.

Table 6.80 "Physical" size of Attribute.

```
00000288    40 00 00 00 00 00 00 00   00 30 00 00 00 00 00 00    @........0......
```

The four bytes at offsets 304 to 311 (black background) at Table 6.81 are recorded as being the real size of the attribute. In this case we see that it is 00000000000026A6h, which equals 9,894 decimal. This is the "logical" size of the file and confirms that value noted in Table 6.74.

The four bytes at offsets 312 to 319 are recorded as being the initialized size of the data stream. It is unclear why this value is required. In this case the value is exactly the same as that for the real size of the attribute.

Table 6.81 "Logical" size of Attribute.

```
00000304    A6 26 00 00 00 00 00 00   A6 26 00 00 00 00 00 00    |&......|&......
```

The Data Attribute Proper – a data run descriptor

The Data Attribute Proper, shown (black background) at Table 6.82, extends, as we note at Table 6.78, from byte offset 320 to byte offset 327. It is a *data run descriptor* that is held in the last few bytes of the Attribute.

Table 6.82 Data run descriptor.

```
00000320    31 03 46 E9 05 00 00 00   FF FF FF FF 82 79 47 11    1.Fé....ÿÿÿÿ,yG.
```

Non-resident attributes are stored in a series of data runs, with each data run specifying the number of contiguous clusters in the run and the starting cluster number for the run. Each data run commences with a one-byte header (which is 00h to mark the end of the series) followed by one or more bytes which specify the number of clusters, which in turn are followed by one or more bytes which specify the starting cluster number. The header is used to specify how many bytes are used in the data run to contain the number of clusters and how many bytes are used in the data run to contain the starting cluster number.

The first nibble of the header byte is used to specify how many bytes are used in the data run to contain the starting cluster number. The second nibble of the header byte is used to specify how many bytes are used in the data run to contain the number of clusters.

Thus, in this case, we have at byte offset 320 the first data run header byte of 31h. The first nibble is 3, indicating that three bytes are used in this data run to contain the starting cluster number. The second nibble is 1, indicating that one byte is used in the data run to contain the number of clusters.

Noting that the bytes which specify the number of clusters come next, we expect to find one byte for this purpose (from the second nibble of the header byte) and that should be at offset 321. We note that it is of value 03h, which indicates that three contiguous clusters are in use for this data run.

We now expect to find three bytes in use (from the first nibble of the header byte) to specify the starting cluster number and this sequence should be from offsets 322 to 324. Here we find the values 46 E9 05h, which when converted from little endian give 05E946h = 387,398 decimal. The data stream therefore starts at cluster 387,398 and extends for three clusters.

It is important to note that the start cluster value represents a *signed* integer. The value as held in the data descriptor *may* have a trailing zero (00h) added to ensure that the leading (sign) bit is zero for positive numbers. This trailing zero will become a leading zero (and hence a positive sign) when the number is re-ordered from little endian for interpretation. It is therefore very important that the correct number of bytes is identified when extraction is taking place. Any further data runs simply follow the current set and are in exactly the same format. Negative numbers are possible as the figure is an offset value and not actually a cluster number. The value in the first data run is the offset from the beginning of the volume. For subsequent runs, the values are an offset from the location of the previous run's first cluster. A fragment of the file *may* therefore be stored in a cluster earlier on the volume than a previously stored fragment. Finally, at offset 325, we note the value 00h for the next header byte. This signifies the end of the data run.

At byte offsets 328 to 331 (black background) at Table 6.83 we find the End of Record Marker followed, in byte offsets 332 to 335, by the Cyclic Redundancy Check.

Table 6.83 End of Record Marker and CRC.

```
00000320   31 03 46 E9 05 00 00 00   FF FF FF FF 82 79 47 11   1.Fé....ÿÿÿÿ‚yG.
```

This completes the deconstruction of an MFT file record with *non-resident* data.

Dealing with Directories

NTFS deals with directories in a similar way to that of files, with each directory having its own MFT record. This record is made up of headers and Attributes, in just the same way as file records, and where file records have either resident or non-resident data associated with them, directories have either resident or non-resident file lists associated with them. A directory listing is re-sorted each time a file is added to or deleted from the directory.

The MFT record containing the directory listing starts in an identical manner to that of any other MFT record. The name of the directory is dealt with in exactly the same way as if it was the name of a file. The Index Root Attribute is introduced after the appropriate File Name Attribute(s).

The directory listing itself is split into a number of parts, similar to a series of Attributes. Within each entry are details of the file to which the entry refers. These details include a pointer to the MFT record for the file itself; thus a link is made from the directory to the file (or to a further subdirectory). As has already been seen above, details within the MFT record for the file point to the "parent" MFT record, which is usually a directory. It is a similar pointer mechanism which is used to establish the directory to file (or subdirectory) relationship.

The Index Root Attribute starts the directory listing system. As with all Attributes the Index Root Attribute always starts with the Attribute Header. This is followed by the Index Root Attribute Proper, which defines the size and shape of the Directory Entries. This is followed by an Index Header and one or more Index Entry Header and Index Entry Data pairs, all of which are part of the Index Root Attribute. The overall construction is as follows:

- AttributeHeader
- Index Root Attribute Proper
- Index Header
- Index Entry Header
- Index Entry Data
- Index Entry Header
- Index Entry Data
- Further Index Entry Header and Index Entry Data pairs
- Index Entry Header [with final entry flag set]

And as normal:

- End of Record marker (FF FF FF FF)
- Error Check Sequence (4 bytes)

Analysis of a Sample MFT Directory Record with Resident Data

In order to compare and contrast MFT file records with MFT directory records, we now select a sample MFT directory record with resident data for further examination, as shown at Table 6.84.

Table 6.84 Sample MFT directory record with resident data.
```
Offset      0  1  2  3  4  5  6  7   8  9 10 11 12 13 14 15
00000000   46 49 4C 45 2A 00 03 00  B4 73 24 01 00 00 00 00   FILE*...´s$.....
00000016   01 00 02 00 30 00 03 00  98 02 00 00 00 04 00 00   ....0...¯.......
```

```
00000032   00 00 00 00 00 00 00 00   04 00 02 00 00 00 00 00   ................
00000048   10 00 00 00 60 00 00 00   00 00 00 00 00 00 00 00   ....`...........
00000064   48 00 00 00 18 00 00 00   5A BF 1E 1B 8F 57 C4 01   H.......Z¿..¸WÄ.
00000080   9C 8C 11 FA 85 57 C4 01   46 01 36 21 8F 57 C4 01   ÉŒ.ú…WÄ.F.6!¸WÄ.
00000096   5E 2D CF 1B 8F 57 C4 01   01 00 00 00 00 00 00 00   ^-Ï.¸WÄ.........
00000112   00 00 00 00 00 00 00 00   00 00 00 00 0B 01 00 00   ................
00000128   00 00 00 00 00 00 00 00   00 00 00 00 00 00 00 00   ................
00000144   30 00 00 00 70 00 00 00   00 00 00 00 00 00 03 00   0...p...........
00000160   52 00 00 00 18 00 01 00   2F 19 00 00 00 00 01 00   R......./.......
00000176   5A BF 1E 1B 8F 57 C4 01   5A BF 1E 1B 8F 57 C4 01   Z¿..¸WÄ.Z¿..¸WÄ.
00000192   5A BF 1E 1B 8F 57 C4 01   5A BF 1E 1B 8F 57 C4 01   Z¿..¸WÄ.Z¿..¸WÄ.
00000208   00 00 00 00 00 00 00 00   00 00 00 00 00 00 00 00   ................
00000224   00 00 00 10 00 00 00 00   08 02 4D 00 59 00 50 00   ..........M.Y.P.
00000240   49 00 43 00 54 00 7E 00   31 00 72 00 65 00 73 00   I.C.T.~.1.r.e.s.
00000256   30 00 00 00 70 00 00 00   00 00 00 00 00 00 02 00   0...p...........
00000272   58 00 00 00 18 00 01 00   2F 19 00 00 00 00 01 00   X......./.......
00000288   5A BF 1E 1B 8F 57 C4 01   5A BF 1E 1B 8F 57 C4 01   Z¿..¸WÄ.Z¿..¸WÄ.
00000304   5A BF 1E 1B 8F 57 C4 01   5A BF 1E 1B 8F 57 C4 01   Z¿..¸WÄ.Z¿..¸WÄ.
00000320   00 00 00 00 00 00 00 00   00 00 00 00 00 00 00 00   ................
00000336   00 00 00 10 00 00 00 00   0B 01 4D 00 79 00 20 00   ..........M.y. .
00000352   50 00 69 00 63 00 74 00   75 00 72 00 65 00 73 00   P.i.c.t.u.r.e.s.
00000368   90 00 00 00 20 01 00 00   00 04 18 00 00 00 01 00   _... ...........
00000384   00 01 00 00 20 00 00 00   24 00 49 00 33 00 30 00   .... ...$.I.3.0.
00000400   30 00 00 00 01 00 00 00   00 10 00 00 01 00 00 00   0...............
00000416   10 00 00 00 F0 00 00 00   F0 00 00 00 00 00 00 00   ....ð...ð.......
00000432   5B 19 00 00 00 00 01 00   68 00 58 00 00 00 00 00   [.......h.X.....
00000448   30 19 00 00 00 00 01 00   80 F3 B4 1B 8F 57 C4 01   0......_ó´.¸WÄ.
00000464   46 01 36 21 8F 57 C4 01   46 01 36 21 8F 57 C4 01   F.6!¸WÄ.F.6!¸WÄ.
00000480   46 01 36 21 8F 57 C4 01   B8 01 00 00 00 00 00 00   F.6!¸WÄ.¸.......
00000496   B6 01 00 00 00 00 00 00   06 00 00 00 00 00 02 00   ¶...............
00000512   0B 03 44 00 65 00 73 00   6B 00 74 00 6F 00 70 00   ..D.e.s.k.t.o.p.
00000528   2E 00 69 00 6E 00 69 00   59 19 00 00 00 00 01 00   ..i.n.i.Y.......
00000544   68 00 56 00 00 00 00 00   30 19 00 00 00 00 01 00   h.V.....0.......
00000560   80 F3 B4 1B 8F 57 C4 01   08 4C 2F DE 85 57 C4 01   _ó´.¸WÄ..L/Þ…WÄ.
00000576   5E 2D CF 1B 8F 57 C4 01   5E 2D CF 1B 8F 57 C4 01   ^-Ï.¸WÄ.^-Ï.¸WÄ.
00000592   00 30 00 00 00 00 00 00   A6 26 00 00 00 00 00 00   .0......¦&......
00000608   20 00 00 00 00 00 00 00   0A 03 53 00 61 00 6D 00    .........S.a.m.
00000624   70 00 6C 00 65 00 2E 00   6A 00 70 00 67 00 00 00   p.l.e...j.p.g...
00000640   00 00 00 00 00 00 00 00   10 00 00 00 02 00 00 00   ................
00000656   FF FF FF FF 82 79 47 11   00 00 00 00 00 00 00 00   ÿÿÿÿ‚yG.........
00000672   00 00 00 00 00 00 00 00   00 00 00 00 00 00 00 00   ................
00000688   00 00 00 00 00 00 00 00   00 00 00 00 00 00 00 00   ................
00000704   00 00 00 00 00 00 00 00   00 00 00 00 00 00 00 00   ................
00000720   00 00 00 00 00 00 00 00   00 00 00 00 00 00 00 00   ................
00000736   00 00 00 00 00 00 00 00   00 00 00 00 00 00 00 00   ................
00000752   00 00 00 00 00 00 00 00   00 00 00 00 00 00 00 00   ................
00000768   00 00 00 00 00 00 00 00   00 00 00 00 00 00 00 00   ................
00000784   00 00 00 00 00 00 00 00   00 00 00 00 00 00 00 00   ................
00000800   00 00 00 00 00 00 00 00   00 00 00 00 00 00 00 00   ................
00000816   00 00 00 00 00 00 00 00   00 00 00 00 00 00 00 00   ................
00000832   00 00 00 00 00 00 00 00   00 00 00 00 00 00 00 00   ................
00000848   00 00 00 00 00 00 00 00   00 00 00 00 00 00 00 00   ................
00000864   00 00 00 00 00 00 00 00   00 00 00 00 00 00 00 00   ................
00000880   00 00 00 00 00 00 00 00   00 00 00 00 00 00 00 00   ................
00000896   00 00 00 00 00 00 00 00   00 00 00 00 00 00 00 00   ................
00000912   00 00 00 00 00 00 00 00   00 00 00 00 00 00 00 00   ................
```

```
00000928   00 00 00 00 00 00 00 00   00 00 00 00 00 00 00 00   ................
00000944   00 00 00 00 00 00 00 00   00 00 00 00 00 00 00 00   ................
00000960   00 00 00 00 00 00 00 00   00 00 00 00 00 00 00 00   ................
00000976   00 00 00 00 00 00 00 00   00 00 00 00 00 00 00 00   ................
00000992   00 00 00 00 00 00 00 00   00 00 00 00 00 00 00 00   ................
00001008   00 00 00 00 00 00 00 00   00 00 00 00 00 00 02 00   ................
```

Normal user access to this directory, via a directory folder view in Windows Explorer, shows at Table 6.85 the file details reported by the operating system, Windows 2000.

Table 6.85 Windows Explorer file directory details.

File Name & Path	\Documents and Settings\NTFS TEST\My Documents \My Pictures
Size (bytes)	0
Last Accessed	21/6/04 12:56
Last Written	21/6/04 11:50
File Created	21/6/04 12:56
Attributes	Read Only bit set

With an image of the system loaded as a virtual disk, forensic software was used to examine the directory details of this directory, with the results as shown at Table 6.86. It should be noted that this is the directory that is the "parent" of the previous file examined, Sample.jpg.

Table 6.86 Forensic software file directory details.

File Name	My Pictures
Last Access	21/06/04 12:56:03
Last Written	21/06/04 11:50:41
File Created	21/06/04 12:56:02
Entry Modified	21/06/04 12:56:12
Logical Size	256
Physical Size	256
Starting Extent	0C-C1616
Physical Location	PS:12991, SO:400
Full Path	\Documents and Settings\NTFS TEST\My Documents \My Pictures
MFT Record Number	6448

Taking it Apart – the FILE Record Header

As with all MFT records, this record starts with a FILE Record Header and the structure and layout of this FILE Record Header is identical to the ones that we have deconstructed. At Table 6.87, we show (black background) the bytes of the FILE Record Header for this sample MFT record from byte offsets 0 to 47. We note that this header starts with the normal "FILE" marker, even though the record is for a directory.

Table 6.87 FILE Record Header.

```
00000000   46 49 4C 45 2A 00 03 00   B4 73 24 01 00 00 00 00   FILE*...´s$.....
00000016   01 00 02 00 30 00 03 00   98 02 00 00 00 04 00 00   ....0...˜.......
00000032   00 00 00 00 00 00 00 00   04 00 02 00 00 00 00 00   ................
```

At Table 6.88 we show the detailed analysis of this File Record Header, using the same descriptors as we used at Table 6.66.

Table 6.88 FILE Record Header – analysis.

Bytes 0 to 3	Start of File Record Header	"FILE"
Bytes 4 and 5	Offset to Update Sequence Number	002Ah = 42
Bytes 6 and 7	Size of Update Sequence	0003h = 3
Bytes 8 to 15	$Logfile Sequence Number	00000000012473B4h
Bytes 16 and 17	Record Use Sequence Number	0001h = 1
Bytes 18 and 19	Hard Link Count	0002h = 2
Bytes 20 and 21	Pointer to First Attribute	0030h = 48
Bytes 22 and 23	Record Flags	0003h = Directory Record in use
Bytes 24 to 27	Logical Size of Record	00000298h = 664
Bytes 28 to 31	Physical Size of Record	00000400h = 1024
Bytes 32 to 39	Base File Reference	0000000000000000h
Bytes 40 and 41	Possible Attribute Count	0004h = 4
Bytes 42 and 43	Update Sequence Number	0002h = 2
Bytes 44 to 47	Update Sequence Array	00 00 00 00

Taking it Apart – the Standard Information Attribute

The start of the Standard Information Attribute is signalled by the identifier 10 00 00 00h at byte offset 48. As with all Attributes, this Standard Information Attribute starts with an Attribute Header.

The Attribute Header

At byte offsets 48 to 71 (black background) at Table 6.89 are the details of this Attribute Header. Its layout is identical to the Attribute Headers that we have encountered and deconstructed above.

Table 6.89 Attribute Header – Standard Information Attribute.

```
00000048  10 00 00 00 60 00 00 00  00 00 00 00 00 00 00 00   ....`...........
00000064  48 00 00 00 18 00 00 00  5A BF 1E 1B 8F 57 C4 01   H.......Z¿.._WÄ.
```

At Table 6.90 is shown the analysis of the Attribute Header for this Standard Information Attribute.

Table 6.90 Attribute Header – analysis.

Bytes 48 to 51	Attribute ID	10 00 00 00
Bytes 52 to 55	Length of Attribute	00000060h = 96 From offset 48 to 143
Byte 56	Resident/Non-Resident Flag	00h = resident
Byte 57	Length of Name of Attribute	00h = no name
Bytes 58 to 59	Offset to Start of Attribute Proper	0000h = not used
Bytes 60 to 61	Flags	0000h = normal
Bytes 62 to 63	Not Yet Known	0000h
Bytes 64 to 67	Length of Attribute Proper	00000048h = 72 From offset 72 to 143
Bytes 68 to 69	Offset to Start of Attribute Proper	0018h = 24 48 + 24 = 72
Byte 70	Indexed flag	00h = not indexed
Byte 71	Padding to 8 byte Boundary	00h

The Standard Information Attribute Proper

The Standard Information Attribute Proper extends from byte offsets 72 to 143 as shown (black background) at Table 6.91.

Table 6.91 Standard Information Attribute Proper.

00000064	48 00 00 00 18 00 00 00	5A BF 1E 1B 8F 57 C4 01	H.......Z¿.._WÄ.
00000080	9C 8C 11 FA 85 57 C4 01	46 01 36 21 8F 57 C4 01	ÉŒ.ú...WÄ.F.6!_WÄ.
00000096	5E 2D CF 1B 8F 57 C4 01	01 00 00 00 00 00 00 00	^-Ï._WÄ.........
00000112	00 00 00 00 00 00 00 00	00 00 00 00 0B 01 00 00	....
00000128	00 00 00 00 00 00 00 00	00 00 00 00 00 00 00 00	....

At Table 6.92 is shown the analysis of the Standard Information Attribute Proper as described in Table 6.70.

Table 6.92 Standard Information Attribute Proper – analysis.

Bytes 72 to 79	Creation Date and Time	21/06/04 12:56:02 GMT
Bytes 80 to 87	Last Modified Date and Time	21/06/04 11:50:41 GMT
Bytes 88 to 95	Last MFT Record Change Date and Time	21/06/04 12:56:12 GMT
Bytes 96 to 103	Last Access Date and Time	21/06/04 12:56:03 GMT
Bytes 104 to 107	File Permissions	01 00 00 00 = read only set
Bytes 108 to 111	Maximum Number of Versions	00000000h = disabled
Bytes 112 to 115	Version Number and Class ID	0000000000000000h
Bytes 120 to 123	Owner ID	00000000h
Bytes 124 to 127	Security ID	0000010Bh
Bytes 128 to 135	Quota Charged	0000000000000000h
Bytes 136 to 143	Update Sequence Number	0000000000000000h

An examination of the reported times and dates by the operating system and by forensic software (see Tables 6.85 and 6.86 respectively) reveals that they are consistent with those recorded here.

Taking it Apart – the File Name Attribute [1]

This is the first of two File Name Attributes that occur in this record. The start of the File Name Attribute is signalled by the identifier 30 00 00 00h at byte offset 144. As with all Attributes, this File Name Attribute starts with an Attribute Header.

The Attribute Header

At byte offsets 144 to 167 (black background) at Table 6.93 are the details of this Attribute Header. Its layout is identical to the Attribute Headers that we have encountered and deconstructed above.

Table 6.93 Attribute Header – File Name Attribute.

00000144	30 00 00 00 70 00 00 00	00 00 00 00 00 00 03 00	0...p.........
00000160	52 00 00 00 18 00 01 00	2F 19 00 00 00 00 01 00	R......./.......

At Table 6.94 is shown the analysis of the Attribute Header for this File Name Attribute.

Table 6.94 Attribute Header – analysis.

Bytes 144 to 147	Attribute ID	30 00 00 00
Bytes 148 to 151	Length of Attribute	00000070h = 112
		From offset 144 to 255
Byte 152	Resident/Non-Resident Flag	00h = resident
Byte 153	Length of Name of Attribute	00h = no name
Bytes 154 to 155	Offset to Start of Attribute Proper	0000h = not used
Bytes 156 to 157	Flags	0000h = normal
Bytes 158 to 159	Not Yet Known	0003h = possible ID
Bytes 160 to 163	Length of Attribute Proper	00000052h = 82
		From offset 168 to 249
Bytes 164 to 165	Offset to Start of Attribute Proper	0018h = 24
		144 + 24 = 168
Byte 166	Indexed flag	01h = indexed
Byte 167	Padding to 8 byte Boundary	00h

The File Name Attribute Proper

The File Name Attribute Proper extends from byte offsets 168 to 249 as shown (black background) at Table 6.95.

Table 6.95 File Name Attribute Proper.

```
00000160   52 00 00 00 18 00 01 00   2F 19 00 00 00 00 01 00   R......./.......
00000176   5A BF 1E 1B 8F 57 C4 01   5A BF 1E 1B 8F 57 C4 01   Z¿.._WÄ.Z¿.._WÄ.
00000192   5A BF 1E 1B 8F 57 C4 01   5A BF 1E 1B 8F 57 C4 01   Z¿.._WÄ.Z¿.._WÄ.
00000208   00 00 00 00 00 00 00 00   00 00 00 00 00 00 00 00   ................
00000224   00 00 00 10 00 00 00 00   08 02 4D 00 59 00 50 00   ..........M.Y.P.
00000240   49 00 43 00 54 00 7E 00   31 00 72 00 65 00 73 00   I.C.T.~.1.r.e.s.
```

At Table 6.96 is shown the analysis of the File Name Attribute Proper as described in Table 6.74.

Table 6.96 File Name Attribute Proper – analysis.

Bytes 168 to 175	Reference to Parent Directory	000100000000192Fh = 6447
		"My Documents"
Bytes 176 to 183	Creation Date and Time	21/06/04 12:56:02 GMT
Bytes 184 to 191	Last Modified Date and Time	21/06/04 12:56:02 GMT
Bytes 192 to 199	Last MFT Record Change Date and Time	21/06/04 12:56:02 GMT
Bytes 200 to 207	Last Access Date and Time	21/06/04 12:56:02 GMT
Bytes 208 to 215	"Physical" Size of File	0000000000000000h = 0
Bytes 216 to 223	"Logical" Size of File	0000000000000000h = 0
Bytes 224 to 227	Flags	00 00 00 10h
Bytes 228 to 231	Extended Attributes and Reparse Points	00000000h
Byte 232	Length of File Name in Characters	08h = 8
Byte 233	Type of File Name	02h = DOS
Bytes 234 to 249	File Name	"MYPICT~1"

As can be seen from Table 6.96, the reference to the parent directory is record number 6447 decimal, and this is identified in the sample MFT as the folder My Documents, which does contain this folder. It should be noted that there are differences in the Last Modified Date and Time, the Last MFT Record Change Date and Time and the Last Access Date and Time recorded in this attribute (Table 6.96) and the equivalent dates and times recorded in the Standard Information Attribute (Table 6.92). As mentioned above, the authors are currently of the view that none of the dates and times in *this* attribute should be relied upon until the rules by which they are updated are fully understood.

It may be noted that the Type of File Name entry here is DOS-compliant (see Table 6.96), indicating that a second LFN File Name Attribute is probably required. It may also be noted that there are six bytes of padding at byte offsets 250 to 255 to bring the next entry onto an 8-byte boundary.

At byte offset 227, part of the four-byte sequence that is set aside for flags, we note a value of 10h. The known range of values for the bytes at offsets 224 to 227 are listed in Table 6.35 with the values of the bytes at 226 and 227 shown as zero in all cases. This is the first occasion on which a value other than zero has been seen in the File Name Attribute at this location. Suspecting that byte 227, or at least one bit within it, might be a flag that marks the record as a directory, a number of experiments were carried out. *Although not documented in any reference seen by the authors, the experiments clearly demonstrated that this value is almost certainly a flag that marks this record as a directory or marks some item peculiar to a directory. It may be noted that the same value also appears in the second File Name Attribute which follows.*

Taking it Apart – the File Name Attribute [2]

This is the second of two File Name Attributes that occur in this record. The start of the File Name Attribute is signalled by the identifier 30 00 00 00h at byte offset 256. As with all Attributes, this File Name Attribute starts with an Attribute Header.

The Attribute Header

At byte offsets 256 to 279 (black background) at Table 6.97 are the details of this Attribute Header. Its layout is identical to the Attribute Headers that we have encountered and deconstructed above.

Table 6.97 Attribute Header – File Name Attribute.

```
00000256  30 00 00 00 70 00 00 00  00 00 00 00 00 00 02 00   0...p...........
00000272  58 00 00 00 18 00 01 00  2F 19 00 00 00 00 01 00   X......./.......
```

At Table 6.98 is shown the analysis of the Attribute Header for this File Name Attribute.

Table 6.98 Attribute Header – analysis.

Bytes 256 to 259	Attribute ID	30 00 00 00
Bytes 260 to 263	Length of Attribute	00000070h = 112
		From offset 256 to 367
Byte 264	Resident/Non-Resident Flag	00h = resident
Byte 265	Length of Name of Attribute	00h = no name
Bytes 266 to 267	Offset to Start of Attribute Proper	0000h = not used
Bytes 268 to 269	Flags	0000h = normal
Bytes 270 to 271	Not Yet Known	0002h = possible ID
Bytes 272 to 275	Length of Attribute Proper	00000058h = 88
		From offset 280 to 367
Bytes 276 to 277	Offset to Start of Attribute Proper	0018h = 24
		256 + 24 = 280
Byte 278	Indexed flag	01h = indexed
Byte 279	Padding to 8 byte Boundary	00h

The File Name Attribute Proper

The File Name Attribute Proper extends from byte offsets 280 to 367 as shown (black background) at Table 6.99.

Table 6.99 File Name Attribute Proper.

```
00000272   58 00 00 00 18 00 01 00   2F 19 00 00 00 00 01 00   X......./.......
00000288   5A BF 1E 1B 8F 57 C4 01   5A BF 1E 1B 8F 57 C4 01   Z¿..˙WÄ.Z¿..˙WÄ.
00000304   5A BF 1E 1B 8F 57 C4 01   5A BF 1E 1B 8F 57 C4 01   Z¿..˙WÄ.Z¿..˙WÄ.
00000320   00 00 00 00 00 00 00 00   00 00 00 00 00 00 00 00   ...............
00000336   00 00 00 10 00 00 00 00   0B 01 4D 00 79 00 20 00   .........M.y. .
00000352   50 00 69 00 63 00 74 00   75 00 72 00 65 00 73 00   P.i.c.t.u.r.e.s.
```

At Table 6.100 is shown the analysis of the File Name Attribute Proper as described in Table 6.74.

Table 6.100 File Name Attribute Proper – analysis.

Bytes 280 to 287	Reference to Parent Directory	000100000000192Fh = 6447 "My Documents"
Bytes 288 to 295	Creation Date and Time	21/06/04 12:56:02 GMT
Bytes 296 to 303	Last Modified Date and Time	21/06/04 12:56:02 GMT
Bytes 304 to 311	Last MFT Record Change Date and Time	21/06/04 12:56:02 GMT
Bytes 312 to 319	Last Access Date and Time	21/06/04 12:56:02 GMT
Bytes 320 to 327	"Physical" Size of File	0000000000000000h = 0
Bytes 328 to 335	"Logical" Size of File	0000000000000000h = 0
Bytes 336 to 339	Flags	00 00 00 10h
Bytes 340 to 343	Extended Attributes and Reparse Points	00000000h
Byte 344	Length of File Name in Characters	0Bh = 11
Byte 345	Type of File Name	01h = Win32
Bytes 346 to 367	File Name	"My Pictures"

As can be seen from Table 6.100, the reference to the parent directory is record number 6447 decimal, and this is identified in the sample MFT as the folder My Documents, which does contain this folder. It should be noted, as explained above, that there are differences in the Last Modified Date and Time, the Last MFT Record Change Date and Time and the Last Access Date and Time recorded in this attribute (Table 6.100) and the equivalent dates and times recorded in the Standard Information Attribute (Table 6.92). None of the dates and times in *this* attribute should be relied upon until the rules by which they are updated are fully understood.

It may be noted that the Type of File Name entry here is Win32-compliant (see Table 6.100) indicating that this is an LFN File Name Attribute. At byte offset 339, part of the four-byte sequence that is set aside for flags, we note a value of 10h and interpret this as a flag that marks the record as a directory (see above). We may also note that no padding bytes are required in this instance.

Taking it Apart – the Index Root Attribute

The start of an Index Root Attribute is signalled by the identifier 90 00 00 00h at byte offset 368. As with all Attributes, this Index Root Attribute starts with an Attribute Header.

The Attribute Header

At byte offsets 368 to 383 (black background) at Table 6.101 are the details of the first part of this Attribute Header. This Attribute Header is interpreted differently from the previous versions analyzed because the Attribute is Named (see Appendix 9 for the template applied).

Table 6.101 Attribute Header – Index Root Attribute – first part.

```
00000368  90 00 00 00 20 01 00 00  00 04 18 00 00 00 01 00   ....  ............
00000384  00 01 00 00 20 00 00 00  24 00 49 00 33 00 30 00   ....  ...$.I.3.0.
```

At Table 6.102 is shown the analysis of the first part of the Attribute Header for the Index Root Attribute.

Table 6.102 Attribute Header – First part – analysis.

Bytes 368 to 371	Attribute ID	90 00 00 00
Bytes 372 to 375	Length of Attribute	00000120h = 288
		From offset 368 to 655
Byte 376	Resident/Non-Resident Flag	00h = resident
Byte 377	Length of Name of Attribute	04h = 4
Bytes 378 to 379	Offset to Name of Attribute	0018h = 24
		368 + 24 = 392
Bytes 380 to 381	Flags	0000h = normal
Bytes 382 to 383	Not Yet Known	0001h = possible ID
Bytes 384 to 387	Length of Attribute Proper	00000100h = 256
		From offset 400 to 655
Bytes 388 to 389	Offset to Start of Attribute Proper	0020h = 32
		368 + 32 = 400
Byte 390	Indexed flag	00h = not indexed
Byte 391	Padding to 8 byte Boundary	00h

This Attribute Header is interpreted differently from what we have seen before, because this Attribute is *named* (see Table 6.102). Byte offsets 392 to 399 (black background) at Table 6.103 contain the details of this name, which is "$I30" in Unicode.

Table 6.103 Attribute Header – Index Root Attribute – second part.

```
00000384  00 01 00 00 20 00 00 00  24 00 49 00 33 00 30 00   ....  ...$.I.3.0.
```

The Index Root

The Index Root Attribute is an Attribute that we have not so far examined. The first four bytes at offsets 400 to 403 (black background) at Table 6.104, identify the *type* of entry as listed in the $AttrDef file (see Table 6.2). In this case we note that 30 00 00 00h is a File Name type.

Table 6.104 Type of entry.

```
00000400  30 00 00 00 01 00 00 00  00 10 00 00 01 00 00 00   0...............
```

Byte offsets 404 to 407 (black background) at Table 6.105 are reported to be an indication of the collation rule. This byte sequence identifies the rule that is to be used to sort the following index entries. If the type is File Name, as is the case here, then the rule COLLATION_FILENAME is used.

Table 6.105 Collation rule.

```
00000400  30 00 00 00 01 00 00 00  00 10 00 00 01 00 00 00   0...............
```

Byte offsets 408 to 411 (black background) at Table 6.106 contain the size of the Index Allocation Entry. The value here of 00001000h is equal to 4096 decimal. A scan of the sample volume reveals that "INDX" files, which are directory listings held as non-resident data in blocks on the "user" area of the disk, are 4096 bytes long. Each block is headed with the four characters "INDX". Any further space that is required by the file is allocated in blocks of the same size, which may or may not be contiguous. It will be seen later that "INDX" files are pointed to by data runs in just the same way as is the file data.

Table 6.106 Size of Index Allocation Entry.
```
00000400    30 00 00 00 01 00 00 00   00 10 00 00 01 00 00 00    0..............
```

Byte offset 412 (black background) at Table 6.107 is declared to be the Number of Clusters per Index Record. It is known from the BPB (see Table 6.1) at byte offset 13h that the cluster size on this disk is eight sectors, and thus this value of 1 equates to 8 × 512 = 4096 bytes. The remaining three bytes, offsets 413 to 415, are padding.

Table 6.107 Number of Clusters per Index Record.
```
00000400    30 00 00 00 01 00 00 00   00 10 00 00 01 00 00 00    0..............
```

The Index Header

The next part of this Attribute is known as the Index Header. Byte offsets 416 to 419 (black background) at Table 6.108 record the offset to the first index entry. In this case the value is 00000010h, which equals 16 decimal. This value therefore points to offset 416 + 16 = 432.

Table 6.108 Offset to first Index Entry.
```
00000416    10 00 00 00 F0 00 00 00   F0 00 00 00 00 00 00 00    ....ð...ð.......
```

Byte offsets 420 to 423 (black background) at Table 6.109 record the total size of the Index Entries. The value 000000F0h is equal to 240 decimal. Applied from the start of this Index Header, the last byte in the index should be at byte offset 416 + 240 − 1 = 655. This coincides with the declaration in the Attribute Header (see Table 6.102).

Table 6.109 Total size of Index Entries.
```
00000416    10 00 00 00 F0 00 00 00   F0 00 00 00 00 00 00 00    ....ð...ð.......
```

The allocated size of the Index Entries is recorded in byte offsets 424 to 427 (black background) at Table 6.110. The value is again 000000F0h which is equal to 240 decimal. This is identical to the total size of the Index Entries seen in Table 6.109 and it is likely that this value will be of more significance in non-resident records.

Table 6.110 Allocated Size of Index Entries.
```
00000416    10 00 00 00 F0 00 00 00   F0 00 00 00 00 00 00 00    ....ð...ð.......
```

Byte offset 428 (black background) at Table 6.111 is reported to be a flag which signals whether the Index is a "Small" index which will fit within the MFT record or a "Large" index that requires an external Index Allocation Unit. In this case 00h signals that this is a "Small" index, whereas 01h would signal it was a "Large" index. Experiments have shown that part directory listings *may* be retained within the MFT record both with and without external "INDX" buffer files. Where both types are present (internal and external) this flag will be set to 01h. Where there are no entries in the listing (an empty directory) or entries are resident only, this flag will be set to 00h. The remaining three bytes at offsets 429 to 431 are undocumented and are likely to be padding.

Table 6.111 Small or Large index flag.
```
00000416    10 00 00 00 F0 00 00 00   F0 00 00 00 00 00 00 00    ....ð...ð.......
```

Index Entries

The next part of the Attribute can be interpreted in a number of different ways, depending upon its content (for details see Appendix 9). In this case, there are three Index Entries and each starts with its own Index Entry Header which is 16 bytes in length. The first two entries do not have the Last Entry flag set; the final entry, which is a null entry, signals that it is also the last entry.

The eight bytes at offsets 432 and 439 (black background) at Table 6.112 point to the MFT record entry for this item. The values are in the same format as we have seen before where we called them "Base File Reference" (see, for example, Table 6.44). The value of the first six bytes 0000195Bh is equal to 6491 decimal, which refers to MFT record number 6491. This record is found to contain the details concerning a file called Desktop.ini.

Table 6.112 MFT reference for this item.
```
00000432    5B 19 00 00 00 00 01 00   68 00 58 00 00 00 00 00    [.......h.X.....
```

The two bytes at offsets 440 and 441 (black background) at Table 6.113 are stated to be the value of the length of the Index Entry, including the Index Entry Header. The value 0068h, which is 104 decimal, indicates that the Index Entry ends at byte 432 + 104 − 1 = 535.

Table 6.113 Length of Index Entry.
```
00000432    5B 19 00 00 00 00 01 00   68 00 58 00 00 00 00 00    [.......h.X.....
```

The two bytes at offsets 442 and 443 (black background) at Table 6.114, are stated to be the length of the stream attached to this Entry. This is the length of the File Name Attribute proper attached to this Index Entry Header. The value here is 0058h, which equals 88 in decimal. The stream starts, according to the specification, at an offset of 16 decimal from the beginning of the Index Entry, which, in this case is at 432 + 16 = 448. It extends to 448 + 88 − 1 = 535.

Table 6.114 Length of stream.
```
00000432    5B 19 00 00 00 00 01 00   68 00 58 00 00 00 00 00    [.......h.X.....
```

The byte at offset 444 (black background) at Table 6.115 is a listing flag byte with values: 00h = Internal MFT listing only, 01h = External "INDX" file exists, 02h = Last Index Entry in directory, and 03h = Internal listing exists and External "INDX" file exists. Here the value is zero, indicating that an internal listing exists.

Table 6.115 Listing flag.
```
00000432    5B 19 00 00 00 00 01 00   68 00 58 00 00 00 00 00    [.......h.X.....
```

There appears to be some confusion over the purpose of this flag (at Table 6.115) and the purpose of the flag in the Index Header (see Table 6.111). A comparison of the two flags across a series of records in the sample MFT revealed the details shown at Table 6.116.

Table 6.116 Comparison of flags.

Index Header *Table 6.111*	Index Entry Header *Table 6.115*	*Findings in MFT Record*
00h	00h	Resident listing only
00h	02h	Final null entry in listing (includes empty listing)
01h	01h	Resident and external listing exists
01h	03h	No resident listing, external listing only exists

The remaining three bytes at offsets 445 to 447 are probably padding. This is the end of the Index Entry Header and the start of the first Index Entry proper.

As noted from Table 6.114, the File Name Type Index Entry stream is from byte offsets 448 to 535, and these are highlighted (black background) at Table 6.117. The data stream for a File Name Type Index Entry appears to be very similar to that for a File Name Attribute proper (see, for example, Table 6.99).

Table 6.117 File Name Type Index Entry.

00000448	30 19 00 00 00 00 01 00 80 F3 B4 1B 8F 57 C4 01	0........ŏ´._WÄ.
00000464	46 01 36 21 8F 57 C4 01 46 01 36 21 8F 57 C4 01	F.6!_WÄ.F.6!_WÄ.
00000480	46 01 36 21 8F 57 C4 01 B8 01 00 00 00 00 00 00	F.6!_WÄ.„.......
00000496	B6 01 00 00 00 00 00 00 06 00 00 00 00 00 02 00	¶..............
00000512	0B 03 44 00 65 00 73 00 6B 00 74 00 6F 00 70 00	..D.e.s.k.t.o.p.
00000528	2E 00 69 00 6E 00 69 00	..i.n.i.

At Table 6.118 is shown the analysis of the File Name Type Index Entry using, as a template, the descriptors from Table 6.100.

Table 6.118 File Name Type Index Entry – analysis.

Bytes 448 to 455	Reference to Parent Directory	0001000000001930h = 6448 "My Pictures"
Bytes 456 to 463	Creation Date and Time	21/06/04 12:56:03 GMT
Bytes 464 to 471	Last Modified Date and Time	21/06/04 12:56:12 GMT
Bytes 472 to 479	Last MFT Record Change Date and Time	21/06/04 12:56:12 GMT
Bytes 480 to 487	Last Access Date and Time	21/06/04 12:56:12 GMT
Bytes 488 to 495	"Physical" Size of File	00000000000001B8h = 440
Bytes 496 to 503	"Logical" Size of File	00000000000001B6h = 438
Bytes 504 to 507	Flags	06 00 00 00h = System, Hidden
Bytes 508 to 511	Extended Attributes and Reparse Points	00000000h
Byte 512	Length of File Name in Characters	0Bh = 11
Byte 513	Type of File Name	03h = Win32 & DOS
Bytes 514 to 535	File Name	"Desktop.ini"

It should be noted that bytes 510 and 511 are shown in Table 6.117 as 02 00h respectively. These are, of course, the Update Sequence Number for this record (see Table 6.88) and they thus need to be replaced, before analysis, by the appropriate values from the Update Sequence Array. In this case, the values are 00 00h and this is what is shown against the Extended Attributes and Reparse Points entry in Table 6.118.

We now repeat this analysis for the second Index Entry, starting with its Index Entry Header at byte offset 536 and continuing to byte offset 551. This is shown (black background) at Table 6.119.

Table 6.119 Index Entry Header.

```
00000528                              59 19 00 00 00 00 01 00          Y.......
00000544   68 00 56 00 00 00 00 00    30 19 00 00 00 00 01 00   h.V.....0.......
```

At Table 6.120 is shown the analysis for the second Index Entry Header. The three bytes at offsets 549 to 551 are probably padding to an 8 byte boundary.

Table 6.120 Index Entry Header – analysis.

Bytes 536 to 543	MFT Reference for this Item	0001000000001959h = 6489 "Sample.jpg"
Bytes 544 to 545	Length of Index Entry	0068h = 104 From offset 536 to 639
Bytes 546 to 547	Length of Stream	0056h = 86 From offset 552 to 637
Byte 548	Listing Flag	00h = resident listing

This is the end of the Index Entry Header and the start of the second Index Entry proper. As noted from Table 6.120, the File Name Type Index Entry stream is from byte offsets 552 to 637, and these are highlighted (black background) at Table 6.121.

Table 6.121 File Name Type Index Entry.

```
00000544   68 00 56 00 00 00 00 00   30 19 00 00 00 00 01 00   h.V.....0.......
00000560   80 F3 B4 1B 8F 57 C4 01   08 4C 2F DE 85 57 C4 01   _ó´._WÄ..L/Þ…WÄ.
00000576   5E 2D CF 1B 8F 57 C4 01   5E 2D CF 1B 8F 57 C4 01   ^-Ï._WÄ.^-Ï._WÄ.
00000592   00 30 00 00 00 00 00 00   A6 26 00 00 00 00 00 00   .0......|&......
00000608   20 00 00 00 00 00 00 00   0A 03 53 00 61 00 6D 00   .........S.a.m.
00000624   70 00 6C 00 65 00 2E 00   6A 00 70 00 67 00 00 00   p.l.e...j.p.g...
```

At Table 6.122 is shown the analysis of the File Name Type Index Entry using, as a template, the descriptors from Table 6.100. The two bytes at offsets 638 and 639 are probably padding to an 8 byte boundary.

Table 6.122 File Name Type Index Entry – analysis.

Bytes 552 to 559	Reference to Parent Directory	0001000000001930h = 6448 "My Pictures"
Bytes 560 to 567	Creation Date and Time	21/06/04 12:56:03 GMT
Bytes 568 to 575	Last Modified Date and Time	21/06/04 11:49:54 GMT
Bytes 576 to 583	Last MFT Record Change Date and Time	21/06/04 12:56:03 GMT
Bytes 584 to 591	Last Access Date and Time	21/06/04 12:56:03 GMT
Bytes 592 to 599	"Physical" Size of File	0000000000003000h = 12,288
Bytes 600 to 607	"Logical" Size of File	00000000000026A6h = 9,894
Bytes 608 to 611	Flags	20 00 00 00h = Archive set
Bytes 612 to 615	Extended Attributes and Reparse Points	00000000h
Byte 616	Length of File Name in Characters	0Ah = 10
Byte 617	Type of File Name	03h = Win32 & DOS
Bytes 618 to 637	File Name	"Sample.jpg"

Finally, we repeat this analysis for the third Index Entry starting with its Index Entry Header at byte offset 640 and continuing to byte offset 655. This is shown (black background) at Table 6.123.

Table 6.123 Index Entry Header.

```
00000640   00 00 00 00 00 00 00 00   10 00 00 00 02 00 00 00   ................
```

At Table 6.124 is shown the analysis for the third Index Entry Header. It is the last Index Entry of zero stream length, as there is no Index Entry following. The three bytes at offsets 653 to 655 are probably padding to an 8 byte boundary.

Table 6.124 Index Entry Header – analysis.

Bytes 640 to 647	MFT Reference for this Item	0000000000000000h = 0
Bytes 648 to 649	Length of Index Entry	0010h = 16
		From offset 640 to 655
Bytes 650 to 651	Length of Stream	0000h = 0
Byte 652	Listing Flag	02h = Last Index Entry

At byte offsets 656 to 659 (black background) in Table 6.125, we find the End of Record Marker followed in byte offsets 660 to 663, the Cyclic Redundancy Check.

Table 6.125 End of Record Marker and CRC.

```
00000656   FF FF FF FF 82 79 47 11   00 00 00 00 00 00 00 00   ÿÿÿÿ‚yG.........
```

External Directory Listings – Creation of "INDX" Files

Taking the directory listing (MFT record number 6448) that we have just examined as a baseline, we now explore the issue of creating an external directory listing, that is, an "INDX" file. By continuing to add files to the My Pictures subdirectory it is apparent that at some stage the listing will become too big to be retained within the one MFT record.

This sample MFT record originally contained details of two files within its directory listing: Desktop.ini and Sample.jpg. We noted the End of Record marker at offset 656 (see Table 6.125) and the FILE Record Header reports the logical size of the record to be 664 bytes in length (see bytes 24 to 27 in Table 6.88). This logical length includes the End of Record Marker and the four check bytes immediately following.

At Table 6.126, we show the details for this same record after further files have been added to the directory. The files added were, in the order shown: MFTtest1.txt, AMFTtst2.txt, ZMFTtst2.txt and JMFTtst2.txt. It was noted that the last file that was added made the listing too big to hold it in the MFT record and this forced the operating system to generate external storage for the entire listing. It was also noted that on each occasion a file was added, the file list was re-sorted. It was to test this effect that we used different characters at the beginning of each file name. Table 6.126 shows the revised MFT record following the addition of the four files, and the subsequent creation of external storage.

Table 6.126 Revised MFT record.

Offset	0	1	2	3	4	5	6	7	8	9	10	11	12	13	14	15	
00000000	46	49	4C	45	2A	00	03	00	C1	36	A0	01	00	00	00	00	FILE*...Á6 .....
00000016	01	00	02	00	30	00	03	00	48	02	00	00	00	04	00	00	....0...H.......
00000032	00	00	00	00	00	00	00	00	07	00	06	00	00	00	00	00	....
00000048	10	00	00	00	60	00	00	00	00	00	00	00	00	00	00	00	....`...........
00000064	48	00	00	00	18	00	00	00	5A	BF	1E	1B	8F	57	C4	01	H.......Z¿.._WÄ.
00000080	E6	F3	4F	E6	51	26	C6	01	E6	F3	4F	E6	51	26	C6	01	æóOæQ&Æ.æóOæQ&Æ.
00000096	E6	F3	4F	E6	51	26	C6	01	01	00	00	00	00	00	00	00	æóOæQ&Æ.........
00000112	00	00	00	00	00	00	00	00	00	00	00	00	0B	01	00	00	....
00000128	00	00	00	00	00	00	00	00	00	00	00	00	00	00	00	00	....
00000144	30	00	00	00	70	00	00	00	00	00	00	00	00	00	03	00	0...p...........
00000160	52	00	00	00	18	00	01	00	2F	19	00	00	00	00	01	00	R......./.......
00000176	5A	BF	1E	1B	8F	57	C4	01	5A	BF	1E	1B	8F	57	C4	01	Z¿.._WÄ.Z¿.._WÄ.

```
00000192   5A BF 1E 1B 8F 57 C4 01   5A BF 1E 1B 8F 57 C4 01   Z¿.._WÄ.Z¿.._WÄ.
00000208   00 00 00 00 00 00 00 00   00 00 00 00 00 00 00 00   ................
00000224   00 00 00 10 00 00 00 00   08 02 4D 00 59 00 50 00   ..........M.Y.P.
00000240   49 00 43 00 54 00 7E 00   31 00 72 00 65 00 73 00   I.C.T.~.1.r.e.s.
00000256   30 00 00 00 70 00 00 00   00 00 00 00 00 00 02 00   0...p...........
00000272   58 00 00 00 18 00 01 00   2F 19 00 00 00 00 01 00   X......./.......
00000288   5A BF 1E 1B 8F 57 C4 01   5A BF 1E 1B 8F 57 C4 01   Z¿.._WÄ.Z¿.._WÄ.
00000304   5A BF 1E 1B 8F 57 C4 01   5A BF 1E 1B 8F 57 C4 01   Z¿.._WÄ.Z¿.._WÄ.
00000320   00 00 00 00 00 00 00 00   00 00 00 00 00 00 00 00   ................
00000336   00 00 00 10 00 00 00 00   0B 01 4D 00 79 00 20 00   ..........M.y. .
00000352   50 00 69 00 63 00 74 00   75 00 72 00 65 00 73 00   P.i.c.t.u.r.e.s.
00000368   90 00 00 00 58 00 00 00   00 04 18 00 00 00 06 00   ...X...........
00000384   38 00 00 00 20 00 00 00   24 00 49 00 33 00 30 00   8... ...$.I.3.0.
00000400   30 00 00 00 01 00 00 00   00 10 00 00 01 00 00 00   0...............
00000416   10 00 00 00 28 00 00 00   28 00 00 00 01 00 00 00   ....(...(.......
00000432   00 00 00 00 00 00 00 00   18 00 00 00 03 00 00 00   ................
00000448   00 00 00 00 00 00 00 00   A0 00 00 00 50 00 00 00   ........ ...P...
00000464   01 04 40 00 00 00 04 00   00 00 00 00 00 00 00 00   ..@.............
00000480   00 00 00 00 00 00 00 00   48 00 00 00 00 00 00 00   ........H.......
00000496   00 10 00 00 00 00 00 00   00 10 00 00 00 00 06 00   ................
00000512   00 10 00 00 00 00 00 00   24 00 49 00 33 00 30 00   ........$.I.3.0.
00000528   31 01 0D FC 04 00 00 00   B0 00 00 00 28 00 00 00   1..ü....°...(...
00000544   00 04 18 00 00 00 05 00   08 00 00 00 20 00 00 00   ............ ...
00000560   24 00 49 00 33 00 30 00   01 00 00 00 00 00 00 00   $.I.3.0.........
00000576   FF FF FF FF 82 79 47 11   46 01 36 21 8F 57 C4 01   ÿÿÿÿ‚yG.F!_WÄ.
00000592   26 97 9A 5F 50 26 C6 01   B8 01 00 00 00 00 00 00   &—š_P&Æ.¸.......
00000608   B6 01 00 00 00 00 00 00   06 00 00 00 00 00 00 00   ¶...............
00000624   0B 03 44 00 65 00 73 00   6B 00 74 00 6F 00 70 00   ..D.e.s.k.t.o.p.
00000640   2E 00 69 00 6E 00 69 00   BF 19 00 00 00 00 02 00   ..i.n.i.¿.......
00000656   70 00 5A 00 00 00 00 00   30 19 00 00 00 00 01 00   p.Z.....0.......
00000672   EA 6D C3 64 50 26 C6 01   00 B2 FB 45 50 26 C6 01   êmÃdP&Æ..²ûEP&Æ.
00000688   EA 6D C3 64 50 26 C6 01   EA 6D C3 64 50 26 C6 01   êmÃdP&Æ.êmÃdP&Æ.
00000704   30 00 00 00 00 00 00 00   2B 00 00 00 00 00 00 00   0.......+.......
00000720   20 00 00 00 00 00 00 00   0C 03 4D 00 46 00 54 00    .........M.F.T.
00000736   74 00 65 00 73 00 74 00   31 00 2E 00 74 00 78 00   t.e.s.t.1...t.x.
00000752   74 00 00 00 00 00 00 00   59 19 00 00 00 00 01 00   t.......Y.......
00000768   68 00 56 00 00 00 00 00   30 19 00 00 00 00 01 00   h.V.....0.......
00000784   80 F3 B4 1B 8F 57 C4 01   08 4C 2F DE 85 57 C4 01   _ó´._WÄ..L/Þ…WÄ.
00000800   5E 2D CF 1B 8F 57 C4 01   5E 2D CF 1B 8F 57 C4 01   ^-Ï._WÄ.^-Ï._WÄ.
00000816   00 30 00 00 00 00 00 00   A6 26 00 00 00 00 00 00   .0......|&......
00000832   20 00 00 00 00 00 00 00   0A 03 53 00 61 00 6D 00    .........S.a.m.
00000848   70 00 6C 00 65 00 2E 00   6A 00 70 00 67 00 00 00   p.l.e...j.p.g...
00000864   C1 19 00 00 00 00 01 00   70 00 5A 00 00 00 00 00   Á.......p.Z.....
00000880   30 19 00 00 00 00 01 00   8A 0C 83 92 51 26 C6 01   0.......Š.ƒ'Q&Æ.
00000896   00 A1 45 84 51 26 C6 01   E4 6E 85 92 51 26 C6 01   .¡E„Q&Æ.änƒ'Q&Æ.
00000912   E4 6E 85 92 51 26 C6 01   30 00 00 00 00 00 00 00   änƒ'Q&Æ.0.......
00000928   2B 00 00 00 00 00 00 00   20 00 00 00 00 00 00 00   +....... .......
00000944   0C 03 5A 00 4D 00 46 00   54 00 74 00 73 00 74 00   ..Z.M.F.T.t.s.t.
00000960   32 00 2E 00 74 00 78 00   74 00 00 00 00 00 00 00   2...t.x.t.......
00000976   00 00 00 00 00 00 00 00   10 00 00 00 02 00 00 00   ................
00000992   FF FF FF FF 82 79 47 11   00 00 00 00 00 00 00 00   ÿÿÿÿ‚yG.........
00001008   00 00 00 00 00 00 00 00   00 00 00 00 00 00 06 00   ................
```

We now examine Table 6.126, using the same section headings as above, and compare the results with our findings for Table 6.84 to establish any major differences that have occurred. In the first section we look at the new FILE Record Header.

The FILE Record Header

At Table 6.127, we show (black background), the bytes of the FILE Record Header for this revised sample MFT record from byte offsets 0 to 47. We note that this header starts with the normal "FILE" marker.

Table 6.127 FILE Record Header.

00000000	46 49 4C 45 2A 00 03 00 C1 36 A0 01 00 00 00 00	FILE*...Á6 .....
00000016	01 00 02 00 30 00 03 00 48 02 00 00 00 04 00 00	....0...H.......
00000032	00 00 00 00 00 00 00 00 07 00 06 00 00 00 00 00	....

At Table 6.128 we show the detailed analysis of this File Record Header, using the same descriptors as we used at Table 6.88. Where the values in Table 6.128 differ from those in Table 6.88, they are highlighted (black background).

Table 6.128 FILE Record Header – analysis.

Bytes 0 to 3	Start of File Record Header	"FILE"
Bytes 4 and 5	Offset to Update Sequence Number	002Ah = 42
Bytes 6 and 7	Size of Update Sequence	0003h = 3
Bytes 8 to 15	$Logfile Sequence Number	0000000001A036C1h
Bytes 16 and 17	Record Use Sequence Number	0001h = 1
Bytes 18 and 19	Hard Link Count	0002h = 2
Bytes 20 and 21	Pointer to First Attribute	0030h = 48
Bytes 22 and 23	Record Flags	0003h = Directory Record in use
Bytes 24 to 27	Logical Size of Record	00000248h = 584
Bytes 28 to 31	Physical Size of Record	00000400h = 1024
Bytes 32 to 39	Base File Reference	0000000000000000h
Bytes 40 and 41	Possible Attribute Count	0007h = 7
Bytes 42 and 43	Update Sequence Number	0006h = 6
Bytes 44 to 47	Update Sequence Array	00 00 00 00

We note that the record has been changed in a number of ways. The logical length is now shown as 584 (bytes 24 to 27), so the End of Record marker is now present at offsets 576 to 579 and the CRC at offsets 580 to 583. A different $Logfile Sequence Number (bytes 8 to 15) has been assigned, and this is expected since it should change for each transaction. Also, as might be expected, the Possible Attribute Count (bytes 40 and 41) and the Update Sequence Number (byte 42 and 43) have been changed.

The Standard Information Attribute

At Table 6.129, we show (black background) the bytes of the Standard Information Attribute (together with its Attribute Header) for this revised sample MFT record from byte offsets 48 to 143.

Table 6.129 Standard Information Attribute.

00000048	10 00 00 00 60 00 00 00 00 00 00 00 00 00 00 00	....`...........
00000064	48 00 00 00 18 00 00 00 5A BF 1E 1B 8F 57 C4 01	H.......Zċ.._WÄ.
00000080	E6 F3 4F E6 51 26 C6 01 E6 F3 4F E6 51 26 C6 01	æóOæQ&Æ.æóOæQ&Æ.
00000096	E6 F3 4F E6 51 26 C6 01 01 00 00 00 00 00 00 00	æóOæQ&Æ.........
00000112	00 00 00 00 00 00 00 00 00 00 00 00 0B 01 00 00	....
00000128	00 00 00 00 00 00 00 00 00 00 00 00 00 00 00 00	....

At Table 6.130 we show the detailed analysis of the Standard Information Attribute, using the same descriptors as we used at Tables 6.90 and 6.92. Where the values in Table 6.130 differ from those in Tables 6.90 and 6.92, they are highlighted (black background).

Table 6.130 Standard Information Attribute – analysis.

Bytes 48 to 51	Attribute ID	10 00 00 00
Bytes 52 to 55	Length of Attribute	00000060h = 96
		From offset 48 to 143
Byte 56	Resident/Non-Resident Flag	00h = resident
Byte 57	Length of Name of Attribute	00h = no name
Bytes 58 to 59	Offset to Start of Attribute Proper	0000h = not used
Bytes 60 to 61	Flags	0000h = normal
Bytes 62 to 63	Not Yet Known	0000h
Bytes 64 to 67	Length of Attribute Proper	00000048h = 72
		From offset 72 to 143
Bytes 68 to 69	Offset to Start of Attribute Proper	0018h = 24
		48 + 24 = 72
Byte 70	Indexed flag	00h = not indexed
Byte 71	Padding to 8 byte Boundary	00h
Bytes 72 to 79	Creation Date and Time	21/06/04 12:56:02 GMT
Bytes 80 to 87	Last Modified Date and Time	31/01/06 10:34:22 GMT
Bytes 88 to 95	Last MFT Record Change Date and Time	31/01/06 10:34:22 GMT
Bytes 96 to 103	Last Access Date and Time	31/01/06 10:34:22 GMT
Bytes 104 to 107	File Permissions	01 00 00 00 = read only set
Bytes 108 to 111	Maximum Number of Versions	00000000h = disabled
Bytes 112 to 115	Version Number and Class ID	0000000000000000h = 0
Byte 120 to 123	Owner ID	00000000h
Bytes 124 to 127	Security ID	0000010Bh
Bytes 128 to 135	Quota Charged	0000000000000000h = 0
Bytes 136 to 143	Update Sequence Number	0000000000000000h = 0

Here we note that the only changes made to the Standard Information Attribute are to the Last Modified Date and Time, the Last MFT Record Change Date and Time and the Last Access Date and Time. We would expect these dates and times to change for each transaction made.

The File Name Attributes

A detailed comparison of the values at byte offsets 144 to 367 in Tables 6.84 and 6.126 show them to be identical, indicating that there have been no changes to either of the File Name Attributes.

The Index Root Attribute

At Table 6.131, we show (black background), the bytes of the Index Root Attribute (together with its Attribute Header) for this revised sample MFT record from byte offsets 368 to 415.

Table 6.131 Index Root Attribute.

```
00000368  90 00 00 00 58 00 00 00  00 04 18 00 00 00 06 00   _...X...........
00000384  38 00 00 00 20 00 00 00  24 00 49 00 33 00 30 00   8... ...$.I.3.0.
00000400  30 00 00 00 01 00 00 00  00 10 00 00 01 00 00 00   0...............
```

At Table 6.132 we show the detailed analysis of the Index Root Attribute, using the same descriptors as we used at Tables 6.102 to 6.107. Where the values in Table 6.132 differ from those in Tables 6.102 to 6.107, they are highlighted (black background).

Table 6.132 Index Root Attribute – analysis.

Bytes 368 to 371	Attribute ID	90 00 00 00
Bytes 372 to 375	Length of Attribute	00000058h = 88
		From offset 368 to 455
Byte 376	Resident/Non-Resident Flag	00h = resident
Byte 377	Length of Name of Attribute	04h = 4
Bytes 378 to 379	Offset to Name of Attribute	0018h = 24
		368 + 24 = 392
Bytes 380 to 381	Flags	0000h = normal
Bytes 382 to 383	Not Yet Known	0006h = possible ID
Bytes 384 to 387	Length of Attribute Proper	00000038h = 56
		From offset 400 to 455
Bytes 388 to 389	Offset to Start of Attribute Proper	0020h = 32
		368 + 32 = 400
Byte 390	Indexed flag	00h = not indexed
Byte 391	Padding to 8 byte Boundary	00h
Bytes 392 to 399	Name of Attribute	"$I30"
Bytes 400 to 403	Type of Entry	30 00 00 00 = File Name
Bytes 404 to 407	Collation Rule	00000001h = 1
Bytes 408 to 411	Size of Index Allocation Entry	00001000h = 4096
Byte 412	Number of Clusters per Index Record	01h = 1
Bytes 413 to 415	Padding to 8 byte Boundary	00 00 00

Here we note that changes have been made to the Length of Attribute (see byte offsets 372 to 375), reducing it from 288 to 88 bytes, and the Length of Attribute Proper (see byte offsets 384 to 387) reducing it from 256 to 56. In addition, the possible attribute ID number (byte offsets 382 to 383) has been changed from 1 to 6.

The Index Header and Index Entry Header

At Table 6.133, we show (black background) the bytes of the Index Header, from offsets 416 to 431, and the bytes of the Index Entry Header from offsets 432 to 447.

Table 6.133 Index Header and Index Entry Header.

00000416	10 00 00 00 28 00 00 00 28 00 00 00 01 00 00 00	....(...(.......
00000432	00 00 00 00 00 00 00 00 18 00 00 00 03 00 00 00	....

At Table 6.134 we show the detailed analysis of the Index Header and Index Entry Header, using the same descriptors as we used at Tables 6.108 to 6.115. Where the values in Table 6.134 differ from those in Tables 6.108 to 6.115, they are highlighted (black background).

Table 6.134 Index Header and Index Entry Header – analysis.

Bytes 416 to 419	Offset to First Index Entry	00000010h = 16
Bytes 420 to 423	Total Size of Index Entries	00000028h = 40
		From 416 to 455
Bytes 424 to 427	Allocated Size of Index Entries	00000028h = 40
Byte 428	Small or Large Index Flag	01h = Large (external)
Bytes 429 to 431	Padding to 8 byte Boundary	00 00 00
Bytes 432 to 439	MFT Reference for this Item	0000000000000000h
Bytes 440 to 441	Length of the Index Entry	0018h = 24
		From 432 to 455

Bytes 442 to 443	Length of Stream	0000h = 0
Byte 444	Listing Flag	03h = No resident External Only
Bytes 445 to 447	Padding to 8 byte Boundary	00 00 00
Bytes 448 to 455	Remainder of Allocated Block	0000000000000000h

Here we note for the Index Header that changes have been made to the Total Size of the Index Entries (see byte offsets 420 to 423) and the Allocated Size of Index Entries (see byte offsets 424 to 427) reducing them both from 240 to 40 bytes. We may also note that the Index Flag (see byte offset 428) now shows a "Large Index" indicating that external storage has been allocated.

For the Index Entry Header, we note that no Base File Reference (see byte offsets 432 to 439) is recorded, that the Length of the Index Entry (see byte offsets 440 to 441) has been reduced from 104 to 24 and that the Length of Stream (see byte offsets 442 to 443) has been reduced from 88 to 0. At byte offset 444, we note that the Listing Flag now shows that there are no resident listings but that an external "INDX" file exists.

Further analysis shows that two new Attributes have been added: an Index Allocation Attribute and a Bitmap Attribute. We consider each of these in detail in the next two sections.

The Index Allocation Attribute

The start of an Index Allocation Attribute is signalled by the identifier A0 00 00 00h at byte offsets 456 to 459. As with all Attributes this Index Allocation Attribute starts with an Attribute Header, the layout of which is identical to one of the Attribute Headers that we have encountered and deconstructed above. The details of this Index Allocation Attribute are shown, from byte offsets 456 to 535 (black background) at Table 6.135.

Table 6.135 Index Allocation Attribute.

```
00000448                                 A0 00 00 00 50 00 00 00       ...P...
00000464   01 04 40 00 00 00 04 00   00 00 00 00 00 00 00 00       ..@...........
00000480   00 00 00 00 00 00 00 00   48 00 00 00 00 00 00 00       ........H.......
00000496   00 10 00 00 00 00 00 00   00 10 00 00 00 00 06 00       ...............
00000512   00 10 00 00 00 00 00 00   24 00 49 00 33 00 30 00       ........$.I.3.0.
00000528   31 01 0D FC 04 00 00 00                                 1..ü....
```

At Table 6.136 we show the detailed analysis of this Index Allocation Attribute. In this case we are examining a non-resident, named Attribute and we follow the layout described in Tables 6.76 to 6.82 for the second part of the Attribute Header.

Table 6.136 Index Allocation Attribute – analysis.

Bytes 456 to 459	Attribute ID	A0 00 00 00
Bytes 460 to 463	Length of Attribute	00000050h = 80 From offset 456 to 535
Byte 464	Resident/Non-Resident Flag	01h = non resident
Byte 465	Length of Name of Attribute	04h = 4
Bytes 466 to 467	Offset to Name of Attribute	0040h = 64 456 + 64 = 520
Bytes 468 to 469	Flags	0000h = normal
Bytes 470 to 471	Not Yet Known	0004h = possible ID
Bytes 472 to 479	Starting VCN	0000000000000000h = 0

Bytes 480 to 487	Last VCN	0000000000000000h = 0
Bytes 488 to 489	Offset to the Data Runs	0048h = 72
		456 + 72 = 528
Bytes 490 to 491	Compression Unit Size	0000h = 0
Bytes 492 to 495	Padding to 8 byte Boundary	00 00 00 00
Bytes 496 to 503	Allocated Size of Attribute	0000000000001000h = 4096
Bytes 504 to 511	Real Size of Attribute	0000000000001000h = 4096
Bytes 512 to 519	Initialized Size of Stream	0000000000001000h = 4096
Bytes 520 to 527	Attribute Name	"$I30"
Bytes 528 to 535	Data Run Descriptor	31 01 0D FC 04 00 00 00h

It should be noted that bytes 510 and 511 are shown in Table 6.135 as 06 00h respectively. These are, of course, the Update Sequence Number for this record (see Table 6.128) and they thus need to be replaced, before analysis, by the appropriate values from the Update Sequence Array. In this case, the values are 00 00h and this is what is included in the value for the Real Size of Attribute entry in Table 6.136.

The Index Allocation Attribute proper is simply the Data Run Descriptor shown starting at offset 528. All that goes before this is the Attribute Header for the Index Allocation Attribute. Using the technique described when examining Table 6.82, this Data Run Descriptor can be analysed as follows:

- The data run header byte, at offset 528, is 31h. This indicates that three bytes are used in this run to contain the starting cluster number and one byte is used to contain the number of clusters.

- The next byte, at offset 529, is 01h and this indicates that the number of clusters is 1.

- The next three bytes, at offsets 530 to 532, when re-ordered from little endian form 04FC0Dh = 326,669 decimal. This is the starting cluster number and so this run is of one cluster at LCN 326,669.

- The next byte, at offset 533, is a null header byte that indicates the end of the runs.

The Bitmap Attribute

The start of a Bitmap Attribute is signalled by the identifier B0 00 00 00h at byte offsets 536 to 539. As with all Attributes this Bitmap Attribute starts with an Attribute Header, the layout of which is identical to one of the Attribute Headers that we have encountered and deconstructed above. The details of this Bitmap Allocation Attribute are shown, from byte offsets 536 to 575 (black background) at Table 6.137.

Table 6.137 Bitmap Attribute.

00000528	B0 00 00 00 28 00 00 00	°...(...
00000544	00 04 18 00 00 00 05 00 08 00 00 00 20 00 00 00	....
00000560	24 00 49 00 33 00 30 00 01 00 00 00 00 00 00 00	$.I.3.0.........

At Table 6.138 we show the detailed analysis of this Bitmap Attribute. In this case we are examining a resident, named Attribute and we follow the layout described in Table 6.102 for the Attribute Header.

Table 6.138 Bitmap Attribute – analysis.

Bytes 536 to 539	Attribute ID	B0 00 00 00
Bytes 540 to 543	Length of Attribute	00000028h = 40
		From offset 536 to 575
Byte 544	Resident/Non-Resident Flag	00h = resident

Byte 545	Length of Name of Attribute	04h = 4
Bytes 546 to 547	Offset to Name of Attribute	0018h = 24
		536 + 24 = 560
Bytes 548 to 549	Flags	0000h = normal
Bytes 550 to 551	Not Yet Known	0005h = possible ID
Bytes 552 to 555	Length of Attribute Proper	00000008h = 8
		From offset 568 to 575
Bytes 556 to 557	Offset to Start of Attribute Proper	0020h = 32
		536 + 32 = 568
Byte 558	Indexed flag	00h = not indexed
Byte 559	Padding to 8 byte Boundary	00h
Bytes 560 to 567	Attribute Name	"$I30"
Bytes 568 to 575	Binary Map	0000000000000001h

The Bitmap Attribute proper occupies bytes 568 to 575 and is a binary map of the allocation areas that are used by the external "INDX" file. At byte offsets 576 to 579 (black background) in Table 6.139 we find the End of Record Marker, followed, in byte offsets 580 to 583, by the Cyclic Redundancy Check.

Table 6.139 End of Record Marker and CRC.

```
00000576   FF FF FF FF 82 79 47 11   46 01 36 21 8F 57 C4 01   ÿÿÿÿ‚yG.6!_WÄ.
```

Discussion

We note, from comparing these two samples of the MFT record, that as files are added to the directory the listings are initially built within the MFT record itself. When no further entries can be added because all space within the MFT record has been used, the MFT directory listing is changed from resident to non-resident. When this occurs, the MFT record is truncated and some of the Index Entries in the Index Root Attribute are overwritten by two new Attributes which define the external storage: the Index Allocation Attribute and the Bitmap Attribute. No directory listing entries (in this case) have been retained as part of the MFT record

It should be noted that, in some cases, directory listings are present both in the MFT record itself and in an external "INDX" file.

The data between the end of the logical record and the end of the record space is known as *MFT Record Slack*. As can be seen in Table 6.126, MFT record slack could still contain much meaningful data. For example, part details of Desktop.ini, and full details of MFTtest1.txt, Sample.jpg and ZMFTtst2.txt are all still accessible from Table 6.126. Such data could well be of some significance in a forensic investigation, as it might be the only record of the file or files having been present on the machine.

Analysis of an "INDX" File

For completeness we now carry out a partial analysis of the external "INDX" file that was created during the production of the Revised MFT Record of Table 6.126. The "INDX" file was found in cluster 326,669 and extends from offset 0 to offset 4095.

The INDX Record Header

At Table 6.140 we show (black background) the bytes of the INDX Record Header from byte offsets 0 to 63. We note that this header, which has some similarities with the FILE Record Header, starts with an "INDX" marker.

Table 6.140 INDX Record Header.

00000000	49 4E 44 58 28 00 09 00 B3 35 A0 01 00 00 00 00 INDX(...⁵5 .....
00000016	00 00 00 00 00 00 00 00 28 00 00 00 C8 02 00 00 ....(...È...
00000032	E8 0F 00 00 00 00 00 00 02 00 01 00 00 00 00 00 ....
00000048	00 00 00 00 00 00 00 00 00 00 00 00 00 00 00 00 ....

At Table 6.141 we show the detailed analysis of this "INDX" Record Header.

Table 6.141 INDX Record Header – analysis.

Bytes 0 to 3	Start of INDX Record Header	"INDX"
Bytes 4 and 5	Offset to Update Sequence Array	0028h = 40
Bytes 6 and 7	Size of Update Sequence Array (words)	0009h = 9
Bytes 8 to 15	$Logfile Sequence Number	0000000001A035B3h
Bytes 16 to 23	Virtual Cluster Number of this Allocation	0000000000000000h
Bytes 24 to 27	Offset to Index Entry Header	00000028h = 40 +24 = 64
Bytes 28 to 31	Offset to End of Final Entry	000002C8h = 712 + 24 −1 = 735
Bytes 32 to 35	Allocated Size of Index Entries	00000FE8h = 4072
		To 4072 + 24 − 1 = 4095
Byte 36	Index Type Flag	00h = small
Byte 37 to 39	Padding to 8 byte Boundary	00 00 00h
Bytes 40 and 41	Update Sequence Number	0002h = 2
Bytes 42 to 59	Update Sequence Array	01 00 00 00 00 00 00 00 00
		00 00 00 00 00 00 00 00 00
Bytes 60 to 63	Padding to 8 byte Boundary	00 00 00 00

The Index Entry Header

At byte offsets 64 to 79 (black background) at Table 6.142, we find the Index Entry Header for the First Index Entry.

Table 6.142 Index Entry Header.

00000064	C0 19 00 00 00 00 01 00 70 00 5A 00 00 00 00 00 À.......p.Z.....

At Table 6.143 is shown the analysis for this first Index Entry Header.

Table 6.143 Index Entry Header – analysis.

Bytes 64 to 71	MFT Reference for this Item	00010000000019C09h
		= 6592 "AMFTtst2.txt"
Bytes 72 to 73	Length of Index Entry	0070h = 112
		From offset 64 to 175
Bytes 74 to 75	Length of Stream	005Ah = 90
		From offset 80 to 169
Byte 76	Listing Flag	00h = resident listing
Bytes 77 to 79	Padding to 8 byte Boundary	00 00 00

The Index Entry

The Index Entry stream, as indicated in Table 6.143, extends from byte offsets 80 to 169, and these are shown (black background) at Table 6.144.

Table 6.144 Index Entry Stream.

```
00000080  30 19 00 00 00 00 01 00  00 15 BF 3C 51 26 C6 01   0.........Â<Q&Æ.
00000096  00 CC 3F 2D 51 26 C6 01  00 15 BF 3C 51 26 C6 01   .Ì?-Q&Æ...Â<Q&Æ.
00000112  00 15 BF 3C 51 26 C6 01  30 00 00 00 00 00 00 00   ..Â<Q&Æ.........
00000128  2B 00 00 00 00 00 00 00  20 00 00 00 00 00 00 00   +....... .......
00000144  0C 03 41 00 4D 00 46 00  54 00 74 00 73 00 74 00   ..A.M.F.T.t.s.t.
00000160  32 00 2E 00 74 00 78 00  74 00 00 00 00 00 02 00   2...t.x.t.......
```

At Table 6.145 is shown the analysis for this first Index Entry stream. This is of a similar form to that for the File Name Attribute Proper (see Table 6.74).

Table 6.145 Index Entry Proper – analysis.

Bytes 80 to 87	Reference to Parent Directory	0001000000001930h = 6448 "My Pictures"
Bytes 88 to 95	Creation Date and Time	31/01/06 10:29:38 GMT
Bytes 96 to 103	Last Modified Date and Time	31/01/06 10:29:12 GMT
Bytes 104 to 111	Last MFT Record Change Date and Time	31/01/06 10:29:38 GMT
Bytes 112 to 119	Last Access Date and Time	31/01/06 10:29:38 GMT
Bytes 120 to 127	"Physical" Size of File	0000000000000030h = 48
Bytes 128 to 135	"Logical" Size of File	000000000000002Bh = 43
Bytes 136 to 139	Flags	20 00 00 00h = archive set
Bytes 140 to 143	Extended Attributes and Reparse Points	00000000h
Byte 144	Length of File Name in Characters	0Ch = 12
Byte 145	Type of File Name	03h = Win32 & DOS
Bytes 146 to 169	File Name	"AMFTtst2.txt"

The next Index Entry Header then follows just as we found in the sample MFT listings.

Some Conclusions of Forensic Significance

From our experiments and from the work of others who have contributed to the analysis of the NTFS system, notably the linux-ntfs project at sourceforge.net, we are able to draw a number of conclusions that we believe have some forensic significance. It should be noted that this work is by no means complete nor are all interpretations that we have made necessarily correct. This is a work in progress, and, as such, should be used as a guideline for forensic practitioners. As always, we strongly recommend that an analyst personally carries out specific experiments to confirm any conclusions that are relied upon in Court.

Dates and Times and DOS Attributes

As the reader will be aware, there are a large number of different dates and times associated with the files and directories within an NTFS system. The questions that arise are which set is the most reliable and accurate, and which set is used by typical forensic software?

A series of experiments were carried out to try to clarify the problem of primacy of dates and times as well as of the DOS attributes. Our initial conclusions are listed below:

- The file dates and times reported by Encase forensic software reflect the entries in the Standard Information Attribute of the entry in the MFT for the file itself. DOS attributes are also read from this Standard Information Attribute.

- The file dates and times reported by the Windows system to a normal user reflect the current data in the Index Entry for that file. DOS attributes are also read from this Index Entry.

- The file dates and times reported by the Windows system rely upon the dates and times (and the DOS attributes) that are in the Standard Information Attribute, being correctly read from that Standard Information Attribute and written to the Index Entry whenever entries are updated.

- However, there is no automatic consistency checking that the file dates and times and the DOS attributes are matched between the Standard Information Attribute and the Index Entry. In fact, no errors were reported by the system when deliberately incorrect and inconsistent values were inserted into the Attributes.

The Update Sequence Array

The use of MD5 (or similar) hash values of files is commonplace within the forensic computing field. It is often the case that the analyst wishes to prove that two files have the same binary image. It may be that two or more files have been found on a volume and their locations or times and dates are relevant, providing they are copies of the same file. It may be that a large number of unlawful images have been found (collections of 25,000 or more are common) and it is required to grade the images for Court purposes. The MD5 hash values of the files can be searched automatically across a database of known images and some unlawful ones can be identified without necessarily having to view them.

It almost goes without saying that the recovery of the file in question from the evidential exhibit must be complete and accurate. Otherwise, the comparison of the file using an MD5 hash will return no match. However, the existence and significance of the update sequence array within NTFS volumes appeared not to have been reported within the forensic computing community until it was first described by the authors following a series of experiments.

As noted above, the final field of the FILE header is used for this "Update Sequence Array" (see Table 6.19). In the case of MFT records with 1024 bytes, the sequence array consists of 4 bytes.

In order to check the consistency of MFT records, and other protected records, NTFS uses a specified value which is placed in the final two bytes of each sector (offsets 510 to 511, and 1022 to 1023 etc.). This value is identified as the "Update Sequence Number" and is stored in byte offsets 42 and 43 of the MFT record. The bytes which originally occupied these end of sector locations are placed in a buffer known as the "Update Sequence Array". There are two sectors in an MFT record and therefore four bytes are replaced.

When the record is read by the operating system the set of two bytes at the end of each sector are checked to ensure that the sector has been read correctly. Once this has been done the original bytes are read from the "Update Sequence Array" and placed into their correct locations in the read data. The operation of this system can be easily checked and tested.

However, this automatic replacement of bytes by the NTFS system means that the forensic recovery of files direct from the MFT record in raw form requires a manual restoration of these update sequence bytes. Analysts must be aware of the update sequence system described above so that recoveries of this type can be made accurately.

It can be seen that if a forensic analyst recovers a file of resident data from the MFT record in raw form, the extraction will still contain the Update Sequence Number in the last two bytes of every sector. Clearly, the problem only arises if the extracted file crosses a sector boundary. An inspection of resident data in the sample MFT shows that the crossing of a sector boundary by a file is a very common occurrence. Should the MD5 hash of the extracted file be compared against a database, or even a single file, no match will be reported. This problem also applies to any record which crosses or reaches a sector boundary, including material obtained from record "slack space" (see discussion below).

There are occasions when this matching of files is of ultimate importance to a prosecution. For instance, a blackmail note created on one machine and then transferred to that of an accomplice for printing or checking can easily tie two defendants together. If the prosecution produces the two files they might look identical, but, if extracted in raw form, the MD5 hashes are unlikely to match. This might be because the sector boundaries occur in different places in the two files, or it might be because the Update Sequence Number is different for each of the two files. This failure of the MD5 hashes to match could easily be seized upon by the defence to suggest unreliability in the prosecution case as a whole and of the forensic examination in particular.

It should be pointed out that the same circumstances equally apply should a raw recovery take place from an NTFS system and the file be compared against the same file stored on a FAT system, which does not replace the end of sector bytes.

It is unfortunate that commonly used forensic software does not report the relocation of end of sector bytes in the MFT when they fall within the data of a file or of an Attribute. This forensic software, in File View, replaces the bytes in their correct locations *but does not report that it has done so.* Stepping through the file in Hexadecimal View, the software reports that the bytes are actually on the physical disk at the end of the affected sectors when they are in fact located within the Update Sequence Array and the bytes in the affected sectors actually contain the Update Sequence Number.

This serves to confirm the authors' view that forensic analysts must have a thorough grounding in the principles of binary storage and disk systems in order to be able to test for themselves what the forensic tools may be telling them.

Identification of Files in Unallocated Space – Deleted Files

When a file is deleted using an NTFS system one byte of the MFT record entry is changed (see Table 6.13) to mark that record as deleted. Although the file itself remains untouched out on the volume, both the record and the area occupied by the file become liable for overwriting. A second pair of bytes is changed, the record use sequence number (see Table 6.10), with the value in this pair being incremented.

If the record entry and the file data have remained untouched since deletion occurred it is a simple matter to recover detail from the record and to extract the file data from its location(s) on the volume.

There are circumstances where data from unallocated space can be connected with some detail from the MFT or external "INDX" files which may have been deleted.

Using the older File Allocation Table (FAT) file system the locations of the file pieces on the volume are stored in a "chain" of entries. When a file is deleted the details of the chain are also destroyed. In the case of a non-fragmented file, recovery is a simple exercise as the starting location and the file size are retained within the directory entry (until that is overwritten) and a contiguous chain of clusters can be followed to the end of the file. In the case of a fragmented file, the first part of the file can be identified, but little clue remains as to the location of further file fragments.

In the NTFS system each and every file fragment is recorded in size and location within the data runs of the MFT record for the file (see Table 6.82). So, even if the early part of a file has been overwritten the remaining parts are still capable of being identified. Knowing the original file size, the extent of overwriting can be established using the data runs and the file size of the "overwriting" file. Any data remaining from the original file can still be recovered, and, depending upon the file type, may be capable of being reconstructed into a meaningful file. The exact identification of the data runs is crucial to this exercise. The reverse is also true. The MFT record, if it still exists, can be tied to data found on the volume by reconstruction of the data runs and searching for the values within the MFT.

When attempting to tie recovered data and MFT records to a directory, a word of warning. The MFT record of the recovered file can be identified to the recovered data by data runs, file size etc., but there is always the possibility that the original MFT record for the directory in which the file resided has also been deleted. Some forensic software makes the assumption that if a directory exists in the MFT record pointed to by the Base File Reference of the file record, then the file did originally belong in that directory. This assumption may well be wrong if the original directory has been deleted and a new one created which happens to use the same record space.

From examination of the sample file set it has been established that the record use sequence number bytes (see Table 6.10) present in the FILE header of a directory record *may* also be used as an identifier of the current incarnation of that directory MFT record. It has also been noted that it is common for files residing in that directory to bear the same value two bytes as the most significant bytes in the Base File Reference field at the beginning of the File Name Attribute (see Table 6.44). Thus, it would seem, the Base File Reference points to the MFT record of the "parent" directory, and the incarnation of that particular record is identified by the record use sequence number (see Table 6.10). This same number is likely to appear as the two unidentified bytes next to the Base File Reference field.

MFT Record Slack Space

A detailed inspection of the sample MFT has shown that a considerable number of records contain material in "slack space". An example of this is the Revised MFT Record which we examined above (see Table 6.126). The End of Record Marker (FF

FF FF FFh) was found starting at offset 576. Beyond that point we noted a number of Index Entries which contain file dates and times, file sizes and file names. These details are all *outside* the current record and are not recognized by the NTFS system. No current forensic software deals with this data or attempts to use it.

If a file is found in unallocated space and it is of evidential value some evidence connecting it with the defendant needs to be found. One favoured defence is the "I bought the disk at a car boot sale", claim, which seeks to suggest that material found in unallocated space was already on the disk when the defendant obtained it, and is the responsibility of some previous owner. Without any evidence to the contrary, the file found in unallocated space could be excluded.

By searching the "slack space" of MFT records it is possible to find full or partial detail of a file *which must have been present on the volume* at the date and time of the entry. If a connection can be made between the file in unallocated space and the detail from "slack space" the file can be dated and the claim can be proved or disproved. To this end the file name and the file size may well assist, particularly if the file appears in some known database using that file name and that file size. The actual location of the file, perhaps within an area occupied by other files of a particular date may also add to the circumstantial evidence.

By way of explanation, it is clear that when populating a directory, the NTFS system acts quite logically. It first creates the directory record within the MFT and then populates it with resident entries until no room is available for further entries. At this point an external "INDX" directory file is created and the record is modified to reflect the existence of this external listing. The entries already present are copied into the new "INDX" file and the End of Record Marker in the MFT record is now set much earlier in the record than previously, since the record no longer contains a list of file entries. The data making up the later file entries in the record are still present but now *outside* the stated length of the record. This leaves an amount of data referring to files in that directory between the new End of Record Marker and the end of the allocated space for that record. This is what we call "MFT Record Slack Space".

MFT Slack Space

When an MFT is created on a volume, about 12.5% of the volume is reserved to provide space for the MFT. This is known as the MFT Zone. The MFT will grow as it is used and, to avoid fragmentation, the MFT Zone is reserved to permit the expansion of the MFT into the unused areas of the Zone. However, should the MFT grow to fill the entire MFT Zone, a further area of the disk will be allocated, resulting in a fragmented MFT.

The MFT will usually start at the same location on the volume, and reformatting of the volume will cause a new MFT to be located starting from the same place. As an MFT is constructed, it is filled from the front. When a new file is created the new MFT record will be placed in the first available slot, either overwriting a deleted record or placed at the current end of the MFT, the MFT file size being adjusted to accommodate the new record. This system can cause a new MFT to be written over an old MFT and, as the old MFT is not usually cleaned, old entries will possibly remain up to the end of the MFT Zone, if the old MFT reached that far. Such entries are fully populated and recoverable, and the data runs may well point to files still present in the now unallocated space of the disk. The recovery of these files using the MFT records from the old MFT will be evidentially reliable, as the records themselves are untouched. The area between the current end of the MFT and the end of the MFT Zone is known as MFT Slack Space.

It is also worth bearing in mind that, as with all Windows systems, bits and pieces of data are written to various areas of the disk without user request or knowledge. The authors have recovered MFT records from unallocated space outside the MFT Zone which have been used to identify files that were present on the volume.

7. The Treatment of PCs

Introduction

Up to this point, we have concentrated in the book on the technical issues: on how computers work and their construction; on how information is stored; and, in particular, on how and where information can be hidden or inadvertently left on hard disk drives. This technical understanding gives us both the knowledge and the confidence that will enable us to find information of evidential value from a PC. However, unless we carry out the investigative processes in ways which guarantee the integrity of that evidence, it is unlikely to be admissible in court. Thus we now need to concern ourselves with perhaps the most important part of all: the processes that we need to carry out and the practices that we need to observe in order to extract information from PCs and present it as admissible evidence in court. In this chapter we are going to consider the treatment of PCs and will be looking at the topics listed below:

- A guide to good practice
- The principles of computer-based evidence
- Search and seizure
- Intelligence, preparation and briefing
- At the search scene
- The operating dilemma
- Shutdown, seizure and transportation
- Computer examinations
- Physical disks and logical drives
- Interpreting partition tables
- Imaging and copying

In the next chapter, we will be looking at the rather different processes involved in the treatment of electronic organizers.

We first look at the principles of computer-based evidence as recommended in the ACPO *Good Practice Guide*. Then we look at the problems of mounting a search and seizure operation and the issues that might occur on site when seizing computers from the premises of a suspect. Guidelines are given for each of the major activities, including the shutdown, seizure and transportation of the equipment. The next section considers the receipt of the equipment into the analyst's laboratory and the process of examination and the production of evidence. An example of a specific disk with a number of partitions set up on it is then described in detail, and full guidance is given on interpreting the host of figures that result. Finally, the issues of imaging and copying are outlined and compared.

■ ■

The ACPO *Good Practice Guide*

The Association of Chief Police Officers (ACPO), in conjunction with the National Hi-Tech Crime Unit (NHCTU)[1] has produced a *Good Practice Guide for Computer Based Electronic Evidence*, the most recent version of which is version 3 dated September 2003 (ACPO, 2003). The document is written as a guide to good practice when dealing with computers and other electronic devices in the possession of a suspect. It is intended for use by officers attending a search and seizure operation, by investigating officers, by computer evidence recovery personnel and by external consulting witnesses. The ACPO *Good Practice Guide* is fully supported by the authors of this book.

The Principles of Computer-Based Evidence

Four principles have been established, and these, together with a brief explanation from the *Good Practice Guide*, are reproduced here, with the kind permission of ACPO:

- *Principle 1*
  No action taken by law enforcement agencies or their agents should change data held on a computer or storage media which may subsequently be relied upon in court.
- *Principle 2*
  In exceptional circumstances, where a person finds it necessary to access original data held on a computer or on storage media, that person must be competent to do so and be able to give evidence explaining the relevance and the implications of their actions.
- *Principle 3*
  An audit trail or other record of all processes applied to computer based electronic evidence should be created and preserved. An independent third party should be able to examine those processes and achieve the same result.
- *Principle 4*
  The person in charge of the investigation (the case officer) has overall responsibility for ensuring that the law and these principles are adhered to.

---

1   The web site http://www.nhtcu.org/ is currently (February 2007) displaying the
    following notice: "The National Hi Tech Crime Unit has now become part of the Serious
    Organised Crime Agency".

Explanation of the Principles

Data held on a computer is no different from information or text contained on a document. For this reason, evidence that is based on a computer or on computer media is subject to the same rules and laws that apply to documentary evidence.

The Doctrine of Documentary evidence may be explained as: "*The onus is on the prosecution to show to the Court that the evidence produced is no more and no less now than when it was first taken into the possession of police*".

Operating systems and other programs frequently alter and add to the contents of the computer's storage space. This happens automatically without the user necessarily being aware that the data has been changed. In order to comply with the principles of computer-based evidence a copy should be made of the entire target device. Partial or selective file copying should not be readily considered as an alternative. The copy or copies should be made onto media that should be retained for examination and subsequent Court use.

In a minority of cases it may not be possible to obtain an image using a recognized imaging device. In these circumstances it may become necessary for the original machine to be accessed to recover the evidence. With this in mind it is essential that any such access is made by a witness who is competent to give evidence to a Court of Law. It is essential to show objectively to a Court that the continuity and integrity of the evidence has been preserved. It is necessary to demonstrate to the Court how evidence has been recovered, showing each process through which the evidence was obtained. Evidence should be preserved to an extent that a third party is able to repeat the same process and arrive at the same result as that presented to a Court.

Search and Seizure

Forensic computing bears a certain similarity to that ancient recipe for jugged hare, the initial line of which optimistically states "First go forth and capture a suitable hare". This chapter, which is primarily aimed at law enforcement personnel, outlines the procedures to be followed for a search and seizure operation where one of the key aims is to take possession of, or image, one or more suspect computers.

The primary objective for an operation of this kind is to secure all evidence in such a manner that its integrity cannot later be challenged and that it is obtained under circumstances which ensure its admissibility in Court.

Pre-Search Intelligence

Whilst it is accepted that there will be occasions when an urgent and immediate search operation is thrust upon the team, most search and seizure tasks should be thoroughly well pre-planned. It is during this stage that as much intelligence as possible is gathered about the premises, the occupants, the users and the computer systems that are located inside. It is vital that the number of computers, their types, operating systems and connections are all known before entry. This will then permit the search team to be prepared with the right equipment and the right expertise, including if necessary any outside experts, and will enable them to deal with the systems correctly and efficiently once entry has been effected.

Some key decisions will have to be made prior to entry. If the premises contain a large network it may well be that it is only possible to target certain specific machines and image those within the time allowed. Such machines will need to be identified prior to the search if at all possible. If seizure of machines is the objective then justification must exist not only for the seizure itself but also for the effect on the suspects once seizure has taken place. It will be rare for a business to continue to operate effectively after its computers have been removed and there are likely to be adverse effects as a result of any on-site imaging or copying.

Intelligence about the actual systems installed in the target premises may indicate the need for an independent expert to be engaged to give advice at the scene. If known individual targets have been identified, consideration could be given to using expertise within the company to assist with advice and information on their systems. Such persons should only be used if it is clear that they have no possible involvement in the matter under investigation. These people are not bound to help and some may even be obstructive because of the disturbance to their workplace.

Contingency planning is also important where information and intelligence is sketchy, incomplete or inadequate. Search team leaders should be in a position to obtain further assistance immediately, in terms of expertise or additional personnel, should they come across unexpected systems at the scene.

The timing of the operation, if possible, should be set outside the normal operating hours of the suspect systems. If an office environment is the target, going in with the cleaner at 7 a.m. is a good idea, since then the premises and the machines can be safely secured before the daily business gets under way.

Pre-Search Preparation

The team allocated to the task of seizing the machines should ensure that they have the following items, in addition to the normal search and seizure equipment:

- *An adequate toolkit*
  This should contain an array of flat and crosshead screwdrivers, a small pair of pliers, wire cutters for cutting cable ties, and a clean 1/2 inch paintbrush for cleaning away dust and dirt.
- *A search kit*
  This should comprise an array of plastic, paper and 'jiffy' bags, adhesive and tie-on labels, tape and elastic bands for securing leads, plastic crates and flat pack boxes for removal of items, and blankets or foam sheets for padding during carriage. Each item, or package of items, should be sealed on seizure, particularly individual computer units containing data storage items. Coloured pens and labels can be used to identify all connections. Plastic bags should not be used for individual packaging of single electronic components as they may create a static charge which could damage the component.
- *Search forms and sketch plan sheets*
  A sketch plan identifying locations of items seized should always be made, and a master property form with associated numbering should be used to list and

identify items against the labels placed on them. All seal numbers must also be listed.

- *Still and video cameras*
  Screenshots of operating machines are useful to prove correct shutdown procedures, and *in situ* pictures are a boon to proving later the proximity of items to suspects and the general layout of the premises. Video is good for recording the removal of complicated connections, although labels should still be used as well.

- *Disk boxes*
  These are for the removal of floppy disks found on the premises. It is essential to ensure that all floppy disks can be identified as to their exact location at seizure.

- *Mobile telephone*
  This is useful to obtain further assistance or advice whilst on-site. It should not be used near computer equipment

- *Storage media*
  A number of clean, blank, floppy disks and USB drives should be prepared beforehand and thoroughly erased to ensure that no previous data is present. These may be used to save files, prior to switching off, on computers found running. Floppy disks are preferable as they leave fewer traces on the home machine. However, it is possible that a computer system being seized has an "on-the-fly" encrypted secure container open at the time of seizure. If this is the case, it would be prudent to copy as much relevant material as possible from the open container to a clean external USB disk drive. Many modern operating systems will permit an external USB drive to be connected whilst the system is still running. However, the person carrying out this process must be equipped and competent to carry out a live seizure, see section below *Machines That Are Switched On (Live Seizure)*

- *A torch*
  Very useful for searching those little unlit places where connecting leads tend to be tucked away.

See also additional items mentioned below for *Machines That Are Switched On (Live Seizure)*.

The Search Briefing

An operational order for any pre-planned search should be prepared, allocating tasks and giving details of the aims and objectives of the search. If computers are involved the person in overall charge must be aware of the ACPO *Good Practice Guide* (ACPO, 2003). All officers who may be involved in the operation should attend the briefing. One possible exception to this may be the computer forensic analysts if it is felt that they should retain a degree of independence from the case itself. Not only should the briefing contain the intelligence information and the logistics of the search, but it must also include a briefing to all officers on the likely presence of computers and the methods of seizure, the staff available to do this, and how they may be contacted. Distinct warnings should be given to discourage enthusiastic and untrained amateurs from tampering with the equipment. Such tampering could lead to contamination of any evidence found and its exclusion from subsequent Court proceedings. Use of samples or some visual representations of the equipment likely to be found will assist in its identification by untrained personnel.

The briefing must include the provisions of any warrant or similar order under which the search and seizure is authorized. It is particularly important that any conditions attached are strictly adhered to.

At the Search Scene

The first priority at the search scene is to gain total control both of the premises and of the occupants. Identification of the numbers and locations of computers present will then permit control to be taken of the computers themselves and their environment. Suspects should be kept clear of all machines and any connections to them, including power, network and telephone. The method and order of seizure can then be assessed and the imaging and copying workload identified if required.

It is not possible in these pages to cover all possible permutations of computers, networks and connections. The advice that follows may need to be modified to allow for the particular configuration faced by the search team. In general terms, where a major network is involved, planning should be done well prior to the search. It is likely that on-site imaging will offer the only reasonable solution to such configurations. For small networks and standalone machines, subject to the issues of disruption to the business already mentioned, seizure is probably the more convenient option, allowing machines to be imaged later and in more controlled circumstances.

To ensure the integrity of any item seized, particularly those items which contain data, security seals should be used on all property containers and the serial numbers entered onto the search log.

The Operating Dilemma

On all occasions where search teams find machines that are switched on and operating they face a dilemma. By allowing the equipment to complete its current task they may gain, or they may lose, evidence. A value judgement has therefore to be undertaken.

As an example, consider a modem or network connection which is operating and is clearly transferring data. It may be that the system is receiving a vital email which contains damning evidence against the suspect. On the other hand it could be receiving a similar email which completely exonerates the suspect from any wrong doing. Added to these possibilities, the file being received might be routine and of no evidential value, but is overwriting some other important evidence on the hard disk. The question is whether to interrupt this transaction or not. Will evidence thereby be gained or lost? That is the dilemma.

The search team need to make a decision immediately, and it should be based on their knowledge of the enquiry and the likelihood of relevant evidence being gained or lost, regardless of whether it benefits the prosecution or the defence. To assist in their decision, they will need to examine the contents of any active computer screens to try to determine what is happening. Needless to say, whatever decision is taken, the circumstances must be recorded in detail.

Machines That Are Switched Off

The following is a list of actions which should be taken, in order, when dealing with machines that are already switched off when their seizure takes place:

1. One of the most important of all steps is to start logging all your actions.
2. Disconnect any external data communication lines, ensuring that such disconnection will not impinge upon the activities of other members of the search team. This will isolate the machine from any external electronic access and help prevent the loss or overwriting of data. If possible, physically trace where the connection goes and note the details. (See also *The Operating Dilemma* section above.)
3. Be satisfied that the computer is actually switched off. Check that it is not in sleep mode or using a blank screen saver. LED indicators on the case of the machine or the monitor may indicate that power is applied. DO NOT SWITCH ON. Be warned that some laptops will power up when the lid is raised
4. Photograph or video the connections *in situ*. Label all cables and sockets so that the machine can be reconstructed exactly as found at a later time. Remove the cables.
5. Remove, package and seal all items, noting individual identification, serial numbers and the like. Sealing an item in front of a suspect is always a good idea. Record all seal and label numbers in the search log.
6. Check the area for sticky notes, diaries, notepads and the like which may have passwords recorded on them. Consider asking the user if passwords are required for the machine or any of the applications and what they are. Note any replies in the log.
7. Consider the seizure of printers and paper samples, if relevant. Some printouts can be associated with a particular printer using forensic techniques. Take advice before the search on this matter.
8. If equipment is to be examined physically for fingerprints, ensure that aluminium powder is not used, as it is a conductor of electricity and can damage the equipment. Any such examination should take place after imaging, and the machine, including the power supply unit, should be thoroughly cleaned internally and externally afterwards. It should then be tested by a competent engineer before it is reused or returned.

Machines That Are Switched On (Immediate Seizure)

The following is a list of actions which should be taken, in order, when dealing with machines which are already switched on, or suspected to be so, when their seizure takes place. This section deals with machines that are seized by personnel who are not competent or equipped for the "Live seizure" process described below.

1. As before, one of the most important steps of all is to start logging all your actions. In particular, note all keystrokes made at the keyboards and all responses that appear on the displays. The use of photographs or video is a distinct advantage in these circumstances.

2. Disconnect any external data communication lines, ensuring that such disconnection will not impinge upon the activities of other members of the search team. This will isolate the machine from any external electronic access and help prevent the loss or overwriting of data. If possible, physically trace where the connection goes and note the details. (See also *The Operating Dilemma* section above.)

3. Check the monitor to confirm that it is actually switched on and powered.

4. If the screen is blank, note that it may be running a blank screen saver.

5. If the DOS prompt, or what appears to be a DOS prompt, is visible, check for the mode of operation. Use the EXIT command to determine whether this is Windows full-screen DOS mode. Record the screen state.

6. If programs are running, note and record screen states and save any open files to floppy disk. DO NOT instigate a write to the hard disk. To avoid any latent automatic actions at shut-down, such as a "wipe" or "clean-up", DO NOT shut down the operating system. Instead, power the machine down by detaching the power connector from the rear of the machine.

7. Proceed as from the fourth item in the section *Machines That Are Switched Off* above.

Machines That Are Switched On (Live Seizure)

If seizing personnel are equipped and competent to carry out a live seizure of data or memory at the time of the operation it is most important that *all* actions are logged, and if possible recorded on video.

If a machine is up and running, there is, as time progresses, the increasing possibility that on-the-fly encryption will be operating. Should this be the case, if the machine is switched off access to any encrypted files or volumes currently accessible will be lost. There is also the possibility, with increasing amounts of memory being present on modern machines, that sizeable amounts of data, including passwords and the occasional "nugget of gold" may be held in volatile RAM.

There are various methods of extracting data from live machines. At the time of writing there are a number of methods under development, one of which involves the use of external USB disk drives with suitable operating systems, as mentioned above. Whichever method is chosen, it is very highly recommended that the method is fully tested *by the operator who will use it* before deployment. It will be this operator who will be questioned in Court regarding the method of acquisition and its effects upon all the data in the machine.

The accurate recording of all actions during this phase of acquisition of the data will permit the later identification of processes and actions which have taken place on the machine and which may have affected the data that has been captured and seized.

The changes to the machine state and the data stored upon it will depend largely on the method of acquisition and the operating system in use. It is thus the case that the method used and its effects upon the machine must be well known to the operator *for each operating system upon which it is to be used.*

In order to carry out any seizure as referred to above additional equipment, storage media, cabling and the like will be required and should be included within the "Pre-Search Preparation" list above.

Once live data acquisition is complete the machine can be dealt with as for *Machines That Are Switched On (Immediate Seizure)* above.

Shutdown Procedures for Servers

It will be very rare that the necessity arises to actually shut down a server, as there are a number of approaches to obtain the required data which do not require the network to be shut down. Such seizures are not within the scope of this book, but include live network acquisitions and seizure of on-site and off-site backup tapes and backup media.

Because servers may be so critical to a business, special procedures need to be observed here.

1. As before, one of the most important steps of all is to start logging all your actions. In particular, note all keystrokes made at the keyboards and all responses that appear on the displays. The use of photographs or video is a distinct advantage in these circumstances.

2. Ensure that the expertise is available for the particular operating system of the server. Note that nearly all server operating systems (Unix, Linux, Windows NT etc.) require to write system information back to the disk before power is turned off. Failure to permit this may result in corrupted disks which could inhibit not only the extraction of evidence but also the restoration of the system for subsequent use by the business.

3. Follow exactly the correct operating system procedure for shutting down the server, then proceed as from the fourth item in the section *Machines That Are Switched Off* above.

Seizure – What Should be Taken

When a system is seized and dismantled, it is essential that it be capable of identical reconstruction. The following items should be taken:

- The main system unit.
- The keyboard and mouse.
- Any external expansion units or cards.
- All connecting leads.
- Any dongles. These are software security devices, often with connectors that are plugged into the parallel port.
- Power supply units, particularly for laptops.

In addition, the following peripheral items may be taken, if deemed relevant. Note that some of these items will have internal batteries and some may not. Consider examining all such items *in situ*.

- Monitors and flat screen panels.
- External media devices, external disk arrays, portable disk enclosures etc.
- Printers. It may be possible to associate output documents with particular printers.
- Modems, network hubs, wireless hubs. Some of these can contain a memory of telephone numbers.
- Scanners.
- Digital cameras and all media. The handbook is also useful.
- PCMCIA cards and leads.

All electronic media found should be taken for examination. In this case, the exhibit bags should be labelled rather than the items themselves. Typical items are:

- Any hard disks not fitted within machines
- All floppy disks.
- Any CD-ROM and CD-RW disks.
- Backup tapes and cartridges of whatever format.
- Video tapes, if a video backup system is fitted.

Other items that may be considered for seizure are as follows. Note that some of these items will have internal batteries and some may not. Consider examining all such items *in situ*.

- Personal organizers, palmtops, PIMs and PDAs together with any connecting cables, power units and cradles. Remember to consider battery replacement if these are retained in storage.
- Mobile telephones. Most of these have a memory of numbers and other data.
- Land line telephones. Some of these have a memory of numbers.
- Answering machines. Some of these have memory.
- Fax machines. Some of these have memory, some retain a duplicate record.
- Dictating machines and tapes.
- Multi-purpose units. That is, combinations of some of the above.

Transport and Storage of IT Equipment

It is important to remember that most IT equipment is susceptible to magnetic fields and therefore removal and storage methods should be such as to avoid exposure to them. There are also considerations with regard to static electrical charges on components which have been separately packaged as well as the effect of condensation on items packaged in plastic bags. Hard disks in particular can be damaged by dropping or other impact. Useful tips for storage as well as removal are as follows:

- Keep all items away from magnetic sources, such as loudspeakers, radios, electrical motors and the like.
- Store at room temperature, not in a damp cellar or garage. Avoid damp and protect from dust.
- Take care when stacking to ensure that fragile items are protected from damage.
- Avoid physical shocks.
- Generally, the use of tough, breathable, paper bags and sacks or aerated plastic bags is the preferred option for most items.

Particular care should be taken with the following items:

- The main system unit. This should be handled with care and kept upright in a secure place when transporting so that it cannot fall over or be subject to shocks.
- Monitors. These are best transported screen down on the back seat of a car and secured by an elasticated strap or something similar.
- Hard disks. For individual components and circuit boards, use anti-static bags or tough paper bags, or wrap in paper and use aerated plastic bags.
- Electronic media such as floppy disks, tape cartridges and so forth. These must not be folded, bent or stored under heavy objects. Do not label the item itself; label the bag in which it is stored.
- Personal organizers, palmtops, PIMs and PDAs. Protect any exposed keyboard from inadvertent pressure. The use of a stiff cardboard sheet around the item can prevent this. Place the organizer in a sealed envelope or something similar to prevent operation through a sealed evidence bag. Consider the need to change batteries regularly. If the organizer is powered by secondary batteries, consider sealing it in its cradle with power cables brought out through the side of the bag so that it can remain on charge.

Practical Notes

Evidence produced from a suspect's computer often tends to be quite damning, and thus it becomes the major target for the defence during the usual round of applications to get evidence excluded. The evidence itself cannot usually be argued with; it is either present on the computer or it is not. The continuity of the evidence, however, must be demonstrable and its integrity unblemished. The use of security seals and a record of their breaking and replacement goes a long way to avoid allegations of the planting of evidence on machines or into images before examination.

One point on warrants arose in the case of R v Du'Kett and others. Lengthy applications were made to exclude all the evidence found on Du'Kett's machines. Du'Kett was the main defendant in a network of software pirates and Cambridgeshire police executed a warrant at his home and seized a number of machines and huge amounts of software. The machines were examined and provided the majority of the evidence and intelligence identifying the other members of the network. It was clear that if the evidence from the first machines examined could be excluded, then all evidence following the information found would also have to be excluded. The defence decided to attack the issue, legality and execution of the warrant. The first target was the formal information document. Having obtained a copy of the police copy of this document they made enquiries of the magistrates' clerk. It was erroneously assumed that the copy they obtained was a copy of the information after the warrant had been issued. It was alleged that the application for the warrant was illegal because the information had not been signed by a magistrate. The original could not be found amongst the Court archives, but eventually the defence accepted that their application was based upon a false assumption and withdrew. The second line of attack followed the ruling of R v Reading Justices [and others], where it was shown that although a warrant was issued to a constable it was effectively executed by others. The constable was simply present whilst the search was carried out. In the Du'Kett case it was alleged that the search was orchestrated by a member of FAST (Federation Against Software Theft), who was present, and that the police officers were simply assisting him. Therefore the execution was unlawful. This application was also withdrawn after argument.

The lessons to be learned from the above are:

- Keep a copy of the original information and mark it as such.
- Provided that the Court agrees, obtain a copy of the information after it has been marked up as the warrant is granted.
- Ensure that any parties, other than those to which the warrant is granted (usually the police), are actually named on the warrant and the reason why they are present is given. This would apply to any external assistants or experts.
- Keep a copy of the warrant itself.
- Keep a copy of the briefing document. This should include the role and reason for the presence of any individual who is named on the warrant. Ensure that during execution the persons to whom the warrant is issued are demonstrably in charge of the search with others purely assisting or advising. The roles must be clear.

Computer Examination – Initial Steps

Having dealt with the seizure of machines in the previous section, this section deals with the reception of the machine at the place of examination, up to the point at which data, which may be of evidential value, is actually examined and analysed.

In our trek from the search and seizure of the machines through the process of their examination to the production of evidential material at Court, it is apparent that we must bear a number of important matters in mind. Of these, the ACPO principles, outlined above, give us the good practice that we must apply to the process of examination. This results in the following:

- The integrity of the original data must be preserved; therefore we will have to use non-intrusive examination techniques (Principle 1).
- If the original data has to be examined, for whatever reason, the analysts must be competent to do so and to give evidence explaining their actions. Trained and qualified staff must be used (Principle 2).

- An audit trail is required and an independent party must be able to reproduce the same actions and get the same result. We must therefore keep a full log of all actions (Principle 3)

The prime objective of the analyst is to recover and secure, from whatever medium is examined, a true copy of the data stored on that medium. This should be done, wherever possible, without any alteration to the original data as a whole. The process for the recovery of evidence is a forensic exercise; thus only forensically sound hardware, software and procedures should be used.

Full records of all actions taken must be kept. It is common that the brief given to the analyst is not as full as it could be, or the suspect may change his explanation at a later stage. Even the recording of a minor matter may play a pivotal part in proving or disproving a claim made by one side or the other. Although not generally aimed at persons who will give expert evidence, this book promotes the principle that a forensic computer analyst will give unbiased evidence or, where required by the Court, expert evidence based upon the facts, and will stand apart from any loyalty to the prosecution or the defence, regardless of who may be the employer.

Reception of Machines and Media

All items should be received in sealed bags. Continuity from person to person should be recorded by the exchange of signatures and a formal identification of the item, particularly the seal number. Local procedures will need to be followed with regard to the detail of the actual records kept, but the log of events of the item for examination should be started at this point and signed appropriately by the person delivering it.

From this stage the security of the item, and any information held upon it, is the responsibility of the person receiving it. Precautions should be taken to ensure that there is no accidental or deliberate tampering and work on, and storage of, these items should be in a secure environment.

Electrical Safety

A brief word on electrical safety is appropriate here. Most organizations employ a Safety at Work Officer, and there may be organizational guidelines in addition to the mandatory regulations. If the analyst is not fully conversant with these, reference should be made to the Safety at Work Officer. It should be noted that different officers actually interpret the regulations in differing ways. Further advice is also available from Local Authority Health and Safety Officers. The analyst might consider obtaining certification in Portable Appliance Testing (IEE, undated) and obtaining a copy of the Electricity at Work Regulations 1989 (HMSO, 1989; HSE Books, 1998; IEE, 1994).

Static Electricity

Many of the components within a computer are susceptible to damage by the discharge of static electricity, particularly the integrated circuits or chips. The analyst should take steps to discharge any body-held static charge prior to any physical examination of a machine simply by touching a known earth connection. In addition, the use of anti-static straps and non-conducting tools will help to minimize the risk of static discharge damage.

External Physical Examination

With the no-cost option of digital photography available, the taking of many photographs during the initial examination phase is of great use when rebuilding a machine or to identify components that were or were not present at the time of seizure.

First record the date and time of the breaking of the seal and then physically examine the item. If there is external damage which may have an effect upon the normal operation of the machine the only real alternative is to remove the medium from the machine and deal with this separately, on a host machine.

The external examination should also include recording details of the machine itself, such as make, model, serial number and any identifying marks, scratches, stickers and the like.

Internal Physical Examination

Before embarking on an internal examination, it is important to bear in mind that the objective is to ensure that the machine is safe for imaging. Any deconstruction or detailed examination of parts should be left until the analyst is satisfied that a good image or images have been obtained. If a component is on the verge of breaking down it is more likely to do so if it is disturbed.

Once the external case has been removed it is a good idea to step back, place hands in pockets and carry out a purely visual inspection first. The majority of PC cases are designed so that most components and contents can be seen without removal of internal items. At this point it should be obvious to the practised eye if there is anything in the case which should not be there. It has been known for drug dealers to record transactions on their computer and place their stock inside the actual machine.

If there is anything in the case which warrants removal as an exhibit it is always better to get a specialist to remove it or at the very least to seek advice from one. If removal has to be done by the analyst then the use of protective rubber gloves is recommended and immediate bagging and sealing of the exhibit should be carried out. Photographs or video which record the item *in situ* and its subsequent removal can be beneficial.

When the visual inspection and record is complete, and subject to the rider at the beginning of this section, a closer inspection can take place, recording the expansion cards and internal devices present. Records should include the details of all hard disks fitted and their specifications, with particular regard to the disk drive parameters, where these are given on the disk. Any unconnected disks are best removed and dealt with on a host machine. Where any internal serial numbers are stated these should be recorded.

Proper recording of the internals of a particular machine can be of importance in demonstrating that the machine was capable of some particular operation, such as being able to play sound files or to connect to the Internet.

Imaging and Copying

Physical Disks and Logical Drives

Before discussing imaging and copying it is important that the reader understands fully the implications of Chapter 5, in particular the principles of CHS and LBA addressing. We must be able to identify the areas on the disk which may hold data to be copied or imaged. The "shape" and size of all hard disks are dictated by the physical characteristics of the disk itself, as specified by the manufacturer. This invariably takes the form of a CHS/LBA statement on the case of the disk and within its own electronics to enable automatic detection by the computer on which it is to be used. At Fig. 7.1 are two examples of labels affixed to hard disks.

Note that many hard disks of a size larger than the CHS limit (8.4 Gbyte) will bear details in the CHS area of the label which refer *only* to the maximum CHS address. Thus a calculation using these parameters will result in a reported size of 8.4 Gbyte, which is actually true: the disk can only address up to that value *in CHS mode*. The actual size of the disk, available with LBA addressing, may be far larger.

The CHS figures shown are the physical parameters of the disk. It is these figures which will be recognized by the machine and recorded internally in the BIOS variables, depending upon whether any translation is required or not. Physical disks are usually referred to by number. For example, when moving between physical and logical views of a disk in Norton Disk Editor, drives are referred to as Hard Disk 1, Hard Disk 2 etc., in physical view, and Disk C, Disk D etc., in logical view.

The difference between the physical disk and the logical drive is a most important concept. The physical disk can be held in your hand; a logical drive is a different animal altogether and is created by partitioning.

Fig. 7.1 Quantum and Seagate disk labels (photograph: Tony Sammes and Brian Jenkinson).

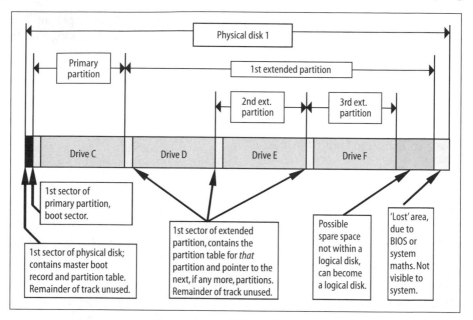

Fig. 7.2 Example partitioned disk.

Partitioning is covered in detail Chapter 5. In short, a physical disk can be partitioned into one or more logical drives. Partitioning, using MS-DOS FDISK or a similar utility, permits users to choose the size of a logical drive or drives which they wish to create on the physical hard disk. It is possible to partition a disk with areas that do not fall within partitions, and so these areas would be unavailable to users. Alternatively, using readily available software, one can move part of the physical disk in and out of a partition at will and thus 'hide' the data contained therein. It thus follows that the forensic computer analyst must be aware of this, and other, possible scenarios and ensure that all the data on a disk is obtained and available for examination and analysis. Some imaging systems permit users to choose the type of image to be taken. Choices involving physical disks and logical drives are available. Users must be fully aware of the meanings of these terms and the implications of each type of image in terms of the data actually captured.

In order to identify the areas of data which may be obtained by an image we will consider the example of a partitioned MS-DOS disk as illustrated in Fig. 7.2.

The diagram is a schematic of what a partitioned DOS disk actually "looks" like. The physical disk extends from the very first sector at CHS 0,0,1 to the end of the disk as reported by the BIOS (see the next section *Interpreting Partition Tables* for an explanation of this). The first logical drive always begins at CHS 0,1,1.

A physical image of this drive should capture all data within the area defined as "Physical Disk", including areas not within a logical drive. The image will thus contain all data from all areas of the disk which are capable of having data stored within them, whether defined for use or not. A logical image of a drive will contain only the data within the area of the defined drive. For example, a logical image of the primary partition in Fig. 7.2 above will only contain the data from the area shown as that allocated to Drive C.

Interpreting Partition Tables

This topic is best illustrated by working through an example. Figure 7.3 is a schematic of a typical (but relatively old) hard disk drive, a Seagate ST3851A with a CHS marking on the case of cylinders 1651, heads 16 and sectors 63. It has been partitioned using MS-DOS 6.22 FDISK to four partitions of 200 Mbyte, 250 Mbyte, 200 Mbyte and 160 Mbyte. The four partition tables are as shown using slightly revised Norton Disk Editor partition table views. We need to remember that cylinders count

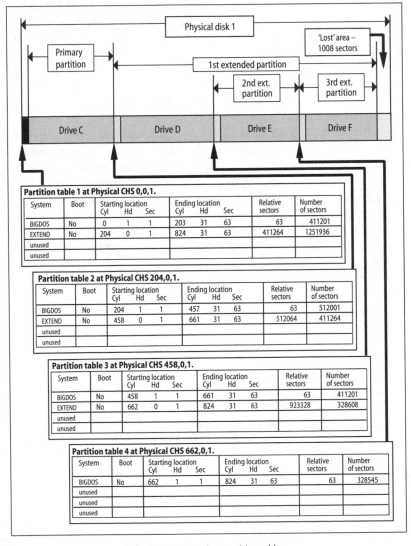

Fig. 7.3 Interpreting partition tables.

from 0, heads from 0 and sectors from 1 in CHS addressing and that Norton Disk Editor uses a different sequence in its tables of Side, Cylinder and Sector. We have re-ordered them in Fig. 7.3 to the more traditional CHS form in an attempt to avoid more confusion than is necessary.

We also need to recall that "Relative Sectors" (see Chapter 5) is the logical block addressing (LBA) sector number from the beginning of the physical disk. For the primary partition, this starts immediately after the Master Boot Record track[2]; all tracks, in this example, being 63 sectors in length[3]. Note that the number is LBA 63 and not LBA 64 because LBA sector counting starts from 0. We should note also that the first extended partition (the container marked EXTEND in partition table 1), by default, extends to the end of that part of the physical disk that is accessible to the BIOS. We will consider this issue further in a moment.

The second and subsequent extended partitions (marked EXTEND in partition tables 2 and 3) are nested within the first extended partition and their "Relative Sectors" declarations each refer to their LBA starting sector relative to the beginning of the first extended partition. However, the three logical partitions (marked BIGDOS in partition tables 2, 3 and 4) have "Relative Sectors" declarations which refer to their starting sector *relative to the beginning of their respective extended partitions* and not to the beginning of the first extended partition. This can be a source of some considerable confusion. In each case, the logical partition starts immediately after the extended partition table track and is at LBA 63 relative to the start of the respective extended partition. Finally, we should note that the CHS addresses of the various boundaries are always at cylinder perimeters.

In order fully to understand and analyse the partition tables we must first know what the physical CHS parameters are. They have already been given as CHS 1651, 16, 63, on the disk label, but we must also know what the BIOS "sees" when it detects the disk. The test machine that was used to create these tables has an autodetecting BIOS, and the disk was actually detected as CHS 825, 32, 63. Using the BIOS detect disk utility gives us three choices, as shown at Table 7.1.

Choice 1 is recommended but it is important to note that the disk size changes between the choices. We know the manufacturer's parameters are given by choice 2 which results in a total disk size of $1651 \times 16 \times 63 = 1,664,208$ sectors. On the other hand, the default values obtained from auto-detection are $825 \times 32 \times 63 = 1,663,200$

Table 7.1 BIOS disk detect options.

Choice	Size (Mbyte)	Cylinders	Heads	Sectors	Type
1	851	825	32	63	LBA
2	852	1651	16	63	NORMAL
3	851	825	32	63	LARGE

---

2 A *track*, you will recall, being one head position of a cylinder.

3 It should be noted that although 63 sectors per track is now the most likely value, some early disks did not conform to this and disks with values from 16 through to 72 sectors per track are known to exist.

sectors. We see, therefore, that there are 1008 sectors, representing some 500 kbytes, which are not addressed by the BIOS. This is the so called 'Lost' area referred to in Fig. 6.3. The differences, as we have seen before, are due to the need for translation of the disk parameters (see Chapter 5). Any physical image that is using the autodetected parameters will not see the "Lost" area. However, imaging a disk in its home machine will usually ensure that the correct[4] parameters are loaded by the BIOS. When hosting a drive elsewhere it is very important to check, if possible, the BIOS and CMOS settings of the home machine to ensure that the correct parameters are used.

Now we know that the disk, as seen by the BIOS, is of a total length of 1,663,200 sectors we can look at the partition tables to check exactly what areas are occupied by logical disks and what areas, if any, fall outside the partitions.

Explanation and notes	**Areas accounted for**
Partition Table 1, at LBA 0, CHS 0, 0, 1	
1. This starts with the master boot record and partition table 1 in the first sector. The remainder (62 sectors) of the track is not used.	LBA 0 to 62 CHS 0, 0, 1 to 0, 0, 63
2. Drive C is defined as starting at LBA 63 and is of 411201 sectors in size.	LBA 63 to 411263 CHS 0, 1, 1 to 203, 31, 63
3. The first extended partition is defined as starting at LBA 411264 and is of 1251936 sectors in size. It thus stretches to end at sector LBA 1663199. Recognizing that LBA counting starts at 0, we note that this therefore uses 1663200 sectors, which is the size that was auto-detected. We therefore now know that the whole physical disk is within partitions. We do not, however, yet know to what extent the logical drives occupy this area. The first logical drive occupying all or part of this extended partition will be declared in a partition table in the first sector of the extended partition, at LBA 411264, CHS 204, 0, 1.	LBA 411264 to 1663199 CHS 204, 0, 1 to 824, 31, 63
Partition Table 2, at LBA 411264, CHS 204, 0, 1	
1. This starts with partition table 2 in the first sector. The remainder (62 sectors) of the track is not used.	LBA 411264 to 411326 CHS 204, 0, 1 to 204, 0, 63
2. Drive D is defined as starting at sector 63 relative to the start of the partition, hence it starts at 411264 + 63 = LBA 411327. It is of 512001 sectors in size.	LBA 411327 to 923327 CHS 204, 1, 1 to 457, 31, 63

---

4 By *correct* here we mean those parameters which were set when the disk was written to by the user.

3. A second extended partition is defined as starting at sector 512064 relative to the start of the extended partition, hence it starts at 411264 + 512064 = LBA 923328. It is of 411264 sectors in size. The second logical drive occupying all or part of this extended partition will be declared in a partition table in the first sector of this extended partition, at LBA 923328, CHS 458, 0, 1.

LBA 923328 to 1334591
CHS 458, 0, 1 to 661, 31, 63

Partition Table 3, at LBA 923328, CHS 458, 0, 1

1. This starts with partition table 3 in the first sector. The remainder (62 sectors) of the track is not used.

LBA 923328 to 923390
CHS 458, 0, 1 to 458, 0, 63

2. Drive E is defined as starting at sector 63 relative to the start of the partition, hence it starts at 923328 + 63 = LBA 923391. It is of 411201 sectors in size.

LBA 923391 to 1334591
CHS 458, 1, 1 to 661, 31, 63

3. A third extended partition is defined as starting at sector 923328 relative to the start of the extended partition, hence it starts at 411264 + 923328 = LBA 1334592. It is of 328608 sectors in size. The third logical drive occupying all or part of this extended partition will be declared in a partition table in the first sector of this extended partition, at LBA 1334592, CHS 662, 0, 1.

LBA 1334592 to 1663199
CHS 662, 0, 1 to 824, 31, 63

Partition Table 4, at LBA 1334592, CHS 662, 0, 1

1. This starts with partition table 4 in the first sector. The remainder (62 sectors) of the track is not used.

LBA 1334592 to 1334654
CHS 662, 0, 1 to 662, 0, 63

2. Drive F is defined as starting at sector 63 relative to the start of the partition, hence it starts at 1334592 + 63 = LBA 1334655. It is of 328545 sectors in size.

LBA 1334655 to 1663199
CHS 662, 1, 1 to 824, 31, 63

We have now accounted for all 1,663,200 sectors (LBA 0 to LBA 1663199) and all 825 cylinders (from zero), 32 heads (from 0) and 63 sectors (from 1). The whole of this disk is addressed within partitions apart from the master boot record and the partition table tracks. Note also the 1008 lost sectors, which have not been addressed by this BIOS. Do note, and be very wary of, the complex counting conventions that have to be used.

Note that a relatively old CHS/LBA disk has been used in this example in order to illustrate BOTH CHS and LBA counting conventions. It is acknowledged by the authors that most hard disks encountered today will be addressed in LBA. However,

CHS cannot be forgotten, as it is used by default together with FAT based file systems on most flash memory devices. It is also worthy of note that many of the most modern operating systems still use CHS to boot and then switch to LBA mode even when using NTFS filing systems.

An Explanation of Imaging

Now that we fully understand the 'shape' and size of the suspect disk we can consider what an image of it actually is. The principle of imaging itself is to obtain all the data present on the disk, whether it be 'live' data or data in an unused area, in such a way that it can be examined as if the original disk itself was being examined. To obtain an image it is normal to use specialist software which reads the suspect disk from its very beginning to its very end, and creates an image file that contains all the data read in the same order. The image file, depending upon format and hardware used, can then be laid down on a disk of similar or larger capacity. Alternatively, the image file(s) can be mounted as a virtual volume on an examination machine. Data appearing in a particular sector of the suspect disk will then appear in the same sector on the target disk or volume.

To give an analogy, taking an image of a disk is similar to taking a copy of a video tape by connecting two tape machines together, recording on one and playing back on the other, and running both tapes from beginning to end. The copy tape (the target) will contain not only the film that was perhaps taped last night but also the adverts before it and, at the end, all the odds and ends of previous recordings, just as on the original tape.

Generally, it is believed that an image of a hard disk drive when it is laid down on another drive is a true 'mirror' image of the original. This is very definitely *not* the case. Where this belief came from is not clear. Possibly it was from one of the manufacturers of imaging hardware and software, where a salesperson's oversimplified explanation of what the product actually did became the prevailing view. It is understandable that such a simplified picture was, and to some extent still is, used to enable non-technical staff to visualize the concepts.

The actual situation is very different. As a result of improved electronics and modern advanced methods of manufacture, defects within the hard disk itself are not seen by the normal user. Although there are minor defects on a vast proportion of new disks, these defects do not detract from the actual storage area of the disk itself. A number of differing methods are used (as we discussed in Chapter 5) to avoid the defective areas by moving the data to another place on the disk. The map of the disk presented to the user takes these areas into account, within the disk electronics, when accessing the sectors and returning the data required. All of this takes place within the disk itself and is totally invisible elsewhere. It therefore follows that although images may be a complete bit-by-bit copy of the electronic patterns on the original disk, it is not necessarily the case (indeed, it is very unlikely) that the data is in exactly the same place on the surface of one of the platters on the image copy as it is on the original disk. It is therefore not a *mirror* image. It should be emphasized that these storage changes from original to image copy are invisible outside of the disk itself, and so have no bearing on the imaging process or on any other operation involving the disk, including forensic examination. However, from the point of view of giving evidence, it is essential that the analyst understands the true nature of the situation, and is thus able to deal with the most searching of technical questions.

There is one further point about knowing the physical size of the suspect disk, and that is knowing the extent of it when the image is laid down on another disk. If the examination software uses a physical address it will, of course, search the whole of the target disk when executed. Such a search will include the area of any larger disk between the end of the image and the end of the disk. Being able to identify the last sector of the image, and thus being able to curtail searching at that point, may save the analyst a lot of search time.

Copying

In some cases it is necessary to copy files from a suspect or target disk to another storage medium. Use of the MS-DOS copy command or drag and drop in Windows[5] is an acceptable practice as the utilities are tried and tested. For floppy disks DISKCOPY is perfectly adequate. It is strongly recommended that any floppy disks or hard drives that are used for temporary storage are completely erased/wiped before use in order to avoid any possible claims of contamination.

A Brief Comparison of Imaging and Copying

In the early days of forensic computing, before imaging was widely available, most recovered evidence was in the form of copied files or raw sectors. When imaging became the norm, the use of copying decreased. Once disks became so large as to cause time constraints on warrants, copying has been re-introduced as a method of capturing data quickly. It is also used as a swift method of obtaining information or intelligence on-site to assist in the identification of target machines and files and permit a focused approach in a time-limited environment. Copying does have some advantages over imaging, and, in this final section we will make a brief comparison of the two.

Imaging	Copying
Images usually need re-loading before viewing can take place.	Copies can be viewed immediately.
Imaging can be a lengthy process.	Copying can be used when convenient or expedient, or, to recover evidence from "unusual" machines or those which are unsuitable for imaging.
Special equipment is required. Solutions are offered which use software alone or specialist hardware and software.	No special equipment or software requirements.

---

5   Though note the problems with copying LFNs in Windows; see Chapter 5.

Imaging	Copying
Can be expensive both in terms of equipment and some media.	Carries no additional costs.
Training in the specific solution is required often at a considerable cost.	Little training required.
Captures and preserves all data on a disk, including deleted files, swap files, slack space, FAT unallocated space and FAT unaddressed space.	Applies to files only.
Reconstructed disk can be "run". Acknowledged as the better solution, preserving date and time stamps and enhancing continuity and integrity of any evidence found.	

References

ACPO (2003) *Good Practice Guide for Computer Based Electronic Evidence V3*, Association of Chief Police Officers (ACPO), National Hi-Tech Crime Unit (NHTCU).

HMSO (1989) *The Electricity at Work Regulations 1989*, Statutory Instrument 1989 635, HMSO, London.

HSE Books (1998) *Memorandum of Guidance on the Electricity at Work Regulations 1989*, HSR 25 HMSO, London.

IEE (undated), *City & Guilds Portable Appliance Testing Course.* See http://www.iee.org/events/courses/short/cg2_gen.cfm.

IEE (1994) *The IEE Code of Practice for In-Service Inspection and Testing of Electrical Equipment*, IEE, London.

8. *The Treatment of Electronic Organizers*

■ ■

Introduction

In this chapter, our main concern is with the extraction of admissible evidence from electronic organizers and *Personal Digital Assistants* (*PDAs*), although other specialist electronic devices may be treated in a similar way. The topics that we will cover are:

- Principles of operation
- Batteries and memories
- Password protection
- Switching on the organizer
- Application of the ACPO guideline principles
- Seizure of organizers
- Examination and what may be possible
- Dealing with the password
- Open heart surgery

We begin by outlining the principles associated with electronic organizers and identifying their major characteristics. We then go on to consider the application of the ACPO *Good Practice Guide* (ACPO, 2003) principles and to recommend some guidelines for seizure of organizers. Finally, we discuss the examination of organizers and look particularly at how admissible evidence might be obtained from protected areas.

■ ■

Electronic Organizers

Electronic organizers range from very small, very cheap devices that can hold no more than a few tens or so of telephone entries, up to large, relatively expensive units that are as powerful as desktop PCs and that can hold vast quantities of text, sound, graphics and other types of computer files. Examples of some typical organizers and PDAs can be seen in Fig. 8.1.

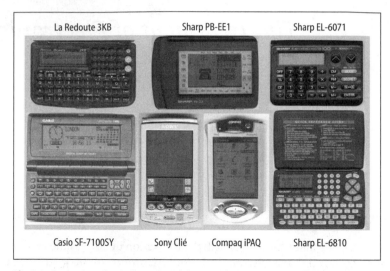

La Redoute 3KB Sharp PB-EE1 Sharp EL-6071

Casio SF-7100SY Sony Clié Compaq iPAQ Sharp EL-6810

Fig. 8.1 A selection of typical organizers (photograph: Tony Sammes and Brian Jenkinson).

Most of the smaller organizers have non-standard operating systems that are often specific not only to the manufacturer but also to the model. For some of the larger organizers and for most PDAs, a number of standard operating systems have come to prominence in recent years.

Possibly the first of these standard operating systems was the Psion "SIBO", said to be named after "Sixteen Bit Organizer" or "Single Board Organizer", and this was used in the Psion 3 range. Psion then developed a new operating system for the Psion 5 which they called "EPOC", a name said to stem from their belief that the world was entering *"a new epoch of personal convenience"*. Subsequently Psion transformed itself, in conjunction with Ericsson, Nokia and Motorola, into a new company called Symbian, and the EPOC operating system has been re-developed and re-branded as "Symbian OS". This operating system is now clearly targeted at the mobile phone and communicator market.

The second major standard operating system is "Palm OS" now produced by PalmSource. This operating system was first developed for the Palm Pilot, a handheld which was initially manufactured by US Robotics before the Palm Computing department was transferred to 3Com. Many subsequent versions of the Palm handheld have used versions of the Palm OS, as have several other handhelds, such as the Sony Clié, the Handspring Visor and the IBM Workpad, to name but three.

Finally, the third major standard operating system is "Windows CE", produced by Microsoft, with the "CE" said to stand for "Compact Edition". Other terms now in use for variations of this series of operating systems include "Windows Mobile Pocket PC" and "Windows Embedded". These operating systems have the benefit of making the organizer or PDA compatible with Windows-based PCs. Such systems often have Windows CE versions of the Microsoft Office suite pre-loaded, with a view to providing a user with mobile use of the Office programs together with facilities for automatic updating and synchronization with their desktop PC system. An organizer that uses the Windows CE system is shown at Fig. 8.2.

Fig. 8.2 A Windows CE organizer – the HP 320 LX (photograph: Tony Sammes and Brian Jenkinson).

Despite the presence of some standard operating systems, there is still an immense variety in the types of electronic organizer and PDA that are available and in the operating systems that they use. This means that the functionality, detailed methods of operation, means of user access and so forth, are typically different for each organizer and PDA. Furthermore, this variety appears still to be increasing rather than converging towards any kind of standard product. This clearly poses a problem for the forensic examiner. Unlike the PC, where a standardized approach to treatment can be taken, most organizers are so different from one another that a standardized approach to treatment is not feasible. A database of organizers, which is known to be incomplete, records over 70 different manufacturers of electronic organizers with more than 450 different models between them, and most of these models are quite different in operation from one another.

Principles of Operation

Electronic organizers may be called Digital Diaries, Palmtops, Handhelds, Memo Masters, Databank Calculators, PDAs and so forth. Although each may have different functionality and may perform differently from one another in detail, all organizers follow a similar basic design. They contain a small microcomputer (marked as CPU in Fig. 8.3) with a miniature keyboard and a display, normally liquid crystal, together with memory chips in which all the information is stored. In short, they are no different, in principle, from the black box model of an information processing system that we met at Fig. 3.20. The amount of memory available for storage, particularly when it is very small, is sometimes indicated in the name of the organizer. An example is the "La Redoute 3KB" (see Fig. 8.1) where 3KB stands for 3 kbyte, and this represents approximately enough storage room for three thousand or so characters of text information. Most organizer memory is volatile and it is usually kept active by

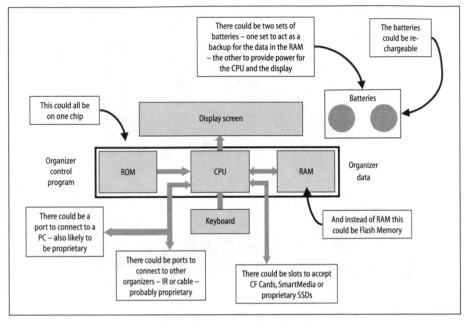

Fig. 8.3 Basic design of an organizer.

batteries. If these fail, all information contained in the organizer could be lost. However, some larger organizers contain a form of flash EEPROM memory which requires no continuous power to retain its contents.

Sometimes there are two sets of batteries: a main set which is designed to run the display, keyboard and microcomputer when the organizer is switched on; and a backup battery which maintains information in the memory if and when the main batteries become discharged. These two sets of batteries can be clearly seen in the example at Fig. 8.4, together with the microcomputer, which in this case uses *chip on*

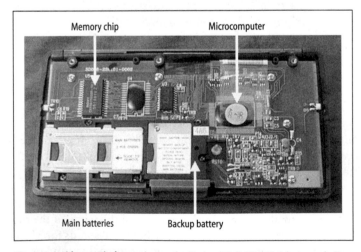

Fig. 8.4 Inside a typical organizer – the Packard Bell DB 128 (photograph: Tony Sammes and Brian Jenkinson).

board (*COB*) technology (see later section) and the memory chip, which here uses a standard *dual in line* (*DIL*) package. This particular memory chip is volatile static random access memory (SRAM) (hence the need for battery backup) and the organizer can store 128 kbyte of information.

Rechargeable Batteries

Many PDAs are designed to be used in conjunction with a laptop or desktop PC. The concept is one where the PDA has its own *cradle*, often connected to the USB port of the PC. This cradle provides a connection to the PC that, given appropriate synchronization software on the PC, will allow automatic backups and file transfers to take place. In addition, the cradle may provide power to the PDA. This design envisages that a user, having taken the PDA to work, would, on returning home fit it into the cradle to allow synchronization and backup of any files changed that day. This has led to many such PDAs being fitted with rechargeable batteries, which are charged up every time the PDA is returned to its cradle. Rechargeable batteries have a life of only a few days, compared with the several weeks of primary cells.

This raises two important points for the seizure of PDAs. The first is to ensure that all associated cables, the cradle, if possible the CD with the PC synchronization and backup software, and the desktop or laptop to which the PDA cradle is connected are all seized together. The second is to check whether the batteries are primary cell or rechargeable. If they are rechargeable, it is important to fit the PDA on its cradle before sealing it in an evidence bag, and to cut a small hole in the bag through which the power cable can be led out and kept connected to an appropriate supply, thus maintaining sufficient charge in the rechargeable batteries.

Two Important Points about Primary Batteries

As mentioned above, most current organizers use SRAM for their internal memory and thus require some form of electrical power to be present at all times if they are to retain the information that they hold. This leads to two important points of which a forensic analyst needs to be aware:

- Just because the display is not working when the organizer is switched on does not mean that all the information is necessarily lost. It may be that the main set of batteries have failed and hence the display cannot operate, but that a backup battery is still active. In this case, on replacing the main batteries we should still be able to recover all the information that is held.

- Removal of all the batteries will normally guarantee a loss of all the information in the memory. We have used the word "normally" here because some systems retain a small charge which will often keep the memory active for several minutes, even with all the batteries removed[1]. However, switching the organizer on when all the batteries are removed will usually dissipate this charge very quickly and

---

1 Some manufacturers rely on this charge to facilitate the changing of a single battery without loss of data.

cause all the information to be lost. It is thus particularly important not to return the organizer to a suspect until forensic analysis has been completed. It is the work of a moment to remove the batteries and thus possibly destroy any incriminating evidence[2].

Memory Extensions

Many of the larger organizers and the PDAs have means by which the internal memory capacity can be extended through the use of add on devices which are also often used for backing up information. In older organizers, these may be proprietary devices called by proprietary names such as "IC Cards", "Solid State Disks" or "Memory Disks" and they may be fitted into plug-in slots on the organizer which are specially designed for this purpose. Such devices may either contain random access memory (RAM) which extends the organizer's capacity, or read-only memory (ROM) programs which extend the organizer's functionality.

These proprietary devices often contain significantly more memory than the organizer itself and it is important that they are recognized and seized with the organizer. The RAM devices may be made up either of standard SRAM memory chips, similar to those in the organizer itself, and fitted with their own integral lithium battery on the device, or they may be a form of early *Flash EEPROM* memory chips that do not require a backup battery. The ROM devices may be one-time-programmable ROM or masked ROM (Psion, 1992), and these also should be seized since they might be needed to interpret user data that has been generated via the extended functionality that they provide.

At Fig. 8.5 is shown a Sharp IQ 8000 organizer, which dates from 1991[3], on top of which has been placed a Sharp IC card. The organizer is a 64 kbyte model and the IC card may be pushed into a slot that is at the rear of the top casing. The IC card may have a list of commands printed on one side that provides a customized touchpad for the functions of the card. The standard touchpad is visible in Fig. 8.5 on the top right-hand side of the organizer. The IC card in this example is a combination card with 64 kbyte of EPROM and 32 kbyte of battery-backed SRAM.

At Fig. 8.6 we have shown a typical solid state disk (SSD), manufactured by Psion PLC, resting on top of the rear casing of a Psion 3a organizer, which dates from 1993. Clearly visible in the figure are the main and backup batteries, as well as the two SSD drive slots, both of which have their doors slightly open. The SSD may be pushed into either slot to give access; in this case to a further 128 kbyte of Flash EEPROM.

In memory terms, the Psion Series 3 range tended to be on the medium to large size compared with other organizers of that period. The one shown in Fig. 8.6 has 2 Mbyte of internal memory and can thus hold close to two million characters of

---

2   An organizer was received for analysis on one occasion where the batteries were neatly sealed in a separate evidence bag so as to prevent any possible leakage to damage the organizer.

3   One of the problems for the forensic analyst is that outdated technology may still be in use by some suspects and we still need to be able to recognize and access it.

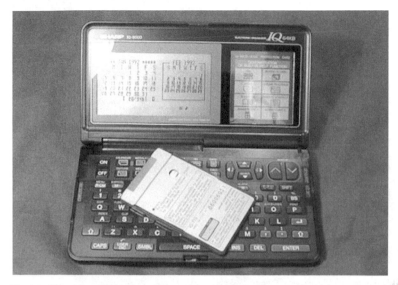

Fig. 8.5 Sharp IC card – the Sharp IQ 8000 (photograph: Tony Sammes and Brian Jenkinson).

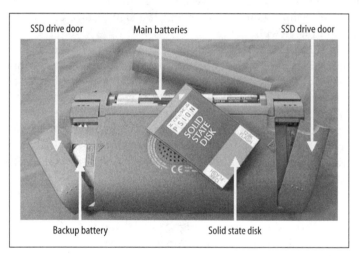

Fig. 8.6 Solid state disks (SSDs) – the Psion 3a (photograph: Tony Sammes and Brian Jenkinson).

information. Although it uses a different operating system (SIBO; see above) from MS-DOS it can be fairly described as a pocket-sized PC.

Most modern organizers and PDAs do not use proprietary memory extension devices, but instead use some form of standard memory card, such as those shown at Fig. 8.7. These are all based on flash memory chips and most appear to a PC, through a suitable interface, as another hard disk drive. There are currently six main memory card *types*: *Compact Flash* (*CF*), *Memory Stick* (*MS*), *Secure Digital* (*SD*), *SmartMedia* (*SM*), *Multimedia* (*MMC*) and *xD Picture* card. A reduced size MMC card (*RS-MMC*) has also been produced.

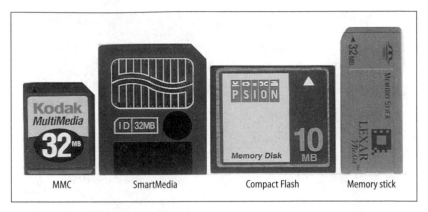

Fig. 8.7 Standard memory cards (photograph: Tony Sammes and Brian Jenkinson).

Significance of Memory Type

In the context of organizers, we have now referred to several different kinds of memory and it is important to understand the significance of each type from a forensic computing viewpoint.

With static RAM (SRAM), the kind of RAM that is to be found in the main memory of most organizers, we must maintain some form of electrical power connected if we are to retain its contents. However, we also have the ability to read from and write to such memory anywhere at will. We can reuse it over and over again for different purposes. We might, through the operating system of the organizer, write a telephone number into one part of the memory and, at some later time, when we no longer require that number, overwrite that part of the memory with details of a memo to do something. SRAM is very flexible and reusable, but it is volatile. If all electrical power is lost, so is all the information that the memory contains.

With the older form of EPROM (erasable programmable read-only memory), such as that referred to in the IC card shown at Fig. 8.5, the memory can be written to (programmed) once using a relatively high voltage[4] and thereafter can only be read from. However, it will retain the programmed information for a very considerable time without the need for any form of power. This class of memory is often known as WORM (write once, read many) memory and the word "erasable" in the name refers to the ability to bulk erase the whole of the memory by subjecting the chip to ultra-violet light. Doing this then allows the EPROM to be reprogrammed with a different set of information. The quartz window which is used to subject the chip to ultraviolet radiation when erasing can just be seen as a small circle on the casing of the IC card in Fig. 8.5. The programming and erasing of this kind of EPROM normally requires specialist equipment and the analyst is unlikely to come across many such EPROMs that have been programmed by a user.

---

4   12.5 V compared with 5 V in the example given. This is normally done using a special EPROM programmer.

However, a slightly more recent form of EPROM no longer requires the use of specialist equipment to program or erase it. Although still a WORM memory, such devices can appear to the user as though they are SRAM. It is an early version of this form of memory which was used by Psion in their Flash SSDs. They were often used for backup purposes and for databases, and Psion wrote file management software which exploited the non-volatility of this early EPROM, without exposing the user to the problems of WORM memory. The file management software achieves this by having a *validity* bit associated with each record stored. When the record is first written the validity bit is not programmed and the record is seen by the file management system to be valid for all subsequent reads. When a change to that record is required, however, a completely new copy of the revised record is written elsewhere and the validity bit of the now outdated record is programmed to make it invalid. In this way, the SSD appears through the file management system to be just like SRAM; changes can be made to records as required. However, it is important to recognize that the same memory locations are not being reused; instead, they are being marked invalid and new memory locations are being used for each change that is made to a record. Two important consequences of this approach result:

- The SSD fills up as records are changed and the actual used space becomes larger than the apparent used space. Eventually, when the SSD is full, consideration has to be given to erasing it. With this form of EPROM[5], erasure of the whole memory is done electrically by applying a high voltage as for writing. In the Psion file management system, this process was known as *formatting*.

- Every change made to the file system is still recorded in the SSD although not accessible through the Psion file management system. Specialist forensic software can be used to access all these changes which may have considerable evidential value.

More recent developments in so-called *flash* technology have led to EPROM chips that can be erased a byte at a time or a block at a time (Micron, 1999a) rather than having to erase the entire chip. We first saw such technology being used in the flash memory of the BIOS on the motherboard of a PC, where infrequent updates from the manufacturer could be easily made. Perhaps most important of all, however, has been the development of the CompactFlash card (Micron, 1999b), which we mentioned above. This consists of flash EPROM memory chips controlled by a complete ATA (IDE) compatible disk controller on the card so that the entire unit appears to be a tiny (at least in form factor) solid state IDE disk. As mentioned in Chapter 4, the largest size of CF card in production at the time of writing (March 2007) is 64 Gbyte. A full and detailed specification (CompactFlash Association, 2004) for such devices has been produced and they are in common use in applications such as digital cameras and mobile phones, as well as electronic organizers. Psion used CompactFlash devices, which they called *Memory Disks*, in the Psion Series 5 range of organizers. However, it should be noted that these memory disks operate just like

---

5 Sometimes referred to as EEPROM, electrically erasable programmable read-only memory.

non-volatile SRAM, so there is no opportunity to access all previous record changes as there was with SSDs.

Perhaps the most important point to come out of this section is a note for arresting officers and search and seizure teams:

- An IC card, or an SSD or a CF memory disk, or an insignificant little MMC card may contain several thousand times the amount of information that is held within the organizer itself.

It should also be noted that some of these memory cards may contain programs rather than provide additional memory. They will normally be marked as such, often with some form of commercial label. They are frequently used for games, spread-sheets, databases (for example, wine, food, route finding and so forth), finance packages, dictionaries and the like.

User Features

The simplest organizer is likely to have a telephone area, a memo area, a schedule or diary area, a calendar and a calculator together with some form of system password protection. Next in complexity might be the inclusion of a clock and an alarm facility. Then, possibly, there might be several telephone and memo areas as well as to do lists and reminder lists with password protection provided for secret and non-secret areas.

More complex still, an organizer might have proprietary word processor, spread-sheet and database applications and might permit additional applications to be downloaded and installed. Finally, there are organizers that are the equivalent of handheld PCs running a standard operating system such as Windows CE and providing support for mini versions of Microsoft Office applications. All of these features are typically accessed differently from model to model.

Password Protection

Most electronic organizers have one or more password-based security features that are intended to protect against unauthorized access to the data held within them. These security features may protect at the level of the *system*, the *file*, the *compartment* or the *record*. From a forensic computing viewpoint, where passwords are not known, it is necessary to defeat such security features if all the evidence is to be accessed. Different approaches may need to be employed against the four different categories of security feature.

At the *system* level, a password may be required before any significant system function can be carried out. This may prevent the operation of an external commu-nications link or deny access to information about the amount of memory in use, as well as preventing any access to the user data held within the organizer.

At the *file* level, a password may be used to generate a key which is then used to apply an encryption algorithm to the file. Usually, a separate one-way hash of the password is also added to the encrypted file. Subsequent decryption occurs only when the correct password is presented and this condition is met when the hash generated using the presented password matches the hash held within the file. The decryption key that is also generated from the presented password is then applied to decrypt the file.

At the *compartment* level two separate areas exist (at least conceptually), and both may hold a number of different record categories, such as telephone, memo and schedule. One area is unprotected and is accessible by default and the other is protected by a password and is inaccessible by default. Presenting the correct password causes the organizer to switch access from the records in the unprotected area to the records in the protected area. Only one of the two areas is accessible at any time.

Finally, at the *record* level, any individual record, be it telephone, memo or schedule, may be "marked" as "secret" or left unmarked. In the default situation, only those records that are not marked as secret are accessible. Presenting the correct password causes the organizer to make accessible *all* records, both secret and non-secret, at the same time.

Switching On the Organizer

The significance of switching on the organizer varies across the entire range. It is important to appreciate that pressing the ON button will always change the internal memory state of the organizer and hence the evidence in some respect or another. The value of each keystroke made on the keyboard is stored in the keyboard buffer of the internal memory, so the act of pressing the ON button itself changes that memory buffer. Although this change is unlikely, in itself, to affect any user data held, what happens thereafter depends on the operating system of the organizer and what other keystrokes are made. If it is a Windows CE operating system, changes to a number of files can take place as the operating system becomes active, in a manner very similar to that of a Windows-based system starting up on a PC. Some other operating systems, which maintain date and time stamping of files, will also change file attributes when those files are opened and closed, again resulting in some aspect of the evidence being changed.

Application of the ACPO *Good Practice Guide* Principles

With a PC, the essential concern, as we saw in Chapter 7, is not to change the evidence on the hard disk and to produce an image which represents its state exactly as it was when seized. With an organizer, there is no hard disk and the concern has to be to change the evidence in the main memory as little as possible, and then only in the certain knowledge of what is happening internally. The possibility of producing an image of the memory rarely exists.

This results in one major difference between the treatment of PCs and the treatment of organizers. To access the organizer it will almost certainly have to be switched on, *which effectively means that Principle 1[6] cannot be complied with.* It is

---

6 Principle 1: No action taken by law enforcement agencies or their agents should change data held on a computer or storage media which may subsequently be relied upon in court.

therefore essential to ensure that Principle 2[7] is complied with because we can rarely image the memory and we thus have to work on the original evidence. This means that the competence of the analyst and Principle 3[8], the generation of a detailed audit trail, are even more important than in the case of the PC.

Guidelines for Seizure

On seizure the organizer should not be switched on. It should be placed in some form of sealed envelope before being put into a sealed evidence bag. This procedure prevents the organizer from being opened and accessed whilst still sealed in the evidence bag, a situation that can easily arise with some organizers.

At Fig. 8.8 we can see clearly how not to do it. This organizer could easily be tampered with by anyone who handles the sealed evidence bag. There can thus be no real guarantee about the continuity of this evidence. Note, however, the earlier comments about fitting organizers with rechargeable batteries into their cradle before sealing into an evidence bag, and passing the power cable out through a hole in the bag.

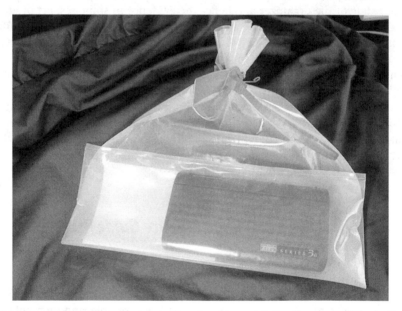

Fig. 8.8 How not to seal an organizer in an evidence bag (photograph: Tony Sammes and Brian Jenkinson).

---

7 Principle 2: In exceptional circumstances, where a person finds it necessary to access original data held on a computer or on storage media, that person must be competent to do so and be able to give evidence explaining the relevance and the implications of their actions.

8 Principle 3: An audit trail or other record of all processes applied to computer-based electronic evidence should be created and preserved. An independent third party should be able to examine those processes and achieve the same result.

If switched on when found, consideration should be given to switching the organizer off using the off switch in order to preserve battery life. A note of the time and date of this process should be made and the organizer should then be packaged and sealed as stated above.

A search should also be conducted for associated devices such as IC Cards, Solid State Disks, and the whole range of memory cards as well as for organizer cradles and for any power and PC connecting cables.

The organizer should never be returned to the accused at the scene or prior to the evidence recovery procedures having been completed. Depressing the RESET button or the removal of all the batteries can result in the complete loss of all information held in the organizer.

A competent person should examine the organizer at an early stage, and should replace the primary batteries as necessary to prevent any loss of evidence. This process should be repeated at regular intervals of a month or so to preserve the evidence until the case is complete. In the case of rechargeable batteries, the organizer should be left on charge. Only a competent person who understands the specific implications of the particular model should access the organizer. As recommended in the Explanation of the Principles (see Chapter 7) it is essential that a witness who is competent to give evidence to a Court of Law makes this access.

It is of paramount importance that anyone handling electronic organizers prior to their examination treats them in such a manner that will give the best opportunity for any recovered data to be admissible in evidence in any later proceedings.

Examination of Organizers and What may be Possible

Provided that either the main or backup batteries are still operational, and the organizer is not faulty, it should be possible to obtain details of all the unprotected information, through the display screen, by normal use of the organizer. This is the recommended approach, since it may be easily audited and repeated by others. This approach also applies to unprotected information in IC cards, SSDs and memory cards, though it may be possible to obtain an image of some of these by treating them as though they were ATA disks. The approach requires that the examiner be thoroughly familiar with the particular organizer, is aware of any alterations to the memory that are unavoidable and is careful to ensure that no inadvertent changes are made. It is vital that a log of all the keystrokes together with any resulting displays is maintained.

It may be possible to obtain some or all of the protected information in the organizer. To achieve this, either the passwords will have to be obtained or the security features of the particular organizer will have to be defeated. There are a number of possible approaches to this problem and these are considered in outline in a later section. Having obtained access to any protected area, the recommended approach is again to access details through the display screen by normal use of the organizer.

Where password-protected information is stored in an encrypted form and the password cannot be obtained, it may be possible to break the encryption by exploiting known weaknesses in the encryption algorithm. This applies only when weak encryption systems have been used.

In most organizers, information is stored in the memory in a very structured way. In particular, it is normally held in the form of a record, and the first part of the record may contain information about how long it is, what type of information it contains, whether or not it is password-protected, and so forth. There may in addition be a marker which indicates that a record has been deleted. When a user deletes information from the organizer, the information itself is rarely removed from memory. Rather, the marker associated with the record is simply set to indicate that the information has been deleted. This is very similar in concept to the deletion of files in FAT-based file systems. It does mean, however, that if we are able to access the memory of the organizer directly, we may be able to restore some of the deleted information. A similar problem to that of undeleting FAT-based files arises here also. The memory space taken up by deleted records will be reused by the organizer when new information is entered and deleted information will eventually be overwritten. This technique also applies to flash SSDs, as we mentioned earlier, and here we can possibly restore deleted files as well as deleted records.

The Trouble with Organizers

From all that has gone before we can now summarize the trouble with organizers so far as the forensic analyst is concerned:

- There is a vast variety of different manufacturers and models.
- Connection to external devices is frequently via non-standard and proprietary connectors and cradles which are often deliberately designed to be incompatible even between models in the same range from the same manufacturer.
- User features are typically different from manufacturer to manufacturer and even from model to model for the same manufacturer.
- Means to access the user features are typically different from manufacturer to manufacturer and from model to model for the same manufacturer.
- Any access, including switching on, alters the memory contents.
- Security features are typically different from manufacturer to manufacturer and from model to model for the same manufacturer.

The consequence of this is that we must obtain, for test purposes, an exact working duplicate of the organizer, together with all its specific connectors and cradles and so forth, for each model that we intend to examine. We need this in order to determine precisely what the user features are; what keystrokes are required to access those user features; what processes will safely (that is, without contaminating any of the evidence) give us access to all the data; and how any security measures in operation may safely be defeated.

In a perfect world, we would buy two samples of every organizer and PDA model as it came off the production line and we would put them away in a big storeroom until we had a case which involved that particular device. Few organizations can afford to do this, and one of the first practical problems with any new organizer case is often in trying to obtain a sample of the organizer for test purposes.

A Set of Protocols

Because of this vast variety of different organizer models we have made no attempt to outline the specific procedure that should be adopted to process any particular model. The required procedures vary greatly from model to model and manufacturer to manufacturer, not only with regard to the keystrokes that need to be entered and the displays that result, but also in the measures that might have to be taken in order to defeat any security features and to access any password-protected areas.

Building on the experience of a large number of past cases, we very early on commenced construction of a database which contains sets of protocols for dealing with specific models of organizer together with photographs of the organizers and details of their characteristics. These sets of protocols utilize the best practice we have so far discovered for each model and these are revised and updated in the light of further experiences with that model.

When a new case comes in, we first need to identify the model, particularly if identifying marks have been erased or there are none present, and this database is our first point of call to see if we have previously worked on this model. We may also compare the new organizer with the photographs in the database to see if it is a re-badged version of a model that we have already dealt with. Finally, the database will also tell us whether or not we have test sample of this organizer in our storeroom.

A generic example of a protocol, in outline, is as follows:

- Identify the organizer and search the database for any prior examples. If found, use latest set of protocols. Obtain test sample.

- Open a new log and note the date and time. Commence a detailed physical external examination of the organizer. Log any noticeable damage and any markings. Open doors to any IC card, SSD drive, memory disk, modem or other card slots. Note the details, including serial numbers and locations, of any IC cards, SSDs, memory disks, modems or other card devices that are found installed. Note the serial number of the organizer, its type and size of RAM. Label the organizer with a signed and dated case identification. Photograph the organizer and associated devices.

- If appropriate, connect a mains adaptor or cradle (do not connect to a PC). Switch on the organizer. Log all keystrokes, the display details and, in particular, the displayed date and time. Also log the current date and time of this action. If appropriate, photograph the screen. Check for any low battery states and replace primary batteries, as necessary, in accordance with the manufacturer's instructions. These should be available from the test sample. Continue to log all keystrokes made throughout. Note whether a system password has been set.

- If a system password is set, then first try any passwords that have been given by the case officer. Log all attempts made and note all results. If this is not successful, then use appropriate measures to attempt to defeat security features. If the organizer has been previously dealt with successfully, details will be in the protocols obtained from the database. If it has not, a series of trials will need to be carried out using the test sample organizer.

- When the system password has been dealt with, log all screen details. With the larger organizers, determine whether the screen is displaying from within an open file. *Do not close any files at this stage.*
- If appropriate, access the system directory and log all file and directory details and in particular all file date and time stamps.
- Note all files that are open together with their displayed details. Try to save copies of open files to a clean pre-prepared IC card, SSD or memory card. Close all open files and log that this has been done. Re-examine the directory structure and note all changes to date, time and size stamps for the closed files.
- Where a personal computer (PC) link to the organizer is available, run diagnostics on the PC and produce a printed copy of the results. If the PC is working correctly, connect to the organizer using the appropriate PC link system. Transfer copies of all files in the organizer to the PC.
- Transfer copies of all files from the PC to the test organizer.
- Commence a detailed examination of each file in the test organizer and in the PC and log all details found. This process is used in order to preserve, as far as possible, the integrity of the evidence organizer. By examining the test organizer, loaded with a copy of the evidence, there is no risk at this stage of inadvertent keystrokes altering the evidence in the evidence organizer.
- Repeat the entire examination using the evidence organizer and compare the results with those logged previously from the test organizer.
- Carry out a diagnostic test on the evidence organizer to establish that it is working correctly. Log all details. If the organizer is not working correctly, try to establish the nature of the failure and make an assessment of what effect, if any, this might have on the information that has been obtained.

Dealing with the Password

There are a number of approaches that can be used to attempt to deal with an unknown password. It is better, however, from an evidential point of view, if the actual password itself can be determined, rather than having to subvert it, because then access to the protected information can be more easily demonstrated to the Court.

The first approach we have called *second guessing*. It is surprising just how often someone who has set a password uses that same password elsewhere in their organizer. As a matter of routine we will examine all the diary entries looking for the pet name of a partner, say, which might turn out to be the key to the protected area. It is useful to have some knowledge of the domestic affairs of the suspect. As well as pet names, we find that nicknames, car numbers, telephone numbers, initials of children in age order and so forth may be used. Many people cannot be bothered with more than one password and they may use the same one for other systems as well. It is therefore worth inquiring whether there are any other organizers involved, as well as whether any PC or Internet account passwords have been determined.

With some organizers, so called *back doors* have been established. These are undocumented key sequences that have probably been provided by the manufacturer in order to aid diagnostic testing and maintenance of the organizer. In some cases they re-boot[9] the organizer into an engineering or service mode. Where we have found these additional facilities, we have sometimes been able to use the manufacturer's diagnostic mode to examine the internal memory, find the password set by the user and then type in that password to unlock the protected area. This must be done with great care. Selecting the wrong diagnostic menu item (and it is not evident what is what since "hidden" menus are often used) might cause the organizer to run, for example, a destructive memory test, causing a total loss of all information.

Many organizers have a copy or *backup mode* whereby some or all of the information held in one organizer can be copied to a second identical or very similar model. The manufacturer normally supplies a suitable connector for this purpose. For those organizers that offer a complete backup, it is sometimes the case that the password will also have been passed between the two organizers during the data transfer. By physically tapping into the connector between the two organizers, it is possible to monitor all signals between them and, using a suitably designed hardware interface and PC program, reconstruct those signals into an image file of all the characters that were passed between the two organizers. The image is often a binary image of all or part of the main memory and will invariably include the password. If we back up the evidence machine to a test machine in this way, we can then simply scan the reconstructed image within the PC to find the password sequence and enter that into the evidence machine. In some cases, where the password is not held in the main organizer memory but instead is held in the on-chip memory of the microcomputer, we do not obtain the password information. However, the image file should contain all the protected as well as the unprotected records and so access to all the evidence is still possible.

Where the organizer has a serial port or a PC link, it is possible that it may respond to what we have called a *magic bullet*. For what we again believe are test and diagnostic purposes, an undocumented character sequence, transmitted into the serial port may cause some organizers to enter a service mode or, in some cases, to send an entire image of its memory back across the link. As in the organizer to organizer backup case, the image may or may not contain the details of the password, depending upon whether it is held in main memory or in the on-chip memory of the microcomputer. However, as before, the image should contain all the protected as well as the unprotected records.

Some organizers which have memory extension slots may treat a fitted memory card in a similar manner to that of a PC with a floppy disk in its A: drive. If this is the case, it may then view the memory card as a "boot" disk. When an organizer is switched on, it effectively performs a "boot" to its internal operating system. If it considers the memory slot as a boot drive, it will first check, on switching on, any memory card that is fitted for a boot loader. If none is found, it will default to the internal operating system, but if a loader is present, it will load and execute the files that are specified by the boot loader. We have had some success in developing boot programs which are designed to access the password location in memory and either display the password on the screen or turn off any "password set" flag before handing

---

9   This is often called "parrot mode" for one well-known PDA.

control back to the internal operating system. By placing such a program on a memory card in the appropriate boot loader format, the card can be used to remove or determine system passwords for the specific organizer model. In practice, each model tends to be different and requires a different program to operate correctly, but clearly a great deal needs to be known about the operating system in order to write programs such as this.

On this point, it is worth noting that the standard operating systems all have *Software Development Kits* (*SDKs*) available for download from the manufacturers' web sites. These contain a wealth of information about the internals of the particular operating system and are intended for use by developers who are producing application software for the particular models of organizers and PDAs that the kits support. In addition, these SDKs may also include *emulators* and *debuggers*. Emulators are programs that run on a software development system, such as a PC, and closely mimic the behaviour of a particular organizer or PDA. They permit a designer to test application software in an environment within which all processes can be observed and monitored. Debuggers are often used to test applications on the actual hardware itself and normally work by downloading a small element of control software into the organizer which then permits remote control and monitoring to take place via the PC running the main debugger software. Usually it will be necessary to switch the organizer into a "debug" mode before the download will be permitted. These facilities can also be used to help defeat security on particular organizers and PDAs.

The use of the Palm OS Debugger to obtain the system password from, for example, the Palm V PDA, has been well documented (Kingpin and Mudge, 2001; Grand, 2002). We demonstrate below an outline of the process that we have used, which is based on the documented approach:

We first set the Palm V into its debug mode by entering the graffiti strokes:

- We then place the Palm V into its cradle, which we have connected to a PC, and then we start the Palm debugger[10] program on the PC.
- Into the Console window of the Palm debugger we enter the command: export 0 "Unsaved Preferences"
- If all goes well, this should result in the uploading of the Palm V file Unsaved Preferences to a predefined folder on the PC. Given that this is successful, the Console window should then look as we have shown in Fig. 8.9.
- We need next to examine the file Unsaved Preferences with a hexadecimal editor in order to find the 32 byte hash of the system password. The hashing process that has been used is weak and can be reversed quite easily (see Kingpin and Mudge, 2001). If we can recognize the hash, we can copy it out and pass it to an

10 The Palm OS Developer Suite can be downloaded from http://www.access-company.com/developers/, and this contains a Palm OS debugger.

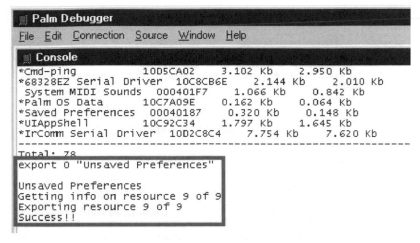

Fig. 8.9 Successful uploading of "Unsaved Preferences".

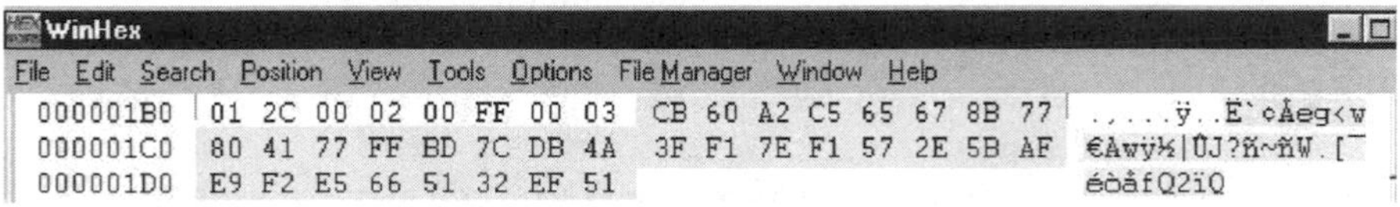

Fig. 8.10 32 byte hash from "Unsaved Preferences".

analysis program which will carry out the reversal process for us. In most cases we have found the hash towards the end of the file, but some trial and error might be required. At Fig. 8.10 we show the 32 byte hash in the Unsaved Preferences file highlighted in a WinHex window.

- The final step is to copy the 32 byte hash out from WinHex and then run, in a DOS box, a program called palmcrypt.exe[11] that has been produced by "@stake Research Labs" for this purpose. The program is executed with a -d switch followed by the 32 bytes of the hash in hexadecimal. Rather than typing all this in, we normally copy the hash using "Copy Block as Hex Values" in WinHex and then paste it into the DOS box after entering the -d switch. The result should look like Fig. 8.11, where we have highlighted in a box the resultant password "13fcfc".

Open Heart Surgery

Finally, if all the foregoing methods fail, we are left only with *open heart surgery*. In this we try to open up the organizer while it is still fully operational and intervene

---

11 Although this program was produced in September 2000 and the @stake website, from which it was freely available, no longer seems to be accessible, a copy of the program was found for free download in February 2007 at http://www.grandideastudio.com/files/security/mobile/palmcrypt.zip.

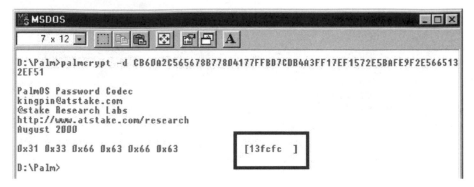

```
MS
DOS  MSDOS                                                    _ □ ✕

  7 x 12 ▾   □ 🖻 🖺  ▣  🖻 🖻  A

D:\Palm>palmcrypt -d CB60A2C565678B77804177FFBD7CDB4A3FF17EF1572E5BAFE9F2E566513
2EF51

PalmOS Password Codec
kingpin@atstake.com
@stake Research Labs
http://www.atstake.com/research
August 2000

0x31 0x33 0x66 0x63 0x66 0x63          [13fcfc   ]

D:\Palm>
```

Fig. 8.11 Determination of password using palmcrypt.

directly in its internal workings. We have, in the past used two different forms of intervention.

- In the first, we established from a very detailed analysis of a test organizer precisely where in the memory of that organizer a flag indicating that the password was set was actually located. Having found the exact place, we connected a specially made piece of electronic hardware to the memory chip which physically changed the password marker in the memory chip from on to off. When the organizer was switched back on, it found that no password had been set.
- The second approach we have used much more frequently. This entails transferring an image of the entire memory of the organizer directly into a PC.

Figure 8.12 demonstrates neatly one of the difficulties with this technique. Here is shown the internal workings of a particular organizer with three battery holders on the left of the diagram. Two of these are for the main batteries and one is for the

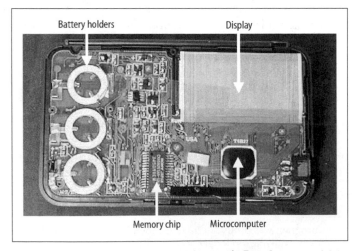

Fig. 8.12 Accessing the memory chip (photograph: Tony Sammes and Brian Jenkinson).

backup battery and as soon as dismantling of the organizer starts, there is a high risk that all the batteries will fall out. For the sake of clarity, we have not shown the details in the figure, but it is essential to connect alternative power supplies to the organizer if the information in the memory is to be retained. This we usually do by soldering external power connections directly on to the printed circuit board as the dismantling process proceeds. As an alternative, we have used electronically controlled machine tools to cut, very accurately, a hole in the rear casing so that we could access the memory chip without having to remove the casing and thus without having to disturb the spring loaded battery carriers.

As can be seen from Fig. 8.12, the memory chip is in a standard DIL package, although the microcomputer itself has been attached to the board using chip on board (COB) technology. It is thus possible to connect to the memory chip using a spring-loaded SOIC connector, and this is shown in place in Fig. 8.13.

In this figure we can see how the SOIC connector sits cleanly over the memory chip and makes contact with each of its legs. The connections, brought out at the top of the clip, are then taken via ribbon cable to a specially designed interface board which in turn is connected to a PC. Specially written programs in the PC are then used to drive the interface board and through it the organizer memory, causing it to read out to the PC all the information contained in the memory chip. What we have done, in effect, is to make the organizer memory an extension of the PC and then simply copied an image of the organizer memory directly to the hard disk of the PC. As in the case of the backup and the magic bullet images, analysis of this image may result in the password being obtained. In any event, both protected and unprotected records are usually stored in the same memory, so access to all the evidence should now be possible.

Problems arise with organizers that use chip on board technology throughout to implement both the microcomputer and the memory, as we see in the example of Fig. 8.14. Making contact with this memory chip is much more difficult. There is no

Fig. 8.13 Connecting to the memory chip (photograph: Tony Sammes and Brian Jenkinson).

Fig. 8.14 Chip on board technology (photograph: Tony Sammes and Brian Jenkinson).

standard form of chip packaging in use here, so we are not able to look up the significance of any of the connections from standard tables; nor are we able to use the very convenient legs of a package to give us relatively easy access to those connections.

The only realistic approach is to try to use a jig, as we have shown in Fig. 8.15. The organizer has been locked into place with a specially drilled sheet of plastic above it and spring-loaded pins have been pushed through the plastic to make contact with specific plated through holes on the printed circuit board. Pins have been positioned to make contact with all the data and address bus lines and these in turn have been connected via ribbon cable to the PC interface. However, a great deal of time and experimentation was required in order to determine which bus line is which so that the spring-loaded pins could be connected to the correct points on the PC interface.

This approach can only be used where the microcomputer and the memory are in separate chips since it is only then that the address and data bus lines have to be implemented as connections on the printed circuit board. Where the memory is on

Fig. 8.15 Using a jig.

Battery holder   Microcomputer and memory

Fig. 8.16 Microcomputer and memory on same chip (photograph: Tony Sammes and Brian Jenkinson).

the same chip as the microcomputer, as is the case in Fig. 8.16, there is no longer any point in trying to access connections on the printed circuit board, since the required buses are all internal to the chip.

This kind of technology continues to pose a problem for the forensic computing analyst, though a number of different approaches are being followed up. One such, for example, involves the removal of the resin from the surface of the chip so that it can be examined under an electron microscope. Using this technique, it may be possible to "see" the charges in the memory and interpret the memory contents directly. It may also be possible to make contact with the internal buses using optical fibres so that appropriate signals, such as "turn off the password bit" could be injected into the chip. A second approach that is under consideration examines the radiated waveforms from the microcomputer under various conditions of operation. An organizer is typically very "noisy" electronically and by converting the noise to sound waves using the superhet principle (an ordinary medium wave or short wave radio receiver provides this capability for most of us) it is possible that different sound patterns could be detected when the microcomputer is carrying out different processes. Perhaps each character of a password, as it is typed in, causes a different noise pattern to occur, depending upon whether it is a correct or incorrect value. The waveforms could also be examined on an oscilloscope to detect useful patterns.

Yet a third approach looks at the performance of the chips when operating outside their designed limits with very high or very low power supply values. Security features have to be designed on the assumption that the device is operating correctly and it is interesting to investigate what happens in various failure modes. We can most easily instigate a failure mode by adjusting the power supply to be outside the working limits of the device. For example, we might find that the minimum voltage at which the microcomputer continues to operate correctly is, say, 1.01 V, whereas the SRAM memory will continue to retain information down to 0.94 V. If we now take the power supply of the organizer down, in steps of 0.01 V say, to 0.98 V, we should have a situation where the memory is still active but the microcomputer has faulted. If we now increase the power supply in steps of 0.01 V there will come a point at which the microcomputer may restart. If, say, the password set bit was remembered by the microcomputer, this process would probably have cleared it and we might find that the system password had been turned off!

Clearly this kind of analysis is very time-consuming, and hence very expensive. Few cases can afford to fund such research. Again, we face that "trouble with organizers": the vast variety with little or no standardization means that every model effectively requires its own mini research project.

JTAG Boundary Scan

As the problems of dealing with chips such as these became more difficult for the forensic analyst, so they were also making life very difficult for the manufacturer in respect of development, testing and diagnosis. With that in mind, a group of companies formed the *Joint Test Access Group* (*JTAG*) with the purpose of agreeing a set of standards for test hardware that would be embedded in future chips. The idea is that a set of *boundary cells* is implemented between the internal elements of the chip and its input and output connections. The cells, when in the normal mode, are inactive and simply permit all input and output signals to pass through. However, when in the test mode, all input signals are captured for analysis and all output signals are preset as appropriate. This is all controlled by software using another microprocessor called the *Test Access Port* (*TAP*) *Controller*. The TAP Controller can itself be given instructions by an external TAP Control device which is connected via a standard five-pin interface on the printed circuit board. The "Standard Test Access Port and Boundary Scan Architecture" IEEE standard was produced in 1990 and this is generally known as "JTAG boundary scan" or "IEEE 1149".

The significance of all of this is that many modern PDAs, for example, are *JTAG compliant* which means that their chips contain boundary cells and TAP controllers and that their PCBs have the five-pin JTAG interface. The IEEE 1149 standard specifies that there are two kinds of instruction – public and private – and that there is a mandatory set of public instructions that must be available on all JTAG-compliant systems. The public instructions are all documented by the chip manufacturers, whereas the private ones are not.

Given that information could be obtained about some of the private instructions, it is possible that security features could be disarmed or defeated using the JTAG interface. For an excellent paper on this subject see Breeuwsma (2006). This is an area for much further work.

A Few Final Words about Electronic Organizers

The electronic organizer can hold very large amounts of information which may have considerable significance from an evidential point of view. To maintain the integrity of this potential evidence, it is essential that the organizer is only accessed by a competent person as explained in Principle 2 of the ACPO Guidelines. The recommendation, following seizure of an electronic organizer, is therefore not to tamper with it in any way but to place it immediately into a sealed envelope and then into a sealed evidence bag (keeping in mind the needs of rechargeable batteries), so that it can be examined by a competent person. However, occasions may arise where the demands of the case require immediate access to the information that may be held in a seized electronic organizer. This has to be an operational decision, where the risk of possible contamination of the evidence is weighed against the importance of immediate intelligence. In order to preserve the evidence, as far as possible, a formal approach should be adopted. All actions taken and the reasons for them should be logged, together with all the keystrokes that were made and all the displays that were obtained. A competent officer might subsequently be able to affirm that no, or limited, contamination had taken place.

References

ACPO (2003) *Good Practice Guide for Computer Based Electronic Evidence V3*, Association of Chief Police Officers (ACPO), National Hi-Tech Crime Unit (NHTCU).

Breeuwsma, M. F. (2006) Forensic imaging of embedded systems using JTAG (boundary-scan), *Digital Investigation*, 3, 32–42.

CompactFlash Association (2004) *CF+ and CompactFlash Specification Revision 3.0*, 12/23/04, CompactFlash Association, PO Box 51537, Palo Alto, CA 94303. URL: http://www.compactflash.org/.

Grand, J. (2002) *Memory Imaging and Forensic Analysis of Palm OS Devices*, @stake, Inc., 196 Broadway, Cambridge, MA 02139.

Kingpin and Mudge (2001), *Security Analysis of the Palm Operating System and its Weaknesses Against Malicious Code Threats*, 10th USENIX Security Symposium, Washington DC, August. URL: http://www.usenix.org/publications/library/proceedings/sec01/kingpin.html.

Microchip (1997) *24LC01B/02B Modules*, Document DS21222A, 8/97, Microchip Technology Incorporated, 2355 West Chandler Blvd, Chandler, AZ 85224-6199. URL: http://www.microchip.com/.

Micron (1999a) *Boot Block Flash Memory*, TN-28-01, FT01. p65 – Rev. 2/99, Micron Technology Inc., 8000 S. Federal Way, PO Box 6, Boise, ID 83707-0006. URL: http://www.micron.com/.

Micron (1999b) *CompactFlash*, FC02. p65 – Rev. 2/99, Micron Technology Inc., 8000 S. Federal Way, PO Box 6, Boise, ID 83707-0006. URL: http://www.micron.com/.

Psion (1992) *'C' Software Development Kit*, Volume II, PLIB Reference, 10 June, Psion PLC.

9. Looking Ahead (Just a Little Bit More)

Introduction

In the first edition of this book, we opened this chapter with these words:

> We have attempted, in this book, to offer a basic foundation for the professional practice of forensic computing. Our aim has been to put in place sufficient theory and good practice as to enable professionals to continue their development from a sound and confident starting point.

None of this has changed for our second edition. Once again, we have had to limit the scope of what we have talked about and there is therefore much that we have not been able to cover in the time and space available. We would like to have included, for example, comprehensive details of CDs and DVDs, their various formats and how to extract forensic information from them. Rather than just an additional chapter, however, we think that this could well be a book in itself. We would like to have included a comprehensive analysis of OLE 2 containers and of Microsoft Office documents, for which we have carried out much research. We have been running courses on these topics, for the past three years, but again we felt that the material would be just too much for a foundation book such as this. Other areas of great interest to us include, for example, details of the various Windows registries and how to deal with fragmented and deleted portions of them; analysis of the recently introduced AOL Topspeed cache; and, the evidence that can be deduced from USB artefacts. However, we had to know where to stop, and we think we have now fitted as much as we safely can into this foundation book, particularly when the radically revised disk chapter and the new work on NTFS are taken into account.

We have started the book with the concepts of information and information storage and we have continued with the fundamental principles that underlie all digital computers. From here on, as in our previous edition, we have tended to concentrate on the personal computer (PC) and, in particular, on the PC running either MS-DOS or one of the Microsoft Windows operating systems. That is not to say that there are no other architectures or operating systems that need to be considered; just that the PC with Microsoft Windows software is still the configuration that the practising forensic computing analyst is most likely to come across today. Cases involving the Apple Macintosh are sometimes met with, as are cases involving PCs which use other operating systems, such as Linux. However, we have to note that the major high street retailers of personal computers are still selling, to an apparently insatiable domestic computer market, large numbers of ever higher and higher performance PCs which are invariably bundled with Microsoft Windows software. It may reasonably be foreseen that most forensic computing analysts will, at some time or another, be coming across some of these PCs in a professional capacity. Although sales of PCs are said to be cooling, the world market for 2007 is predicted[1] to be 254 million units and this represents a 10.5% growth over 2006. It is this continuing trend, we would claim, that justifies the approach we have taken in the book to concentrate upon the PC as the example system.

However, other systems, although possibly different in detail, do not in any way detract from the principles that we have established for the PC and so the theoretical and procedural groundings of the early chapters are all still applicable.

What this chapter is about, however, are issues that may change the ways in which we currently deal with PCs (and other electronic devices) because of overriding technical or legal issues. The "looking ahead" is very deliberately "just a little bit more" because the status and application of this technology beyond a few months or so is notoriously difficult to predict. Well-known authoritative statements from the past, explaining, for example, that computers may weigh no more than 1.5 tons[2], that there is a world market for maybe five computers[3], and that there is no reason anyone would want a computer in their home[4], only serve to illustrate this point. We have tried here to be fair and make comment, in passing, on some of our own earlier views from the first edition version of this chapter.

Bigger and Bigger Disks

In this very spirit of fairness, we felt that we had to repeat the original opening sentence of this section from the first edition and follow that up with a comparable statement from the marketplace of today. Our statement back in January 2000 was:

> At the time of writing [January 2000], an advertisement[5] in a national newspaper offers a 600 MHz PC with 128 Mbyte of RAM and a 27 Gbyte hard disk for just over £1500.

---

1 See http://www.channelregister.co.uk/2006/03/28/idc_pc_shipments/.

2 "Computers in the future may weigh no more than 1.5 tons" *Popular Mechanics*, forecasting the relentless march of science, 1949.

3 "I think there is a world market for maybe five computers"; Thomas Watson, chairman of IBM, 1943.

4 "There is no reason anyone would want a computer in their home"; Ken Olson, president, chairman and founder of Digital Equipment Corp., 1977.

5 Time Computers Ltd, *The Express*, Tuesday 4 January 2000, p. 49.

We should compare this with an advertisement[6] noted, in April 2006, for a 3.20 GHz Pentium 4 system with 1024 Mbyte of RAM and a 250 Gbyte serial ATA hard disk for under £1000. This is over 5 times the speed, 8 times the RAM size and nearly 10 times the hard disk capacity for two thirds of the price. Clearly the trend of putting high-performance PCs within the financial reach of most ordinary people is not just continuing, but accelerating. However, it is still the size of the hard disk that poses one of the greatest potential problems for the forensic computing analyst.

Although we were aware of many apocryphal stories about the quantity of paper such disk sizes can represent, we felt, for the first edition of the book, that we should provide an authenticated version. We started with a 500 sheet pack of 80 g A4 paper and found this to be 2.25 inches thick. A typical page, with 1 inch margins all round, was filled with 12 point characters and this was found to contain 3,600 of them. We were thus able to determine that 2.25 inches of paper, or 500 sheets, assuming that we print on one side only, represents 500 × 3,600 = 1,800,000 characters, or, in computing terms, 1,800,000 bytes. From this, we could establish that 1,000,000 bytes represents 2.25/1.8 = 1.25 inches.

We can therefore state that 250 Gbyte, which is 250 × 1024 × 1024 × 1024 and is equal to 268,435,456,000 bytes, represents 268,435.456 × 1.25 inches of paper. This is 335,544.32 inches or 33,5544.32/12 = 27,962 feet of paper. In other words, 250 Gbyte of information represents a column of A4 paper nearly 28,000 feet high.

To put this height into context, Nelson's Column, in Trafalgar Square, London is a mere 170 feet high and equates to only 1.5 Gbyte; Big Ben at 320 feet equates to about 2.8 Gbyte and the Eiffel Tower at 1050 feet equates to about 9.4 Gbyte (see Fig. 9.1). There are no buildings or monuments that are anything like as high as 250 Gbyte, the nearest object of comparable height being Mount Everest at 29,028 feet, which is

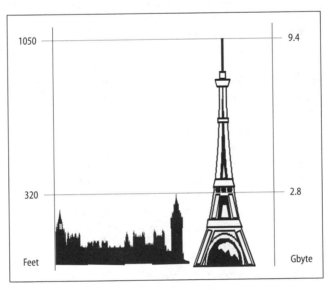

Fig. 9.1 Heights in Gbyte.

---

6 See http://www1.euro.dell.com/content/products/features.aspx/dimen_xps600

equivalent to about 260 Gbyte. A useful rule of thumb to remember for this height analogy is that "1 Gbyte represents a column of A4 paper about 110 feet high".

Although this rule of thumb is helpful in giving us some meaningful capacity metric for disks of a few Gbyte in size, once we exceed about a thousand feet in height the analogy tends to lose its significance. We felt that another analogy might be more appropriate for the much larger disks of today. Here we conceive of laying the column of A4 paper down along a road and converting distances from feet to miles. The value 250 Gbyte then equates to 27,962 feet = 27,962/5,280 = 5.3 miles, and the associated rule of thumb can be simply expressed as "approximately 50 Gbyte to the mile". The 1.6 TByte hard disk that is now available off the shelf can therefore be equated with a horizontal column of paper approximately 32 miles long.

Another useful metric is related to the time needed to read what is contained in such enormous repositories. If we consider the 250 Gbyte hard disk again we note from above that it is 268,435,456,000 bytes in size, and, since there are 3,600 characters to a page (also from above) this represents 74,565,404 pages of A4 text (from 268,435,456,000/3,600). Given that we can possibly read a page of A4 text in a minute and that we are prepared to work 8 hours a day, 300 days a year doing nothing but this, then it would take us 74,565,404/(60 × 8 × 300) = over 517 years to read it all.

The days when the investigating officer could say "...just print out all that's on the disk and I will decide what is relevant" have long gone. It is today quite impractical to consider printing out anything but a very tiny fraction of the information that might be held on the hard disk. Quite apart from the impossible problems of producing and handling columns of paper that may be several miles in length, investigating officers would be faced with the prospect of possibly hundreds of person-years of effort in just trying to read it all! Indulging further in this fantasy world, it is not difficult to imagine a Computer Crime Unit conversation along the following lines: "George, go and fetch me the top sheet of the printout, will you?"; "OK Guv, but you do realize that's a round trip of twenty miles – do I get expenses?".

We suggested in the first edition that this unprecedented and seemingly endless increase in the size of hard disks would cause us problems, and this has proved to be the case. Unfortunately, seven years on we still have no easy answers. The role of the forensic computing analyst has had to change quite radically, largely because of the disk size problem. In the very beginning, the role was simply that of a technician who arranged for all of the data to be produced to the investigating officer in an accessible form. Now the role has had to become that of an experienced examiner who must assist the investigating officer in finding, identifying and extracting from the disk (or, preferably, an image of the disk – but see later) all the evidence that is pertinent to the investigation. The ability to search acres of haystacks and chance upon, in a sensible time frame, the few needles that are present would appear to be a major asset. Often, also, the analyst of today will be required to try to establish the provenance of a piece of evidence that is to be relied upon, and this will entail attempting to determine all the different processes that may have taken place to cause that piece of evidence to arise.

These examination processes require specialist tools as well as a clear understanding of the fundamentals in order to use them effectively. Some tools and techniques are available that can help to reduce the search space that has to be examined. For example, databases containing hash signatures of all known standard software files can be run against the disk image and all successful hits can be ruled out of any further searches. Similarly, databases containing hash signatures of known unlawful files can be run against the disk image and successful hits ruled in for further examination. This is common practice and can be made part of standard operating procedures. Much more difficult is looking for something on a very large disk for which you have no clear search clue; a passphrase perhaps, or a incriminating shortcut that has been deleted from the desktop. There is no point in carrying out generic, broad-based searches across 250 Gbyte of hard disk if all you have is the vain hope that you might find something amongst all those useless hits that it is going to take you several hours to acquire. What has happened in practice is that many of the most effective analysts seem to have acquired a "nose" from their experience of working on many cases, and this gives them an edge in knowing what to look for and where to look for it. Perhaps this is the only practical solution to the big disk problem.

Many analysts write their own tools to solve specific problems, and these are increasingly being shared around the community. However, this too poses a problem, which is only just beginning to be addressed. Should not all such tools, including mainstream commercial products, be accredited, by some recognized body, so that the integrity of evidence obtained using them can be demonstrated in Court? Much good work along these lines is taking place in the USA with the Computer Forensics Tool Testing (CFTT) Project[7] of the National Institute of Standards and Technology but we are not aware of any similar work in the UK.

To Image or not to Image?

There are other legal traps here for the unwary. Simply looking on the hard disk for information that could support a prosecution by the investigating officer is seen by some as unacceptable. There may reside on the hard disk evidence that could equally well demonstrate the innocence of the accused, and the view is that this too should be looked for and retrieved. Where the size of the hard disk is small enough, or the quantity of information held is very limited, printouts of all the evidence can be produced, with copies going to both the prosecution and the defence. Here the problem does not arise as both parties have access to everything. Some now argue that, in the case of much larger disks, containing much greater quantities of information, it is sufficient for both parties to receive a certified image[8] of the disk and for each then to access from their image whatever they require. However, this too may not be possible or practical in the future. The standard CD-ROM, which has been the most frequently used medium for certified images in the past, can only store some 700 Mbyte, so, for a 27 Gbyte hard disk, we require some 40 CD-ROMs for each image. DVDs are now cheap enough to provide a more practical alternative, though, even at 4.7 Gbyte each, we might require 40 or more[9] for our 250 Gbyte hard disk. More

---

7 See http://www.cftt.nist.gov/.

8 The imaging software should be accredited.

9 Depending upon the degree of compression that has been used in the image.

significant, however, is the view held by some authorities that imaging is no longer the appropriate approach.

This view is held not just because of the practical problems of imaging very large disks, but also because of the legal and ethical issues of seizing such vast quantities of information, much of which is unlikely to be relevant to the case. This issue is particularly pertinent where *legal privilege* is involved and where it is essential that only relevant evidence is accessed.

What might replace imaging is difficult to see. Imaging has a number of very real advantages. By taking identical and unmodifiable certified images of the disk at the time of seizure and passing a copy to prosecution and a copy to defence we can be certain of the integrity of the evidence, given that the imaging tool is accredited. Analysts can examine the image without fear of corrupting the evidence and can also, if required, generate additional hard disk "clone" versions from their image for examining files and executing software packages on a test machine. Perhaps equally important, where a business is involved, the PC with its hard disk can be returned to the user so that work may continue as soon as the imaging is complete. If a non-imaging approach were to be adopted, the PC could not be returned to the user until *analysis* was complete, which for a large hard disk might take many weeks.

Perhaps the most effective solution, particularly where legal privilege is involved, is for a Court to authorize and oversee the imaging of the hard disks, so that the evidence is captured and retained with a high degree of integrity, and then for the Court to decide what parts of the image are to be made available to the various parties.

Live System Analysis

In addition to this imaging issue, many now believe that some form of "live analysis" may be appropriate on some systems at the time of seizure. Previous thinking had invariably recommended an immediate shutdown or a "pulling of the plug" on systems that were found to be active at the time of seizure. Whilst many accepted that it was appropriate to "move the mouse" or "touch the keyboard" to test whether a blank screen was a result of a screen saver before shutting down, having recorded or photographed the screen details that resulted, the next action would normally be to switch the system off. This was done in order to change the evidence as little as possible before imaging took place.

That thinking has now changed, particularly in respect of secure containers. These are files that appear as virtual disks on the system. They are often very large in size, and they use strong encryption to secure all the data in the file. Without access to the passphrase or key, the likelihood of being able to access the plaintext data is vanishingly small, so if it can be established that a container such as this is currently open on the live system, an opportunity to access the data is afforded that is unlikely ever again to be repeated. The advent of "hot swap" USB external hard disk drives has meant that an examiner can connect one of these to a live system and copy out significant amounts of data from the live system without having to reboot. It is important to log all the actions taken because this will cause changes to many of the system files, but it may be argued that the value of the data accessed could well offset the loss of integrity.

Others believe that this process could be taken further. The entire RAM could be examined or copied out, and this might contain evidential artefacts that would be lost on switch-off. Network connectivity, including mounted network file systems, could also be examined on a live system. This is an area of current research, and we may expect to see much more on live analysis in the future.

Networked Systems Add to the Problems

A 250 Gbyte hard disk on a standalone computer may seem problematic enough, but this can be magnified many times over where a network of computers is involved. Here we may have very many hard disk servers, each of which has far more capacity than the standalone disk, and each of which is accessible from any point in the network. To confound the problem, some or all of these servers may be in the jurisdictions of other nations, geographically separate from the systems that are being seized and subject to quite different legal systems.

In such cases, imaging of anything other than the local disks is unlikely to be feasible, and making accesses beyond the local system may not even be legal. Current thinking tends to favour the seeking of guidance from the local systems administration staff, where they are not involved in the case, and selectively accessing only material which is relevant to the case, thereby occasioning minimum disruption to the network and the business. Live access of relevant data can often be carried out with such assistance, obtaining across the network partial file backup sets from the appropriate servers. An explanation of a such method is given in Birch (2006). Backup tapes made by the organization are another important potential source of evidence.

Where this cannot be done, perhaps because the local systems administration staff are themselves involved, then disconnecting the external network, closing the local systems down and imaging the hard disks that are accessible seems to be the only fallback position.

Encryption

The final issue we consider in this brief look ahead is the problem of encryption. Although the capability has been around for a long time, we are now beginning to see more and more cases where strong encryption has been used. There is now a wide variety of user-friendly programs available that enable strong encryption to be applied securely to files, to email messages, and to entire virtual disks with little or no knowledge or effort required by the user.

We will mention first weak encryption. For some time, several word processor, spreadsheet and other similar office application programs incorporated a form of built-in encryption which was activated by means of a password. As we described in Chapter 8, when a file is password-protected it is saved in an encrypted form and a secure hash of the password is saved with it. Subsequent decryption occurs only when the correct password is presented and this condition is met when the hash generated using the presented password matches the hash held within the file. The decryption key that is also generated from the presented password is then applied to decrypt the file. Two possible weaknesses are present in these early systems. Firstly, the application programs tended to use encryption algorithms that are often unpublished and cryptographically weak; that is, they contain flaws that permit cryptanalysts to perform decryption without a knowledge of the password. The limited protection offered by such algorithms often relies upon the fact that the algorithm is unknown, even though this can always be established by reverse engineering the code. Secondly, it is possible to generate a table[10] of all possible passwords and their hashes (so-called *Rainbow Tables*) and use these to look up the particular password from its hash. A number of companies still sell software products which can be used to break these weak algorithms quite quickly or, alternatively, retrieve the original password from its hash in the file.

In the case of strong encryption, the algorithm is published and is well known and does not rely upon any obfuscation for protection. Indeed, the view of the cryptographic community is that publication of the algorithm permits peer review to take place and allows any possible weaknesses to be thoroughly explored. Algorithms that have continued to remain unbroken in such a spotlight can therefore justifiably claim the title "strong". In addition, the Rainbow Tables approach can be defeated quite easily by adding a *salt* to the password, which then makes the generation of the tables impractical since a separate set of tables would be required for each salt value.

Despite concerns by some nations about the misuse of cryptography, software products incorporating strong encryption are now widely available throughout the world. Indeed, almost all the encryption algorithms are available as source code computer programs on the Internet. Forensic computing analysts are particularly likely to encounter the effects of these algorithms in three main areas: email messages, encrypted files on a hard disk and encrypted volumes on a hard disk. In what follows we mention a variety of specific software products. In doing so, we are not in any way endorsing a particular product, rather simply using it as an exemplar with which we are familiar for the particular kind of functionality that it exhibits.

Encryption of Email

Perhaps the best known of the email encryption systems is Pretty Good Privacy or PGP (Garfinkel, 1995). At Fig. 9.2 we have shown a block diagram view of a PGP email message being passed from Ted (on the left-hand side of the figure) to Alice (on the right-hand side of the figure). PGP is not a cryptographic algorithm; rather, it is a system for managing cryptographic keys and messages.

---

10 In fact, although all passwords and their hashes are initially generated, only a small proportion are stored in the tables (of the order of 1 in 10,000), and this is done in such a way that all other passwords and hashes can be generated relatively quickly from the tables using as few as 10,000 hash operations. See Oechslin (2005) for further details.

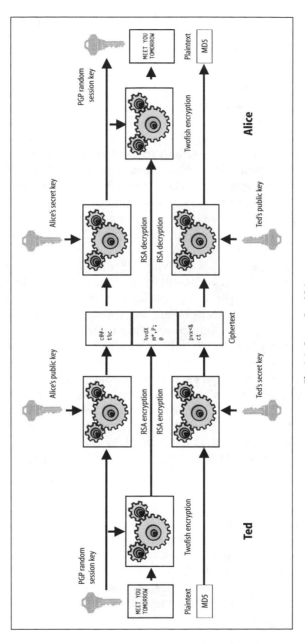

Fig. 9.2 Pretty Good Privacy.

PGP uses two forms of encryption: private key (also known as symmetric) encryption and public key (also known as asymmetric) encryption. With private key encryption, the same secret key is used both to encrypt the plain text message to ciphertext and to decrypt the ciphertext back to the original plain text. The problem with this, however, is how do you securely distribute your secret key to your distant correspondent so that they can decrypt your messages? With public key encryption, a pair of different (but mathematically related) keys are generated. One (the public key) is used to encrypt the plain text message to ciphertext and the other (the secret key) is used to decrypt the ciphertext back to the original plain text. Key distribution is solved here by a user, having generated a key pair, quite openly distributing the public key of the pair to all potential correspondents, whilst retaining the secret key safely locked away. Only this secret key will decrypt messages that have been encrypted with the public key and so only the user, with access to the secret key, will be able to decrypt them. The problem here, however, is that the mathematical computations that are involved in public key encryption and decryption are several thousand times slower than the equivalent computations for private key encryption. Even relatively short messages therefore take an unacceptably long period of time to encrypt and decrypt using public key cryptography.

PGP overcomes both the problems of key distribution and performance by using the two methods together. At Fig. 9.2 we note, on the left-hand side, that Ted wishes to send the message "MEET YOU TOMORROW" to Alice. We first assume that Alice has used her PGP system to generate a public key encryption key pair, and has distributed her public key to, among others, Ted. She will, of course, have retained her secret key safely locked away where only she can access it. In order to send the message from Ted, his PGP system will automatically generate a random "session key" of, say, 128 bits and then use (for example) the Twofish[11] private key encryption algorithm with this session key to encrypt the message "MEET YOU TOMORROW" to ciphertext. In parallel, PGP also takes the random session key and encrypts that using (for example) the RSA[12] public key encryption system and Alice's public key to produce a ciphertext version of the session key. If Bob wishes to *sign* his message, the PGP system will also form an MD5 signature of the original plain text message and then encrypt the resulting 128 bit MD5 value using RSA public key encryption and his own secret key, which he must specifically authorise.

The three pieces of ciphertext, one being the private key encryption of the message "MEET YOU TOMORROW", one being the public key encryption, using Alice's public key, of the random session key, and one being the public key encryption, using Bob's secret key, of the MD5 signature are now merged and transmitted as one out onto the open network.

On receipt by Alice, her PGP system demerges the three parts and uses her secret key, which she must specifically authorize, together with the RSA public key decryption algorithm to convert the enciphered session key back to its original

---

11 See Twofish: A New Block Cipher, Bruce Schneier, http://www.schneier.com/twofish.html.

12 Named after its three inventors: Ron Rivest, Adi Shamir and Leonard Adelman. For details see Schneier (1996), pp. 466–74.

value. The PGP system then uses this decrypted session key together with the Twofish private key decryption algorithm to convert the ciphertext of the message back to the original plain text as shown. An MD5 signature is then generated from this resulting plain text. Finally, the PGP system uses Bob's public key and the RSA public key decryption algorithm to decrypt the enciphered MD5 signature and the system compares the two MD5 signatures for compliance. If they are identical, Alice knows (with one proviso) that the message could only have come from Bob. That is because only Bob holds the secret key which matches his public key and so only he could have encrypted the MD5 signature. The proviso, of course, is that Alice can trust that the public key she has really did come from Bob. If she received it from him personally then that is probably the most effective basis for trust.

From the viewpoint of the practical forensic computing analyst, there is very little that can be done about breaking the encryption of either of these algorithms. However, given access to Alice's computer, the most profitable approach would be to try to establish the passphrase that protects Alice's *secret key ring*: that is, the place where PGP keeps her secret keys. This is normally in a .skr file, which itself is encrypted using a strong encryption algorithm. Given successful access to the keyring, PGP could then be used to decrypt all messages sent to Alice that have been encrypted using her public key.

It used to be the case that Windows "front ends", produced by third parties, would be used with the then somewhat complex DOS-based version of PGP. Often such front ends had poor security features and passwords and passphrases entered through them could be found, for example, in the swap file or in unallocated space. Regrettably for the forensic analyst that has now all changed, and modern Windows-based versions of PGP do not make these kinds of fundamental security mistakes. Without knowledge of the passphrase, a well-managed PGP system has become effectively impossible to access, and the best hope is that the user has done something foolish that compromises his password or his system.

Hiding Folders and Encrypting Files

There is now a wide variety of user-friendly programs which users might employ to make access by others to their files more difficult. Some allow individual files or complete folders of files to be hidden on the hard disk, whilst others encrypt files and folders. The first of these is exemplified by Magic Folders[13], a program which makes selected folders on the hard disk and all the files within those folders invisible to all applications. Folders and files cannot be deleted, viewed, modified or executed, and to all intents and purposes they do not exist. Through the use of a password, however, normal and complete access can be restored. From a forensic computing viewpoint, however, there should be no real problem with accessing the hidden files or folders. The file data remains on the hard disk in its original form; only the operating system (and thus all applications that use the operating system for file access) are convinced that the files do not exist. Programs that access the disk directly and, in particular, disk editing tools will readily find the hidden files.

---

13 See PC-Magic Software at http://www.pc-magic.com/.

Presumably, for this reason, the same company produces an enhanced product called Encrypted Magic Folders, which, in addition to the hiding of files and folders, also encrypts and decrypts the files as they are accessed. This means that the files always remain on the hard disk in an encrypted form. This is quite different from other systems whereby a file is either all completely in an encrypted form or all completely in a plain text form. PC-Magic have developed their own encryption algorithms which operate at the byte level and ensure that only the sequence of bytes that has currently been requested by the access is decrypted and passed to the file system. Since these are not published algorithms it is not known how difficult or otherwise it may be to break this encryption. However, attempting to obtain the password is still probably the most effective policy.

An alternative approach is exemplified by programs such as Cryptext, which, although now dated, can still be found for free download[14] from the Internet. This uses a strong cryptographic algorithm, RC4[15] to encrypt a specified file and overwrite the plain text version on the hard disk. Again, a password is used to control access to the process and a hashed version of this password is stored with the file, using the SHA-1[16] algorithm. Decryption occurs when the correct password is given and the encrypted version is then converted to plain text and this plain text is used to overwrite the encrypted version on the hard disk. These facilities are made readily accessible to the user by means of a right mouse button click on a file that displays a menu providing "encrypt" and "decrypt" options. Again, the most effective policy is probably to attempt to obtain the password. However, where plain text is overwritten by ciphertext, the work of Peter Gutmann (1996) may be of interest. In his paper he describes how it may be possible to access information from a hard disk after it has been overwritten with new information. This would be of particular value where a plain text version of a file is overwritten by the encrypted version.

Hard Disk Encryption on the Fly

The final technique that we will mention here concerns encrypting a hard disk or a hard disk partition "on the fly". This technique works by producing an encrypted container file which, using special software drivers, can then be mounted to appear to the operating system as a virtual drive with its own drive letter. The drive is made accessible by means of a password and then all accesses typically pass through the driver, which encrypts on writing to the disk and decrypts on reading from it. That is, plain text is converted to cipher text on being written to the disk and cipher text is converted to plain text on being read from the disk. This is precisely what PGPdisk does. In the case of the BestCrypt[17] product this driver uses the Rijndael encryption

---

14 See, for example, http://www.fusionsource.com/downloads/encrypt.html.

15 "RC" apparently refers to "Ron's Code" or "Rivest Cipher", after the designer Ron Rivest. For details, see Schneier (1996), pp. 318 and 397.

16 Secure Hash Algorithm. For details, see Schneier (1996), pp. 442–5.

17 See Jetico, Inc. at http://www.jetico.com/.

algorithm[18], which has been selected by NIST as an *Advanced Encryption Standard* (*AES*), and E4M (Encryption for the Masses) is a similar *On The Fly Encryption* (*OTFE*) product, as is Scramdisk, which apparently consumed it[19].

Since the first edition this area has become ever more difficult, and our concerns are that it will get even worse in the future. Windows Vista[20], the latest generation of operating system from Microsoft, just released in January 2007, has built-in OTFE which could ensure that the entire disk remains encrypted with a strong encryption algorithm at all times. The word currently about is that this feature will be turned off by default for non-corporate versions but that it would not be difficult for any user to turn it on. However, we may hope that some users will perceive the risk to their valuable data as too great. Forgetting a password, a minor failure of the hard disk, a sudden power outage; these could all possibly result in users never seeing their data again. Before OTFE, one could hope for some data recovery from hard disk failures; with OTFE it would seem to be a near impossible task.

A Final Word

The technology in this field is still advancing at an unprecedented rate and we can see clearly that the task of the forensic computing analyst is going to become ever more challenging. We believe that a good grasp of the theoretical and practical principles along the lines that we have presented in this book is an essential prerequisite for the professional analyst. However, we also believe that what we have talked about here is only the beginning, and that there is much, much more to do. We hope that our readers will find, as we most certainly do, that they have entered one of the most stimulating, exciting and rewarding disciplines that there is today. We look forward to working with you in tackling some of those very difficult problems that the discipline is about to face.

References

Birch, P. (2006) *An Investigation of the Novell Netware Storage Services (NSS) 6 File Storage System, with a View to Establishing A Method of Forensically Capturing Data From Netware 6 NSS Volumes*, MSc Thesis, Cranfield University.

Garfinkel, S. (1995) *PGP – Pretty Good Privacy*, O'Reilly & Associates Inc., San Francisco.

Gutmann, P. (1996) Secure deletion of data from magnetic and solid-state memory, *Sixth USENIX Security Symposium Proceedings*, San Jose, CA, 22–25 July. See also http://www.cs.auckland.ac.nz/~pgut001/pubs/secure_del.html.

---

18 See http://www.iaik.tu-graz.ac.at/research/krypto/AES/old/%7Erijmen/rijndael/ and http://www.iaik.tu-graz.ac.at/research/krypto/AES/.

19 See http://www.samsimpson.com/cryptography/scramdisk/.

20 See http://www.microsoft.com/windows/products/windowsvista/default.mspx.

Oechslin, P. (2005) *Password Cracking: Rainbow Tables Explained*, The International Information Systems Security Certification Consortium, Mar–Apr 2005 Newsletter. URL: https://www.isc2.org/cgi-bin/content.cgi?page=738.

Schneier, B. (1996) *Applied Cryptography, Protocols, Algorithms and Source Code in C*, John Wiley & Sons, New York.

Bibliography

ACPO (2003) *Good Practice Guide for Computer Based Electronic Evidence V3*, Association of Chief Police Officers (ACPO), National Hi-Tech Crime Unit (NHTCU).

Adams, C. K. (1981) *Master Handbook of Microprocessor Chips*, Tab Books Inc, Pennsylvania.

Aikenhead, M. (1995) Legal knowledge based systems: some observations for the future, *Web Journal of Current Legal Issues*, [1995] 2 Web JCLI, 19 May. URL: http://webjcli.ncl.ac.uk/articles2/aiken2.html.

Akdeniz, Y. (1996) Section 3 of the Computer Misuse Act 1990: an antidote for computer viruses!, *Web Journal of Current Legal Issues*, [1996] 3 Web JCLI, 24 May. URL: http://webjcli.ncl.ac.uk/1996/issue3/akdeniz3.html.

Akdeniz, Y. (1997) UK government policy on encryption, *Web Journal of Current Legal Issues*, [1997] 1 Web JCLI, 28 February. URL: http://webjcli.ncl.ac.uk/1997/issue1/akdeniz1.html.

Anderson, M. R. (1996) Erased files often aren't, *Government Technology Magazine*, November. URL: http://www.govtech.net/magazine/story.php?id=95238. No longer available.

ANSI (1996) *ANSI X3.279-1996 – AT Attachment Interface with Extensions (ATA-2)*, ANSI, 11 West 42nd Street, New York, URL: http://alpha1.dyns.net/files/Drive/d0948r4c.pdf.

Apple Computer Inc. (1999) *More About IEEE 1394 and FireWire*. URL: http://developer.apple.com/hardware/FireWire/More_about_Firewire.htm. No longer available.

Apple Computer Inc. (2006) *Device Drivers FireWire*. URL: http://developer.apple.com/hardwaredrivers/fireWire/Index.html.

ASUS (2005) *ASUS Motherboard A8N32-SLI*, E2280, Second Edition V2, October 2005, ASUSTeK Computer Inc.

Atzberger, P. and Zolli, A. (1996) Portable Network Graphics, *Trincoll Journal*. URL: http://www.webtechniques.com/archives/1996/12/zolli/.

Avanstar Inc. (undated) *QuickView Plus from Stellent Corporation*, republished under licence by Avantstar, Inc., Corporate Headquarters, 18986 Lake Drive East, Chanhassen, MN 55317, USA. URL: http://www.avantstar.com/.

Barrett, N. (1997) *Digital Crime – Policing the Cybernation*, Kogan Page, London.

Binary Research (1997) Ghost URL: http://www.ghostsoft.com/.

Birch, P. (2006) *An Investigation of the Novell Netware Storage Services (NSS) 6 File Storage System, with a View to Establishing A Method of Forensically Capturing Data From Netware 6 NSS Volumes*, MSc Thesis, Cranfield University.

Blackstock, S. (undated) *LZW and GIF explained*. URL: http://www.cis.udel.edu/~amer/CISC651/lzw.and.gif.explained.html.

Borland (1994) *Borland C++ User's Guide, Version 4.5*, Borland International, Inc., 100 Borland Way, PO Box 660001, Scotts Valley, CA 95067-0001.

Born, G. (1997) *The File Formats Handbook*. International Thompson Publishing, London.

Bowker, A. L. and Drinkard, L. N. (1996) Downloading: using computer software as an investigative tool, *Law Enforcement Bulletin*, Federal Bureau of Investigation, June. URL: http://www.fbi.gov/publications/leb/1996/june961.txt.

Brouwer, A. E. (2004) *Partition Types: List of Partition Identifiers for PCs*. URL: http://www.win.tue.nl/~aeb/linux/partitions/partition_types-1.html.

Brown, C. L. T. (2004) *Exchangeable Image file Format (ExIF)*, Technical White Paper, Technology Pathways LLC, 12 October. URL: http://www.TechPathways.com/uploads/Exif.pdf.

Brown, S. (1998) *Hard Disk Partitioning, Why and How (for MS-DOS/Windows PCs)*, 18 November. URL: http://members.tripod.com/~diligent/hd-partn.htm.

Chandler, D. (1994) *Semiotics for Beginners*, University of Wales, Aberystwyth. URL: http://www.aber.ac.uk/media/Documents/S4B/semiotic.html.

Choo, A. L.-T. and Mellors, M. (1995) Undercover police operations and what the suspect said (or didn't say), *Web Journal of Current Legal Issues*, [1995] 2 Web JCLI, 19 May, URL: http://webjcli.ncl.ac.uk/articles2/choo2.html.

Clarke, A. R. M. and Powys-Lybbe, D. (1986) *The Amstrad CP/M Plus*, MML Systems Ltd, London.

Clede, B. (1993) Investigating computer crime is every department's concern, *Law and Order*, July, URL: http://ourworld.Compuserve.com/homepages/BillC/compcrim.htm. No longer available.

Collins, R. (2003) *Dr Dobbs Microprocessor Resources, Protected Mode Basics*, Copyright © 2003 *Dr. Dobb's Journal*. URL: http://www.x86.org/articles/pmbasics/.

CompactFlash Association (1999), *CF+ and CompactFlash Specification Revision 1.4*, 7/99, CompactFlash Association, P.O. Box 51537, Palo Alto, CA. URL: http://www.compactflash.org/.

CompactFlash Association (2004), *CF+ and CompactFlash Specification Revision 3.0*, 12/23/04, CompactFlash Association, P.O. Box 51537, Palo Alto, CA. URL: http://www.compactflash.org/.

Computers & Law (1996) Discovery of computer data, *Computers & Law*, Spring. URL: http://wings.buffalo.edu/law/Complaw/CompLawPapers/printup.htm. No longer available.

Corel (1997) *WordPerfect Document File Format*, Corel WordPerfect Suite 8 Software Development Kit, in Corel/SDKs/Suite8/DOCS/B_1DOCIN.HTM.

Committee of Ministers (1995) *Concerning Problems of Criminal Procedure Law Connected with Information Technology*, Recommendation No. R (95) 13 of the Committee of Ministers to Member States, Council of Europe, 11 September. URL: http://www.privacy.org/pi/intl_orgs/coe/info_tech_1995.html.

Compaq (1997a) *Power-on Self-Test (POST)*, 17 March. URL: http://172.18.229.243/support/techzone/solutions/post.html. No longer available.

Compaq (1997b) *Power-on Self-Test Messages*, 17 March. URL: http://www.cnunix.com/ftp/Compaq/post_msgs.htm.

Cramer, J. (1997) Legal research on the Internet, *Computers & Law*, 28 April. URL: http://wings.buffalo.edu/Complaw/CompLawPapers/cramer.htm. No longer available.

Darwin, I. F. (1992) *file(0) synopsis*. URL: http://unixhelp.ed.ac.uk/CGI/man-cgi?file.

Davis, M. (1999) *Forms of Unicode*, President of the Unicode Consortium, IBM, 1 September. Downloaded from: http://icu.sourceforge.net/docs/papers/forms_of_unicode/.

Dees, T. M. (1994) Dealing with computer evidence, Originally published in *Law Enforcement Technology*, **21**(8), 48. URL: http://www.rrinvestigations.com/articles/computer-evidence.htm. No longer available online.

Department of Justice (1994) *Federal Guidelines for Searching and Seizing Computers*, US Department of Justice, Criminal Division, Office of Professional Development and Training, July. URL: http://www.epic.org/security/computer_search_guidelines.txt.

Deutsch, P. (1996) *RFC 1952, GZIP file format specification version 4.3*, Network Working Group, May.

Deyring, K.-P. (ed.) (2003) *Serial ATA: High Speed Serialized AT Attachment, Revision 1.0a*, 7 January.

Digital Research Inc. (1987) *Operator's and Programmer's Guide for the Amstrad CPC6128 and PCW8256*, William Heinemann Ltd, London.

Dockery, M. (1995) *Digital Discovery and Recovery: a New Kind of Evidence Gathering*, Dockery Associates, Indianapolis. URL: http://www.pimall.com/nais/n.digit.discer.html.

Downing, R. (1995) *Magill* and the Software Directive: are they interoperable?, *Web Journal of Current Legal Issues*, [1995] 4 Web JCLI, 28 September 1995, URL: `http://webjcli.ncl.ac.uk/articles4/downing4.html`.

Duncan, R. (1988) *Advanced MS-DOS Programming*, Microsoft Press, Redmond, WA.

Elonex (1995) *Elonex MT-500/I System Board Configuration Guide*, August, Elonex plc, 2 Apsley Way, London NW2 7LF.

Elonex (1997) *MS-5156 User's Manual, Rev 1.21*, September.

EMS (1987), *LOTUS(R)/INTEL(R)/MICROSOFT(R), EXPANDED MEMORY SPECIFICATION [1]*, Version 4.0, 300275-005, October. Copyright © 1987, Lotus Development Corporation, Intel Corporation, Microsoft Corporation.

EPIC (1994) EPIC analysis of new Justice department guidelines on searching and seizing computers, *Criminal Law Reporter*, **56**(12) (21 December). URL: `http://cpsr.org/prevsite/cpsr/privacy/epic/guidelines_analysis.txt`.

Falbo, F. R. (1997) *The Ref – Hardware Specs at Your Fingertips*, 1 September. URL: `http://www.boutell.com/lsm/lsmbyid.cgi/001627`.

Feldman, M. (ed.) (undated) *Graphics File Formats*, URL: `http://www.sjhf.net/Article/fileformat/graphics/200608/180.html`.

Finch, S. G. (ed.) (1995) *Information Technology – AT Attachment Interface with Extensions (ATA-2)*, Working Draft, Proposed American National Standard, X3T10 948D, Revision 3, 17 January. URL: `http://alpha1.dyns.net/files/Drive/d0948r4c.pdf`.

Free Software Foundation (2006) *Why There Are No GIF files on GNU Web Pages*, 28 February. `http://www.gnu.org/philosophy/gif.html`.

Freer, J. (1987) *Systems Design with Advanced Microprocessors*, Pitman, Computer Systems Series, London.

Garfinkel, S. (1995) *PGP – Pretty Good Privacy*, O'Reilly & Associates Inc., San Francisco.

Gilbert, H. (1996) *Surviving the Next Operating System*. URL: `http://pclt.cis.yale.edu/pclt/OPSYS/Default.htm`.

Grand, J. (2002) *Memory Imaging and Forensic Analysis of Palm OS Devices*, @stake, Inc., 196 Broadway, Cambridge, MA.

Gutmann, P. (1996) Secure deletion of data from magnetic and solid-state memory, *Sixth USENIX Security Symposium Proceedings*, San Jose, CA, 22–25 July. See also `http://www.cs.auckland.ac.nz/~pgut001/pubs/secure_del.html`.

Hamilton, E. (1992) *JPEG File Interchange Fomat Version 1.02*, C-Cube Microsystems, 1778 McCarthy Boulevard, Milpitas, CA.

Hinckley, K. (1995) *The GIF Format as Intellectual Property*. URL: `http://www.utopia.com/`. No longer available.

HMSO (1989) *The Electricity at Work Regulations 1989*, Statutory Instrument 1989 635, HMSO, London.

Hoey, A. (1996) Analysis of The Police and Criminal Evidence Act, s.69 – Computer Generated Evidence, *Web Journal of Current Legal Issues*, [1996] 1 Web JCLI, 25 January. URL: `http://webjcli.ncl.ac.uk/1996/issue1/hoey1.html`.

Hoffman, G. (1995) *Computer Crime – Legal Enforcement in the Age of the Internet*. URL: `http://www.privnet.com/~hoffmang/jomc191/paper.html`. No longer available.

HSE Books (1998) *Memorandum of Guidance on the Electricity at Work Regulations 1989*, HSR 25, HMSO, London.

IBM (undated) *Understanding EDO (Hyper Page Mode)*, IBM Applications Note, International Business Machines Corp. URL: `http://www.chips.ibm.com/`. No longer available.

IBM (1995) *No-ID Sector Format*, Dr Steven R Hetzler, IBM Research Division, Almaden Research Center, San Jose, CA. URL: Now Hitachi – see `http://www.hitachigst.com/hdd/ipl/oem/tech/noid.htm`.

IBM (1996a) Synchronous DRAMs: the DRAM of the future, *IBM MicroNews*, First Quarter, 4–6.

IBM (1996b) *Understanding DRAM Operation*, IBM Applications Note, 12/96, International Business Machines Corp. URL: `http://www.cs.albany.edu/~sdc/CSI404/dramop.pdf`.

IBM (1996c) *Understanding VRAM and SGRAM Operation,* IBM Applications Note, 12/96, International Business Machines Corp. URL: http://www.ee.surrey.ac.uk/Personal/R.Webb/l3a15/extras/vrmsgrm.pdf.

IBM (1997) *Understanding Static RAM Operation,* IBM Applications Note, 03/97, International Business Machines Corp. URL: http://www.ee.surrey.ac.uk/Personal/R.Webb/l3a15/extras/sramop.pdf.

IBM (1998a) *Getting beyond the ATA 8.4 GB limit,* Dr Steven R Hetzler, IBM Storage Systems Division, 5600 Cottle Road, San Jose, CA. URL: http://www.storage.ibm.com/hardsoft/diskdrdl/library/8.4gb.htm. No longer available.

IBM (1998b) *IBM Deskstar 25GP and Deskstar 22GXP Hard Disk Drives,* IBM Storage Systems Division, 5600 Cottle Road, San Jose, CA. Now Hitachi – see http://www.hitachigst.com/tech/techlib.nsf/techdocs/85256AB8006A31E587256A79006E5943/$file/djna_ds.pdf.

IBM (1999) *Disk Manager (version 9.47),* 25 March. IBM Storage Systems Division, 5600 Cottle Road, San Jose, CA. Now Hitachi – see http://www.hitachigst.com/hdd/support/download.htm #Diskmanager.

IEE (undated) *City & Guilds Portable Appliance Testing Course.* URL: http://www.iee.org/events/courses/short/cg2_gen.cfm.

IEE (1994) *The IEE Code of Practice for In-Service Inspection and Testing of Electrical Equipment,* IEE, London.

Intel (1979) *The 8086 Family User's Manual,* October, Intel Corporation.

Intel (1997) *Intel Architecture Software Developer's Manual,* Volume 2: Instruction Set Reference, Order Number 243191. URL: http://www.intel.com/.

Intel (1998a) *SE440BX Motherboard Technical Product Specification,* March, Intel Corporation, PO Box 5937, Denver, CO.

Intel (1998b) *SE440BX Motherboard Technical Product Guide,* February, Intel Corporation, PO Box 5937, Denver, CO.

ISO (undated) ISO DIS 10918-1.

Jenkinson, B. L. (2005) The structure and operation of the master file table within a Windows 2000 NTFS environment, *MSc Thesis,* Cranfield University.

Kahn, J. R. (1989) *Implications of Computer Technology and Use for the Law of Evidence.* URL (now only available in French): http://www.masse.org/cic97bar.htm.

Kegel, D. (1997) *Dan Kegel's Fast Hard Drives Page,* 19 April, URL: http://www.kegel.com/drives/.

Khambata, A. J. (1982) *Microprocessors/Microcomputers Architecture, Software, and Systems,* John Wiley & Sons, Chichester.

Kingpin and Mudge (2001), *Security Analysis of the Palm Operating System and its Weaknesses Against Malicious Code Threats,* 10th USENIX Security Symposium, Washington DC, August. URL: http://www.usenix.org/publications/library/proceedings/sec01/kingpin.html.

Kozierok, C. M. (2001) *The PC Guide,* Site Version: 2.2.0 – Version Date: 17 April. URL: http://www.PCGuide.com/.

Kuhn, M. (2005) *UTF-8 and Unicode FAQ,* 02/02/2005, http://www.cl.cam.ac.uk/~mgk25/unicode.html.

Lambert, M. (1995), Circular extended partitions: round and round with DOS, *Virus Bulletin,* September, p. 14. Mike Lambert, Virus Bulletin Ltd, The Quadrant, Abingdon, Oxfordshire, OX14 3YS.

Lambert, M. and Moore, C. (1992) *Circular Extended Partitions: A DOS Vulnerability or When the Magic Floppy Won't Boot,* Mike Lambert, Before Disaster Strikes, 1153 Dublin Place, Herndon, VA 22070, and Charles Moore, Automation Mentors, Inc., 12220 Wye Oak Commons, Burke, VA 22015.

Lamers, L. J. (ed.) (1994), *Information Technology – AT Attachment Interface for Disk Drives,* Working Draft, Proposed American National Standard, X3T10 719D, Revision 4c.

Landis, H. (1995a) *ATA/ATA-1/ATA-2/IDE/EIDE/etc FAQ Part 1 of ? – The Basics,* Version 0b, 7 February. URL: http://www.ata-atapi.com/hiwfaq.htm.

Landis, H. (1995b) *How It Works – BIOS Types, CHS Translation, LBA and Other Good Stuff*, Version 4a. URL: http://www.ata-atapi.com/hiwchs.htm.

Landis, H. (1995c) *How It Works – DOS Floppy Disk Boot Sector, Version 1a*. URL: http://www.ata-atapi.com/hiwdos.htm.

Landis, H. (1995d), *How It Works – OS2 Boot Sector*, Version 1a. URL: http://www.ata-atapi.com/hiwfos2.htm.

Landis, H. (1997), *How It Works – Master Boot Record*, Version 1b. hiw@sugs.talisman.com.

Landis, H. (1998a) *ATA News*, February. hiw@sugs.talisman.com.

Landis, H. (1998b) *Facts and Fiction (FnF)*, February. hiw@sugs.talisman.com.

Landis, H. (1998c) *How it Works – Partition Tables*, Version 1e and Version 1h. hiw@sugs.talisman.com.

Landis, H. (1999a) *ATADRVR ATA/ATAPI Low-level Driver, User's Guide, Version 13H*, atadrvr@sugs.talisman.com.

Landis, H. (1999b) *Using DMA with ATA or ATAPI*. atadrvr@sugs.talisman.com.

Landis, H. (1999c) *Using PIO with ATA or ATAPI*. atadrvr@sugs.talisman.com.

Landis, H. (2001) *How It Works: CHS Translation*. http://www.ata-atapi.com/.

Landis, H. (2005) *Information, Test Software and Consulting Services for Developers of Products using ATA (PATA, IDE/EIDE), Serial ATA (SATA), ATAPI, and CE-ATA and Other ATA Related Interfaces*, 27 October. URL: http://www.ata-atapi.com/.

Lash, A. (1995) Time to call in the cybertroops, *Open Computing*, July, URL: http://www.wcmh.com/oc/features/previous/9507insb.html#cybertroops. No longer available.

Leach, P. J. (1998) *UUIDs and GUIDs*, Internet Draft, Network Working Group, Microsoft, Rich Salz, Certco, 4 February. URL: http://www.opengroup.org/dce/info/draft-leach-uuids-guids-01.txt.

Leach, P., Mealling, M. and Salz, R. (2004) *A UUID URN Namespace*, Internet Draft, Network Working Group, December. URL: http://tools.ietf.org/id/draft-mealling-uuid-urn-05.txt.

Liebenau, J. and Backhouse, J. (1990), *Understanding Information An Introduction*, Macmillan Press, London.

Lim, W. and Valentino, R. (1996) *comp.sys.ibm.pc.hardware, Frequently Asked Questions (Draft)*, 30-8-96. URL: http://www.faqs.org/faqs/pc-hardware-faq/.

Lord, D. (1991) *Gander for Windows*. URL: http://www.medical-papers.com/download/GANDER.EXE/.

Majors, N. (1996) *Technicians' Guide to PC Hard Disk Subsystems*, Data Recovery Labs, 26 February. URL: http://www.programmersheaven.com/download/1471/download.aspx.

Mares, D. (2006) *Computer Forensics and Data Analysis*, Mares and Company, LLC, PO Box 464429, Lawrenceville, GA. URL: http://www.dmares.com/.

Maxtor (1996) *Maxtor's CrystalMax 1080 Model Number 84320A8*, Rev A 3/18/96. URL: http://www.mysimon.com/Hard-Drives/9025-11620_8-20142861.html.

Maxtor (2001) *Big Drives: Breaking the 137 Gigabyte Barrier*, Maxtor Corporation. URL: http://www.maxtor.com/products/bigdrive/whitepaper.htm. No longer available.

Maxtor (2003) *DiamondMax Plus 9 Specification*, Maxtor Corporation, 500 McCarthy Boulevard, Milpitas, CA. DS-DiamondMaxPlus9-5/03-CL.

McCarvel, R. T. (1996) *Taking the Fourth Amendment to Bits: The Department of Justice Guidelines for Computer Searches and Seizures*, 17 October. URL: http://www.seanet.com/~rod/comp_4a.html.

McLean, P. T. (ed.) (1995) *Information technology – AT Attachment-3 Interface (ATA-3)*, Working Draft, X3T10 2008D, Revision 5, 6 October. URL: http://alpha1.dyns.net/files/Drive/ATA-3.pdf.

McLean, P. T. (ed.) (1999) *Information Technology – AT Attachment with Packet Interface – 5 (ATA/ATAPI-5)*, Working Draft, T13 1321D, Revision 1c, 31 August.

McLean, P. T. (ed.) (2001) *Information Technology - AT Attachment with Packet Interface – 6 (ATA/ATAPI-6)*, Working Draft, T13 1410D, Revision 1e, 26 June.

Mellanox (2002) *Understanding PCI Bus, PCI-Express and InfiniBand Architecture*, White Paper, Rev 1-20, Mellanox Technologies Inc., 2900 Stender Way, Santa Clara, CA. URL: http://www.mellanox.com/.

Messmer, H.-P. (2002) *The Indispensable PC Hardware Book*, 4th edn, Addison-Wesley, Reading, MA.

Microchip (1997) *24LC01B/02B Modules, Document DS21222A*, 8/97, Microchip Technology Incorporated, 2355 West Chandler Boulevard, Chandler, AZ. URL: http://www.microchip.com/.

Micro Firmware (1998a) *Issues with Hard Drives over 4GB*, Micro Firmware Tech Support, 330 W Gray Street, Norman, Oklahoma. URL: http://www.allensmith.net/Storage/firmware/over4gb.htm.

Micro Firmware (1998b) *Notes on Installing Hard Drives Larger Than 2 Gigabytes*, Micro Firmware Tech Support, 330 W Gray Street, Norman, Oklahoma. URL: http://www.allensmith.net/Storage/firmware/over2gb.htm.

Micro Firmware (1998c) *Problems with New Partition Types Used by WIN95 FDISK*, Micro Firmware Tech Support, 330 W Gray Street, Norman, Oklahoma. URL: http://web.archive.org/web/20040215073614/www.firmware.com/support/bios/w95partn.htm.

Micro Firmware (1998d) *Some Technical Info on Hard Drives*, Micro Firmware Tech Support, Micro Firmware Tech Support, 330 W Gray Street, Norman, Oklahoma. URL: http://web.archive.org/web/20031206050206/www.firmware.com/support/bios/hdtech.htm.

Micron (1999a) *Boot Block Flash Memory, TN-28-01, FT01.p65 – Rev. 2/99*, Micron Technology Inc., 8000 S. Federal Way, PO Box 6, Boise, ID. URL: http://www.micron.com/.

Micron (1999b) *CompactFlash, FC02.p65 – Rev. 2/99*, Micron Technology Inc, 8000 S. Federal Way, PO Box 6, Boise, ID 83707-0006. URL: http://www.allensmith.net/Storage/HDDlimit/FAT16.htm.

Microsoft Corporation (1999a) *Description of FAT32 File System*, Article ID: Q154997, 8 August. URL: http://support.microsoft.com/support/kb/Q154997.

Microsoft Corporation (1999b) *Problems Accessing FAT16 Drives Larger Than 2 GB*, Article ID: Q127851, 15 January. URL: http://support.microsoft.com/support/kb/articles/Q127/8/51.asp.

Microsoft Corporation (2000) *Microsoft Extensible Firmware Initiative FAT32 File System Specification*, FAT: General Overview of On-Disk Format, Version 1.03, Hardware White Paper, 6 December. Microsoft Corporation.

Microsoft Corporation (2003) *Serial ATA in the Microsoft Operating System Environment*, Microsoft Corporation, 18 July. URL: http://www.microsoft.com/whdc/device/storage/serialATA_FAQ.mspx.

Microsoft Corporation (2004) *Compound File Binary File Format*. Issued under licence to the Advanced Authoring Format (AAF) Association and currently available as Low-Level Container Specification v1.0.1 at http://www.aafassociation.org/html/specs/aafcontainerspec-v1.0.1.pdf.

MicroSystems (undated) *POST CODE MASTER Version 1.40*, MicroSystems Development, Inc. 4100 Moorpark Ave. Suite #104, San Jose, CA 95117.

Moher, R. K. (1996) Computer crime: tips on securing and recovering electronic data, *New York Law Journal*, 17 December. URL: http://www.ljextra.com/securitynet/articles/121796s2.html. No longer available.

Mosteller, T. (1995) *CMOSRAM2.EXE*. Tellerware, 1872 Rampart Lane, Lansdale, PA 19446-5051.

Mueller, S. (1998) *Upgrading and Repairing PCs*, 8th edn, Macmillan Computer Publishing, New York.

Murray, J. D. and vanRyper, W. (1996) *Encyclopedia of Graphics File Formats*, O'Reilly & Associates, Sebastopol, CA.

National Committee on Information Technology Standards (NCITS) (1998) *Technical Committee T13 AT Attachment*. URL: http://www.ncits.org/.

National Computer Security Center (undated) *A Guide to Understanding Data Remanence in Automated Information Systems*, National Computer Security Center, NCSC-TG-025, Library No. 5-236,082, Version-2. URL: http://crypto-systems.com/datarem.html.

Norton, P. (1988a) *The Norton Disk Companion*, Peter Norton Computing Inc.

Norton, P. (1988b) *The Norton Trouble Shooting Guide for Disks*, Peter Norton Computing Inc.

Norton, P. and Goodman, J. (1997) *Peter Norton's Inside the PC*, 7th edn, SAMS Publishing, Indianapolis.

Oechslin, P. (2005) *Password Cracking: Rainbow Tables Explained*, The International Information Systems Security Certification Consortium, Mar–Apr 2005 Newsletter. URL: https://www.isc2.org/cgi-bin/content.cgi?page=738.

Ogren, J. (undated) *ST506/412 Connector*, URL: http://www.cc86.org/~pjf/hwb/co_ST506.html.

Patterson, D. A., Gibson, G. A. and Katz, R. H. (1988) A case for redundant arrays of inexpensive disks (RAID). *SIGMOD Conference*, pp. 109–116.

Peacock, C. (2005) *USB in a Nutshell, Making Sense of the USB Standard*, 15 June. URL: http://www.beyondlogic.org/usbnutshell/usb1.htm.

Phoenix (1995) *BIOS Enhanced Disk Drive Specification Version 1.1*, 9 May. Phoenix Technologies Ltd, 2575 McCabe Way, Irvine, CA. URL: http://www.phoenix.com/.

Phoenix (1998) *BIOS Enhanced Disk Drive Specification, Version 3.0*, 12 March. Phoenix Technologies Ltd, 2575 McCabe Way, Irvine, CA. URL: http://www.phoenix.com/.

PKWARE Inc. (2006) *APPNOTE.TXT - .ZIP File Format Specification*, Version: 6.3.0, Revised: 29 September. URL: http://www.pkware.com/documents/casestudies/APPNOTE.TXT

Pollitt, M. M. (undated a) *A Five-Step Approach to Forensic Examinations*, Federal Bureau of Investigation, Baltimore, MD.

Pollitt, M. M. (undated b) *Computer Forensics: An Approach to Evidence in Cyberspace*, Federal Bureau of Investigation, Baltimore, MD.

Pollitt, M. M. (1995a) Forensic use of a peer to peer network, *Second International Conference on Computer Evidence*, Baltimore, MD, 10–15 April.

Pollitt, M. M. (1995b) Principles, practices, and procedures: an approach to standards in computer forensics, *Second International Conference on Computer Evidence*, Baltimore, Maryland, 10–15 April 1995. Federal Bureau of Investigation, Baltimore, MD.

Postuma, P. (1995) *BIOS Reporter, version 1.1*. ppostuma@nbnet.nb.ca, 16 Fullyer Drive, Quispamsis, NB, Canada E2G 1Y7.

PowerQuest (1996) *PartitionMagic 3.0 User Guide*, PowerQuest Corporation, 1083 N State Street, Orem, UT. Now Symantec – see http://www. symantec.com/techsupp/home_homeoffice/products/pmagic/pmagic_8/manuals.html.

PowerQuest (1997) *Primary, Extended, Logical, Free Space! What Do I Need!*, PowerQuest Corporation, 1083 N State Street, Orem, UT. URL: http://support.powerquest.com/logical.htm. No longer available.

PowerQuest (1998) *BootMagic User Guide*, PowerQuest Corporation, PO Box 1911, Orem, UT. URL: http://www.powerquest.com/.

Pratt, T. (2003) *Serial ATA Interface on Client Systems*, Dell White Paper, June. http://www.dell.com/r&d/.

Psion (1992) *'C' Software Development Kit*, Volume II, PLIB Reference, 10 June. Psion PLC.

Quantum (1996) *Quantum Fireball™ 1.0/1.2/1.7/2.1/2.5/3.2/3.8 GB AT Product Manual*, Chapter 5, Table 5.1, Quantum Corporation, October. URL: http://www.quantum.com/.

Quantum (1997a) *An Immediate Solution to Breaking the 528 MB DOS Barrier*. Quantum Corporation. URL: http://www.karmaint.com.tr/qntm_528mb1.html. No longer available.

Quantum (1997b) *Ultra AT – A Quantum White Paper*, Quantum Corporation. URL: http://www.quantum.com/.

Quantum (1999) *Breaking the 2.1 Gigabyte Barrier*. Quantum Corporation, URL: http://www.quantum.com/.

Quinlan, D. (1996) *magic-numbers: file(1) specification*. URL: http://www.catb.org/~esr/magic-numbers/mail-archive/0016.html.

Raymond, E. S. (1996) *rfc-draft*. URL: http://www.catb.org/~esr/magic-numbers/rfc-draft.

Raymond, E. S. (1997) *The Magic Numbers Group Home Page*. URL: http://www.catb.org/~esr/magic-numbers/.

Risley, D. (1997) *PC Mechanic, Hard Drives*. URL: http://pcmech.pair.com/hdindex.htm.

Rodrigue, J.-P. (undated) *What is BIOS? (Mini FAQ)*. URL: http://www.sysopt.com/tutorials/article.php/3552511.

Rodrigue, J.-P. and Croucher, P. (1997) *The BIOS Survival Guide*. URL: http://www.cacs.louisiana.edu/~mgr/404/burks/pcinfo/hardware/bios_sg/bios_sg.htm.

Rosch, W. L. (2002) *Hardware Bible*, Electronic Edition, 12 December. URL: http://safari.quepublishing.com/0789728591/pref01.

Rosenblatt, K. S. (1996) How to investigate computer intrusion: a checklist, *Government Technology*, October. URL: http://www.infosyssec.org/infosyssec/cheklist.htm.

R v Aslett (2002), IN THE CROWN COURT AT MANCHESTER, T2001/0383, Wednesday 25th September, 2002, BEFORE: HIS HONOUR JUDGE GEAKE, *REGINA -v- JONATHAN ASLETT*, Transcript of the Official Palantype Note of Cater Walsh & Co., Suite, 410, Crown House, Kidderminster, DY10 2DH.

Schneier, B. (1996) *Applied Cryptography, Protocols, Algorithms and Source Code in C*, John Wiley & Sons, New York.

Schwartz, M. (1997a) *Elser Word convertress*. URL: http://user.cs.tu-berlin.de/~schwartz/pmh/elser/elser.html.

Schwartz, M. (1997b) *LAOLA file system*. URL: http://user.cs.tu-berlin.de/~schwartz/pmh/guide.html.

Seagate (1991a) *Specifications for ST-506*. URL: http://www.seagate.com/support/disc/specs/mfm/st412.html.

Seagate (1991b) *Specifications for ST-412*. URL: http://www.seagate.com/support/disc/specs/mfm/st506.html.

Seagate (1994) *FIND-ATA.EXE v1.0, An ATA Interface Identify Drive Utility*, Seagate Technology Inc., B-5 Technical Support, 920 Disc Drive, Scotts Valley, CA. URL: http://www.infoatec.it/download/findat10.zip.

Seagate (1995a) *NFDisc v1.20, Partition Record Display and Maintenance*, Seagate Technology Inc. URL: http://www.seagate-asia.com/sgt/korea/discutil.jsp.

Seagate (1995b) *SGATFMT4.EXE v4.0, Seagate Format Drive Utility*. URL: http://www.infoatec.it/download/sgatfmt4.zip.

Seagate (1996) *FindSector v1.0, Sector Level Display and Maintenance*. URL: http://ptm2.cc.utu.fi/ftp/hd-cd-fd/tools/FINDSECT.TXT.

Seagate (1997a) *Cheetah 4.5- to 9.1-Gbyte capacity disc drives*. URL: http://www.seagate.com/. No longer available.

Seagate (1997b) *Low-level Formatting an ATA (IDE) Hard Drive*, Seagate Technology, Inc, B-5 Technical Support, 920 Disc Drive, Scotts Valley, CA. URL: http://www.seagate.com/ww/v/index.jsp?vgnextoid=95f0781e73d5d010VgnVCM100000dd0 4090aRCRD&locale=en-US.

Seagate (1997c) *Seagate Fast ATA/Fast ATA-2 Fact Sheet*, Seagate Technology, Corporate Communications. URL: http://www.seagate.com/support/kb/disc/fastfs.html.

Seagate (1998a) *DiscWizard*. URL: http://www.seagate.com/www/en-us/support/downloads/discwizard.

Seagate (1998b) *FAQ Disk Manager Basics, BIOS Limitations*, Seagate Technology. URL: http://www.seagate.com/support/kb/disc/bioslmt.html.

Seagate (1998c) *Ultra ATA Advanced ATA Sorage Interface*. URL: http://www.seagate.com/support/kb/disc/ultra_ata_faq.html.

Silverglate, H. A. and Viles, T. C. (1991) *Constitutional, Legal, and Ethical Considerations for Dealing with Electronic Files in the Age of Cyberspace*. Federal Enforcement Conference, Washington, DC, 16–17 May. URL: http://www.eff.org/pub/Global/USA/Legal/search_and_seizure.speech. No longer available.

Smith, R. E. (1997) *Internet Cryptography*, Addison-Wesley, Reading, MA.

Solutions by Design (1997) *Hard Disk Sub-Systems*, Solutions by Design (Australia) Pty Ltd, 22 August. URL: http://www.solbydes.com.au/sbd/hdtech1.htm. No longer available.

Sommer, P. (1995) *Forensic Computing CSRC Research Project*, URL: http://csrc.lse.ac.uk/csrc/forncomp.htm. No longer available.

Steunebrink, J. (1997) *The BIOS IDE Harddisk Limitations*. URL: http://www.inter.nl.net/hcc/J.Steunebrink/bioslim.htm

Stevens, C. E. (1995) *BIOS Enhanced Disk Drive Specification Version 1.1*, Phoenix Technologies Ltd, 9 May. URL: http://www.phoenix.com/NR/rdonlyres/19FEBD17-DB40-413C-A0B1-1F3F560E222F/0/specsedd30.pdf.

Stevens, C. E. (ed.) (2005) *Information Technology – AT Attachment – 8 ATA/ATAPI Command Set (ATA8-ACS)*, Working Draft, T13 Project 1699D, Revision 1e, 20 June.

Stevens, C. E. and Broyles, P. J. (1997) *ATAPI Removable Media Device BIOS Specification Version 1.0*, Compaq Computer Corporation and Phoenix Technologies Ltd, 30 January. URL: http://www.phoenix.com/NR/rdonlyres/EDD1AAA0-177E-4024-A0B1-E4BD06B673F7/0/specsatapi.pdf.

Stockton, J. R. (2005) *Date and Time Scales*. URL: http://www.merlyn.demon.co.uk/dayscale.htm.

Stone, R. (1995) Exclusion of evidence under Section 78 of the Police and Criminal Evidence Act: practice and principles, *Web Journal of Current Legal Issues*, [1995] 3 Web JCLI, 18 July. URL: http://webjcli.ncl.ac.uk/articles3/stone3.html.

Storage Networking Industry Association (2004) *Common RAID Disk Data Format Specification*, Revision 01.00.00, 14 December. http://www.snia.org/tech_activities/ddftwg.

Susskind, R. (1996) *The Future of Law: Facing the Challenges of Information Technology*, Oxford University Press, Oxford. Review article by: Charlesworth, A. (1997), *Web Journal of Current Legal Issues*, [1997] 3 Web JCLI, 30 June. URL: http://webjcli.ncl.ac.uk/1997/issue3/charles3.html.

Symantec (1995) *Norton Utilities for Windows 95 User's Guide*, Symantec Corporation, Peter Norton Group, 10201 Torre Avenue, Cupertino, CA.

Symantec (1999) *Norton Utilities Version 4, User's Guide, Norton Disk Editor*, Symantec Corporation, Peter Norton Group, 10201 Torre Avenue, Cupertino, CA.

Tauritz, D. R. (1995) *EIDE/MIO Mini FAQ v0.2*, 15 January. URL: http://margo.student.utwente.nl/el/pc/hd-info/minieide.zip.

Tischer, M. and Jennrich, B. (1996) *PC Intern, The Encyclopedia of System Programming*, Abacus, Data Becker Edition.

Townsend, S. and Hale, B. (1996) *Post Memory Manager Specification Version 1.0*, Phoenix Technologies Ltd and Intel Corporation, 20 September. URL: http://www.phoenix.com/NR/rdonlyres/873A00CF-33AC-4775-B77E-08E7B9754993/0/specspmm101.pdf.

UN (1994) *International Review of Criminal Policy – United Nations Manual on the Prevention and Control of Computer-related Crime*. URL: http://www.uncjin.org/Documents/EighthCongress.html.

Unisys (undated) *License Information on GIF and Other LZW-based Technologies*. URL: http://www.unisys.com/about__unisys/lzw.

USB (1998) *Universal Serial Bus Specification, Revision 1.1*, 23 September. Compaq Computer Corporation, Intel Corporation, Microsoft Corporation, NEC Corporation. URL: http://www.usbman.com/WebDrivers/usbpdffiles/USB%20Specification.pdf.

USB (2000) *Universal Serial Bus Specification Revision 2.0*, Compaq, Hewlett-Packard, Intel, Lucent, Microsoft, NEC, Philips, 27 April. URL: http://www.usb.org/developers/docs/usb_20_05122006.zip.

van Staten, E. (1997) *Harddrive Related Terms and Tricks*, 16 April. URL: http://www.computercraft.com/docs/evsterms.html.

Vidström, A. (2005) *Computer Forensics and the ATA Interface*, Technical Report FOI-R--1638--SE, February 2005, 1650-1942, Swedish Defence Research Agency, Command and Control Systems, Box 1165, SE-581 11 LINKÖPING, Sweden.

von Neumann, J. (1945), *First Draft of a Report on the EDVAC*, 30 June. Contract No W-670-ORD-492, Moore School of Electrical Engineering, University of Pennsylvania, Philadelphia.

Wehman, J. and Haan, P. (1998) *The Enhanced IDE/Fast-ATA/ATA-2 FAQ*, V1.92, 23/1/1998. URL: http://burks.brighton.ac.uk/burks/pcinfo/hardware/atafaq/atafq.htm.

Weitz, H. (1997) Trial practice in the computer age: use of computer-generated evidence, *Web Law Review*, Winter. URL: http://www.eaglelink.com/law-review/3w97.html.

Western Digital (undated a) *Enhanced IDE Implementation Guide, Version 5*. Western Digital Corporation, 8105 Irvine Center Drive, Irvine, CA. URL: http://www.wdc.com/.

Western Digital (undated b) *User's Guide WD1003V-MM1 Winchester Disk Controller (also MM2, SR1 and SR2)*. Western Digital Corporation, 8105 Irvine Center Drive, Irvine, CA. URL: http://www.wdc.com/.

Western Digital (1997a) *Drive Parameters*, 25 March. Western Digital Corporation, 8105 Irvine Center Drive, Irvine, CA. URL: http://www.wdc.com/.

Western Digital (1997b) *Enhanced IDE Interface*, Western Digital Corporation, 8105 Irvine Center Drive, Irvine, CA. URL: http://www.wdc.com/.

Western Digital (1998a) *8.4 GB Capacity Barrier*, Western Digital Corporation, 8105 Irvine Center Drive, Irvine, CA. URL: http://www.wdc.com/.

Western Digital (1998b) *Large Disk Integration*, 10/07/1998, Western Digital Corporation, 8105 Irvine Center Drive, Irvine, CA. URL: http://www.wdc.com/.

Western Digital (1999) *EZ-Drive FAQ Sheet*, 9 March, 8105 Irvine Center Drive, Irvine, CA. URL: http://www.wdc.com/.

Williams, R. (1996) *Data Powers of Ten*. Although the original page has now expired, a similar version is available at URL: http://www2.sims.berkeley.edu/research/projects/how-much-info/datapowers.html.

XMS (1991), *eXtended Memory Specification (XMS), ver 3.0*, January 1991. Copyright © 1988, Microsoft Corporation, Lotus Development Corporation, Intel Corporation, and AST Research, Inc.

Zacker, C. (1995) *Upgrading and Repairing Networks*, Que, San Francisco, CA. URL: http://www.quepublishing.com/bookstore/product.asp?isbn=0789701812&redir=1&rl=1

Zander, M. (1985) *The Police & Criminal Evidence Act 1984*, Sweet & Maxwell Limited, London.

Ziv, J. and Lempel, A. (1977) A universal algorithm for sequential data compression, *IEEE Transactions on Information Theory*, **23**(3), 337–343.

Appendix 1. *Common Character Codes*

American Standard Code for Information Interchange (ASCII)

This is by far the most common of the character codes. It was originally defined as a 7 bit code (hexadecimal 00 to 7F) and includes a number of control characters (00h to 1Fh) that were used with teleprinter and communications terminals. It is listed below in decimal, hexadecimal and octal.

Dec	Hex	Oct	Char	Dec	Hex	Oct	Char	Dec	Hex	Oct	Char	Dec	Hex	Oct	Char
0	00	000	NUL	32	20	040	SP	64	40	100	@	96	60	140	`
1	01	001	SOH	33	21	041	!	65	41	101	A	97	61	141	a
2	02	002	STX	34	22	042	"	66	42	102	B	98	62	142	b
3	03	003	ETX	35	23	043	#	67	43	103	C	99	63	143	c
4	04	004	EOT	36	24	044	$	68	44	104	D	100	64	144	d
5	05	005	ENQ	37	25	045	%	69	45	105	E	101	65	145	e
6	06	006	ACK	38	26	046	&	70	46	106	F	102	66	146	f
7	07	007	BEL	39	27	047	'	71	47	107	G	103	67	147	g
8	08	010	BS	40	28	050	(	72	48	110	H	104	68	150	h
9	09	011	TAB	41	29	051	)	73	49	111	I	105	69	151	i
10	0A	012	LF	42	2A	052	*	74	4A	112	J	106	6A	152	j
11	0B	013	VT	43	2B	053	+	75	4B	113	K	107	6B	153	k
12	0C	014	FF	44	2C	054	,	76	4C	114	L	108	6C	154	l
13	0D	015	CR	45	2D	055	-	77	4D	115	M	109	6D	155	m
14	0E	016	SO	46	2E	056	.	78	4E	116	N	110	6E	156	n
15	0F	017	SI	47	2F	057	/	79	4F	117	O	111	6F	157	o
16	10	020	DLE	48	30	060	0	80	50	120	P	112	70	160	p
17	11	021	DC1	49	31	061	1	81	51	121	Q	113	71	161	q
18	12	022	DC2	50	32	062	2	82	52	122	R	114	72	162	r
19	13	023	DC3	51	33	063	3	83	53	123	S	115	73	163	s
20	14	024	DC4	52	34	064	4	84	54	124	T	116	74	164	t
21	15	025	NAK	53	35	065	5	85	55	125	U	117	75	165	u
22	16	026	SYN	54	36	066	6	86	56	126	V	118	76	166	v
23	17	027	ETB	55	37	067	7	87	57	127	W	119	77	167	w
24	18	030	CAN	56	38	070	8	88	58	130	X	120	78	170	x
25	19	031	EM	57	39	071	9	89	59	131	Y	121	79	171	y
26	1A	032	SUB	58	3A	072	:	90	5A	132	Z	122	7A	172	z
27	1B	033	ESC	59	3B	073	;	91	5B	133	[	123	7B	173	{
28	1C	034	FS	60	3C	074	<	92	5C	134	\	124	7C	174	|
29	1D	035	GS	61	3D	075	=	93	5D	135	]	125	7D	175	}
30	1E	036	RS	62	3E	076	>	94	5E	136	^	126	7E	176	~
31	1F	037	US	63	3F	077	?	95	5F	137	_	127	7F	177	DEL

Windows ANSI Character Set

A number of different extensions have been made to the original ASCII character set to utilize the codes from 80h to FFh. One that is often met with is the Windows ANSI character set. The range from 00h to 7Fh is as for the ASCII character set. The extended portion of the set is shown below with blanks for codes that do not display.

Dec	Hex	Oct	Char	Dec	Hex	Oct	Char	Dec	Hex	Oct	Char	Dec	Hex	Oct	Char
128	80	200		160	A0	240		192	C0	300	À	224	E0	340	à
129	81	201		161	A1	241	¡	193	C1	301	Á	225	E1	341	á
130	82	202	‚	162	A2	242	¢	194	C2	302	Â	226	E2	342	â
131	83	203	ƒ	163	A3	243	£	195	C3	303	Ã	227	E3	343	ã
132	84	204	„	164	A4	244	¤	196	C4	304	Ä	228	E4	344	ä
133	85	205	…	165	A5	245	¥	197	C5	305	Å	229	E5	345	å
134	86	206	†	166	A6	246	¦	198	C6	306	Æ	230	E6	346	æ
135	87	207	‡	167	A7	247	§	199	C7	307	Ç	231	E7	347	ç
136	88	210	ˆ	168	A8	250	¨	200	C8	310	È	232	E8	350	è
137	89	211	‰	169	A9	251	©	201	C9	311	É	233	E9	351	é
138	8A	212	Š	170	AA	252	ª	202	CA	312	Ê	234	EA	352	ê
139	8B	213	‹	171	AB	253	«	203	CB	313	Ë	235	EB	353	ë
140	8C	214	Œ	172	AC	254	¬	204	CC	314	Ì	236	EC	354	ì
141	8D	215		173	AD	255		205	CD	315	Í	237	ED	355	í
142	8E	216		174	AE	256	®	206	CE	316	Î	238	EE	356	î
143	8F	217		175	AF	257	¯	207	CF	317	Ï	239	EF	357	ï
144	90	220		176	B0	260	°	208	D0	320	Ð	240	F0	360	ð
145	91	221	'	177	B1	261	±	209	D1	321	Ñ	241	F1	361	ñ
146	92	222	'	178	B2	262	²	210	D2	322	Ò	242	F2	362	ò
147	93	223	"	179	B3	263	³	211	D3	323	Ó	243	F3	363	ó
148	94	224	"	180	B4	264	´	212	D4	324	Ô	244	F4	364	ô
149	95	225	•	181	B5	265	µ	213	D5	325	Õ	245	F5	365	õ
150	96	226	–	182	B6	266	¶	214	D6	326	Ö	246	F6	366	ö
151	97	227	—	183	B7	267	·	215	D7	327	×	247	F7	367	÷
152	98	230	˜	184	B8	270	¸	216	D8	330	Ø	248	F8	370	ø
153	99	231	™	185	B9	271	¹	217	D9	331	Ù	249	F9	371	ù
154	9A	232	š	186	BA	272	º	218	DA	332	Ú	250	FA	372	ú
155	9B	233	›	187	BB	273	»	219	DB	333	Û	251	FB	373	û
156	9C	234	œ	188	BC	274	¼	220	DC	334	Ü	252	FC	374	ü
157	9D	235		189	BD	275	½	221	DD	335	Ý	253	FD	375	ý
158	9E	236		190	BE	276	¾	222	DE	336	Þ	254	FE	376	þ
159	9F	237	Ÿ	191	BF	277	¿	223	DF	337	ß	255	FF	377	ÿ

IBM Extended ASCII Character Set

Another extension that is often met with is the IBM Extended ASCII Character set. This extended set includes the familiar line drawing characters and is shown below.

Dec	Hex	Oct	Char	Dec	Hex	Oct	Char	Dec	Hex	Oct	Char	Dec	Hex	Oct	Char
128	80	200	Ç	160	A0	240	á	192	C0	300	└	224	E0	340	α
129	81	201	ü	161	A1	241	í	193	C1	301	┴	225	E1	341	β
130	82	202	é	162	A2	242	ó	194	C2	302	┬	226	E2	342	Γ
131	83	203	â	163	A3	243	ú	195	C3	303	├	227	E3	343	π
132	84	204	ä	164	A4	244	ñ	196	C4	304	─	228	E4	344	Σ
133	85	205	à	165	A5	245	Ñ	197	C5	305	┼	229	E5	345	σ
134	86	206	å	166	A6	246	ª	198	C6	306	╞	230	E6	346	µ
135	87	207	ç	167	A7	247	º	199	C7	307	╟	231	E7	347	τ
136	88	210	ê	168	A8	250	¿	200	C8	310	╚	232	E8	350	Φ
137	89	211	ë	169	A9	251	⌐	201	C9	311	╔	233	E9	351	Θ
138	8A	212	è	170	AA	252	¬	202	CA	312	╩	234	EA	352	Ω
139	8B	213	ï	171	AB	253	½	203	CB	313	╦	235	EB	353	δ
140	8C	214	î	172	AC	254	¼	204	CC	314	╠	236	EC	354	∞
141	8D	215	ì	173	AD	255	¡	205	CD	315	═	237	ED	355	φ
142	8E	216	Ä	174	AE	256	«	206	CE	316	╬	238	EE	356	∈
143	8F	217	Å	175	AF	257	»	207	CF	317	╧	239	EF	357	∩
144	90	220	É	176	B0	260	░	208	D0	320	╨	240	F0	360	≡
145	91	221	æ	177	B1	261	▒	209	D1	321	╤	241	F1	361	±
146	92	222	Æ	178	B2	262	▓	210	D2	322	╥	242	F2	362	≥
147	93	223	ô	179	B3	263	│	211	D3	323	╙	243	F3	363	≤
148	94	224	ö	180	B4	264	┤	212	D4	324	╘	244	F4	364	⌠
149	95	225	ò	181	B5	265	╡	213	D5	325	╒	245	F5	365	⌡
150	96	226	û	182	B6	266	╢	214	D6	326	╓	246	F6	366	÷
151	97	227	ù	183	B7	267	╖	215	D7	327	╫	247	F7	367	≈
152	98	230	ÿ	184	B8	270	╕	216	D8	330	╪	248	F8	370	°
153	99	231	Ö	185	B9	271	╣	217	D9	331	┘	249	F9	371	•
154	9A	232	Ü	186	BA	272	║	218	DA	332	┌	250	FA	372	·
155	9B	233	¢	187	BB	273	╗	219	DB	333	█	251	FB	373	√
156	9C	234	£	188	BC	274	╝	220	DC	334	▄	252	FC	374	ⁿ
157	9D	235	¥	189	BD	275	╜	221	DD	335	▌	253	FD	375	²
158	9E	236	₧	190	BE	276	╛	222	DE	336	▐	254	FE	376	■
159	9F	237	ƒ	191	BF	277	┐	223	DF	337	▀	255	FF	377	□

In addition to the codes from 80h to FFh, the IBM Extended Character set, also defines printable codes for the control characters from 00h to 1Fh. These are shown in this next table:

Dec	Hex	Oct	Char	Dec	Hex	Oct	Char	Dec	Hex	Oct	Char	Dec	Hex	Oct	Char
0	00	000		1	01	001	☺	2	02	002	☻	3	03	003	♥
4	04	004	♦	5	05	005	♣	6	06	006	♠	7	07	007	•
8	08	010	◘	9	09	011	○	10	0A	012	◙	11	0B	013	♂
12	0C	014	♀	13	0D	015	♪	14	0E	016	♫	15	0F	017	☼
16	10	020	►	17	11	021	◄	18	12	022	↕	19	13	023	‼
20	14	024	¶	21	15	025	§	22	16	026	▬	23	17	027	↨
24	18	030	↑	25	19	031	↓	26	1A	032	→	27	1B	033	←
28	1C	034	∟	29	1D	035	↔	30	1E	036	▲	31	1F	037	▼

Windows Unicode

As the development of the Universal Character Set (UCS) and Unicode progressed, Microsoft selected UCS-2 to be the Windows version of Unicode. This is essentially a 16 bit, two byte character code, and, for English language use, it is simply the equivalent ASCII code byte with a leading 00H byte. For PC systems, of course, the two bytes will be held little endian, so the 00H byte will be seen to be stored in the higher address of the pair.

It should be noted that UCS-2 is not quite the same as UTF-16 (Unicode Transformation Format – 16), though for our practical purposes it would mostly appear to be so. UTF-16, however, permits what are known as *surrogate pairs* which are particular 16 bit codes that signal that there are more than two bytes associated with the character. This produces what is in effect a 21 bit Unicode. Surrogate pairs are specifically prohibited by UCS-2, which is strictly a 16 bit Unicode.

Appendix 2. *Some Common File Format Signatures*

Hex signature	File Type	Description
xx[1] xx xx xx AF 11	FLI	Graphics – Autodesk Animator
xx xx xx xx AF 12	FLC	Graphics – Autodesk 3D Studio
xx xx 2D 6C 68 35 2D	LZH	Archive – LHA archive file
- l h 5 -		
00	PIF	Windows – Program Information File
00 00 00 02	MAC	Graphics – MAC Picture format
00 00 01 00	ICO	Graphics – Windows icon format
00 00 01 Bx	MPG	MPEG Video File
00 00 02 00	CUR	Graphics – Windows cursor file
00 00 02 00 04 04	WKS	Spreadsheet – Lotus 1-2-3
00 00 02 00 05 04	WRK	Spreadsheet – Symphony
00 00 02 00 06 04	WK1	Spreadsheet – Lotus 1-2-3
00 00 02 00 06 04	WR1	Spreadsheet – Symphony
00 00 1A 00 00 10	WK3	Spreadsheet – LOTUS 1-2-3
00 00 1A 00 02 10	WK4	Spreadsheet – LOTUS 1-2-3
00 01 00 00 53 74 61 72	MDB	Database – Microsoft Access File
S t a r		
64 61 72 64 20 4A 65 74		
d a r d J e t		
20 44 42		
D B		
00 01 00 08	IMG	Graphics – GEM Image format
00 06 15 61 00 00 00 02	DB	Database – Netscape Navigator (v4)
00 00 04 D2 00 00 10 00		
01 00 00 00	PIC	Spreadsheet graph – Lotus 1-2-3
01 00 00 00	EMF	Enhanced Windows Meta File (print spooler)
02	DBF	Database – dBASE II
03	DBF	Database – dBASE III
03	DBF	Database – dBASE IV
03	DBF	Database – FoxPro
09 00 04 00 07 00 01 00		Spreadsheet – Excel BIFF2[2]
09 02 06 00 00 00 01 00		Spreadsheet – Excel BIFF3
09 04 06 00 00 04 00 01	XLW	Spreadsheet – Excel BIFF4
0A	PCX	Graphics – ZSOFT Paintbrush
11 00 00 00 53 43 43 41	PF	Windows Prefetch File
S C C A		
1F 8B 08	GZ	Archive – GZIP archive file

Hex signature	File Type	Description
1F 9D 90	TAR.Z	Archive – Compressed tape archive file
21 42 44 4E ! B D N	PST	Microsoft Outlook file
25 50 44 46 % P D F	PDF	Adobe Portable Document Format file
2E 73 6E 64 . s n d		Sound – NeXt/Sun audio format
2E 52 4D 46 . R M F	RM	Real Media file
30 00 00 00 4C 66 4C 65 0 L f L e	EVT	Windows Event Viewer file
31 BE 00 00 00 AB	DOC	Word processor – MS Word 4
31 BE 00 00 00 AB	WRI	Word processor – MS Write
32 BE 00 00 00 AB	WRI	Word processor – MS Write
34 12	PIC	Graphics – PC Paint
38 42 50 53 8 B P S	PSD	Graphics – Adobe Photoshop
3A DE 68 B1	DCX	Graphics – CAS fax format
3F 5F 03 00 ? _	HLP	Windows Help file
41 48 A H	PAL, PIC	Graphics – Dr Halo format
42 4D B M	BMP	Graphics – Windows bitmap
43 52 45 47 C R E G	DAT	Windows 9x Registry files
43 54 4D 46 C T M F	CMF	Sound – Creative music format
43 57 53 C W S	SWF	Shockwave Flash file
43 72 65 61 74 69 76 65 C r e a t i v e 20 56 6f 69 63 65 20 46 V o i c e F 69 6c 65 1A i l e	VOC	Sound – Creative voice format
44 61 6E 4D D a n M	MSP	Graphics – Windows Paint
45 59 45 53 E Y E S	CE1, CE2	Graphics – ComputerEyes format
46 4F 52 4D F O R M	LBM	Graphics – Interchange file format
46 57 53 F W S	SWF	Shockwave Flash file
47 49 46 38 37 61 G I F 8 7 a	GIF	Graphics – graphics interchange format
47 49 46 38 39 61 G I F 8 9 a	GIF	Graphics – graphics interchange format
49 42 4B 1A I B K	IBK	Sound – Soundblaster instrument bank
49 49 2A 00 I I	TIF	Graphics – tag image file format Intel (little endian)
49 4d 44 43 I M D C	IC1, IC2, IC3	Graphics – Atari Imagic film format

Hex signature	File Type	Description
4C 00 00 00 L	LNK	Microsoft Windows Shortcut file
4C 69 6E 53 L i n S	MSP	Graphics – Windows 3.x Paint
4D 47 43 M G C	CRD	Database – Windows 3.x Cardfile
4D 4D M M	TIF	Graphics – tag image file format Motorola (big endian)
4D 53 43 46 M S C F	CAB	Microsoft Cabinet file
4D 53 43 46 M S C F	PPZ	Microsoft Powerpoint Packaged file
4D 54 68 64 M T h d	MID	Sound – standard MIDI format
4d 5A M Z	EXE, DLL, DVR, COM, SYS	Executable files
50 4B P K	ZIP	Archive – Pkzip archive file
50 4D 43 43 P M C C	GRP	General – Windows group file
50 C3	CLP	Graphics – Windows 3.x clipboard
52 45 47 45 44 49 64 R E G E D I T	REG	Windows Registry Editor files (text)
52 49 46 46 xx xx xx xx R I F F 41 56 49 20 4C 49 53 54 A V I L I S T	AVI	Graphics – Resource interchange file format (RIFF) wrapping Audio/video interleaved file
52 49 46 46 xx xx xx xx R I F F 52 4d 49 44 64 61 74 61 R M I D d a t a	RMI	Sound – Resource interchange file Windows MIDI file
52 49 46 46 xx xx xx xx R I F F 57 41 56 45 66 6D 74 20 W A V E f m t	WAV	Sound – Resource interchange file format (RIFF) wrapping Windows WAVE file
53 42 49 1A S B I	SBI	Sound – Soundblaster instrument format
56 44 56 49 V D V I	AVS	Graphics – Intel digital video interface
59 A6 6A 95	RAS	Graphics – SUN raster format
5A 4F 4F 20 Z O O	ZOO	Archive – Zoo archive file
5F 43 41 53 45 5F _ C A S E _	CAS, CBK	EnCase v 3 Case file. EnCase v 4 and 5 use OLE 2 Container file (see below)
xx xx xx xx 6D 6F 6F 76 m o o v	MOV	Graphics – Apple QuickTime movie file
72 65 67 66 r e g f	\<none\>	Windows Registry Hive file
7B	DBF	Database – dBASE 1V
7B 5C 72 74 66 31 { \ r t f 1	RTF	Word processor – rich text format
83	DBF	Database – dBASE III

Hex signature	File Type	Description
83	DBF	Database – dBASE IV
83	DBF	Database – FoxPro
8B	DBF	Database – FoxPro
89 50 4E 47 0D 0A P N G	PNG	Graphics – Portable Network Graphics file
95 01	SKR	PGP Secret Key Ring
99 00	PKR	PGP Public Key Ring
99 01	PKR	PGP Public Key Ring
9 B A5	DOC	Word processor – Winword 1.0
B5 A2 B0 B3 B3 B0 A2 B5	CAL	Calendar – Windows 3.x calendar
BA BE EB EA	ANI	Graphics – NEOchrome animation
CF AD 12 FE	DBX	Microsoft Outlook Express
D0 CF 11 E0 A1 B1 1A E1		OLE 2 Container file (structured storage) used by a variety of applications – in particular most Microsoft Office documents
D7 CD C6 9A	WMF	Graphics – Windows metafile format
DB A5	DOC	Word processor – Winword 2.0
E3 82 85 96	PWL	Windows Password file
F5	DBF	Database – FoxPro
FE DB	SEQ	Graphics – Cyber paint
FE DC	SEQ	Graphics – Cyber paint
FF 57 50 43 -1 W P C	WPD	Word processor – WordPerfect
FF 57 50 43 -1 W P C	WPG	Graphics – WordPerfect Graphic
FF D8 FF E0 xx xx 4A 46 49 46 J F I F	JPG	Graphics – JPEG/JFIF format
FF D8 FF E1 xx xx 45 78 69 66 E x i f	JPG	Graphics – JPEG/Exif format – digital camera
FF FF	GEM	Graphics – GEM Metafile format
FF FF FF FF	SYS	Executable system file

1   "xx" is used to indicate "don't care". In other words, we have for this case four leading bytes whose values can be anything (don't care) followed by af 11.

2   Excel binary interchange format

Note: Some of the updates to this Appendix have been obtained, with thanks, from the web page of Gary C. Kessler at http://www.garykessler.net/library/file_sigs.html dated 25 January 2007.

Appendix 3. *A Typical[1] Set of POST Codes*

Hex code	Description of POST operation
02h	Verify real mode
03h	Disable non-maskable interrupt (NMI)
04h	Get processor type
06h	Initialize system hardware
08h	Initialize chipset with initial POST values
09h	Set IN POST flag
0Ah	Initialize CPU registers
0Bh	Enable CPU cache
0Ch	Initialize caches to initial POST values
0Eh	Initialize I/O component
0Fh	Initialize the local bus IDE
10h	Initialize power management
11h	Load alternate registers with initial POST values
12h	Restore CPU control word during warm boot
13h	Initialize PCI bus mastering devices
14h	Initialize keyboard controller
16h	BIOS ROM checksum
17h	Initialize cache betore memory autosize
18h	8254 timer initialization
1Ah	8237 DMA controller initialization
1Ch	Reset programmable interrupt controller
20h	Test DRAM refresh
22h	Test keyboard controller
24h	Set ES segment register to 4 GB
26h	Enable A20 line
28h	Autosize DRAM
29h	Initialize POST memory manager
2Ah	Clear 512 KB base RAM
2Ch	RAM failure on address line xxxx
2Eh	RAM failure on data bits xxxx of low byte of memory bus
2Fh	Enable cache before system BIOS shadow
30h	RAM failure on data bits xxxx of high byte of memory bus
32h	Test CPU bus-clock frequency
33h	Initialize POST dispatch manager
34h	Test CMOS RAM
35h	Initialize alternate chipset registers
36h	Warm start shut down
37h	Reinitialize the chipset (motherboard only)
38h	Shadow system BIOS ROM
39h	Reinitialize the cache (motherboard only)
3Ah	Autosize cache

Hex code	Description of POST operation
3Ch	Configure advanced chipset registers
3Dh	Load alternate registers with CMOS values
40h	Set Initial CPU speed
42h	Initialize interrupt vectors
44h	Initialize BIOS interrupts
45h	POST device initialization
46h	Check ROM copyright notice
47h	Initialize manager for PCI option ROMs
48h	Check video configuration against CMOS RAM data
49h	Initialize PCI bus and devices
4Ah	Initialize all video adapters in system
4Bh	Display QuietBoot screen
4Ch	Shadow video BIOS ROM
4Eh	Display BIOS copyright notice
50h	Display CPU type and speed
51h	Initialize EISA motherboard
52h	Test keyboard
54h	Set key click if enabled
56h	Enable keyboard
58h	Test for unexpected interrupts
59h	Initialize POST display service
5Ah	Display prompt "Press F2 to enter SETUP"
5Bh	Disable CPU cache
5Ch	Test RAM between 512 and 640 KB
60h	Test extended memory
62h	Test extended memory address lines
64h	Jump to UserPatchl
66h	Configure advanced cache registers
67h	Initialize multiprocessor APIC
68h	Enable external and processor caches
69h	Setup System Management Mode (SMM) area
6Ah	Display external L2 cache size
6Ch	Display shadow-area message
6Eh	Display possible high address for UMB recovery
70h	Display error messages
72h	Check for configuration errors
74h	Test real-time clock
76h	Check for keyboard errors
7Ah	Test for key lock on
7Ch	Set up hardware interrupt vectors
7Eh	Initialize coprocessor if present
80h	Disable onboard Super I/O ports and IRQs
8lh	Late POST device initialization
82h	Detect and install external RS232 ports
83h	Configure non-MCD IDE controllers
84h	Detect and install external parallel ports
85h	initialize PC-compatibie PnP ISA devices
86h	Re-initialize onboard I/O ports
87h	Configure motherboard configurable devices
88h	Initialize BIOS Data Area
89h	Enable Non-Maskable Interrupts (NMIs)
8Ah	Initialize extended BIOS data area
8Bh	Test and initialize PS/2 mouse
8Ch	Initialize diskette controller
8Fh	Determine number of ATA drives

Hex code	Description of POST operation
90h	Initialize hard-disk controllers
9lh	Initialize local-bus hard-disk controllers
92h	Jump to UserPatch2
93h	Build MPTABLE for multiprocessor boards
94h	Disable A20 address line (ReI. 5.1 and earlier)
95h	install CD-ROM for boot
96h	Clear huge ES segment register
97h	Fix up multiprocessor table
98h	Search for option ROMs
99h	Check for SMART Drive
9Ah	Shadow option ROMs
9Ch	Set up power management
9Eh	Enable hardware interrupts
9Fh	Determine number of ATA and SCSI drives
A0h	Set time of day
A2h	Check key lock
A4h	Initialize typematic rate
A8h	Erase F2 prompt
AAh	Scan for F2 key stroke
ACh	Enter SETUP
AEh	Clear IN POST flag
B0h	Check for errors
B2h	POST done - prepare to boot operating system
B4h	One short beep before boot
B5h	Terminate QuietBoot
B6h	Check password (optional)
B8h	Clear global descriptor table
B9h	Clean up all graphics
BAh	Initialize DMI parameters
BBh	Initialize PnP Option ROMs
BCh	Clear parity checkers
BDh	Display MultiBoot menu
BEh	Clear screen (optional)
BFh	Check virus and backup reminders
C0h	Try to boot with INT 19h
Clh	Initialize POST Error Manager (PEM)
C2h	Initialize error logging
C3h	Initialize error display function
C4h	Initialize system error handler

1. These codes are taken from the SE440BX Motherboard Technical Product Specification, by permission of Intel Corporation.

Appendix 4. *Typical BIOS Beep Codes and Error Messages*

Intel[1] SE440BX Motherboard

Beep code	POST code	Explanation
1-2-2-3	16h	BIOS ROM checksum
1-3-1-1	20h	Test DRAM refresh
1-3-1-3	22h	Test Keyboard Controller
1-3-3-1	28h	Autosize DRAM
1-3-3-2	29h	Initialize POST Memory Manager
1-3-3-3	2Ah	Clear 512 KB base RAM
1-3-4-1	2Ch	RAM failure on address line xxxx
1-3-4-3	2Eh	RAM failure on data bits xxxx of low byte of memory bus
1-4-1-1	30h	RAM failure on data bits xxxx of high byte of memory bus
2-1-2-2	45h	POST device initialization
2-1-2-3	46h	Check ROM copyright notice
2-2-3-1	58h	Test for unexpected interrupts
2-2-4-1	5Ch	Test RAM between 512 and 640 KB
1-2	98h	Search for option ROMs. One long, two short beeps on checksum failure

One long beep followed by several short beeps indicates a video problem.
One short beep indicates that POST completed normally.

Error message	Explanation
Diskette drive A error	Drive A is present but fails the POST diskette tests. Check that the drive is defined with the proper diskette type in Setup and that the diskette drive is installed correctly.
Extended RAM Failed at offset :nnnn	Extended memory not working or not configured properly at offset nnnn.
Failing Bits: nnnn	The hexadecimal number nnnn is a map of the bits at the RAM address (System, Extended, or Shadow memory) that failed the memory test. Each 1 in the map indicates a failed bit.
Fixed Disk 0 Failure or Fixed Disk 1 Failure or Fixed Disk Controller Failure	Fixed disk is not working or not configured properly. Check to see if fixed disk installed properly. Run Setup to be sure the fixed-disk type is correctly identified.

Error message	Explanation
Incorrect Drive A type – run SETUP	Type of diskette drive for drive A not correctly identified in Setup.
Invalid NVRAM media type	Problem with NVRAM (CMOS) access.
Keyboard controller error	The keyboard controller failed test. Try replacing the keyboard.
Keyboard error	Keyboard not working.
Keyboard error nn	BIOS discovered a stuck key and displayed the scan code nn for the stuck key.
Keyboard locked – Unlock key switch	Unlock the system to proceed.
Monitor type does not match CMOS – Run SETUP	Monitor type not correctly identified in Setup.
Operating system not found	Operating system cannot be located on either drive A or drive C. Enter Setup and see if fixed disk and drive A are properly identified.
Parity Check 1	Parity error found in the system bus. BIOS attempts to locate the address and display it on the screen. If it cannot locate the address, it displays ????.
Parity Check 2	Parity error found in the I/O bus. BIOS attempts to locate the address and display it on the screen. If it cannot locate the address, it displays ????.
Press <F1> to resume, <F2> to Setup	Displayed after any recoverable error message. Press <F1> to start the boot process or <F2> to enter Setup and change any settings.
Real-time clock error	Real-time clock fails BIOS test. May require motherboard repair.
Shadow RAM Failed at offset: nnnn	Shadow RAM failed at offset nnnn of the 64 KB block at which the error was detected.
System battery is dead – Replace and run SETUP	The CMOS clock battery indicator shows the battery is dead. Replace the battery and run Setup to reconfigure the system.
System cache error – Cache disabled	RAM cache failed the BIOS test. BIOS disabled the cache.
System CMOS checksum bad – run SETUP	System CMOS RAM has been corrupted or modified incorrectly, perhaps by an application program that changes data stored in CMOS. Run Setup and reconfigure the system either by getting the default values and/or making your own selections.
System RAM Failed at offset: nnnn	System RAM failed at offset nnnn of the 64 KB block at which the error was detected.
System timer error	The timer test failed. Requires repair of system motherboard.

Elonex² MT-500/I System Board

Beeps	Error message	Description
1 beep	Refresh Failure.	The memory refresh circuitry on the motherboard is faulty.
2 beeps	Parity Error.	Parity error in the first 64KB of memory.
3 beeps	Base 64KB Memory Failure.	Memory failure in the first 64KB of memory.
4 beeps	Timer Not operational.	Memory failure in the first 64KB of memory, or Timer 1 on the motherboard is not functioning.
5 beeps	Processor Error.	The CPU on the board generated an error.
6 beeps	8042 Gate A20 Failure.	The keyboard controller may be bad. The BIOS cannot switch to protected mode.
7 beeps	Processor Exception Interrupt Error.	The CPU generated an exception interrupt
8 beeps	Display Memory Read/Write Error.	The system video adapter is either missing or its memory is faulty. This is not a fatal error.
9 beeps	ROM Checksum Error.	The ROM checksum value does not match the value encoded in the BIOS.
10 beeps	CMOS Shutdown Register Read/Write Error.	The shutdown register for CMOS RAM failed.
11 beeps	Cache Error/External Cache Bad.	The external cache is faulty.

Error message	Explanation
8042 Gate – A20 Error	Gate A20 on the keyboard controller (8042) is not working.
Address Line Short!	Error in the address decoding circuitry on the motherboard.
Cache Memory Bad, Do Not Enable Cache!	Cache memory is defective.
CH-2 Timer Error	Most systems include two timers. There is an error in timer 2.
CMOS Battery State Low	CMOS RAM is powered by a battery. The battery power is low.
CMOS Checksum Failure	After CMOS RAM values are saved, a checksum value is generated for error checking. The previous value is different from the current value. Run Setup.
CMOS System Options Not Set	The values stored in CMOS RAM are either corrupt or nonexistent. Run Setup.
CMOS Display Type Mismatch	The video type in CMOS RAM does not match the one detected by the BIOS. Run Setup.
CMOS Memory Size Mismatch	The amount of memory on the motherboard is different than the amount in CMOS RAM. Run Setup.
CMOS Time and Date Not Set	Run Setup to set the date and time in CMOS RAM.
Diskette Boot Failure	The boot disk in floppy drive A: is corrupt. It cannot be used to boot the system. Use another boot disk and follow the screen instructions.

Error message	Explanation
Display Switch Not Proper	Some systems require that a video switch on the motherboard be set to either colour or monochrome. Turn the system off, set the switch, then power on.
DMA Error	Error in the DMA (Direct Memory Access) controller.
DMA #1 Error	Error in the master DMA channel.
DMA #2 Error	Error in the slave DMA channel.
FDD Controller Failure	The BIOS cannot communicate with the floppy disk drive controller.
HDD Controller Failure	The BIOS cannot communicate with the hard disk drive controller.
INTR #1 Error	Interrupt channel 1 failed POST.
INTR #2 Error	Interrupt channel 2 failed POST.
Invalid Boot Diskette	The BIOS can read in floppy drive A: but cannot boot the system.
Keyboard is locked... Unlock It	The keyboard lock on the system is engaged. The system must be unlocked to continue.
Keyboard Error	There is a timing problem with the keyboard.
KB/Interface Error	There is an error in the keyboard connector.
Off Board Parity Error	Parity error in memory installed in an expansion slot. The format is: OFF BOARD PARITY ERROR ADDR (HEX) = (XXXX). *XXXX* is the hex address where the error occurred.
On Board Parity Error	Parity error in motherboard memory. The format is: ON BOARD PARITY ERROR ADDR (HEX) = (XXXX). *XXXX* is the hex address where the error occurred.
Parity Error ????	Parity error in system memory at an unknown address.

1. These beep codes and error messages are taken from the SE440BX Motherboard Product Guide, by permission of Intel Corporation.
2. These beep codes and error messages are taken from the MT-500/I Series Configuration Guide, by kind permission of Elonex plc.

Appendix 5. Disk Partition Table Types

Type	Use
00	Unused partition table entry
01	DOS, Primary Partition (FAT12, <16MB)
02	XENIX root file system
03	XENIX /usr file system
04	DOS 3.0+, Primary Partition (FAT16, >=16MB and <32MB)
05	DOS 3.3+, Extended Partition using standard INT 13h
06	DOS 3.31, Primary Partition (FAT16, >32MB) using standard INT 13h
07	OS/2 IFS (HPFS), Windows NT NTFS, QNX.x pre-1988, Advanced UNIX
08	OS/2 (v1.0-1.3 only), AIX boot partition, SplitDrive, Commodore DOS, DELL partition spanning multiple drives, QNX 1.x and 2.x ("qny")
09	AIX – data partition, Coherent file system, QNX 1.x and 2.x ("qnz")
0A	OS/2 Boot Manager, OPUS (Open Parallel Unisys Server), Coherent swap partition
0B	Windows 95 OSR2 FAT32 partition
0C	Windows 95 OSR2 FAT32 partition LBA-mapped using INT 13h extensions
0D	Possibly a type 07 LBA
0E	Windows 95 DOS FAT16 partition LBA-mapped using INT 13h extensions – else same as 06
0F	Windows 95 Extended partition LBA-mapped using INT 13h Extensions – else same as 05
10	OPUS
11	Hidden DOS FAT12, OS/2 Boot Manager: Inactive type 01[1], Leading Edge DOS 3.x logically sectored FAT[2]
12	Compaq configuration/diagnostics partition
13	Reliable Systems FTFS
14	Hidden DOS FAT16 < 32MB, OS/2 Boot Manager: Inactive type 04, Novell DOS 7.0 FDISK, AST DOS with logically sectored FAT
15	–
16	Hidden DOS FAT16, partition >= 32 MB, OS/2 Boot Manager: Inactive type 06
17	Hidden Windows NT NTFS, OS/2 Boot Manager: Inactive type 07
18	AST SmartSleep partition or AST Windows swap file, Compaq system diagnostics
19	Unused – claimed for Willowtech Photon coS (completely optimized system)
1A	–
1B	Hidden Windows 95 OSR2 FAT32
1C	Hidden Windows 95 OSR2 FAT32 LBA-mapped
1E	Hidden Windows 95 FAT16 LBA-mapped
1F	Hidden LBA DOS Extended partition
20	Unused – claimed for Willowsoft Overture File System (OFS1)
21	Officially listed as reserved (HP Volume Expansion, SpeedStor variant), Claimed for Oxygen FSo2

Type	Use
22	Oxygen Extended
23	Reserved
24	NEC DOS 3.x
25	–
26	Reserved
27	–
28	–
29	–
2A	AtheOS File System (AFS)
2B	SyllableSecure (SylStor)
2C	–
to	–
30	–
31	Reserved
32	NOS
33	Reserved
34	Reserved
35	JFS on OS/2 or eCS
36	Reserved
37	–
38	THEOS ver 3.2 2GB partition
39	Plan 9 partition, THEOS ver 4 spanned partition
3A	THEOS ver 4 4GB partition
3B	THEOS ver 4 extended partition
3C	PowerQuest PartitionMagic recovery partition
3D	Hidden NetWare
3E	–
3F	–
40	VENIX 80286
41	Personal RISC Boot, PowerPC boot, PTS-DOS 6.70 & BootWizard: Alternative Linux, Minix, and DR-DOS
42	Secure File System (Peter Gutmann), Windows 2000 (NT 5): Dynamic extended partition, PTS-DOS 6.70 & BootWizard: Alternative Linux swap and DR-DOS
43	PTS-DOS 6.70 & BootWizard: DR-DOS, Alternative Linux native file system (EXT2fs)
44	GoBack partition
45	Priam, EUMEL/Elan, Boot-US boot manager
46	EUMEL/Elan
47	EUMEL/Elan
48	EUMEL/Elan
49	–
4A	ALFS/THIN lightweight filesystem for DOS, AdaOS Aquila (withdrawn)
4B	–
4C	Oberon partition
4D	QNX 4.x
4E	QNX 4.x 2nd part
4F	QNX 4.x 3rd part, Oberon partition
50	OnTrack Disk Manager read-only DOS partition, Lynx RTOS, Native Oberon (alt)
51	OnTrack Disk Manager read/write DOS partition, Novell
52	CP/M, Microport System V/386
53	OnTrack Disk Manager write-only partition
54	OnTrack Disk Manager non-DOS partition (DDO)
55	Micro House EZ-Drive non-DOS partition

Type	Use
56	Golden Bow VFeature partition, DM converted to EZ-BIOS, AT&T MS-DOS 3.x logically sectored FAT
57	DrivePro, VNDI partition
58	–
59	–
5A	–
5B	–
5C	Priam EDISK
5D	–
5E	–
5F	–
60	–
61	Storage Dimensions SpeedStor partition
62	–
63	UNIX System V/386, Mach, MtXinu BSD 4.3 on Mach, GNU HURD
64	SpeedStor, Novell Netware 286, 2.xx, PC-ARMOUR protected partition
65	Novell Netware 386, 3.xx or 4.xx
66	Novell Netware SMS partition
67	Novell Netware
68	Novell Netware
69	Novell Netware 5+, Novell Storage Systems (NSS)
6A	–
to	–
6F	–
70	DiskSecure Multi-Boot
71	Reserved
72	–
73	Reserved
74	Reserved, Scramdisk partition
75	PC/IX IBM
76	Reserved
77	M2FS/M2CS partition, VNDI partition
78	XOSL FS
79	–
7A	–
7B	–
7C	–
7D	–
7E	Unused
7F	Unused
80	Minix (ver. 1.4a and earlier)
81	Minix (ver. 1.4b and later), Mitac Advanced Disk Manager, Linux
82	Prime, Linux swap, Solaris UNIX
83	Linux native
84	OS/2 hiding a type 04 partition, APM hibernation, can be used by Win98
85	Linux Extended
86	FAT16 volume/stripe set[3], Old Linux RAID partition
87	NTFS volume/stripe set, HPFS FT mirrored partition (see 86)
88	Linux plaintext partition table
89	–
8A	Linux kernel partition
8B	FAT32 volume/stripe set (see 86)
8C	FAT32 volume/stripe set using INT 13h extensions (see 86)
8D	Free FDISK hidden primary DOS FAT12 partition[4]
8E	Linux Logical Volume Manager partition

Type	Use
8F	–
90	Free FDISK hidden primary DOS FAT16 partition (see 8D)
91	Free FDISK hidden DOS extended partition (see 8D)
92	Free FDISK hidden primary DOS large FAT16 partition (see 8D)
93	Amoeba file system, Hidden Linux native partition
94	Amoeba bad block table
95	MIT EXOPC native partition
96	–
97	Free FDISK hidden primary DOS FAT32 partition (see 8D)
98	Free FDISK hidden primary DOS FAT32 partition (LBA) (see 8D), Datalight ROM-DOS Super-Boot partition
99	DCE376 logical drive Mylex EISA SCSI
9A	Free FDISK hidden primary DOS FAT16 partition (LBA) (see 8D)
9B	Free FDISK hidden DOS extended partition (see 8D)
9C	–
9D	–
9E	–
9F	BSD/OS
A0	Laptop hibernation partition, IBM Thinkpad, Phoenix NoteBios, Toshiba and Sony VAIO
A1	Laptop hibernation partition, NEC 6000H notebook, HP Volume Expansion (SpeedStor variant)
A2	–
A3	HP Volume Expansion (SpeedStor variant)
A4	HP Volume Expansion (SpeedStor variant)
A5	BSD/386, 386BSD, NetBSD, FreeBSD
A6	OpenBSD, HP Volume Expansion (SpeedStor variant)
A7	NeXTStep partition
A8	Mac OS-X
A9	NetBSD
AA	Olivetti DOS with FAT12
AB	Mac OS-X boot partition, GO! partition
AC	–
AD	–
AE	ShagOS file syatem
AF	ShagOS swap partition
B0	BootStar Dummy (part of DriveStar disk image by Star-Tools GmbH)
B1	HP Volume Expansion (SpeedStor variant)
B2	–
B3	HP Volume Expansion (SpeedStor variant)
B4	HP Volume Expansion (SpeedStor variant)
B5	–
B6	HP Volume Expansion (SpeedStor variant), Corrupted Windows NT mirror set (master), FAT16
B7	BSDI BSD/386 file system or secondary swap, Corrupted Windows NT mirror set (master), NTFS
B8	BSDI BSD/386 swap or secondary file system
B9	–
BA	–
BB	PTS BootWizard hidden
BC	–
BD	–
BE	Solaris 8 boot partition
BF	New Solaris x86 partition

Type	Use
C0	CTOS, REAL/32 secure small partition, NTFT partition, Novell DOS/OpenDOS/ DR-OpenDOS/DR-DOS secured partition
C1	DR-DOS LOGIN.EXE-secured FAT12
C2	Unused – Reserved for DR-DOS 7+, Hidden Linux
C3	Reserved for DR-DOS 7+, Hidden Linux swap
C4	DR-DOS LOGIN.EXE-secured FAT16, < 32 M
C5	DR-DOS LOGIN.EXE-secured extended
C6	DR-DOS LOGIN.EXE-secured FAT16 >= 32M, Windows NT corrupted FAT16 volume/stripe (V/S) set
C7	HPFS FT disabled mirrored partition, Cyrnix Boot, Windows NT corrupted NTFS volume/stripe (V/S) set
C8	Reserved for DR-DOS 7+
C9	Reserved for DR-DOS 7+
CA	Reserved for DR-DOS 7+
CB	DR-DOS 7.04+ secured FAT32 (CHS)
CC	DR-DOS 7.04+ secured FAT32X (LBA)
CD	Reserved for DR-DOS 7+, CTOS Memdump
CE	DR-DOS 7.04+ secured FAT16X (LBA)
CF	DR-DOS 7.04+ secured extended partition (LBA)
D0	Multiuser DOS secured partition, REAL/32 secure big partition
D1	Old Multiuser DOS secured FAT12
D2	–
D3	–
D4	Old Multiuser DOS secured FAT16 (<32M)
D5	Old Multiuser DOS secured extended partition
D6	Old Multiuser DOS secured FAT16 (BIGDOS >= 32 M)
D7	–
D8	CP/M 86
D9	–
DA	Non-FS Data
DB	CP/M, Concurrent CP/M, Concurrent DOS, CTOS (Convergent Technologies OS), KDG Telemer=try SCPU boot
DC	–
DD	Hidden CTOS Memdump
DE	Dell PowerEdge Server utilities partition
DF	BootIt EMBRM, DG/UX virtual disk manager partition
E0	Reserved for ST AVFS
E1	DOS access or SpeedStor FAT12 extended partition
E2	DOS read-only (Florian Painke's XFDISK 1.0.4)
E3	Storage Dimensions, DOS read-only
E4	SpeedStor FAT16 extended partition
E5	Tandy DOS with logically sectored FAT
E6	Storage Dimensions SpeedStor
E7	–
to	–
EA	–
EB	BeOS file system
EC	SkyOS SkyFS
ED	Reserved for Matthias Paul's Sprytix
EE	Indication that this legacy MBR is followed by an Extensible Firmware Interface (EFI) header.
EF	Partition that contains an EFI file system
F0	Linux/PA-RISC boot loader
F1	SpeedStor Storage Dimensions
F2	DOS 3.3+ secondary partition, Unisys DOS with logical sectored FAT

Type	Use
F3	SpeedStor Storage Dimensions
F4	SpeedStor Storage Dimensions large partition, Prologue single volume partition
F5	Prologue multi-volume partition
F6	Storage Dimensions SpeedStor
F7	Unused – planned for O.S.G. EFAT
F8	–
F9	pCache
FA	Bochs
FB	VMware file system partition
FC	VMware swap partition
FD	Reserved for FreeDOS (http://www.freedos.org/), Linux RAID partition
FE	LANstep, IBM PS/2 IML (Initial Microcode Load) partition, Storage Dimensions SpeedStor (>1024 cylinder), Windows NT Disk Administrator hidden partition, Linux Logical Volume Manager partition (old)
FF	Xenix bad-block table

1   When OS/2 boot manager boots a DOS partition it hides all other primary DOS partitions except for the one that is booted. It does this by adding 10h to the other partition types; hence 01, 04, 06 and 07 become 11, 14, 16 and 17.

2   A logically sectored FAT is a FAT12 or FAT16 partition where the sector size is larger than the usual 512 bytes, up to a maximum of 8192 bytes.

3   Windows NT4 adds 80 to the partition type for partitions that are part of a fault tolerant set giving 86, 87, 8B and 8C.

4   Free FDISK hides types 01, 04, 05, 06, 0B, 0C, 0E and 0F by adding 8C.

This information has been obtained from the following sources:

1. Landis, H. (2002) *How It Works: Partition Tables,* 18 December, URL: http://www.ata-atapi.com/hiwtab.htm.
2. Seagate (1995) *NFDisc v1.20, Partition Record display and maintenance.* URL: http://www.seagate-asia.com/sgt/korea/discutil.jsp.
3. van Staten, E. (1997) *Harddrive Related Terms and Tricks,* 16 April. URL: http://www.computercraft.com/docs/evsterms.html.
4. Wirzenius, L. (1997) *Partition Types (from Linux FDISK),* 4 May, http://ceu.fi.udc.es/docs/sag-0.4/node38.html.
5. http://www.mossywell.com/boot-sequence/
6. Brouwer, A. E. (2005) *Partition Types: List of Partition Identifiers for PCs.* URL: http://www.win.tue.nl/~aeb/linux/partitions/partition_types-1.htm.

Appendix 6. *Extended Partitions*

Introduction

There appear to be two views commonly held in the literature about how extended partitions are constructed, although we were not able to find any definitive specifications. One view holds that extended partitions are constructed as "nested boxes", as we have shown in the upper section of Fig. A6.1. In this view, each extended partition (shown in light grey) is a box that contains all subordinate extended partitions as well as the logical partitions (shown in dark grey) nested one inside the other. The reader will note that, for clarity in the figure, we have shown the boxes one beneath the other rather than one inside the other as they should be.

The other view holds that extended partitions are constructed as "chained boxes" where each extended partition, except for the outer one, just contains the next logical partition. We have shown this view in the lower section of Fig. A6.1.

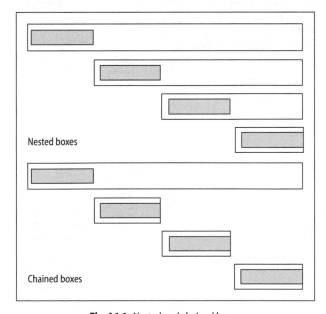

Nested boxes

Chained boxes

Fig. A6.1 Nested and chained boxes.

In order to determine what approach is in use in the systems which we come across, we carried out experiments to determine the actual structures that result when FDISK and PartitionMagic are used successively to partition the same hard disk. The disk we used was a Quantum Pioneer SG 1.0A which had a manufacturer's label marked "C/H/S 1.0GB 2097/16/63". This indicates a maximum possible capacity of:

$$2097 \times 16 \times 63 = 2,113,776 \text{ sectors}$$
$$2,113,776 \times 512 = 1,082,253,312 \text{ bytes}$$
$$1,082,253,312 / (1024 \times 1024) = 1032.12 \text{ Mbyte}$$

The disk was partitioned, on each occasion, with a primary DOS partition of 504.0 Mbyte and an extended DOS partition of the remaining space which was reported as 525.7 Mbyte. The extended partition was then further partitioned into three logical partitions of 246.1 Mbyte, 246.1 Mbyte and 33.4 Mbyte respectively. It is this disk which was used as the example for Fig. 5.29 repeated here as Fig. A6.2 for convenience.

The partitioning process was carried out using, in the first instance, PQMAGICT.EXE (PartitionMagic by Powerquest Version 3.03.256) and then, after deleting all partitions, using FDISK.EXE (MS-DOS Version 6). The results obtained from both partitioning processes were found to be identical in terms of the partition tables that were produced. Norton Disk Editor was used to analyse these partition tables and both hexadecimal and partition table views were obtained.

It may be noted that this hard disk has not been partitioned right to the very end of all the available physical sectors, although the maximum number of sectors that were accessible to the partitioning programs was used. The last partitioned CHS address is

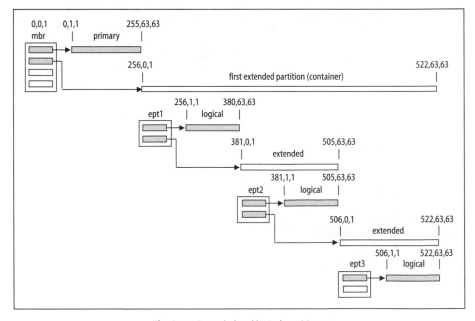

Fig. A6.2 Extended and logical partitions.

```
Physical Sector:     Cyl  0, Side 0, Sector 1
+------+----+--------------------+--------------------+----------+----------+
|      |    | Starting Location  |  Ending Location   | Relative | Number of |
|System|Boot|Side Cylinder Sector|Side Cylinder Sector| Sectors  | Sectors  |
+------+----+--------------------+--------------------+----------+----------+
|BIGDOS| Yes|   1     0       1  | 63   255     63  |       63 |  1032129 |
|EXTEND| No |   0   256       1  | 63   522     63  |  1032192 |  1076544 |
|unused| No |   0     0       0  |  0     0      0  |        0 |        0 |
|unused| No |   0     0       0  |  0     0      0  |        0 |        0 |
+------+----+--------------------+--------------------+----------+----------+
```

Fig. A6.3 Partition table for master boot record.

seen to be 522, 63, 63, which gives the number of available sectors as $523 \times 64 \times 63 = 2,108,736$[1]. This may be confirmed from the Master Boot Record partition table, Fig. A6.3, where the number of sectors on the disk can be calculated as 63 + 1,032,129 (BIGDOS) + 1,076,544 (EXTEND) = 2,108,736. This compares with the 2,113,776 sectors calculated from the physical number of cylinders, heads and sectors as given on the manufacturer's label. The difference of 5040 sectors arises for two reasons: firstly, because the CHS translation algorithm uses bit shifting and divides cylinders by 4 and multiplies heads by 4. This results in the loss of one cylinder (1008 sectors) in translation because 2097 is not exactly divisible by 4 but gives 524 with a remainder of 1. The last translated CHS address is therefore 523, 63, 63. This leads to the second reason for the loss: FDISK and PartitionMagic have not utilized the whole of the translated disk but have partitioned only to CHS 522, 63, 63. This is equivalent to the loss of four real cylinders (4032 sectors), which, together with 1008 sectors makes up the missing total of 5040 sectors.

Results

When we examined the partition tables, we noted that both PartitionMagic and FDISK gave exactly the same results, as shown in Figs. A6.4–A6.10.

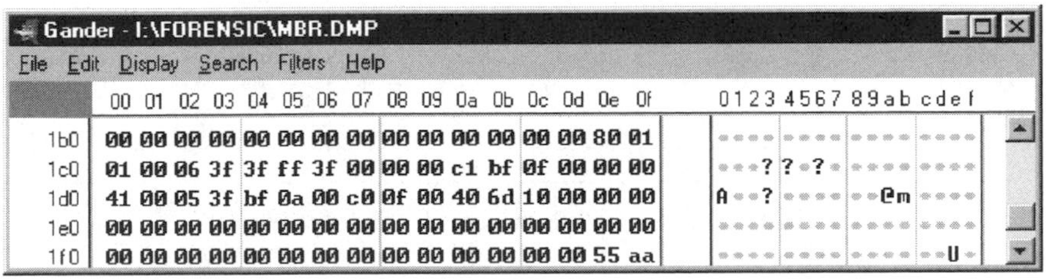

Fig. A6.4 Partition table for master boot record – hexadecimal.

---

1   The reader will recall that cylinders and heads in CHS addresses are counted from 0 and not 1.

```
Physical Sector:     Cyl  256, Side 0, Sector 1
+------+----+--------------------+--------------------+-----------+-----------+
|      |    | Starting Location  |  Ending Location   | Relative  | Number of |
|System|Boot|Side Cylinder Sector|Side Cylinder Sector|  Sectors  |  Sectors  |
+------+----+--------------------+--------------------+-----------+-----------+
|BIGDOS| No |  1    256      1   | 63    380     63   |      63   |   503937  |
|EXTEND| No |  0    381      1   | 63    505     63   |  504000   |   504000  |
|unused| No |  0     0       0   |  0     0       0   |       0   |        0  |
|unused| No |  0     0       0   |  0     0       0   |       0   |        0  |
+------+----+--------------------+--------------------+-----------+-----------+
```

Fig. A6.5 Partition table for the first extended partition.

From these experiments it is evident that the system in use here is the "chained boxes" construction. In all the hard disk analysis case work that the authors have carried out over the past decade, neither has come across anything other than the "chained boxes" construction approach for extended partitions.

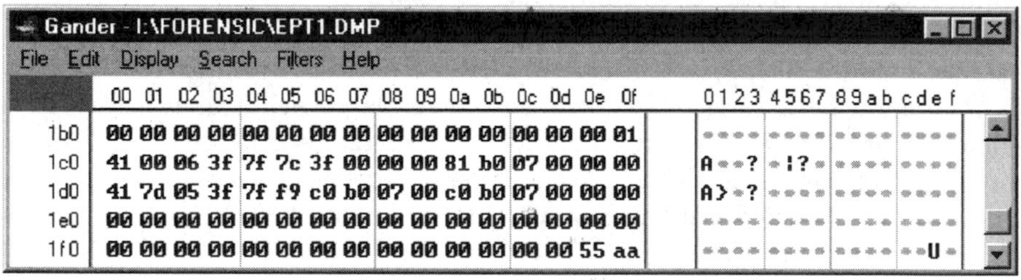

Fig. A6.6 Partition table for the first extended partition – hexadecimal.

```
Physical Sector:     Cyl  381, Side 0, Sector 1
+------+----+--------------------+--------------------+-----------+-----------+
|      |    | Starting Location  |  Ending Location   | Relative  | Number of |
|System|Boot|Side Cylinder Sector|Side Cylinder Sector|  Sectors  |  Sectors  |
+------+----+--------------------+--------------------+-----------+-----------+
|BIGDOS| No |  1    381      1   | 63    505     63   |      63   |   503937  |
|EXTEND| No |  0    506      1   | 63    522     63   | 1008000   |    68544  |
|unused| No |  0     0       0   |  0     0       0   |       0   |        0  |
|unused| No |  0     0       0   |  0     0       0   |       0   |        0  |
+------+----+--------------------+--------------------+-----------+-----------+
```

Fig. A6.7 Partition table for the second extended partition.

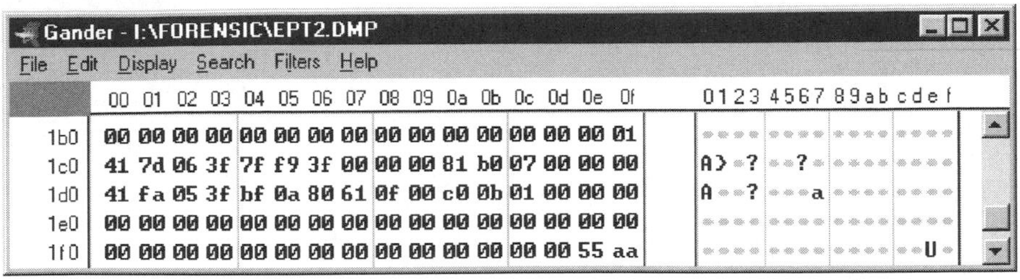

Fig. A6.8 Partition table for the second extended partition – hexadecimal.

```
Physical Sector:    Cyl 506, Side 0, Sector 1
+------+----+--------------------+--------------------+----------+----------+
|      |    | Starting Location  | Ending Location    | Relative | Number of|
|System|Boot|Side Cylinder Sector|Side Cylinder Sector| Sectors  | Sectors  |
+------+----+--------------------+--------------------+----------+----------+
|BIGDOS| No |  1    506    1     | 63    522    63    |    63    |  68481   |
|unused| No |  0     0     0     |  0     0     0     |     0    |     0    |
|unused| No |  0     0     0     |  0     0     0     |     0    |     0    |
|unused| No |  0     0     0     |  0     0     0     |     0    |     0    |
+------+----+--------------------+--------------------+----------+----------+
```

Fig. A6.9 Partition table for the third extended partition.

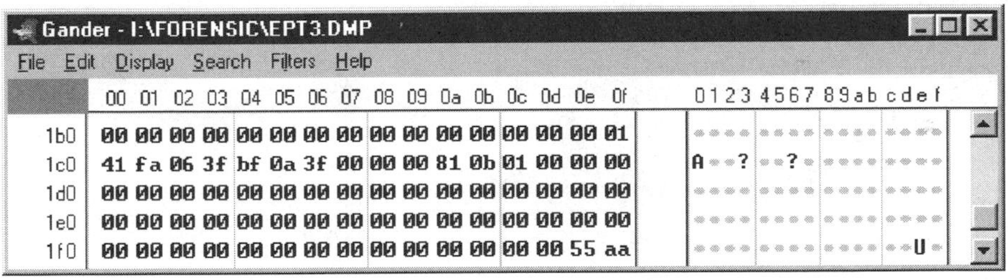

Fig. A6.10 Partition table for the third extended partition – hexadecimal.

Appendix 7. *Registers and Order Code for the Intel 8086*

Intel 8086 Registers

The Intel 8086 has eight general purpose registers which are 16 bits (two bytes or one word) in size. They are known as: AX, BX, CX, DX, SI, DI, BP, and SP (stack pointer). The first four, AX, BX, CX and DX may also be addressed as eight general purpose 8 bit (one byte) registers AH, AL, BH, BL, CH, CL, DH, and DL. There are also 4 segment registers which are 16 bits (two bytes or one word) in size. These are known as: CS (code segment), DS (data segment), ES (extra segment), and SS (stack segment). Additional instruction code details for the P5 processor have been added to this list, see Intel (1997).

Intel 8086 Hexadecimal Order Code

Hex	Instruction	Description
00	ADD	Add byte register into byte
01	ADD	Add word register into word
02	ADD	Add byte into byte register
03	ADD	Add word into word register
04	ADD	Add immediate byte into AL
05	ADD	Add immediate word into AX
06	PUSH ES	Push ES onto stack
07	POP ES	Pop ES from stack
08	OR	Logical OR byte register into byte
09	OR	Logical OR word register into word
0A	OR	Logical OR byte into byte register
0B	OR	Logical OR word into word register
0C	OR	Logical OR immediate byte into AL
0D	OR	Logical OR immediate word into AX
0E	PUSH CS	Push CS onto stack
0F	BSF	Bit Scan Forward
	BSR	Bit Scan Reverse
	BSWAP	Byte Swap
	BT	Bit Test
	BTC	Bit Test and Complement
	BTR	Bit Test and Reset

Hex	Instruction	Description
	BTS	Bit Test and Set
10	ADC	Add with carry byte register into byte
11	ADC	Add with carry word register into word
12	ADC	Add with carry byte into byte register
13	ADC	Add with carry word into word register
14	ADC	Add with carry immediate byte into AL
15	ADC	Add with carry immediate word into AX
16	PUSH SS	Push SS onto stack
17	POP SS	Pop SS from stack
18	SBB	Subtract with borrow
19	SBB	Subtract with borrow word register from word
1A	SBB	Subtract with borrow byte from byte register
1B	SBB	Subtract with borrow word from word register
1C	SBB	Subtract with borrow immediate byte from AL
1D	SBB	Subtract with borrow immediate word from AX
1E	PUSH DS	Push DS onto stack
1F	POP DS	Pop DS from stack
20	AND	Logical AND byte register into byte
21	AND	Logical AND word register into word
22	AND	Logical AND byte into byte register
23	AND	Logical AND word into word register
24	AND	Logical AND immediate byte into AL
25	AND	Logical AND immediate word into AX
26		ES segment override
27	DAA	Decimal adjust AL after addition
28	SUB	Subtract byte register from byte
29	SUB	Subtract word register from word
2A	SUB	Subtract byte from byte register
2B	SUB	Subtract word from word register
2C	SUB	Subtract immediate byte from AL
2D	SUB	Subtract immediate word from AX
2E		CS segment override
2F	DAS	Decimal adjust AL after subtraction
30	XOR	Exclusive OR byte register into byte
31	XOR	Exclusive OR word register into word
32	XOR	Exclusive OR byte into byte register
33	XOR	Exclusive OR word into word register
34	XOR	Exclusive OR immediate byte into AL
35	XOR	Exclusive OR immediate word into AX
36		SS segment override
37	AAA	ASCII adjust AL after addition
38	CMP	Subtract byte register from byte for compare
39	CMP	Subtract word register from word for compare
3A	CMP	Subtract byte from byte register for compare
3B	CMP	Subtract word from word register for compare
3C	CMP	Subtract immediate byte from AL for compare
3D	CMP	Subtract immediate word from AX for compare
3E		DS segment override
3F	AAS	ASCII adjust AL after subtraction
40	INC	Increment word register 0 by 1
41	INC	Increment word register 1 by 1
42	INC	Increment word register 2 by 1
43	INC	Increment word register 3 by 1
44	INC	Increment word register 4 by 1
45	INC	Increment word register 5 by 1

Hex	Instruction	Description
46	INC	Increment word register 6 by 1
47	INC	Increment word register 7 by 1
48	DEC	Decrement word register 0 by 1
49	DEC	Decrement word register 1 by 1
4A	DEC	Decrement word register 2 by 1
4B	DEC	Decrement word register 3 by 1
4C	DEC	Decrement word register 4 by 1
4D	DEC	Decrement word register 5 by 1
4E	DEC	Decrement word register 6 by 1
4F	DEC	Decrement word register 7 by 1
50	PUSH	Push word register 0 onto stack
51	PUSH	Push word register 1 onto stack
52	PUSH	Push word register 2 onto stack
53	PUSH	Push word register 3 onto stack
54	PUSH	Push word register 4 onto stack
55	PUSH	Push word register 5 onto stack
56	PUSH	Push word register 6 onto stack
57	PUSH	Push word register 7 onto stack
58	POP	Pop word register 0 from stack
59	POP	Pop word register 1 from stack
5A	POP	Pop word register 2 from stack
5B	POP	Pop word register 3 from stack
5C	POP	Pop word register 4 from stack
5D	POP	Pop word register 5 from stack
5E	POP	Pop word register 6 from stack
5F	POP	Pop word register 7 from stack
60	PUSHA/PUSHAD	Push All General Registers
61	POPA/POPAD	Pop All General Registers
62	BOUND	Check Array Against Bounds
63	ARPL	Adjust RPL Field of Selector
64		FS segment override
65		GS segment override
66		operand size
67		address size
68	PUSH	Push imm16/32
69	IMUL	Signed Multiply
6A	PUSH	Push imm8
6B	IMUL	Signed Multiply
6C	INS	Input Byte from Port
6D	INS	Input Word from Port
6E	OUTS	Output Byte to Port
6F	OUTS	Output Word to Port
70	JO	Jump short if overflow
71	JNO	Jump short if not overflow
72	JB	Jump short if below
	JC	Jump short if carry
	JNAE	Jump short if not above or equal
73	JAE	Jump short if above or equal
	JNB	Jump short if not below
	JNC	Jump short if not carry
74	JE	Jump short if equal
	JZ	Jump short if zero
75	JNE	Jump short if not equal
	JNZ	Jump short if not zero
76	JBE	Jump short if below or equal

Hex	Instruction	Description
	JNA	Jump short if not above
77	JA	Jump short if above
	JNBE	Jump short if not below or equal
78	JS	Jump short if sign
79	JNS	Jump short if not sign
7A	JP	Jump short if parity
	JPE	Jump short if parity even
7B	JPO	Jump short if parity odd
	JNP	Jump short if not parity
7C	JL	Jump short if less
	JNGE	Jump short if not greater or equal
7D	JGE	Jump short if greater or equal
	JNL	Jump short if not less
7E	JLE	Jump short if less or equal
	JNG	Jump short if not greater
7F	JG	Jump short if greater
	JNLE	Jump short if not less or equal
80 /0	ADD	Add immediate byte into byte
80 /1	OR	Logical OR immediate byte into byte
80 /2	ADC	Add with carry immediate byte into byte
80 /3	SBB	Subtract with borrow immediate byte from byte
80 /4	AND	Logical AND immediate byte into byte
80 /5	UB	Subtract immediate byte from byte
80 /6	XOR	Exclusive OR immediate byte into byte
80 /7	CMP	Subtract immediate byte from byte for compare
81 /0	ADD	Add immediate word into word
81 /1	OR	Logical OR immediate word into word
81 /2	ADC	Add with carry immediate word into word
81 /3	SBB	Subtract with borrow immediate word from word
81 /4	AND	Logical AND immediate word into word
81 /5	SUB	Subtract immediate word from word
81 /6	XOR	Exclusive OR immediate word into word
81 /7	CMP	Subtract immediate word from word for compare
82		
83 /0	ADD	Add immediate byte into word
83 /1	OR	Logical OR immediate byte into word
83 /2	ADC	Add with carry immediate byte into word
83 /3	SBB	Subtract with borrow immediate byte from word
83 /4	AND	Logical AND immediate byte into word
83 /5	SUB	Subtract immediate byte from word
83 /6	XOR	Exclusive OR immediate byte into word
83 /7	CMP	Subtract immediate byte from word for compare
84	TEST	AND byte register with byte for flags
85	TEST	AND word register with word for flags
86	XCHG	Exchange byte register with byte
87	XCHG	Exchange word register with word
88	MOV	Move byte register into byte
89	MOV	Move word register into word
8A	MOV	Move byte into byte register
8B	MOV	Move word into word register
8C /0	MOV	Move ES into word
8C /1	MOV	Move CS into word
8C /2	MOV	Move SS into word
8C /3	MOV	Move DS into word
8D	LEA	Calculate offset and place in word register

Hex	Instruction	Description
8E /0	MOV	Move memory word into ES
	MOV	Move word register into ES
8E /2	MOV	Move memory word into SS
	MOV	Move word register into SS
8E /3	MOV	Move memory word into DS
	MOV	Move word register into DS
8F	POP	Pop memory word from stack
90	NOP	No Operation
91		
92		
93		
94		
95		
96		
97		
98	CBW	Convert byte into word
99	CWD	Convert word to doubleword
9A	CALL	Call far segment, immediate 4 byte address
9B	WAIT	Wait until BUSY inactive
9C	PUSHF	Push flags onto stack
9D	POPF	Pop flags from stack
9E	SAHF	Store AH into flags
9F	LAHF	Load AH with flags
A0	MOV	Move byte, offset immediated word, into AL
A1	MOV	Move word, offset immediate word, into AX
A2	MOV	Move AL into byte, offset immediate word
A3	MOV	Move AX into word, offset immediate word
A4	MOVS	Move byte [SI] to ES:[DI]
	MOVSB	Move byte DS:[SI] to ES:[DI]
A5	MOVS	Move word [SI] to ES:[DI]
	MOVSW	Move word DS:[SI] to ES:[DI]
A6	CMPS	Compare bytes ES:[DI] from [SI]
	CMPSB	Compare bytes ES:[DI] from DS:[SI]
A7	CMPS	Compare words ES:[DI] from [SI]
	CMPSW	Compare words ES:[DI] from DS:[SI]
A8	TEST	AND immediate byte into AL for flags
A9	TEST	AND immediate word into AX for flags
AA	STOS	Store AL to byte [DI], advance DI
	STOSB	Store AL to byte ES:[DI], advance DI
AB	STOS	Store AX to word [DI], advance DI
	STOSW	Store AX to word ES:[DI], advance DI
AC	LODS	Load byte [SI] into AL, advance SI
	LODSB	Load byte [SI] into AL, advance SI
AD	LODS	Load word [SI] into AX, advance SI
	LODSW	Load word [SI] into AX, advance SI
AE	SCAS	Compare bytes AL ES:[DI], advance DI
	SCASB	Compare bytes AX ES:[DI], advance DI
AF	SCAS	Compare words AL ES:[DI], advance DI
	SCASW	Compare words AX ES:[DI], advance DI
B0	MOV	Move immediate byte into byte register 0
B1	MOV	Move immediate byte into byte register 1
B2	MOV	Move immediate byte into byte register 2
B3	MOV	Move immediate byte into byte register 3
B4	MOV	Move immediate byte into byte register 4
B5	MOV	Move immediate byte into byte register 5

Hex	Instruction	Description
B6	MOV	Move immediate byte into byte register 6
B7	MOV	Move immediate byte into byte register 7
B8	MOV	Move immediate word into word register 0
B9	MOV	Move immediate word into word register 1
BA	MOV	Move immediate word into word register 2
BB	MOV	Move immediate word into word register 3
BC	MOV	Move immediate word into word register 4
BD	MOV	Move immediate word into word register 5
BE	MOV	Move immediate word into word register 6
BF	MOV	Move immediate word into word register 7
C0	Rxy	Rotate various left or right
C1	Rxy	Rotate various left or right
C2	RET	Return near
C3	RET	Return near
C3	RET	Return near
C4	LES	Load doubleword into ES and word register
C5	LDS	Load doubleword into DS and word register
C6	MOV	Move immediate byte into byte
C7	MOV	Move immediate word into word
C8	ENTER	Create a stack frame for a procedure
C9	LEAVE	Set SP to BP, then pop BP
CA	RETF	Return far
CB	RETF	Return far
CC	INT 3	Interrupt 3
CD	INT	Interrupt number immediate byte
CE	INTO	Interrupt 4 if overflow is set
CF	IRET	Interrupt return
D0 /0	ROL	Rotate 8 bit byte left once
D0 /1	ROR	Rotate 8 bit byte right once
D0 /2	RCL	Rotate 9 bit quantity left once
D0 /3	RCR	Rotate 9 bit quantity right once
D0 /4	SAL	Multiply byte by 2, once
	SHL	Multiply byte by 2, once
D0 /5	SHR	Unsigned divide byte by 2, once
D0 /7	SAR	Signed divide byte by 2, once
D1 /0	ROL	Rotate 16 bit word left once
D1 /1	ROR	Rotate 16 bit word right once
D1 /2	RCL	Rotate 17 bit quantity left once
D1 /3	RCR	Rotate 17 bit quantity right once
D1 /4	SAL	Multiply word by 2, once
	SHL	Multiply word by 2, once
D1 /5	SHR	Unsigned divide word by 2, once
D1 /7	SAR	Signed divide word by 2, once
D2 /0	ROL	Rotate 8 bit byte left CL times
D2 /1	ROR	Rotate 8 bit byte right CL times
D2 /2	RCL	Rotate 9 bit quantity left CL times
D2 /3	RCR	Rotate 9 bit quantity right CL times
D2 /4	SAL	Multiply byte by 2, CL times
	SHL	Multiply byte by 2, CL times
D2 /5	SHR	Unsigned divide byte by 2, CL times
D2 /7	SAR	Signed divide byte by 2, CL times
D3 /0	ROL	Rotate 16 bit word left CL times
D3 /1	ROR	Rotate 16 bit word right CL times
D3 /2	RCL	Rotate 17 bit quantity left CL times
D3 /3	RCR	Rotate 17 bit quantity right CL times

Hex	Instruction	Description
D3 /4	SAL	Multiply word by 2, CL times
	SHL	Multiply word by 2, CL times
D3 /5	SHR	Unsigned divide word by 2, CL times
D3 /7	SAR	Signed divide word by 2, CL times
D4	AAM	ASCII adjust after multiply
D5	AAD	ASCII adjust before division
D6	SALC	Set AL on Carry
D7	XLAT	Set AL to memory byte [BX + unsigned AL]
D7	XLATB	Set AL to memory byte DS:[BX + unsigned AL]
D8		Floating Point Escape opcode
D9		Floating Point Escape opcode
DA		Floating Point Escape opcode
DB		Floating Point Escape opcode
DC		Floating Point Escape opcode
DD		Floating Point Escape opcode
DE		Floating Point Escape opcode
DF		Floating Point Escape opcode
E0	LOOPNE	jump short if CX/=0 and not equal
	LOOPNZ	jump short if CX/=0 and ZF=0
E1	LOOPE	jump short if CX/=0 and equal
	LOOPZ	jump short if CX/=0 and zero
E2	LOOP	jump short if CX/=0
E3	JCXZ	Jump short if CX register is zero
E4	IN	Input byte from immediate port into AL
E5	IN	Input word from immediate port into AX
E6	OUT	Output byte AL to immediate port
E7	OUT	Output word AX to immediate port
E8	CALL	Call near
E9	JMP	Jump near
EA	JMP	Jump far
EB	JMP	Jump short
EC	IN	Input byte from port DX into AL
ED	IN	Input word from port DX into AX
EE	OUT	Output byte AL to port number DX
EF	OUT	Output word AX to port number DX
F0	LOCK	Assert BUSLOCK signal
F1	ICEBP	In-Circuit-Emulator Breakpoint
F2	REPNE	Repeat following CX times or until ZF=1
	REPNZ	Repeat following CX times or until ZF=1
F3	REP	Repeat following CX times
	REPE	Repeat following CX times or until ZF=0
	REPZ	Repeat following CX times or until ZF=0
F4	HLT	Halt
F5	CMC	Complement carry flag
F6 /0	TEST	AND immediate byte with byte for flags
F6 /2	NOT	Reverse each bit of byte
F6 /3	NEG	Two's complement negate byte
F6 /4	MUL	Unsigned multiply (AX = AL * byte)
F6 /5	IMUL	Signed multiply (AX = AL * byte)
F6 /6	DIV	Unsigned divide AX by byte
F6 /7	IDIV	Signed divide AX by byte
F7 /0	TEST	AND immediate word with word for flags
F7 /2	NOT	Reverse each bit of word
F7 /3	NEG	Two's complement negate word
F7 /4	MUL	Unsigned multiply (DXAX = AX * word)

Hex	Instruction	Description
F7 /5	IMUL	Signed multiply (DXAX = AX * word)
F7 /6	DIV	Unsigned divide DXAX by word
F7 /7	IDIV	Signed divide DXAX by word
F8	CLC	Clear carry flag
F9	STC	Set carry flag
FA	CLI	Clear interrupt enable flag
FB	STI	Set interrupt enable flag
FC	CLD	Clear direction flag
FD	STD	Set direction flag
FE /0	INC	Increment byte by 1
FE /1	DEC	Decrement byte by 1
FF /0	INC	Increment word by 1
FF /1	DEC	Decrement word by 1
FF /2	CALL	Call near, offset absolute at word
FF /3	CALL	Call far segment, address at doubleword
FF /4	JMP	Jump near to word (absolute offset)
FF /5	JMP	Jump far
FF /6	PUSH	Set [SP 2] to memory word

Reference

1. Intel (1997), Intel Architecture Software Developer's Manual, Volume 2: Instruction Set Reference, Order Number 243191, URL: http://www.intel.com/.

Appendix 8. NTFS Boot Sector and BIOS Parameter Block

This appendix contains details of the boot sector and the BIOS parameter block for NTFS volumes. Boot sectors and BIOS parameter blocks have been considered in some detail in Chapter 5, but these are for FAT file systems. The details given here are specific to NTFS volumes and should be related to the analysis carried out in Chapter 6.

Layout of Boot Sector on NTFS Volumes

At Table A8.1 is shown the outline layout of the 512 byte NTFS boot sector. Highlighted in italic text are the two main areas that are expanded in Table A8.2 below: namely, the BIOS parameter block and the Extended BIOS parameter block.

Table A8.1 NTFS boot sector layout.

Byte offset (decimal)	Byte offset (hex)	Length in bytes	Use
0–2	00–02	3	Jump instruction to bootstrap code
3–10	03–0A	8	OEM ID
11–35	*0B–23*	*25*	*BIOS parameter block*
36–83	*24–53*	*48*	*Extended BIOS parameter block*
84–509	54–01FD	426	Bootstrap code
510–511	01FE–01FF	2	End of sector signature

Layout of BIOS Parameter Block and Extended BIOS Parameter Block

The two values marked with an asterisk (*) in Table A8.2 are signed 8 bit numbers which may be used in two different ways. If the numbers in these fields are positive (between 00–7Fh) they define how many *clusters* there are for each MFT record or

387

Table A8.2 BIOS Parameter block and extended BIOS parameter block.

Byte offset (decimal)	Byte offset (hex)	Length in bytes	Use
11–12	0B–0C	2	Number of bytes per sector, usually 512
13	0D	1	Number of sectors per cluster
14–15	0E–0F	2	Number of reserved sectors, usually 0.
16–20	10–14	5	Use not specified but must be 0.
21	15	1	Media descriptor
22–23	16–17	2	Use not specified but must be 0.
24–31	18–1F	8	Not used
32–35	20–23	4	Use not specified but must be 0.
36–39	24–27	4	Not used
40–47	28–2F	8	Total number of sectors on volume
48–55	30–37	8	Logical cluster number for start of $MFT
56–63	38–3F	8	Logical cluster number for start of $MFTMirr
64	40	1	Size of MFT record in clusters, usually 1024*
65–67	41–43	3	Not used
68	44	1	Size of index buffer, "INDX file" in clusters*
69–71	45–47	3	Not used
72–79	48–4F	8	Volume serial number
80–83	50–53	4	Not used

INDX file. If the numbers are negative (80–FFh) they define how many *bytes* there are for each MFT record or INDX file.

The actual value is calculated by raising 2 to the power of the absolute value of this number. Thus, if offset byte 64 contains, as it does in the sample BPB, the value F6h, then the 8 bit signed value of the number, F6, is −10 and its absolute value is 10. Thus the number of *bytes* (because it is negative) in each MFT record entry is $2^{10} = 1024$ bytes. This conforms with current experience that all systems seen to date have a 1024 byte record size.

The detail in this appendix has been obtained from: http://www.microsoft.com/resources/documentation/Windows/XP/all/reskit/en-us/Default.asp?url=/resources/documentation/Windows/XP/all/reskit/en-us/prkd_tro_ilxl.asp.

Appendix 9. *MFT Header and Attribute Maps*

This appendix contains details of the MFT Header and the Attributes for NTFS volumes.

MFT Attribute Identifiers

The values for the MFT Attribute Identifiers are as listed in Table A9.1.

Table A9.1 MFT Attribute Identifiers.

Standard_Information	ID	10 00 00 00
Attribute_List	ID	20 00 00 00
File_Name	ID	30 00 00 00
Object_ID	ID	40 00 00 00
Security_Descriptor	ID	50 00 00 00
Volume_Name	ID	60 00 00 00
Volume_Information	ID	70 00 00 00
Data	ID	80 00 00 00
Index_Root	ID	90 00 00 00
Index_Allocation	ID	A0 00 00 00
Bitmap	ID	B0 00 00 00
Reparse_Point	ID	C0 00 00 00
EA_Information	ID	D0 00 00 00
EA	ID	E0 00 00 00
Logged_Utility_Stream	ID	00 00 00 00

MFT Record Structure

All MFT records in the sample MFT have the structure shown in Table A9.2.

Table A9.2 MFT record structure.

File Record Header
Standard Attribute Header
Attribute Proper
Standard Attribute Header
Attribute Proper
And so on
End of Record marker (FF FF FF FFh)
Error Check Sequence (4 bytes)

The FILE Record Header

It should be noted that the Windows XP version of this Header is 8 bytes longer than the Windows 2000 version. The reason for this is that in Windows XP a new field has been added to contain the MFT Record Number. The details of the Windows 2000 version are given in Table A9.3 and the changes for the Windows XP version are given in Table A9.4 below.

Table A9.3 FILE Record Header – Windows 2000.

Byte offset (decimal)	Byte offset (hex)	Length in bytes	Use	Notes (where value is mentioned bytes are in little endian format)
0–3	00–03	4	Identification String "FILE"	Appears at the head of all MFT record entries.
4–5	04–05	2	Offset to the Update Sequence Array in bytes	The value of these two bytes is the number of bytes from the beginning of the header to the first byte of the update sequence array. The offset is calculated by adding this value to the offset of the first byte of the header.
6–7	06–07	2	Length of Update Sequence	The Update Sequence Array is 6 bytes in length for 1024 byte record MFT. This value always appears to be 3 in such an MFT. Possibly a count of length in words.
8–15	08–0F	8	Reportedly the $Logfile sequence number (not confirmed)	Use is not defined, probably used to index changes to the record in $Logfile
16–17	10–11	2	Record Use Sequence Number	Starts at 1 on first use and incremented when the record is marked as deleted.
18–19	12–13	2	Hard Link Count (not confirmed)	Count of hard links associated with the entry.
20–21	14–15	2	Offset to First Attribute in bytes	The value of these two bytes is the number of bytes from the beginning of the header to the first byte of the Attribute following it. The offset is calculated by adding this value to the offset of the first byte of the header.
22–23	16–17	2	Record Status Flags	Records the status of the record: 00 00 = deleted file record 01 00 = file record in use 02 00 = deleted directory record 03 00 = directory record in use
24–27	18–1B	4	"Logical" size of the record in bytes	The value of these four bytes is the count, in bytes, of the record from the first byte of this header to the last byte of the error check sequence. The error check sequence of 4 bytes follows the End of Record marker of FF FF FF FFh.

Byte offset (decimal)	Byte offset (hex)	Length in bytes	Use	Notes (where value is mentioned bytes are in little endian format)
28–31	1C–1F	4	"Physical" size of the record in bytes	The value of these bytes is the actual size, in bytes, of the allocated size of the record. This is known as the "Physical" Size. It is fixed in the BIOS Parameter Block of the Boot Record. In most cases it is 1024 bytes.
32–39	20–27	8	1. Base File Reference 2. Unknown – possibly an ID sequence number	This field is used to store a Base File Reference Number probably in the first six (least significant) bytes. It is used for records where there are more Attributes than can fit into a single record. In the second or subsequent records these bytes contain a value which is the number of the MFT record in which the "parent" record resides. The use of an ID sequence number in the remaining bytes is uncertain but there is a consistent use of low two-byte values in the most significant pair. This two-byte value is the same in all records referring to the same "parent" record.
40–41	28–29	2	Next Attribute ID number	The value of these two bytes is the number to be allocated to the next Attribute to be added to this record. It is not a value that equates to the number of Attributes already present in the record plus one. It appears to be incremented as each Attribute is added, but not decremented when one is removed.
42–43 (see notes below)	2A–2B	2	The Update Sequence Array Part 1 – The Update Sequence Number	The number occupying these two bytes is used as a test value for the reading of the record. It appears here, and is seeded into the final two bytes of each SECTOR of the record. In a 1024 byte record this is at bytes offset 510, 511, 1022 and 1023. The data which should occupy these bytes is placed in the Update Sequence Array Part 2 in that order. When a record is read into memory the value of the Update Sequence Number is compared against the four bytes at 510, 511, 1022 and 1023. If a match is made the read is successful and the four bytes in memory are replaced by the four bytes from the Update Sequence Array Part 2, thus replacing the seeded values with the correct ones for the data set required.

Byte offset (decimal)	Byte offset (hex)	Length in bytes	Use	Notes (where value is mentioned bytes are in little endian format)
44–47	2C–2F	4	The Update Sequence Array Part 2 – The Array	These four bytes are the bytes from offsets 510, 511, 1022 and 1023 of the record which have been replaced by the Update Sequence Number for integrity testing.

It should be noted that the use of the words "sequence number" only implies the use of a number which is incremented; it is not a definitive title. The location of Part 1 of the Update Sequence Array is pointed to by the value of the bytes at offsets 4 and 5 of this header. Table A9.3 refers to a Windows 2000 installation. In the case of a Windows XP installation the location pointed to by these bytes is 6 bytes further on due to inclusion of a field for the MFT Record Number. The final section of the Windows XP header is as shown at Table A9.4.

Table A9.4 FILE Record Header – final section for Windows XP.

Byte offset (decimal)	Byte offset (hex)	Length in bytes	Use	Notes (where value is mentioned bytes are in little endian format)
42–43	2A–2B			Unused
44–47	2C–2F	4	MFT Record Number (XP)	These four bytes store the MFT Record Number for THIS record. The Record Number can be calculated by identifying the offset value in bytes of the start of the record from the start of the MFT and dividing by the record size (usually 1024).
48–49	30–31	2	The Update Sequence Array Part 1 – The Update Sequence Number	The number occupying these two bytes is used as a test value for the reading of the record. It appears here, and is seeded into the final two bytes of each SECTOR of the record. In a 1024 byte record this is at bytes offset 510, 511, 1022 and 1023. The data which should occupy these bytes is placed in the Update Sequence Array Part 2 in that order. When a record is read into memory the value of the Update Sequence Number is compared against the four bytes at 510, 511, 1022 and 1023. If a match is made the read is successful and the four bytes in memory are replaced by the four bytes from the Update Sequence Array Part 2, thus replacing the seeded values with the correct ones for the data set required.

Byte offset (decimal)	Byte offset (hex)	Length in bytes	Use	Notes (where value is mentioned bytes are in little endian format)
50–53	32–35	4	The Update Sequence Array Part 2 – The Array	These four bytes are the bytes from offsets 510, 511, 1022 and 1023 of the record which have been replaced by the Update Sequence Number for integrity testing.
54–55	36–37	2	Padding to 8 byte boundary	

The Attribute Header

There are four types of Attribute Header: Type 1 is Resident, Un-Named; Type 2 is Non-Resident, Un-Named; Type 3 is Resident, Named; and Type 4 is Non-Resident, Named. Each of these headers differs from one another and so full details of each are given in the four tables below.

Attribute Header – Type 1

This Attribute Header is Resident (given by byte offset 8 = 00h) and Un-Named (given by byte offset 9 = 00h).

Table A9.5 Attribute Header – Type 1 – Resident, Un-Named.

Byte offset (decimal)	Byte offset (hex)	Length in bytes	Use	Notes (where value is mentioned bytes are in little endian format)
0–3	00–03	4	Attribute Identifier	A four-byte Identification number, this is the ID as defined in $AttrDef for each Attribute type. This value identifies the layout of the Attribute following this header.
4–7	04–07	4	Length of Current Attribute in bytes	The value of these two bytes is the number of bytes making up the length of this Attribute, including this header. It can also be used to calculate the location of the first byte of the next Attribute, or End of Record Marker, by adding this value to the offset of the first byte of the header.
8	8	1	Non-Resident Flag	Value 00 = Resident Attribute Value 01 = Non-Resident Attribute TO APPLY THIS TEMPLATE THIS BYTE MUST BE STORING THE VALUE 00h.

Byte offset (decimal)	Byte offset (hex)	Length in bytes	Use	Notes (where value is mentioned bytes are in little endian format)
9	9	1	Length of Attribute Name in Characters	Note that in Unicode two bytes are used to store each character value, thus a name length of 4 will occupy 8 bytes. TO APPLY THIS TEMPLATE THIS BYTE MUST BE STORING THE VALUE 00h.
10–11	0A–0B	2	Offset to Start of Attribute Proper in bytes	The value of these two bytes is the number of bytes from the beginning of the header to the first byte of the Attribute proper following it. The offset is calculated by adding this value to the offset of the first byte of the header. (NOT ALWAYS USED)
12–13	0C–0D	2	Data Status Flags	Value 01 00h = Compressed Value 40 00h = Encrypted Value 80 00h = Sparse (Used in Data Attribute)
14–15	0E–0F	2	Reportedly an Attribute ID number (not confirmed)	May be used for a number of purposes not yet identified, in particular as a flag for virus infected/ cleaned files
16–19	10–13	4	Length of the Attribute Proper in bytes	The value of these four bytes is the number of bytes making up the length of the Attribute Proper. Added to the length of the header it gives the total length of the Attribute as defined at offsets 4–7.
20–21	14–15	2	Offset to Start of Attribute Proper in bytes	The value of these two bytes is the number of bytes from the beginning of the header to the first byte of the Attribute proper following it. The offset is calculated by adding this value to the offset of the first byte of the header.
22	16	1	Indexed flag (not confirmed)	
23	17	1	Padding to 8 byte boundary	Unused.

Attribute Header – Type 2

This Attribute Header is Non-Resident (given by byte offset 8 = 01h) and Un-Named (given by byte offset 9 = 00h).

Table A9.6 Attribute Header – Type 2 – Non-Resident, Un-Named.

Byte offset (decimal)	Byte offset (hex)	Length in bytes	Use	Notes (where value is mentioned bytes are in little endian format)
0–3	00–03	4	Attribute Identifier	A four-byte Identification number, this is the ID as defined in $AttrDef for each Attribute type. This value identifies the layout of the Attribute following this header.
4–7	04–07	4	Length of Current Attribute in bytes	The value of these two bytes is the number of bytes making up the length of this Attribute, including this header. It can also be used to calculate the location of the first byte of the next Attribute, or End of Record Marker, by adding this value to the offset of the first byte of the header.
8	8	1	Non-Resident Flag	Value 00 = Resident Attribute Value 01 = Non-Resident Attribute TO APPLY THIS TEMPLATE THIS BYTE MUST BE STORING THE VALUE 01h.
9	9	1	Length of Name in Characters	Note that in Unicode two bytes are used to store each character value, thus a name length of 4 will occupy 8 bytes. TO APPLY THIS TEMPLATE THIS BYTE MUST BE STORING THE VALUE 00h.
10–11	0A–0B	2	Offset to Start of the Name of the Attribute, in bytes	The value of these two bytes is the number of bytes from the beginning of the header to the first byte of the Attribute's Name. That location is calculated by adding this value to the offset of the first byte of the header. (Should be zero – un-named)
12–13	0C–0D	2	Data Status Flags	Value 01 00h = Compressed Value 40 00h = Encrypted Value 80 00h = Sparse (Used in Data Attribute)
14–15	0E–0F	2	Reportedly an Attribute ID number (not confirmed)	May be used for a number of purposes not yet identified, in particular as a flag for virus infected/cleaned files.
16–23	10–17	8	Starting Virtual Cluster Number	NTFS uses mapping of Real Clusters to Virtual Clusters, the value of the Starting Virtual Cluster should normally be 00h.
24–31	18–1F	8	Ending Virtual Cluster Number	Virtual Clusters are the same size as clusters on the disk.

Byte offset (decimal)	Byte offset (hex)	Length in bytes	Use	Notes (where value is mentioned bytes are in little endian format)
32–33	20–22	2	Offset to the start of the Data Run Sequence(s), in bytes	The value of these two bytes is the number of bytes from the beginning of the header to the first byte of the Data Run Sequence(s). The offset is calculated by adding this value to the offset of the first byte of the header.
34–35	22–23	2	Compression Unit Size	Use of this field to identify compression is confirmed but the method has not been explored.
36–39	24–27	4	Padding to 8 byte boundary	
40–47	28–2F	8	The "Physical" size of the Attribute, in bytes	Physical size in the case of non-resident data means the size in bytes of the storage block(s) allocated for the storage of the data.
48–55	30–37	8	The "Logical" size of the Attribute, in bytes	Logical size in the case of non-resident data means the actual size in bytes of the data itself.
56–63	38–3F	8	The initialized data size of the stream, in bytes	In most cases this is the same size as the Logical size of the data, its use is uncertain.
64 on	40 on	Varies	The Data Run Sequence (This is the Data Attribute Proper but is included here for simplicity)	There can be almost any number of data runs for a fragmented file. Their make up and size are governed by the first byte in the sequence. See "Data Runs – an Example" below. Remember, any successive data runs are addressed as an offset from the start of the previous one.

Data Runs – an Example

For Non-Resident Attributes, a Data Run Sequence is required (see byte offset 64 in Table A9.6). An example of such a sequence is given in Fig. A9.1.

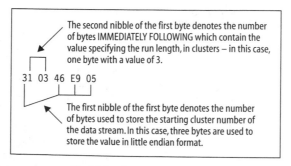

Fig. A9.1　Data runs – an example.

Evaluating a data run such as:

31 01 DA 85 02 11 18 50 11 01 30

gives us the following:

a run length of 01 clusters from 0285DA h = 165,388
a run length of 18h = 24 clusters from 0285DAh + 50h = 165,418
a run length of 01 clusters from 0285DAh + 50h + 30h = 165,466

Attribute Header – Type 3

This Attribute Header is Resident (given by byte offset 8 = 00h) and Named (given by byte offset 9 > 00h).

Table A9.7 Attribute Header – Type 3 – Resident, Named.

Byte offset (decimal)	Byte offset (hex)	Length in bytes	Use	Notes (where value is mentioned bytes are in little endian format)
0–3	00–03	4	Attribute Identifier	A four-byte Identification number, this is the ID as defined in $AttrDef for each Attribute type. This value identifies the layout of the Attribute following this header.
4–7	04–07	4	Length of Current Attribute in bytes	The value of these two bytes is the number of bytes making up the length of this Attribute, including this header. It can also be used to calculate the location of the first byte of the next Attribute, or End of Record Marker, by adding this value to the offset of the first byte of the header.
8	8	1	Non-Resident Flag	Value 00 = Resident Attribute Value 01 = Non-Resident Attribute TO APPLY THIS TEMPLATE THIS BYTE MUST BE STORING THE VALUE 00h.
9	9	1	Length of Name in Characters (N = number of bytes occupied)	Note that in Unicode two bytes are used to store each character value; thus a name length of 4 will occupy 8 bytes. TO APPLY THIS TEMPLATE THIS BYTE MUST BE STORING A VALUE GREATER THAN 00h.
10–11	0A–0B	2	Offset to Start of the Name of the Attribute, in bytes	The value of these two bytes is the number of bytes from the beginning of the header to the first byte of the Attribute's Name. That location is calculated by adding this value to the offset of the first byte of the header.

Byte offset (decimal)	Byte offset (hex)	Length in bytes	Use	Notes (where value is mentioned bytes are in little endian format)
12–13	0C–0D	2	Data Status Flags	Value 01 00h = Compressed Value 40 00h = Encrypted Value 80 00h = Sparse (Used in Data Attribute)
14–15	0E–0F	2	Reportedly an Attribute ID number (not confirmed)	May be used for a number of purposes not yet identified, in particular as a flag for virus infected/cleaned files
16–19	10–13	4	Length of the Attribute Proper in bytes	The value of these four bytes is the number of bytes making up the length of the Attribute Proper. Added to the length of the header it gives the total length of the Attribute as defined at offsets 4–7.
20–21	14–15	2	Offset to Start of Attribute Proper in bytes	The value of these two bytes is the number of bytes from the beginning of the header to the first byte of the Attribute proper following it. The offset is calculated by adding this value to the offset of the first byte of the header.
22	16	1	Indexed flag (not confirmed)	
23	17	1	Padding to 8 byte boundary	
24 on	18 on	N	Name of Attribute in Unicode (padded to 8 byte boundary}	Note that in Unicode two bytes are used to store each character value, thus a name length of 4 will occupy 8 bytes.

Attribute Header – Type 4

This Attribute Header is Non-Resident (given by byte offset 8 = 01h) and Named (given by byte offset 9 > 00h).

Table A9.8 Attribute Header – Type 4 – Non-Resident, Named.

Byte offset (decimal)	Byte offset (hex)	Length in bytes	Use	Notes (where value is mentioned bytes are in little endian format)
0–3	00–03	4	Attribute Identifier	A four-byte Identification number, this is the ID as defined in $AttrDef for each Attribute type. This value identifies the layout of the Attribute following this header.

Byte offset (decimal)	Byte offset (hex)	Length in bytes	Use	Notes (where value is mentioned bytes are in little endian format)
4–7	04–07	4	Length of Current Attribute in bytes	The value of these two bytes is the number of bytes making up the length of this Attribute, including this header. It can also be used to calculate the location of the first byte of the next Attribute, or End of Record Marker, by adding this value to the offset of the first byte of the header.
8	8	1	Non-Resident Flag	Value 00 = Resident Attribute Value 01 = Non-Resident Attribute TO APPLY THIS TEMPLATE THIS BYTE MUST BE STORING THE VALUE 01h.
9	9	1	Length of Name in Characters (N = number of bytes occupied)	Note that in Unicode two bytes are used to store each character value, thus a name length of 4 will occupy 8 bytes. TO APPLY THIS TEMPLATE THIS BYTE MUST BE STORING A VALUE GREATER THAN 00h.
10–11	0A–0B	2	Offset to Start of the Name of the Attribute, in bytes	The value of these two bytes is the number of bytes from the beginning of the header to the first byte of the Attribute Name. That location is calculated by adding this value to the offset of the first byte of the header.
12–13	0C–0D	2	Data Status Flags	Value 01 00h = Compressed Value 40 00h = Encrypted Value 80 00h = Sparse (Used in Data Attribute)
14–15	0E–0F	2	Reportedly an Attribute ID number (not confirmed)	May be used for a number of purposes not yet identified, in particular as a flag for virus infected/ cleaned files.
16–23	10–17	8	Starting Virtual Cluster Number	NTFS uses mapping of Real Clusters to Virtual Clusters, the value of the Starting Virtual Cluster should normally be 00h.
24–31	18–1F	8	Ending Virtual Cluster Number	Virtual Clusters are the same size as clusters on the disk.
32–33	20–22	2	Offset to the start of the Data Run Sequence(s), in bytes	The value of these two bytes is the number of bytes from the beginning of the header to the first byte of the Data Run Sequence(s). The offset is calculated by adding this value to the offset of the first byte of the header.

Byte offset (decimal)	Byte offset (hex)	Length in bytes	Use	Notes (where value is mentioned bytes are in little endian format)
34–35	22–23	2	Compression Unit Size	Use of this field to identify compression is confirmed but the method has not been explored.
36–39	24–27	4	Padding to 8 byte boundary	
40–47	28–2F	8	The "Physical" size of the Attribute, in bytes	Physical size in the case of non-resident data means the size in bytes of the storage block(s) allocated for the storage of the data.
48–55	30–37	8	The "Logical" size of the Attribute, in bytes	Logical size in the case of non-resident data means the actual size in bytes of the data itself.
56–63	38–3F	8	The initialized data size of the stream, in bytes	In most cases this is the same size as the Logical size of the data, its use is uncertain.
64 on	40 on	N	Name of Attribute in Unicode (padded to 8 byte boundary}	Note that in Unicode two bytes are used to store each character value, thus a name length of 4 will occupy 8 bytes.
64+N on	40+N on	Varies	The Data Run Sequence (This is the Data Attribute Proper but is included here for simplicity)	There can be almost any number of data runs for a fragmented file. Their make up and size are governed by the first byte in the sequence. See Example.

The Standard Information Attribute (ID = 10 00 00 00h)

The Attribute Proper is preceded by one of the Attribute Headers of Types 1 to 4 above.

Table A9.9   The Standard Information Attribute.

Byte offset (decimal)	Byte offset (hex)	Length in bytes	Use	Notes (where value is mentioned bytes are in little endian format)
0–7	0–7	8	Created Time/Date in "FileTime" format	This entry refers to the item subject of the record as a whole, be it a file or directory. It is the most reliable, being the first one to be updated with any change, other dates and times receive copies of this entry to update them.

Byte offset (decimal)	Byte offset (hex)	Length in bytes	Use	Notes (where value is mentioned bytes are in little endian format)
8–15	8–0F	8	Last Modified Time/Date in "FileTime" format	This entry refers to the item subject of the record as a whole, be it a file or directory. It is the most reliable, being the first one to be updated with any change, other dates and times receive copies of this entry to update them.
16–23	10–17	8	Last MFT Record Update Time/Date in "FileTime" format	This entry refers to the item subject of the record as a whole, be it a file or directory. It is the most reliable of its type, being the first one to be updated with any change, other dates and times receive copies of this entry to update them. THE UPDATE OF THIS ENTRY HAS BEEN SHOWN TO BE UNRELIABLE: changes can be made to the MFT entry without this field being updated.
24–31	18–1F	8	Last Access Time/Date in "FileTime" format	This entry refers to the item subject of the record as a whole, be it a file or directory. It is the most reliable, being the first one to be updated with any change, other dates and times receive copies of this entry to update them.
32–35	20–23	4	DOS File Permissions Binary Flags (Old Style DOS Attributes)	01 00 00 00 = Read Only 02 00 00 00 = Hidden 04 00 00 00 = System 20 00 00 00 = Archive 40 00 00 00 = Device* 80 00 00 00 = Normal* 00 01 00 00 = Sparse File* 00 04 00 00 = Reparse Point 00 08 00 00 = Compressed 00 10 00 00 = Offline* 00 20 00 00 = Not Content Indexed* 00 40 00 00 = Encrypted * = not tested
36–39	24–27	4	Reportedly a value for the Maximum Number of Versions (not confirmed)	Probably used for version control of multiple copies of files used by multiple users on a network.
40–47	28–2F	8	Reportedly Version Number and Class ID (not confirmed)	Probably used for version control of multiple copies of files used by multiple users on a network.
48–51	30–33	4	Reportedly an Owner ID field (not confirmed)	Probably used for access control of multiple users on a network.
52–55	34–37	4	Reportedly a Security ID (not confirmed)	Probably used for access control of multiple users on a network.

Byte offset (decimal)	Byte offset (hex)	Length in bytes	Use	Notes (where value is mentioned bytes are in little endian format)
56–63	38–3F	8	Reportedly Quota Charged Value (not confirmed)	Probably used on networked systems to control storage space allocated to users.
64–72	40–47	8	Reportedly a $USNJRNL update sequence number	Claimed to be the Update Sequence Number for the file $USNJRNL. When of zero value it is likely that the $USNJRNL function has not been activated.

The File Name Attribute (ID = 30 00 00 00h)

The Attribute Proper is preceded by one of the Attribute Headers of Types 1 to 4 above.

Table A9.10 The File Name Attribute.

Byte offset (decimal)	Byte offset (hex)	Length in bytes	Use	Notes (where value is mentioned bytes are in little endian format)
0–7	0–7	8	1. Base File Reference 2. Unknown – possibly an ID sequence number	This field is used to store a Base File Reference Number probably in the first six (least significant) bytes. It is used to indicate the MFT record number of the "parent" directory. If the file resides in the ROOT directory this value will usually be 05h. The use of an ID sequence number in the remaining bytes is uncertain but there is a consistent use of low two-byte values in the most significant pair. This two-byte value is the same in all records referring to the same "parent" directory record. It is suggested that this value is the current value present in the Record Use Sequence Number of the "parent" directory MFT record at the time of the creation of THIS record and can thus identify THIS record to a particular incarnation of the MFT record to which it points.
8–15	8–0F	8	Created Time/Date in "FileTime" format	This entry refers to the item subject of the record as a whole, be it a file or directory. Located in this Attribute it is NOT the most reliable. Experiments have shown that this entry is not updated even when the filename is changed.

Byte offset (decimal)	Byte offset (hex)	Length in bytes	Use	Notes (where value is mentioned bytes are in little endian format)
16–23	10–17	8	Last Modified Time/Date in "FileTime" format	This entry refers to the item subject of the record as a whole, be it a file or directory. Located in this Attribute it is NOT the most reliable. Experiments have shown that this entry is not updated even when the filename is changed.
24–31	18–1F	8	Last MFT Record Update Time/Date in 'FileTime' format	This entry refers to the item subject of the record as a whole, be it a file or directory. Located in this Attribute it is NOT the most reliable. Experiments have shown that this entry is not updated even when the filename is changed.
32–39	20–27	8	Last Access Time/Date in 'FileTime' format	This entry refers to the item subject of the record as a whole, be it a file or directory. Located in this Attribute it is NOT the most reliable. Experiments have shown that this entry is not updated even when the filename is changed.
40–47	28–2F	8	The 'Physical' size of the file, in bytes	Physical size means the size in bytes of the storage block(s) allocated for the storage of the data.
48–55	30–37	8	The 'Logical' size of the file, in bytes	Logical size means the actual size in bytes of the data itself.
56–59	38–3B	4	DOS File Permissions Binary Flags (Old Style DOS Attributes)	01 00 00 00 = Read Only 02 00 00 00 = Hidden 04 00 00 00 = System 20 00 00 00 = Archive 40 00 00 00 = Device* 80 00 00 00 = Normal* 00 01 00 00 = Sparse File* 00 04 00 00 = Reparse Point 00 08 00 00 = Compressed 00 10 00 00 = Offline* 00 20 00 00 = Not Content Indexed* 00 40 00 00 = Encrypted * = not tested
60–63	3C–3F	4	Reportedly used by Extended Attributes and Reparse Points (not confirmed)	
64	40	1	Length of File Name in Characters (N = number of bytes occupied)	File names can be stored in DOS format and Unicode format. Note that in Unicode two bytes are used to store each character value, thus a name length of 4 will occupy 8 bytes.

Byte offset (decimal)	Byte offset (hex)	Length in bytes	Use	Notes (where value is mentioned bytes are in little endian format)
65	41	1	Type of Filename, in binary flag format.	00 = Posix Type 01 = Win32 Type Long File Name (Unicode) 02 = DOS Type Short File Name (8:3) 03 = Win32 & DOS; both names are identical, only the DOS-compliant short name is used.
66 on	42 on	N	File Name in text format	File name length is not fixed, one byte for the length restricts long file names to 256 bytes of storage (in Unicode 128 characters). This field is usually padded to the next 8-byte boundary.

The Data Attribute (ID = 80 00 00 00h)

The Attribute Proper is preceded by one of the Attribute Headers of Types 1 to 4 above.

Table A9.11 The Data Attribute.

Byte offset (decimal)	Byte offset (hex)	Length in bytes	Use	Notes (where value is mentioned bytes are in little endian format)
0 on	0 on	N	Data to length N bytes	The data simply follows the Standard Attribute Header. The length of the data is defined within the header.

The Index Root Attribute (ID = 90 00 00 00h)

The Attribute Proper is preceded by one of the Attribute Headers of Types 1 to 4 above. This is followed by the Index Root Attribute proper which defines the size and shape of the Directory Entries. This is followed by an Index Header and one or more Index Entry Header/Index Entry Data pairs, all of which are part of the Index Root Attribute. The overall construction is as shown at Table A9.12.

Table A9.12 The Index Root Attribute.

Attribute Header
Index Root Attribute Proper
Index Header
Index Entry Header
Index Entry Data
Index Entry Header
Index Entry Data
etc.
Index Entry Header (with final entry flag set)

Construction of the Index Root Attribute Proper

Table A9.13 The Index Root Attribute Proper.

Byte offset (decimal)	Byte offset (hex)	Length in bytes	Use	Notes (where value is mentioned bytes are in little endian format)
0–3	0–3	4	Type Declaration	The type of Index Root is declared here using the values specified in the $AttrDef file. For Directories this entry will usually define a File Name type and the entries in the index will follow the structure of a File Name Attribute.
4–7	4–7	4	Collation Rule	The number stored here will define the method used to sort the entries. If of File Name Type, the rule will be Collation_Filename.
8–11	8–0B	4	Size of Allocated Space for the Attribute, in bytes	Appears to default to 4096 bytes even when the data is resident. 4096 bytes is the block size for external "INDX" files when the data becomes too big to retain within the MFT.
12	0C	1	Number of clusters per Index Record	Appears to default to the number of clusters in a 4096 byte block even when the data is resident. 4096 bytes is the block size for external "INDX" files when the data becomes too big to retain within the MFT. Sectors per cluster is available for all disks in the BIOS Parameter Block at offset 0Bh.

Construction of the Index Header

Table A9.14 The Index Header.

Byte offset (decimal)	Byte offset (hex)	Length in bytes	Use	Notes (where value is mentioned bytes are in little endian format)
0–3	0–3	4	Offset to first Index Entry, in bytes	The value of these four bytes is the number of bytes from the beginning of this header to the first byte of the first Index Entry Header. That location is calculated by adding this value to the offset of the first byte of this header.
4–7	4–7	4	Total size of Index Entries, in bytes	The value of these four bytes is the number of bytes from the beginning of this header to the last byte of the FINAL Index Entry.

Byte offset (decimal)	Byte offset (hex)	Length in bytes	Use	Notes (where value is mentioned bytes are in little endian format)
8–11	8–0B	4	The Allocated size of the Index Entries in bytes	The amount of space in bytes allocated for the storage of the Index Entries
12	0C	1	Listing Flag	See table below for values

Listing Flags in the Index Header and the Index Entry Header

Table A9.15 Listing flags in the Index Header and the Index Entry Header.

Index Header Byte Offset 12	Index Entry Header Byte Offset 12	
00h	00h	Resident listing only
00h	02h	Final null entry in listing (includes empty listing)
01h	01h	Resident and external listing exists
01h	03h	No resident listing, external listing only exists

Construction of the Index Entry Header

Note that the final entry in the Index Root Attribute is usually a null entry, consisting of this header (see Table A9.16) only with byte offset 12 set to indicate its status as the last entry (see flags of Table A9.15). No data is attached to the listing.

Table A9.16 The Index Entry Header.

Byte offset (decimal)	Byte offset (hex)	Length in bytes	Use	Notes (where value is mentioned bytes are in little endian format)
0–7	0–7	8	1. Base File Reference 2. Unknown – possibly an ID sequence number	This field is used to store a Base File Reference Number probably in the first four (least significant bytes). These bytes contain a value which is the number of the MFT record in which the "parent" record resides. The use of an ID sequence number in the remaining bytes is uncertain but there is a consistent use of low two-byte values in the most significant pair. This two-byte value is the same in all records referring to the same "parent" record.
8–9	8–9	2	Size of the Index Entry, in bytes	The value of these two bytes is the number of bytes from the beginning of this header to the last byte of this Index Entry, includes the Entry and this header.

| 10–11 | 0A–0B | 2 | Size of the Index Entry stream, in bytes | The value of these two bytes is the number of bytes from the beginning of the Index Entry attached to this header, to the last byte of the Index Entry. |
| 12 | 0C | 1 | Listing Flag | See Table A9.15 for values |

Construction – Index Entry Data – Index Entry Header Listing Flag = 01h

Table A9.17 Index Entry Data – Listing Flag = 01h.

Byte offset (decimal)	Byte offset (hex)	Length in bytes	Use	Notes (where value is mentioned bytes are in little endian format)
0 on	0 on	8	Index VCN	Virtual Cluster Number in Index for the Entry data

Construction – Index Entry Data – Index Entry Header Listing Flag <> 01h

Table A9.18 Index Entry Data – Listing Flag <> 01h.

Byte offset (decimal)	Byte offset (hex)	Length in bytes	Use	Notes (where value is mentioned bytes are in little endian format)
0 on	0 on	Varies	As Declared Attribute Type in the Index Root Attribute proper, offsets 0–3.	In most cases, for Directories, this will be an identical layout to a File Name Attribute Proper as laid out above.

The Index Allocation Attribute (ID = A0 00 00 00h)

As with all Attributes the Index Allocation Attribute proper is preceded by one of the Attribute Headers of Types 1 to 4 above. This is followed by the Index Allocation Proper which contains only a series of one or more Data Run Sequences as described above at Table A9.6 and Fig. A9.1.

Construction of the Index Allocation Proper

Table A9.19 The Index Allocation Attribute Proper.

Byte offset (decimal)	Byte offset (hex)	Length in bytes	Use	Notes (where value is mentioned bytes are in little endian format)
0 on	0 on	Varies	Data Run Sequence(s)	See Data Run Example at Fig. A9.1 above

The Bitmap Attribute (ID = B0 00 00 00h)

The Attribute Proper is preceded by one of the Attribute Headers of Types 1 to 4 above.

Table A9.20   The Bitmap Attribute Proper.

Byte offset (decimal)	Byte offset (hex)	Length in bytes	Use	Notes (where value is mentioned bytes are in little endian format)
0 on	0 on	Varies	Binary Fields	Binary Map of Attribute Space

The Attribute List (ID = 20 00 00 00h)

As with all Attributes, an Attribute List always starts with Standard Header. Following the header the construction of fields is as follows.

Table A9.21   The Attribute List.

Byte offset (dec)	Byte offset (hex)	Length in bytes	Use	Notes (where value is mentioned bytes are in little endian format)
0–3	00–03	4	Attribute Identifier	A four-byte Identification number, this is the ID as defined in $AttrDef for each Attribute type. This value identifies the layout of the Attribute following this header.
4–5	04–05	2	Length of Current Attribute in bytes	The value of these two bytes is the number of bytes making up the length of this Attribute, including this header. It can also be used to calculate the location of the first byte of the next Attribute, or End of Record Marker, by adding this value to the offset of the first byte of the header.
6	06	1	Length of Name in Characters (N = number of bytes occupied)	Note that in Unicode two bytes are used to store each character value; thus a name length of 4 will occupy 8 bytes.
7	07	1	Offset to Start of the Name of the Attribute, in bytes	The value of these two bytes is the number of bytes from the beginning of the header to the first byte of the Attribute Proper following it. The offset is calculated by adding this value to the offset of the first byte of the header.
8–15	08–0F	8	Starting Virtual Cluster Number	NTFS uses mapping of Real Clusters to Virtual Clusters, the value of the Starting Virtual Cluster should normally be 00h.

Byte offset (dec)	Byte offset (hex)	Length in bytes	Use	Notes (where value is mentioned bytes are in little endian format)
16–23	10–17	8	1. Base File Reference 2. Unknown – possibly an ID sequence number	This field is used to store a Base File Reference Number probably in the first four or six (least significant) bytes. In this location the number appears to be a pointer to the record number which contains the Attribute being declared in the list. The actual use of the additional two bytes is unclear but they do appear to be identical to the Record Use Sequence Number of the "parent" record.
24–25	18–19	2	Reportedly an Attribute ID number (not confirmed)	May be used for a number of purposes not yet identified, in particular as a flag for virus infected/ cleaned files.
26 on	1A on	N	Name of Attribute in Unicode (padded to 8 byte boundary)	Note that in Unicode two bytes are used to store each character value; thus a name length of 4 will occupy 8 bytes.

INDX Files

This is the construction of the INDX Record Header. It appears at the front of each "INDX" file. This is followed by one or more Index Entry Header/Index Entry Data pairs, similar to the latter part of the Index Root Attribute seen above (see Table A9.12).

Table A9.22   INDX files.

Byte offset (decimal)	Byte offset (hex)	Length in bytes	Use	Notes (where value is mentioned bytes are in little endian format)
0–3	00–03	4	Identification String "INDX"	Appears at the head of all INDX record files.
4–5	04–05	2	Offset to the Update Sequence Array in bytes	The value of these two bytes is the number of bytes from the beginning of the header to the first byte of the update sequence array. The offset is calculated by adding this value to the offset of the first byte of the header.
6–7	06–07	2	Length of Update Sequence	The Update Sequence Array is 18 bytes in length for 4096 byte INDX file.
8–15	08–0F	8	Reportedly the $Logfile sequence number (not confirmed)	Use is not defined, probably used to index changes in $Logfile

Byte offset (decimal)	Byte offset (hex)	Length in bytes	Use	Notes (where value is mentioned bytes are in little endian format)
16–23	10–17	8	Virtual Cluster Number of this Allocation	The Virtual Cluster Number of this INDX file in the whole Allocation
24–27	18–1B	4	Offset to first Index Entry, in bytes	The value of these four bytes is the number of bytes from the beginning of this header to the first byte of the first Index Entry Header. That location is calculated by adding this value to the offset of the first byte of this header.
28–31	1C–1F	4	Total size of Index Entries, in bytes	The value of these four bytes is the number of bytes from the beginning of this header to the last byte of the FINAL Index Entry.
32–35	20–23	4	The Allocated size of the Index Entries in bytes	The amount of space in bytes allocated for the storage of the Index Entries
36	24	1	Listing Flag	As in Index Header – see Table A9.14
37–39	25–27	3	Padding to 8-byte Boundary	
40–41	28–29	2	The Update Sequence Array Part 1 The Update Sequence Number	The number occupying these two bytes is used as a test value for the reading of the file. It appears here, and is seeded into the final two bytes of each SECTOR of the 4096 byte file. The data which should occupy these bytes is placed in the Update Sequence Array Part 2 in that order. When a record is read into memory the value of the Update Sequence Number is compared against the final 2 bytes of each sector of the file. If a match is made the read is successful and the tested bytes in memory are replaced by the bytes from the Update Sequence Array Part 2, thus replacing the seeded values with the correct ones for the data set required.
42–59	2A–3B	18	The Update Sequence Array Part 2 – The Array	These 18 bytes are the bytes from the final two bytes of each sector of the file which have been replaced by the Update Sequence Number for integrity testing.
60–63	3C–3F	4	Padding to 8-byte Boundary	

Appendix 10. *The Relationship Between CHS and LBA Addressing*

As we explained in Chapter 5, the ATA-6 (McLean, 2001, p. 21) specification states that CHS translation is now obsolete, in the following words: "*All devices shall support LBA translation. In standards ATA/ATAPI-5 and earlier, a CHS translation was defined. This translation is obsolete but may be implemented as defined in ATA/ATAPI-5*".

We list in Chapter 5 a number of reasons why it is essential for forensic computing analysts to continue to have a good knowledge of both CHS and LBA addressing and an understanding of the relationship between them. Referring back to the relevant sections of the ATA-5 (McLean, 1999, pp. 19 and 20) specification we may note the following statements:

"*Logical sectors on the device shall be linearly mapped with the first LBA addressed sector (sector 0) being the same sector as the first logical CHS addressed sector (cylinder 0, head 0, sector 1).*"

"*The following is always true for LBA numbers less than or equal to 16,514,064 for devices supporting the current CHS translation: LBA = (((cylinder_number * heads_per_cylinder) + head_number) * sectors_per_track) + sector_number – 1.*"

An Illustrative Example

At Fig. A10.1 we show diagrammatically a simplified disk of two platters and hence four heads (which are labelled 0 to 3) and of two cylinders (which are labelled 0 and 1) that has been divided up into 8 sectors per track (which are labelled 1 to 8). Given this configuration, the formula for LBA, specified above, may be rewritten as:

$$LBA = \text{Cylinder [C]} \times \text{Number of Heads [4]} \times \text{Number of Sectors per Track [8]}$$
$$+ \text{Head [H]} \times \text{Number of Sectors per Track [8]}$$
$$+ \text{Sector [S]} - 1$$

Using this formula we note that a CHS address of (1, 0, 5) becomes:

$$LBA = 1 \times 4 \times 8 = 32$$
$$+ 0 \times 8 = 0$$
$$+ 5 - 1 = 4$$
$$= 36$$

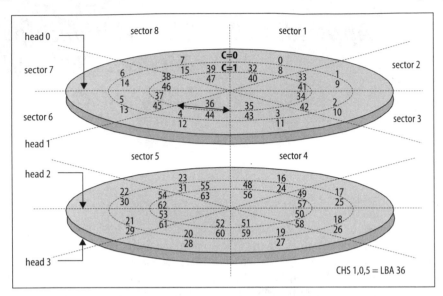

Fig. A10.1 Two disk platters showing the relationship between CHS and LBA addressing.

If we examine the diagram we can see that this is the case. Starting from CHS (0, 0, 1), we know that this is defined as LBA 0. On the diagram we can see that for the dotted oval C = 0, on the upper surface of the upper platter (head 0) within the arc for sector 1 there is the number 0, symbolizing LBA 0. As we progress round this oval (track) in a clockwise direction, we note that within each new sector arc the number increments by 1 resulting in LBA 1, 2, 3 etc., up to LBA 7. On reaching LBA 7, we have completed all the sectors on this first, uppermost track and the next step is to switch to the next head (head 1) which causes us to access the track on the underside of the upper platter. Continuing in a clockwise direction, we note that for CHS (0, 1, 1) we are at LBA 8 (the number immediately underneath the 0 of LBA 0). Once again we can see how continuing round the track, incrementing by 1 through each sector arc, we access LBA 9, 10, 11 etc., up to LBA 15.

At LBA 15, we have once again completed all the sectors on this second underneath track and the next step is to switch to the next head (head 2) which causes us to access the track on the upperside of the lower platter. The first sector of this track is LBA 16 and, as we continue round clockwise, we note that we access in turn LBA 17, 18, 19 etc., up to LBA 23. At LBA 23 we have again accessed all the sectors on this track and so the next step is to switch to the next and last head (head 3). This causes us to access the track on the underside of the lower platter and we can see that the first sector CHS (0, 3, 1) is LBA 24. Now we continue round, accessing in turn, LBA 25, 26, 27 etc., up to LBA 31.

By LBA 31 we have utilized all four heads and have thus completed a cylinder. The next step must be to move the head assembly to the next cylinder position (C = 1) and start again with the first head (head 0). This is what we see as the second dotted oval on the uppermost surface of the upper platter. The CHS address (1, 0, 1) is clearly LBA 32 and, as we move round clockwise we access LBA 33, 34, 35 etc. Marked with a double arrow line is LBA 36 and it is clear from the diagram that this is CHS $(1, 0, 5)$ as we calculated above.

References

McLean, P. T. (ed.) (1999) *Information Technology – AT Attachment with Packet Interface – 5 (ATA/ATAPI-5)*, Working Draft, T13 1321D, Revision 1c, 31 August.

McLean, P. T. (ed.) (2001) *Information Technology - AT Attachment with Packet Interface – 6 (ATA/ATAPI-6)*, Working Draft, T13 1410D, Revision 1e, 26 June.

Appendix 11. *Alternate Data Streams – a Brief Explanation*

Historical Note

During the development of OS/2 in the late 1980s, IBM and Microsoft included within their new *High Performance File System* (*HPFS*) an implementation of *forks* as part of the file storage mechanism. These forks were known as *extended attributes*. When, in 1993 Microsoft released Windows NT, with the new NTFS filing system, the use of forks within the file storage system was retained and the facility was renamed *Alternate Data Streams*. These streams were designed mainly to allow for metadata, comprising information about the file, to be added to a file record so that the file information could also be made available when the file itself is accessed. We will see how this works in the examples that follow.

Alternate Data Stream in Place of Thumbs.db

In the particular case of Windows 2000, Alternate Data Streams are generated in place of Thumbs.db files when the "View|Thumbnails" menu item is selected in Explorer and the file system is NTFS. To demonstrate this, we have taken a sample from a Windows 2000 NTFS system, and considered a normal .jpg file, NuggetofGold.jpg, which has not yet been looked at using "View|Thumbnails" in Explorer. Some of the details reported by Encase are shown at Fig. A11.1.

From the Encase entry, we note that the MFT record number for NuggetofGold.jpg is 16086 (not shown in Fig. A11.1) and we list at Table A11.1 the details of that MFT record.

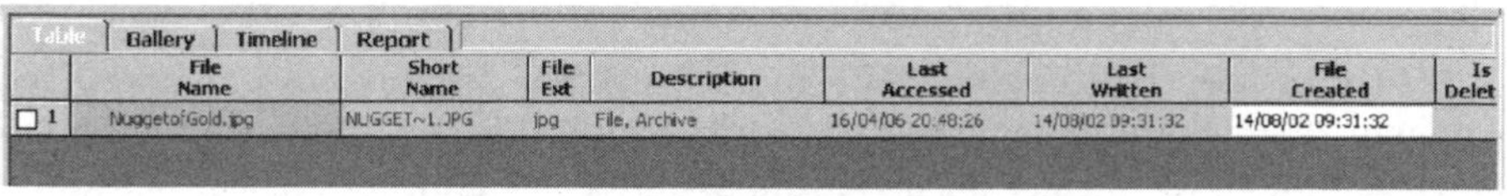

	File Name	Short Name	File Ext	Description	Last Accessed	Last Written	File Created	Is Delet
☐ 1	NuggetofGold.jpg	NUGGET~1.JPG	jpg	File, Archive	16/04/06 20:48:26	14/08/02 09:31:32	14/08/02 09:31:32	

Fig. A11.1 Encase details of NuggetofGold.jpg.

Table A11.1 Details of MFT record for NuggetofGold.jpg – 16086.

Offset	0	1	2	3	4	5	6	7	8	9	10	11	12	13	14	15	
00000000	46	49	4C	45	2A	00	03	00	9C	B5	07	DF	00	00	00	00	FILE*...oμ.ß....
00000016	05	00	02	00	30	00	01	00	E0	01	00	00	00	04	00	00	....O...à.......
00000032	00	00	00	00	00	00	00	00	0B	00	05	00	00	00	00	00	....
00000048	10	00	00	00	60	00	00	00	00	00	00	00	00	00	00	00	....`...........
00000064	48	00	00	00	18	00	00	00	00	32	F6	5F	75	43	C2	01	H........2ö_uCÂ.
00000080	00	32	F6	5F	75	43	C2	01	70	A0	06	1C	97	61	C6	01	.2ö_uCÂ.p ..-aÆ.
00000096	70	A0	06	1C	97	61	C6	01	20	00	00	00	00	00	00	00	p ..-aÆ. ....
00000112	00	00	00	00	00	00	00	00	00	00	00	00	0F	01	00	00	....
00000128	00	00	00	00	00	00	00	00	00	00	00	00	00	00	00	00	....
00000144	30	00	00	00	78	00	00	00	00	00	00	00	00	00	0A	00	0...x...........
00000160	5A	00	00	00	18	00	01	00	41	08	00	00	00	00	10	00	Z.......A.......
00000176	00	32	F6	5F	75	43	C2	01	00	32	F6	5F	75	43	C2	01	.2ö_uCÂ..2ö_uCÂ.
00000192	C0	08	BB	1A	97	61	C6	01	C0	08	BB	1A	97	61	C6	01	À.».-aÆ.À.».-aÆ.
00000208	00	A0	02	00	00	00	00	00	CE	9F	02	00	00	00	00	00	. ...ÎY......
00000224	20	00	00	00	00	00	00	00	0C	02	4E	00	55	00	47	00	.........N.U.G.
00000240	47	00	45	00	54	00	7E	00	31	00	2E	00	4A	00	50	00	G.E.T.~.1...J.P.
00000256	47	00	2E	00	6A	00	70	00	30	00	00	00	80	00	00	00	G...j.p.0... ...
00000272	00	00	00	00	00	00	09	00	62	00	00	00	18	00	01	00	........b.......
00000288	41	08	00	00	00	00	10	00	00	32	F6	5F	75	43	C2	01	A........2ö_uCÂ.
00000304	00	32	F6	5F	75	43	C2	01	C0	08	BB	1A	97	61	C6	01	.2ö_uCÂ.À.».-aÆ.
00000320	C0	08	BB	1A	97	61	C6	01	00	A0	02	00	00	00	00	00	À.».-aÆ.. ......
00000336	CE	9F	02	00	00	00	00	00	20	00	00	00	00	00	00	00	ÎY...... ....
00000352	10	01	4E	00	75	00	67	00	67	00	65	00	74	00	6F	00	..N.u.g.g.e.t.o.
00000368	66	00	47	00	6F	00	6C	00	64	00	2E	00	6A	00	70	00	f.G.o.l.d...j.p.
00000384	67	00	00	00	50	00	00	00	80	00	00	00	50	00	00	00	g...P... ...P...
00000400	01	00	00	00	00	00	04	00	00	00	00	00	00	00	00	00	....
00000416	29	00	00	00	00	00	00	00	40	00	00	00	00	00	00	00	).......@.......
00000432	00	A0	02	00	00	00	00	00	CE	9F	02	00	00	00	00	00	. ...ÎY......
00000448	CE	9F	02	00	00	00	00	00	31	10	A6	6F	2C	31	10	C5	ÎY......1.¦o,1.Å
00000464	DE	07	31	0A	54	EE	F5	00	FF	FF	FF	FF	82	79	47	11	Þ.1.Tîõ.ÿÿÿÿ'yG.

A top-level analysis of the MFT record at Table A11.1 is given below at Table A11.2. We note that the padding after the file name contains 'slack' remnants.

Table A11.2 Top level analysis for NuggetofGold.jpg – 16086.

File Record Header	bytes 0 to 47
Standard Information Attribute (Attribute Header)	bytes 48 to 71
Standard Information Attribute Proper	bytes 72 to 143
File Name Attribute (Attribute Header)	bytes 144 to 167
File Name Attribute Proper	bytes 168 to 263 (includes padding at bytes 260–263)
File Name Attribute (Attribute Header)	bytes 264 to 287
File Name Attribute Proper	bytes 288 to 391 (includes padding at bytes 386–391)
Data Attribute (Attribute Header)	bytes 392 to 455
Data Attribute Proper (data run)	bytes 456 to 471 (3 runs of 5 bytes) (includes padding at byte 471)
End of Record Marker	bytes 472 on

As can be seen by using the MFT maps provided elsewhere in this book (see Appendix 9) this record is as expected for a "normal" JPEG image file. As mentioned above, although the file has been viewed, Explorer has only, so far, been set to the menu item "View|Details". If we now change that view by selecting the menu item

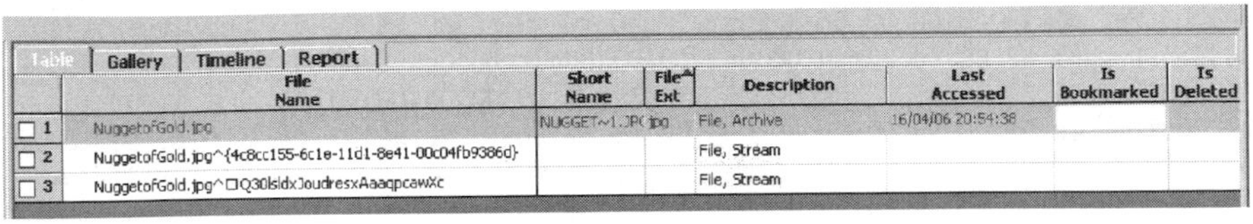

	File Name	Short Name	File Ext	Description	Last Accessed	Is Bookmarked	Is Deleted
☐ 1	NuggetofGold.jpg	NUGGET~1.JPG	jpg	File, Archive	16/04/06 20:54:38		
☐ 2	NuggetofGold.jpg^{4c8cc155-6c1e-11d1-8e41-00c04fb9386d}			File, Stream			
☐ 3	NuggetofGold.jpg^☐Q30IsidxJoudresxAaaqpcewXc			File, Stream			

Fig. A11.2 Two additional streams.

"View|Thumbnails" and using that, access the file NuggetofGold.jpg, the MFT record automatically gains two ADS streams. We see this from the Encase record, which now shows two additional streams (see Fig. A11.2).

Examination shows that there is no Thumbs.db file in this folder, and that this has been replaced by the use of two Alternate Data Streams for each file. The stream at item 2 above is an identifier; it has no further data associated with it. Experiments have demonstrated that this identifier does not change between directories or machines. A thumbnail version of the JPEG file is now specified by the stream identified by the string "Joudres" within its name. This thumbnail data is non-resident and is stored elsewhere on the disk. All three entries are seen to bear the same MFT file identification number. If we now look at the MFT record again, we note the detail shown at Table A11.3 below.

Table A11.3 Details of MFT record with Alternate Data Streams – 16086.

```
Offset      0  1  2  3  4  5  6  7   8  9 10 11 12 13 14 15
00000000   46 49 4C 45 2A 00 03 00  45 52 09 DF 00 00 00 00   FILE*...ER.ß....
00000016   05 00 02 00 30 00 01 00  D0 02 00 00 00 04 00 00   ....0...Ð.......
00000032   00 00 00 00 00 00 00 00  12 00 06 00 00 00 00 00   ................
00000048   10 00 00 00 60 00 00 00  00 00 00 00 00 00 00 00   ....`...........
00000064   48 00 00 00 18 00 00 00  00 32 F6 5F 75 43 C2 01   H........2ö_uCÂ.
00000080   00 32 F6 5F 75 43 C2 01  F0 7C BD F9 97 61 C6 01   .2ö_uCÂ.ð|½ü-aÆ.
00000096   F0 7C BD F9 97 61 C6 01  20 00 00 00 00 00 00 00   ð|½ü-aÆ. .......
00000112   00 00 00 00 00 00 00 00  00 00 00 00 0F 01 00 00   ................
00000128   00 00 00 00 00 00 00 00  00 00 00 00 00 00 00 00   ................
00000144   30 00 00 00 78 00 00 00  00 00 00 00 00 00 0A 00   0...x...........
00000160   5A 00 00 00 18 00 01 00  41 08 00 00 00 00 10 00   Z.......A.......
00000176   00 32 F6 5F 75 43 C2 01  00 32 F6 5F 75 43 C2 01   .2ö_uCÂ..2ö_uCÂ.
00000192   C0 08 BB 1A 97 61 C6 01  C0 08 BB 1A 97 61 C6 01   À.».-aÆ.À.».-aÆ.
00000208   00 A0 02 00 00 00 00 00  CE 9F 02 00 00 00 00 00   . ......ÎY......
00000224   20 00 00 00 00 00 00 00  0C 02 4E 00 55 00 47 00    .........N.U.G.
00000240   47 00 45 00 54 00 7E 00  31 00 2E 00 4A 00 50 00   G.E.T.~.1...J.P.
00000256   47 00 2E 00 6A 00 70 00  30 00 00 00 80 00 00 00   G...j.p.0... ...
00000272   00 00 00 00 00 00 09 00  62 00 00 00 18 00 01 00   ........b.......
00000288   41 08 00 00 00 00 10 00  00 32 F6 5F 75 43 C2 01   A........2ö_uCÂ.
00000304   00 32 F6 5F 75 43 C2 01  C0 08 BB 1A 97 61 C6 01   .2ö_uCÂ.À.».-aÆ.
00000320   C0 08 BB 1A 97 61 C6 01  00 A0 02 00 00 00 00 00   À.».-aÆ.. ......
00000336   CE 9F 02 00 00 00 00 00  20 00 00 00 00 00 00 00   ÎY...... .......
00000352   10 01 4E 00 75 00 67 00  67 00 65 00 74 00 6F 00   ..N.u.g.g.e.t.o.
00000368   66 00 47 00 6F 00 6C 00  64 00 2E 00 6A 00 70 00   f.G.o.l.d...j.p.
00000384   67 00 00 00 50 00 00 00  80 00 00 00 50 00 00 00   g...P... .P...
00000400   01 00 00 00 00 00 04 00  00 00 00 00 00 00 00 00   ................
00000416   29 00 00 00 00 00 00 00  40 00 00 00 00 00 00 00   ).......@.......
00000432   00 A0 02 00 00 00 00 00  CE 9F 02 00 00 00 00 00   . ......ÎY......
00000448   CE 9F 02 00 00 00 00 00  31 10 A6 6F 2C 31 10 C5   ÎY......1.¦o,1.Å
00000464   DE 07 31 0A 54 EE F5 00  80 00 00 00 88 00 00 00   Þ.1.Tîõ. ...^...
```

```
00000480  01 1B 40 00 00 00 0F 00   00 00 00 00 00 00 00 00   ..@.............
00000496  01 00 00 00 00 00 00 00   78 00 00 00 00 00 06 00   ........x.......
00000512  00 20 00 00 00 00 00 00   28 1A 00 00 00 00 00 00   . ......(.......
00000528  28 1A 00 00 00 00 00 00   05 00 51 00 33 00 30 00   (.........Q.3.0.
00000544  6C 00 73 00 6C 00 64 00   78 00 4A 00 6F 00 75 00   l.s.l.d.x.J.o.u.
00000560  64 00 72 00 65 00 73 00   78 00 41 00 61 00 61 00   d.r.e.s.x.A.a.a.
00000576  71 00 70 00 63 00 61 00   77 00 58 00 63 00 63 00   q.p.c.a.w.X.c.c.
00000592  31 01 EF 74 33 21 01 11   0B 00 00 00 FF FF FF FF   1.ït3!......ÿÿÿÿ
00000608  80 00 00 00 68 00 00 00   00 26 18 00 00 00 0B 00   ...h....&......
00000624  00 00 00 00 68 00 00 00   7B 00 34 00 63 00 38 00   ...h...{.4.c.8.
00000640  63 00 63 00 31 00 35 00   35 00 2D 00 36 00 63 00   c.c.1.5.5.-.6.c.
00000656  31 00 65 00 2D 00 31 00   31 00 64 00 31 00 2D 00   1.e.-.1.1.d.1.-.
00000672  38 00 65 00 34 00 31 00   2D 00 30 00 30 00 63 00   8.e.4.1.-.0.0.c.
00000688  30 00 34 00 66 00 62 00   39 00 33 00 38 00 36 00   0.4.f.b.9.3.8.6.
00000704  64 00 7D 00 00 00 00 00   FF FF FF FF 82 79 47 11   d.}.....ÿÿÿÿ'yG.
```

A top level analysis of the MFT record at Table A11.3 is given below at Table A11.4.

Table A11.4 Top level analysis for `NuggetofGold.jpg` with Alternate Data Streams – 16086.

File Record Header bytes 0 to 47	
Standard Information Attribute (Attribute Header)	bytes 48 to 71
Standard Information Attribute Proper	bytes 72 to 143
File Name Attribute (Attribute Header)	bytes 144 to 167
File Name Attribute Proper	bytes 168 to 263 (includes padding at bytes 260–263)
File Name Attribute (Attribute Header)	bytes 264 to 287
File Name Attribute Proper	bytes 288 to 391 (includes padding at bytes 386–391)
Data Attribute (Attribute Header)	bytes 392 to 455
Data Attribute Proper (data run)	bytes 456 to 471 (3 runs of 5 bytes) (includes padding at byte 471)
Data Attribute (Attribute Header)	bytes 472 to 591 (includes padding at bytes 589–590)
Data Attribute Proper (data run)	bytes 592 to 607 (includes padding at bytes 601 to 607)
Data Attribute (Attribute Header)	bytes 608 to 707 (Resident, no data!)
Padding	bytes 708 to 711
End of Record Marker	bytes 712 on

We note that the record is identical to the point where the original record data ends. Two new data attributes have been added, the first of which includes the data run for the thumbnail. The second is only a header as no data exists to append to it.

Further Use of Alternate Data Streams

If we access the file in Explorer and right-click on it to obtain the Properties window we see the display shown at Fig. A11.3.

We note that some details are extracted by Explorer from the directory entry, some details in the Properties window are extracted from the file itself and some brief details are shown in the bottom bar.

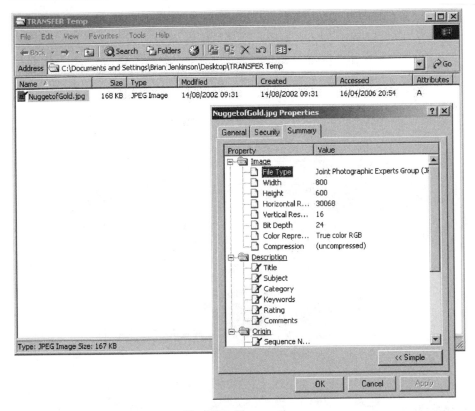

Fig. A11.3 File properties.

If we now use the Properties window to add some further detail as shown at Fig. A11.4 and we then view the results in Explorer, we see the display shown at Fig. A11.5.

We can see in Fig. A11.5 that the new detail entered now appears in the bottom bar. This material has not been added to the file itself; rather, two further Alternate Data Streams have been generated. We see this in the Encase view of the file at Fig. A11.6.

Examination of the streams shows that "SummaryInformation" contains the details, in text form, from the fields Title, Subject, Author, Keywords and Comments, and that "DocumentSummaryInformation" contains details from the Category field.

Hiding a Picture (or Other Item)

It is quite simple for users to add their own Alternate Data Streams without using the Properties window. In order to add a "hidden" picture image to this record, which is accessible via the original "Nugget of Gold" picture, a new Alternate Data Stream can be readily inserted. Given that a file hiddenpic1.jpg has been created, its contents are simply added by using a command line as follows:

```
notepad [Path]hiddenpic1.jpg>[Path]nuggetofgold.jpg:hiddenpic1.jpg
```

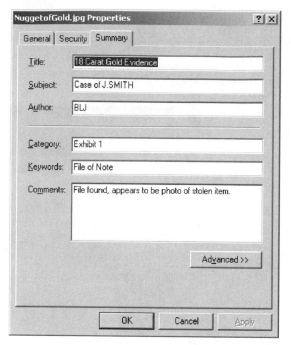

Figure A11.4 Adding file properties.

Fig. A11.5 Effect of added properties.

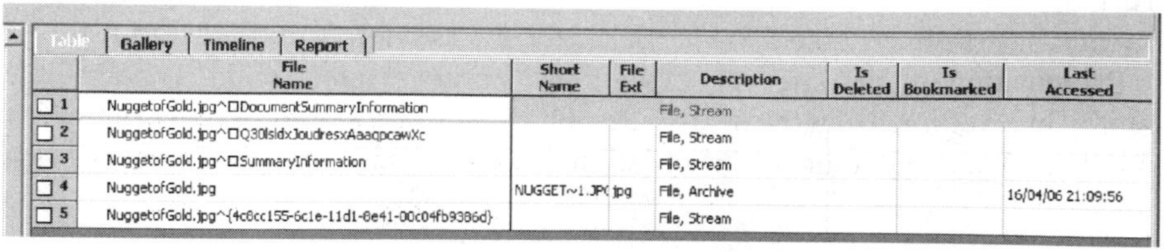

	File Name	Short Name	File Ext	Description	Is Deleted	Is Bookmarked	Last Accessed
☐ 1	NuggetofGold.jpg^☐DocumentSummaryInformation			File, Stream			
☐ 2	NuggetofGold.jpg^☐Q30IsldxJoudresxAaaqpcawXc			File, Stream			
☐ 3	NuggetofGold.jpg^☐SummaryInformation			File, Stream			
☐ 4	NuggetofGold.jpg	NUGGET~1.JP(	jpg	File, Archive			16/04/06 21:09:56
☐ 5	NuggetofGold.jpg^{4c8cc155-6c1e-11d1-8e41-00c04fb9386d}			File, Stream			

Fig. A11.6 Encase view of added properties.

Note that there is one space only in this command line, immediately after the word notepad and that [Path] is the full pathname to the files. We can see in Encase that another ADS, NuggetofGold.jpg^ hiddenpic1.jpg, has been added to the list (see Fig. A11.7).

We now look at what has happened in the MFT record as a result of these changes (see Table A11.5).

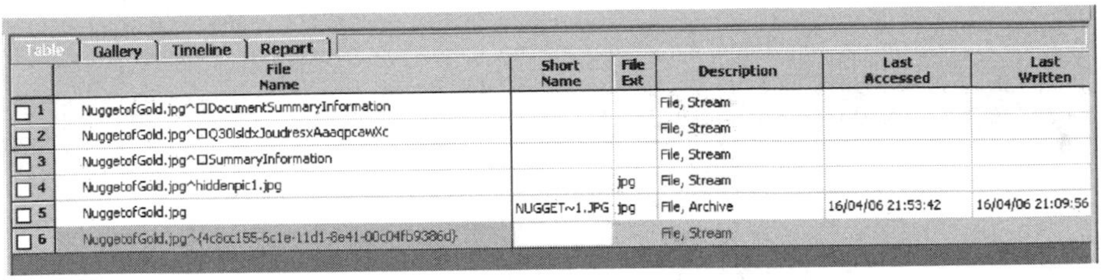

	File Name	Short Name	File Ext	Description	Last Accessed	Last Written
☐ 1	NuggetofGold.jpg^□DocumentSummaryInformation			File, Stream		
☐ 2	NuggetofGold.jpg^□Q30lsldxJoudresxAaaqpcawXc			File, Stream		
☐ 3	NuggetofGold.jpg^□SummaryInformation			File, Stream		
☐ 4	NuggetofGold.jpg^hiddenpic1.jpg		jpg	File, Stream		
☐ 5	NuggetofGold.jpg	NUGGET~1.JPG	jpg	File, Archive	16/04/06 21:53:42	16/04/06 21:09:56
☐ 6	NuggetofGold.jpg^{4c8cc155-5c1e-11d1-8e41-00c04fb9386d}			File, Stream		

Fig. A11.7   Encase view of another ADS.

Table A11.5   Details of MFT record as a result of changes – 16086.

```
Offset      0  1  2  3  4  5  6  7    8  9 10 11 12 13 14 15
00000000   46 49 4C 45 2A 00 03 00   D2 99 12 DF 00 00 00 00   FILE*...ÒT.ß....
00000016   05 00 02 00 30 00 01 00   60 03 00 00 00 04 00 00   ....0...`.......
00000032   00 00 00 00 00 00 00 00   27 00 08 00 61 00 00 00   .........'...a...
00000048   10 00 00 00 60 00 00 00   00 00 00 00 00 00 00 00   ....`...........
00000064   48 00 00 00 18 00 00 00   00 32 F6 5F 75 43 C2 01   H........2ö_uCÂ.
00000080   D0 3D 23 1D 9A 61 C6 01   A0 1B 3C 96 A0 61 C6 01   Ð=#..saÆ. .<- aÆ.
00000096   30 32 17 3A A0 61 C6 01   20 00 00 00 00 00 00 00   02.: aÆ. .......
00000112   00 00 00 00 00 00 00 00   00 00 00 00 0F 01 00 00   ................
00000128   00 00 00 00 00 00 00 00   00 00 00 00 00 00 00 00   ................
00000144   20 00 00 00 18 02 00 00   00 00 00 00 00 00 1A 00    ...............
00000160   00 02 00 00 18 00 00 00   10 00 00 00 20 00 00 1A   ............ ....
00000176   00 00 00 00 00 00 00 00   D6 3E 00 00 00 00 05 00   ........Ö>......
00000192   00 00 02 0E 47 73 74 68   30 00 00 00 20 00 00 1A   ....Gsth0... ...
00000208   00 00 00 00 00 00 00 00   D6 3E 00 00 00 00 05 00   ........Ö>......
00000224   0A 00 02 0D 47 6C 61 35   30 00 00 00 20 00 00 1A   ....Gla50... ...
00000240   00 00 00 00 00 00 00 00   04 3F 00 00 00 00 05 00   .........?......
00000256   00 00 00 00 A8 22 6B E2   80 00 00 00 20 00 00 1A   ....@"kâ ... ...
00000272   00 00 00 00 00 00 00 00   04 3F 00 00 00 00 05 00   .........?......
00000288   01 00 01 00 01 00 00 00   80 00 00 00 50 00 1B 1A   ........ ...P...
00000304   00 00 00 00 00 00 00 00   04 3F 00 00 00 00 05 00   .........?......
00000320   06 00 05 00 44 00 6F 00   63 00 75 00 6D 00 65 00   ....D.o.c.u.m.e.
00000336   6E 00 74 00 53 00 75 00   6D 00 6D 00 61 00 72 00   n.t.S.u.m.m.a.r.
00000352   79 00 49 00 6E 00 66 00   6F 00 72 00 6D 00 61 00   y.I.n.f.o.r.m.a.
00000368   74 00 69 00 6F 00 6E 00   80 00 00 00 50 00 1B 1A   t.i.o.n. ...P...
00000384   00 00 00 00 00 00 00 00   04 3F 00 00 00 00 05 00   .........?......
00000400   03 00 05 00 51 00 33 00   30 00 6C 00 73 00 6C 00   ....Q.3.0.l.s.l.
00000416   64 00 78 00 4A 00 6F 00   75 00 64 00 72 00 65 00   d.x.J.o.u.d.r.e.
00000432   73 00 78 00 41 00 61 00   61 00 71 00 70 00 63 00   s.x.A.a.a.q.p.c.
00000448   61 00 77 00 58 00 63 00   80 00 00 00 40 00 13 1A   a.w.X.c. ...@...
00000464   00 00 00 00 00 00 00 00   04 3F 00 00 00 00 05 00   .........?......
00000480   04 00 05 00 53 00 75 00   6D 00 6D 00 61 00 72 00   ....S.u.m.m.a.r.
00000496   79 00 49 00 6E 00 66 00   6F 00 72 00 6D 00 08 00   y.I.n.f.o.r.m...
00000512   74 00 69 00 6F 00 6E 00   80 00 00 00 38 00 0E 1A   t.i.o.n. ...8...
00000528   00 00 00 00 00 00 00 00   D6 3E 00 00 00 00 05 00   ........Ö>......
00000544   26 00 68 00 69 00 64 00   64 00 65 00 6E 00 70 00   &.h.i.d.d.e.n.p.
00000560   69 00 63 00 31 00 2E 00   6A 00 70 00 67 00 00 00   i.c.1...j.p.g...
00000576   80 00 00 00 68 00 26 1A   00 00 00 00 00 00 00 00    ...h.&.........
00000592   04 3F 00 00 00 00 05 00   05 00 7B 00 34 00 63 00   .?........{.4.c.
00000608   38 00 63 00 63 00 31 00   35 00 35 00 2D 00 36 00   8.c.c.1.5.5.-.6.
00000624   63 00 31 00 65 00 2D 00   31 00 31 00 64 00 31 00   c.1.e.-.1.1.d.1.
00000640   2D 00 38 00 65 00 34 00   31 00 2D 00 30 00 30 00   -.8.e.4.1.-.0.0.
```

```
00000656   63 00 30 00 34 00 66 00   62 00 39 00 33 00 38 00   c.0.4.f.b.9.3.8.
00000672   36 00 64 00 7D 00 B2 E2 30   00 00 00 78 00 00 00   6.d.}.²â0...x...
00000688   00 00 00 00 00 00 0A 00 5A   00 00 00 18 00 01 00   ........Z.......
00000704   41 08 00 00 00 00 10 00 00   32 F6 5F 75 43 C2 01   A........2ö_uCÂ.
00000720   00 32 F6 5F 75 43 C2 01 C0   08 BB 1A 97 61 C6 01   .2ö_uCÂ.Â.».-aÆ.
00000736   C0 08 BB 1A 97 61 C6 01 00   A0 02 00 00 00 00 00   Â.».-aÆ..  ......
00000752   CE 9F 02 00 00 00 00 00 20   00 00 00 00 00 00 00   ÎŸ......  ......
00000768   0C 02 4E 00 55 00 47 00 47   00 45 00 54 00 7E 00   ..N.U.G.G.E.T.~.
00000784   31 00 2E 00 4A 00 50 00 47   00 2E 00 6A 00 70 00   1...J.P.G...j.p.
00000800   80 00 00 00 38 00 00 00 00   0E 18 00 00 00 26 00   ...8.........&.
00000816   00 00 00 00 38 00 00 00 68   00 69 00 64 00 64 00   ....8...h.i.d.d.
00000832   65 00 6E 00 70 00 69 00 63   00 31 00 2E 00 6A 00   e.n.p.i.c.1...j.
00000848   70 00 67 00 00 00 00 00 FF   FF FF FF 80 00 00 00   p.g.....ÿÿÿÿ ...
```

A top-level analysis of the MFT record at Table A11.5 is given at Table A11.6.

Table A11.6 Top level analysis for NuggetofGold.jpg as a result of changes – 16086.

File Record Header	bytes 0 to 47
Standard Information Attribute (Attribute Header)	bytes 48 to 71
Standard Information Attribute Proper	bytes 72 to 143
Attribute List (Attribute Header)	bytes 144 to 167
Attribute List Proper	bytes 168 to 679
Includes: SIA	bytes 168 to 199 [D6 3E=16086]
File Name	bytes 200 to 231 [D6 3E=16086]
File Name	bytes 232 to 263 [04 3F = 16132]
Data	bytes 264 to 295 [04 3F = 16132]
Data	bytes 296 to 375 [04 3F = 16132]
Data	bytes 376 to 455 [04 3F = 16132]
Data	bytes 456 to 519 [04 3F = 16132]
Data	bytes 520 to 575 [D6 3E=16086]
Data	bytes 576 to 679 [04 3F = 16132]
File Name Attribute (Attribute Header)	bytes 680 to 703
File Name Attribute Proper	bytes 704 to 799 (includes padding at bytes 794–799)
Data Attribute (Attribute Header)	bytes 800 to 855 (no data!) (includes padding at bytes 852 to 855)
End of Record Marker	bytes 856 on

In this instance, we have added to Table A11.6 the record pointers from within the Attribute List and these are 16086 (this MFT record) and 16132. Things have now got a little bit complicated. The original MFT record (16086) can no longer hold all of the attributes for this file, so a further MFT record has had to be created as record number 16132. The pointers indicate that now one File Name Attribute and one Data Attribute are in record 16086 and that one File Name Attribute and five Data Attributes are in record 16132. Our detailed analysis shows that this is correct.

Having examined MFT record 16086 at Table A11.5 above, we now look at MFT record 16132 at Table A11.7:

Table A11.7 Details of new MFT record as a result of changes – 16132.

```
Offset      0  1  2  3  4  5  6  7   8  9 10 11 12 13 14 15
00000000   46 49 4C 45 2A 00 03 00   60 21 1E DF 00 00 00 00   FILE*...`!.ß....
00000016   05 00 00 00 30 00 01 00   E0 02 00 00 00 04 00 00   ....0...à.......
00000032   D6 3E 00 00 00 00 05 00   07 00 0A 00 04 00 00 00   Ö>.............
00000048   30 00 00 00 80 00 00 00   00 00 00 00 00 00 00 00   0... ..........
00000064   62 00 00 00 18 00 01 00   41 08 00 00 00 00 10 00   b.......A.......
```

```
00000080    00 32 F6 5F 75 43 C2 01    00 32 F6 5F 75 43 C2 01    .2ö_uCÂ..2ö_uCÂ.
00000096    C0 08 BB 1A 97 61 C6 01    C0 08 BB 1A 97 61 C6 01    Â.».-aÆ.Â.».-aÆ.
00000112    00 A0 02 00 00 00 00 00    CE 9F 02 00 00 00 00 00    . .....ÎY......
00000128    20 00 00 00 00 00 00 00    10 01 4E 00 75 00 67 00     .........N.u.g.
00000144    67 00 65 00 74 00 6F 00    66 00 47 00 6F 00 6C 00    g.e.t.o.f.G.o.l.
00000160    64 00 2E 00 6A 00 70 00    67 00 00 00 50 00 00 00    d...j.p.g...P...
00000176    80 00 00 00 50 00 00 00    01 00 00 00 00 00 01 00    ...P...........
00000192    00 00 00 00 00 00 00 00    29 00 00 00 00 00 00 00    ........).......
00000208    40 00 00 00 00 00 00 00    00 A0 02 00 00 00 00 00    @........ .....
00000224    CE 9F 02 00 00 00 00 00    CE 9F 02 00 00 00 00 00    ÎY......ÎY......
00000240    31 10 A6 6F 2C 31 10 C5    DE 07 31 0A 54 EE F5 00    1.¦o,1.ÅÞ.1.Tîõ.
00000256    80 00 00 00 80 00 00 00    01 1B 40 00 00 00 06 00    ... .....@.....
00000272    00 00 00 00 00 00 00 00    00 00 00 00 00 00 00 00    ................
00000288    78 00 00 00 00 00 00 00    00 10 00 00 00 00 00 00    x...............
00000304    7C 00 00 00 00 00 00 00    7C 00 00 00 00 00 00 00    |.......|.......
00000320    05 00 44 00 6F 00 63 00    75 00 6D 00 65 00 6E 00    ..D.o.c.u.m.e.n.
00000336    74 00 53 00 75 00 6D 00    6D 00 61 00 72 00 79 00    t.S.u.m.m.a.r.y.
00000352    49 00 6E 00 66 00 6F 00    72 00 6D 00 61 00 74 00    I.n.f.o.r.m.a.t.
00000368    69 00 6F 00 6E 00 63 00    31 01 2C 6F 28 00 00 00    i.o.n.c.1.,o(...
00000384    80 00 00 00 80 00 00 00    01 1B 40 00 00 00 03 00    ... .....@.....
00000400    00 00 00 00 00 00 00 00    01 00 00 00 00 00 00 00    ................
00000416    78 00 00 00 00 00 00 00    00 20 00 00 00 00 00 00    x........ ......
00000432    28 1A 00 00 00 00 00 00    28 1A 00 00 00 00 00 00    (.......(.......
00000448    05 00 51 00 33 00 30 00    6C 00 73 00 6C 00 64 00    ..Q.3.0.l.s.l.d.
00000464    78 00 4A 00 6F 00 75 00    64 00 72 00 65 00 73 00    x.J.o.u.d.r.e.s.
00000480    78 00 41 00 61 00 61 00    71 00 70 00 63 00 61 00    x.A.a.a.q.p.c.a.
00000496    77 00 58 00 63 00 63 00    31 02 BE 68 2E 00 0A 00    w.X.c.c.1.¾h....
00000512    80 00 00 00 70 00 00 00    01 13 40 00 00 00 04 00    ...p.....@.....
00000528    00 00 00 00 00 00 00 00    00 00 00 00 00 00 00 00    ................
00000544    68 00 00 00 00 00 00 00    00 10 00 00 00 00 00 00    h...............
00000560    1C 01 00 00 00 00 00 00    1C 01 00 00 00 00 00 00    ................
00000576    05 00 53 00 75 00 6D 00    6D 00 61 00 72 00 79 00    ..S.u.m.m.a.r.y.
00000592    49 00 6E 00 66 00 6F 00    72 00 6D 00 61 00 74 00    I.n.f.o.r.m.a.t.
00000608    69 00 6F 00 6E 00 61 00    31 01 A9 67 28 00 00 00    i.o.n.a.1.©g(...
00000624    80 00 00 00 68 00 00 00    00 26 18 00 00 00 05 00    ...h....&......
00000640    00 00 00 00 68 00 00 00    7B 00 34 00 63 00 38 00    ....h...{.4.c.8.
00000656    63 00 63 00 31 00 35 00    35 00 2D 00 36 00 63 00    c.c.1.5.5.-.6.c.
00000672    31 00 65 00 2D 00 31 00    31 00 64 00 31 00 2D 00    1.e.-.1.1.d.1.-.
00000688    38 00 65 00 34 00 31 00    2D 00 30 00 30 00 63 00    8.e.4.1.-.0.0.c.
00000704    30 00 34 00 66 00 62 00    39 00 33 00 38 00 36 00    0.4.f.b.9.3.8.6.
00000720    64 00 7D 00 00 00 00 00    FF FF FF FF 82 79 47 11    d.}.....ÿÿÿÿ'yG.
```

A top level analysis of the MFT record at Table A11.7 is given below at Table A11.8.

Table A11.8 Top level analysis for NuggetofGold.jpg as a result of changes – 16132.

File Record Header	bytes 0 to 47
File Name Attribute (Attribute Header)	bytes 48 to 71
File Name Attribute Proper	bytes 72 to 175 (includes padding at bytes 170–175)
Data Attribute (Attribute Header)	bytes 176 to 239
Data Attribute Proper (data run)	bytes 240 to 255 (3 runs of 5 bytes) (includes padding at byte 255)
Data Attribute (Attribute Header)	bytes 256 to 375 (includes padding at byte 374–375)
Data Attribute Proper (data run)	bytes 376 to 383 (1 runs of 5 bytes) (includes padding at byte 381–383)

Data Attribute (Attribute Header)	bytes 384 to 503 (includes padding at byte 501–502)
Data Attribute Proper (data run)	bytes 504 to 511 (1 runs of 5 bytes) (includes padding at byte 509–511)
Data Attribute (Attribute Header)	bytes 512 to 615 (includes padding at byte 614–615)
Data Attribute Proper (data run)	bytes 616 to 623 (1 runs of 5 bytes) (includes padding at byte 621–623)
Data Attribute (Attribute Header)	bytes 624 to 727 (no data!) (includes padding at byte 724–727)
End of Record Marker	bytes 728 on

Note that even though entries are made in the second MFT record all references to the items are directed to the "parent" record, number 16086. It is this number that appears in Encase against each reference.

Answers to Exercises

Chapter 2

2.1 (a) 01010111 01110110
- (1) 30295
- (2) +30295
- (3) 22390
- (4) +22390
- (5) +87 and +118
- (6) 87.4609375
- (7) 5776
- (8) 5776
- (9) W v

(b) 10000000 01111111
- (1) 32640
- (2) +32640
- (3) 32895
- (4) –32641
- (5) –128 and +127
- (6) 128.49609375
- (7) 807?
- (8) 807F
- (9) ? ?

(c) 01000110 01011001
- (1) 22854
- (2) +22854
- (3) 18009
- (4) +18009
- (5) +70 and +89
- (6) 70.34765625
- (7) 4659
- (8) 4659
- (9) F Y

(d) 0000101 10001000
- (1) 34821
- (2) –30715
- (3) 1416
- (4) +1416

   (5) +5 and −120
   (6) 5.53125
   (7) 0588
   (8) 0588
   (9) ? ?
(e)   00110111 10011001
   (1) 39223
   (2) −26313
   (3) 14233
   (4) +14233
   (5) +55 and −103
   (6) 55.59765625
   (7) 3799
   (8) 3799
   (9) 7 ?
(f)   01110010 00111111
   (1) 16242
   (2) +16242
   (3) 29247
   (4) +29247
   (5) +114 and +63
   (6) 114.24609375
   (7) 723?
   (8) 723F
   (9) r ?
(g)   10010001 01000010
   (1) 17041
   (2) +17041
   (3) 37186
   (4) −28350
   (5) −111 and +66
   (6) 145.2578125
   (7) 9142
   (8) 9142
   (9) ? B
(h)   01010101 01100001
   (1) 24917
   (2) +24917
   (3) 21857
   (4) +21857
   (5) +85 and +97
   (6) 85.37890625
   (7) 5561
   (8) 5561
   (9) U a

2.2   (a) 01000011 01111111

(b) 00011000 10101011
(c) 01000010 01111010
(d) 00011001 00000100
(e) 01001010 00001100
(f) 11011111 11001000
(g) 11111100 11000100
(h) 01100111 11000000

2.3 (a) 01000001 01000000 00000000 00000000
     (b) 01000001 10000000 00000000 00000000
     (c) 01000010 11111110 00000000 00000000
     (d) 11000010 11111110 00000000 00000000

2.4 (a) +24.75
     (b) –24.75
     (c) +1986.0
     (d) –5025.0

2.5 (a) This is confirmed as a graphics file of GIF format by the file signature "GIF89a" at address 00H to 05H.
     (b) The image width is at address 06H of value 80 02 which in little endian becomes 0280H and is equal to 640 in decimal. Similarly, the image height is at address 08H of value e0 01 which in little endian becomes 01e0H and is equal to 480 in decimal.
     (c) This is a colour image. The global colour table starts at address 0dH and although the first triple is 00 00 00, the second is 80 00 00 which, because all values are not the same, is not a grey-scale value.

Chapter 3

3.1 Table 3A.1 is the finger check table for Question 1. The counter register starts at 31, referring to the instruction "load 07" and the execution of this results in the gp register being set to 03H. Meanwhile, the counter register has been stepped to 33. The next instruction, at 33, is "add 07" and the result of this execution is that 03H is added to 03H in the gp register giving 06H. Again, the counter register has been stepped, now to 35, and so the instruction "add 07" is

Table 3A.1 Finger check of Exercise 3.1.

Counter register	Doing		Using code	gp	Address	
	Code	Action			07	08
31	01	load	07	03	03	01
33	04	add	07	06	03	01
35	04	add	07	09	03	01
37	02	store	08	09	03	09
39						

executed, resulting once again in 03H being added to the gp register now to give 09H. Again, the counter register has been stepped, now to 37, and so the instruction "store 08" is executed. This results in the value in the gp register, 09H, being put into memory address 8. The counter register is now at 39, where we leave the example. The overall effect of this sequence is to multiply the value in address 07 by 3 (using successive addition) and to place the result in address 08.

3.2 Below is listed the complete finger check table for this code and data sequence: As can be seen, the final value of memory address 09 is 08. The sequence in memory address 09 is seen to be: 2, 3, 5, 8 ... which is the Fibonacci number sequence.

Counter register	Doing		Using code	gp	Address					
	Code	Action			05	06	07	08	09	0a
31	01	load	05	04	04	00	01	01	00	01
33	02	store	06	04	04	04	01	01	00	01
35	01	load	07	01	04	04	01	01	00	01
37	04	add	08	02	04	04	01	01	00	01
39	02	store	09	02	04	04	01	01	02	01
3b	01	load	08	01	04	04	01	01	02	01
3d	02	store	07	01	04	04	01	01	02	01
3f	01	load	09	02	04	04	01	01	02	01
41	02	store	08	02	04	04	01	02	02	01
43	01	load	06	04	04	04	01	02	02	01
45	05	subtract	0a	03	04	04	01	02	02	01
47	02	store	06	03	04	03	01	02	02	01
49	08	jbnz	16	03	04	03	01	02	02	01
4b–16=35	01	load	07	01	04	03	01	02	02	01
37	04	add	08	03	04	03	01	02	02	01
39	02	store	09	03	04	03	01	02	03	01
3b	01	load	08	02	04	03	01	02	03	01
3d	02	store	07	02	04	03	02	02	03	01
3f	01	load	09	03	04	03	02	02	03	01
41	02	store	08	03	04	03	02	03	03	01
43	01	load	06	03	04	03	02	03	03	01
45	05	subtract	0a	02	04	03	02	03	03	01
47	02	store	06	02	04	02	02	03	03	01
49	08	jbnz	16	02	04	02	02	03	03	01
4b–16=35	01	load	07	02	04	02	02	03	03	01
37	04	add	08	05	04	02	02	03	03	01
39	02	store	09	05	04	02	02	03	05	01
3b	01	load	08	03	04	02	02	03	05	01
3d	02	store	07	03	04	02	03	03	05	01
3f	01	load	09	05	04	02	03	03	05	01
41	02	store	08	05	04	02	03	05	05	01
43	01	load	06	02	04	02	03	05	05	01
45	05	subtract	0a	01	04	02	03	05	05	01
47	02	store	06	01	04	01	03	05	05	01
49	08	jbnz	16	01	04	01	03	05	05	01
4b–16=35	01	load	07	03	04	01	03	05	05	01
37	04	add	08	08	04	01	03	05	05	01
39	02	store	09	08	04	01	03	05	08	01

3b	01	load	08	05	04	01	03	05	08	01
3d	02	store	07	05	04	01	05	05	08	01
3f	01	load	09	08	04	01	05	05	08	01
41	02	store	08	08	04	01	05	08	08	01
43	01	load	06	01	04	01	05	08	08	01
45	05	subtract	0a	00	04	01	05	08	08	01
47	02	store	06	00	04	00	05	08	08	01
49	08	jbnz	16	00	04	00	05	08	08	01
4b										

3.3 The program code and data segments for Exercise 3.3 are as shown in Fig. 3A.1.

program				data	
Memory address	Doing code	Using code		Memory address	Value
31	01	05		05	03
33	02	08		06	07
35	01	0a		07	00
37	02	07		08	00
39	01	07		09	01
3b	04	06		0a	00
3d	02	07			
3f	01	08			
41	05	09			
43	02	08			
45	08	0e			
47					

Fig. 3A.1 Program and data for Exercise 3.3.

For completeness, the finger check table for the above example is also shown as follows:

Counter register	Doing		Using code	gp	Address					
	Code	Action			05	06	07	08	09	0a
31	01	load	05	03	03	07	00	00	01	00
33	02	store	08	03	03	07	00	03	01	00
35	01	load	0a	00	03	07	00	03	01	00
37	02	store	07	00	03	07	00	03	01	00
39	01	load	07	00	03	07	00	03	01	00
3b	04	add	06	07	03	07	00	03	01	00
3d	02	store	07	07	03	07	07	03	01	00
3f	01	load	08	03	03	07	07	03	01	00
41	05	subtract	09	02	03	07	07	03	01	00
43	02	store	08	02	03	07	07	02	01	00
45	08	jbnz	0e	02	03	07	07	02	01	00
47–0e=39	01	load	07	07	03	07	07	02	01	00
3b	04	add	06	0e	03	07	07	02	01	00
3d	02	store	07	0e	03	07	0e	02	01	00

Counter register	Doing		Using code	gp	Address					
	Code	Action			05	06	07	08	09	0a
3f	01	load	08	02	03	07	0e	02	01	00
41	05	subtract	09	01	03	07	0e	02	01	00
43	02	store	08	01	03	07	0e	01	01	00
45	08	jbnz	0e	01	03	07	0e	01	01	00
47–0e=39	01	load	07	0e	03	07	0e	01	01	00
3b	04	add	06	15	03	07	0e	01	01	00
3d	02	store	07	15	03	07	15	01	01	00
3f	01	load	08	01	03	07	15	01	01	00
41	05	subtract	09	00	03	07	15	01	01	00
43	02	store	08	00	03	07	15	00	01	00
45	08	jbnz	0e	00	03	07	15	01	01	00
47										

As can be seen, the value in memory address 07 is 15H, which is 21 decimal, and this is the result of multiplying 7 by 3.

Chapter 5

5.1 From Fig. 5A.1 it can be seen that the RLL encoded signal forms the three RLL chunks 0010, 11, and 0010 resulting in the binary code 0 0101 1001 0. This is the hexadecimal value 59h with leading and trailing zeros, as was used in the example of Fig. 5.6. 59h is the ASCII code for the character "Y". Also shown in the diagram is the equivalent MFM encoding.

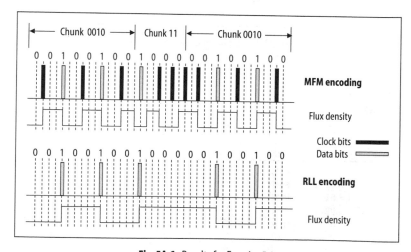

Fig. 5A.1 Results for Exercise 5.1.

5.2 The three byte capacities of Fig. 5A.2 are calculated as follows: for "Hardware" 2097 × 16 × 63 × 512 = 1 082 253 312; for "DOS" 524 × 64 × 63 × 512 = 1 081 737 216; and for "Current", the same as "Hardware". The LBA mode number of sectors is calculated from 2097 × 16 × 63 = 2 113 776. The translated

```
Drive: QUANTUM Pioneer SG 1.0A              Port: Primary (01F0h)
            Hardware      DOS        Current      Max ECC: 4 bytes
Cylinders: 2097           524        2097
    Heads: 16             64         16
  Sectors: 63             63         63
 Capacity: 1,082,253,312  1,081,737,216  1,082,253,312
            LBA Mode:    Yes        2113776
```

Fig. 5A.2 Results for Exercise 5.2.

number of sectors accessible is $524 \times 64 \times 63 = 2\ 112\ 768$ resulting in a loss of 1008 sectors.

5.3 Given a Logical Block Address of 1,045,721 for a disk which has 16 heads and 63 sectors per track, the values of the equivalent CHS address are calculated as follows:

$C = 1,045,721/(16 \times 63) = 1037$

$H = (1,045,721 \bmod (16 \times 63))/63 = 425/63 = 6$

$S = ((1,045,721 \bmod (16 \times 63)) \bmod 63) + 1 = (425 \bmod 63) + 1 = 47 + 1 = 48$

The LBA address is calculated from the CHS address as follows:

$LBA = (1037 \times 16 \times 63) + 6 \times 63 + 48 - 1 = 1,045,296 + 378 + 47 = 1,045,721$

5.4 The Seagate ST38410A hard disk drive is marked C 8391, H 16, S 63 and therefore has a total number of sectors of $8391 \times 16 \times 83 = 8,458,128$.

(a) Standard bit shifting requires the smallest power of two divided into the C value that gives $C < 1024$. In this case that is 16, resulting in translated values of $C = 8391/16 = 524$, $H = 16 \times 16 = 256$, and $S = 63$. The total number of translated sectors is $524 \times 256 \times 63 = 8,451,072$.

(b) Revised ECHS is used when there are problems with H values of 256 (as in this case). Cylinders are first multiplied by 16/15 to give $C = 8391 \times 16/15 = 8950$ and heads are set $H = 15$. The revised cylinder values are then divided, as before, by the smallest power of two that gives $C < 1024$. Again this is 16, resulting in translated values of $C = 8950/16 = 559$, $H = 15 \times 16 = 240$, and $S = 63$. The total number of translated sectors is $559 \times 240 \times 63 = 8,452,080$.

(c) Revised LBA Assisted requires the total disk capacity to be determined as $8391 \times 16 \times 63 \times 512 = 4,330,561,536$, and this when divided by $1024 \times 1024 = 4129.95$ Mbyte. This value is then looked up in Table 5.12, where it is seen to fall within the entry $4032 < cap < 8032.5$ Mbyte. As a result, $C = 4,330,561,536/(63 \times 255 \times 512) = 526$, $H = 255$, and $S = 63$. The total number of translated sectors is $526 \times 255 \times 63 = 8,450,190$.

5.5 The meaning of the second entry in the partition table at Fig. 5.26 is as follows. At 1ceh the value 00h identifies this as a non active partition. The following three bytes, at 1cfh to 1d1h, describe the starting CHS address of this active partition as cylinders 256, heads 0, sectors 1, in the following way:

Address	Value	Interpretation		Result	
1cfh	00h	= 00000000	= heads	= 0	H
1d0h	41h	= 000001	= sectors	= 1	S
		01	= cylinders		
1d1h	00h	= 00000000	= cylinders	= 256	C

At 1d2h we note that the partition type is 05h, which is an extended DOS partition. Then the three bytes at 1d3h to 1d5h describe the CHS address of the end of the partition as cylinders 522, heads 63 and sectors 63 in the following way:

Address	Value	Interpretation		Result	
1d3h	3fh	= 00111111	= heads	= 63	H
1d4h	bfh	= 111111	= sectors	= 63	S
		10	= cylinders		
1d5h	0ah	= 00001010	= cylinder	= 522	C

Starting at 1d6h we have the four bytes of the LBA address as 00 c0 0f 00. Recalling that this number is held in little endian format, we reorder these to be 00 0f c0 00 and calculate the number as fc000h = LBA 1 032 192. Similarly, at 1dah we have the four bytes of the partition size as 40 6d 10 00 and again, reordering these results in 00 10 6d 40 which is 106d40h = 1 076 544 sectors. With a sector size of 512 bytes this gives us 1 076 544 × 512/(1024 × 1024) = 525.65 Mbyte. These results are confirmed by the EXTEND entry in Fig. 5.27.

5.6   At offsets a0–a7h of Fig. 5.38 is the directory filename SUB1 padded out with spaces and at offsets a8–aah are a further three spaces for the directory extension. At offset abh is the file attributes byte of value 10h and this represents a subdirectory entry. Offsets ac–b1h are not used and are set to 00h. However, at offsets b2–b3h is the last access date of 270fh in little endian. In binary this is 0010 0111 0000 1111 and when divided up as in Fig. 5.37 this is equivalent to 0010011 years from 1980, 1000 number of month, and 01111 day of month, giving us 1999/8/15. At offsets b6–b7h is the time of the last update as 5020h. In binary this is 0101 0000 0010 0000 and when divided up as in figure 5.36, this is equivalent to 01010 hours, 000001 minutes, and 00000 × 2 seconds giving us 10:01:00. Similarly, the date of the last update is at offsets b8–b9h and is again 270fh in little endian, resulting in a date of 1999/8/15. At offsets 1ba–bbh is the first cluster number in little endian, that is 001b, which is 27 in decimal, and finally, at offsets bc–bfh is the file size of 0.

5.7   Name: THISIS~1TXT

1st char	T	01010100
rotate		00101010
char	H	01001000
sum		01110010
		-------------------------

rotate		00111001
char	I	01001001
sum		10000010

----

rotate		01000001
char	S	01010011
sum		10010100

----

rotate		01001010
char	I	01001001
sum		10010011

----

rotate		11001001
char	S	01010011
sum		00011100

----

rotate		00001110
char	~	01111110
sum		10001100

----

rotate		01000110
char	1	00110001
sum		01110111

----

rotate		10111011
char	T	01010100
sum		00001111

----

rotate		10000111
char	X	01011000
sum		11011111

----

rotate		11101111	
char	T	01010100	
sum		01000011	= 43h

5.8   The additional time and date fields start at offset cch with the reserved byte
       00h. At offset cdh is the 10 millisecond units past creation time of 5ch which is
       equivalent to decimal 92, giving 920 milliseconds. At offsets ce–cfh is the file
       creation time of 5297h in little endian. In binary this is 0101 0010 1001 0111 and
       when divided up as in Fig. 5.37 this is equivalent to 01010 hours, 010100
       minutes, and 10111 × 2 seconds, giving us 10:20:46. Similarly the creation date
       is at offsets d0–d1h and is 270fh in little endian. In binary this is 0010 0111 0000
       1111, and when divided up as in Fig. 5.37 this is equivalent to 0010011 years
       from 1980, 1000 number of month, and 01111 day of month, giving us 1999/8/
       15. The last access date is at offsets d2–d3h and is again 270fh, resulting in 1999/

8/15. Finally, at offsets d4–d5h is the high word of the start cluster number for FAT32 systems that is 0000h here.

Glossary

2's complement

See two's complement.

A20

Address line 20. The segment:offset memory addressing architecture permits physical addresses up to 1 megabyte plus 64 kilobytes less 16 bytes. In the original 8088 processor, physical memory addresses could only extend to 1 byte below the 1 megabyte mark and any addresses above that value "wrapped around" to the beginning of memory again. Some early programs were written to take advantage of this feature. The 80286 and higher Intel processors, however, give access to physical addresses in real mode up to the limit of the segment:offset memory addressing architecture, and programs which expect wraparound are thus incompatible. To provide full compatibility with the 8088, circuitry is included in many systems which permits the twenty-first address line (A20) to be disabled, thus causing wraparound. *See also* HMA; Real mode.

ACPO

Association of Chief Police Officers.

AGP

Accelerated Graphics Port. A local video bus, and its connector, that provides improved graphics performance over a normal PCI connection. AGP is now being replaced by PCI Express x16. *See* PCI; PCI Express.

Allocation unit

An MS-DOS file system memory unit consisting of a number of disk sectors. Also known as a cluster.

ANSI

American National Standards Institute.

ARLL

Advanced Run Length Limited. An encoding method used to store information magnetically on the surface of a disk.

ASCII

American Standard Code for Information Interchange. Character code in common use.

ASCIIZ

An ASCII string of characters which is terminated by an all zeros byte.

ATA

AT Attachment. ATA defines a standard specification for connecting hard disk drives to the PC. Further updates to the standard include ATA-2 through to ATA-7.

ATAPI

ATA Packet Interface. A standard that permits CD-ROM and tape drives to be connected to the IDE (ATA) interface.

Back door

A feature left in a system for the convenience of designers and testers which may be used to defeat the security system.

BCD

Binary Coded Decimal. A format used for representing decimal numbers.

BCAI

Byte Count After Index. A code used in hard disks to identify the position in bytes on the disk relative to an index mark. *See* BFI.

Beep code

A specific set of beeps sent to the PC loudspeaker when a POST diagnostic fails.

BFI

Bytes From Index. A code used in hard disks to identify the position in bytes on the disk relative to an index mark. *See* BCAI.

Big endian

A method of forming a number from two or more bytes taken together. The highest valued bits are taken as being in the lowest valued address.

BIOS

Basic Input–Output System. The name given to the system programs which provide basic input and output functions for the PC. Usually held in ROM or flash EPROM.

Bit

Binary digit. The elementary unit of information storage.

Boot

To "boot" is to execute the "bootstrap" code. The bootstrap is that sequence of code which is initiated at the instant of switching on the PC and which causes it to load its working programs. The word stems from the phrase: "to pull oneself up by one's bootstraps".

Boot record

See boot sector

Boot sector

The first sector in a partition or on a floppy disk that contains the bootstrap loader code for the particular operating system. Also known as the boot record.

Boundary cells

See JTAG.

BPB

BIOS Parameter Block. Located within the boot record, this contains essential data about the volume.

Bus

A set of parallel wires (or tracks on a printed circuit board) which connects one part of the PC to another.

Bus mastering

A mechanism whereby the memory and input–output devices, as well as the processor, can take control of the buses. *See also* DMA.

Byte

A group of 8 bits taken together. The fundamental unit of memory addressing.

Cache

Caching is a method of increasing performance by keeping frequently used data in more rapidly accessible and faster storage.

CCITT

International Telegraph and Telephone Consultative Committee.

CD-R

See CD-ROM.

CD-ROM

Compact Disc Read-Only Memory. A means of storing up to 700 Mbyte of data on a disk which is very similar in appearance and method of working to an audio CD. Originally this was a read-only system (hence CD-ROM), but there are now writable (write-once) CDs (CD-R) and re-writable CDs (CD-RW).

CD-RW

See CD-ROM.

CF card

Compact Flash card. A standard form of flash EPROM memory system, configured to function like an ATA disk drive. Used in some PDAs and cameras.

Chipset

Often used to refer specifically to the set of controller chips on the motherboard of a PC. *See also* Northbridge and Southbridge.

CHS

Cylinder Head Sector. The original form for addressing sectors on a disk. *See also* LBA.

CISC

Complex Instruction Set Computer. Microprocessors which have a large and complex set of instruction codes. *See also* RISC.

Clean boot

A boot that carries out all the POST/boot activities from the very beginning of the sequence using a floppy disk that has been constructed to ensure that none of the hard disks is written to. *See also* Boot.

Cluster
A file system allocation unit. It consists of a number of disk sectors.

CMOS
Complementary Metal-Oxide Semiconductor. A type of integrated circuit design and fabrication known for its low power consumption.

CMOS RAM
A small amount of memory in the real-time clock chip that is preserved by the clock battery and is used for storing system configuration information.

COB
Chip On Board. A form of technology where the chip (or die) is connected directly to the printed circuit board without being packaged. A blob of resin is then placed over the die to protect it. Also known as Direct Chip Attach (DCA).

Cold boot
A boot that carries out all the POST/boot activities from the very beginning of the sequence. The system is starting from cold. *See also* Boot.

CP/M
Control Program for Microcomputers. An operating system developed for the 8 bit Intel 8080 processor.

CRC
Cyclic Redundancy Check. A form of checksum used to detect certain kinds of error.

Cylinder
The narrow cylinder strip swept out at a particular head assembly position on all surfaces of all platters during one rotation of the disk. *See* Head; Sector; Track.

DAM
Data Address Mark. A low-level format marker on a disk surface.

Daughterboard
A subordinate printed circuit board (PCB) that connects, often at right angles, to the motherboard in a PC. Sometimes known as a riser board.

DCA
Direct Chip Attach. A form of technology where the chip (or die) is connected directly to the printed circuit board without being packaged. A blob of resin is then placed over the die to protect it. Also known as Chip On Board (COB).

DCO
Device Configuration Overlay. An overlay that can be set on a hard disk drive to alter its working modes and features, including changing its apparent capacity.

DDO
Dynamic Drive Overlay. Software that is resident on a hard disk and automatically loaded during the bootstrap sequence to provide CHS translation.

DDR

Double Data Rate. A method of doubling the performance of SDRAM by using both the rising and falling edges of a clock pulse to transfer data. DDR2 and DDR3 technologies have also been announced. *See* SDRAM.

Defect Lists

Lists that are internal to a hard disk drive and that identify bad sectors. The P-List is the primary list generated during manufacture of the disk, and the G-List is the grown defect list generated whilst the disk is in use.

Defrag

Defragment. The process of reordering data on a disk in order to improve the efficiency of access.

DEG

The UK Digital Evidence Group

DIL

Dual In-Line. A form of PC chip packaging and the socket for it.

DIMM

Dual In-line Memory Module. A small printed circuit board mounted with several memory chips which may be locked into a socket on the motherboard of a PC. *See also* SIMM; SODIMM.

DIP

Dual In-line Package. *See* DIL.

Disk ID

A four-byte value written to the master boot record of a hard disk to act as an ID. Also known as the NT Serial Number.

DMA

Direct Memory Access. A means by which input–output devices and the internal memory unit can perform data transfer operations independently of the processor. The logic circuitry which provides this capability.

DOS

This strictly refers to any Disk Operating System, but it is often used as a synonym for MS-DOS. *See* MS-DOS.

DRAM

Dynamic Random Access Memory. A form of RAM that requires continuous refreshing, hence the word "dynamic". *See* SRAM.

DVD

Digital Versatile Disc or Digital Video Disc. A successor to the CD-ROM, and generally backwards compatible with it. This technology currently has a storage capacity of up to 17 Gbyte.

EBCDIC

Extended Binary Coded Decimal Interchange Code. A less commonly used character code from IBM.

ECC

Error-Correcting Code. A set of check bytes used to detect and correct certain kinds of errors.

ECHS

Extended CHS. The facility offered by a BIOS which incorporates CHS translation software.

EDO

Extended Data Out (sometimes called Hyper Page Mode). An architecture for DRAMs.

EEPROM

Electrically Erasable PROM. Read-only memory that can be repeatedly programmed, completely erased electrically and reprogrammed.

EIDE

Enhanced IDE. A standard originally used by Western Digital to refer to systems with ATA-2, ATAPI and dual IDE/ATA host adaptor facilities. Now in common use.

EISA

Extended Industry Standard Architecture. An improved version of the ISA standard PC bus architecture.

Enhanced BIOS

A BIOS that incorporates the INT 13h extensions.

EMM

Expanded Memory Manager. *See* Expanded memory.

EMS

Expanded Memory System. *See* Expanded memory.

EPROM

Erasable PROM. Read-only memory that can be repeatedly programmed, completely erased and reprogrammed.

ESDI

Enhanced Small Device Interface. A disk standard that was designed to improve on the ST412/506 interface. Now effectively obsolete.

Exif

Exchangeable Image File Format. This is a picture format that has been designed to allow camera and image metadata to be embedded in JPEG files. *See* JPEG.

Expanded memory

A design developed by Lotus, Intel and Microsoft for accessing more than one megabyte of memory by bank-switching additional memory into the one megabyte real mode address space. LIM EMS stands for Lotus–Intel–Microsoft Expanded Memory System.

Expansion slots
The slots on a PC where expansion cards can be fitted to provide additional functionality.

Exponent
Part of a floating point number.

Extended memory
Memory above the one megabyte address. Apart from the High Memory Area (*see* HMA), extended memory is only accessible when the processor is in protected mode.

Extended partition
A construct on a hard disk designed to contain one or more logical partitions.

FAT
File Allocation Table. A disk resource allocation mechanism first used by the MS-DOS file system. The file system itself. *See also* NTFS; FAT12, FAT16, FAT32.

FAT12, FAT16, FAT32
Types of FAT-based file systems using 12, 16 and 32 bit entries in the file allocation tables, respectively. *See also* NTFS; FAT.

FCFC
Forensic Computing Foundation Course. Postgraduate level course run by Cranfield University in conjunction with the UK Digital Evidence Group.

FCG
The UK Joint Agency Forensic Computer Group. Now named the Digital Evidence Group.

FDC
Floppy Disk Controller.

File signature
Unique character sequence embedded at the beginning of a file which may be used to identify the type of file. Sometimes called the magic number.

Firewire
A serial bus technology designed primarily for high-performance audio and video multimedia applications. Sometimes known as i.Link and IEEE-1394.

Flash EPROM
EEPROM chips that permit erasure and reprogramming at the level of the block or the byte rather than having to erase the entire chip first.

Floating point
A binary representation of numbers held in scientific notation form.

FM
Frequency Modulation. An encoding method used to store information magnetically on the surface of a disk.

Form factor
The physical shape and size of a packaged chip or a disk.

FPM
Fast Page Mode. An architecture for DRAMs.

FSB
Front Side Bus. The high-performance bus that connects the Northbridge chip to the processor. *See* Northbridge.

GIF
Graphic Interchange Format. A commonly used graphics file format. Picture files of that type.

Gigabyte
A unit of memory of value 2^{30} or 1,073,741,824 bytes.

GUI
Graphical User Interface. A user interface which provides graphical elements such as windows, icons, menus and pointers (WIMP) to control PC applications.

GUID
Globally Unique Identifier. An identifier that is unique across both space and time.

Gzip
A commonly used free archive file format.

Head
The magnetic read–write heads of a disk drive. The particular head number currently active. *See* Cylinder; Sector; Track.

Head assembly
Mechanical assembly to which the heads of a hard disk unit are connected.

Hex
Abbreviation for numbers shown in the hexadecimal number system.

High-level format
The process of establishing a file system on a disk. *See* low-level format.

HMA
High Memory Area. The area of memory (64 kilobyte less 16 bytes in size) that is located in the PC memory map immediately above the 1 megabyte address. *See also* A20.

HOL
High-Order Language. A high-level programming language.

HPA
Host Protected Area. An area that can be reserved on a hard disk drive by instructing the controller to reduce the value of the maximum addressable sector.

HPM

Hyper Page Mode (sometimes called Extended Data Out). An architecture for DRAMs.

IAM

Index Address Mark. A low-level format marker on a disk surface.

IC Card

Proprietary name for an organizer memory card.

IDAM

ID Address Mark. A low-level format marker on a disk surface.

IDE

Integrated Drive Electronics, Intelligent Disk Electronics and similar interpretations. A hard drive interface standard. More usually now referred to as AT Attachment or ATA.

IDE

Integrated Development Environment. A set of integrated programming tools for use by a programmer.

IEEE 1394

See Firewire.

IEEE 754

Definition of standard floating point number formats.

i.Link

See Firewire.

INT

Software interrupt instruction code.

Interrupt vector

A four-byte segment:offset address pointer to interrupt handling code.

I/O port address

The physical address (or range of addresses) that are assigned to a hardware device and which permit control instructions and data to be exchanged with that device.

IRQ

Interrupt request channel. The physical channel number assigned to a hardware device which permits interrupts to be passed from that device.

ISA

Industry Standard Architecture. A defined standard PC bus architecture which formalized and updated the PC-AT architecture.

ISO

International Organization for Standardization.

JFIF

JPEG File Interchange Format. A graphics file format. A picture file that conforms to the JFIF specifications. *See* JPEG.

JTAG

Joint Test Access Group. A group set up to agree standards for the embedding of test facilities into electronic chips. These take the form of boundary cells which are controlled by a Test Access Port and this permits test and diagnostic commands to be sent to the chip and data to be received from it.

JPEG

Joint Photographic Experts Group. A graphics standards committee. A picture file that conforms to the JPEG specifications.

Kilobyte

A unit of memory of value 2^{10} or 1024 bytes.

LBA

Logical Block Addressing. An alternative system for addressing sectors on a disk. *See* CHS.

L-CHS

Logical CHS address. The translated CHS address at the INT 13 interface. *See* CHS.

LCD Panel

Liquid Crystal Display Panel. A flat screen technology used for modern display devices.

LFN

Long File Name. A file name that can be up to 255 characters in length. *See also* SFN.

Little endian

A method of forming a number from two or more bytes taken together. The lowest valued bits are taken as being in the lowest valued address.

Local bus

Internal connection made between the processor bus and some expansion slots to improve graphics and disk performance. *See* VL-Bus; AGP

Logical partition

A partition or volume on a hard disk that is contained within an extended partition.

Low-level format

The process of placing address and structure markers on a disk. *See* high-level format.

LSN

Logical Sector Number. Sector numbers counting from 0 from the beginning of a volume.

LZW

Lempel–Ziv–Welch. A file compression system named after its designers.

Magic number

A synonym for "file signature". Unique character sequence embedded at the beginning of a file which may be used to identify the type of file.

Mantissa

Part of a floating point number.

Master boot record

The first sector on a hard disk containing the partition table and the code which is used to analyse it.

MCA

Micro Channel Architecture. A proprietary IBM PC bus architecture.

Megabyte

A unit of memory of value 2^{20} or 1,048,576 bytes.

Memory disk

Proprietary name for an organizer flash memory card.

Memory stick

A proprietary form of flash EPROM memory system, normally configured to function like an ATA disk drive.

MFM

Modified Frequency Modulation. An encoding method used to store information magnetically on the surface of a disk.

MFT

Master File Table. Database that contains details of all the files on an NTFS file system. *See* NTFS.

MIPs

Millions of Instructions Per Second. Sometimes used as a measure of processor performance.

MMC

Multi Media Card. A standard form of flash EPROM memory system, configured to function like an ATA disk drive. Used in some PDAs and cameras.

MMIO

Memory Mapped Input Output. A technique where I/O port addresses are allocated space in the normal main memory map.

MMX

Multimedia extensions. An additional set of instructions designed for multimedia use and built into the later Intel Pentium processors.

Motherboard

The main printed circuit board of a PC to which all other elements are connected.

MS-DOS

The Microsoft Disk Operating System. An early command line-based operating system found in most PCs.

MZR

Multiple Zone Recording. This is a system where different tracks on the surface of a disk have different numbers of sectors per track. *See also* ZBR; ZCAV.

Nibble

4 bits taken together. Half a byte.

Northbridge

One of the two standard controller chips on the motherboard of a PC. The higher performance bridge that links processor, caches and main memory. *See also* Chipset; Southbridge.

NTFS

New Technology File System. Type of file system intended to be an improvement over the FAT based file systems. *See also* FAT12, FAT16, FAT32; FAT.

NT Serial Number

A four-byte value written to the master boot record of a hard disk to act as an ID. Also known as the Disk ID.

Object code

The code executed by the target machine. Typically this will have been generated by a compiling system from source code written by a programmer.

Partition

A logical volume established on a hard disk.

PATA

Parallel ATA. The original ATA standard that uses a parallel IDE cable to connect disk drives to the motherboard. Now qualified by the word "parallel" to distinguish it from the newer *serial* ATA standard. *See also* ATA; SATA.

PC

Personal Computer.

PC-AT

Personal Computer – Advanced Technology. The later architecture of the PC on which most modern PC systems are based.

PCB

Printed Circuit Board.

P-CHS

Physical CHS address. The CHS address at the physical disk. *See* CHS.

PCI

Peripheral Component Interconnect. A standard PC parallel bus architecture designed by Intel for the Pentium range of processors.

PCI Express
Peripheral Component Interconnect Express. A more recent PC serial bus architecture that operates over one or more serial *lanes*.

PC-XT
Personal Computer – Extended Technology. The earlier architecture of the PC.

PDA
Personal Digital Assistant. A form of personal electronic organizer.

Petabyte
A unit of memory of value 2^{50} or 1,125,899,906,842,624 bytes

PGA
Pin Grid Array. A type of PC chip packaging and the socket for it.

PGP
Pretty Good Privacy. A personal encryption system.

PIO
Programmed Input–Output. A means of data transfer that is carried out directly by the central processor. *See* DMA.

Platter
A thin disk coated with magnetic material which forms two surfaces of a hard disk unit.

PLCC
Plastic Leaded Chip Carrier. A form of PC chip packaging and the socket for it.

PGA
Pin Grid Array. A form of processor chip packaging and the socket for it.

PNG
Portable Network Graphic. A relatively new graphics file format.

PnP
Plug and Play. Automatic detection and allocation of those resources (IRQs, I/O Addresses, DMA channels) that are required by a hardware device.

POST
Power-On Self Test. The sequence of tests that are executed when power is first switched on to the PC.

POST code
A specific code that is sent to an I/O port when a POST diagnostic fails.

PROM
Programmable ROM. Read-only memory that can be programmed after manufacture.

Protected Mode
One of the operating modes of the 80286 and higher Intel processors, in which a more complex addressing architecture than the segment:offset system of real

mode is used and the CPU enforces protection mechanisms designed to prevent one program from disrupting another. *See also* Real mode; Virtual-86 mode.

PS/2

A standard connector and socket used, typically, for the mouse and the keyboard.

RAID

Redundant Array of Inexpensive (or Independent) Disks. A set of disk drives that are used together to provide improved performance and reliability.

RAM

Random Access Memory. The main (volatile) memory of the PC.

Real number

Synonym for floating point number.

Real mode

One of the operating modes of the 80286 and higher Intel processors, and the only operating mode of the 8088, 8086, 80186 and 80188 processors. In this mode, used by MS-DOS, all addresses specified by programs must correspond directly to real physical addresses in the first 1 Mbyte of memory (thus the name Real Address Mode) and utilize the segment:offset addressing architecture. *See also* Protected Mode; Virtual-86 Mode.

Resident data

File data in an NTFS system that is held within the body of the MFT record. *See* NTFS; MFT.

RISC

Reduced Instruction Set Computer. Microprocessors which have a small reduced set of instruction codes. *See also* CISC.

Riser board

A subordinate printed circuit board that connects, often at right angles, to the motherboard in a PC. Sometimes known as a daughterboard.

RLL

Run Length Limited. An encoding method used to store information magnetically on the surface of a disk.

ROM

Read-Only Memory. Non-volatile memory that cannot (normally) be changed. Used to contain, for example, the BIOS in a PC.

RSA

Rivest (Ron), Shamir (Adi), Adelman (Leonard). Inventors of the RSA security algorithm.

RS-MMC

Reduced Size Multi Media Card. A standard form of flash EPROM memory system, configured to function like an ATA disk drive. Used in some PDAs and cameras.

RTF

Rich Text Format. A standard word processor file format.

SATA

Serial ATA. The original ATA standard uses a parallel IDE cable to connect disk drives to the motherboard. This newer standard uses serial cables. *See also* ATA; PATA.

SCSI

Small Computer Systems Interface. A standard expansion bus typically used to connect a number of devices, such as hard disks, tape drives and CD-ROMs, to a computer.

SDC

Secure Digital. A standard form of flash EPROM memory system, configured to function like an ATA disk drive. Used in some PDAs and cameras. Has built-in security features.

SDRAM

Synchronous DRAM. DRAM that operates synchronously with the processor clock.

SEC

Single Edge Connector. A form of processor chip packaging and the socket for it.

Sector

For the purposes of addressing, a disk track is divided into a number of equal sized sectors. *See* Cylinder; Head; Track.

Service Area

Area on a hard disk drive that contains service data such as defect lists and the controller firmware.

SETUP

A program within BIOS that can be accessed during the boot sequence by pressing a specific set of keys and which enables CMOS settings to be changed. *See* CMOS RAM.

SFN

Short File Name. A file name that conforms to the original DOS standard of a maximum of 8 characters for the file name and a maximum of 3 characters for the file type. *See also* LFN.

SGRAM

Synchronous Graphics RAM. DRAM designed for graphics use with a high-speed serial port and which operates synchronously with the processor clock.

Shadow RAM

RAM used to hold copies of some or all of the BIOS code in order to achieve performance improvements.

Side

Term used by Norton to refer to a head. *See* Head.

SIMM
Single In-line Memory Module. A small printed circuit board mounted with several memory chips which may be locked into a socket on the motherboard of a PC. *See* DIMM.

Slack space
The space from the end of a file to the end of the last cluster containing the file.

SLI
Scalable Link Interface. A technology that permits more than one graphics card to be used in parallel to improve overall graphics performance.

Slots 1 and 2 and A and B
The SEC form factors of some Intel Pentium II and III microprocessors (Slots 1 and 2) and their equivalents from other manufacturers (Slots A and B). *See* SEC.

SMART
Self-Monitoring and Reporting Technology. A self-monitoring and reporting system found on modern hard drives.

SmartMedia
A standard form of flash EPROM memory system. Used in some PDAs and cameras.

Sockets 1 to 8
The form factors of many microprocessors from the 80486 to the Pentium Pro.

SODIMM
Small Outline Dual In-line Memory Module. A small printed circuit board mounted with several memory chips which may be locked into a socket on the motherboard of a PC. *See also* SIMM; DIMM.

SOIC
Small Outline Integrated Circuit. A form of PC chip packaging and the socket for it.

Source code
The original code written by the programmer. *See* Object code.

Southbridge
One of the two standard controller chips on the motherboard of a PC. The lower performance bridge that links the expansion buses and the I/O devices. *See also* Chipset; Northbridge.

SPGA
Staggered Pin Grid Array. A form of processor chip packaging and the socket for it.

SRAM
Static Random Access Memory. A form of RAM that does not require refreshing, hence the word "static". *See* DRAM.

SSD

Solid State Disk. Proprietary name for an organizer memory card.

ST412/506

Early *de facto* standard for connecting hard disk drives to their controllers.

TAP

Test Access Port. *See* JTAG.

Terabyte

A unit of memory of value 2^{40} or 1,099,511,627,776 bytes

Thumb drive

A solid state memory device, usually of Flash EPROM, that is configured to function like an ATA disk drive and is connected via a USB port.

TIFF

Tagged Image File Format. A graphics file format. Picture files of that type.

TQFP

Thin Quad Flat Plastic. A form of PC chip packaging and the socket for it.

Track

The narrow circular strip swept out at a particular head assembly position on one surface of a platter during one rotation of the disk. *See* Cylinder; Head; Sector.

Trash blocks

Unused areas within a document that may contain information unrelated to the document but of forensic significance.

two's complement

A format used for representing binary numbers with negative values.

UCS-2

Universal Character Set 2. A 16 bit two-byte character code which is the Microsoft Windows version of Unicode. *See* Unicode.

UDMA

Ultra Direct Memory Access. *See* Ultra-DMA

Ultra-ATA

Ultra-AT Attachment. *See* Ultra-DMA.

Ultra-DMA

An ATA standard that permits high-performance transfer rates and disk sizes that are greater than the 8.4 Gbyte limit. Also known as Ultra-ATA, Ultra33, Ultra66, UDMA etc.

UMB

Upper Memory Block. Blocks of memory above the 640 kbyte address in the 1 Mbyte main memory map.

Unicode

A range of multibyte character codes of which the Windows version of Unicode is probably the best known. This is a 16 bit two-byte version. *See* UCS-2.

USB

Universal Serial Bus. A bus architecture that permits up to 127 peripheral devices to be daisy-chained on to a high-speed serial bus.

UTF-16

Unicode Transformation Format 16. A multibyte character code that is mainly 16 bit two-byte, but permits surrogate pairs which signal sequences of more than two bytes. This produces what is in effect a 21 bit Unicode. *See also* Unicode; UCS-2.

VDU

Visual Display Unit. The once standard display unit of a PC. Now often replaced by a flat screen LCD panel.

VESA

Video Electronics Standards Association. The organization which designed the VESA Local Bus to improve disk and graphics performance on systems that, at the time, were ISA or EISA bus-based. *See* VL-bus; ISA; EISA.

Virtual-86 mode

One of the operating modes of the 80386 and higher Intel processors in which user programs run as if the CPU were in real mode, while providing the protection and the address capabilities of protected mode to a supervisor program which oversees each of the 8086 virtual environments in which the user programs are running. *See also* Protected mode; Real mode.

VL-Bus

VESA Local Bus. An interim PC bus architecture designed by VESA for better graphics and disk performance. Used the local bus concept and was superseded by the PCI bus.

von Neumann, John

Famous mathematician credited (though some dispute this) with the invention of the stored program concept. A machine architecture which implements this concept.

VRAM

Video RAM. DRAM designed for graphics use with a high-speed serial port.

Warm boot

A boot that carries out the boot activities from part way though the sequence, often bypassing all of the POST. The system is starting from warm. *See also* Boot.

WIMP

Windows, Icons, Menus, Pointers. A Graphical User Interface (GUI) which provides graphic elements such as windows, icons menus and pointers to control PC applications.

Winchester Drive

A term that is said to have originated from an early IBM drive that had 30 megabytes of removable media and 30 megabytes of fixed media. This gave rise to the name "30–30", which is the calibre of the famous rifle made by the Winchester gun factory. The term "Winchester" then became synonymous with a PC hard drive.

Word

16 bits taken together. Two bytes. *See* Big endian; Little endian.

WORM

Write Once, Read Many times memory. Used to be applied to optical and early CD-ROM devices that could not be changed once written.

xD Picture Card

A standard form of flash EPROM memory system, designed for use in cameras.

ZBR

Zoned Bit Recording. This is a system where different tracks on the surface of a disk have different numbers of sectors per track. *See also* MZR and ZCAV.

ZCAV

Zoned Constant Angular Velocity. This is a system where different tracks on the surface of a disk have different numbers of sectors per track. *See also* ZBR and MZR.

ZIF

Zero Insertion Force. Refers to a PC chip socket which has a locking and unlocking device and for which zero force is needed to insert or remove a chip.

Zip

A commonly used proprietary archive file format.

ZIP disk

A proprietary form of large (100–250 Mbyte) floppy-type disk.

Index